LORD BEAVERBROOK

LORD BEAVERBROOK
A Life

by
Anne Chisholm and Michael Davie

ALFRED A. KNOPF
New York   1993

THIS IS A BORZOI BOOK
PUBLISHED BY ALFRED A. KNOPF, INC.

*The authors and publisher would like to thank the following
for allowing the use of copyright photographs:*

Centre for the Study of Cartoons and Caricature, University of Kent at Canterbury,
Condé Nast, Country Life, Express Newspapers, House of Lords Record Office,
Hulton-Deutsch Collection, Mrs. Zenia Lester, the Estate of the late Lady
McLintock, National Portrait Gallery (London), Popperfoto, Press Association,
Robert Hunt Library, Trustees of the Broadlands Archives, Colin Vines.

Chisholm, Anne.
Lord Beaverbrook: a life / Anne Chisholm and Michael Davie.—
1st American ed.
p.   cm.
Includes bibliographical references and index.
ISBN 0-394-56879-6
1. Beaverbrook, Max Aitken, Baron, 1879-1964. 2. Great Britain—
Politics and government—20th century. 3. Newspaper publishing—
Great Britain—History—20th century. 4. Publishers and publishing—
Great Britain—Biography. 5. Politicians—Great Britain—Biography.
I. Davie, Michael. II. Title.
DA566.9.B37C49 1993
941.082'092—dc20
[B]   92-54282
                                                 CIP

Manufactured in the United States of America

FIRST AMERICAN EDITION

CONTENTS

ACKNOWLEDGEMENTS

We must first thank the Clerk of the Records of the House of Lords and the Beaverbrook Foundation for permission to quote from the Beaverbrook Papers, the Bonar Law Papers, and the Wargrave Papers in the custody of the House of Lords Record Office.

Although this biography is in no sense authorized, the third Baron Beaverbrook, the first Baron Beaverbrook's grandson, raised no objection to the project, and we have had substantial and generous help from members of Beaverbrook's family: his daughter the late Mrs Janet Kidd; his niece the late Lady McLintock; his nephews Alan Ramsay of Dunbar and Allan Aitken of Montreal; his granddaughters Lady Jean Campbell, the Hon. Mrs Christopher Smallwood (Kirsty Aitken), and the Hon. Laura Aitken; his grandsons Timothy Aitken and William Montagu; his daughter-in-law Lady (Violet) Aitken; the widow of his nephew Sir William Aitken MP, Lady (Penelope) Aitken; his great-nephew Jonathan Aitken MP; and the first Lady Beaverbrook's niece, Mrs Jehanne Warwick of Montreal.

We are particularly indebted to Mrs K. V. Bligh, Assistant Archivist at the House of Lords Record Office, and Miss Mary Flagg, Manager and Research Officer at the Harriett Irving Library of the University of New Brunswick, for their patience and prolonged assistance. We would also like to thank the Churchill Archives Settlement; Churchill Archives Centre, Churchill College, Cambridge; and Winston S. Churchill, MP.

The late Lady McLintock and Alan Ramsay read and commented on the first two chapters. Christopher Armstrong and H. V. Nelles, professors of history at York University, Toronto, read and commented on chapter three. Dr Cameron Hazlehurst of the Australian National University gave us expert guidance on the politics of the First World War and the 1920s. Dr Stuart Ball of the University of Leicester read and commented on the account of the Empire Crusade in chapters fourteen and fifteen. Dr Martin Gilbert read and made many suggestions for improving those parts of the book that describe relations between Beaverbrook and Churchill, in chapters four, seven, eight, twelve, sixteen, eighteen, nineteen, and twenty. Philip Ziegler read and commented on the section about the abdication of King Edward VIII in chapter sixteen, and Dr Richard Cockett on the appeasement passages in the same chapter. Mervyn Jones, former assistant editor of *Tribune*, read the sections about Beaverbrook and the left. Lieutenant-General Sir Ian Jacob read and commented on sections about military strategy in the Second World War; Mme Josephine Champsaur (née Rosenberg), Beaverbrook's secretary from 1953-1959, read and commented on the last two chapters. Jeremy Hardie ACA read and commented on Appendix A. We list these debts not to excuse omissions or blunders, which are of course ours alone, but to record our gratitude to academics and other busy people who were kind enough to find the time to improve our work.

We must further thank the following for their help: the Hon. David Astor, former editor of the *Observer*; Emeritus Professor Dr Alfred G. Bailey of the University of New Brunswick; J. R. A. Bailey; the Hon. Mrs Sarah Baring; Antony Beevor; Miss Sally Belfrage; Sir Isaiah Berlin; Lord Blake; the Hon. Lady Bowater; Alan Brien; Dr Christian Carritt; Dame Barbara Cartland; Mme Josephine Champsaur; the late Sir Eric Cheadle; A. H. T. Chisholm; Colin Chisholm; Lady Mary Clive; the Hon. Artemis Cooper; Mrs J. P. Crichton, Hon. Librarian of the Hopetoun House Preservation Trust; Arthur Crook; Sir Michael Culme-Seymour; Mrs Peter Davie; Dr Dido Davies, the biographer of William Gerhardie; Lady d'Avigdor-Goldsmid; Joseph X. Dever; Lord James Douglas-Hamilton MP; Miss Virginia Duigan; Robert Edwards, former editor of the *Daily Express*; David Elliot, the grandson of R. D. Blumenfeld; Lady Elton (née Sheila Lambert); the late Miss Gwen Ffrangçon-Davies; the Hon. Daphne Fielding; the Rt Hon. Michael Foot MP; Alastair Forbes; Professor Roy Foster; Milton Gendel; Miss Victoria Glendinning; Professor Alfred A. Gollin; Mrs Margaret Gordon, the widow of John Gordon, former editor-in-chief of the *Sunday Express*; Lord Granard; Lord Grantley; Dennis Morgan Griffiths, historian of the *Evening Standard* and formerly production manager of the *Daily Express*; Mrs Pamela Harriman; Harold Harris; Christopher Hawtree; Dr Timothy Healy; Michael Holroyd; Anthony Howard; Mrs Döe Howard; Lieutenant-General Sir Ian Jacob; Lord Jay; Miss Tjebbelina Kits; the late Miss Toto Koopman; Mrs Zenia Lester; Ian G. Lumsden, curator of the Beaverbrook Art Gallery; Mrs Betty MacArthur; Norman Mailer; the late Sir John Martin; Sir Peter Masefield; the Reverend John H. McIndoe; Mrs Sheila McNeil; the Hon. John Montagu and Caroline Montagu; Brian Moore; Dr Janet Morgan; Mrs Ann Moyal; Mrs Anne Moynihan, daughter of the late Sir James Dunn; Mrs Verily Paget; Jeffrey Potter, the biographer of Dorothy Schiff; David Pryce-Jones; Mrs Kent Rhodes; John Ross Robertson, the son of E. J. Robertson; Lady Sibell Rowley (née Lygon); Anthony and Sally Sampson; John Sancton, formerly Brigadier Michael Wardell's deputy on the *Daily Gleaner* of Fredericton; Lord Shawcross; Professor Robert Skidelsky; Lady Soames; Professor Hugh Stephenson; Mrs Eva Taylor; John Terraine; George Malcolm Thomson; Colin Vines; Timothy Wardell; Alan Watkins; the late Sam White; Charles Wintour, former editor of the *Evening Standard*; Mrs Anne Wollheim; Mrs Patrick Wolrige-Gordon

Acknowledgements

(Ann Howard, daughter of the late Peter Howard); Lord Wyatt of Weeford; Lord Young of Dartington.

Before the late A. J. P. Taylor's last illness, he encouraged us by saying that there was room for another biography of Beaverbrook besides his own: a characteristically generous statement that has often sustained us.

Further thanks are due. Simon Davie's assiduous research in the files of Beaverbrook newspapers and elsewhere has been invaluable. Faith Evans made many shrewd and fruitful observations on the draft. At Random House, Roddy Bloomfield was the most encouraging of publishers, Louise Speller consistently helpful, and Charles Elliott of Alfred A. Knopf and the Bodley Head a tower of strength. We thank Douglas Matthews, the Librarian at the indispensable London Library for compiling the index.

For permission to quote from unpublished documents or letters we are grateful to the following: Emeritus Professor Alfred G. Bailey (Bailey family papers); Cambridge University Library and Anne Amyes (William Gerhardie papers); the estate of Charles Carrington (Carrington papers); Arthur Crook (Stanley Morison papers); the Rt Hon. Michael Foot MP (his letters); Milton Gendel (Montagu letters); Lord Grantley (Jean Norton's diaries); Dr Timothy Healy (Healy letters); the Hopetoun Papers Trust, Hopetoun House, South Queensferry, Scotland (papers of the Marquess of Linlithgow); Bruce Hunter, David Higham Associates (Driberg papers); Mrs Döe Howard (Peter Howard papers); Mrs Sheila McNeil (Hector McNeil letters); the Trustees of the Liddell Hart Centre for Military Archives; The National Trust (Kipling papers); Lord Norwich and the Hon. Artemis Cooper (Lady Diana Cooper letters); Mrs Verily Paget (Sir Samuel Hoare's papers); Lord Shawcross (his letters); Mrs Eva Taylor (A. J. P. Taylor letters); John D. Teskey, Director of Libraries (Fredericton), University of New Brunswick (documents in the Harriet Irving Library); Timothy Wardell (Wardell papers); Lord Wyatt (his letters); Dr Percy M. Young and the Trustees of the Estate of the late Harriet Cohen (Harriet Cohen letters).

LORD BEAVERBROOK

INTRODUCTION
A VISIT TO
LA CAPPONCINA
1956

IN THE SUMMER of 1956 the 1st Baron Beaverbrook, aged seventy-seven, had reached the stage of life that comes to all adventurers when the facts of their careers begin to vanish into the mists of legend. His great days were over, but he was still treated with circumspection because of the power, erratically exercised, of his hugely successful newspapers – the *Daily Express*, *Sunday Express*, and *Evening Standard*. His reputation, to say the least, was uneven. Some admired him as a journalistic genius and for his part in winning the Second World War. To others he was a pre-war appeaser, a malign influence on Churchill, a self-aggrandizing newspaper proprietor and a corrupter of young journalists. Most liberals and Labour sympathizers detested the way he used his power; but a handful of prominent left-wingers saw him, mysteriously, as the enemy, like them, of the British establishment. Others again dismissed him as a figure of fun.

One of the authors of this book, Michael Davie, was then a reporter on the *Observer*. One Saturday afternoon, a few hours before the paper went to press, the news editor belatedly realized that the newly-weds of the decade, Marilyn Monroe and Arthur Miller, had arrived at London airport to an hysterical reception. The reporter was handed a sheaf of Press Association copy and told to produce six hundred words for page one, which he did, making the point that few intellectuals in history could ever have been as widely envied as Miller. Beaverbrook read the story and possibly, remembering his past, felt a twinge of this universal masculine emotion. At all events, he was not too old or too jaded to have lost his lifelong impulse to tempt people into his web. So a week later, just after Nasser seized the Suez Canal, the reporter found himself whisked out to the Beaverbrook villa in the south of France – flattered, and alarmed, but above all surprised that a man who had entered British public life almost fifty years earlier, who had served in the Cabinet in both world wars, who had been on close terms with Northcliffe, Churchill, Lloyd George and Roosevelt, who was generally believed to have made possible the victorious Battle of Britain, and who had drunk and negotiated with Stalin

1

while German troops advanced on the suburbs of Moscow, could still be alert to a flicker of reporting talent he thought he had spotted in a trivial story published by a newspaper he did not own.

Few people encountered Beaverbrook and came away unimpressed; although the reporter declined the job, that visit eventually led to this book. Immediately afterwards, he typed out some notes. Here, slightly cut but with nothing added except brief explanations of names, is what he saw and heard that summer weekend thirty-six years ago.

Met at Nice airport by a young man who introduced himself simply by saying, 'I'm Raymond.' Thirtyish, white shirt, sandals. He in turn introduced me to a thin brown woman with a pointed face who was apparently a French countess. Car driven by silent chauffeur wearing dark glasses and blue serge suit. *En route*, the Countess announced herself as very old friend of Lord Beaverbrook and spoke of him with respect. She said nothing of interest, except that Cocteau lived down there and had scrawled murals all over the wall of the house in which he had been ill.

Half-hour drive. Villa Beaverbrook – 'La Capponcina' – no less imposing than I'd expected. Courtyard scattered with cars, all his. Cloisters, fountain, flowers, coolness. Long white corridor decorated with medieval carvings. Raymond said these had been picked up by Molyneux, from whom Beaverbrook had bought the villa in 1939. Raymond now began to fit into place. He was the valet. From behind a door came a low rasp. Raymond listened at the door and said that 'he' was on the phone to London so we had better wait. Said: 'I never bathe in the West Indies. All those *sandflies*. And the blacks. I don't like blacks.'

The rasp stopped. Raymond opened the door and showed me in. Whirl of a skirt leaving the room; little gnarled figure advanced holding out a hand. 'Did you have a good journey?' I told him it had been a bad journey. 'Were you on time?' No. He said BOAC were never on time (it had been BEA). He was wearing sandals, white socks, white trousers of some roughish material, a white shirt open at the neck and a bush shirt over the top. The room was lined with books, including a complete set, as it appeared, of the *Revue des Deux Mondes* elaborately bound in orangey leather, presumably a Molyneux acquisition. This was Beaverbrook's study. In the middle was an upright desk, where Beaverbrook stood to work.

'Come and sit down.' He drew up a chair to within four feet of himself. This was the interview. 'What are the papers saying?' His voice was very strong, very Canadian. He seemed relaxed, his hands dangling on his lap. I said I'd seen only the *Sunday Times*, *Observer* and *Sunday Express*: that the *ST* and *Observer* didn't want to use force over Suez but that Hugh Fraser MP in the *Sunday Express* evidently thought we should use force at once. 'What else are they saying?' I mentioned one or two things. 'So the *Sunday Times* doesn't want to go to war. What do they want to do?'

Questioned me about myself. 'Do you want to go to New York?' I said I hadn't had an offer yet. He grinned. He said: 'We want to dev-e-lop the New York letter on the *Evening Standard*.' He asked if I read Sam White from Paris. I said I did and he praised him. 'We'll go out of doors. Do you want a hat?' He put on a pair of dark glasses and a straw hat and led the way outside.

A fat man in dark blue trousers and dark blue shirt came up. His stomach was showing, sprinkled with fair hair. Lord Rosebery. 'Rose-berry', as Beaverbrook pronounced it, introducing me [6th Earl, aged seventy-four, very rich; Liberal MP 1906–10; DSO 1918; racehorse owner]. At once Beaverbrook's attention was caught by the swimming pool a few yards from the house and he went off to gaze into its depths. I stayed with Rosebery and we could hear Beaverbrook shouting, 'The pool is dirty. We shall have to empty the pool.'

A veranda runs along the front of the house, roofed by a vine at one end and a wisteria at the other. Chairs and a table scattered with, naturally, all the Sunday papers and *Time* and a copy of *Nice Matin*. Rosebery took me off past the pool to a path on the other side. The Mediterranean a long way below, hazy horizon, Monte Carlo to the left. Wholly isolated. No signs from here that the coast had been touched by tourists. Rosebery started talking about cricket. Man of extreme geniality; probably the model for the Earl of Emsworth.

Beaverbrook had disappeared. Rosebery said he thought we might have a drink (it was now half past four) and led the way to a scullery, where Raymond was sitting reading the *Sunday Dispatch* ('Oh I read all the papers') and a large man in an apron was polishing glasses. 'A drink? Certainly me lord.' The butler reached into a cupboard for a bottle, and poured two glasses half full of whisky. Rosebery directed the operation with care. He tried his glass. Too much whisky, he said, taking another hefty drink. The butler put in more soda. 'Now there's too little whisky.' The butler added more whisky.

Rosebery led the way back to the veranda and sat down. He said that John Hislop had been staying with him and had written an article about his horses in the *Sporting Life*. He didn't think it a very exciting article; fumbled through the papers to try to find it. The sun blazed down, the whisky disappeared, a gardener went by with a hose, Beaverbrook no-where to be seen. A pretty girl came up: Miss Rosenberg, Beaverbrook's secretary. Rosebery decided he'd go and have a lie down. The Countess seemed to be lying down too.

Beaverbrook reappeared and said he was going down to the rose garden. He shouted for Raymond, and Raymond appeared carrying a pair of white gardening gloves and secateurs. Beaverbrook pulled on the gloves, took the secateurs, did not thank Raymond, and led the way through the garden. We negotiated, by means of stepping stones, a lawn of verbena. 'Don't tread on the blue grass. If anyone treads on the blue grass he is

3

hanged from the highest tower in Monte Carlo.'

The rose garden, dry and secluded, was enclosed by four walls. 'Isn't this a beautiful place?' Beaverbrook stepped up on to the bed on the left of the entrance and began to clip off the heads of dying roses. He said he did this every afternoon; he was getting to be an old man and this was about as much exercise as he could manage. He cut the roses and tossed them on to the paved path one by one. Raymond, he said, came round afterwards and collected them and arranged the petals very beautifully.

He clipped at a rose that collapsed. 'It disintegrates. It falls away into little pieces.' He had a verbal trick of repeating the sense of an idea in two ways. He worked on round the beds, intent.

He asked: 'Do you go down to the stone? Do you make up your own page?' I said I did. He went on: 'Has his lordship gone up to rest?' I said he had. 'That's what happens to you when you get old.'

He enquired if I liked being a journalist. I said I did. 'Great fun, isn't it?' He gave a big grin, as if we were conspirators against the world.

He began to talk about newspapers. He said the *Guardian* was a good paper but not a complete paper. He said he thought highly of Alastair Cooke, and found the *Guardian*'s French coverage very good. He said *The Times* was a much improved paper. Haley [Sir William Haley, the editor] was a good man. 'Do you read Oliver Edwards?' Surprised that his reading extended to Haley's pseudonymous books column, I said I found it unreadable. 'Ohhh no, it's nart unreadable. It can be read. And everyone knows it's Haley and that's how everyone knows he's damn dull.'

He asked if I'd ever been to America. 'Fascinating country,' he said. He went on clipping away and I wondered if he was about to make an offer. 'New York is very expensive,' he said. 'Very expensive, expensive, expensive.' Now it's coming, I thought: an offer that will stagger me by being either very big or very small. The paths were strewn with roses. He said nothing.

He talked about various journalists who had worked with him. He knew all the names of the *Express* American staff and how the offices in New York and Washington operated. He said if I went to America I must come home again. 'Don't stay in America.' Many journalists went out and never returned, which in his view was a loss to Britain. 'Many of the top journalists received their training in our office.'

He spoke of Hugh Massingham, the *Observer*'s political correspondent. 'A very good friend of mine.' His column was always worth reading and well informed. He said, 'the *Observer* is a good paper.' Of David Astor [the editor] he said: 'He has flair. It's not all done by luck.'

By now his hat was right on the back of his head. He seemed wholly at peace with the world, liking to talk about 'the journalists'.

His conversation proceeds by direct questions. The result is that anyone with him is naturally led to ask direct questions in return. He does not mind this. I asked about Onassis. 'Oh, he's an amusing dog. An amusing dog. He takes care to get hold of arl the important people who come into the bailiwick. Takes the ladies out in his yacht. I think Niarchos is better at the game than the other one.'

He talked about horse racing. He was against it. 'They think nothing of arranging a dishonest race. Never get mixed up in horse racing.'

He had completed the beds round the side and got up on the central bed. 'Do you go to church?' he asked. 'Oh, Church of England. I see the Church of England is making overtures to the Church of Scotland. The Church of Scotland will not be swallowed up. "Call me a thief, a rogue or a scoundrel, but never call me bishop." That was one of Wesley's more extravagant sayings.' He grinned at me.

I asked who was the greatest journalist he had ever known. 'Political journalist? Garvin. He gave the Conservatives a motto every week. He had great influence. J. A. Spender was a great political journalist. He wrote for the *Westminster Gazette*.' I said I had read the life of him by Wilson Harris. 'Aaah yes. Wilson Harris was damn dull. Damn dull,' he said, and chuckled. He started back up the steps to the villa. 'Never get dull.'

Back on the terrace he shouted for Raymond, who came out and took away his gloves and secateurs. He told Raymond he had left the roses for him to arrange. Then he went indoors. I asked Raymond if he knew whether I was staying the night or not. 'I've asked his lordship three times and all he says is that it's his decision and he's got a right to make up his own mind in his own time.'

I sat under the wisteria and shuffled through a mangled heap of Sunday papers, *Time* and *Newsweek*. Lord Rosebery appeared in a bath robe and went off to the pool. Miss Rosenberg followed him.

The Countess came out and sat down [she was not a countess, but Mme Marie-Edmée Escarra, who was helping Beaverbrook buy pictures for an art gallery he was giving to his native New Brunswick, the latest of his many benefactions to the province. She was also his mistress]. Beaverbrook came out and asked her to 'get the folder'. She went inside and came out again carrying a concertina file. Beaverbrook opened it and pulled out a sheaf of photographs of paintings. He put them on his knee and went through them, giving his view on each one, naming the painter if he knew, guessing if he didn't, and then turning the photograph over to see if he had been right. I glimpsed Stubbs, Gainsborough, Paul Nash and some Canadian painters.

He came to a painting by Lucian Freud.

'Zat is Frood,' said the Countess over his shoulder.

'Not Frood,' said Beaverbrook. 'Fried.'

He turned over some hundred photographs with assiduity and absorption, occasionally handing me one he thought of special quality. 'Great painting,' he would say.

The Countess went off, and the four of us went into the sitting room for a rum cocktail mixed by Beaverbrook with ice and limes and a lot of

5

stirring. Miss Rosenberg was sitting in a beach shirt and Rosebery in his bath robe. 'Miss Rosenberg, are you wearing a bathing costume?' She said she wasn't. 'Harry, are you wearing a bathing costume?' Rosebery said he wasn't either. 'A man once walked across this carpet in his (dripping) bathing costume and I had to send away and have another one spun.' He talked about the pool and how long it would take to empty.

Dinner time. Beaverbrook asked me if I had anything to change into, and I said I had just a suit, and he said a suit would do very well. He called the butler and asked him to take me down to a little pavilion, below the terrace away from the house, which had a big bed in a small room and next door a bathroom. The windows opened directly on to the Mediterranean. Wondering how long I had for a bath, I asked whether Lord Beaverbrook was punctual as a rule. Very punctual indeed.

By the time I got back up to the house, at one minute to eight, the others were waiting. Beaverbrook led off down the corridor, through the dining room, and out on to a little patio with some stone walls and a plain wooden table laid for dinner. Yellow basket chairs with yellow cushions.

The Countess sat at the head of the table, Rosebery on her left, Beaverbrook on her right and me on Beaverbrook's right opposite Miss Rosenberg.

Rosebery said: 'You know, when my father was Prime Minister he had to write to Queen Victoria every night in his own handwriting; there were no typewriters or anything like that and it used to take a tremendous time.' The French lady asked what he wrote about. 'Oh he had to tell her what had happened in the House and what had been going on in the Cabinet and so on. Tremendous amount of work – at the end of the day too, you know. You used to keep a diary didn't you Max? Keep a record of what you'd been doing, speeches and so on, so that you'd always be able to look it up if anyone said anything?' Beaverbrook, in a white dinner jacket, was non-committal.

Rosebery and Beaverbrook talked about Lady Flora Hastings. 'The question was,' said Beaverbrook, 'whether Lady Flora Hastings was or was not a virgin.' Rosebery tried to recall the details of this old scandal, when one of Queen Victoria's ladies-in-waiting started to look as if she were going to have a baby. He tried to remember the name of the doctor. 'You know who it was Max; what was his name?' 'Doctor Morell,' said Beaverbrook. They argued over the details of the case. 'She . . . was . . . not . . . a virgin,' said Beaverbrook, spacing out the words. 'You're the first person who's ever denied that she was a virgin,' said Rosebery. 'She had a cyst.' 'Nevertheless she was not a virgin.' They wrangled about the point until Beaverbrook said: 'After your behaviour over the last ten minutes, Harry, I'm going to pay you the greatest compliment I can pay a man. You remind me of my granddaughter.'

Rosebery said of someone that he had reported Rosebery and three other members of his club to the secretary because they were playing cards for five bob and the club rules said you were only supposed to play for half a crown. 'He went to prison soon afterwards and we were awfully pleased. Can't remember why he went though. Do you remember Max?' Beaverbrook (with great emphasis): 'He stole money from the people.' Rosebery mentioned a pre-World War I financial scandal. Beaverbrook remembered every detail.

Once, when the Countess said something, Beaverbrook put his head on one side and called out: 'Whaaat? I can't hear you.'

His meal seemed to run on parallel lines to ours. Raymond kept bringing him little plates of this and that, and he drank a different wine.

He said the crest on the plates was that of Lord Grantley [Richard Norton, 6th Baron Grantley, 1892–1954, businessman and film producer, who in 1919 married Jean Kinloch, later Beaverbrook's mistress]. 'He was a great wit.'

The Countess asked who was the Queen's adviser. 'Oh she has a private secretary you know, fellow called Adeane,' said Rosebery. Yes, but who advised her? 'Lord Mountbatten,' said Beaverbrook without raising his eyes from his plate. But on politics. . . ? 'Laaard Mountbatten.'

After coffee Beaverbrook led us back to the sitting room, where he went straight to a radiogram and put on, very loud, a long-playing record of *My Fair Lady*. Then he led the way out to the veranda and sat down in the basket chair. The music blared out and he sat there with his lids lowered looking like a very rich and wicked Buddha, immobile. It was too noisy to talk. When the record had passed his favourite song – 'Wiv a little bit of luck' – Beaverbrook got up, went inside, and put the needle back so that it played the song again. 'Very good song,' he said.

Before the record had finished he got up and said he was going to bed.

Next morning I was having breakfast alone on the patio when Beaverbrook appeared, again in white from head to foot. 'Did you sleep well? Come and join me when you've finished breakfast.' He took me again into the secret citadel of the walled rose garden, then on to a little balcony overlooking the sea. I asked if he bathed. He said he used to, but lately had had eczema. I asked if he preferred the south of France to his other houses. He said he didn't; he thought he preferred Nassau. He liked the sun.

He walked me round the swimming pool, inviting me to guess how long it would take to fill. He said Michael Foot was the ablest journalist he knew. He asked me if I knew the publisher of *Reader's Digest*: 'He said to me: "Max, aren't you sorry for all the people in the world who aren't journalists?" ' He spoke of *Time* and *Life*. I said some of their correspondents seemed uneasy, though well paid, about the way their copy was changed in the head office. He said, without blinking an eyelid, 'That is a weakness. It destroys the confidence of the man on the spot.' He said you couldn't run a newspaper as a philanthropic enterprise. 'To be a successful newspaper proprietor you need prejudice and breadth of vision.

7

It's a rare combination.' He said of the *Evening Standard*'s woman in New York, Evelyn Irons: 'She's very good on the news. A good newswoman. But she's not so good on the features.' He sat down on a swinging couch affair. 'D'you want to go to New York?' I said I would have to think about it. 'You should not hesitate. You should throw yourself into a new project with energy and enthusiasm.' He said I should let the editor of the *Evening Standard* know my decision. He spoke of the Art Gallery in New Brunswick. I asked if he found that the price of paintings went up when it was known that he was in the market for so many. No, not if you went to reputable dealers. He said it was foolish to hold on to your money when you were getting old. He was giving his away. He said he got more pleasure out of the Gallery now than from anything else.

We went back to the veranda and Lord Rosebery. Had Beaverbrook heard that Aldrich, the American ambassador in London, was going home? 'Yes.'

'What's your view of him?'

'Deaf and dumb.'

'You know, they say no woman is safe with him.'

'Yaas, he knows the language of love.'

They spoke of Lord Curzon. I asked whether Curzon was an insolent man. 'No,' said Beaverbrook, 'he was not insolent but he was stately. He had a great wit in Cabinet. F. E. Smith [later Lord Birkenhead] after the First War was defending the Armenians in Cabinet with great eloquence, extolling their physical courage. He challenged Curzon to name a single battle they had lost. Curzon said: "Can you name a single battle that they won?" India disrupted his character. After India, he thought he was the vice-regent of God on earth.'

Rosebery: 'I know he was fearfully mean. Do you know he once asked me to sell him a cob. Well, I didn't want to sell it particularly but I let him have it for £120. A long time afterwards I had a letter from him saying he had finished with the cob and he proposed to send it back and would I let him have his £120.'

Beaverbrook said: 'Churchill and I are the only two survivors of [Lloyd] George's cabinet. Churchill's in very good health. I haven't been feeling too good lately.'

Beaverbrook said to Rosebery: 'It is a very curious phenomenon, the London press. The *Observer* is for the blacks, and the *Spectator* is for the buggers.' Rosebery asked about the source of Ian Gilmour's money [the *Spectator*'s owner], and spoke vaguely about a homosexual Gilmour uncle. 'Now we know,' said Beaverbrook, 'why the *Spectator* is for the buggers.'

Rosebery wandered off and Beaverbrook asked me how much money I got. I told him. 'How do you live on it?' He didn't think there was a single person in a good position at the *Daily Express* who received as little. 'We have a top-hat pension scheme. For one of our top men like John Gordon [editor-in-chief of the *Sunday Express*] we must pay two or three thousand a year.' He made notes on a little pad on the arm of his chair.

Michael Foot, his wife Jill Craigie, and their daughter came to lunch. Mrs Foot said she had been reading the manuscript of a new Beaverbrook book [*Men and Power*]. She said the Tories wouldn't like it. 'The Tories never like what I do,' he said, grinning happily. Foot asked him about the day's news, but he said the office hadn't called. He seemed disappointed.

After lunch Rosebery and I had to leave – Rosebery for Goodwood where he had a horse running. Beaverbrook handed me an envelope containing tapes and asked me to deliver it to the *Express* in London. He came out to the car to see us off. The last I saw of him he was disappearing into the purple and flame flowers, white hat tipped on the back of his head, making, I suppose, for the dictaphone or tape recorder.

A whole generation later, when the idea of writing a new biography of Lord Beaverbrook occurred to us, we disinterred the yellowing pages of notes from 1956 and kept them by us while researching and writing this book. A surprising number of Beaverbrook's essential attributes, both serious and trivial, manifested themselves during that short visit. Apart from his enthusiasm for newspapers and journalists he displayed his lifelong dread of dullness, which conditioned his life as well as his papers; his instinctive belief in personality as the clue to history and current events; his exceptional memory, especially for financial and sexual scandal; and his keen interest in gossip. Many, though not all, of the key characters in his life made an appearance in his table talk – Lloyd George, Churchill; his favourite left-wing journalist, Michael Foot, turned up; his favourite grandchild, Lady Jean Campbell, was mentioned; dinner was eaten off plates that had belonged to his *maîtresse en titre* for twenty years, Jean Norton. As always after he had become rich, he had around him pretty women and eccentric servants whom he treated, as he did everyone else, with a mixture of charm, courtesy and ruthlessness. His interest in religion, his dislike of racing, his faddiness over his food, his determination to make his own daiquiris, were all characteristic and, to his intimates, familiar.

This book has been written to explore those 1956 observations, and to reconsider the impact of Beaverbrook's powerful and seductive personality in the context of his life and times. Our aim has also been to re-examine the legends and the reputation, the dark side as well as the light. Enough time has now elapsed, we hope, for the caricature images of Beaverbrook to be replaced by a calmer portrait by authors who were never beholden to him professionally or personally, one of whom never met him. We have also tried to suggest some answers to what is perhaps the most interesting question of all: how was it that an outsider like Beaverbrook could penetrate with such speed and apparent ease the heart of British politics, journalism and social life, and stay there for fifty years? By examining the qualities and the weapons he deployed to such effect we hope to throw light not only on Beaverbrook himself but on the circles in which he operated and the society in which he lived.

CHAPTER 1

SON OF THE MANSE
1879–1900

LIKE MANY MEN who make a fortune quickly, Beaverbrook did his best to create his own legend. He claimed that his Scottish forebears had been 'agricultural labourers' and told stories about how, brought up in fearful deprivation as the son of the manse in the Canadian backwoods, he was compelled to walk to school barefoot. Thereby he added extra drama to what the editor of a Canadian journal once described as 'the most spectacular success story of the century . . . the New Brunswick boy who became a multi-millionaire before he was 30'.[1]

In England Beaverbrook has often been seen as a lone adventurer, someone who arrived in London from nowhere. In fact he was part of a huge Aitken clan; his father was one of ten children, and so was Max himself. His second youngest sister used to send all her nephews, nieces and grandchildren £1 at Christmas. At the end of her life, in 1972, she was distributing £104.[2]

The family came from Torphichen in West Fife. A Torphichen minister, consulting baptismal registers, once traced it back to 1613. This information allowed Beaverbrook to take a swipe at the grandest political dynasty in Britain, whose members had for forty years treated him with aristocratic disdain. 'I am descended from eight or ten generations of agricultural labourers,' he boasted, 'therefore I feel quite equal to the Cecil family with this difference, that *none* of my ancestors stole church funds.' But the Aitkens were not 'agricultural labourers' or 'peasant people', as he also called them; they were tenant farmers as far back as 1720, and perhaps even before that. Their landlords were the earls of Hopetoun. Documents at Hopetoun House, the seat of the Marquess of Linlithgow (the 7th earl became a marquess in 1901), show that in the mid-nineteenth century Beaverbrook's grandfather, Robert Aitken, was doing well and was about to do better. He was renting a farm of 'about 99 acres Scottish measure' whose full name was Wester Tartraven and Lime Craig of Silvermine – Silvermine for short; it was so called because silver had once been extracted from a nearby glen under royal charter from James VI. Robert's

11

widowed mother lived in a new steading on the property, and a cousin in one of the farm cottages she had repaired at her own expense.

The soil hereabouts is poor, impacted clay on limestone, and the rise in the Aitkens' fortunes came not from farming but from industry's growing demand for lime. In 1841, the Hopetoun estate factor wrote a confident memorandum to the earl about Robert Aitken's prospects. Silvermine included a lime quarry; so did an adjacent property owned by a Colonel Hamilton Ferrier. But the Ferrier quarry was worked out, which meant that 'the sales from the Tartraven one may be considerably increased'. The estate would have to enlarge the lime kilns 'to enable the tenant to carry on the workings to a greater extent', but the capital expenditure would profit the earl as well as his tenant since, as the factor suggested, a new lease could be pegged to rising sales. The memorandum concluded: 'Robert Aitken is a very steady and industrious man, is married and has five or six children. He has always paid the Rent most regularly. His father and grandfather were also tenants on the Tartraven Estate.' He was certainly meticulous about money. In 1853 he wrote a reasonably literate letter to the factor to say that he and his wife had been going over their accounts and discovered that the factor, in a rent transaction, had given them a pound too much change: 'I return you the pound with great pleasure,' he wrote.[3] Robert Aitken's success with his lime quarries enabled him to buy property in Bathgate, the nearest market town to Silvermine; his wife was a Bathgate girl. Beaverbrook's father, William Cuthbert Aitken, born on 28 February 1834, was their third child and first son.

Beaverbrook once motored up to Scotland to see where his father had come from. Torphichen is about halfway between Glasgow and Edinburgh, and he later described how, one Sunday morning as the congregation was leaving Torphichen kirk after the service, he encountered the beadle, a retired saddler, who turned out to be a distant Aitken cousin. 'He showed me many gravestones bearing my family's name, though none marked my ancestors.' Aitken is a common surname in these parts. Nevertheless, the young Canadian was 'deeply moved' to see for the first time 'the land of my fathers', and recalled (he said) the lines of Sir Walter Scott:

> Breathes there the man, with soul so dead,
> Who never to himself has said,
> This is my own, my native land!

The beadle took him off to his cottage, which, otherwise bare, contained a huge mahogany four-poster bed. The beadle said proudly that the bed had been slept in by Norman Macleod, the nineteenth-century journalist and champion of the Church of Scotland. The jaunt became still more memorable when the old fellow took him to the ancestral home of Silvermine.

There it stood, deserted and almost tumbledown, with the land gone out of cultivation. . . . The cottage, all on one floor with beds built into the walls of living room and kitchen, was a stone structure of forbidding appearance. The byre adjoined the house and was of the same materials. Here, in these crowded quarters of this small and rather dark house, a family of several sons and daughters had dwelt together. They would be required to work the fields at an early age. The land looked to me of stern and harsh fertility, suitable only for simple crops such as buckwheat.

As so often in the Beaverbrook canon, his account is striking but not altogether accurate. He conveyed the impression that Torphichen was a miserable and isolated community entirely populated by peasants, whereas in truth it had strong European connections reaching back to the twelfth century, when the Knights of St John of Jerusalem, the crusading Hospitallers, made it their Scottish headquarters. A Lord Torphichen, whose title dates from 1564, still owns property in the village. The substantial and evocative remains of the Preceptory, now carefully maintained by the Secretary of State for Scotland, rise up just off the village square. Attached to this noble medieval ruin is the parish church, built in 1756, with plain box pews and the raised pulpit from which Beaverbrook's father is reported to have preached his first sermon.

The beadle cannot have been a very well-informed guide, since he failed to show Beaverbrook, near the entrance to the church, a prominent gravestone whose inscription reads:

Erected by John Aitken Silvermine
in memory of Margaret his daughter
who died 1803 aged 13
William his son died 24 January 1833 aged 14
John died 1836 aged 35.

A later addition records that John Aitken died in 1840, aged eighty-eight, and his wife Elizabeth Donaldson in 1857, aged eighty. John Aitken was the father of Robert Aitken, and thus Beaverbrook's great-grandfather.

The Preceptory is not the only local link with the remote past. Torphichen is set in rolling countryside, and a mile outside the village is a gigantic mound called Cairnpapple, a very ancient burial site. Silvermine lies in the shadow of this great tump: the low rectangular house, typical of the region, its byre and its mill survive.

From this rather bleak but by no means isolated spot Beaverbrook's father went at the age of eight to Bathgate Academy, an imposing and gloomy granite building near the middle of the town. Aged sixteen, already identified as 'a man o' pairts', he moved on to the University of Edinburgh. 'I was under the impression,' a Canadian friend of Beaverbrook's said, 'from hearing Lord Beaverbrook talk about him, that he walked to Edinburgh University every Monday morning carrying his bag of oatmeal to feed himself for the week. He may have, but if he did, it was because the family was careful and lived frugally.'

William Aitken, indeed, had the best university education Scotland could offer: a four-year arts course, followed by four years of divinity, subsidized by the Church of Scotland, during which he was required to study Latin, Greek, logic, moral philosophy, theology, practical divinity, church history and Hebrew. After rigorous examinations, he was finally licensed in September 1858 to preach the gospel by the presiding minister of the Church of Scotland in the name and by the authority of the Presbytery of Linlithgow. (Silvermine was in the parish of Linlithgow, though the Aitkens worshipped in Torphichen which was much closer.)

He was now twenty-four, and did not find a church for the next six years. Nothing is known of how he earned a living – perhaps as a private tutor, perhaps as a teacher – during that time. At last, on 2 August 1864, the Presbytery of Linlithgow was notified that the General Assembly's Colonial Committee had appointed Mr William Aitken to be minister of the church at Cobourg, a prosperous health resort on the shores of Lake Ontario.

Two weeks later, in St Michael's church in Linlithgow, he delivered the prescribed discourses, read Greek and Hebrew, and was questioned about divinity and church history. The Presbytery then agreed to proceed to his ordination. Having answered further questions satisfactorily, 'he was by solemn prayer and imposition of the hands of the Presbytery set apart to the office of the Holy Ministry'.[4]

Aitken owed his appointment, and Beaverbrook his Canadian origins, to the Great Disruption in the Church of Scotland. The dispute turned on who was to have most say in the appointment of a minister – the congregation or the patrons, usually landlords, whose rights of nomination were protected by statute. In 1843, matters came to a disastrous head when two-fifths of the ministers walked out of the General Assembly in Edinburgh and processed down Hanover Street to Canonmills through cheering crowds to set up the Free Church of Scotland. The split caused depths of bitterness difficult for later generations to appreciate. For a time, the Church of Scotland looked as if it might shrivel to a rump: many of its most active and respected members seceded, and so did a third of its congregations; a Free Church was established on the Aitkens' doorstep, in Torphichen. By the time William Aitken was awaiting a call, the Church of Scotland had become deeply worried by the success of the Free Church in Canada. It therefore offered to subsidize ministers who were prepared to cross the Atlantic. Aitken was one of them.

Like other young men before and since, he was bowled over by his first impressions of the United States; and his reactions were not in the least puritanical. Someone in Boston gave him a bottle of whisky, which he appreciated; his dinner in the hotel was 'sumptuous'; and he was waited on by 'a regiment of the prettiest girls I ever saw . . . as dark as midnight, and fiery as gunpowder. . . . One especially, a very pretty girl – an angel. . . . I fell over head and ears in love with her.'

He soon came down to earth when he reached Cobourg. A long letter of March 1865 to a friend back home described his 'very considerable difficulties'. His predecessor as minister, the congregation and the church trustees had all transferred their allegiance to the Free Church; they 'refused to open the Church for me'. Litigation started. Besides, he could not afford a house or servant, and his lodgings were inadequate. He proposed to bring out his younger sister Ann: 'I can't do without somebody of the female order – it's impossible'. He was offered but declined an alternative post in Peterborough: he did not fancy living 'in the back-woods surrounded by wolves and bears and Indians'.

Luckily his suffering did not last long. Before the year was out, he received and accepted a call from the parish of Vaughan in Maple, Ontario, where he stayed for fifteen years. His great stroke of good fortune was to meet and marry, soon after his move, Jane Noble. She was only eighteen, and at the time of the marriage she looked, as the minister later told one of his sons, 'like a little Dresden doll'. Beaverbrook used to maintain that whereas the dour side of his character came from the Aitkens, it was his Celtic strain, inherited from his Irish mother, that gave him the side that 'gets up and dances'. This mixture, he claimed, was a clue to his character. It was said of the Aitkens that they would not move five miles for £100, provided they could scratch a living where they were; but the Nobles were more enterprising, and Beaverbrook's ruthlessness and acumen seem to have come from that side of the family. His mother's father, Joseph Noble, was a tough, hard Ulsterman of plantation stock. He and his younger brother emigrated from County Tyrone to Ontario in the 1840s, taking their workmen with them. Joseph settled in Maple, which had a large West Highlands population (the church held a service in Gaelic every Sunday afternoon), and his brother founded Nobleton, the next township to the west.

Gradually Joseph bought up most of Maple. He was a rigid Orangeman, with a capacity for whisky and an uncontrollable temper, and family tradition has it that on Orange anniversaries he used to ride a white horse in processions through Toronto and afterwards roam the streets, drunk, looking for Papists to assault. Papists being rare in Toronto, he would attack Protestants instead. This formidable man married into a most respectable family. Sarah Macquarrie was descended from the chiefs of Ulva, off the southern coast of Mull. In 1773, Boswell and Dr Johnson met the chief of the clan on their tour to the Hebrides, and he told them that his family had owned Ulva for nine hundred years; to their surprise, they found him a most polite and civilized gentleman. The Macquarries arrived in Ontario after a Hector Macquarrie and his wife emigrated to the United States in 1802 from the island of Mull; during the War of 1812, like other loyalists, they moved north to Canada, acquiring a farm outside Maple.

Joseph Noble died a rich man, leaving his brother-in-law, Archie Macquarrie, as executor. But Joseph's eldest son Arthur – Beaverbrook's uncle – was a rogue, with a taste for gambling, horses and women. His mother doted on him; when Archie told her that her son was robbing the estate she refused to believe him, and Archie resigned. Arthur went from bad to worse. Ann Aitken had come out from Scotland to look after the minister, and Arthur married her. He transmitted to her the venereal disease from which he himself died a few years afterwards.[5]

This family scandal was accompanied by a family tragedy. Jane Noble and William Aitken were married in 1867. In all they were to have ten children, five of whom arrived in Maple. Max was the fifth, born on 25 May 1879. An older child, Katie, died of diphtheria at the age of six. It was the combination of her death and the scandal of Arthur Noble that made the Aitkens decide to move right away from Maple. In his memoirs, Beaverbrook refers to his maternal grandfather only as 'a prosperous storekeeper and farmer', and not at all to the Macquarries, his Aunt Ann or his Uncle Arthur.

HIS FATHER AND MOTHER

Ten months after Max was born, his father received the call from Newcastle. Here was the event that gave Beaverbrook's life its most consistent thread. Newcastle is in northern New Brunswick, and New Brunswick is one of the Maritime Provinces, so called because they border the Gulf of St Lawrence on the Atlantic. The geography of the Maritimes, jutting out from the extreme north-east of the continent, makes them almost an appendage of Canada, divided from the rest of the country by the mighty St Lawrence river. They have not had much to boast about – no Rocky Mountains or wheat belt – and have depended on logging and fish. So they have never been rich. A ditty about the Jones Boys, who work all night and work all day but still can't make that sawmill pay, was a feature of Beaverbrook's lifelong repertoire. The skies are enormous, and the winters hard and long, until in May the days become blue and clear and the region wakes up for the brilliant summer and fall. Two facts about the Maritimes shaped Beaverbrook's outlook and career. They looked naturally to the old country. Their ports were the focus for transatlantic shipping: Halifax to Liverpool was one of the great sea routes, the shortest link between the Old World and the New. The British Navy had a base in Halifax, which was also the site of the British Army's North American garrison. The other fact, particularly worrying in New Brunswick, which shares a long border with the state of Maine, was the growing industrial power of the giant to the south. The last thing the Maritimes wanted, having wrested the region from the French, was to lose their independence to the Americans. Soldiers from the Maritimes formed part of the Canadian force that inflicted the first defeat on the American armed forces in the War of 1812, and burned Washington.

Thereafter Canada's main external problem was to protect herself against the southern juggernaut. Maps of the North American railway systems in the late nineteenth century vividly make the point: the American lines reach up like greedy fingers to the Canadian border, where they have been stopped; then from east to west, not up and down, stretches the Canadian Pacific Railway (completed when Beaverbrook was six), a deliberate attempt to direct trade towards the British Isles and away from the United States. Trade barriers and tariff walls were part of the Canadian way of life. For over a century, encompassing Beaverbrook's whole career, the argument that preoccupied Canada was whether a Free Trade agreement with the United States – also known as 'reciprocity' – would enlarge Canada's wealth by bringing in American capital, or whether it would smother Canada's infant industries and threaten Canadian culture and nationhood.

The move from Maple to Newcastle was, for William Aitken, a considerable step up. Newcastle by 1880 had become the centre of Presbyterianism to the north of the important Miramichi river, and St James church was one of the best-endowed in New Brunswick. Competition from would-be ministers was strong. Candidates who had 'presented' themselves were invited to conduct divine service on different Sundays; then the members of the congregation who had 'heard' them, women as well as men, voted by writing on a slip of paper their own name and that of their preferred minister. William Aitken swept in with an unusually large majority: 129 votes for him and only 10 for all the other candidates together. The post carried an annual salary of $1200, a free house and the use of the Glebe Lot, a piece of land given to the church by a local businessman originally from Edinburgh.[6] The Glebe Lot became the site of the Sinclair ice rink, built by Lord Beaverbrook.

Newcastle is remote even today. In 1880 it was little more than a frontier settlement, the population mainly Scots and Irish, with a scattering of French and Indians. Even in the early years of this century the Aitken family used to talk about 'going down to Canada' when they went to Montreal. The surrounding country is very heavily forested and flat, and the Miramichi, the cause of the town's existence, is big and broad, deep enough for freighters to dock near the middle of the town and so convey a sense of the inhospitable North Atlantic lying just over the horizon. While Beaverbrook was growing up, down the river every spring came the thousands of logs that had been cut and stacked on its banks in the winter months. On the town's edge today is the world's largest pulp and coated-paper mill.

Although the Aitkens arrived in Newcastle a century after its foundation they soon acquired close links with its history, especially through the Davidson family. The founding father of Newcastle was an adventurous fisherman from Inverness, William Davidson. Apart from isolated groups of Indians, the first settlers along the Miramichi were French. In 1690 an English fleet from Boston conquered Acadia, now Nova Scotia, thus beginning the long struggle between Britain and France for control of the continent that ended only in 1763. Victorious, and seeking to consolidate their hold, the British government quickly instituted a scheme to settle English-speaking Protestants on land from which the French, mainly Roman Catholics, had been expelled, in some cases brutally, during the wars. This colonization policy formed the character of the region: predominantly Scottish, Protestant, anti-French and patriotic. The alert Davidson saw his chance; two years after the peace, out from Scotland to look for opportunities, he found a likely spot on the Miramichi for a salmon-fishing industry and applied successfully to the British government for a grant of 100,000 acres. He was probably the first English-speaking settler on the river. His deed included the proviso that '25,000 acres each year for the first four years be settled in the proportion of one Protestant person for every 200 acres'.[7]

Davidson recruited settlers from his native land, who would also help him run the salmon-fishing business. He exported Miramichi salmon to the West Indies; and on the return voyage the ships carried sugar, molasses and rum to the settlements on the Miramichi. When the scattered early Presbyterian congregations in New Brunswick took picnics to church to fortify themselves in the lunch interval between the first and second parts of the service, they often included jugs of West Indian rum. Besides salmon, Davidson saw the possibilities in lumber; he supplied spars to the Royal Navy, and pioneered the replacement of the huge old six- or eight-foot saws, worked by hand, with power-driven sawmills. When Newcastle was founded in 1790, the site chosen for the first courthouse and gaol was occupied by two cabins owned by Davidson. That is the site now called Beaverbrook Square.

Davidson's descendants became pillars of St James church; his grandson, a capable lawyer, became the Reverend William Aitken's closest friend. When Davidson died, Aitken delivered a eulogy that struck those present as unusually emotional for so reserved a man. The founding father was buried not in Newcastle but at Wilson's Point (named after yet another Scotsman, from Orkney), where two branches of the Miramichi meet. Wilson's Point was bought by Beaverbrook after the Second World War and presented to the province as a park.

Beaverbrook knew the history of all the makers of New Brunswick and came to regard himself as their successor. It is not surprising that his particular hero was Peter Mitchell, born in Newcastle in 1824, who became premier of New Brunswick and a father of Canadian confederation: 'a rough, blunt, and daring man'. As an entrepreneur, he built up a large shipbuilding business; and he owned and edited a newspaper, the *Montreal Herald*. As a politician, he was a patriot with a vision of Canada's promise. As an orator, he was unrivalled. He died in 1899 in the Windsor

Hotel in Montreal, and although he did not share his wife's enthusiasm for the temperance cause and was notoriously unfaithful to her (an illegitimate son discovered only at the age of twenty-one that Mitchell was his father) he was buried in the cemetery of St James church, of which he had been a trustee, by the Reverend William Aitken.[8] Max Aitken was then twenty. The inscription on the stone monument that Beaverbrook erected to his memory in Beaverbrook Square has a Beaverbrookian ring: 'Timber Merchant, Shipbuilder, Orator, and Statesman, he gave vigorous leadership to the public and commercial life of his Country'.

It was another substantial shipbuilder who built Max's boyhood home, the house that William Aitken and his family moved into in 1880. It was only three years old when the shipbuilder sold it to the congregation of St James, and sufficiently prominent to be singled out and depicted in the corner of a contemporary map of Newcastle. Now known as the Old Manse, it is still one of the largest houses in the district, in the best part of town, standing on a ridge and, with its mansard roof, looking much more French than English. The largest room in the Aitkens' day was the double parlour on the ground floor, comfortably furnished by the Aitkens at their own expense with flowered wallpaper and portraits. The smallest was the bedroom that Max shared with one of his brothers on the top floor, with a view down towards the port and the sailing ships trading with the West Indies. At the back of the house was a barn: like all Newcastle families, the Aitkens kept livestock. Unlike many other families, they employed servants inside and out. All in all, the manse was a spacious, solid, comfortable family home.

Newcastle has grown sideways rather than upwards, and church spires still dominate the skyline. St James church, five minutes' walk from the manse, remains one of the prettiest examples of colonial architecture, white and elegant, in New Brunswick. It was opened in 1828 to replace an earlier church destroyed by fire, a constant hazard in these parts, and although the original box pews and inside gallery have disappeared, the finely proportioned entrance and spire survive unchanged.[9]

More of Max Aitken's childhood than he would have wished was spent inside this building. His father made him pump the organ by hand during services, which was hard work. That organ, the second one used in St James church – until 1872 Presbyterians frowned on organs as 'carnal' – is now in retirement at a church in Black River. Its successor was a grander instrument, a Casavant pipe organ given by Beaverbrook at a cost of $6000 and bearing a brass plaque with the inscription: 'IN MEMORY OF THE REV. WILLIAM AITKEN. For twenty three years Minister of this Church. I give thy voice to speak now his is still. Beaverbrook, Nov. 1919'. (He cribbed the 'I give' quotation from Blenheim Palace.) Later, Beaverbrook paid for the organ to be fitted with an electro-pneumatic action. He never forgot his servitude. When he gave the church eleven new bells (the largest bell bears the same quotation from Blenheim as the himself selected the cylinders containing the hymn tunes played by the bells. He told the Reverend D. F. Hoddinott, one of his father's successors, that he especially wanted the tune of 'Art thou weary, heavy-laden?' The hymn represented, he said, his physical state as pumpboy during his father's ministry.

For Beaverbrook, even more than for most men, the relationship with his father, and what his father stood for dominated his life. Mr Hoddinott wrote of Beaverbrook in 1978: 'Some years before his death he asked [me] to accompany him to Saint James church. As we sat in that beautiful and historic edifice he talked freely of his father and spoke with animation concerning his reading of the scriptures and his preaching. In the course of the conversation he remarked: "When my father stood up to read the scriptures and to preach it was as if God Almighty was speaking." '[10]

The Reverend William Aitken certainly looked the part, with his grim expression and long, beautifully brushed white beard. His appearance proclaimed his respect for his calling; years later, members of the congregation remembered that he would dress with care not only for services but also when he went to call on parishioners; they particularly recalled his black gloves. After William retired, when he was on holiday in Florida at his son's expense, Max suggested that he should have his portrait painted; he replied solemnly that 'having spent a long life in the laborious efforts to extend the kingdom of Christ, I should deem it essential, if my appearance is to be perpetuated, it must be in my official costume in my robes of office'; and he had neither gown nor bands nor cassock with him.

His congregation found him reserved, but he was well respected, especially for his sermons – eloquent performances lasting more than half an hour and delivered, as required by the Presbyterian Church, which prided itself on this difference from the Church of England, without notes. Sometimes he preached anti-Catholic sermons; sometimes he mocked the Baptist doctrine of total submersion. Once, in his fervour, he beat the sides of his pulpit with such emphasis that a section fell off. 'He preached hell and damnation with a Calvinistic fervour,' a parishioner remembered.[11] Yet he was unusually ecumenically-minded at a time when the various churches were fiercely competitive, and often swopped pulpits with the Methodists. His accent was distinctly Scottish: 'Very guid', he would say, and roll his 'r's when he said 'prayer'.[12]

At home with his family he was much less stern and unforgiving than he was in his sermons. 'He was a dreamer,' said Jean McLintock, a grand-daughter who was brought up by him and his wife. He was not ambitious. Much of his leisure he spent in his study with his books – he read both Latin and Greek for pleasure – and his pipe; neighbours often noticed his lamp burning late at night. Orthodox Presbyterian standards were maintained in the manse: prayers before and after meals; church every Sunday; no card games. But he did not oppress the children. 'Ha, ha! little girls!' he would exclaim in a 'rather preoccupied way' when he encountered them, sometimes handing out peppermints kept in his pocket. He did not object to cards in other people's houses. He was indulgent towards dancing. He played chess, pressing his reluctant eldest son, Traven, to take him on when he was only seven or eight; more surprisingly, he played with the local Roman Catholic priest, Father Patrick Dixon. And he rarely scolded the children: 'Tut, tut, tut, tut,' he would say. The family called him 'papa', with the accent on the second syllable.

'Mama', also with the accent on the second syllable, was 'the stronger character', Jean McLintock considered. Beaverbrook said he never noticed 'any evidence of warmth' between his parents, though he could not remember any quarrels either; his mother always called his father 'Mr Aitken'. The marriage may have been undemonstrative, but it is clear that Jane Aitken was devoted to her husband, as he was to her. She survived him by fourteen years and wore widow's weeds until she died at the age of seventy-eight. As the wife of the minister of St James she was automatically one of the town's leading citizens, and she played her full part, arranging sewing parties at the manse, giving tea parties on the lawn in summer, and organizing dances in the double parlour. She was a good cook. Everyone who knew her regarded her as a highly efficient manager, running the house and family, ambitious for her children and standing no nonsense from the congregation. Her response to whispered disapproval about dancing in the manse was to hold a special dance and send out printed invitations. After her husband retired they were very short of money, but as her eldest daughter, Rahno, testified she never complained.

BOYHOOD

'Life', Beaverbrook wrote lugubriously in his old age,

> was rough in New Brunswick in the last quarter of the last century. In the towns of the Province there was no electric light. The telephone was still a rare and novel instrument. There were no lavatories. There was no sewage system. Drinking water had to be brought from the well. For fuel we depended on birch logs from the forest. Thus it was that the pump and the hand-saw were the portion of every boy in the Province, and many of a girl as well. The Church Services, Sunday School, and other church activities provided most of the social life of the community.

His tribulations with the organ were no doubt real. But his stories about having to look after the family cow and 'most reluctantly' to hoe the weeds 'on many a summer evening' were exaggerated, and so were his accounts of the family's poverty. Jean McLintock, who was very fond of her Uncle Max, described as 'preposterous' the stories he used to tell her about going to school barefoot because the family was so poor; to prove her point, she produced a photograph showing him, as a boy, in a velvet suit. She also inherited a diary kept by her Aunt Rahno, Max's eldest sister. Rahno spent six years at school and university in Edinburgh and in 1896 went back to Scotland with her father for his health, which again suggests that the family when hardly poverty-stricken. Beaverbrook modified the shoes story when he came to write about his early days, saying that he went shoeless for comfort.

'I was a conspicuously naughty and idle boy,' he wrote. There, he was accurate. All his life he liked to stir up trouble. He always looked mischievous, with his big head and mouth and his wide, wicked-looking grin. Asked once why he had fought another boy, he said, 'He called me "moccasin-mouth".' A Newcastle tradesman remembered walking behind Max and a group of his friends and overhearing them discuss the power of God. One of them said to Max: 'He couldn't make your mouth any bigger without removing your ears.' The boy was usually dishevelled, his light-coloured hair seldom combed or cut. He would never, a contemporary complained, 'polish himself up'.

His school, Harkins Academy, was the church's school. It was open to all, and supplied an orthodox education which included Latin. 'It was a good form of education,' Beaverbrook wrote, 'surpassing that given at public schools (Eton, etc.) in England. There was free contact with every class in the community. That was very valuable. It gave the child a wider knowledge of human nature, a better understanding of the rules of the game, and a deeper sympathy with the disabilities and misfortunes of his neighbours.' He may have learnt 'the rules of the game' at Harkins, but he learned little else. The school's register of attendance shows that 'W. Max Aitken' (who later appears as 'Maxie Aitken'), aged thirteen, was 'tardy' twenty-one times during the first term of 1893. Nobody else, out of forty-six pupils, had anything like such a bad record; the nearest contender was 'tardy' only eleven times.[13]

His first principal, Dr Philip Cox, later a professor of biology at the University of New Brunswick, remembered him as 'bright and interesting, of a quick, nervous turn of mind. . . . He was not regarded as a clever student, but only as a fair average, though unquestionably he possessed a marked talent for mathematics.' Mathematics was the only subject on which Max seemed able or willing to concentrate. 'He impressed me as being an absent-minded boy, as if he was always thinking of something beyond the confines of the classroom, perhaps of the next prank.' Cox remembered Max devising a new, improved version of 'the ordinary pin trap', whereby a pin was held in position by a piece of cork and placed on a bench for someone to sit on. This was often spotted, so Max invented a method of bending the pin 'in such a way that it could be placed on the seat with the point upwards and not be seen. It proved very successful.' His victims were 'invariably the dull, more studious pupils who were not inclined to enter into the conspiracies against the teachers'.

As he grew older, he became more idle. Cox's successor was Dr F. P. Yortson.

I tried every method of persuasion to induce him to learn his lessons, or at least to pay ordinary attention to his work, but without any success whatever . . . I punished him [slapping him on the hand with a leather strap] because day after day he came not knowing his lessons. Not only that: he would deliberately refuse to do the ordinary work of the school. I would say to the class that I wanted them to do such and such a problem. . . . Max would promptly fold his arms, sit back and not raise his pencil.

The young Max was not, however, entirely without intellectual interests – or so he claimed: at the manse, in a lair constructed out of the woodpile in the cellar, next to the furnace (he seems to have felt the cold), he read Scott, Thackeray and Stevenson – 'in limited measure' – but not Dickens, whom he 'could not abide', then or later. Apart from the mathematics, the single time he impressed any of his teachers was when he turned in an essay on Warren Hastings that astonished, by its literary talent, both Dr Yortson and the Reverend William Aitken. Yortson thought it a 'masterpiece' for a sixteen-year-old.[14]

Max was as difficult at home as he was at school. He misbehaved in church, sometimes sitting in the gallery (with a 'coloured boy') instead of the family pew, and falling asleep when he was supposed to be pumping the organ. Once he ran away, and was discovered hiding in the woods. When the Christian Temperance Union – the temperance 'fanatics', he called them – met in the Temperance Hall on freezing winter nights, he used to creep in and secretly turn off the gas heating. When he threw stones at one of the sisters in the Catholic convent next door to the manse, his mother spanked him in front of them.

He spent little time with his father, and his mother was a busy woman. Young Max, in the middle of the family, was often bored, and conscious that other families – particularly the Corbetts who lived across the road – were less severely disciplined than the Aitken children. 'This family was most attractive in its domestic relations,' he recalled sixty years on. Mrs Corbett protected and comforted him when he was in trouble, and he stayed the night with the Corbetts when he deemed it prudent not to go home; besides, Mrs Corbett was more generous with the butter than Mrs Aitken. (Out of the blue, in 1929, his boyhood friend Will Corbett had a cable from Max 'saying that he was making me an annuity of a thousand dollars a year for the rest of my life; was I ever surprised, and glad of that gift!')

He puzzled and sometimes annoyed his elder brothers and sisters; Rahno was once so angry with him that she threw him downstairs. Misapprehensions between them evidently persisted until olive branches were exchanged in 1904, when Rahno – by then a hospital superintendent in Montreal – wrote to tell him: 'Like many others I have never understood you altho, dear boy I have tried to . . . since you were a little chap I had the idea that I was the sister you had no use for – if I can ever make up to you for the past please let me do so. You can understand it's hard for

23

me to write this letter it would be ten times harder to say.'[15] His younger brother described him as 'a fiend to live with'. A neighbour remembered that Max was 'often a trouble to his mother, who took a stick to him frequently'; she saw him quite often sobbing after being punished by his mother, his hand in front of his face.[16] From his other-worldly, gentle father Max inherited a never entirely suppressed apprehension that he might one day have to account to a higher power. His mother's legacy is less easily discerned, although it was in part physical: like his sister Rahno, he was to inherit her asthma. It is tempting to suppose, besides, that his later relations with women were affected by an instinctive determination never to allow them his mother's power to hurt or humiliate him, in public or in private.

Max was not merely naughty; he was also sensitive, nervous and volatile. He suffered, he said, from an 'anxiety complex'. Rahno was engaged to a Newcastle youth who died suddenly. The young Max was 'terrified', but his mother, herself 'in grief and misery', did not 'give any attention to my panic'. Max became subject 'often and again' to 'unreasoning fear'. The funerals of Newcastle children 'brought on tempests of despair in my tortured brain'. His father conducted the services, and Max was often called on to act as pallbearer.

> At the graveside I had much difficulty in suppressing a sense of panic bordering on hysteria, and my relief was brief when we returned from the churchyard. We pallbearers usually wore white cotton gloves, served out by Colonel Maltby, the undertaker. These mementos of gloom I carried home and hid in a little loft over the wing of our house. One day I collected the set of gloves and burned them in a frying pan in the barn loft, at the risk of setting the whole place on fire.

A marked preoccupation with illness and death remained with him.

Another trait showed itself early: he was exceptionally observant, especially of weakness. Dr Yortson sounds as if he was haunted for life by his memory of the 'small, white-faced little boy sitting in the front row on the left hand side of the top desk'. This description was given exactly sixty years later.

> He never took his eyes off me. Every movement of mine was recorded and his impressions transmitted to the rest of the school by winks, whispers or gestures. . . . He seemed to have the most diabolical ingenuity in knowing exactly the thing to do or say that would annoy me most. . . . He simply had me sized up so accurately that he knew exactly every weak point in my character. . . . I had a bad habit of gritting my teeth when I was annoyed. He spotted this at once and would imitate the gesture every time I looked at him. At that time moustaches were just becoming fashionable and I was beginning to grow one. Every morning when I came into school and stood before my desk Max would promptly telegraph to the rest of the school how

many more hairs I had grown during the night. He did this by signals on his fingers when he thought I was not looking his way.

Max felt, he said later, unappreciated. His parents and teachers did not understand his restlessness; their moral standards were too high, their discipline too severe. Few of them spotted the lad who, through sheer application and hard work as well as ingenuity, would make a fortune in the decade after he left school. Father Dixon, the Catholic priest who played chess with his father, saw his promise, but Cox and Yortson did not. Yet the evidence was there, if his elders had considered what he was up to – not at home or in school, but 'on the streets', as he put it. He was a champion at guessing games with marbles that involved bluff. He was always on the lookout for ways of making money and showed a 'premature capacity for snatching at the main chance'. He hung about the house of a Mr Call at mail times, to take his letters to the post (five cents). He searched for and destroyed potato bugs (two cents per can). He kept hens in the manse barn and sold the eggs. He acquired a newspaper round, delivering and selling the two newspapers published two hundred miles away in St John – Newcastle was too small to have its own daily paper. Then he became the St John *Daily Sun*'s Newcastle correspondent, paid a dollar a column. Next he became the *Sun*'s salesman of subscriptions in the Newcastle area, and was announced in the paper as such on 21 October 1893. He was fourteen. He sold his first subscription to Dr Yortson for $3. He was supposed to keep a dollar as commission and send the other $2 to the *Sun*, but Yortson learned later that he held the money back, and other subscriptions as well, because he had not been paid for his news items. The paper tried to collect its money from his father, claiming that he was legally responsible for his son's debts; but Max possessed a letter from the editor saying that they would pay him for contributions at the regular rates, which they had failed to do. So he paid himself out of the subscriptions he had solicited and collected, and learned early on that keeping pieces of paper was an important element of the art of self-defence.

Had he not been driven by the urgent need for money he would probably, he thought later, have gone straight into journalism; but the prospects in New Brunswick were 'less than nothing'. While working for the *Daily Sun* he started and ran a school newspaper, the *Leader*, which sold for a cent and was abruptly shut down when the Reverend William Aitken discovered his son desecrating the Sabbath by working on it at 2 a.m. one Sunday morning. The *Leader* could be sharp: 'There is in Grade 8 a little cur who cannot take a hint. He is becoming a nuisance to one and all.' During the paper's brief life, the boy who helped to distribute the first issue was lucky enough to be tipped 25 cents by a customer. Max, who found no such customer on his route, decided that it would be a good idea to switch routes to distribute the second issue. One further glimpse of the young Max's pride and anxiety about money comes from a contemporary who remembered him falling over while skating and being helped up and brushed down by a woman; Max felt he should reward her, but only had two cents; he gave them to her with the promise, 'When I get rich I'll give you more!'[17]

His father was one of those who did not recognize his talents. A dignified figure himself, William Aitken did not approve of his son selling newspapers. Max used to rush into a shop and duck down with a big bundle of papers under his arm if he saw his father coming. When Max ran away, it was his father who came to bring him home. When he stayed with the Corbetts it was his father who would come over and ask Will (in a kindly way) if he had seen 'that scoundrel son of mine'. Dr Yortson reported that at the time of the Warren Hastings essay Max's father was 'almost in despair' about his son's lack of application and indiscipline. The other children were all heading for or at universities, but Max was the odd one out; he alone was not university material. He left high school early. Aged sixteen, he sat the entrance exam for Dalhousie University in Halifax, where his eldest brother Traven – considered the brilliant one – had read law. According to Max's own account, he did well for the first two days but on the third, which was Greek and Latin, his 'hostility to these dead languages' overwhelmed him and he sent back the paper with a message to the examiners saying he did not want a university career after all since it 'involved unnecessary and even useless labour in futile educational pursuits'. But he held it against Dalhousie that it had refused him admittance, which was one reason why in later life he helped to build up the University of New Brunswick as a rival; had he deliberately sabotaged his chances, he would have had no cause for resentment. If he did behave as he claimed, he was committing the most fundamental act of rebellion thus far against his parents: defiance of his mother, who sought a good education for all her children, as well as of his father, the Greek and Latin scholar. His patient father next tried to persuade him to become a bank clerk with the Bank of Nova Scotia, but Max, using tactics of passive resistance, refused. Instead, he took a humiliating job in Newcastle as an assistant in Mr E. Lee Street's drugstore. His wage was $1 a week, and he spent much of his time washing empty bottles. A contemporary remembered how Max found some old bottles of lotion abandoned in the basement. He polished them up, affixed new labels and sold them.[18]

This was the lowest point of his youth. A rigorous Presbyterian upbringing lays fearful emphasis on the commandment 'to honour thy father and thy mother that thy days may be long upon the land which the Lord thy God giveth thee', and by its 'implicit threat that lack of respect for one's parents could lead to a short life'.[19] He had been named William after his father; Maxwell was his second name. But by the time he failed to get into Dalhousie and returned to Newcastle to 'another cycle of disgrace with criticism' he knew that he had inherited none of his father's characteristics and had brought him only worry and disappointment. Max grew up imprinted with his father's hellfire message, but temperamentally incapable of living by his father's rules and standards. He respected education and books – and took pride later in his father's learning – but as an adolescent was too impatient to benefit from them. At the age of sixteen, escape from the drugstore, and no doubt from the limitations of the manse and the town as well, 'became an obsession'.

BOWLING ALLEY AND BROTHEL

He bought his freedom by borrowing money from a local lumberman, Edward Sinclair. His new idea was to turn himself into a lawyer by becoming articled to a rising barrister, nine years older than himself, whom he had met on a Miramichi steamboat. This was Richard Bedford Bennett, later Prime Minister of Canada. To the young Max, Bennett was a hero, perhaps because he was Max's exact opposite: tall, slight, freckled, austere, forbidding, parsimonious and tight-fisted; a deeply religious and belligerent Methodist who taught at Sunday School, always carried a Bible, and deplored card games, dancing, smoking and drinking.

His air of self-confidence and aura of future eminence were infectious, and in November 1895 Max followed him across the river to Chatham, a little town of a few hundred people where Bennett worked in the law office of L. J. Tweedie. The building survives: a modest wooden house in the main street backing almost on to the river. A plaque (unveiled by Beaverbrook) reads: 'In This Building Richard Bedford Bennett First Viscount Bennett And William Maxwell Aitken First Baron Beaverbrook Were Articled With The Hon. L. J. Tweedie LL. D. For the Study of Law. Erected by the Citizens of Chatham'. The plaque might have added that Lemuel J. Tweedie rose to be Lieutenant Governor and then Premier of New Brunswick. He came from a prominent family of politicians and clergymen. His cousin of a younger generation, R. A. Tweedie, worked as a private secretary to successive premiers of New Brunswick and, after the Second World War, for Beaverbrook. He once asked Beaverbrook what sort of man L. J. Tweedie was. 'Very vain,' Beaverbrook replied; he required a lot of attention and service which kept the young Max constantly on the hop. 'I made up my mind,' Beaverbrook continued, 'that one day I would have me a Tweedie of my own to bounce around, and that is why I have you.' Of this chilling remark R. A. Tweedie says: 'There was more truth than poetry in that observation.'[20]

In Chatham, Max lived in a hotel called the Adams House, where he met a lively clerk, H. E. Borradaile, who worked for the Bank of Montreal next door. Borradaile was twenty-one and started by patronizing the sixteen-year-old, but he soon learned better. Both felt oppressed by poverty, and Borradaile became aware, through the bank, that the main lumber companies of the region bought large quantities of beans and tinned meats from Armour in Chicago, dealing direct with Armour's head office 1200 miles away. He mentioned this fact to Max, who at once spotted an opportunity for a Canadian middleman. He got Borradaile to write to Armour, on Bank of Montreal writing paper, suggesting that their business could be expanded if they appointed Canadian agents who knew the local market to act for them in the whole of New Brunswick. To Borradaile's surprise, Armour agreed. Borradaile wrote out his resignation from the bank, and he and Max prepared to go into business together as Borradaile & Aitken. Drawing up partnership papers, however, 'we were almost at once at loggerheads, and the first and only row I had with Max ended by my tearing up my resignation – and that was that'. This was not the last time that an Aitken business associate complained that Max wanted too large a slice of the cake.

Years later Borradaile lunched with L. J. Tweedie at the Savoy Hotel in London. Tweedie told him: 'You know, Borradaile, if you and Max had gone on with that partnership you would have owned, not Chatham, but the whole of New Brunswick! Do you know that after he had been in my office for a month I was not sure whether he was working for me or I for him.'

Borradaile had another memory of Max in Chatham:

> In the coldest part of winter the river froze over to a depth of three or four feet, and in the spring when the ice was breaking up provided an awe-inspiring sight. It travelled at about the rate of the hour-hand of a watch and as it moved out to the mouth of the river huge blocks of ice piled up slowly but relentlessly along the shore, making a queer noise and sweeping all before it. Once, as Max and I were watching, it took a huge fir tree that was growing by the shore as if it were a tiny fern and tossed it roots and all on to the heap of ice ever moving on and on. Max turned to me and said, 'If I could harness that power, there would be nothing I could not do.'[21]

Courage, restlessness and untiring energy were the qualities of Max in his teens. On the side, he became the local correspondent for the *Montreal Star* and an agent for the Great West Life Insurance Company – 'in this I was of great help', Borradaile recalled, 'as the Bank of Montreal clerks were little tin gods in these small towns and my recommendation carried weight'. This was Aitken's first experience of selling insurance. He was also collecting debts for a Newcastle doctor: on 30 November 1896 he wrote to tell him that he had collected one debt of $1.50. Fifty cents were due for costs, and 10 cents for commission, which meant '60 cents for me and 90 cents for you. How is that for a start as a lawyer. Hold the funds Dr and I will make a haul from you when I go up.' Max enjoyed being a dun. 'Send me that bill against R. W. McL. I would like to collect it. Also some more bills. Has Johnston paid up yet? If not I will draw up some bogus papers and scare the life from him.'[22]

He was too bumptious for some. The young men in Chatham had their social centre, the Cypress Club, which Aitken tried to join. Disliking his 'forward manner' and 'everlasting push', a majority voted against him. Then a friend, Albert McClellan, became club president, and promised his fellow members, who warned him that Max would want to run things, that he would keep him in hand. However, Aitken had scarcely joined when he decided the club needed a newspaper rack, ordered one from St John, and presented the club with a bill for $6. Friends and enemies alike complained, whereat Max said he would pay the bill himself. Resentment turned miraculously to approbation: it was an example of what largesse could do. McClellan said later he never found out where Max got the $6: 'the poor little beggar hadn't a damn cent'. His salary was very small, and he had no help from home.[23]

When he grew rich, he used to bore his guests by showing them time after time the film *Destry Rides Again*, in which Marlene Dietrich sits on the bar of a Wild West saloon in net stockings and sings about 'the boys in the back room'. The Adams House had a Back Room. Admission to this select group was not by vote, but by the key and whim of the room clerk. It sounds livelier than the Cypress Club. One fellow guest, a Miramichi lumberman, had had a thumb cut off by a buzz saw. Early every morning, rubbing his stump, he would start the day in the Back Room by mixing himself an eye-opener of sugar, enough hot water to melt the sugar, Angostura bitters and De Kuyper gin. In the summer, the boys in the Back Room would hire a horse and buggy and drive off to country dances, called 'Bonnet Hops', having learnt their whereabouts from 'the village fiddler'. They went uninvited, but 'the lumberjacks were always glad to see us . . . for we went well supplied with refreshments from the little Back Room'. It was all very different from life at the manse in Newcastle. The wider world of Chatham was not very wide, but it was Max's first taste of freedom.

It also gave him his first experience of politics, when he persuaded a hesitant Bennett to stand for election as a Chatham alderman. He next coaxed his friend J. L. Stewart, the proprietor of the *Chatham World*, into printing election leaflets. Then he borrowed Bennett's bicycle and toured the town delivering the leaflets. Bennett won, by a single vote, and Max took the credit; but the new alderman was not pleased when he became aware that his seventeen-year-old campaign manager had made all kinds of unauthorized promises on his behalf.

Before long, Bennett decided that Chatham was too small for him and took a job in a law firm in Calgary, Alberta, two thousand miles to the west. Max assumed that he would now move from his own little office at the back of the wooden building to Bennett's room at the front, with the expectation of a partnership. He imagined a new nameplate, 'Tweedie & Aitken', on the office door. Instead, Tweedie passed him over in favour of another would-be lawyer from Newcastle, Charlie Mitchell, the nephew of New Brunswick's former Premier and a university graduate. That was the end of Max's hopes in Chatham. He felt the humiliation all the more sharply because his supplanter came from his home town. 'Misery and despair overwhelmed me.'

But he persisted with his idea of becoming a lawyer. Since leaving school, though careless of his popularity with contemporaries, he had begun to see the sense of cultivating well-placed elders. He now turned to a county court judge, who advised him to make a change. Max thereupon wrote to a lawyer, John Montgomery, in St John, a much bigger and more important commercial centre than Chatham, who wrote back to say there would 'not be the slightest difficulty in the world in getting into a Saint John law firm', but, he added in a disheartening postscript, 'as a rule Law Students in this City receive no pay'; they might make $2 or $3 a week typing, or writing law reports for the newpapers, but 'I suppose you would want pay enough to cover your board and this is where the difficulty comes in'.[24] Max took a chance. He scraped up the train fare to St John, taking his few possessions and his one suit with him, and settled down at a desk in the genial Montgomery's office. There was not enough work for Montgomery, let alone Max, and although he registered at the Law School and even attended lectures, his legal career made little progress. Instead, he spent much of his energy paying for his board by selling insurance – fire, accident, anything he could get hold of. His morale remained low. The size and bustle of St John excited him, with its 'exceedingly bright lights' and the 'great plate glass windows with the rich display of goods', but he was always broke, often lunching off a single apple, and he was homesick and lonely, making no friends among the young.

One older friend he did have, a marine insurance agent. Every winter in St John was enlivened by a big night of merry-making known as the Assembly, a grand ball to which all the gilded youth of the city were invited. Max had no social connections, but his friend said he would put his name forward for an invitation. Max took waltzing lessons and hired evening dress, but the invitation failed to arrive. All day he waited; his friend had no news. Max got dressed; unable to afford cuff-links, he used safety pins instead. Still the invitation did not come. So Max changed out of his evening dress into his only suit and went out into the streets and walked past the Assembly Hall, hearing the sound of the waltz and meditating on 'my unhappy and wretched loneliness'. Years later, he told the novelist Barbara Cartland that he had not been sent an invitation because the Assembly organizers learned that he had once sold newspapers in the street, and they could not invite newsboys.[25]

Max stayed in St John for six months, and then made up his mind to follow Bennett to Calgary. Bennett had corresponded with the Reverend William Aitken about the idea of sending Max to university to take a proper law course, but Aitken thought – rightly – that the time was past for any such remedy. Max, he wrote to Bennett, had now, at the age of eighteen, 'got a taste for business and a liking for the business intercourse of the world. I believe he could no more set himself down to a course of theoretical study than he could take (or rather think of taking) a journey to the moon.' At college he would only learn 'indolent habits'. The minister nevertheless thanked Bennett warmly for his kind interest in Max, who was always the better for having someone near him to whom he could look with respect and for guidance (another shrewd observation), and wished that Bennett was still in Chatham to impart to his son 'ambitions and energies and moral motives'. But although Max was not university material, wherever he went – to Chatham, to St John, and now to Calgary – he took with him his little bookcase and a handful of books. He remembered that bookcase in his old age, as Citizen Kane remembered his childhood sleigh, Rosebud.

In Calgary he had a second taste of practical politics, more serious than the first, when he helped to run Bennett's 1898 campaign for the Legislative Assembly of the North-West Territories. But despite the opportunities he saw in the expanding West he lacked any set purpose or plan of action: with a friend, he bought (with borrowed money) and sold (at a profit) a bowling alley; he moved to Edmonton and traded in meat (at a loss). In Edmonton, he encountered a man with whom he formed a lifelong association – James Dunn, later a financier and industrialist with a raffish reputation, a baronet and a multi-millionaire. The pair had first met as boys when they explored the beaches of New Brunswick together during summer holidays. Dunn was five years older than Max, but they found a mutual bond in anti-Sabbatarianism. Max's father made them attend his open-air services; and Dunn's mother, a telegraph operator who brought James up when his father died after falling into Bathurst harbour while trying to free a log-jam, was so strict a Presbyterian that she forbade her son even to whittle sticks on Sundays. In Edmonton he was working for a law firm (he had read law at Dalhousie), but had decided he had picked the wrong part of Canada. Montreal, with its banks and brokers, was the city of opportunity. 'The West must pay tribute to the East', he told Max, 'and I'm off to the East where I can collect tribute': a neat and accurate comment on the financial structure of the Canadian economy at the turn of the century, and a perception that helped both men make their fortunes.

They may not have spent all their time in Edmonton discussing economic geography. Rebecca West fell in love with Beaverbrook in the twenties and wrote a novel about it, abandoned and unpublished in her lifetime.[26] In the book, the Beaverbrook character, 'Pitt', tells his lover that 'Sir Jack Murphy' – plainly based on Sir James Dunn – has a hold over him from the past. When 'Pitt' was a young man, out in California, 'they laughed at me because I was so short and such a funny-looking little devil . . . and I wanted money and I wanted drink and I wanted women. I wanted all the things that other men seemed to get for the asking.' A friend left a fur coat with him for safekeeping; desperate for money, he sold it. 'I spent that money giving a grand dinner at the Poodle Dog and having two of the best women in the best whorehouse in the town.' They told him they liked small men. His friend reappeared and charged 'Pitt' with theft. 'Murphy' got him out of gaol.

This passage in West's novel is obviously based on what Beaverbrook told her about his early life. The episode might be a Beaverbrook fantasy embroidered by the novelist; but the young Max was certainly conscious of his size – he was five foot seven inches – and thought himself unattractive, while Dunn was tall, a dandy and in Max's eyes 'exceedingly good-looking'. It is not at all unlikely that in faraway Edmonton, influenced and protected by the older and more worldly-wise Dunn – who had already made one trip to London – young Max discovered for the first time the pleasures of adult bad behaviour.

At all events, Dunn changed Max's mind about the relative advantages of East and West. Dunn went east to Montreal, and Max, having borrowed the train fare from a friendly bank manager, retreated to St John, stopping in Toronto and Montreal to collect insurance agencies before setting up as a full-time insurance agent – the only business he knew. By his own account, during this phase of his life, approaching twenty-one, he did little except waste his time, playing billiards and trying to beat the odds at dice and poker. Then, on his twenty-first birthday, he had what he liked to look back on as his 'conversion'.

CHAPTER 2

THE MONEY SPINNER
1901–1906

TO CELEBRATE his coming of age on 25 May 1900, Max Aitken went on a three-day fishing party with friends and 'an ample supply of whisky'. Among those present, he wrote later, was 'a lad of energetic temperament' from Nova Scotia who had plunged into business in the United States.

> Something in the expatriated lad's manner and way of talking, his delineation of new ideas of effort and achievement set the match to the tow of latent and fiery ambition which must have been present below the threshold in the mind of one of his hearers. The next morning I announced abruptly that I was going back to work and left the party. 'Now farewell horses, dances, songs and delight', sang the gypsy poet. I never loafed again. I seemed to shake off in an hour of reflection the careless habits of my early years . . . the idler became a demonic worker; the spendthrift a rigid economist; the man of casual habits, punctual, exact and unswerving in attention to business.

To illustrate the full extent of this transformation, he said he even gave up poker. 'From the moment of my "Conversion", I laid down my hand at poker and refused to pick it up again' – apart from being briefly tempted on the day of Queen Victoria's funeral, when he found himself marooned in Cape Breton, but 'the cards failed to hold my attention'. When writing the account of his conversion he must have forgotten how much poker he played in 1903, as recorded by him in a surviving diary.[1] Beaverbrook enjoyed drama and liked to see his life marked by dramatic turning points. He used to tell an improbable story about how he was turned from a stupid boy into a clever boy by being run over by a horse-drawn mowing machine; at the age of seventy-five he claimed he still bore the cog marks of its wheel on his ear.

But something undoubtedly happened in his twenty-first year to make him stir himself. His first key decision, which largely determined the direction of his moneymaking, was to move to Halifax: 'following the advice given by Tennyson in The Northern Farmer I decided to "go where money is".' He rented a back room in the Halifax Hotel as a base, and went on the road as an insurance agent and salesman.

It was a good moment in Canadian history to set out to make as much money as possible as quickly as possible, which was Aitken's aim for the next ten years. Canada was booming, and the businessmen of Halifax were becoming more ambitious. With a population in 1901 of 40,832, Halifax owed its importance to its harbour, which is long, narrow and safe: hence the city's role as a military fortress, garrisoned by the British Army until 1906, and its strong connections with the British Isles, cemented by much marrying of Halifax girls to British soldiers and sailors. Hence too its prominence as the leading commercial centre east of Montreal. The port gave birth to the transatlantic shipping business – the most successful Haligonian of all was Samuel Cunard – and it was also, like Newcastle but on a larger scale, the centre of a long-established trade with the West Indies, with the islands exporting sugar and rum, and Canada exporting fish. To service this trade, Halifax banks had established branches in some of the islands, including Cuba and Trinidad. At the time that Aitken rented his back room, the money-men in Halifax had just begun to look south for profits more substantial than could be made from the sale of fish.

Around the turn of the century, Canadians were starting to play a leading part in establishing utilities – telephones, gas, tramways, hydro-electric plants – in Latin America and the Caribbean. American capitalists, who would otherwise have been their competitors, were fully occupied with the modernization of their own exploding cities. Canadian engineering and financial skills were the equal of the Americans', and greatly superior to those of countries further south, where the cities were also beginning to expand. If the Canadians could get into those markets, they could expect higher profits than they could make at home.

The first Canadian venture was the construction in 1897 of a hydro-electric plant to supply light and power to Kingston, Jamaica, and to electrify a tramway there. It was a small project, but successful enough quickly enough to encourage others to take the hint. Stimulated by a restless, grandiose-minded genius of a Yankee engineer named F. S. Pearson, Canadian money also financed an extremely profitable operation that replaced the mule-drawn public transport of Sao Paulo, Brazil, with an electric railway – so profitable indeed that the promoters' main worry was that the Brazilian government would find out how much money they were extracting from the country. That project was largely financed from Toronto. In Halifax the 'men of fortune', as Max Aitken called them, tended to look more favourably on the West Indies than on Latin America. They knew more about the West Indies, for one thing, through their fish trade. For another, instead of having to struggle with a foreign language and erratic Latin American politicians, in the West Indies they could expect to benefit from the local knowledge of the Halifax branch banks and the benevolence of British colonial governors, who could usually be relied on to prefer Canadian developers to Americans.

But where was the risk capital to come from to exploit the new opportunities? The stock exchanges of Montreal and Toronto were small and primitive, of little use as a source of new funds. London had put money into one of F. S. Pearson's biggest schemes, in Rio de Janeiro, but was much less inclined to take a flier on the profitability of tramways in Trinidad being built by a company in Nova Scotia. This is where the young Aitken stepped in; and so did James Dunn and another future multi-millionaire, Izaak Walton Killam – all three of them players in the West Indian fund-raising business that became 'something of a school for budding capitalists'.[2]

After he set up shop in the Halifax Hotel, Aitken met a lawyer who became one of his business allies: W. B. Ross. Just before Aitken's 'conversion', in March 1900 Ross had signed up as a member of the happy syndicate that backed F. S. Pearson's railway in Sao Paulo. Ross now told Aitken about another Pearson project in Brazil. Aitken did his financial homework. Then he applied to a Montreal stockbroker, Burnett & Co., for bonds to sell on commission.

Aitken knew, from his time on the road as an insurance salesman, where the 'pools of money' in the Maritimes were to be found: under the beds of the citizens of Nova Scotia and New Brunswick – the doctors and lawyers and sea captains who had been doing well since the beginning of the Canadian boom. They were a canny group, certainly not gamblers, and most of them had never invested in anything more adventurous than a municipal bond. Good arguments were required to induce them to invest in a faraway place, however attractive the interest rates. All his life Max Aitken could rely on his powers of persuasion. When his targets opened their doors, they found on the doorstep a grinning little figure with a silver tongue that they, like many others later, found hard to resist. Aitken has been called 'the first bond salesman in Canada'. A new business need had called into existence a new profession, and one that precisely suited the talents of its earliest practitioner.

The Aitken masterstroke was to contrive to get in with the dominant Halifax group led by John F. Stairs. The Stairs family, from northern Ireland via Philadelphia, was rich. When one member of the family died, leaving $900,000, Aitken described the estate as 'very big' for Canada. One young Stairs was at New College, Oxford. John F. Stairs, a slight figure with a neat beard, was universally respected and known throughout Atlantic Canada: the dominant figure in the Union Bank of Halifax, the largest ship-chandler in Halifax, and the president of the most important industrial company in the region, Nova Scotia Steel and Coal. He was also a leading local conservative, and strong supporter of the protectionist views of Joseph Chamberlain, the English radical Conservative and prophet of the Empire.

There are two versions of how he and Aitken met. Aitken said they met on a train. Another version says they met when Aitken tried to sell Stairs a typewriter. At all events, the persistent young Max made an impression, as he usually did, and Stairs asked if he would like to work for him. The story was told afterwards by Stairs's grandson.

'What's my first job?'
'Well,' said the old man with a grin on his face, 'I want you to go to Windsor and steal a bank.'
'How?' asked Max in a quiet voice.
'With a velvet glove, my boy, just a velvet glove,' said Mr Stairs.
That night Max dined at the Stairs house, and after dinner they sat talking far into the night. The following day Max set off for Windsor.
The Commercial Bank of Windsor was a very old and small country bank, owned by four or five crusty old men; and the Union Bank had wanted to get control for a long time. Several weeks passed, and eventually Max went back to Halifax with proxies for control. This was his first really important financial success, and many years afterwards he confirmed the essential facts as related above. Stairs rewarded him with his first $10,000, as a fee.[3]

By 1902, Aitken's link with the Stairs group was solidly forged. The circle included B. F. Pearson (not to be confused with the American F. S. Pearson), a company promoter and well-connected lawyer whose law firm employed two young men of outstanding talent, R. E. Harris, who later became Chief Justice of Nova Scotia, and C. H. Cahan, later a member of R. B. Bennett's government in Ottawa. In 1900, these men had started an electricity undertaking in British Guiana, Demerara Electric, and in 1901 had persuaded the governor of Trinidad and the Colonial Office to allow them to do the same in that island. They were also looking at a much more ambitious F. S. Pearson project in Mexico. At first they used Aitken as an odd job man. In May 1902 he was writing to R. E. Harris about amalgamating two pulp mills. Next, the directors of the Munro Wire Works were meeting in his rooms to discuss the year's profits. September was a good month for Aitken. Stairs told him that the 'Scotia' – Nova Scotia Steel and Coal – dividend would be 2½ per cent for the half-year. Next day, Aitken bought Scotia shares. On 13 September he recorded in his diary: 'Met R. E. Harris & E. H. Cahan [sic] and discussed Mexican Water Power. I am to have right to dispose of 85,000 bonds & stock at 95, with 2½ per cent commission to me. After that probably 85,000 on same terms. Will probably make a pot of money on Mexican Light and Power.'
At the time Aitken was gloating over these arrangements, however, the Mexican project was little more than a gleam in F. S. Pearson's eye. His ambition was to harness a spectacular waterfall to a powerhouse that would transmit electricity to Mexico City, a hundred miles away; the scheme envisaged the diversion of a river and the construction of a tunnel through remote and rugged country, quite apart from the need to reach agreement with the Mexican government. He secured an option on the waterpower concession only on 11 March 1902. No work had begun by September.

Mexican Light and Power was not incorporated – by Harris and Cahan – until October. Still, persuading himself that he was going to make 'a pot of money' on what at that stage, and for a long time afterwards, was a purely speculative venture, was no doubt an essential preliminary to marketing the 'stuff' with conviction. 'Stuff' was the disrespectful collective noun applied by Aitken and his associates to the bonds and stock they were selling.

Also in September 1902, Aitken was involved in a plot to take over an insurance company. He wrote to B. Hal Brown of London and Lancashire Life in Montreal: 'I am writing to you today after the most thorough deliberation. I am placing in your hands information with which you could in a word destroy my purposes. My people here have urged me to consider well before writing and this I have done. I depend entirely upon your integrity.' He meant 'lack of integrity', since he wanted Brown to enter an alliance with him while concealing the fact from his employers. The plot was for Canadian interests to 'secure' London and Lancashire. Aitken had arranged the finances, he told Brown, and had obtained a list of the shareholders from London. Two courses of action were possible: to buy up the shares individually and 'secretly'; or to approach the directors and ask them to make a sale. Which was it to be? He reassured Brown about his own job. 'I have always arranged matters with a view to leaving the management in your hands, and, in fact, making you a party to the scheme. . . . We are in your hands . . . but there are some men I trust in every emergency.' Then came a sweetener: 'N. S. Steel at 112 to 113 is a good purchase for probable advance within three or four weeks. This letter is strictly confidential.'[4] The investment tip was a characteristic Aitken touch – good for Brown, and, since a little extra push from Montreal would do no harm to Scotia's price, for Aitken's nine-day-old stake as well. The flattery was also characteristic; he was learning how to make people feel special.

Aitken was behaving with new-found confidence, and not without reason. Stairs, having formed a view, was not easily shifted; and Stairs believed in Aitken. One proof of it came in the winter of 1902, when Stairs and his associates were trying to buy the main lumber business on the Nashwaak and St John rivers, as the first step towards the creation of a big pulp concern. The problem was that the mind of the eighty-two-year-old lumberman who owned the business, Alexander Gibson, was as confused as his debts and finances. The banks were closing in, but Stairs and Harris could get no sense out of him. Finally, having conferred all day with Aitken, they sent him down to Fredericton to see if he could succeed where they had failed. The aged patriarch, with his long white beard and long black shoes, reminded him of Brigham Young and Buffalo Bill. Aitken could not persuade him to relinquish any of his authority, either – instead, he asked Aitken to reorganize the business for him – but it was a complex and important negotiation for an experienced businessman like

Stairs to entrust to a twenty-three-year-old.[5] At last, Aitken had found a fatherly mentor who appreciated his talents.

His real father's powers began to fail just as his son's fortunes began to rise. The congregation of St James reluctantly concluded that their minister was too old and his sermons too repetitive. 'Sermons were produced in an atmosphere of anxiety,' his son wrote. What was worse, the minister began to suffer from aphasia. 'He would be standing in his pulpit delivering his sermon. Suddenly he would find himself at a loss for words. For a full minute he would be unable to utter a syllable. It was distressing for my mother who sat in the Minister's Pew, always upset if an attack developed; and quite happy if the sermon finished with no untoward event.' Finally, the congregation voted at their annual meeting to ask the minister to retire; and he did so, in April 1902.

'ROYAL SECURITIES WAS ME'

It was a great advantage in every way to have Stairs as a patron; even so, Aitken established himself in the business and social circles of Halifax, and contracted fruitful alliances in Toronto and Montreal, with extraordinary speed. 'If London was "The City" of western capitalism at the turn of the century', Christopher Armstrong and H. V. Nelles have written, 'Canada was one of its outlying villages. . . . Despite the growing volume of business, the Canadian financial world remained little more than a village in actual physical size, consisting of a few streets, fifty or so major banks and financial houses, and perhaps no more than forty key individuals.' Eastern Canada dominated the country, and the power centres of eastern Canada were the banks, especially the Bank of Montreal, the insurance companies and the mighty Canadian Pacific Railway. Politicians and businessmen were closely intertwined; the industrialists and financiers, all known to one another, largely wrote their own rules – and the rules were much less strict than those that applied, for instance, in London. 'Those people did things you couldn't even think of doing today,' a director of the Royal Bank of Canada remarked not long ago.

It was a world that the newly ambitious young Aitken was well equipped to infiltrate. Energy, quick wits and confidence were what mattered; and those were his principal qualities. His Scottish ancestry was an asset, too, since many of the key players were Scotsmen.

His diary for 1903 contains brief entries of a life that was gathering pace. 'I am away from Halifax a great deal,' he wrote in January. On 30 September he sailed as a guest of the Royal Navy aboard HMS *Retribution* from Halifax to Boston. He was in New York on 4 and 5 October, then back to Boston on the 6th, and on to Montreal the same day. On the 8th he returned to Boston, and on the 9th he went to New York. On the 11th he was in Toronto. Then back to Montreal, and so on. On Saturdays, he sometimes worked all day. The social round, when he was in Halifax, was intense. He gave dinners at the Halifax Hotel, the City Club and the Halifax Club (3 November: '16 present. Very expensive'). Two colonels and the consul general were among his occasional guests. He took parties to the theatre. He went to the regatta, the opera and, occasionally, to church. He played golf, a lot of bridge – five days out of seven between 6 and 12 September – and a good deal of poker, noting precisely his wins and losses. One evening in March he won $34.75 at poker – a tidy sum.

He entertained his father and his sister Jean when they visited and may not have mentioned the poker. His father after he went home, wrote to Max: 'You are doing well – that I could plainly see. I sincerely hope that you will go on from prosperity to greater prosperity. You spoke to me declaring your firm belief that principle and uprightness are at the root of a prosperous and manly life. You are quite right.'

Perhaps encouraged by Max's declaration, the minister sent him thirty or forty books 'which you will find interesting in your leisure hours', including *Daniel Deronda*, Wilkie Collins, Boswell's *Life of Johnson*, Wordsworth's Poems, *Don Quixote* ('greatest of all novels'), and *Electric Science* by F. C. Bakewell. Three months later, finding himself short of money in his retirement, he sent off another forty volumes, this time religious books, which he asked his son to sell: 'I don't want too high a price – just a decent moderate price and no more.'

Max's parents, like everyone else, found it difficult to keep in touch with their elusive son. His father soon wrote again:

> We had heard that you had been seen in Montreal of late, and we had expected that you would drop in on us. . . . Just come to see us when you can make it most convenient. We will be glad to see you at any time. You cannot take us unawares or amiss. . . . I hope you are getting on well in Halifax, attending church regularly and at all times behaving like a good Christian. . . . You are not very old yet, but I am fully persuaded that you will keep yourself dignified and do your best as a Christian and a gentleman and no fear but you will get on well. I am so happy to think that there is not a black sheep in all my family.

The implication was that Max had been, or would have been, the black sheep.

He saw the Stairs family regularly, sailing on their yacht, giving a small dinner for John F. Stairs, going to a Jim Stairs picnic ('afterwards poker my rooms'), accompanying Mrs Stairs to church, and, towards the end of the year, seeing a lot of Miss Stairs: her card-playing 'euchre party' of 8 December sounds decorous. She was not the only girl in his life. 14 February: 'Spent evening Miss Glover.' 15 February: 'At Miss Glover's tonight.' 22 March: 'Called on Miss Crawford.' 8 July: 'Went on Arm and to Williams Lake – Miss White.' The Arm was a beautiful inlet near the entrance to Halifax harbour. 2 August: 'Took Miss Brophy on the Arm today.' 12 August: 'Took Margaret White to theatre.' 2 September: 'On the Arm this evening with Miss Steiner.' 3 September: 'On Arm this afternoon with Miss Steiner.' 21 September: 'Took Miss Foster to Academy tonight.'

Nor did he slow down for holidays. He spent Christmas Eve 1903 at the Stairs house in Halifax, left by train for Amherst on Christmas Day to dine with his business friend D. W. Robb, went on to Newcastle to see his parents that evening, and left on Boxing Day for Montreal, staying at his regular Montreal base, the Windsor Hotel. On New Year's Eve there was a charity ball at the hotel. 'Went to balcony and looked on for a short time. Bed at 1230 p.m.'

Early in 1903 he acquired a secretary and for the first time began to keep 'recognised accounts'. On 26 May he wrote in his diary: 'Played golf this afternoon. Organised Royal Securities Co. Ltd. today. Mr Stairs President – I am Sec'y.' Had he foreseen the glorious future of RSC he would have made its organization the lead item, since the company was to become the most successful financial operation in Canada: the main instrument first of Aitken's fortune and then of Killam's. Besides Stairs, the board of RSC consisted of George Stairs, a brother of John, and the lawyers Harris and Cahan. It was capitalized with $50,000 worth of $100 shares, and given the power to act for its founders as 'investors, capitalists, financiers, concessionaires, brokers and agents'.

There was nothing royal about Royal Securities. Stairs and his friends set it up to fill the gap between the cash they themselves could spare for their new companies and what the companies needed; the method was to sell stocks and shares to the public by direct approach, and it was the first company of that kind in the country. Essentially, RSC institutionalized what Aitken had been doing already, tramping the Maritimes and knocking on doors. This was the firm he later called 'the money spinner'. He said further: 'Royal Securities was me.'

Its first success was the Trinidad Electric Company, created by the Stairs group in 1901 to build a new electricity plant in Port of Spain and to replace mule transport with trolley cars. By the middle of 1903, despite recent riots, the business was beginning to move. The trolleys, the local manager reported, seemed fuller than those in Halifax.

There was a standard financing method for this kind of promotion. The company issued bonds with a par value greater than the sum needed to carry out the necessary work, together with common stock of comparable par value. Underwriters took the bonds and tried to market them at about 90 per cent of par. To make the deal more attractive, the common stock was given away free with the bonds as a bonus, with the insiders getting more favourable treatment than outsiders. If all went according to plan, the money raised by the sale of bonds would allow operations to start, and the operations would generate enough revenue to pay the interest on the bonds, and to begin to pay dividends on the common stock. The bonds had to be fed on to the market slowly, to prevent wild price swings being caused by speculators. Once the bonds had been placed with 'real investors', the promoters could begin to 'make a market' in the stock and sell it off to sea captains and the like. This is where the money was made, since the insiders had acquired the stock for nothing.

Aitken did not invent this method of company promotion, but he turned it into a fine art, as his handling of Trinidad Electric showed. It did not get off to a flying start, partly because of the riots and partly because the first stockbroking firm he approached to help launch the company's wares on the public was suspended, following a brief stock market depression. However, the climate soon improved. In mid-1903, with good news arriving from the local manager, Aitken told his associates that Trinidad was doing well enough to be in a position to pay the 5 per cent interest on its $720,000 of bonds, and 7 per cent on its $1,032,000 par value of common stock. The stage was thus set to go public.

In September, Aitken told W. D. Ross, a Toronto banker, that he had decided to float a public issue of Trinidad bonds, which, following normal practice, would have to be completed before a listing of Trinidad stock. At that stage, Royal Securities held $100,000 par value worth of bonds, and options on a further $100,000. Aitken set about collecting further options, offering those bondholders who did not want to keep bonds as a long-term investment 95 per cent of their par value, with the aim of selling them at 97 per cent. At the same time, he began to organize a 'pool' in the common stock. A 'pool' was a collection of people who recognized that it was in all their interests to allow a 'pool manager' to establish, by judicious buying and selling, a genuine, orderly market for the company's offerings before they themselves tried to sell their holdings. Otherwise, untutored persons might sell as soon as the stock advanced a point or two, and tutored persons might be able to drive the price of the stock down to suit their own purposes. Any market manipulation was going to be done by insiders, not outsiders. Aitken explained his intentions in 'the matter of Trinidad Electric stock' in a letter to D. W. Robb of 23 December. 'We desire to avoid speculative holdings. With this end in view, we will endeavour to govern the advances and declines in Market quotations. . . . We intend to make extensive purchases on our own account from time to time when this stock needs protection. . . .'[6] The stock was to be distributed gradually, and the pool members had agreed not to sell or buy in the market until the pool was dissolved on 1 July 1904, which would give six months for the distribution. By that time a genuine market should have been established, and the insiders, Aitken among them, could offload.

All went smoothly. The Port of Spain 'blacks' continued to pack the trolleys, the financial press in eastern Canada was fed some optimistic items, profits for the year were $103,230, and on 11 December the Trinidad directors announced a 5 per cent dividend. By the time dealings began on the Montreal Stock Exchange on Christmas Eve, the public was in a receptive state of mind.

With things going well, Trinidad Electric (president: John F. Stairs) released some more common stock to Royal Securities (president: John F. Stairs). On 1 October 1904, Aitken moved to strengthen his personal grip on the new profit centre. He proposed to Trinidad that he should take over their $125,000 debts, supply them with four 'nine-bench Open Vestibule Electric Tram Cars' and 2800 feet of steel rails, and build a new house for the manager in Port of Spain. In return, he wanted '$168,000 of shares of the common stock of your company to be issued to me and also the bonds in the Union Bank held by it'. A deal went through, with Aitken getting 100 bonds at par value of $480 and 27,500 shares. Putting together the options secured earlier by Royal Securities and his own holdings, Aitken now 'could control almost all the company's stock'. As soon as his Trinidad deal was signed, he set about disposing of $500,000 par value worth of shares at prices ranging from $75 to $85. At the end of the year, Trinidad's annual profits were up again to $117,065, and year by year they continued to rise, proving once again that there is nothing quite so satisfactory as a monopoly – or as it was more politely described in the case of Trinidad Electric, an 'exclusive franchise'. Aitken was excited by the progress at Trinidad Electric, by his own profits and the satisfied purchasers. Thanks to the enthusiasm for trolley travel on the part of the citizens of Port of Spain, he learned his first lesson about the blessings of monopoly and the possible rewards of company promotion.

Trinidad was Aitken's first success, but it was accompanied by his first crisis. He and Stairs were in Toronto on business in mid-September 1904 when Stairs fell ill and soon afterwards died. Aitken by this time was almost part of the Stairs family; it was he who chose the biblical quotation for Stairs's tombstone: 'What doth the Lord require of thee, but to do justly, and to love mercy, and to walk humbly with thy God?' He did what he could to comfort Mrs Stairs, who was devastated by her husband's death. So was Aitken, though not for long. In his memoirs, he said that 'the death of Mr Stairs affected me so deeply that it was impossible to get down to my tasks'. The records do not quite support this account. On 30 September in a letter about the funeral he described how 'poor Mr Harris sobbed like a little child when the great gathering of people sang "Nearer My God to Thee". My own usefulness seems now to be ended although it will be only too soon when I will have recovered from this way of thinking, and devote myself as strenuously to our business affairs.'[7] He was right. Next day, he put his proposal to Trinidad Electric for acquiring common stock.

In any case, he could not afford to indulge his grief. Stairs was not quite such a masterful businessman as had been thought. As head of the Union Bank he had been planning a merger of local banks, and to that end had bought a large block of shares in the People's Bank of Halifax (where Aitken kept a private account). The insiders now learned that the People's Bank, unknown to Stairs, had been the victim of a massive fraud and had lost $450,000, exhausting its surplus. For years it had been issuing false balance sheets. If its customers became aware of the true position before defences were shored up, the effect on both its finances and on those of the Union Bank 'could not be measured'. Harris, George Stairs and Aitken took over the liability for John F. Stairs's shares in the People's Bank. But People's wanted to sell itself to the Bank of Montreal, on disastrous terms. Stairs, Harris and Aitken went to Montreal to demand a better price. Edward Clouston, the head of the Bank of Montreal, refused. George Stairs, furious, stormed out of Clouston's office threatening to appeal to the federal government. The great banker reflected and relented, sending a message to the Stairs deputation saying he wished to see 'the young fellow with the big head'. Aitken negotiated better terms.[8]

John F. Stairs had also left Nova Scotia Steel in trouble. A building programme had far exceeded the estimates. The company's liquid capital was exhausted, and it had contracted large debts. When he fell ill, in September 1904, he had been engaged in restructuring the company. With Stairs immobilized, the risk was that the company might have to pass its dividend, crippling the money-raising he had planned. Aitken and W. D. Ross quickly stepped in, taking over $160,000 of Scotia's debts. On 20 September Ross wrote to Aitken saying, 'I think we can probably congratulate ourselves on having saved the company from a serious financial catastrophe'.[9] But they had applied only a tourniquet; much larger sums were needed to complete the programme. The directors, 'in a dither . . . like lost sheep', asked Aitken to solve their problem. According to Aitken, Harris asked him to make his help conditional on Harris becoming president; in return, Harris would see that he became a Scotia director. Aitken agreed. His solution was to buy 1,500,000 of second mortgage bonds for $1,250,000, borrowing the money from two banks and pledging everything he owned as security: 'a daring act'. Then Harris double-crossed him: he became president of Scotia, but he did not make Aitken a director. It was 'a bitter setback and a real betrayal'. But though he neither forgave nor forgot Harris's treachery, his own position strengthened in the confused aftermath of his patron's death. He was, he told Ross on 28 October, to be paid $10,000 for one year's service handling a pool in the Scotia bonds; with Ross, he underwrote the bond sale, which went so well that he made his first serious 'pot of money' from it – 'short of $200,000', he reckoned. By the end of the year he and Ross, on the basis of a 'vastly improved' forecast for steel sales in 1905, were relishing the prospect of 'a killing in Scotia common'. Nor did Stairs's death weaken Aitken's association with Trinidad Electric. Aitken's other friend named Ross, W. B., took over the vacant chairmanship, and Aitken put in another old friend as a director – J. L. Stewart, the owner of the little newspaper in Chatham, 'to represent my interests'.

More and more, Aitken dominated Stairs's other legacy, Royal

Securities: expanding its range of business, taking on extra staff and, in 1905, opening a branch office in Montreal. The firm had come into being, as an RSC booklet noted wistfully in 1963, at a time of 'superlative opportunities for the investment of capital', as Canada discovered the full range of her resources.[10] Aitken was willing to look at anything. He lent money, thought about possible tram franchises in Britain, considered a land speculation deal in the Canadian north-west, encouraged Havelock Mineral Springs ('I am of the opinion that a very good market might be secured for your mineral water'), investigated the costs of shipping wheat to see if he could do it more cheaply, involved himself with the Munro Wire Works – 'Everything in Wire and Bedding' – and invested a small sum in a boot and shoe company because those who ran it, though without any experience of management, were 'all young, and pretty bright and active'; he was banking on the individuals, and on the 'certainty that the East must manufacture that which it consumes'. He put money into a patent medicine company, makers of Minard's Liniment ('the great internal remedy for man and beast'), Honey Balsam, Minard's Family Pills and Nelson's Cherokee Vermifuge. These products did good business in the back country, and Aitken signed up the foreman on a five-year contract at $75 a month: 'This man', he wrote solemnly to Ross, 'is in possession of the secret process of the manufacture of the liniment'.

Increasingly, people approached him with ideas – to start a new telephone company in St John after the New Brunswick Telephone Company jacked up its rates, to finance a new machine to print a French weekly journal in Bathurst, to back a patent and surefire method of keeping eggs fresh – or to propose deals or seek help with mergers, sales or financing. One man who tried to sell him something was his old benefactor Edward Sinclair, who offered him his lumber business for between $300,000 and $400,000, a deal on which he, Max, would 'clean up' some $30,000 to $40,000; Max turned him down, but he did offer to act as go-between with a man in Toronto who 'has been distinctly successful in selling lumber properties'.[11] Aitken's circle of contacts, in every sort of business, large and small, grew wider every month, and he never stopped travelling and working. On 3 April 1905 he cancelled his subscription to the *Presbyterian Witness*, but it is doubtful whether for some time he had had much opportunity of reading it.

BUSINESS METHODS

In the course of this frenetic activity, Aitken adopted the business methods that stayed with him all his life. At the age of seventy-seven, in his study at La Capponcina in the south of France, he used to rap out letters and instructions to his secretary while standing at a lectern. It was a habit he had acquired fifty years earlier, after he moved his headquarters from Halifax to Montreal. 'It was my custom to stand all day at a lectern in the general office, surrounded by staff. A private office is an inviting place for lengthy conversations. Business is more swiftly dispatched if there are no easy chairs.' As he worked, he scrumpled up pieces of paper and threw them on the floor – another habit that lasted.

One member of his staff was Izaak Walton Killam, who joined Royal Securities in 1904 and learned a lot from Aitken; he once said, after he himself became Canada's leading financier, that if he envied Beaverbrook for any one thing it was his ability to say things clearly in a few words. After 1903, when he acquired a secretary, every piece of his business or family correspondence was normally kept or filed, though there has been some filleting. From the beginning, the Aitken letters are shorter, usually much shorter, than the others. Even at twenty-two he was not afraid to be forthright: asked to help in a merger, he wrote back saying of the Starr Manufacturing Company: ' . . . the directors are not competent business men and the management is entirely worthless'. He was decisive. A friend from Fredericton described a visit to his office:

'The morning mail was on his desk – thirty or forty letters. Aitken went through them like a bullet out of a gun. Do this, do that, he barked out to his secretary and then turned with a smile – "Now, Loring! What can I do for you?" '[12]

His treatment of subordinates – secretaries, editors, air marshals – stayed much the same, too. He harried them. He must have been a good talent-spotter, since three or four of the young men he hired in the early days of Royal Securities became highly successful – Killam, who left $83 million, most conspicuously. His Chatham banking friend, Borradaile, described how Aitken invited him to stay in Halifax, and after a few days asked him to come to the office, as he was seeing a young man and would like Borradaile's opinion.

> When I got to the office – which was about ten feet square with one desk and two chairs – I found that Max was out and the young man was sitting at the desk, smoking a pipe and reading a paper. He introduced himself and apologised for Max, who had had to dash out, but would be back shortly. The young man was Izaak Walton Killam. Knowing Max so well I was sure he never did anything without a purpose. I wondered what it was all about. When at last Max had returned and Killam had gone, he asked me what I thought of him. I said that he seemed a very nice boy but would never set the Thames on fire. How wrong I was! . . . The meeting in that small office was to decide whether to take me back into the fold or to take Killam.[13]

Killam, then nineteen, was working as a bank teller at $750 a year. Aitken paid him $3000 to join Royal Securities as a salesman. It was too much. Killam spent his time playing bridge, not knocking on doors. After a year, Aitken cut his salary to $1500 with a share of the profits: 'A change came over him the next day; the bridge table was forsaken.' At the end of Killam's second year, he earned more than $6000. That did not stop

Killam complaining: 'the matter of salary is one which I have frequently brought to your attention,' he wrote. 'Am tired out each night,' he told Aitken from Fredericton, after calling on twenty-five to thirty people in two days. 'I am glad to hear you are working hard,' was Aitken's response. Aitken pursued Killam with messages all round the Maritimes:

> I would like to know if you are getting down to your office all right at nine o'clock in the morning. . . . I beg to say that you absolutely must keep the expenses of your Saint John office down. . . . The Saint John mailing list is thoroughly inadequate. . . . I beg to point out to you that the securities you sell consist largely in issues which we do not press very hard. On the other hand smaller issues, in which there is a very much better profit for us, are not sold as largely by you.

Then, when Killam seemed to be on the verge of resignation, Aitken reassured him, telling him he was sure that if he attended 'very strictly' to business he would 'very shortly reap the results'.[14] Aitken had (and retained) a good poker player's judgement of when someone was bluffing and when he was not. Aitken lent Killam money to keep him, which taught Killam a lesson: later, he himself always underpaid his senior people, but bought securities for them cheaply while charging them interest on the loans; they made a lot of money in the long run, but until the long run arrived they had to go on working for Killam.

He was not the only Aitken employee to complain about being underpaid; so did Aitken's secretary, to no avail. Aitken was quite prepared to lend money to his staff, but never, at least in the early days, without security. His usual device was to hold the borrower's insurance policies, assigned to him, as collateral against the loan. One practice he adopted early and stuck to was to promote from within, perhaps remembering his own disappointment when Charlie Mitchell was brought in over his head in the Chatham law firm. 'I do not like to take persons from outside and promote them over the heads of those already in our employ . . .', he told Fred Burrill in the Royal Securities office. 'I am sure it will make the organisation stronger and better if we can always feel that each employee we take in will not be set aside by the introduction of new men, but that all are working for promotion.'[15] He harassed his employees, but with outward politeness. 'I suggest' was a common preamble to an instruction.

Then, as later, he kept on the move. People never knew where he was. Even his secretary sometimes lost him. Sinclair the lumberman could not find him when he was trying to sell Aitken his business: 'I was in Halifax to see you, but couldn't find out where you were, or when you would be back.' Meetings at railway stations were commonplace, as he hurried through Fredericton or Amherst. Telegrams were his indispensable instrument, often written in code. At the end of 1903 he fired off two or three telegrams every day as he bought and sold Scotia stock, using three stockbrokers so that nobody would know what he was up to in the market. 'It is my experience over many years that it is best to buy and hold on. Moving in and out of the market is never as satisfactory,' he wrote at the end of his life. That was not his original investment philosophy. As he wrote to a fellow investor in Nova Scotia Steel in June 1903, 'Scotia is selling at 92 and of course it is very much below value. . . . At the same time a profit is a profit.'[16] However, he rarely dipped in and out of stocks he knew nothing about; and he certainly knew about Scotia. 'Do not forget to let me know if any movement is proposed in Scotia shares,' Ross wrote to him.[17] He told Stewart to buy and hang on to Scotia shares in the winter of 1904. Before long, he said, they would be paying a 10 per cent dividend and selling at 110. He added that he was not supposed to be giving Stewart such tips.

He was fired by the same passion and need for inside information about business and finance that he later acquired for the workings of the British Cabinet. He travelled to meet people face to face – a poker player's instinct; rarely did he finance a company unless he knew its owners or managers. 'I do not buy stock in any company whatsoever unless I am directly connected,' he wrote in 1907.[18] Knowledge picked up on his travels, sparingly dispensed, helped him to keep in with older and more sedentary associates, confined to their banks or offices, who in turn rewarded him with their own gossip about the Canadian financial village.

With all his associates, he took trouble. Towards John F. Stairs, one of the few people to whom he wrote long letters, he was always deferential. Everyone else he treated as an equal. He was not afraid of rows. W. D. Ross complained vigorously when Aitken took too much for granted before the Scotia bond issue of 1904. 'I fail to see why I should be asked to boost up Scotia bonds in order to make flotation successful', Ross wrote. 'Surely I have done enough'.[19] Ross purred with gratitude, however, when Aitken gave him a private early warning about Scotia's bad results in 1905 (Stewart, we must hope, had got out by then, since Scotia shares dropped to the fifties). Aitken's launch of one particular company, Porto Rico, in 1907 produced rows with everybody, especially Harris, because Aitken thought they were being mean and greedy about lending him money. But he invariably moved quickly to patch up the rifts. Usually he was reasonably open with his associates, but he did not always tell them the truth. He told one stockbroking firm that he would deal exclusively with them, while continuing to deal with others. He dealt on his own account in shares that Royal Securities was interested in. After he acquired control of Demerara Electric as a member of a syndicate, he sailed close to the wind when he instructed the manager on the spot to feed all information to him personally, not to the other members of the syndicate.[20]

Aitken could be cunning. Seeking to buy a well-established electricity company in Truro, Nova Scotia, from someone called Chambers, he instructed his agent on the spot, T. G. McMullen, to do so by 'bluff'. First,

McMullen should tell Chambers that he and Aitken were proposing to start a second electricity company in the town, but aiming at a different market; thus 'we hope we could get along together in an amicable spirit'. Next, McMullen should 'intimate' to Chambers that McMullen-Aitken would be producing electricity by waterpower, which would mean that the new-comers would get all the big contracts because they 'could supply power at so much less than he could, using coal'. Finally, McMullen should send a water engineer to Truro, to examine the waterpower: his presence would 'lend great credence to that story'.[21] This bluff, Aitken calculated, would so unnerve Chambers that he would decide, believing the future expansion of his business to be blocked, to throw in his hand and sell.

He showed exceptional pernicketiness about money. He was always writing to the railway company to get back the price of an unused railway ticket, or telling his staff to economize on envelopes and querying the amount spent on postage. He told a member of the Halifax office that when writing a letter of more than two pages the first page could be on the firm's engraved headed paper, but the following sheets must be on cheaper, unheaded paper. 'We supply our offices with cheaper quality of paper for inter-office paper, and I have to request that you use paper of this description when addressing me.'[22] He checked in detail the expenses sent in by his travelling salesmen, and often queried them.

He first appreciated the power of newspapers when he saw how they could be used to promote an Aitken cause. He was ready to manipulate his associates provided they did not realize what was happening, as he did over Demerara Electric; and he soon learned how he might manipulate the general public as well. Aitken prepared for the public sale of Trinidad stock by getting a puff printed in the *Halifax Herald*, which, conveniently, already had a stake in Trinidad. Then he sent the article to Ross in Toronto, asking him to have it published in the Toronto papers, 'paying for the information [*sic*] if necessary'. He must have meant 'insertion'. Ross arranged for it to appear in *The News*, one of Toronto's dailies. 'I am not putting this particular article in any of the other papers as it might appear to be inserted for the purpose of booming the stock, but if you will send me any other articles or facts in connection with the Company from time to time I shall be glad to see that they appear in different papers at different times.' Aitken told Ross to be sure to send him 'a memo of the expenses that you have been put to', adding, 'we will do these things in a more systemised manner after a little while'.[23]

But the clearest early traces of the later master of popular newspapers are to be seen in the way he tackled a company prospectus. In those days no law governed these documents; a company promoter, like a newspaper publisher, could feed the public anything he liked. The Aitken method was similar in both cases: cheer people up, give them hope, and select the ingredients accordingly.

The sixteen-page Porto Rico prospectus was produced jointly by Aitken and Toronto stockbroker A. E. Ames, an old associate, and took three months of letter-writing and proof-swopping to complete. The pattern of these exchanges was strikingly similar to innumerable later exchanges between Beaverbrook and his editors. On 25 April Aitken received and returned the first set of proofs: 'I have made numerous alterations.' Next day, he said he did not 'care for' the idea of a picture of a sugar mill. 'Why not put in a picture of San Juan City from the harbour?' Ames at once put in hand the harbour picture, but nevertheless sent Aitken a proof of a picture of the sugar mill: ' . . . it struck me as a good thing to have in, being typical of the principal industry of the island, and having an air of substantiality'. Next day Aitken said he thought the mill picture was 'exceedingly good', and 'would suggest that it be inserted'. But the view of San Juan City 'will make a valuable addition to the prospectus'.

A more awkward problem was the figures. If the prospectus candidly listed exactly how much stock Aitken and his friends had acquired in buying the company, it would show rather too clearly that $222,000 of bonus stock was going to the promoters, who of course included Aitken and Ames. 'My idea', wrote Ames, 'is not to deceive the investor, but a fair remuneration of the promoters is objected to by some', and it would therefore be best to avoid 'parading this feature'. Aitken did not demur. They also agreed that the map should show 'macadam roads completed and under construction, to indicate that the country is opened up rather than of a desert character, while the names of places suggest population'. Another railroad, owned not by Canadians but by Americans, it was deemed prudent to omit from the map altogether. Aitken next 'suggested' the 'striking out' of the view of the 'Modern Tobacco Factory' as it was 'not very interesting'. Ames, like Beaverbrook's editors later on, accepted all 'suggestions'.

Aitken watched every detail. 'I think there should be a comma'; certain letters were 'out of line'. The pictures should be at the back of the prospectus, because the pictures, if interspersed with reading matter, 'might distract attention while a salesman is going over it with a prospective investor'. On 15 May Aitken submitted the prospectus to a directors' meeting. Afterwards he wrote to Ames: 'The population was stated by Mr Ross as 55,000 instead of 65,000, but I declined to accept his estimate'. Aitken's final stroke came on 9 July. 'The prospectus is all right,' he wrote to Ames; but he avoided taking any responsibility for it. 'I am not passing upon the prospectus as an officer of the Porto Rico Railways Co, and would like you to be responsible for its accuracy. Will you be good enough to send me a copy of this letter to Montreal for my files.'[24]

He was learning to cover his tracks. The editor of the *Halifax Herald*, W. R. McCurdy, was an Aitken ally, and Aitken got him to write an article for a circular produced by the West Indian Committee in London to encourage interest in the region. Aitken wanted McCurdy to lament the lack of trade between Canada and the West Indies. 'Such should not be

lition', he wrote to McCurdy in unusually foggy prose, 'and is due
ou may say in your opinion to a lack of proper transportational
between Canada and the British West Indies.' McCurdy duly
repeated to London: 'Such should not be the case, and that it is so is due
largely, I believe, to a lack of proper transport facilities between Canada
and the West Indies.' The article went on to argue that Canada should
subsidize a shipping line operating out of Halifax, the natural terminus.
Aitken told McCurdy that his reason for asking him to write 'all this' was
that he was interested in a project along these lines and the article, 'while
I have no doubt in accord with your views on the subject, will also serve
my purpose at the present moment. Of course this is confidential.'

About the companies he controlled, outsiders, including actual or
potential investors, were allowed to know only what Aitken wanted
known. Instructing Fred Burrill of his Halifax office to send the monthly
gross and net receipts of Trinidad and Demerara to the West Indian
Committee in London (he was seeking to attract the attention of British
investors), he added: 'When these receipts show increases over the
corresponding months of last year, please properly state such increases.
But if the increases do not occur, please do not refer to the results of the
corresponding month of the preceding year. Please let me know if you
understand this all right.' Burrill understood perfectly. 'We note that in
the event of a deficit . . . such is to be suppressed, whereas, in the event
of an increase, we are to call special attention to same. I beg to state that
this has been our custom all along in sending these earnings to the various
papers and individuals.'[25]

CHAPTER 3

MARRIAGE AND MERGERS
1906–1910

IN THE HECTIC early years of the century, when Aitken was making his fortune, his private life took on a pattern that never changed. Uncertain of his power to please, he thought that money was his only asset. His beneficiaries, in varying degrees, became his dependants. There was nothing automatic about a first-generation millionaire Maritimer deploying his money in this way. James Dunn and Izaak Walton Killam rarely gave a cent to anybody.

Aitken's first beneficiaries were his family, and his first pensioners were his parents. Nobody in the family, including himself, had suspected that the wayward Max might turn into a master-financier, and his unexpected success transformed his relations with its members. From being the child who did not fit in, a puzzle to his brothers and sisters and an anxiety to his parents, he became the family's pivot.

When Max began his rise, which may be dated to the incorporation of Royal Securities in 1903, his father was drawing a retirement stipend of $200, which represented less than half the salary of a Royal Securities stenographer. The eldest boy, Traven, had read law at Dalhousie and gone west to Nevada to seek his fortune, with indifferent results. The second son, Magnus, known as Mauns, had a modest post with the Royal Bank of Canada in Antigonish. Max's immediate younger brother, Arthur, was studying to become a doctor. The youngest boy, Allan Anderson, also known as Buddie or Bud, was a semi-invalid. Of the girls, both the eldest, Rahno, and the second girl, Annie Anderson, known as Nan, were working in hospitals. The two youngest children, Jean, an exceptionally pretty girl known as Gyp, and Laura, born when her mother was fifty, were still at school. There was no hardship in the family, but equally there was little prospect that any of them would lead anything other than a modest middle-class life.

Max started to help his family quietly, doing what he could as soon as he could. At first, he made small loans in response to particular requests; for instance, a loan to Mauns charged at the unbrotherly rate of 6 per cent.

51

Slowly the scale of his benefactions increased. But he did not treat everyone alike. For his parents, he met every need. His first sizeable outlay was a retirement house he built for them in Newcastle, a property which they named Torphichen; the children became joint owners. Besides the house, he gave his parents clothes – a coat for his mother ('. . . the moment it arrived Mama put on her things and went out calling to show off her finery') and a hat, suit and fur-lined overcoat for his father, after Rahno had reported that he was 'very very poorly clothed'. He paid for an operation on his mother's rheumatic hands, and built an extension to Torphichen when his father found it hard to climb the stairs.

To his elder sisters he gave presents of money for holidays, and, when Rahno became engaged in 1906, $500 for her wedding 'preparations'. He paid the school fees of the younger girls. When Arthur was going through medical school in Illinois, Max paid his fees too. He paid virtually all the expenses of his sickly brother. Towards Mauns he behaved like a bank manager, not giving him any presents but always being prepared to help on certain conditions. To Traven, recognizing his ability, he offered not cash but jobs.

Except when money was needed to tide someone over an illness, when he always told them to spend whatever was necessary, help was usually accompanied by exhortations. He told Mauns sternly that he must not 'discount the future' by spending more than he earned, and implied that the money might dry up if he did. He lectured Traven about the road to prosperity: 'My advice is that only one thing counts, and that thing is absolutely necessary, namely, hard work. Nothing else is any good.' He tried to persuade the youngest girls to keep accounts of their spending; but when they failed he remained indulgent. Allan, in California for his health at Max's expense, was required to submit detailed expenses every week: 'Ticket to Long Beach $1.50; socks $1.00; gloves $1.00; laundry .90.'

Although Max paid all manner of bills for the family, he took no part in decisions. Rahno was in charge of Gyp's career, and if Rahno thought Gyp should train to become a librarian ('so many nice girls do that nowadays'), so be it. He rarely wrote letters of any length to his family, although they did to him. As he became more important and busier, he used his secretary as a family manager. One peculiar result was that his mother received letters purporting to have been written by the secretary that had in fact been dictated by her son. When the girls ran out of pocket money, they wrote to the secretary. Laura wrote from Trafalgar School in Montreal: 'Dear Miss Tobin, Would you please send me a cheque for $25 for I am quite out of pocket money. My brother told me to write.'

Max saw his family only occasionally, and rarely for long. In April 1905, Gyp complained that she had not seen him since the previous August. When he went home, it was usually for one night only. A letter of 1905 from Allan Davidson, the Newcastle lawyer and his father's close friend, described how he had run into Torphichen to 'burn some tobacco with Mr

Aitken' and found Mr and Mrs Aitken 'warmed through and through by having you to themselves for even a few hours'.[1]

His family were not alone in benefiting from his success. Max helped people get jobs: the nephew of a clergyman who asked him to put in a word for the nephew at a bank; a friend of Traven's who wanted to work in the Robb Engineering Company's machine shops; a waiter at the Halifax Club who wanted to move to Montreal: 'thoroughly honest and I think perhaps the best waiter we ever had', said Aitken's reference. After John F. Stairs died he employed his son, even though, as Mrs Stairs remarked, Max didn't really like him; she thought the Nova Scotia Steel people might have done more for him for his father's sake, 'so I am glad that you have not changed'. When Aitken's boyhood friend from Newcastle, Will Corbett, asked for help, he told him he could have as much money as he wanted. But when disinclined to lend money or back a business scheme, Max soon developed a standard alibi: ' . . . my resources are taxed to the utmost of my capacity'.[2]

Although his tastes could not yet be described as extravagant, he quickly learned to spend money on himself as well as others. He stayed at the hotels where businessmen were expected to stay – the Windsor in Montreal or the Waldorf in New York. When he rented an apartment after he left the Halifax Hotel he insisted on a wood-burning fire, and was ready to pay whatever it would cost to install. In 1905 he built himself a house on a prime site in Halifax, overlooking the Arm; it was not much more than a cottage, but he hired a housekeeper, bought a yacht that he converted to a 'gasolene launch' and then a 'first rate canoe and dinghy'.

Aitken was ready to pay for what he wanted; what he absolutely could not tolerate was any suspicion that someone was getting the better of him, or that he was being denied his rights: hence battles with the railways to get rebates on unused tickets, and threats to go elsewhere when hotels put up their rates. From shopkeepers, he was always trying to extract a discount. In November 1905 he negotiated a price of $15 for a watch priced at $16.75, then tried to get an additional discount of 10 per cent.

His most absurd yet characteristic battles were with his tailor, Gibb & Co. of Montreal and the Royal Exchange, London. As a newcomer to Halifax society, Aitken began to take more interest in his clothes. He bought handkerchiefs marked with his initials and ordered a hatbox from London. Then he started to complain – for instance, that the 'tails cross behind' on his 'dress coat', to which the tailor implausibly replied that his size had changed. In November 1905 Aitken's patience snapped. He had had a new suit made and

> . . . the coat . . . is more lopsided and out of proportion than it is possible
> to imagine, unless the coat was made with the aim of creating a monstrosity.
> I have been under the impression that a good deal of the trouble with the
> last two or three suits is owing to my own bad temper, consequently I got a

friend who is noted for his even temper to look at the last suit which you made for me, and when I told him it had come from your workshops, it seemed to him incredible.

Gibb & Co. sent an emollient reply. Aitken partly backed down: 'I probably was a little bit hasty, refusing to take the last suit of clothes you made me. In the little dark closet where you try my clothes on, I do not have the chance to see whether they fit or not, but when I get the suit out in the broad daylight, I very soon discover the defects.'

The truce did not last long. The tailor sent in a bill for $503 which listed, among other items: 'Fine White Diamond Quilting Dress Vest, $8; Black Beaver Chesterfield, Lined Extra Fine Mink, Extra Fine Otter Collar, Cuffs and Lapels, $375; Drab whipcord riding breeches remodelled, $4.00; Repairing Cleaning & Pressing Grey Llama Wrapper, 75c.' Aitken went through every item with a pencil, making sure the tailor had given him a 10 per cent discount on all items, including an umbrella. He then sent the tailor not $503 but $498.98, having corrected the sums and crossed out the 'llama wrapper' charge: 'I do not own a grey llama wrapper.' The tailor replied that it was not worth troubling about the 75 cents, but he would nevertheless mention that the wrapper had been bought by Mr Aitken the previous spring. Aitken wrote back: 'I would like to know what the word wrapper means, as this may be a name which you give to something which I call differently. As far as I know, I have never owned anything which I would call a grey llama wrapper. The price of seventy five cents is a small matter, but I must be just, as I insist upon being justly done by.' That was the point. The tailor replied as if to an idiot child: 'We will try to explain it to you, as to the meaning of grey llama. "Grey" stands for the colour, viz:– black and white; "llama" for the quality of wool the goods are made of and should be of very soft nature, and to the touch, something similar to wash leather. "Wrapper" means a medium weight overcoat.' He enclosed a sample of cloth 'for your further guidance'. Two days later Aitken capitulated in one sentence, without apology: 'I now enclose seventy five cents.'[3]

His temperament was not serene. Besides his perpetual restlessness, every now and again he would be plunged in self-pity, usually when he was not making money. Then he would complain about how hard he worked on others' behalf, how little he was appreciated and how poorly he was rewarded. When one of his company promotions ran into trouble, it was usually someone else's fault.

Aitken seems to have been as surprised as his friends when he briefly interrupted his business deals and his disputes with Gibb & Co. in order to get married. On 29 January 1906, in the Garrison Chapel in Halifax, a 'very quiet' wedding ceremony reported briefly by the *Halifax Morning Chronicle* was attended by his mother, his brother Traven and forty-three other guests, among them his old friend the marine insurance agent from

St John and a Stairs as groomsman. The bride was Gladys Drury, a girl universally liked and universally thought beautiful. She was very young, eighteen to his twenty-six, with long auburn hair and green eyes. The new Mrs Aitken 'wore a going-away gown of hunter's green and green chiffon hat, and carried a bouquet of white roses'.

The Drurys were a cut above the Aitkens. The bride's distinguished father, Lieutenant-Colonel (later Brigadier-General) Charles Drury, had lately been appointed to a coveted post demanding social as well as military accomplishments: he was the first Canadian to command the Halifax garrison after the British Army relinquished its responsibilities. Gladys was one of three sisters, all regarded as beauties. Aitken said he first saw her when she dined with her family at the Halifax Hotel. Her father had taken up his new appointment, but 'could not afford to live in the Headquarters provided for his illustrious predecessors, mostly wealthy members of aristocratic English dynasties'. One of these predecessors was Queen Victoria's father, the Duke of Kent. The colonel, dependent on his salary, housed his family in the hotel. Aitken saw his chance: 'My dining place was forthwith transferred from the Halifax Club to the Halifax Hotel.' His daughter Janet told a different story: she said he met Gladys in church.[4] At any rate, she seemed to him to be 'a child', with 'no experience of the world'. He may also have been attracted by her social position. What did she see in him? Possibly what many other women saw: energy; generosity; someone who liked and thought he needed women; someone who was never dull and could support her; someone with a future.

One of Gladys's sisters, Arabella, later looked back on 'those happy days in Halifax at the dreadful hotel – when we used to giggle and tickle you! and I was so amused when I asked you what you would do when you grew up and you said well it might surprise you to know that I am going into English politics and I may one day be Prime Minister of England!! We laughed because we thought you were joking – but I realize now that you were in earnest.'[5]

Once Gladys accepted Aitken's proposal of marriage, he acted with his usual despatch. The Montreal papers published the engagement announcement on 28 December 1905. But he showed a curious reluctance to tell his friends precisely what was happening. It was as late as 20 January, nine days before the wedding, that he telegraphed an architect friend in Montreal, Sam Finley, to ask him to be an usher. Finley wrote back, saying that of course he would be 'on deck to see you through all right, but for Heaven's sake let us know the day if you know it yourself! but I wouldn't be the least bit surprised if you didn't definitely decide till about an hour before! You certainly are the most erratic chap I ever met.' W. D. Ross had the same complaint: 'You did not say positively 29th or 30th or what hour.' On 23 January, a St John broker wrote to Aitken in Halifax: 'I note you state you will be here Tuesday January 30th for sure. There must be something exceptional or why this positiveness?' His business associates thought he had done well to marry a Drury: 'I remember Miss Drury as a little child, as her father Col. Drury was a gentleman I have always admired, and held in the very highest esteem,' a manager of the Mutual Life Assurance Company told him.[6]

In a diary entry on his wedding day, Aitken used a peculiar word; he hoped the 'experiment' would be successful. He wrote in a draft section of his memoirs that he 'had not married under any very compelling desire for marriage. It had been to some extent a matter of convenience with me.' He was eligible 'and a good deal sought after'; and he had been told that if he was proposing to move for business reasons to Montreal, as he was, then he must have a family. The decision to marry may also have been connected with his health, which was already, as it remained, a constant preoccupation. Often in 1905 he had felt depressed and ill, taking to his bed and imagining all kinds of dire complaints. Was anything wrong with him? Was he lonelier than he realized, or suppressing disquiet at moving so rapidly and successfully away from the values of the manse? Friends and colleagues told him he was suffering only from overwork, and his doctor diagnosed his trouble as 'neurasthenic'. It was not long after the onset of a particularly bad attack of depression that he met Gladys Drury. He ascribed to this meeting the recovery of his energy and spirits.

Having recovered them, he subordinated his marriage to his business plans, rather than vice versa. The St John broker now learned the reason for Aitken's 'positiveness'. All along, he had planned to visit St John on the day after his wedding to inspect the Royal Securities branch there, in the Canada Life building, where Killam was in charge. He concluded that the office arrangements were good, but that 'probably Killam spends too much of his time in the office, and not enough time in looking for clients outside'.[7] This was not a problem that would have worried most people married the previous day.

MONTREAL

Immediately after the marriage, having checked up on Killam in St John, Mr and Mrs Aitken left Halifax for good and settled in Montreal. By the time of their move the city was established as the financial and commercial capital of Canada, and its principal port of entry. The population was some 405,000 and three-fifths of it was French; but the thin upper crust were united by one key credential: they spoke English. To protect their identity, they nurtured the British connection. Sir Hugh Graham, a leading newspaper proprietor, dressed his chauffeur in the costume of a British coachman. The core of the city remained conveniently small, character- ized, as in the days of fur traders and missionaries, by the proximity of God and Mammon. The temples of the worshippers of Mammon were scarcely less grandiose than those of the worshippers of God. In the Place d'Armes, home of the Montreal Trust Company that Aitken bought in 1906, the Gothic parish church of Notre Dame, able to seat a vast congregation, faced the mighty Bank of Montreal, built in the style of ancient Rome. The new Montreal Stock Exchange, where the members kept their hats on while they traded, had been modelled on a temple in Tivoli, outside Rome, by an architect from New York. In Dominion Square, the Roman Catholic cathedral imitated, at half the size, St Peter's, Rome; but it was rivalled, on the south side, by the Romanesque Windsor Street railway station, the land gateway to the continent, and by the adjacent Windsor Hotel, where the marble had not been stinted. This was the arena to which Aitken had come, as he wrote later, to compete with 'men of wider experience, higher prestige, and extensive capital resources', or, as he wrote of them at the time, 'sharks'.

He moved with Gladys first into the Windsor Hotel and then into an apartment in the upper-crust Sherbrooke Street, and went to work at the Royal Securities office in St James Street, near the Bank of Montreal and the St James's Club, to which all the village elders belonged and which he soon joined. His annual salary, as vice president of Royal Securities with, in effect, sole executive responsibility, was $4000. It was a modest figure that reflected the almost unlimited opportunities the job had given him for making money on the side. By his own reckoning he was worth, at the beginning of 1906, $700,000; this sum can be put into contemporary perspective by the letter, already quoted, that he wrote in June 1906, in which he referred to estates of 'more than $1,000,000' and 'more than $900,000' as 'very big estates for this country'.

During the next five years Aitken's moneymaking energies – despite a financial panic, moments of despair and a genuine illness – were even more obsessively deployed than they had been in the previous five. He floated companies in the Caribbean; bought and sold the Montreal Trust Company (making a $200,000 profit in a year); got out of and then back into Royal Securities; bought Montreal Rolling Mills, a steel company dealing in finished products; 'built the bastions of present-day industrial Canada'[8] by putting through mergers of a number of small companies into a few big ones: the Canada Cement Company, the Steel Company of Canada, the Canadian Car and Foundry Company; launched the Calgary Power Company; started off Western Canada Power with the building of a hydroelectric plant in British Columbia; set up the Montreal Engineering Company as a subsidiary to manage public utilities; started a weekly magazine; nearly succeeded in buying the *Montreal Gazette*; conducted the first large public financing of the infant Canadian newsprint industry by placing, in London, £1,000,000 worth of first mortgage bonds of Price Brothers & Co. to pay for a new mill; and briefly acquired control of Rolls Royce. He also continued to deal on the stock market, especially in Nova Scotia Steel where a cheerful young member of the Stairs family, new to the firm ('work is certainly hell'), supplied him with inside information.[9]

From the middle of 1905 until after he moved to Montreal he spent much of his time gazing south, scanning the Caribbean, Central America and South America for another proposition that would perform as well as Trinidad Electric and the relaunched Demerara. Selling bonds and stocks for other companies was all very well, but the real money was to be made by starting and promoting one's own projects. In July 1905 he went to San Juan in Puerto Rico with his banker friend W. D. Ross and his stockbroker ally A. E. Ames, but nothing came of the visit. In November, he told Ross he planned to go in the new year to Guatemala, where he was interested in a street railway franchise. About the same time he proposed to investigate prospects in Matanzas in Cuba, but the visit fell through. The chief engineer of Trinidad Electric, Fred Teele, was sent to Brazil to look into trams, electricity and gas in Pernambuco, again without results. An agent was despatched to Colombia to examine a railroad project, but – not surprisingly, having encountered an outbreak of yellow fever – he strongly advised Aitken to steer well clear of this 'dead country' and recommended Venezuela instead. In January 1906 Aitken was complaining that he had not made any money for a long time: 'I am almost in despair.' Then his hopes soared as he thought he had spotted a winner in the trams of Quito in Ecuador; he had received 'a very full and complete report and a very promising one'. There was one snag: 'Unfortunately, that country is now in a state of revolution.' He thought somebody must be organizing revolutions behind his back to spite him, since he had been about to invest in Colombia when the same thing happened. Aitken cast his net wider and wider, even into tinpot British Honduras, whence he received a report and a map, but again without results.

At last, opportunity knocked. On 13 February 1906 he arrived in Havana on a honeymoon that doubled as a business trip, or vice versa. Canadian interests were already well represented in Cuba: Sir William Van Horne, the great Canadian railway builder, had constructed the first railway system in 'that lovable island' after he retired from Canadian Pacific; like other entrepreneurs from the frozen north he enjoyed doing business in the sunshine and in 1902 had opened the new railway's headquarters in Camaguey. Aitken took with him, besides his wife, the engineer Fred Teele from Trinidad; a week after his arrival he wrote a long letter home to his Canadian associates saying that he was negotiating to set up a combined tramways and electric lighting company in Santiago de Cuba, at one end of the Van Horne railway. He was impressed by what he saw: 'The island of Cuba is enjoying wonderful prosperity. . . . Except in the buildings Cuba will compare favourably with Canada in every respect barring morals.'[10] The Santiago negotiations fell through, but on a further visit, in April, he nailed down a more promising deal. He wrote on 8 May to the J. G. White company in New York, an important engineering firm with Caribbean interests:

While in Cuba, I bought the Puerto Principe Electric Light Company, for the sum of $300,000. This Lighting Company is in the City of Camaguey. Its net earnings for the last year amounted to $31,750.00. The year before its earnings amounted to slightly over $23,000.00. The Company has installed 60 arc lights and about 5,800 incandescent lights. The plant operates only from sunset to midnight.

I bought 200 acres of land in the City of Camaguey, and 217 acres to the north of Sir William Van Horne's Car Works. The Van Horne Car Works are a short distance away from the city. I bought the old Mule Tram Franchise, and I acquired the Electric Railway Franchise, in an almost completed condition. . . . I am not going to be in a hurry to construct the tram lines, but at present will operate the Electric Light Plant. When the tramlines are constructed, they will pass through the lands which I have purchased. On account of the congested condition of the population of the City, I expect to make a very good profit out of selling building lots.[11]

So it proved, for cities were growing fast and land prices booming. But before the profit could start to flow work was delayed by an uprising, which was put down by American troops, and Aitken's local business partner, Roberto Betancourt, had to get round some 'objectionable' local ordinances. He explained his methods to Aitken. 'I have secured the promise of several of my friends to the effect that our plans will be approved as submitted by us, and to that effect we are to meet in my office with the Mayor, so that at the session [of the Municipality] in which they come up, there will be no discussion of them, they having been arranged before then. You must give me very material help with this land scheme if you wish it to be a success.'[12] What form this 'material help' should take, Betancourt evidently thought it unnecessary to spell out.

Aitken had scarcely floated Camaguey, setting up four separate companies for the purpose, when he applied the brakes. He also held up operations in Mexico, where a young man was looking for prospects on Aitken's behalf. A big new deal had come up in Puerto Rico. The J. G. White company of New York held a stake in Porto Rico Power and Light, which supplied electricity to San Juan. Now they proposed to float a new enterprise to buy up the local tramway operator, greatly extend the tramlines and develop a hydroelectric site near the city. But they were engineers rather than financiers. Aitken and his friends therefore set up the new company, Porto Rico Railways, to finance these plans, with J. G. White being given a share in the company and a contract to develop the trams and build the electricity plant.

It was a bigger flotation than Royal Securities was used to, requiring the issue of $650,000 worth of 5 per cent bonds at 90 per cent with 100 per cent bonus stock, with $220,000 worth of bonus stock for the insiders. Aitken got $30,000 for arranging the deal, and he also bought some land, for the same reasons that he bought land in Camaguey. The issue got off to a slow start; Killam, beating the Maritime back roads, reported that 'business has not been up to much';[13] James Harding, who had been sent to open an experimental one-man Royal Securities office in London in the spring of 1906 (Aitken's first London venture), found the 'lack of interest' among London stockbrokers 'highly discouraging', as one by one they sent back the Porto Rico prospectus prepared by Aitken and Ames with such care. However, the larger Canadian investors were impressed, and by the fall of 1906 the issue was oversubscribed. In October, the motormen and conductors on the San Juan trams were put into uniform for the first time. In a fit of euphoria, the scheme was expanded and another bond issue made, this time with a par value of $800,000. Aitken and his wife took some important investors from Toronto on a conducted tour.

Then came a near disaster: the recession of early 1907. The subscribers to the first bond issue failed to pay up; and J. G. White reported cost over-runs on the construction work. Cash was urgently needed: another $500,000. Aitken was furious, both with the backsliders and with his associates: so furious that in September 1907 he resigned – the first of his many resignations – and only the urging of W. D. Ross forced him to change his mind. He was no sooner back in charge when the financial panic of October 1907 struck. Most of the Porto Rico money was on deposit in New York with the Trust Company of America, which closed its doors. Aitken was staying at the Waldorf Hotel and saw the queues of worried depositors. His account written half a century later exudes genuine alarm:

> Disaster! What could be done? Who would help me? Money must be found at once to pay wages and salaries in Porto Rico. Failure would mean workmen's liens and winding up proceedings. Default! What a terrible prospect. Failure! Doubts would arise about the concerns financed by me. . . . A financial house of high repute was my first life line. There I appeared and waited for the arrival of the partner most likely to hear my plea. Explanations were simple and my misfortune easily understood. But money was almost unobtainable. Rates of interest were prohibitive. Security made little difference. Would my personal credit gain me a temporary loan? I got it! The price was high and part of my own equity was added to the charge. No matter. I had escaped the whirlwind.

The crisis provoked quarrels with Ross, who turned down Aitken's request for credit; with J. G. White, who refused to guarantee that there would be no more cost over-runs; and with Ames, who complained to Aitken that it was his own fault that 'we fell somewhat behind in placing our securities', because Aitken had decided the date of the second bond issue unilaterally, despite promises of consultation. Nevertheless, Ames went on, 'you dunned us unmercifully by letter and by telegram and personally in my office' and 'arbitrarily withheld for months the bonus stock to which we were entitled'. Matters got worse before they got better, but by the autumn of 1908 prospects were bright. Porto Rico Railways became and continued to be a prosperous concern – apart from a hiccup in 1913 when Aitken had to guarantee the dividend – until it was nationalized in 1944.

So it went on, with trips planned and cancelled, companies incorporated, 'electric propositions' investigated, and a typical, farcical dispute with a bookshop in Boston that sent him a guide not to Colombia but to the District of Columbia. He had a bright idea a day. Without warning, he sent Betancourt a 'cinema machine' so that people would use the trams to go and see it; Betancourt protested, but the idea worked. Most of his ideas did.

HUSBAND AND SON

As he grew richer, Aitken became more and more self-absorbed. During this roller-coaster decade, he put himself and his preoccupations first. This is not to say that he neglected his responsibilities; on the contrary, he dealt with his personal relationships as if they consisted of responsibilities and nothing else – as if, once he had provided material support to friends or family, displays of affection, solicitude or intimacy were optional extras to be fitted in if and when other demands on his time allowed, which they rarely did.

He had no long-range marriage strategy, any more than he had a long-range business strategy. As a newly-wed husband, he made forward plans that were erratic, to say the least. His honeymoon was simply a truncated version of a business trip originally planned to take in Cuba, Venezuela and then England; and it was revised for business, not marital, reasons. No sooner was he back in Montreal after his second trip to Cuba than he thought about buying a large house in Halifax – one of the finest in the city, the estate agent told him, with stables for three horses and room for two or three carriages, and a bargain at $8500.

His health again worried him. On 26 June 1906, he told a Newcastle correspondent that he was 'going away on July 14 for a long time and will be unable to take up any new business. . . . I have been in very bad health for some time.' To W. D. Ross he complained of 'severe attacks of intestinal trouble' and loss of weight; he was down to 122 lb. Ross told him, as his friends always did when he gave them the details of his state of health, that his sole trouble was overwork and mental strain over the large sums of money he was handling. George Stairs chided him for 'neglecting the ordinary rules of health – for instance irregularity in your meals'. Stairs continued: 'I know men in England carrying on businesses of large magnitude and requiring great thoughts, and yet these men take time for a comfortable lunch in the middle of the day – and at 5.30 leave their offices for home. It is not a sign of a good businessman to see him neglecting the laws of health.' Aitken paid no heed. A planned trip to England in 1906, to sell shares, had to be cancelled when he was struck down with appendicitis in Montreal. On 21 September he was operated on, the surgeon telling him that his appendix had been the cause of his internal troubles of the past two years. (Exactly fifty years later the patient was still complaining that the surgeon's fee, $500, had been too high.) Three weeks later Aitken was let out of hospital and went to New York, where he felt the same old symptoms. The doctors decided that he was 'suffering from Gastritis of the stomach and intestines . . . and a disposition to adhesions' – not surprising, since the Montreal doctors had kept him immobile in bed for twenty days after the operation – and put him back in hospital for a month. He wrote to Dr Curry in Halifax:

> I have already told Dr Quintard that I thought that in your opinion my condition was brought about by overwork and hallucinations with possibly too great business strain at the time of the death of the late Mr Stairs and events which followed it that winter. I told him I had gone to you when I believed I had heart disease, and you had dispelled that illusion, and many others which I have entertained in the last three years.[14]

For years he continued to worry about his heart, with little reason.

Aitken went on to consult Dr Curry about Gladys. As a result of 'my operation and my subsequent more serious illness she sustained a nervous collapse. The pains for which you treated her during the summer became so severe that she had to take to her bed in the same hospital with me, at Dr Quintard's private hospital. . . . I think perhaps with her all she requires is that treatment which you give to all persons suffering from nervousness.' Dr Curry wrote back to say he had presumed Mrs Aitken's illness arose from the 'mental strain' she underwent during Max's illness.

None of this interrupted for long his attention to business. From hospital he continued to harry his Royal Securities staff by letter and telegram, warning them not to assume that because he was in hospital he did not need to know of their activities: 'Please understand that no detail is too small to advise me of, as I wish [to be] kept closely in touch with the office.' He found the anxious solicitude of Gladys oppressive and, having first assured himself that 'analysis of stomach content' was within the powers of Halifax medical men, took her there. He wanted to get back to work. Gladys's first married Christmas was not romantic. On Christmas Eve her husband telegraphed Dr Quintard in New York: 'stomach wash this morning much worse than ever previously. Contents highly coloured. On removal of tube small substance appearing to be blood in lower end of tube. . . . Do you consider blood serious?' Later the same day he telegraphed again: 'analyst says no blood but I don't believe him'. Dr Quintard telegraphed back: 'Symptoms not significant'.[15]

By 29 December Aitken had cheered up. Although 'the contents of my stomach never looked to be as bad when I was in New York', there was no sign of blood. 'The stomach pump is not used as efficiently or as gently as Dr Halsey was accustomed to do, but New York is the home of luxuries even in stomach pumps. I go out every day at three o'clock and ride for an hour and a half. I do not come into my office until eleven in the morning, and I am on the whole a wonderfully well behaved person.' He planned to go south in January to recuperate: to Puerto Rico. 'I am leaving Mrs Aitken behind because she seems to be getting on so well here. Her family is in mourning and not going out at all and consequently she has no temptation to over-exert herself. I am too busy to spend a great deal of time with her and consequently do not worry her as I used to do in New York.'

He wrote later that his illness left him so depressed for so long that, 'feeling that there was no objective in life', he considered giving up 'the cares of business' altogether and retiring to a farm in Alberta. He certainly thought about 'going away for six months or more' at the beginning of 1907, or so he told R. E. Harris. 'But youth and vitality worked their miracle.'

He gave Gladys a fur coat and an account at a jewellers; their plans changed and she went with him to Puerto Rico. The birth of their first child, Janet, on 9 July 1908, he said, 'increased the intimacy of our relationship'. Of all inconvenient places, the cottage on the Arm had been chosen for this 'monumental event', and the gynaecologist predictably missed it, since he had to come out from the city by boat.

In her autobiography, Janet fantasized about the scene on the night of her birth: a happy family gathering for a bonfire party attended by her mother's two devoted brothers and one of her beautiful sisters, by three of Janet's Aitken aunts – Rahno, Gyp and Laura – and by her uncle Allan. She imagined her mother staring from her bedroom window into the darkness to pick out her father, not yet thirty, with his 'big head, wide grin, and neat feet', in the flickering light of the fire. 'Probably' he was talking to R. B. Bennett or Sir Robert Borden, two future Canadian Prime Ministers. Or perhaps he was handing a glass to his 'old school friend' [sic] Sir James Dunn. 'And she would have heard them laughing. They laughed a lot in those days, my father and his friends', as 'they helped themselves and each other to the power and the wealth that dangled before them like so much ripe fruit on a tree'.[16] The last phrase, at least, was accurate.

Aitken returned to his fruit-picking in Montreal soon after the birth. Less than a month later, on the morning of 7 August, Gladys sent a telegram from Halifax to his office: 'When are you coming home? Baby and I have come to town and will stay until you return. Gladys.' At 11.45 a.m. Aitken replied: 'What do you mean by telegram? Do I understand that you or your baby are ill? W. M. Aitken.' (This reply was charged to the firm.) Gladys: 'Both very well. Cottage too lonely.' Aitken, at 5.45 p.m.: 'I am leaving for Halifax tonight on Ocean Limited.'[17] Back in Montreal, he informed her on 28 August by telegram that he was going to England in September. The 'increased intimacy' did not include consultation. For once Aitken's often-planned first visit to England did not fall through; Gladys accompanied him, though not the two-month-old baby daughter. By the time they returned, Aitken had collected 'a pocketful of orders for Canadian securities' and made his first contact with the political life of England by calling on Andrew Bonar Law, an up-and-coming New Brunswick-born Conservative MP, to sell him some bonds. This meeting was no accident; Aitken had planned it in Canada, asking R. E. Harris to give him an introduction. Gladys had shown herself well able to hold her own in London society, but she was soon back in Halifax, staying with Mrs Stairs, who found the baby growing sweeter every day, while Aitken was once again in Halifax, immersed in business.

When someone congratulated Aitken's mother on her brilliant son, she replied, 'Which one?'; but her husband treated Max's success like the return of the prodigal. Much correspondence survives from the minister to 'my dear Max', but almost none from son to father. The themes are constant: requests for the son to come and see his parents; news of ailments; congratulations on successes; gratitude for his generosity; exhortations to the pursuit of a Christian life.

At least father and son shared a keen interest in health. 'Health after all is the main thing,' declared the minister, ' . . . so amid all that demands your attention let that be the chief demand' – advice that, as usual, the son ignored. 'Do come soon,' his father wrote. 'I want to have a long chat with you. The house you know is very empty now.' In the winter of 1906 the minister's health was troubling him and he thanked Max for proposing that he and Mrs Aitken should go to Bermuda, 'or some other genial health resort', but he felt too old. Traven by this time had gone West to seek his fortune; his wife had died and he left his two small girls in Newcastle. Gladys offered to look after them, but it was decided that they should live with their grandparents. Next year the flow of books resumed, forty volumes sent from Newcastle to Montreal – not, this time, for sale but for Max to read: 'I know you will like them.' The consignment included Chambers' *Encyclopaedia of English Literature* ('you will find it very useful'); Swift's *Tale of a Tub*, containing 'a good deal of Swift's rough humour'; a history of the Highlands ('an old book which was in my father's home as far back as I can remember'); and Dante, who 'is of course splendid'.

Finally, in 1907, the minister and his wife agreed to winter in the south. Mrs Aitken wrote to Max to tell him it was the first time his father had been away from Newcastle for any length of time since he had gone to Scotland eleven years earlier. From the Hotel Alcazar, St Augustine, Florida, William Aitken wrote on Christmas Eve to say, 'I hardly know how to thank you sufficiently for your kindness' in sending him to 'this most genial climate. To Anderson [Allan Anderson, the youngest boy], in his sickly, broken down condition, it is simply invaluable.' Traven's little girls went too; Jean McLintock remembered her grandfather's delight in the family's special private coach attached to the train, and how he invited friends to dine luxuriously on board during the stop in Baltimore.

William Aitken never took his son's largesse for granted. On 23 April

1908 he wrote to thank Max for providing the use of a horse and carriage. He had kept two horses in his first parish at Vaughan, and regarded himself as 'no mean judge of horseflesh'. But he did not need a full-time driver. He knew his son liked the family to tell him exactly how they spent his money. 'I shall take and keep a note of the times we have a driver.'

By 1909 the whole family was feeling the effects of Max's bounty. He paid for another long holiday in St Augustine, Florida, for his parents and Allan; 'should you not like your room at the Magnolia Hotel when you arrive,' his secretary wrote to his mother, 'it will be quite easy for me to change same, as we have paid a good price'; she enclosed $75 in American bills for immediate expenses, and explained that more money would be available in St Augustine. He paid Gyp's fees at the college in Pasadena, California, where she was training to be a librarian, and gave her an allowance. He paid for Laura at the University of Toronto. Mauns in 1909 was working at the Royal Bank of Canada branch office in Bathurst, New Brunswick, with a family of three children to support; Max lent him $1995, the exact size of the loan that Mauns asked for, but made Mauns assign his life insurance policies to him as collateral. Traven was working in a law office in Calgary, Alberta; Aitken put business his way. He sent cheques to Nan. When Rahno's doctor husband fell seriously ill with kidney trouble in California, Max's secretary wrote to say that 'Mr Aitken does not wish Dr Walker to worry about monetary matters in his present state of health', and Aitken paid out accordingly.

His generosity aroused universal and constant gratitude. 'I am sure there never was another boy as good to his people as you are', Nan wrote in 1909. After his secretary wrote to his mother in September 1909 to inform her that money had been paid into the Royal Bank of Canada in Newcastle for herself and Mr Aitken, and that there would 'always be money in these accounts and that you can always draw against same', his mother wrote back: ' . . . please thank Mr Aitken from me for his unlimited kindness'. She wrote to Max three months later: 'I don't know what we should have done without you. You certainly have been a good son to us.' Mauns wrote of 'kindness which I will never forget'. Gyp and Laura sent loving thank you letters. 'I do not know how to thank you,' wrote Allan from California, after Max offered to buy him a horse and buggy. 'Will it be all the same to you if I get a small single-seated automobile instead? . . . The people here use autos a great deal.'

Aitken was at his best when trouble struck. Then, as later, his first instinct was, 'Need any money?' When Rahno's husband died in California he cabled: 'Very very sorry indeed to hear about Horatio. Gladys and I sympathise with you very deeply. Can we do anything for you here? How much money shall I telegraph you? Would you like me to send someone out to you, and who?'[18]

The minister, now seventy-four, took a more and more unrealistic view of his son's way of life. On 4 January 1909, when Max was at his busiest, more books arrived from Newcastle. 'They are mostly relating to old important eras of the days that are long gone – the reformation era etc. – and of course are very interesting. I know you will enjoy looking into them now and again.' He enclosed a list of books sent, thirty-three in all, including Buchanan's *History of Scotland* in four volumes, *Essay on the Reformation* by Mackay in one volume, the Bible, the *Life of Thomas Bateman*, Rawlinson's *Ancient Egypt* in two volumes, and the *Pontificate of Leo X* in six volumes.

As William Aitken grew older, his travels became more ambitious, not less. On 11 March 1909, he wrote from Florida to say that he and his wife were planning to go to Washington – 'we are anxious to see the American Capital City. Then on to New York, and a day or two there – then on to Montreal', where Max, unknown to his father, was plotting the biggest deal of his career thus far, the formation of the Canada Cement Company.

THE CANADA CEMENT AFFAIR

By this time Aitken, though regarded warily by a few, and still barely thirty, had established a reputation among the insiders of eastern Canada as an exceptionally energetic and ingenious financier. Sir Herbert Holt, president of the Royal Bank of Canada, gave him the seal of approval by joining the board of Royal Securities; Sir Edward Clouston of the Bank of Montreal, recently knighted, looked on him with equal favour. With his high collar, loose tie and tiepin, his apparent deference to his elders, and his beautiful and well-connected wife, Aitken was on top of the world, embarking on what he called his 'first real big year'. The year 1909 was indeed big. By the time it ended, he had brought off a nationwide coup by merging the principal cement companies in Canada, with profit to himself. He had also realized that comparably glorious opportunities existed in other industries. During the rapid Canadian boom, all sorts of independent new enterprises had popped up in different parts of a huge and financially unsophisticated country. Aitken's methods were usually devious, but his ideas were always simple. He perceived the obvious and seductive fact that these enterprises – cement first, then steel, paper, power, grain – could make more money, and perhaps become more efficient, if they combined.

His initial merger, however, nearly brought him down. This became known as the Canada Cement affair and it had its origins in early 1909. The outlines of a murky operation, whose true nature will never now be known, are as follows; details will be found in the appendix on p. 529.

By 1909, the cement industry in Canada was in grave trouble. Cement, naturally, had boomed in line with the rest of the Canadian economy, but overproduction and the establishment of new companies meant that the producers were cutting one another's throats and in most cases losing a great deal of money.

At that point, an industrialist named Joseph Irvin formed a syndic merge a handful of these companies. He was head of two prof companies and a third that was going bankrupt: Exshaw. A merger, Irvin calculated, would save Exshaw and take care of its debts to the Bank of Montreal. Sir Edward Clouston at the bank approved the plan.

Aitken was brought into play by Clouston for reasons that remain obscure. First Aitken joined the Irvin syndicate, whose members thought they must admit him in order to stay on terms with Clouston and the bank to which they owed money. Then Aitken captured control of the syndicate by packing it with his own associates. Next, on his own initiative, he organized a far bigger merger than Irvin had dreamed of. He put together all the leading cement mills in the country, who could easily see the commercial advantages of the near-monopoly that he proposed. The new company he had called into being, Canada Cement, was launched in September 1909.

Irvin was on the board. So was the grand old man of the Canadian Pacific Railway, Sir Sandford Fleming, the president of the three companies run by Irvin. Both men had a personal financial stake in Exshaw. But after Canada Cement was launched Aitken refused to include Exshaw on the terms sought by Irvin and his associates. They said they were victims of an Aitken double-cross. He had pretended that he would take up the options he held on all three of their companies, but, having scooped up the two strong ones, had left out the weak one, thus wrecking the original merger idea. They also complained that the Bank of Montreal had failed to keep its promise to ensure the inclusion of Exshaw.

Fleming attacked Aitken privately, and then in 1911 publicly, with coast-to-coast newspaper coverage. By that time Aitken had moved to London. Fleming charged that Aitken had bought the merged companies for some $14,000,000, informed the shareholders that he had paid over $27,000,000, and issued himself with bonds and shares far in excess of the companies' true cost. Alleging that 'capital [had been] misappropriated on an enormous scale', Sir Sandford appealed to two successive Canadian Prime Ministers for action, the Liberal Wilfred Laurier and the Conservative Robert Borden, but they parried his demands – Borden, perhaps, because Aitken was a secret contributor to Conservative election funds. From London, Aitken reacted with a mixture of caution and bravado. Publicly, he flatly denied that he had made large sums out of the merger. Privately, he organized the concealment and destruction of documents, and caused the company through which he had arranged the merger to disappear altogether. In Canada, the Bank of Montreal brought an action against the Fleming interests for the repayment of debt. Preliminary hearings were held, at which Irvin and his associates expanded their allegations against Aitken. But in November 1913 the case was settled out of court – with Aitken making a secret cash contribution to the settlement – shortly before he was due to appear as a witness.

Rage though he might, and did, at the self-interest, jealousy, political bias, spite, dishonesty and blackmailing tactics of his accusers, Aitken never succeeded in dispersing the cloud of suspicion that enveloped him after the Canada Cement affair became public knowledge in 1911. His departure from Canada for London in 1910 was always, and still is, seen to be connected with his apprehension about that gathering cloud.

CHAPTER 4
THE PLUNGE INTO POLITICS
1910–1912

THE SUCCESSFUL FINANCIER from the New World arrived in England on his second visit in the spring of 1910. 'I had been reading the London newspapers and the exciting political situation over Chamberlain's plan for a united Empire filled me with enthusiasm,' he recalled with uncharacteristic vagueness. 'Surely this was a vision of splendour and as always my admiration was aroused and I was fired with a desire to take part in such a glamorous adventure. Why not try to set up a movement in Canada to cooperate with the British Tory Party which had by this time adopted Chamberlain's programme?'

Aitken's immediate purpose was less lofty: to raise $5,000,000 to finance the acquisition of a steel company, Montreal Rolling Mills, as a prelude to his creation of a Canadian steel combine, and he was in London for only a week. Their son Max was barely two months old, but Gladys made the voyage with her husband. 'I informed my wife that I was leaving on a journey to London. She informed me that her duty to her husband conflicted with her devotion to her young daughter and newborn son. She must make a sacrifice. And I was not the victim.' Aitken's mother was brought down from New Brunswick to look after the household. The crossing, in the last week of April, was stormy; but Aitken was cheered by 'the presence beside me of my beautiful and vivacious companion'. During his busy week, he called again on Bonar Law: 'Our meeting was cordial but for the second time I did not succeed in arousing his enthusiasm.' He tried and failed to pay his respects to Joseph Chamberlain: 'He was not unwilling to encourage a young supporter from abroad but a stroke had put an end to his political career, though the fiction of his leadership was still maintained.' After a week he described as 'restless' – but it was crowned with success, as he borrowed his $5,000,000 from Parr's Bank against his personal securities – the Aitkens sailed home again, leaving on 7 May, the day after the death of Edward VII. 'The whole nation was in mourning,' Aitken recalled, 'which impressed me as an admirable though solemn demonstration of loyalty and devotion to the

69

monarchy. And of course the monarch was inevitably associated with my conception of a United Empire: Canada and the Dominions, Crown Colonies and India, in one customs union, and under one crown.'

Despite the apparent immutability of the monarchy and the Empire, Britain in 1910 was in political turmoil, and the cracks in the splendid façade opened up opportunities for energetic adventurers like Max Aitken. Both the territory of the country and its constitution were under threat. The Liberal government under Herbert Asquith was fighting to negotiate Home Rule for Ireland against bitter opposition; and David Lloyd George, Asquith's radical Welsh Chancellor, was planning social reforms that would lead to deadlock in Parliament. The Conservative Party under Arthur Balfour was still split by the issue that had given the Liberals a landslide victory in 1906: Free Trade versus Tariff Reform.

Aitken had no interest in Ireland or constitutional matters, but his instinctive wish to strengthen the bonds of Empire predisposed him towards Tariff Reform and Imperial Preference. In 1910 these issues aroused as much heart-searching as Britain's relations with Europe half a century later, posing deep questions of national identity and self-interest. The principal ideas behind Tariff Reform were likely to appeal to Aitken: first, to revitalize the British Empire, increasingly threatened by two powerful rivals for world trade and political power – the United States and Germany; and second, to help create jobs inside a self-contained market for British and colonial raw materials and finished products.

The threat produced a prolonged battle for the soul of the Conservative Party between the Free Traders, led by the aristocratic Cecil family – Balfour was a cousin of the Cecils – and the Tariff Reformers, a newer breed of Conservative, with manufacturing interests to protect. Some of the steam went out of it when in July 1906, the day after his seventieth birthday, the prophet and leader of Tariff Reform, Joseph Chamberlain, suffered a stroke that effectively removed him from public life. His main disciples, his son Austen and the comparative newcomer Bonar Law, were less inspiring figures. Nevertheless the party remained deeply divided between those who were convinced that Tariff Reform could win the next election, and those who were equally convinced that the higher food prices implied by this policy must prove an electoral disaster.

By the time of Aitken's third visit, later in 1910, the nation was moving towards a constitutional crisis that overshadowed such matters. In November 1909 the House of Lords threw out Lloyd George's People's Budget – an event unprecedented in British political history. Parliament was immediately dissolved. At the general election of January 1910, the 'Peers v. People' election, Asquith retained his majority in the Commons only with the support of the Irish Nationalists. The new Parliament was dominated by the constitutional question; Asquith was determined that the Lords should be curbed, and in April the Parliament Bill removing their power to dismiss legislation passed the House of Commons. Another election was called, to decide once and for all whether the Lords should lose their powers. Parliament was dissolved on 28 November. These events gave Aitken his chance to enter British politics; and the Conservative Party was his natural political destination. His political friends and connections in Canada were conservative; his record and standing as a rich financier, coupled with an emotional commitment to the Empire rooted in his Maritime background, made his allegiance inevitable. He was never drawn towards, nor indeed pursued by, the old High Tory, aristocratic wing of the Conservatives; they distrusted him and he despised them. He much enjoyed describing how when he first met Balfour all the Conservative leader wanted to talk about was the stock market.[1] The Conservatism that attracted Aitken in 1910 has been summed up as 'the imperialist Conservatism of Rhodes and Chamberlain, the creed of the successful industrialists, of the engineers and technicians who were opening up a new world by their enterprise and their not always overscrupulous vigour – the Conservatism of which Rudyard Kipling was both prophet and high priest'.[2]

BONAR LAW AND KIPLING

In July 1910 the Aitkens again left Montreal together on their way to London, with high hopes. 'Without doubt a longing to take part in the Empire plan was a controlling desire,' he wrote, adding disarmingly, 'But my ignorance of British public life was immense and my vanity led me to foolish conclusions. My success in making mergers in Canada had turned out so wonderfully well. Why not exercise the same talent in making a worthy contribution to the effort of bringing all the Empire units into one commercial combine?' It is not likely that he had decided to abandon finance for politics; his most immediate business in London was once again to raise money, this time for the development of the Canadian newsprint industry. He later drew a moving picture of the excited young couple, as they arrived in New York to board the *Lusitania*, discussing where his destiny lay. 'Would I turn again to finance? No! I said to my wife. "No!" said she. We would go forward to find, if possible, a place in the great conception, the mighty plan for a United Empire.'

Arriving in London in late July, they found many people away for the holidays, and business, politics and social life suspended. They took a flat in Cavendish Square. Aitken went for a third time to call on Bonar Law, but the house was closed; he kept boredom and uncertainty at bay by acquiring the Rolls Royce motor car company, on the market after the death of Charles Stewart Rolls in an air crash. ('Meanwhile there was money to invest. Capital should not be idle.') He visited the land of his forebears. In the early autumn, over lunch with another business acquaintance, an influential Conservative Member of Parliament, Edward

Goulding, Aitken again met Bonar Law. This time, the two men took a liking to each other.

They were both of Scottish extraction, born and raised in New Brunswick, both had fathers who were Presbyterian ministers, and both had made successful careers in business. In Bonar Law Aitken found someone from familiar territory; someone else who had spent his childhood listening to scarifying sermons, helping with the chores and skating all winter on frozen rivers. He also found a man, at the heart of Conservative Party politics and a leading Tariff Reformer, who was not an upper-class Englishman with inherited land or wealth, but a business-man with experience of investment and finance. Here the resemblance ends. Aitken was twenty-one years younger; in character and temperament they were opposites. Bonar Law, with his long oval face, solemn expression and drooping moustache, was as cautious and pessimistic as Aitken was adventurous and optimistic. Moreover, Bonar Law's life as a young man had been very different from Aitken's.

His mother had died when he was two, and Bonar Law left Canada for good with his maternal aunt when he was twelve to live with her in Glasgow. At sixteen he left school and started work in his cousin's merchant bank; his formative years were spent in the utmost respectability, among the well-off but deeply unostentatious Scottish middle-class business community. He played golf and bridge and enjoyed milk, with gingerbread, as a nightcap. His only indulgence was nicotine: he became a heavy pipe and cigar smoker. Bonar Law impressed the tough Glasgow business community, and in 1886, when he was twenty-seven, was offered a partnership in the leading iron merchants William Jacks, where he spent ten successful years.

In 1891 he married a Glasgow shipbroker's daughter, to whom he was devoted: they had seven children. Five years later he inherited a substantial sum of money and decided to stand for Parliament, and in 1900 he became the Conservative member for the Blackfriars division of Glasgow. Balfour made him Parliamentary Secretary at the Board of Trade in 1902; he was noticeable in the House of Commons for his phenomenal memory, although an unexciting speaker. In the Liberal landslide of 1906 he lost his seat, but was soon found another, at Dulwich in south London. In 1909 he finally moved from Scotland to London, to a large house off Edwardes Square, Pembroke Lodge, where he could be close to the centre of events; but he disliked society and preferred to live quietly at home with his large family.

Bonar Law's background, political career and opinions all made him an obvious target for Aitken's attentions; and a personal tragedy made him more responsive to a new friendship than he might otherwise have been. In October 1909, his wife Annie had suddenly fallen ill and died. She was forty-two; their youngest child was only five. Bonar Law, who had always had a melancholy streak, sank into depression and lethargy. Aitken's energy and admiration were a distraction and a tonic. He was able to cheer Bonar Law, perhaps because he had no connection with the past. As he recalled, 'It seems that almost at once he was telling me the most intimate details of his life. He spoke so frankly and plainly that there was no doubt that he was making me his confidant.' Aitken was flattered in his turn. He himself was well aware of the incongruities in the friendship. He described an early lunch with Bonar Law:

> . . . the food was not very good, and I noticed with a little annoyance that I was given one glass of whisky and water, whereas my host helped himself twice to what appeared to be a special whisky out of his own bottle. This keeping of a special tap in one's own house is a thing that I have a prejudice against.
> It was a week after that when I found out that he was a teetotaller and his 'special whisky' was a bottle of lime juice. I had remorse for my lack of charity. Henceforward I saw more of him and it was plain that my conversation amused him.
> Next, to my surprise I found him dining with me. But perhaps his surprise was greater than mine for he never dined with anyone if he could help it.[3]

Bonar Law's friends and family were surprised too, and not all of them were pleased by the new arrival in the inner circle. His sister Mary, who had taken over the administration of the household after Mrs Law's death, told him, 'I don't care about [for] the growing influence of Max Aitken here.' Bonar Law was lying on a sofa reading; he took off his glasses and said quietly, 'Do let me like him.'[4] She did, and in time became devoted to him herself.

Money as well as politics drew Bonar Law and Aitken together. In October 1909, Bonar Law put $5000 into Royal Securities. In 1910, Aitken had his Price Brothers bonds to sell; and on 20 October Bonar Law put in £100,000, a very large sum. From then on, they had constant financial dealings with each other. It has been calculated that Bonar Law 'probably benefited to the extent of some £10,000 a year, of course tax free'.[5] He was an early investor in Canada Cement and bought into other companies in which Aitken was heavily involved; for his part Aitken was soon buying copper futures and pig iron warrants through William Jacks. Bonar Law was rich already, and understood financial markets; his links with Aitken did not lead to dependence. With others, it was to be rather different. From the very first months of his arrival in England Aitken managed to combine politics, friendship and money in a peculiarly potent cocktail. He liked deploying his money-making skills on behalf of his new friends, and the access such transactions required was useful to him. If there was a clear element of self-interest in Aitken's pursuit of Bonar Law's friendship, there was also genuine liking and respect. Bonar Law was modest, scrupulous and steady; Aitken admired such qualities in his new mentor all the more because he did not share them.

To Bonar Law, Aitken appeared an excellent prospect for the Tariff Reform wing of the party. In the month that he invested his £100,000 he wrote to tell Aitken that he had asked Conservative Central Office 'about any suitable seats available'.[6]

Bonar Law was not the only wily Conservative eager to attract Aitken's dynamism and millions into the party. So was Edward Goulding, a less prominent politician than Bonar Law but even better fitted to be sponsor and guide to an aspirant MP. Known to his friends as Paddy, Goulding was a tall, thin, genial figure, a wealthy Anglo-Irishman (his father had been MP for Cork) educated at Cambridge. He had been in Parliament almost continuously since 1895 and, as a passionate admirer of Joseph Chamberlain, was entirely committed to imperialism and social reform. He was a founder member of the Tariff Reform League, and had been chairman of its Organization Department since 1904. Chamberlain called him the best organizer he had ever known, and J. L. Garvin, the editor of the *Observer*, described him as 'a legend behind the scenes and a power in politics without being either a minister or a force in debate. . . . There never was a more potent backbencher in the House of Commons; nor a surer, shrewder manager of human nature in the lobbies and the dining room.'[7] Aitken learned a great deal from Goulding, as he told him decades later: 'In politics I am the product of your encouragement. You had the foresight to know that I could do something. . . .'

In 1910 Goulding was forty-eight and a bachelor, with a large and agreeable house, Wargrave Hall, on the Thames in Berkshire. There, with his sister as hostess, he would give weekend house parties, especially during the summer when he loved to show guests, usually politicians and journalists, his rose garden and to arrange bridge games or picnics on the river. He was close to Bonar Law; Garvin; H. A. Gwynne, editor of the fiercely Conservative *Morning Post*; R. D. Blumenfeld, the respected American-born editor of the ailing *Daily Express*; Hugh Chisholm, of the *St James's Gazette* and a prominent Tariff Reformer; F. E. Smith, the barrister and rising star of the Tories; and Sir Edward Carson, the formidable leader of the Ulster Unionists. Unlike Bonar Law, Goulding was sociable and gregarious and loved to bring people together. Like Bonar Law, he very soon benefited from the Aitken connection; after Aitken acquired Rolls Royce in the summer of 1910 he put Goulding on the board, where he remained for the rest of his life, though Aitken soon sold out.

The first time Aitken signed the visitors' book at Wargrave (giving his address simply as 'Montreal') was on 27 September 1910; Gladys had already returned to Canada and the children. In the same month Goulding gave a lunch party in honour of Balfour and Bonar Law; Aitken was invited and found himself sitting next to Blumenfeld, who recorded his impressions. 'A comparative youth, carelessly dressed, with tousled hair, searching eyes, alternately hard and twinkling, and a large full-lipped mouth which made him look cold and forbidding in repose, and extraordinarily attractive when it spread itself in a smile over his colourless face.' During lunch Aitken remarked to Blumenfeld, almost casually: 'I am going into Parliament. I am going to pick out a good, sound Liberal seat and turn it over to the Unionist Party.'[8] Soon afterwards, as Aitken himself put it: ' . . . under Bonar Law's patronage . . . I took the plunge into public life, seeking at once an opportunity to stand for parliament. An opening arose in North Cumberland, a constituency centring on Carlisle.' In fact it was Goulding who proposed the Cumberland seat, though no doubt with Bonar Law's approval, in a letter dated 8 October: 'I have heard of a possible constituency which I think is worth your careful consideration and which we might get you the offer of,' Goulding wrote, advising Aitken to refer for more information to the secretary of the Tariff Reform League. According to Aitken, he went up to Carlisle for a week, feeling decidedly nervous: 'Anxiety and even fear obsessed me – and why not? I had never made a speech. My knowledge of politics was confined to the Empire issue.' The aspiring candidate was relieved not to be asked to speak in public.

By this time everyone knew that the rich young Canadian was on the lookout for a seat, and that with his connections and wealth he was likely to find one and fight it on Tariff Reform at the next election. On 22 October he wrote to R. B. Bennett in Canada: 'I believe I am being selected on my merits or supposed merits. They say money does not count but I am sometimes suspicious.'[9]

At the same time that Aitken was impressing politicians and editors, he was making friends with the outstanding writer of the day, a connection that added greatly to Aitken's prestige both in England and in Canada. He became a close family friend of the great poet of the Empire, Rudyard Kipling.

Kipling then was not only a towering literary figure: he stood for, and indeed had helped to create, the imperialist fervour that lay behind Joseph Chamberlain's political campaign. In his novels, stories and poems he celebrated the Empire, its administrators, soldiers, camp followers and subjects; he believed in hierarchy and authority, and never questioned the right of the British to rule much of the world. He was politically inept, yet frequently consulted by statesmen and journalists. In 1910 he was at the height of his powers and fame. His poem 'Recessional', written for Queen Victoria's Jubilee in 1897, had become the unofficial imperial anthem; in 1907 he became the first English writer to be awarded the Nobel Prize for Literature. He lived in Sussex with his two children and his American wife, Carrie.

Kipling judged all politicians by how they stood on the Empire. He had written a poem in praise of Chamberlain's vision, and another, 'Our Lady of the Snows', on the unpromising topic of the Canadian Preferential Tariff of 1897:

A Nation spoke to a Nation
A Queen sent word to a Throne:
Daughter am I in my mother's house,
But mistress in my own.
The gates are mine to open,
As the gates are mine to close,
And I set my house in order,
Said our Lady of the Snows.

He knew and admired Canada, and it was not surprising that he was impressed by a dynamic young Canadian prepared to build a political career on imperial links. In 1906, in a letter to H. A. Gwynne, Kipling had written:

I am glad you have seen the politicians at close quarters. They are a macaroni-backed crew, even the best of them, and they will follow only winning causes. You must wake up some of the young men on our side. Our great weakness, of course, is that we have no understudy to Chamberlain, and I think that is due to the way in which the inner caste of Conservatives has stifled and hampered the young blood. Can't you find a young 'un and enthuse him?[10]

Perhaps he thought Aitken was such a young 'un.

Aitken and Kipling first met in the autumn of 1910. A very formal letter survives, drawing Kipling's attention to an article attacking reciprocity – the proposal, backed by the Liberals in Canada, to lower tariffs by mutual agreement between Canada and the United States, which was naturally anathema to believers in Imperial Preference. Before long they were on much closer terms.

'AN OUTSIDE MAN'

Early in November, with an election in prospect, events took a turn that gave Aitken his chance of entering Parliament, in a country where he was not even entitled to vote, sooner than he could possibly have anticipated. Lord Derby, the political overlord of Lancashire, felt strongly that it would be good for the Conservative Party if Bonar Law gave up his safe seat in Dulwich and went all out for a Tariff Reform victory in the traditional Free Trade stronghold around Manchester. Bonar Law was ready to do so, and was offered Ashton-under-Lyne, but eventually the choice fell on North West Manchester, an even more marginal seat. Ashton-under-Lyne was thus left without a candidate; whereupon Bonar Law wrote, on 14 November, to the chairman of the Conservative Association:

As regards your constituency, if you want an outside man, there is a young friend of mine who, I think, would make a very good candidate. He is a young Canadian, not much over 30, who without any outside help has made a large fortune; he is a keen imperialist and for that reason wants to stand for Parliament. He has not had any political experience, but he has a distinct personality and, I believe, would be attractive in any constituency.

With characteristic ambivalence Bonar Law went on: 'Of course I always think that a good local man is to be preferred but if you have to go outside, it might be worthwhile to think of my friend. . . .'[11]

What happened next is obscure, partly because Aitken's own account is not strictly accurate. According to him, a deputation from Ashton-under-Lyne came to London on a Saturday and lunched with him and Bonar Law at Pembroke Lodge. 'Bonar Law drank his lime juice as usual. Others, including myself, took to the excellent and possibly overproof Scotch whisky. . . . When Bonar Law repeated his refusal, not for the first time, the company was startled by my question – "Why not me?" ' In Aitken's version he was really hoping for the seat Bonar Law had abandoned, Dulwich, and, by the morning after, had cold feet about offering to take on the much trickier Lancashire seat; but, when Bonar Law 'gave me a severe lecture early on Sunday morning on the necessity for continuity in conduct and behaviour in political relationships' (a line that rings true), he realized that 'my fate was determined'.

As so often with Aitken, the reality behind his rearrangement of the facts was less sunny. An undated letter to Bonar Law shows that Aitken had mixed feelings about the whole enterprise:

> The central office has ignored my offer to serve the party in the interests of Tariff Reform and Preference from the period of my first visit until three days ago. . . . Now that the election is impending I am offered a seat intended by the office for a labour candidate. . . . I cannot accept further humiliation at the hands of a body which cannot accept proffered services in the spirit in which I approached the subject.[12]

His phrase 'labour candidate' meant a working-class Conservative; Goulding was one of the leaders of a drive to field more such candidates. Aitken, for all his political inexperience and eagerness, could not tolerate being manoeuvred by anyone. He preferred to do the manoeuvring himself.

By the third week of November the die was cast. On the 20th Aitken sent a telegram to Goulding: 'The Mayor and Councillor Shaw are entirely too persuasive. Gwynne has joined their forces. I am ready to accept if you and F. E. Smith will guarantee to address a meeting warranted to be not less than 3,000 on Monday November 28th . . . unless you and Smith give me a warranty the deal is off.' Aitken felt the need of heavyweight support; star speakers at public meetings were important, and he doubted his own ability to dominate an audience. On the same day, another telegram went off from Gwynne to Kipling, although he was known to detest public appearances: 'Aitken standing for Ashton-under-Lyne six miles from Manchester you promised make speech during election. Suggest you make it for Aitken. . . .'[13]

Goulding, already in his own constituency, Worcester, wrote back in calm and encouraging tones:

> You are a fine chap and will win Ashton on your own. Of course I'll speak for you on 28th but you only want one outside speaker besides yourself and Cousins. . . . Mind you – the *candidate* is the man that is in the footlights – your own personality will do the trick – if you are having Law one night that is splendid – but my advice is don't have too many big guns to detract from the biggest gun – yourself. . . .

Meanwhile in Ashton-under-Lyne the leading Conservative paper, the *Reporter*, informed its readers on 21 November that William Maxwell Aitken was 'secured' as the Conservative candidate; reminded them that the election was to take place 'on Saturday week, December 3rd'; and announced that 'Mr Aitken last week cabled from London to New Brunswick for his wife, and Mrs Aitken is expected to arrive at Fishguard today'. The paper went on to outline the candidate's background, not very accurately: 'Mr Aitken has achieved a remarkably brilliant career as a commercial man. After being at school for some time he studied law with Governor Tweedy and then occupied a prominent position in the Brunswick Government.' The fact was that the Conservative officials of Ashton-under-Lyne, let alone the voters, knew nothing about Aitken except that he was Canadian, rich and a protégé of Bonar Law; even so, they knew more about him than he knew about them. Aitken had about ten days to win the seat. In later years he liked to remark: 'Manchester was my political cradle, and it rocked a good deal.'[14]

Ashton-under-Lyne is today engulfed in the grim urban sprawl of outer Manchester. In 1910 it was a somewhat undistinguished cotton town, with some depressing slum terraces, and Conservative Party activists of the solid, bourgeois sort – doctors, clergymen, teachers. The sitting MP was a Liberal, an important local figure and owner of a chain of grocery stores, who had held the seat in February by only 293 votes. According to contemporary press reports, 'When it was known that an unknown Canadian was coming the Liberals sent up a shout of laughter.' 'We want no foreigner,' wrote 'A Patriot': 'A Lancashire man for a Lancashire seat.' 'Who is Mr Aitken?' his opponents asked repeatedly, and mocked his rasping Canadian accent and his talk of dollars and cents. A Liberal versifier published a verse with the refrain:

> So back you must go, William, over the water
> We are able to govern our own little show.

The Conservatives countered quickly; the *Reporter* announced 'A Popular Refrain: All the Children in Ashton are singing it.

Yip i addy i ay, i ay;
Yip i addy i ay;
Vote for Aitken on polling day
He's the man and he's come to stay . . .'

Two legends grew up round the Ashton-under-Lyne campaign of 1910; that Aitken introduced startlingly new and efficient methods of campaigning, and that he poured money into securing victory by any means, including bribery. Certainly Aitken organized his campaign, based at the Midland Hotel, with style and efficiency, and he could afford to spend money; but he took care to discover the legal limitations on campaign spending. No details of the expenses of the campaign survive, but there is a letter of 21 November from Aitken to Goulding asking him to contribute via the Tariff Reform League, and adding, 'I suppose I am precluded now from making any contributions on my own account at all.' Aitken could afford to pay for copious campaign literature, and to provide a fleet of cars for canvassing and the transport of voters to the polls; and he paid for a large eve-of-poll party for some two thousand Conservative women at the biggest Ashton hotel: since women did not then have the vote, this could not be regarded as 'treating'.

Aitken did everything he could to procure good publicity in the local press; on 14 November, well before he accepted the nomination, he instructed his secretary in Canada, Miss de Gruchy: 'Get articles privately prepared dealing with constructive work tramways water power industrials. Omit combines financial operations. Do not deal in figures. Riches beneficial. . . . Do not omit Mrs Aitken who is very important. . . .'[15] His ruse was to plant material in the Canadian press so that it could be reproduced in the English papers. While Aitken wanted to be seen as the sturdy industrialist, rather than the devious financier, the Liberals naturally tried to present him as a ruthless millionaire speculator. A rumour spread that he had cornered cotton and wheat, thereby increasing unemployment in Lancashire. Fun was poked at the way he pronounced cotton as 'carton'; but he soon learned how to deal with such tactics. 'Lancashire audiences I know want to hear about their cotton – I am still pronouncing it as I used to (laughter) – still the foreigner (laughter). . . .' As for the rumour, he was forthright: 'I have never bought or sold a bale of cotton, I have never bought or sold a bushel of wheat.' This may have been true; the next sentence was perhaps not: 'I have never carried on any speculative transaction and I have never engaged in any speculative enterprise.' Posters appeared in Ashton offering £1000 reward to anyone who could prove the allegation. When he was attacked for being a millionaire, he had an answer ready: 'It is said that I am a rich man. . . . I am quite rich enough to be able to devote myself to the service of my country if I get the chance. . . .'

As for the brilliant new campaign methods, it is hard to see how much reorganization could be achieved in ten days. But to one contemporary reporter he did seem a different kind of candidate.

> He has set a new fashion in electioneering, a fashion likely to spread far. . . .
> He planned the election exactly as though it were some great new business enterprise. Everyone who has had anything to do with elections knows that much slackness prevails. Whole sections of voters are left untouched; others are canvassed half a dozen times over. At Ashton-under-Lyne, these things did not happen. A system of checks, accountancy and book-keeping was installed. Every man's work was supervised, and every man's work had to be done.

Goulding was doubtless gratified to learn that his protégé had taken his advice so seriously. He wrote to Aitken again on 26 November: 'I do hope that you are canvassing. Many votes are got that way. Your sympathy and breeziness would accomplish much and if Mrs Aitkin [sic] would do the same it would be grand. You are going to win. . . . Get the *Daily Express* each day – splendid tips for speeches – also try and visit workshops daily. . . .'

Gladys Aitken, after her dash from Montreal, proved a real asset during the campaign. Aitken reckoned that she was a better speaker than he was; Goulding urged that she be as active as possible; Bonar Law glumly advised her not to wear her best clothes on the platform, but apparently she paid no attention. In those days, the candidate's wife was expected to add glamour and charm to the all-male business of elections, and to influence other women to influence their men. Gladys, with her tall, glowing presence and her Canadian ease, made a great impact. 'A fine, handsome Canadian,' the *Reporter* called her. Her husband was described as 'spare, lithe-limbed . . . of sallow complexion and frank open countenance, radiant with smiles'.

Aitken found speech-making hard. He was used to being in control, knowing his subject, facts and figures at his fingertips; at election meetings there was always the fear that he might be asked a question he could not answer. He stuck, as far as possible, to his chosen topic: the Empire and how to strengthen it. He issued a manifesto:

> A crisis has arrived which is without parallel in the annals of the British Empire. The Liberals have decided on a rush Election in the hope that the question of paramount importance to all Britons – namely, the solidarity of our Empire – may be overlooked. Electors! The position is grave and calls for your most serious consideration. You must think now, and think aright. Britain stands FIRST NOW in the unity of nations. See to it, men of Britain, that she stands FIRST ALWAYS.

A contemporary verbatim report of one of his speeches does not suggest a natural orator.

. . . those who have travelled over the possessions of Great Britain on the American continent instantly realise that Britain's position in regard to her possessions there is greater and better than that of the United States. Don't be deceived. They haven't developed as the American states have developed, but that's very largely our own fault and we're going to remedy it. Britain has her possessions in every part of the world, she has land in four continents. England, however, is not today the leading nation of all the world. Twenty-five years ago she was first in the production of steel; today she is third. . . .

When he was asked for his views about the reform of the House of Lords, he did not pretend he had any. 'He said frankly he was not immensely interested in it. It did not give any employment. . . .' On one occasion he dried up completely during a speech, and simply said, in a shaking voice: 'If I could make you men of Ashton realise what this Empire of ours means, there would not be one Radical left in the place.' When Bonar Law came to speak, he told the audience: 'Mr Aitken has never had any experience of making speeches; but he has had experience of things more difficult than making speeches.' F. E. Smith tackled with barrister-like deftness the awkward matter of Aitken being an outsider and a millionaire: quoting Burns, he simply said: 'A man's a man for a' that.'

The evening before the poll, 2 December, the Aitken campaign reached its climax with a torchlit procession led by the 'Imps' – the young men of the Junior Imperialist League – down the High Street. A huge magic lantern erected in the Market Square threw Aitken's portrait on to a screen erected on the side of the George and Dragon Hotel. Next day, fleets of cars ferried his supporters to the polls; when Aitken found some of the drivers sitting down to a meal in the hotel he flew into a rage and shouted at them to get out into the streets again. He and Gladys 'drove about continuously during the day in open carriages decked with party colours'.

At 9.15 p.m. the result was announced by Major Pownall, 'who rushed down the steps of the Town Hall in great glee and shouted to the expectant crowd Aitken, Aitken'. He had won by 196 votes, out of a total vote of 7892. 'Hats and sticks were waved enthusiastically and weird blue lights were thrown into the air and illuminated the surroundings,' wrote the *Reporter*. Aitken then appeared, declined to make a speech, and threaded his way through the crowds to the Central Conservative Club, where he appeared at a window to wave to the cheering throng. Gladys was with him and 'in view of the assembled multitude, threw her arms around her husband's neck and kissed him'. Aitken then managed a few words: 'I am now a Lancashire man,' he shouted, 'a Lancashire man from Canada.'

Among the congratulations that reached him (and the local newspapers) was a cable from the Premier of New Brunswick: 'I hope you will have as distinguished a career as New Brunswick's great son – Bonar Law.' Aitken himself sent off a jubilant cable to Goulding, whose poll was not due until 5 December: 'You may think this Ashton affair can be attributed wholly to you but my wife shares the honour with you . . . when does Worcester come off, can I assist?' On 4 December Goulding wrote back: 'A thousand and the heartiest congratulations on your great victory – it is splendid – the one bright thing.' (Bonar Law had been narrowly beaten at Manchester; but he won a by-election at Bootle six weeks later.) 'I poll tomorrow and I hope to be right. I have gone boldly for Tariff – it will be a grand thing to have you to work with in the House. . . .' But in the country as a whole, the result of the December election was very little different from February: the Liberals were strengthened in their determination to curb the powers of the House of Lords.

'WHO IS MR AITKEN?'

Victory at Ashton-under-Lyne brought Aitken national publicity for the first time in Britain. 'Who is Mr Aitken?' asked the *Daily Mail*.

> Picture to yourself a man of thirty one, scarce looking his years, of slight physique and with a face browned by early life in the province of woods and streams and sea. He is full of nervous energy. His large eyes, his strong lips and active manner tell of one unusually keen, quick and responsive. . . . And here, in Mr Max Aitken, we have a new figure in English politics. His campaign of Imperialism, efficiency and social reform will not be confined to Ashton. It is not without significance that one of the most striking victories of the campaign has been won by a newcomer from overseas, who looks on our problems and opportunities with the fresh and broad vision of the illimitable West.

When the *Daily Express* asked Aitken to tell the readers how he had achieved his dramatic success, he cabled confidently: 'Victory due to brilliant organisation and Tariff Reform.' Congratulations and requests for interviews flowed in; on the day after the poll the mighty press baron, Northcliffe, inventor of mass circulation newspapers in Britain, instructed a young reporter on the *Daily Mail* to go immediately to Manchester to talk to 'a very remarkable young Canadian. . . . He is Bonar Law's friend and he will be a big new figure in British politics.' Aitken made a lasting impact on the reporter. 'What impressed me most was his dynamic force. . . . He was intensely alive, and conveyed a sense of dominating vitality.' Aitken also showed signs of having a sense of humour, 'a rare gift in a newly-rich man planning a career'.[16] But by the time the article was reproduced in Canada, the new MP was suffering a reaction. 'A Nervous Breakdown,' said a *Toronto Star* headline, 'He is at Present Recuperating After the Stress of the Campaign.' In the wake of a great effort, Aitken was always liable to fall ill and summon the doctors. Nevertheless he managed to attend two celebration banquets, one in Ashton – a triumphant occasion despite the absence of Lord Derby, whom Aitken declined to invite in retaliation for his lack of support during the campaign – and another in London, where some of the Tory old guard apparently found his after-dinner speech bumptious.

For all the praise and excitement, however, Aitken realized very quickly that the life of an MP had its drawbacks. He found himself enmeshed in a party machine that seldom worked as he thought it should, and his new prominence exposed him to scrutiny he did not always welcome. A letter to Goulding on 14 December radiates polite fury: 'I regret exceedingly that the Tariff Reform League went to the expense of sending literature into Ashton on the eve of the poll . . . as I did not conduct any meetings on December 2nd I regret that the four speakers were wasted that day. . . . I must again revert to the position I so reluctantly gave up of declining to discuss the Tariff Reform League beyond thanking the organisation for all their assistance in Ashton.' He went on with some force: 'You will bear in mind I am new to politics and I have to inform you it is customary in my business to freely discuss the weakness of organisation without bitterness and in the hope that improvement may result. In my business also I have never found an organisation in which there was not room for improvement.' A remark in a letter to Bonar Law of the same date evidently reflects his tussle with the League: 'It is different in business, isn't it?'

More serious was the spate of sneering that broke out in the Liberal press, especially in the Manchester area, about the way the election had been conducted. Readers' letters, mostly anonymous, used phrases such as 'the voters' blatant prostitution'; 'degrading practices introduced by both parties'; and 'The fact is admitted by honest electors of either political faith that soulless pariahs openly sell their votes to the highest bidder.' Aitken was a political novice, he had won by a narrow margin, and he was a millionaire; conclusions were drawn. More ominous was the rumour that the Liberals intended to file a petition to overturn the result on grounds of corruption. Despite reassurances from legal and political advisers Aitken was clearly worried by the threat, and was fretting over it when he and Gladys went off to the south of France for Christmas. He announced that he was going on doctor's orders, to recover from the exertions of the campaign.

Before leaving, however, he was able on behalf of one of his new friends to turn his mind to business; Kipling sought his advice about investing part of his considerable literary earnings in Canadian bonds, adding, 'It's a shame to worry you when you are just drawing breath.' On 21 December Aitken replied that he had

. . . taken the liberty of cabling to the Montreal Trust Co. to say that any order from you must be very carefully executed. . . . The Directors of the Montreal Trust Company represent the best commercial element in Canada and I am sure that every one of them would rather do anything than lose a penny of your money, and your money particularly. I can write you this way now because I live in England and have resigned from the Board of the Trust Company . . . if you will do me the honour to consult me again, I will be only too glad to give you the benefit of my knowledge of Canadian conditions.

This exchange marks the beginning of a voluminous correspondence about Kipling's finances, with which Aitken gave a great deal of help over the next few years. The letter was signed by a secretary, who added at the foot: 'Under medical orders Mr Aitken has been enjoined complete rest and has gone away.' Kipling immediately wrote back, sounding faintly embarrassed:

> Dear Aitken, (I think we will drop the Mister)
> You are more than good to bother to write to me now, when you are paying the penalty of a plunge into our quiet hum-drum English politics. You must have had a hell and a half of a time but what specially cheered me is that you seem to have won out on straight business talk – pure Tariff Reform. It's a huge victory in every point of view and I *do* hope Canada will see it. Evidently your cables have touched the spot for the old 'Montrust' is jumping quite lively at the end of the wires. . . . Now you get fit again and when you feel you are all right take a fortnight or three weeks in Switzerland and find out what a Canadian winter with all the luxuries really means. It's the best pick me up in the world.

All his life, however, Aitken preferred the sun to mountains and snow.

From Cannes he was in correspondence with one of his lawyers about his election expenses, which, he was told, 'are well within the allowance and I do not think will be queried. . . . You can sign your declaration before any English JP and I expect that there are many in Cannes.' On 4 January, evidently in answer to further anxious enquiries from Aitken, the lawyer wrote again: 'The time for filing a petition on the grounds of corrupt practices has gone, as this must be done within 21 days . . . a petition can now only be founded on illegal practices and expenditures based on the agent's accounts.' Aitken's agent, J. C. Buckley, had submitted the accounts and all was in order; 'I cannot gather that there is any evidence of anything wrong having been done. . . . I hope that you are rapidly throwing off the effect of the election strain.' But Aitken remained sensitive about his alleged malpractices. He wrote later to Will Andrew, owner of the *Reporter*: 'I do not care one bit for my place in Parliament if it is to be won with the same amount of mental anguish and humiliation which I suffered in the last election . . . both you and I have pledged our words that corruption in Ashton is going to be cleaned up. . . .' While he was in the south of France he executed one important piece of business. He gave R. D. Blumenfeld a subsidy for the troubled *Daily Express*.

'SQUIRMING OUT OF THE BAZAARS'

By early February the Aitkens were back in London, where the duties of an MP and his wife awaited them. At first they took a flat in Knightsbridge; Aitken also found it convenient to keep rooms at the Hyde Park Hotel. His City office was in Lombard Street. Copious constituency correspondence proves that he and Gladys did their very best, especially in the first year or two, to meet the demands made on them. It was not easy: Ashton was five hours by train from London, and they had no knowledge of the district, the people or what was expected of them. A flood of requests poured in: to join local societies, attend and open bazaars, become patrons of pageants, judge dog shows, grace annual dinners and balls, present prizes, watch football matches. Aitken found such occasions testing, and frequently proposed Gladys in his place. As he wrote plaintively to a local worthy: 'I am very unwilling to get into the habit of opening Bazaars and attending football matches, although I know it is my duty to appear among my constituents. I have great difficulty squirming out of the Bazaars and I am afraid I have done so at my wife's expense. . . .'

Nearly always, a donation or subscription was involved. The Conservative agent, to whom Aitken's London office forwarded all such requests, applied a simple rule of thumb: Conservative-run organizations got a guinea, others 10s 6d. The agent also kept his eye on press notices of local deaths, making sure that his MP responded appropriately. Thus: 'I enclose invoice for Robert Winterbotham's wreath – may I order for Col. Pearson and Commander H – they are not quite dead yet, but expected to go off this weekend?'

There was also a steady flow of begging letters from individuals. All were looked into; Aitken was prepared to be generous, but hated being taken for granted. He used a network of local informants to vet each request, and frequently asked for a second opinion. As he wrote primly to one of his regular checkers, the Secretary of the Ashton-under-Lyne Trades and Labour Council: 'There is nothing I dislike so much as giving money to unworthy persons who merely spend the money in drink, and I sometimes get very disappointed with my efforts on account of the various mistakes I make.' Often he would ask his agents to give a needy family food or clothes rather than cash. More than one struggling clergyman, possibly after hearing that their MP was a son of the manse, wrote painfully humble requests for financial help; in such cases, Aitken was always kind. At the same time, he liked to keep control; in one case, where he ended up paying for the education of a clergyman's son who wrote him touching schoolboy letters of gratitude, a letter went back in reply to say that the benefactor 'will be glad to hear from him how he progresses; and when he is earning sufficient money, and it is convenient for him to do so, will be pleased to have the return of this amount'.

Aitken refused to let his generosity be defined on partisan lines. All the churches, chapels and convents that approached him received the same sum. As for requests for help in emigrating to Canada: 'My attitude is to assist Liberals as well as Conservatives without any enquiry as to their political views. . . . I am aware that in sending Conservatives to Canada I am depriving myself of votes, but in this respect I am utterly indifferent.' He was also aware that his political opponents would jump at any chance to revive the corruption charge. Writing to a supporter, he took a robust line:

> I know that the Radicals will shout that I am corrupting the constituency and that sort of thing, but really I do not mind criticism. The dogs have been yelping about my heels for about ten years now and their howling disturbs me no longer. I want to go straight on doing what I think is right, regardless of public opinion. I have not given a sovereign in Ashton for every £5 I gave in Montreal. Of course I regard Ashton as my home. The people adopted me and I will be dutiful until they kick me out.

Aitken's initial response to the would-be emigrants was to help everyone. The earliest applicants were the luckiest; they were sent their fares and told to report to Gladys's brother Victor Drury at the Royal Securities Corporation in Montreal, who would help them to find a job. Word spread rapidly round Ashton; Montreal began to feel the strain. When the streets in Canada turned out not to be paved with gold, complaints came back to parents and friends. Within six months, Aitken was exasperated. He wrote in July 1911 to G. H. Coop, Chairman of Ashton Conservative Association: 'I experience considerable trouble from one or two of the persons I have sent out to Canada; they have not made good, and cannot hold their jobs, and are everlastingly bothering my office, and one good man's time is taken up almost entirely in looking after them.' He suggested that prospective emigrants should consider their health and qualifications, and save up to buy their own fares; but nothing stopped the flow. As another Ashton worthy wrote to Aitken: 'The glamour of Canada is over Ashton and everyone who goes expects that he is straightaway going to make a fortune. . . . The real trouble is that people in this district regard you as superhuman . . . and think the mention of your name ought to spare them any effort on their own part.' Gradually the tide slackened; but not before a society had been formed in Montreal of immigrants from Ashton-under-Lyne.

Apart from helping individuals, the Aitkens gave generous assistance to groups of Ashton people, especially poor children. In March 1912 a prolonged coal strike led to real hardship among Lancashire mining families. Aitken instructed his team to provide a hot meal daily for the miners' children. The considerable organization required fell to the lot of Councillor Shaw, president of the District Infirmary, which the Aitkens also subsidized. Aitken took a keen interest in the menus provided for the children, and wrote to Shaw: 'I would also like children of men not belonging to unions to be treated as well as children of Trade Unionists. . . . I want the little ones to have plenty to eat every day.' With the help of the Salvation Army, Shaw saw that they did. On 20 March 1912, 375 children sat down to eat in two halls; Shaw reported a number waiting outside. They were given hot-pot and bread, pea soup, currant pudding and potato pie. Two days later, nearly 600 children arrived, and on the next Sunday 750 (stewed meat and potato followed by rice pudding). Within a week, nearly 1000 children were arriving to be fed; even after the strike was over, Shaw and his helpers could not stop the children coming. They decided to make Easter the occasion for a final banquet: fish and potato pie and buns. Afterwards the children gave three cheers for the Aitkens; the local press was encouraged to take photographs. 'Your kind action is receiving great praise in the town,' Shaw wrote. That Christmas, he received a handsome gold pencil case; the Aitkens also endowed a cot in his name at the Infirmary, which pleased him even more: 'Your noble and gracious act will always be deeply engraved in my heart.'

The Aitkens also enjoyed giving the local youngsters a good time. In the years before the First World War a total of about five thousand children were given a day out in the country, with a special train, a picnic, organized games and a small present to take home. Everyone was aware of the need to avoid doing anything that smacked of 'treating'; Boy Scouts rather than 'Imps' helped look after the children, and in the summer of 1912 a plan for a huge garden party for all the constituents – some four or five thousand people – was abruptly cancelled on legal advice. Any such party, Aitken was informed, 'would be extremely dangerous . . . might amount to the offence of general treating, which is a corrupt practice and if established would render your next election void'. The local Liberal Party was already planning its attack for his next campaign.

Such constraints no doubt seemed insulting and tiresome. When Aitken felt unappreciated he often succumbed to bouts of self-pity, or ill-health, often accompanied by threats to withdraw altogether from whatever activity had depressed him. During his short time as an MP he often thought of giving up. A mere ten weeks after his election, he wrote to a friend: 'I must get another candidate who is prepared to give a great deal of time to the Ashton-under-Lyne constituency or devote a great deal of time to it myself. The latter is almost impossible at present on account of my business interests, which I am not prepared to sacrifice.' Sometimes it was business, sometimes his health, and increasingly his political and social activities in London that caused him to break his promises. His instinct was to say yes at first and then withdraw later; this often led to recriminations. One example is typical. In February 1912 he was expected at the Annual Social of the Ashton-under-Lyne Conservative and Unionist Women's Association, run by a Mrs Neild. As the occasion approached, he made his excuses; the Whips would not hear of him leaving London. Mrs Neild was not pleased; she complained to Coop, who wrote in desperation to Aitken: 'I am afraid you are making a very great mistake. . . . I do really seriously suggest you should be present next Tuesday, even at the expense of disobeying the whips.' Aitken wrote back crisply that he knew where his priorities lay and expected his constituents to allow him to use his judgement. 'If they are dissatisfied with their Member I will be the first to give them an opportunity of selecting another.' He did, however, write an apology to Mrs Neild, explaining that, much as he would have preferred the Women's Association Annual Social, his parliamentary duties had to come first. She wrote back menacingly: 'We must always do our duty first and Pleasure after. I hope many a time to see you with us.'

SIR MAXWELL AND 'PUBLIC EVIL'

As a Member of Parliament at Westminster, Aitken failed to impress his contemporaries. His personality and influence, so strong outside the House, were oddly muted and ineffective inside it. The excitement of politics for Aitken came from outside Parliament and behind the scenes. Being an MP was a useful credential; he liked being a member of the club as long as he did not have to spend much time there. Towards the Conservative party manager, Arthur Steel-Maitland, he was often disrespectful. 'I am not at all interested', he wrote in August 1911, 'in wasting time in futile opposition to Radical measures in the House of Commons.' To the unease of Central Office he promoted a New York banking friend, Otto Kahn, as prospective candidate for Gorton, a neighbouring constituency. Kahn, whose strong German accent, Aitken assured sceptics, would be no more of an electoral liability than his own Canadian twang, contributed generously to the funds but repeatedly failed to find time to visit Gorton; eventually he withdrew.

To a dedicated House of Commons man like Goulding, Aitken was a disappointment. Goulding was constantly hunting for his protégé, reproving him for cutting appointments, and urging him to attend and to speak more. Thus he wrote encouragingly to Aitken in late May 1911, after rebuking him gently for missing a meeting: 'Bonar told me that you spoke A1 at Manchester and surprised him. I spoke to him and FE about your maiden speech – but both were strongly of opinion that as you have left it over so long much better to wait a bit longer and speak on the Colonial vote or when the Conference will be discussed, which must be pretty soon. FE spoke most warmly about you. . . .'

Aitken did, however, quickly make contacts at Westminster, and not only in his own party. He was never really a wholehearted party man, and several of his new cronies were outsiders or mavericks, men prepared to break rules in order to achieve power and get things done. The ambitious, explosive F. E. Smith, for instance, later the 1st Earl of Birkenhead, Conservative MP for a Liverpool constituency and the outstanding barrister of his day, was the son of an estate agent. Smith was very close to Winston Churchill, whose ducal background was far from modest, but who was regarded by orthodox Tories with horror; he was a passionate Free Trader who had left the Conservatives for the Liberals in 1904 over Tariff Reform, and was widely seen as an unreliable opportunist. Aitken was soon on friendly terms with Churchill, despite opposing views; the Canadian was an early recruit to the Other Club, the distinguished dining club for insiders founded by Smith and Churchill in 1911. When Parliament was in session the Other Club met fortnightly, usually at the Savoy, and was dedicated to fierce political argument across party lines. Soon Aitken was seeing much of Smith, spending evenings with him drinking and gambling; both were passionate and competitive bridge players. Before long Aitken was making Smith extra money – he both earned and spent a fortune – by investing on his behalf. At Westminster Aitken was also impressed early on with the man the Conservative Party most hated, Lloyd George, and he soon took a great liking to Tim Healy, the eloquent, wily Irish Nationalist MP who had spent his entire political career fighting for Home Rule against the Tories. All these men were older than he was – the youngest of them, Churchill, was five years older – all of them were unconventional, and none of them was rich.

In his first four months in the House Aitken spoke only once, to ask a question about trade with Japan. Thereafter, during the six years he was an MP, his contributions were few, and restricted to trade and finance. His maiden speech, when he eventually steeled himself to deliver it on 20 July 1911, was hardly electrifying. He took Goulding's advice and chose a subject on which he was well qualified – trade with the West Indies. He attacked the government for not doing more to encourage imperial trade, and warned that the United States was doing far more: 'The field requires to be tilled if good results are to be obtained, and it seems a great pity that the American government should go on tilling its tropical field while Great Britain fails to do so.' Although his speech was described by the *Morning Post* as being 'of great power and lucidity', it made little stir elsewhere.

Aitken's unimpressive parliamentary performance in the first six months of 1911 is less surprising when events in Canada are taken into account. First, encouraged by the leader of the Canadian Conservative Party, Robert Borden, he conceived the extraordinary notion of abandoning Westminster and going into politics in Canada, where a general election was in the offing. He wrote to a Montreal lawyer on 3 April saying that Borden wanted him to lead the Conservative Party in New Brunswick and to accept office if the Conservatives won: 'I have practically decided to accede to his request.' On 12 May, however, the Canada Cement row burst into the open when Sir Sandford Fleming made public his charges; and

d himself fighting for his life under savage and sustained attack.
g able to savour his new role as an MP, Aitken had to protect
changed his mind about going into Canadian politics, telling
on that as 'the principal figure in the anti-Trust agitation' stirred up by
the cement monopoly he had best keep clear. However, he went on, he had
told Allan Davidson in Newcastle that he would 'provide the entire election
expenses' for the local Conservative candidate; 'I have made it a condition
that he shall deny that the money comes from me.' The uproar in Canada
began to muddy the political waters at Westminster and Ashton-under-
Lyne. Although Aitken tried to take a bold line, especially in the
constituency – where reports of the huge profits he had made from the
cement deal brought him a flood of begging letters – two letters to political
friends show how anxious he really felt. Early in May 1911 (his letter is
undated; the reply is dated 5 May) he wrote a long letter to Churchill,
offering to arrange a visit to Canada for him. He went on:

> There is an objection to me you must know about. I created all the big trusts
> in Canada. None of them are bad trusts but the Western farmers attack me
> very often and sometimes very offensively. I don't care. But you might not
> like an intimate connection. I can best illustrate the position when I tell you
> that my relation to Canada was in a small way the same as Morgan's relation
> to America. I'm done now and in fact for eighteen months past I have
> steadily pulled out. . . . If you don't mind the objection I would take care
> to relieve you from the incubus if it developed. And if you are to be my
> guest it won't so appear. Probably it doesn't make any difference at all and
> I exaggerate it. . . . Please don't tell anybody I admitted I organised any
> trusts, and please forgive me for this very long letter.'[17]

His letter demonstrates a combination of innocence – Churchill was, after
all, a political opponent, and even if a personal friend a very recent one
– unease and guile. The proposed visit never took place. Later in 1911,
Churchill proposed Aitken for a government job on the Imperial Trade
Commission: 'He is really a very advanced Liberal and it is only accident
that sent him into politics on the Tory side.' Asquith replied with distaste:
'Aitken is quite impossible. I take it that his Canadian record is of the
shadiest. . . .'[18]

To Goulding, who sent him a letter of encouragement, Aitken wrote on
25 May:

> I am so pleased to get your letter . . . it came at a time when I was feeling
> rather blue and cheered me up very much indeed.
> I am under very heavy fire, and must forgo everything for the moment,
> so that I can keep a good return fire going. The Canadian public is laughing
> at the attacks being made on me, but the radical press are making the most
> of it. . . . Please do not say anything to any person, and particularly don't
> let anybody know I am taking the slightest notice of it, because I must keep
> an undisturbed exterior.

He repeated, to emphasize why he could not be more active in Parliament, 'You will therefore understand why I will forgo everything for the moment.'

Paradoxically, the eruption of the scandal coincided with Aitken becoming a knight in the 1911 Coronation honours. On 20 April, as he wrote to Borden in Canada, the Unionist Chief Whip, Acland Hood, had called on him and offered him a knighthood 'for the purpose of rewarding me for services to come and to the Unionist Party and not to the Canadian party'.[19] Apart from the obvious reason – that he was rich enough to contribute large sums to party funds – it is hard to see why Aitken deserved a knighthood after less than six undistinguished months in Parliament. He hinted to Canadian correspondents that he had introduced new methods in his constituency and was likely to be made head of the new Unionist Central Office; neither was so.

Aitken did not accept the knighthood without considerable hesitation and manoeuvring. He summoned H. A. Gwynne and asked him whether he should accept; Gwynne thought he had convinced him he should not. Aitken wrote to Borden: 'None of the people who expect to get Front Bench rank in England will accept Knighthoods or Baronetcies, and I must modestly admit that I am generally regarded as a Front Bench probable.' He appeared to want Borden to decide for him: 'I imagine a Knighthood is of enormous political benefit in Canada, and for that reason I have really signified my acceptance. . . . If you write in opposition to my accepting, please put your letter in such a shape that I can show it to Sir Alexander Acland Hood.'[20] Borden replied, unhelpfully, on 1 May: 'I do not think the acceptance or non-acceptance of the knighthood would materially affect the Canadian situation.' When Aitken accepted, he told his Canadian friends he felt obliged to do so because of his position in British public life, and his British friends the reverse. Writing to Bonar Law to congratulate him on being made a Privy Councillor, he said: 'But I do want you to realise that I am deeply grateful to you for my own affair. Hood did me the kindness but you made it possible and in my selfish way I want you to know that I am always ready to serve you not because of what you've done for me but because you are yourself.'[21]

In Ashton-under-Lyne, naturally, the elevation of their MP was greeted with approbation and pride. In Canada, some of the press was scathing. The *Toronto Globe* wrote: 'Everywhere people are asking what Sir Max Aitken has done, or what hidden and mysterious power he wields that he should be selected for the honour of knighthood. . . .' The *Ottawa Journal*, with the Canada Cement affair in mind, went much further: 'Why has a gentleman who has contributed to do public evil, and never done anything else of note except get rich out of the evil, been selected for honour at the hands of the crown?' And in his own patch, Montreal, the *Witness* asked: 'Can anyone guess the answer to the question why an archmergerer, a wholesale stock waterer, should be created a knight?

There are thousands of people in Canada who have done more to deserve such honour, if honour it may be called.'

Abuse from Canada had one lasting result: it helped to settle Aitken on the other side of the Atlantic. At this time, and for some time to come, he was the opportunist, not the careful planner. By the early summer of 1911 the two children, Max, aged one, and Janet, aged three, had arrived from Montreal. Wanting to establish their young family in the country not too far from London, the Aitkens at first rented a house in Surrey, Worplesdon Manor. The pattern of their future life soon emerged: there was always a flat, a hotel suite or later a house or two in town, but Gladys and the children were based in the country, where, especially at weekends and during holidays, the Aitkens would entertain. Although for a time during 1911 and 1912 Aitken toyed with the idea of finding a house near Ashton-under-Lyne, and even asked his agents to inspect one or two, nothing came of it; neither he nor Gladys can have cared much for the idea of life in suburban Lancashire.

Aitken already knew how agreeable and useful a large house within easy reach of Westminster and the City could be. The country weekend was in its heyday, and had become the setting for more significant activities than the traditional aristocratic pastimes of shooting, cards and flirtation. Press lords and politicians as well as great landowners and hostesses arranged weekend parties: Goulding had Wargrave, Asquith had The Wharf, F. E. Smith had Charlton, Northcliffe had Sutton Place, the Astors had Cliveden and, in the autumn of 1911, the Aitkens acquired Cherkley Court, near Leatherhead in Surrey. Aitken paid £25,000 and the house was bought in Gladys's name.[22] For the next fifty-three years Cherkley saw as much political, social and sexual intrigue as any house in England. It was also to be the one settled, permanent home Aitken had, the house where his children grew up, a base for his and Gladys's Canadian relations and friends, and the one place he always returned to in bad times and good.

A large grey stone house of some thirty bedrooms, built in the 1870s for a Birmingham ironmaster, Cherkley was solid rather than graceful. It had a porticoed entrance, a tower, a separate stable block and a terrace looking on to the garden; the position, on a ridge of wooded hills, and the views south into Sussex were exceptionally fine. It was easy to reach from London – an hour by road, or train to Leatherhead. Although hardly remote, Cherkley was secluded, up a mile-long drive of beeches and maples, and the grounds contained some of the most ancient yew trees in southern England. The estate was said to contain neolithic remains and a stretch of the Pilgrims' Way. There was good golf nearby and riding; the Aitkens put in a swimming pool and tennis court. The house and grounds were in a poor state and the new owners employed G. H. Coop, chairman of the Ashton-under-Lyne Unionist Party, who was a plumber and electrician, and also Buckley, the agent, who ran a building company, to put in central heating, electricity and modern plumbing; this arrangement led first to pleasure and gratitude, then to much correspondence and eventually to tension and recriminations. Carrie Kipling and Gladys Aitken, by now good friends, planned the decoration and furnishings together; the Aitkens' daughter Janet remembered from her childhood 'deep armchairs and sofas in brocades of flaming colours'. Bonar Law gave Aitken books for his new library, and wrote to him:

> In our relationship all the giving has been on your side that is quite right [*sic*] for you have plenty to spare but I wanted to give you something to note the fact that you have taken possession of your estate. I could think of nothing better than books and I have sent some to Cherkley. They bulk large but are not of much value. They are all however books which I like and if you have any of them already bring them in and I shall change them.[23]

In the early days at Cherkley, Bonar Law and his six children, whose ages in 1911 ranged from the late teens to six, were frequent weekend guests. Later, Law's daughter Isabel recalled their visits. 'My father was a constant guest. Lunch on Saturday or Sunday, a game of tennis or bridge – often both – and back to London for dinner.' They were invited several years running to spend Christmas at Cherkley; Isabel remembered 'the happy atmosphere . . . Gladys was so beautiful with her lovely dark red hair, pretty figure, lovely complexion and happy expression . . . she took me with her into Dorking to get extra decorations and a Christmas tree.'[24] Gladys Aitken put family life above everything else; the motherless Law family were in good hands at Cherkley, which Janet Aitken also remembered as 'a child's paradise'. As she grew up, walks in the gardens with a nurse were replaced by donkey rides, a longed-for pony, hide-and-seek in the woods and a tree house where Tim Healy would leave her presents from 'the little people'. Healy was more fun than Bonar Law, whom she christened Mr Smoke because he always had a pipe or a cigar in his mouth.

The Kiplings came often to Cherkley with their two children, John and Elsie. In 1911 they and the Laws spent Christmas there together; Carrie Kipling noted in her diary: '. . . many children. Twentytwo for dinner, 17 in the house'.[25] Kipling composed a poem for the new visitors' book, drawing a somewhat incongruous analogy between the refurbished Surrey mansion and primitive man:

> This is the prayer the Cave Man prayed
> When first his household fire he lit. . . .
> The loneliest of all things made
> He lights his fire at eventide
> And prays as his first fathers prayed
> For friends to gather there beside.
> And that is why I send this tome
> Of virgin pages fitly wrought
> To hold the names of all who come

Beneath your roof at Cherkley Court
Oh long, long may the record run,
And you enjoy until it ends
The Four Best Gifts beneath the Sun,
Love, Peace and Health and Honest Friends.[26]

In March 1912 the Aitkens' third and last child was born; he was christened Peter Rudyard Aitken. Kipling was one of his godfathers, and Edward Goulding wrote Aitken an emotional letter of congratulation on the birth of 'the guard to the king!'. He praised Gladys extravagantly: 'She is a great lady – looks ability style – if ever I am fortunate enough to meet my mate I hope that she will be your wife's model; you are a lucky young fellow and deserve it.'[27]

The friendship between Kipling and Aitken grew, stimulated by mutual admiration and mutual interests. Kipling no doubt enjoyed advising the dynamic young operator, while for Aitken to enjoy the confidence of the great Kipling, philosopher and voice of the Empire, must have been intoxicating. Wives and children played a part, although Janet Aitken recalled Kipling as 'Mr Sad', because 'he had a drooping moustache and never seemed to smile.' Max and Gladys Aitken went on motoring trips with the Kiplings; once they spent a few days driving in Normandy together. Kipling bought a Rolls Royce, and invoked Aitken's influence when it went wrong. Aitken always remembered his talks with the writer: 'Kipling would ask me to tell him my account of a book I had read. And he liked very much my dramatisation of Bible stories. In the spring of the year we walked over the downs at Cherkley, making bonfires here and there of rough grass. . . . A Roman road runs through Cherkley. His stories of the Roman occupation fascinated me. When we went walking together I always made a point of taking him to the Roman road.' Kipling would sit up late at Cherkley talking and drinking with Aitken, to Carrie's displeasure.[28]

It is striking, however, that in the many letters they exchanged before the First World War the main topic is money. The forceful Carrie Kipling has usually been credited with managing their finances, but Kipling's own letters to Aitken show a detailed grasp of financial matters. He had made and was still making a very great deal of money out of his writing; he was a rich man by 1902. It was important to him to deploy his money sensibly, and Aitken was happy to help. Six months after they met, he virtuously explained his position when forwarding a letter of advice to Kipling from Royal Securities. 'I want you to understand that I am President of the Royal Securities Corporation which writes me this letter . . . I am not interested in any of the companies whose securities I recommend, and, in fact, decline to recommend securities of any Company in which I am interested.' (This was not his practice with Bonar Law.)

Alongside money matters, their correspondence contains many political exchanges. Kipling was profoundly ambivalent about politics and politicians; he called political life 'a dog's life without a dog's decencies'.[29] At the same time he enjoyed influence, and liked to know what was going on. He had a rising Conservative politician in his own family; in one of his earliest letters to Aitken (in which he accepts an offer to underwrite $50,000 worth of Canadian Steel Bonds) in March 1911 he wrote: 'I do hope you have made acquaintance in the House with my cousin Stanley Baldwin – MP for Mid Worcestershire. . . . I think you'll find him a delightful fellow as well as a man of business.' He went on: 'Don't mind if you find the House, at first, about as stimulating as a Fundy fog-bank and as easy to handle as a mudfence in thaw. All the chaps, except the abject fools, feel that at the first go. Then they get their second wind. Of course the whole secret of government is to prevent that damned House doing anything at all; but in these days alas that is not possible so one tries to minimize the harm it does.'

From the start of their friendship Aitken tried to stimulate Kipling to write poems or make statements that could be used to promote Anglo-Canadian links; but Kipling always refused to write to order, which was why he declined to be Poet Laureate. 'Now as to those Canadian verses,' he wrote. 'Do you suppose that if I could have done a set fit for the job I wouldn't have turned them in long ago? I've tried and tried again but I can't hit the line I want and a misfire now would be worse than nothing at all.' He directed Aitken instead to some old lines – 'The people of my own blood, They may do ill or well, But they tell the lies I am wonted to – They are used to the lies I tell, And we do not need interpreters When we go to buy or sell' – which can hardly have struck the right note.

Sometimes political and financial interests appeared to conflict; but Aitken was undaunted. In early September 1911, during the run-up to the Canadian election, Kipling wrote an open letter to the *Montreal Star*, condemning in intemperate terms the proposed reciprocity agreement between the USA and Canada. He included the bizarre suggestion that such an agreement could lead to Canada being 'compelled later on to admit reciprocity in the murder rate of the United States'. Kipling was fervently anti-American at this time, much given to contrasting the tidy, law-abiding, God- and Empire-fearing Canadians with the chaotic, materialistic Americans. A week after his letter appeared, Aitken wrote to him gleefully 'about the excitement your message created in Canada. The Liberals have gone mad over your reference to the high murder rate on the American side.' In the same letter, he strongly recommended Kipling to invest in American securities. 'I invest considerable money for my friends in the United States,' he said, 'and just last evening Bonar Law and I were talking over the position of Canadian and American railroads.' He himself had £75,000 in Chesapeake and Ohio bonds, and offered to get £1950 worth for Kipling, adding: 'If you have too great an objection to investment in Americans, I will gladly choose you some Canadian Bonds, but I really think you will make no mistake in distributing your American investments just a little over United States enterprises as well as Canadian enterprises.' As for the Canadian election campaign: 'I would hate to tell you how much money I have spent. . . . Public sentiment undoubtedly favours the Conservatives, and the party with the most money will win. Such is democracy.'

Aitken also used Kipling as a source of inspiration and telling phrases for his own speeches, especially concerning Free Trade, which Kipling presented as the ruin of the nation and an invitation to Socialism. 'If you allow a man to be chased from trade to trade long enough he will end up on the street corner. And that is where the Socialist is waiting for him. . . . The Socialist is like the fly that produces sleeping-sickness in South Africa. He cannot live in a decently clean and healthy district.' As for Lloyd George's Insurance Bill, then going through Parliament, 'We have turned our back on the greatest Empire that has ever been allowed to come into existence, for the lofty amusement of filching half-pennies from house-maids.' Aitken sometimes used Kipling's notes: a jubilant cable dated 30 September 1911 reads: 'With your brains and my voice, I made a first rate speech on Thursday night.'

When Kipling was moved to express in verse his feelings about current political events, Aitken was ready and eager to exploit the results. In April 1912 his poem 'Ulster', a passionate denunciation of Home Rule, was published in several countries to coincide with a speech by Bonar Law at a huge, dramatic Unionist demonstration in Belfast. Law stood on a platform with Sir Edward Carson and some seventy MPs, beneath what was said to be the largest Union Jack ever made, while a hundred thousand Irish Unionists marched past in military formation. It was an uncharacteristically stirring speech; 'Once again you hold the pass for the Empire,' Law told the throng. 'You are a besieged city.' Kipling's poem, which Aitken deployed in Canada, was thought even at the time to go a bit far:

> We know the war prepared
> On every peaceful home
> We know the hells declared
> For such as serve not Rome. . . .

As a Catholic Conservative MP wrote in protest to the *Morning Post*: 'This is a direct appeal to ignorance and a deliberate attempt to foster religious hatred.'[30]

In so far as Aitken encouraged Kipling to pronounce on political matters, and then helped to publicize the results, it is doubtful whether he did either his friend or the cause concerned much good in the long run. Kipling became so identified with the extreme right wing of Conservatism that his popularity and standing as a wise man began to wane. The political game of manoeuvrings and compromise, which attracted Aitken, was alien to Kipling; he despised it. When he spoke out, it was from burning moral conviction – never a comfortable ingredient in political life, and not one that Aitken was much given to.

CHAPTER 5

'THE GIDDY HEIGHTS OF JOURNALISM' 1910–1912

AITKEN'S ENTRY into British politics was noisy and abrupt. His entry into British newspapers was much more private and gradual, though he was moving on both fronts at the same time. Newspapers had always attracted him. Before he settled in England he had delivered newspapers, produced his own schoolboy paper, worked as small-town stringer and used newspapers to boost companies he was promoting. His first newspaper investment was a small stake in the *St John Standard*, and as soon as he had made his killings of 1909 he started his own publication. In the first week of January 1910 he told his friend J. L. Stewart of the *Chatham World*:

> I have given some young cubs leave to fritter my money away on a weekly magazine called the *Canadian Century*, which makes its first appearance on Friday. I can't get away from my earliest inclinations which were always in the direction of the giddy heights of journalism. . . . Like the organ grinder who inherited a fortune, and thereafter hated the sound of a 'hurdy gurdy', I have come to my inheritance, and I am determined to taboo all financial matters from the columns of the *Canadian Century*. . . .[1]

Aitken was the dominant shareholder, but three business associates – Izaak Walton Killam of Royal Securities, Clouston of the Bank of Montreal, and the banker W. D. Ross – also had small stakes. The *Canadian Century* – ' "Canada for the Canadians" was the watchword' – was intended to occupy the same place in Canadian life that influential small-circulation publications like the *Westminster Gazette* occupied in Britain.

Restless as ever, he had barely started his weekly magazine before in February 1910 he tried to land a much bigger fish – the *Montreal Gazette*, the only English-language morning paper in the city. The deal fell through only because any change of ownership had to be approved both by the

Bank of Montreal and by the Canadian Pacific Railway, and though the Bank approved the CPR did not – 'no doubt', Aitken thought, because of the early rumblings of the cement row.

Four months later, the *Montreal Herald* building collapsed after a fire, facing the proprietor, who was inadequately insured, with ruin. The ashes were scarcely cold before Aitken put $150,000 into the paper and rescued him.[2] There was a price. The *Herald*, one of Montreal's evening papers, supported Sir Wilfred Laurier's Liberal government. Thereafter, it was 'persuaded' to support the Conservatives.

By the autumn of the same year, Aitken had his eye on a British newspaper. At Edward Goulding's lunch party where he first got on terms with Bonar Law, his opening words to his fellow guest Ralph Blumenfeld, even before he startled him by disclosing his political ambitions, were about the *Daily Express*. According to Blumenfeld, Aitken came up to him, introduced himself and said, 'You're Blumenfeld, aren't you? How much do you want for your paper?' 'Not so fast,' Blumenfeld replied.[3] Blumenfeld was struck by Aitken's giant urchin smile and stream of questions, and concluded that he showed 'a natural aptitude for politics and newspapers'. Part of that aptitude was his passion for being well informed. The *Express* might not be for sale, but it was in financial straits. The paper had been founded in 1900 by a semi-literate product of Winchester College, Arthur Pearson, as a direct challenge to Northcliffe's phenomenally successful *Daily Mail*, begun four years earlier. Pearson himself had originally been hailed as a budding Northcliffe; but in 1908 he had gone virtually blind and turned the *Express* into a public company, making Blumenfeld general manager as well as editor, and selling a large stake to George Lawson Johnston, the proprietor of Bovril. Despite Blumenfeld's efforts, the *Express* had made little progress. He invested heavily in new machinery in early 1910, and although with a daily sale of 400,000 copies the circulation was up, so were production and distribution costs – and profits were down, making shareholders disinclined to advance the resources the paper needed to attack the *Daily Mail*. Blumenfeld tried to borrow in the City, but found its conditions too limiting. In the winter of 1910 he accordingly sought the advice of his friend and political ally Bonar Law, who said the Conservative Party would help; but Blumenfeld thought that taking money from that source would undermine his own independence and his paper's credibility. Bonar Law then had another idea: his busy new acquaintance Aitken.

Aitken had moved from Cannes to Monte Carlo as he recovered, over Christmas and the New Year, from his exhausting election campaign; there Blumenfeld appeared on the steps of the casino – an appropriate meeting place – and handed him a letter from Bonar Law setting out reasons why he should help its bearer. Aitken took Blumenfeld back to his hotel and wrote him a cheque for £25,000, without collateral. It was exceedingly rare for Aitken to lend money without security. The loan, however, ensured the continued support of the *Express* for Bonar Law; and it also bound Blumenfeld to Aitken. Soon afterwards Blumenfeld wrote in his diary: 'He . . . insists that he and I are going to do big things together.'

THE MENTOR: R. D. BLUMENFELD

To R. D. B. from Rudyard Kipling
Who once had served to the sultry hour
When roaring like a gale,
The Harrild and the Hoe devour
The league-long paper bale
And has lit his pipe in the morning calm
That follows the midnight stress:
He has sold his soul to the old black art
Men call the Daily Press.

The Monte Carlo cheque was Aitken's entry fee to popular journalism in Britain, and a milestone in the history of mass-circulation newspapers. He credited Blumenfeld with having 'laid the foundation of the whole structure and the entire character of the *Express*'.[4] 'Blum', he said on another occasion, 'taught me the business of journalism.'[5]

Blumenfeld was another transplanted North American who had made his own way to the top; more important, Blumenfeld was a product of American, not British, journalism. He was fifteen years older than Aitken – born in 1864 in Watertown, Wisconsin, where his father, who had been a printing apprentice in Stuttgart at the age of thirteen, owned a print shop and ran *Der Weltbürger*, one of the first German-language papers in the Middle West. The son left home early, worked for papers in Kansas City and San Francisco, and arrived in New York, aged eighteen, as a 'good reporter'. At the age of twenty-three, he was sent to London by the United Press news agency to cover Queen Victoria's Golden Jubilee; then he was hired by the *New York Herald*, the most profitable newspaper in the world.

The founder of the *Herald* is given credit for having invented news in the modern sense. James Gordon Bennett was a Scotsman who went to Washington when its population was three thousand, walked uninvited into offices and told his readers, in irreverent prose, what their government was up to. Unlike English papers, the *Herald* was aimed – like the *Daily Express* later – at readers in all stations of life, 'the journeyman and his employer, the clerk and his principal'. It reported not only murders – while other papers were still publishing only court reports, Bennett went to the scene of the crime and described the corpses – but also Wall Street prices. The *Herald* was the first paper to identify and exploit the public appetite for gossip about high society; and it gave advice to the lovelorn. But news came first: to cover the Civil War, Bennett employed two dozen correspondents.

By the time Blumenfeld joined the paper it was in the hands of Bennett's grotesquely spoilt and self-willed son, James Gordon Bennett Junior, who lived on the Champs-Elysées with his Pekinese, owned a palazzo in Venice and a castle in Scotland, and sailed about in yachts, with a cow to supply fresh milk, calling himself 'Commodore'. He pioneered the absentee proprietorial tyranny, made possible by faster communications, later refined by Beaverbrook. 'I want one feature article a day,' he instructed his staff. 'If I say the feature is to be black beetles, black beetles it's going to be.' But he had flair, as Blumenfeld acknowledged. He sent Mark Twain to report on the West, and H. M. Stanley to find Dr Livingstone. He signed up Marconi and his new wireless apparatus to guarantee the *Herald* first news of the America's Cup. He wanted 'all points of the day's news without the verbiage', and told his managing editor: 'Never spare expense when the news justifies it. Whenever there is an important piece of news I want the *Herald* to have the best and fullest account of it. Another point which I think you understand is letting a thing drop the moment public interest in it begins to flag. The instant you see a sensation is dead, drop it and start in on something new.'[6] That was the authentic voice of the modern newspaper manager – in 1882. No British newspaper – despite stirrings at the *Daily Telegraph* – thought in such crisp terms for another fourteen years, and no British newspaper acted on the spare-no-expense principle before the heyday of the *Daily Express*.

American and British schools of journalism diverged long before 1882. One of Blumenfeld's heroes was Charles A. Dana of the *New York Sun*, the radical who hired Karl Marx as his London correspondent and became a member of Lincoln's Cabinet. In 1850 Dana described the contrast between American and European, especially British, journalism. In Europe, the papers were class-ridden: the writers polished up their 'elaborate essays' as if they were academics, not journalists, and addressed themselves only to the top layer of society. In America, speed and brevity were the thing, aimed at everybody, with no muffling rhetoric. Blumenfeld admired the way Dana 'paid as much attention to the style and manner of a police court report or an auction sale as he did to the leading article'.

In 1890, Bennett sent Blumenfeld to head the *Herald* office in London and to rescue a British Sunday offshoot of the Paris *Herald* – the forerunner of today's *International Herald Tribune*. Blumenfeld tried American tricks, introducing a racing competition, 'a prize for the reader who gives the best solution in football', and a page for children; but although the circulation rose to 60,000 – more than the combined circulation of the *Observer, Sunday Times, Reynolds' News* and *Sunday Dispatch* – in 1892 Bennett suddenly shut it down.

By then, Blumenfeld was fully aware of the gulf between American and British journalistic enterprise. When Baring's Bank collapsed, threatening financial panic, Blumenfeld suggested to *The Times* that they might perhaps send a reporter to the Bank of England to find out if it was coming

101

to the rescue; *The Times* replied that the Bank, if and when it made a move, would undoubtedly issue an official statement. Blumenfeld put on his bowler hat, went round to the Bank, saw the governor, helped him concoct a statement to avert the crisis, filed the story, and walked back to *The Times* where he took pleasure in telling the managing director, Moberly Bell, that his paper and every other paper in London had been scooped by the *New York Herald*.

In the United States, newspapers were revolutionized by growing literacy and shrinking production costs. Large circulations became the goal. Intensified competition centred on news, snappily presented with larger headlines. Inconsequential titbits added spice. More space was given to finance and sport. The interview became common; so did the description of personalities. Journalism became far less literary, as the transmission of news, the printing presses and the means of distribution all speeded up. Rising circulations and new possibilities of profit both made and attracted millionaires.

Blumenfeld welcomed the 'new journalism', as Matthew Arnold sardonically called it, when British conservatism finally responded to the same pressures that had caused the newspaper revolution in the United States. In New York, the launch in 1896 of the *Daily Mail*, costing a halfpenny, would scarcely have caused a stir. In Britain, where half a dozen solemn political organs – *The Times, Daily Telegraph, Morning Post, Daily News, Daily Chronicle*, and *Standard* – competed sleepily every morning for the attention of the bourgeoisie, its impact was electrifying: as orders poured in after the first issue, Alfred Harmsworth (later Lord Northcliffe) made his famous remark, 'We have struck a goldmine!' Before long, helped by the Boer War, the *Daily Mail* was selling an unprecedented million copies a day.

Blumenfeld joined in the excitement. He had resigned from the *Herald* in 1900, exasperated beyond endurance by the 'Oriental despot', as he called Bennett, when in a Fleet Street barber's shop he met Harmsworth, who offered him a job as the *Daily Mail* news editor. By comparison with Bennett as an employer, Harmsworth seemed normal. Harmsworth trusted Blumenfeld. He sent him off to try to buy *The Times*, telling him he could go up to £1,000,000. When Blumenfeld reported failure, Harmsworth said, 'Never mind. We'll get it sooner or later,' as he did eight years later for £320,000. Blumenfeld nevertheless felt unappreciated at the *Mail*, and in 1902 went to work for Pearson first as foreign editor and then as editor of the *Daily Express*. Pearson had visited New York to study American techniques: the *Express* was the first paper in Britain to put news on the front page. To Pearson, as to Aitken later, Blumenfeld was an invaluable catch not only because he understood the 'new journalism', but because he understood Harmsworth, the new genius of mass circulation.

When Aitken met him, Blumenfeld had been at the *Express* for eight years, and after twenty years in London knew everyone; and everyone liked him, with his Anglicized accent, Frenchified moustache and London-style wing collars. He was, Beaverbrook wrote, 'the only newspaper man, in my experience, who was the object of the affection and devotion of the entire political community'.[7] Gladstone had asked him to stay at his country home, Hawarden. He knew the coming young men in politics – the men Aitken was going to deal with – years before Aitken heard their names. He became a friend of Tim Healy in 1890. He came across Churchill in 1900, aged twenty-five and 'radiating self-confidence'. He met Bonar Law when he became a new MP: 'a Canadian who is in the metal business in Scotland. . . . A quiet unassuming man with no trace of a Transatlantic accent. Mitchell-Thomson [Sir Mitchell Mitchell-Thomson, a solicitor of the Bank of Scotland] says he is a mountain of common sense, with an uncanny genius for facts and figures, and that he is a most convincing speaker.' In 1908 he 'met Rudyard Kipling with his cousin, Stanley Baldwin, the young ironmaster from the West Country, who hopes one day to get into Parliament like his father before him . . . rather shy . . . not at all politician-like in his manner, and I do not suppose he will ever do more than follow his leader if he gets in . . . badly dressed'.

Such connections with leading politicians had one far-reaching result, for it is almost certainly true, as Blumenfeld claimed, and as he told his son, that it was he who 'educated' Aitken about Tariff Reform.[8] Blumenfeld knew Joseph Chamberlain well. He himself had been converted to the cause by the plight of the homeless he talked to on the Embankment in the early hours as he walked home from the office. Chamberlain persuaded him that tariff barriers would produce jobs, which inspired Blumenfeld to invent the slogan, 'Tariff Reform Means Work For All'; and it was Blumenfeld who, in 1903, secretly arranged the meeting between Chamberlain and Arthur Pearson that caused an excited Pearson to wake up Blumenfeld next morning and tell him that the *Daily Express* was going to back Chamberlain: it was the first paper in London to do so.

Blumenfeld took tea with Madame Blavatsky, the theosophist; played pool in Chelsea with Mark Twain; lunched with W. S. Gilbert, who, 'like most successful men, ate sparingly and spoke a good deal about his digestion'; learned from Arthur Sullivan that he hoped for a success with *The Gondoliers*; listened to Joe Lyons's ambitious plans for teashops; and met Todd Sloan, the American jockey who was introducing a new style of crouching in the saddle. These were not the sort of people that Garvin or Gwynne consorted with. Blumenfeld was interested in politics, and taken seriously by politicians, but he also had the good popular journalist's indiscriminate curiosity (noting in 1890 'a new drink called Martini Cocktail') and an American alertness to new trends, though he usually misjudged them. He thought underground trains would never catch on because they were unhealthy.

He was more prescient about the impact of new technology on the newspaper industry: Linotype machines to replace the hand-setting of type; news tickers; Marconigrams. As soon as he saw, in Paris, 'autocars' delivering newspapers – the first newspaper vans – he advocated their introduction to London. He was the first person to speak on the transatlantic telephone (and to employ the preliminaries still common today: can you hear me? what's the time with you? what's the weather like?).[9] Aitken could not have handed a cheque to a better mentor.

APPRENTICE PROPRIETOR

Even as he was investing in a London paper, Aitken was becoming increasingly exasperated by his magazine in Canada. The *Canadian Century* was indeed feeble. It managed to achieve a circulation of 5550 after six months, and no doubt had he stayed in Canada Aitken would have made a success of it; instead, he complained across the Atlantic to A. R. Doble of Royal Securities, who was keeping an eye on the magazine, that it was 'barren of ideas, damned by the obvious and commonplace'. Nor was the paper much help in support of Aitken causes. Doble warned him in September 1910 that 'everybody here thinks there is imminent danger of Laurier getting drawn into a reciprocity measure this coming session, which is going to hurt some of your infant industries'. Removal of Canada–United States tariff barriers might indeed be expected to expose the Aitken combines – cement, steel, paper – to severe competition. The *Century* was told to keep 'hammering away' against reciprocity, but even this simple instruction was mishandled. Doble sketched out an editorial and assumed that it would be tidied up before publication; instead, he told his employer, it had been published exactly as written – except for the punctuation, which had been omitted.

In January 1911 Aitken told Doble: 'The *Canadian Century* is no good. It is getting worse and worse in my opinion.' Doble was experiencing the frustrations of newspaper bosses down the ages. 'I am continually telephoning suggestions to him [the editor] and look in vain to see the results in print,' he told Aitken. 'For instance, the other day the RV hospital had a man who had been swallowing three-inch wire nails at a vaudeville show in the East End, and after locating a bunch of them in his insides by the x ray, the doctors took them out, including one which got sidetracked to his kidney.' Doble arranged with the hospital superintendent to give the story and an X-ray picture to the *Century* exclusively. The editor promised to send a man up the same afternoon. 'That was two weeks ago.' The reporter, Doble discovered, 'forgot his assignment'.[10]

More important fish were frying in London. Aitken seemed to be on the verge of buying the *Express*. In March 1911 he was in negotiations with Pearson, and told Goulding that 'the matter' was coming to a head. Goulding encouraged him, saying he much hoped he would become 'Boss of the *Express*'. In late June, Goulding evidently thought Aitken had succeeded in buying the paper: 'I am very glad about the *Express* as I am confident that you and Blum can make it a great organ.'[11]

There is a mystery here. It has been surmised that during this period Aitken was acting not on his own but as a secret conduit for Conservative Party funds to friendly but ailing papers. It would not be surprising if this was so, and it may have been the real reason for his knighthood. Today even the most corrupt party manager would hesitate before covertly putting party money into a newspaper; however before 1914 the Conservative Party secretly financed several papers, while the Liberals used party funds to buy the *Westminster Gazette*, whose revered editor, J. A. Spender, universally regarded as a pillar of integrity, knew about these secret arrangements, though his readers did not.[12] (Spender turned down a knighthood from Campbell-Bannerman in 1906 and a baronetcy from Asquith in 1916 on the grounds that a political journalist must on no account compromise his independence.) However, Goulding was in a position to know whether Aitken was acting on his own behalf or the party's in his *Express* dealings, and he certainly believed, as his letters to Aitken demonstrate, that Aitken wanted to buy the paper for himself. On this occasion, he failed.

No doubt for that reason, he was soon trying to buy the *Standard*, a solid, family-owned morning paper with a distinguished history, somewhat in the style of *The Times*. The *Standard* had started to lose readers round the turn of the century partly because the 'new journalism' had passed it by and partly because, though a Conservative paper, it had opposed Joseph Chamberlain and Tariff Reform; at least, that was Blumenfeld's opinion. In 1904, together with its sister paper, the *Evening Standard*, it was bought by Pearson, who at once with Blumenfeld's advice changed its policy and its editor. In 1910, after his eyesight had failed, Pearson sold it to a mercurial proprietor named Davison Dalziel (later Lord Dalziel of Wooler), to whom Aitken made approaches. Kipling wrote to Aitken on 9 March 1911 saying he 'very greatly' hoped that he would be able to get the *Standard*, adding: 'I just pray your £10,000 cheque will soften his heart, if he has one. Evidently he has no brains.'[13] Aitken's negotiations once again came to nothing.

He was still busy with the Canadian press. Putting on a different hat, he tried to merge the two big papers in Montreal, the *Herald* (in which he still had a $150,000 stake) and the *Daily Star*, in order to create a monopoly paper dominating the city. All the owners would have had to do thereafter, like the owners of other Canadian combines that Aitken had put together, would have been to listen to the cash register. But the owner of the *Star*, Sir Hugh Graham (later Lord Atholstan), loved newspapers more than money. He told Aitken, who reported his sentiments to the owner of the *Herald*, that 'he would rather make $200,000 out of a newspaper than make $1,000,000 out of a hardware shop' – Aitken, in some moods, would have said the same.[14] Aitken thought he saw an opportunity, which also had obvious commercial benefits, to create a powerful megaphone for the

Conservative voice during the run-up to the coming election. Failing that, he pressed Graham on Imperial Preference. The *Star* was already campaigning against 'the American agreement' – reciprocity. Could Graham and the *Star* go a step further, and 'force the issue at the Canadian polls to the point of demanding a preference from Britain'? Thus on both sides of the Atlantic Aitken worked to promote the same cause. He was still feeling his way, though, or pretended to be. In March 1911 he asked Graham, in tones of unusual humility, whether he would mind if from time to time he sought his advice on Imperial Preference and related subjects, 'because I am entirely inexperienced and must sometimes necessarily blunder into very faulty positions'.[15]

In London, word soon got round that the new Canadian millionaire MP might be persuaded to lose some money in newspapers. He became the target for every hard-pressed journalist or owner in the city. Horatio Bottomley, journalist and demagogue, wrote to say that his *John Bull* sold nearly a million a week and made £50,000 a year – yet was in temporary difficulties. He needed to raise £20,000–£25,000. Aitken drafted a reply saying he might help, but thought better of it and instead pleaded ill-health – wisely, since Bottomley later went to prison for fraud. In March 1911 T. P. O'Connor, an outstanding popular journalist, had another idea. Why did not Aitken set up a company to publish *T. P.'s Magazine*? All it would take was £10,000, plus £50 a month for O'Connor. Aitken did not bite. In May, O'Connor wrote again. Odhams, the biggest newspaper printers in London, were thinking of expanding and raising more capital. Why did not Aitken finance or promote a new company himself and perhaps go on the board of Odhams? T. P. would give him the printing of *T. P.'s Weekly* and *T. P.'s Magazine*. 'It would bring you at once in touch with the whole newspaper world and put you on the inside track of what was going on. . . . You would be able to develop something larger later on.' O'Connor ended optimistically: 'Finally, I would be glad if you would send me a cheque for a thousand pounds for the shares in *T. P.'s Weekly* as it requires a little finance at the present moment.'

Owners and editors of illustrated papers also had Aitken in their sights. Would he care to join in 'plans' for the *Sphere* and *Tatler*? No, he was not interested; he was 'not very well'. Would he like, for £5000, 'an opportunity to acquire a controlling interest' in 'the acknowledged Social Journal in this kingdom', the *World*? He was not interested. Would he care to take over a financial paper, the *Citizen*, which needed only £350 purchase price and £1000 capital to make it 'the greatest financial paper in the kingdom'? No, he was 'not feeling well'.[16]

However, he was feeling well enough to take effective control of the *Globe*, the oldest of London's seven evening newspapers, founded in 1803 and printed on pink paper. Numerous rich proprietors had owned it over the years. Goulding thought it scarcely worth bothering about compared to the *Express*, but in 1911 Aitken put up £15,000, the Unionists £25,000, and together they bought the paper from one of the newly rich Harmsworth brothers, Hildebrand.[17]

At the same time, his patience with the *Canadian Century* was finally running out. 'I refuse to be connected with a failure,' he told Doble. In August 1911 he read the latest balance sheet. 'Management hopeless,' he wrote. 'We are sending good money after bad.' In September, he refused to go on and sold.

The *Globe*, though unsuccessful, gave Aitken useful practice in dealing with advertisers and editors, like a young fighter testing his skills in the amateur ring before turning professional. Under Aitken's guidance, the *Globe* editor interviewed Aitken's new friend Gordon Selfridge, the store owner; an advertisement followed. Aitken briefed the City editor, A. J. Sharwood, on Brazilian railways; an article duly appeared. Aitken said the article was 'very good'; but the 'Market Report yesterday was about as bad as possible'. He sent Sharwood a 'suggestion for your personal paragraph' – probably the dullest news item he ever sent any of his editors: 'Mr R. Home Smith of Toronto, who is well-known in Real Estate and financial circles there, is spending a few weeks in England.' In February 1914 Sharwood proposed that Aitken should put up the money to lift the paper 'right out of the ruck of the evenings' and turn it into a 'first-class evening financial';[18] evidently he did not understand that the *Globe*'s main interest for Aitken was political, though he trod warily – sitting on the fence, for instance, over the dubious ministerial share-dealings of the Marconi scandal despite the urgings of Kipling, who told him that the fence 'is very crowded already'.[19]

It was his experience at the *Globe* that made Aitken realize that the game was up for traditional politically sophisticated evening journals such as the *Westminster Gazette, Pall Mall Gazette* and the *Globe* itself – papers which concentrated on views rather than news and catered for a small circle of insiders. The *Globe*, he told Kipling in November 1913, 'can be of no great political influence until the circulation reaches a decent figure'.[20] One of his motives – and one of the Conservative Party's – for putting money into the paper in the first place had been to provide a home for Blumenfeld if the *Express* proved past saving; and it was to Blumenfeld that Aitken turned to make the *Globe* more popular. Blumenfeld revamped the make-up, banished editorials from the front page, started a women's page and sharpened up the attacks on the Liberals; the circulation responded, rising from some 20,000 in 1912 to 36,950 in 1914. But it was still puny by comparison with the *Star*'s 500,000, and the *Evening News*'s 600,000. In May 1914, Aitken wrote to Kipling: 'I have refused to advance the *Globe* newspaper any more money . . . Blumenfeld could not change the organisation and it is steadily losing a thousand pounds a month.'[21] Aitken finally contrived to pass on his interest in the *Globe*, using the Unionist press bureau chief as intermediary, to a Birmingham industrialist, Dudley Docker.

The *Globe* had been a joint venture between Conservative Party managers and Aitken. These two parties, and Blumenfeld, now began an intricate triangular dance round the *Daily Express* that lasted four years – much longer than any of Aitken's other takeovers. Blumenfeld's position was straightforward: he needed financial backing, but he did not want to lose financial control, which he equated with editorial independence. The Conservative Central Office managers desperately wanted the *Express* to survive, as it could be relied on for loyal support; but although they regarded Blumenfeld as a first-rate editor, they thought him a poor businessman – with reason; as he often said, he 'hated business'. They were therefore prepared to back the *Express* – with party funds, or money from rich supporters, or a combination of the two – provided they could name their own business manager. Then there was Aitken, theoretically an ally of Central Office but increasingly mistrusted by them as time went by, and increasingly looked to by Blumenfeld as his saviour.

The money put into the *Express* in 1911 was not enough, and the triangular dance began on 29 May 1912 when *The Times* reported that the paper was in receivership and its creditors were claiming £31,698. No one was more alarmed than the Conservative party manager, Arthur Steel-Maitland. 'The *Express* is of very great value to us', he wrote. 'I really think it would be a disaster if [it] were lost.' With Oliver Locker-Lampson, a young Etonian MP, he accordingly put together a rescue plan that envisaged the buying out of existing shareholders by rich party backers, the retention of Blumenfeld – 'the finest editor in England' – cost reductions of at least £5000 a year, the injection of £30,000 new capital, and the 'reconstruction of business management'. Thus for between £50,000 and £60,000 the party would be able 'to retain the only halfpenny paper [it] possesses in London'; it would cost far more than that, Steel-Maitland calculated, to launch a successor. As always, Blumenfeld feared loss of control: 'I beg of you to stand by me,' he wrote to Bonar Law. He then proposed a counter-plan, whereby he would buy a controlling interest for £20,000 – probably with money from Aitken – and Central Office would find £40,000 from party supporters. That would have given Blumenfeld the control he wanted: 'I must have the final word. My authority must be unquestioned and if that is not accorded, please count me out.'

Aitken now told Blumenfeld that he and his powerful American banker friend Otto Kahn were ready to buy the paper outright. Blumenfeld informed Central Office, who urged him to trust them instead; they would guarantee him editorial independence. To stop Aitken, Locker-Lampson took control of a large block of shares he had previously arranged to acquire from Pearson and had been holding for Blumenfeld. He accused Blumenfeld of going back on a promise not to consult Aitken, and warned him that Aitken's motives were suspect. 'Aitken never intended to give you absolute control of the *Daily Express* if either he or his friend [Otto

Kahn] had purchased it'; instead, said Locker-Lampson, he planned to manipulate it through its editor. Furious, Blumenfeld threatened legal action and appealed to Bonar Law. Law refused to take sides. It was an impasse.

Next, Aitken moved again in Blumenfeld's support, increasing his own stake. He bought shares from Johnston of Bovril, still the principal shareholder, and secretly lent Blumenfeld £40,000. Locker-Lampson, thwarted, now withdrew, leaving Steel-Maitland and his rich party allies to sort out the mess.[22]

They did so. By the end of August 1912, the *Express* had a new structure: Blumenfeld was chairman, and among the new shareholders were the railway magnate, Sir Alexander Henderson, the Duke of Westminster and Lord Howard de Walden, with Steel-Maitland putting up nearly half the £47,500 needed to buy out the old shareholders, probably from party funds. From outside, it looked as if Blumenfeld had won total control; in fact, the *Express* had been rescued by the Conservative Party. But Aitken still had a stake, and Blumenfeld's ear; and he bided his time.

Thus in two and a half years Aitken had started a magazine, tried to buy three papers, bought one paper, and tried and failed to create a monopoly paper in Montreal. In each case his motive was political; it had not taken him long in England to realize that newspapers were power – or rather, with the example of Northcliffe before him, that big-circulation papers were power.

CHAPTER 6

THE HERMIT CRAB
1911–1914

EARLY IN OCTOBER 1911 Aitken set off again for Canada, accompanied by Edward Goulding. In the aftermath of the Canadian election they wanted to see the victorious Borden, discuss the next moves towards Tariff Reform and raise the vexed question of food taxes; with the Canada Cement scandal still bubbling, Aitken may well have felt the need of support from a leading British politician and businessman of evident rectitude and impeccable credentials.

The political scene they left in London was also bubbling. On the eve of his departure Aitken wrote to Kipling:

> Bonar Law has come to the conclusion that Balfour's position is very dangerous. Bonar is loyal to his leader, but admits that he may owe his allegiance elsewhere in the near future. I hear that the effective opposition intends to consolidate on Austin [*sic*]. I had a letter from Garvin this morning, and he says he is applying himself to breaking the back of his new task. I have no doubt in my own mind that his new task is a new leader.

Balfour was carrying the blame for the long series of disasters that had befallen the Conservative Party since 1906, and was rumoured to be thinking of resignation. There were two clear candidates for the succession: Austen Chamberlain, generally acknowledged to be a decent but ineffective politician; and Walter Long, a Tory of the old school, a country squire with a large backwoods following. Neither seemed ideal, but both had committed supporters; the last thing the party needed was a damaging split.

Who first mooted the possibility of Bonar Law standing for the leadership? It cannot have been Goulding, for he, at the start, was a Chamberlain man. Aitken was certainly one of the earliest Law promoters. From the *Lusitania*, he wrote to Bonar Law. Despite a tentative opening, the letter radiates confidence.

110

My dear Bonar,

I hope you like your own name in my handwriting – if not I will call you AB. . . . Goulding and I have had a row, first night on board, and none since. He hasn't bored me a bit. I can't answer vice versa. Our quarrel was over politics. He is a canvassing agent for Austen – or was. I told him Smith [F. E. Smith] had no chance at all and he agreed. I then said you had some chance even if only an off chance. He agreed. Then I charged him with disloyalty and further argued that, if Garvin and Smith now came out or came out at the critical moment for you, that you would win. He straightway wrote to Garvin, posted his letter at Queenstown and since has talked of no other thing.

I have stated that you told me you would take the leadership if the chance offered. That your present line of conduct was your best plan for winning, etc. He urged you promised Austen you wouldn't contest first place with him. I ridiculed this statement, if made, having any effect on your friends, using the obvious arguments.

I didn't know what influence Paddy [Goulding] had with Garvin and Smith. If he has enough influence and strength to persevere something may come of this. I build no hopes on him. Smith dominates him entirely and I would rather deal with Smith. . . . yours faithfully, W. M. Aitken.[1]

Clearly Aitken felt little awe towards other leading Tories. The references to Goulding have a brisk, almost patronizing tone. The letter also shows that on his friend's behalf Aitken was decisive and unscrupulous. Bonar Law's undertaking to Austen Chamberlain was real, and to break it would be a serious matter. Aitken brushed it aside almost casually, thereby showing Bonar Law the way out; what would be the point of declining to stand himself if his friends were determined to run him anyway? Aitken's role, from this moment on, was to do for Bonar Law what Law appeared reluctant to do for himself: push, scheme and make the most of every opportunity.

Early in November events speeded up. Aitken returned from Canada on the 7th. On the 8th, after Balfour resigned, Chamberlain and Long agreed that while neither was prepared to withdraw in favour of the other, both would withdraw if a strong third candidate emerged. This agreement gave Bonar Law and Aitken their chance. Late that evening, after speaking, along with Austen Chamberlain, at a big Tariff Reform League dinner, Bonar Law decided to let his name go forward.

The Chief Whip set up a meeting at the Carlton Club, at noon on Monday, 13 November, of all Conservative and Unionist MPs. Thus Aitken had a weekend during which to ensure Bonar Law's success. The chances did not look good. Out of 280 Conservative MPs, only 40 were firm Law supporters. Aitken's first task was to keep Bonar Law's nerve steady when he looked like losing it. He soon realized that his man's best chance lay in deadlock between Long and Chamberlain, and therefore urged Bonar Law's supporters to vote not for him, when the time came, but for whichever of the rivals seemed the weaker. Aitken was also busy drumming up press support for Bonar Law, as an exchange of telegrams between him and Kipling over the crucial weekend indicates. Aitken needed Kipling to throw his weight behind Law with the important editors: hence this wire, undated: '. . . Northcliffe doing very well for us but Gwynne trying to remain neutral and doing badly. Can you force him at least as far as *Times* attitude.' In a wire dated 9 November Kipling said: 'Very good will do my best quietly let me have news as it comes along hope you fit.' A later wire shows that Kipling duly put pressure on Gwynne: '. . . have however wired Gwynne to back him as soundest tariff reform fewest enemies and specially acceptable dominions present juncture.'

Meanwhile Goulding was under pressure from the Chamberlain faction, who were indignant, with some reason, at Bonar Law's disregard for his promise. One MP wrote to Goulding asking him to persuade Law to stand down: 'I do not think he has a chance of election, and his standing may gravely prejudice Austen's chances and in any case cannot fail to leave a nasty taste.'[2] Goulding showed the letter to Law, who fell into indecision and drafted a reply which indicated that, if his candidature was indeed spoiling Chamberlain's chances, he would withdraw. However, before sending it he showed it to the one man he must have known would not approve. On the Friday morning, 10 November, he took it round to Aitken in Knightsbridge.

Somebody once said of Aitken that he always knew political dynamite when he saw it. He knew that if word got around that Bonar Law was wavering, their cause was lost. After a heated argument, Aitken and Law composed another letter, much shorter and firmer than the first. There is an Aitken-like clarity about it: 'My position is very simple. I have not sought and do not seek the leadership, but friends of mine have asked me whether I would accept the position, if it were offered to me, and I have said that I would. . . . I am quite satisfied that the fact that my name is put forward will not affect Chamberlain any more than it will affect Long.'[3]

When Chamberlain realized that Bonar Law was serious, and that Long would not give way, he decided to withdraw if Long would do the same. Long agreed. After a further attack of scruples, Bonar Law accepted the nomination. On Monday the 13th Aitken accompanied his man to the Carlton Club. He feared that the new leader might be too modest and self-deprecating, and told him, 'You are a great man now. You must talk like a great man, behave like a great man.' The reply perhaps exemplifies why Aitken admired Bonar Law and why Bonar Law owed so much to Aitken: 'If I am a great man, then a good many great men must have been frauds.'[4]

In the long run, Bonar Law's accession to the leadership probably saved the unity of the Conservative Party. But the way in which he became leader has continued to be seen by Conservative historians as 'among the most extraordinary transactions in recent English politics.'[5] As the man at his elbow, Aitken earned himself the beginning of his reputation as a sinister power behind the scenes. Balfour's secretary wrote to his master during the leadership contest:

> Much intrigue has been at work . . . Bonar Law's own methods are open to much criticism. In this struggle I am told that he has been run by Mr Max Aitken, the little Canadian adventurer who sits for Ashton-under-Lyne, introduced into that seat by him. Aitken practically owns the *Daily Express* and the *Daily Express* has run Bonar Law for the last two days for all it is worth. The real Bonar Law appears to be a man of boundless ambition untempered by any particularly nice feelings. It is a revelation.[6]

Aitken at first sought a reward. He wired to his Canadian friend J. D. Hazen, a former Premier of New Brunswick and now a minister in Borden's government, on 18 November: 'I am very anxious to obtain appointment as Parliamentary Secretary. Will you ask Borden to send private and personal message to Bonar Law recommending me.' On 22 November Borden obediently wrote to Bonar Law: 'Several of my friends have asked me to write to you with regard to Sir W. M. Aitken. I hesitate to offer any suggestion, as obviously it should have little weight in such a matter; but perhaps I may venture to say that if he should be chosen as your Parliamentary Secretary, the selection would be favourably regarded here.' In the meantime, Aitken had changed his mind. Any such appointment would focus more attention on him; did he really want it? He wired Hazen on 23 November telling him, perhaps prematurely, that he had turned down the position on 'account of uncertainty concerning Fleming' – in other words the Canada Cement affair.[7] Presumably Bonar Law and Aitken talked the matter over; on 9 December Bonar Law wrote to Borden:

> As regards Sir Max Aitken, he is the most intimate personal friend I have in the House of Commons (in spite of the comparatively short time I have known him) and not only for that reason but because of his remarkable force and ability, I should have preferred him as my Secretary to anyone else. Since I got my appointment also he has been assisting me in the most effective way, but he does not himself wish to be publicly announced as one of my secretaries, and he desires to continue to help me without any public announcement. . . . Later on if he should desire to have his connection with me made public I shall be delighted to announce it.[8]

Aitken remained Bonar Law's close friend and political and financial adviser; no detail of Bonar Law's life was too minor for his attention. He even found him a butler for Pembroke Lodge. Aitken was constantly to be found at Bonar Law's house, as F. E. Smith observed in an ominous little verse:

> Round Pembroke Lodge in Edwardes Square
> Like rooks the claimants caw,

While Aitken keeps with gargoyle stare
His vigil over Law.[9]

'AITKEN IS OUR LEADER'

If Aitken had expected that, with Bonar Law as leader, the fight to align the party solidly behind Tariff Reform would be easier, he soon realized his mistake. During 1912 Bonar Law, like Balfour before him, found the question of food taxes a huge problem. To the wholehearted Tariff Reformer, food taxes were essential; Imperial Preference could not be a reality unless non-imperial imports, especially foodstuffs, were taxed. To most of the Tory Party, even those otherwise sympathetic to the imperial cause, food taxes were electoral suicide, and other issues, principally Ireland and the future of the Union, mattered far more.

Aitken now devised a plan for strengthening the food tax case: he played the Canadian card. With Aitken acting as go-between, the Canadian Prime Minister was invited to visit England during the summer. Clearly, the stronger the Canadian demand for food taxes, the easier for Bonar Law to appeal to imperialist loyalties. In June, Borden arrived and was duly invited to Cherkley, where in long discussions with Bonar Law he made a powerful case for food taxes. Aitken kept Kipling informed, and told him later that year:

> Borden agreed with Bonar Law at my house that in the next Budget he would refer to the offer emanating not only from the United States but from Germany for Preferential Trade relations with Canada and that he would indicate that the policy of the present administration in Canada is to patiently wait for the present for a policy of Preferential Trade relations with Great Britain.
>
> I cannot overstate the satisfaction which Bonar Law got from his discussion with Borden, and I frankly state that Borden has gone much further than I ever expected.

In the summer of 1912 Aitken returned to Canada, this time accompanied by F. E. Smith and a parliamentary delegation. Among his purposes was to ensure that Borden stayed in line and, as he told Kipling, to whip up support in Canada for Borden's policy. During his month-long visit he also managed to put through the largest real estate deal ever done in Montreal and, in Calgary, to buy over a hundred grain elevators and a flour mill in association with his old friend R. B. Bennett, by now one of Calgary's MPs. Before leaving Canada he formed a company to expand Toronto Structural Steel, and set up two huge power schemes (never to be realized) to dam the St Lawrence river. Clearly his days as a Canadian financier were not over yet. During 1912 he also acquired control of a bank in London that had a long connection with the West Indies, the Colonial Bank.

At this point, Aitken was in an extraordinary position. The outcome of the Canada Cement row was still uncertain. Nevertheless, apart from his business coups he was manipulating, on two continents, two political leaders and two great political parties. His goal was in sight: a really effective bond between Canada and Britain based on preferential tariffs.

By the late autumn triumph had turned to confusion and near disaster, as the Free Traders in the party turned on food taxes with open ferocity. The uproar, led by the Cecils and Lord Derby, came close to splitting the party and brought Bonar Law to the brink of resignation only a year after Aitken had helped him to the leadership, and only five months after he and Borden had forged the crucial alliance. Aitken fought back: in December he organized a huge meeting in Ashton-under-Lyne at which Bonar Law spoke on Tariff Reform and proclaimed, to a large audience carefully packed with supporters, that he did not intend to impose food taxes unless the Empire demanded them, and so proposed to call a colonial conference to consider the matter. Aitken and his constituency workers made Bonar Law's appearance into a thrilling, if faintly inappropriate, occasion crowned by a torchlit procession with the leader carried shoulder-high back to the train for London.

But despite all his efforts, Aitken could not hope to contain the passions of the Free Traders. As he wrote later, 'I had hoped that Bonar Law's speech would forestall the mutiny but instead it brought the mutiny to a head.'[10] Northcliffe ran a damaging newspaper campaign against what he christened stomach taxes; Lord Derby and the Lancashire Free Trade lobby were up in arms. By Christmas, which the Laws again spent at Cherkley, the picture was black. F. E. Smith, from his own Christmas gathering among the Churchills at Blenheim, wrote warning Bonar Law in dramatic terms that disaster was looming and that all Aitken's wiles were needed.

What followed is still obscure, but shows Aitken at his most devious. With Bonar Law apparently caught by his commitment to food taxes, and resignation the only honourable course if he could not carry the party with him, someone thought of a possible way out. A memorandum pleading with the leader to remain in place and accept a modification of the food tax policy was signed by all the party's MPs except six. Bonar Law took the opportunity offered him. He stayed on, and Tariff Reform was shelved.

And where was Aitken meanwhile? By his own account he remained loyal to food taxes, declined to sign the memorandum, and for a time fell out seriously with his friend and leader. 'For the first time in my life I could not march with Law,' he wrote later. 'I should have been false to my lifelong convictions and to my public if I had ratted on Imperial Preference. . . .'[11] Most historians have accepted this version of events; but it has recently been pointed out that a copy of the memorandum has survived in the Crawford and Balcarres Papers and that Aitken's signature is on it.[12] Certainly there is evidence that at the time other food taxers, including Goulding, felt Aitken had betrayed them. Goulding wrote to Garvin on 11 January 1913: 'Bonar Law has under the influence of his young Canadian friend lost his nerve . . .' and Garvin a few days later, wrote savagely to the proprietor of the *Observer*, Waldorf Astor:

> It becomes pretty clear that we have been played with and that Aitken is our leader. . . . Morally, that is in respect of will and decision – there is no Bonar Law but only a receptacle which must always be inhabited by another personality. The Hermit Crab in this case is Aitken, always putting himself into the other man's ear, and swaying in his sinister, insistent way as he likes that strange enfeebled mass of timidity and ambition.[13]

If, as now appears, Aitken supported the move to get his leader off the hook, he presumably took the risk of lying about the episode later on in order to give his actions consistency with his greatest source of pride, the one cause he never abandoned, Tariff Reform and Imperial Preference. The method used to offer Bonar Law a way out was oddly similar to the excuse Aitken had provided at the outset of the leadership contest the previous year; and in the long term the most important consideration for Aitken was to ensure that Bonar Law remained as leader.

Nevertheless, the collapse of his high hopes for the great Anglo-Canadian political merger no doubt lay behind an acute spell of anxiety about his health during the spring and summer of 1913. In May, he announced while on a visit to Ashton-under-Lyne that he felt he should step down. 'I have been a failure as a Member of Parliament,' he told a meeting, to cries of 'Oh no! Not at all!' 'I have had one illness after another, and I have been quite unable to attend to my parliamentary duties. . . .'[14] After heartfelt reassurances from his supporters he decided not to resign yet, but in July he spent some weeks undergoing tests in a clinic in Munich. The doctors there found nothing physically wrong; when Bonar Law heard the good news he wrote to Aitken: 'I always thought that what was wrong with you was chiefly nervous and I still think that is at the bottom of it.'[15] Even so, when planning another early autumn trip to Canada Aitken asked Dr Thomas Horder, who had become his preferred London doctor, whether he would be prepared to travel with him and look after him; but the cost of securing the doctor's exclusive services proved prohibitive, and Aitken started to feel better.

'MY POOR OLD FATHER'

For some years the Reverend William Aitken had also been prone to bouts of ill-health, when he would write despairingly to his son, as in 1909 when a spell of deafness led him to complain: 'I can now take part in no social conversation. . . . It is almost unbearable.' He wondered whether it would be wise even to attempt another journey south for the winter; 'As regards the old minister of Newcastle, his wisdom is quietly and patiently to "bide his time" which cannot now be long, in the midst of his loved and loving old Parishioners.' However, pressed by Max to think of his ailing son Allan Anderson, he decided that perhaps he could manage another trip after all: he was 'most willing to sacrifice every feeling of comfort to the restoration of poor Anderson's health . . . I should like on this occasion to go to Bermuda . . . or Nassau or one of those West Indian islands.' In February 1910 he wrote: 'God has been especially kind to me' – Max, too, he might have added, for the minister was then in South Carolina.

During these years, Aitken heard something about his father that made a deep impression on him. It was rumoured in Newcastle that the retired minister was experiencing doubts about his faith, and questioning the orthodoxy of the Presbyterian Church. A family friend whose great-grandmother was a devout Anglican remembers hearing that the Reverend Aitken paid her frequent visits to talk over his spiritual crisis.[16] Something about the idea that his father's stern faith weakened before he died appealed to Aitken, partly just as a telling story. Aitken behaved with steady generosity and kindness to his parents; at the same time, he came to enjoying pointing out how easy it was to persuade even the most upright and unworldly to share in the pleasures that money could buy. Moreover, the less rock-like the father's faith turned out to be, the less guilt the son need feel about his own backslidings. Doubts or not, the Reverend Aitken consistently urged his son (ineffectively) to attend church with his children; 'This above all else,' he wrote in April 1911, 'will ensure you the esteem, confidence and trust of your fellow men.'

Aitken's attitude to his father became increasingly complex, as a mysterious letter to Kipling of July 1912 shows. 'I hope I will not be imposing upon you', he wrote,

> in sending you the enclosed letter in order that you may realise what a kindness you have done to my poor old father in sending him the book. I ought to explain that my father had an accident some years ago, and that he lost his memory for immediate events for a time, and that his memory returned again after a few years. He is very old nearly ninety and quite blind. The man who writes the letter to me is a country barrister, and has been my father's constant and intimate friend for more than forty years.
>
> My father has written you in my care, but as he is quite blind and does not realise that his letters cannot be read, his letters are not sent on. He behaves like a little child with the book and shows it to all his friends as his greatest treasure.

Even allowing for the possibility that he dictated it in a hurry, Aitken's letter is a puzzling mixture of fact and invention. His father was not 'nearly ninety', but seventy-eight. Although he had indeed broken his thigh bone the previous winter, the accident did not lead to loss of memory; presumably Max had in mind the aphasia of 1902. The oddest assertion is that his father is quite blind and his letters unreadable. Max had just had

117

a letter from his father in his own hand from Newcastle and dated 3 July; it was, and is, entirely legible and makes appropriate references to Kipling. 'I had the other day a present from Rudyard Kipling of his new book, *Rewards and Fairies*. . . . Do you often see R. K.? I think I would like to see him. He is unquestionably one of the first writers if not the *very first* of the day.'

Why should Max mislead Kipling about his father's condition? Why did he not say that his father was delighted to have the book, and pass on to Kipling the compliments in the letter he had just received? Did he simply want to move Kipling to sympathy for the decrepit father and admiration for the tender-hearted son? Or was it that he felt proprietorial about his friendship with the great writer and did not want his father and Kipling to develop, even by letter, a relationship independent of himself? Four months later, the allegedly blind and senile nonagenarian was asking his son's opinion of Home Rule, reporting that his damaged leg was much better, and adding cheerfully, 'Why, it is even possible that I might once more see old Scotland.' He never did so; he died in December 1913.

UP TO THE BRINK

At the time of his father's death Aitken found himself caught up in the central drama of political and national life in the pre-war years – the Irish Question. He used to say, later on, that he intended to write a full account of his involvement in the Irish saga, but he never did. His personal allegiances complicated the matter; Bonar Law was passionately committed to Ulster, as was F. E. Smith, but Tim Healy influenced him powerfully in the other direction. Kipling was of course even more hostile to Home Rule and any form of compromise than Law; the ferocity and irrationality of Kipling's views gradually left Aitken behind. Later he wrote judiciously:

A generation which did not participate in the Home Rule struggle of the years 1910–1914 will be unable to understand that intense bitterness of sentiment it evoked in Liberal and Conservative minds alike. . . . I can perhaps explain the intensity of this feeling as well as any man because I acted as an intermediary in practically all the negotiations for a compromise settlement . . . . In all such transactions one felt the complete lack of understanding of, or sympathy for, the standpoint of the opposite side.

By the autumn of 1913, both Asquith and Bonar Law were looking for a way through the dangerous Irish maze. Both had somewhat miscalculated: Asquith in hoping that once the Home Rule Bill was introduced a sense of realism would bring its opponents in both countries into line, and Bonar Law in thinking that he could use Ulster's loyalist belligerence to block Home Rule without bringing the country to the brink of civil war.

Bonar Law agreed. It was essential for their encounter to be kept absolutely secret, to avoid inflaming their followers. Showing his total confidence in Aitken, Bonar Law suggested Cherkley, 'the house of a friend of mine . . . quite isolated, and the only risk of publicity would be through the servants which in this case would not be great'.[17] Demonstrating considerable confidence in Aitken himself, Asquith acquiesced; he arrived after lunch on 14 October, and found Bonar Law playing double dummy bridge with their host.

Aitken later described his efforts to break the ice. Bonar Law's mood was 'harsh' and he was not responsive to Asquith's small talk about the fine view. 'Unfortunately,' wrote Aitken, 'this kind of observation never had the slightest effect in rousing Bonar Law's interest.' Aitken launched into a long anecdote about a *Daily Express* reporter just back from Belfast, where he had been subjected to much hymn singing, who found himself kept waiting to see Blumenfeld, the *Express* editor, and finally sent in a rhyme:

> Oh God, our help in ages past,
> Our hope for years to come,
> Chuck out the dirty beasts within,
> And let me see my Blum.

'Humour came to the rescue', wrote Aitken, 'and a contact of personality was instantly established'. He went on to summarize his lifelong tactics as a conciliator.

> The leaders of parties live their lives among supporters, friends and subordinates who share their views and intensify their natural bias. When they meet their opponents it is as open foes in debate. In the course of time they lose their sense of perspective and become harsh and unbending in their attitude towards the viewpoint of the other side. This is especially the case with serious and honest men, and the only method of relieving the tension between them when they meet personally is to introduce some touch of humour or interest which makes them feel that the stage enemy may after all be human.

He added, provocatively: 'My own experience is that negotiations proceed better and national interests are more readily served when the negotiators on both sides are not too serious.'

There is no evidence that he was present when Bonar Law and Asquith got down to business, or that he played any part other than stage manager in their encounters. Both leaders wrote full private accounts to their closest aides and neither mentioned Aitken. No doubt he did talk the matter over intensively with Bonar Law, and he always said that he was himself in favour of compromise.

Three meetings were held at Cherkley in late 1913 between Asquith and

Bonar Law: on 14 October, 6 November and 9 December. At all three, the argument revolved around 'exclusion', whereby Ulster would be left out of the arrangements for self-government for the rest of Ireland. After the first meeting, Bonar Law agreed to try to sell the idea to the Tories; after the second, Asquith apparently agreed to ask his Cabinet to consider excluding either four or six counties, with an option for Ulster to join the rest of the country later on. At the third meeting it became clear that neither man could deliver his followers; the Cherkley talks ended in deadlock. In January 1914 Bonar Law publicly acknowledged that all attempts at compromise had failed. George V's Secretary, Lord Stamford-ham, wrote to Bonar Law: 'The King . . . takes comfort in the fact that . . . the two parties have come nearer than could have been expected. . . .' In the end the way ahead for Ireland, after much further tension and bloodshed, was not very far from the exclusion proposals discussed at Cherkley; although, given the subsequent history of Ulster in the later twentieth century, it has never been appropriate to consider the Irish Question solved.

It continued to obsess politicians until the eve of the First World War. Bonar Law took little interest in Europe, and Aitken also 'found it hard to grasp that the war peril was an actual thing'.[18] In July 1914 Aitken was again in action as messenger between Bonar Law and the Liberals, who had asked the King to call a conference; Bonar Law was unenthusiastic, but complied. The Buckingham Palace Conference opened on 21 July, and ended in failure three days later. Soon afterwards, the last few days of peace found Aitken at the centre of events.

At Goulding's house at Wargrave, Bonar Law, Sir Edward Carson, F. E. Smith and Aitken gathered for the weekend of Friday, 31 July. There, amid the late roses, they had expected to plan the Conservative Party's next moves on Ireland; but events in Europe were accelerating. War between France and Germany seemed inevitable. Aitken recalled that he arrived 'very late' to find 'the conference . . . involved in a discussion of the attitude the Opposition should adopt towards the war and the Government. While this was proceeding news reached us of acute dissensions in the Cabinet on the subject of British intervention.' Despite Britain's clear treaty obligation to Belgium, a substantial section of Asquith's Cabinet, including Lloyd George, was opposed to war. Churchill, then First Lord of the Admiralty, who felt strongly that not to fight would be dishonourable and wrong, was in close touch with F. E. Smith, and had asked him to propose to Bonar Law that if some of the Liberal Cabinet resigned, which seemed likely, the Tories should step in to support Asquith in a war coalition. Although Bonar Law felt, as did most of the Tory Party, that Britain should fight, he was suspicious of Churchill; as Aitken wrote later: 'He objected to Mr Churchill as the medium, and commented on the fact that overtures were made through him. This method of indirect communication so common in political circles never suited Bonar Law, and he would take no action.' It must be said, however, that he frequently allowed others, Aitken in particular, to use such methods on his own behalf.

On the Saturday morning, according to Aitken, everybody at Wargrave except Bonar Law wanted to drive back to London at once to await developments; Bonar Law cautiously insisted that they wait until the afternoon, when Aitken's cars conveyed them all to town. Aitken's own account of the next day or two is vivid, and shows him impressed by Bonar Law's refusal to contemplate a coalition, but drawn to the more dramatic, energetic approach of Smith and Churchill. Back in London, Churchill tried to persuade Bonar Law to dine with him and Sir Edward Grey, the Foreign Secretary, but Bonar Law declined and withdrew to Pembroke Lodge to confer with his senior Tory colleagues, Balfour and Lord Lansdowne. Aitken was unable to resist when Smith offered to take him round to see Churchill after dinner; as he put it,

I had been dazzled by the brilliant powers of the young Liberal leader. I had dined at his house, had talked with him unreservedly – of course with plenty of display on his part of that kind of wit which contains the promise of coming intimacy. . . . None the less, I was so far living in the Bonar Law atmosphere of suspicion, that when Birkenhead offered to take me to Churchill's house at the Admiralty . . . I went frankly as a critic.

Soon after Aitken arrived, a message came that the German ultimatum to Russia was postponed. 'I ignorantly regarded it as an omen of peace and rejoiced in the prospect of escaping a European war.' Churchill, naturally, disagreed: '. . . he argued that the German menace had to be faced and fought out some time or another'. A game of bridge was started; Aitken was cut out and looked on. 'Suddenly an immense despatch box was brought into the room.' Aitken, with a reporter's instincts, noticed that the single sheet of paper Churchill took from it looked disproportionately small, as did the one-line message: Germany had declared war on Russia. He watched closely as Churchill rang for a servant, changed out of his dinner jacket and left the room to mobilize the Fleet. Churchill seemed oddly calm; 'He went straight out', wrote Aitken, 'like a man going to a well-accustomed job.' He handed over his cards to Aitken, who found himself 'in an extremely unfavourable tactical position'. They waited for Churchill to come back, but he never did; '. . . it was nearly morning when we left for our homes'.

On Sunday morning, Aitken went to Pembroke Lodge and helped Bonar Law write to Asquith defining the Tories' attitude to the looming outbreak of war. Law offered unhesitating support and said that it would be 'fatal to the honour and security of the United Kingdom' if Great Britain failed to support France and Russia. Aitken himself, he said, delivered this crucial letter to Downing Street. That night, he dined at the House of Commons in the company of Liberal politicians for the first time:

'This was the beginning of the breaking of many bonds and the binding of new ones – associations were formed which led men into strange paths never before contemplated.' The next day, Monday, 3 August, when it became clear that the Germans were about to march through neutral Belgium, all but the most fervently pacifist Liberals were united in outrage, and by 4 August the country was at war with Germany.

COLLARING GOLD

If Aitken's published writings give a stirring account of his public and political activities during the run-up to the war, his correspondence with Kipling was much less elevated. In July 1914 the Kipling family went on holiday to Kessingland Grange, a lonely house on the Norfolk coast near Lowestoft, which they borrowed from their friend Rider Haggard. Kipling had for some time been urging England to rearm, introduce conscription and beware of the Hun, but like most of the politicians and journalists that summer he was still obsessed with the Ulster crisis, which he thought could well encourage German aggression. As war came closer, he was in constant touch with Aitken; the national drama did not blot out their financial dealings. On 29 July Aitken wrote to Kipling: '. . . if we are to have a European war the advantage to Canada and America will be enormous. The price of wheat will go up and America will have a period of great prosperity . . . we are making very big profits every day the panic lasts. If European war follows we will get Crimean war prices. It's an ill wind etc.' That same day he sent Kipling an excited wire: 'If you want to see the real thing in the way of panic come to the city now.' Two days later: 'Bank Act suspended Martial law declared in Germany New York Stock exchange closed' and 'Shall I try to collar you some gold this is biggest panic in world's history.' Meanwhile Kipling was writing to Blumenfeld, on the day war was eventually declared, of his contempt for the hesitations of the Liberals: '. . . I somehow fancy that these sons of Belial will wriggle out of the mess after all. . . . How the Teuton must despise us – and how justly!'[19] On the following day, 5 August, Kipling wrote to Aitken asking for £50 in gold to pay bills. He went on:

> You know we look out on the north sea here and the whole drama of naval war seems to be being acted just over the skyline. Destroyers are patrolling the coast now and tonight the lights will be put out all along the coast – occasionally we see cruisers tearing past and flashing signals to the destroyers. It's a little bit strange at first but, like all human experiences, in a few days we shall feel as tho we had never lived any other life. Best love to you all.

On 10 August John Kipling, not yet seventeen, went up to London to volunteer.

Even after the family returned to Sussex, Kipling was still worrying about cash and food; Aitken helped him with both, sending £100 in a parcel and consignments of bacon and flour. By the end of August Kipling was, as his wife wrote to Sir Max, 'hard at work on some verses. . . . What paper ought they to appear in in Canada? . . . I do not apologise for troubling you because I know you will be glad to have them appear in Canada. . . .' On 1 September Aitken offered the verses, in return for 'a substantial contribution' to Mrs Kipling's fund for Belgian nurses, to the *Montreal Star*; on the 3rd they appeared in *The Times* and all over the world, striking a memorably heroic note:

> For all we have and are
> For all our children's fate
> Stand up and meet the war
> The Hun is at the gate.

The last two lines soon became famous:

> What stands if freedom fall?
> Who dies if England live?

One of the last letters Aitken wrote to Kipling in 1914 struck a less heroic but no less ominous note: 'Money is very cheap and trade is falling off so fast that I cannot see any reason for higher rates. Of course, this does not apply to the armaments trade.'

CHAPTER 7

A CANADIAN IN FLANDERS
1914–1916

THE WAR BROUGHT Aitken extraordinary opportunities, but its first months were a time of confusion as he tried to find a role in the huge drama building up on the flat plains of Flanders. His financial affairs, after a flurry of activity as war broke out, were to remain quiescent for the next four years (although he continued to run the Colonial Bank). He deposited £5000 in the local bank at Ashton-under-Lyne as a gesture of confidence and tried, without success, to interest Asquith in a non-profitmaking scheme whereby the Alberta Grain Company, which he and R. B. Bennett controlled, would operate on behalf of the British government to collect and ship Canadian grain to Britain.[1] If he had imagined that his business skills would be sought after in the national crisis, he was wrong – although F. E. Smith, faced with the prospect of losing his large income from the Bar, came to him for help. Aitken immediately guaranteed him an overdraft of £7000.[2] After only four years in England, he was already linked by financial dealings with the leader of the Conservative Party, two powerful MPs (Smith and Goulding), the Empire's most revered poet and one of Fleet Street's best-respected editors.

To Aitken's surprise, the outbreak of war did not immediately overshadow all domestic politics. He found himself out of sympathy with Bonar Law, who remained obsessed with Ireland: in Aitken's opinion, 'much water had to flow under many bridges and rivers of blood over the fields of Europe before the question could be raised again. . . . I thought Bonar Law had lost his sense of proportion. . . . He thought differently, and was quite angry with me for maintaining the opposite view.'[3]

On 26 September 1914 Aitken sailed for Canada, accompanied by Tim Healy. F. E. Smith sent him an emotional wire: 'Goodbye my dear friend I have a great affection for you Fred.'[4] (The overdraft had been agreed the day before.) Aitken's purpose was to survey his own and his friends' business interests (he told Kipling) and to assess Canada's response to the war. He and Healy made recruiting speeches, and in talks with his Canadian political friends, especially Borden, the Prime Minister, and Sam

Hughes, the eccentric and emotional Minister for Militia and Defence, his own contribution to the war was on the agenda. He was still leaving open the possibility of going into Canadian politics, and put the considerable sum of $20,000 into keeping the Northumberland County constituency in New Brunswick warm for himself. But with a large Canadian force on the point of sailing for England there was evidently scope for Aitken, with his powerful connections in both places, to play a crucial part in relations between Canada and the mother country.

On 3 October, 30,000 Canadian troops sailed for England – the largest force ever to have crossed from the New World to the Old. Two weeks later they were camped on Salisbury Plain under the command of an Englishman, Lieutenant-General Edwin Alderson. While the Canadians prepared to leave for France, where the opposing armies were already settling into a grim pattern of trench warfare, Aitken looked for a job that would enable him to join them. Most of his friends were similarly occupied; they all wanted to be in uniform. Gladys was helping with relief for Belgium and the reorganization of hospitals in Surrey and Ashton-under-Lyne; her sister-in-law Laura Aitken arrived to drive an ambulance in France; and Allan Aitken, his health restored, came over with the Canadian Army. Aitken was at home at Cherkley for the first Christmas of the war. Bonar Law, with his two sons of military age, and the Kiplings, whose son John had managed to scrape a commission in the Irish Guards, joined the party. It was the last of the cheerful joint family gatherings.

Aitken now learned that the newly-created post of 'Canadian Eye Witness' at the front would provide him with the credentials to go to France, attach himself to GHQ, accompany and observe Canadian and other troops, and report their manoeuvres and battles back to Canada – all without himself having to become part of any military hierarchy. By the end of 1914 he badly wanted the job. He cabled Sam Hughes: 'Most important section of London Press agrees to give me opportunity to describe Canadian mobilisation in series of illustrated articles and Kipling has promised to help me. . . . May I have appointment now and may I go on with my articles which I am certain will be of service in the whole Canadian situation. . . .' But awkward questions were raised about how a British MP, resident in England, could represent Canada. The next cable proposed a solution: 'Hazen will telegraph you that I will be candidate in New Brunswick next election will this be sufficient . . .' accompanied by a message from a supporter: 'Max Aitken is in bad hole because Bonar Law and Smith stated he had appointment as Canadian Eye Witness and statement has been published in his constituency. . . . He is best possible man and his publicity will do Canada great deal of good including immigration and he will spend money freely. . . .'

Early in January 1915, after he had seen in the New Year with F. E. Smith at the Ritz in Paris, Aitken's appointment came through. He was given the honorary rank of lieutenant-colonel and 'appointed to take charge of the work connected with records generally appertaining to the Canadian Overseas Expeditionary Force, and particularly the reporting of casualties'. As his cable to Hughes shows, from the first Aitken intended to use the Eye Witness post as a base for reporting the war himself. Generals and politicians were trying hard to control, if not to prevent, the flow of information from France. Reporters were not allowed at the front at all. Over dinner at the Other Club Kitchener, the Secretary for War, made F. E. Smith Director of the Press Bureau – an appointment described as 'typical of the slapdash way that the mobilisation of British society was hastily improvised at the outbreak of war'.[5] Kitchener wanted the Press muzzled. Even the more enlightened members of the government, such as Churchill, envisaged the Press Bureau as merely an information office producing officially sanctioned news. Meanwhile leading journalists, like Colonel Charles à Court Repington of *The Times*, were protesting at the folly of misleading the anxious public with reassurances that were shown up as lies when the wounded came home. Concessions were made, and Smith resigned, but British war correspondents were still severely restricted; they were not allowed, for example, to give the names of individuals or regiments, and censorship was harsh. A separate system governed cables going overseas, however, and Aitken proceeded to take full advantage of it.

He set up a London office at his own expense at his business address in the City, 3 Lombard Street. From the start, he was determined to compile proper records; he discovered in January 1915 that the records kept by the War Office about Canadian troops were 'in a state of chaos' – as he informed Hughes. In France, he rented a house and provided his own transport and staff. Affluent officers without front-line responsibilities could, and did, have a convivial time; luxuries were supplied from home, and leave in Paris or London was easily arranged. F. E. Smith took three horses with him.

During 1915 and 1916, as well as writing about Canadian exploits for the press, Aitken sent daily cables in code to Borden and Hughes about the progress of the war. Mrs Kipling noted in her diary that he frequently called on 'Rud' for help. As a war correspondent, Aitken made his name with his story of the outstanding courage of the 1st Canadian Division at the second battle of Ypres in April 1915, when a small Canadian unit held firm against a greatly superior German force using, for the first time, the terrible new weapon, gas; this episode, graphically described by Aitken, caught the imagination of the British as well as the Canadian public. Aitken argued constantly with the censors, and after a year thought he had not done badly. 'I succeeded in securing relaxation of the censorship,' he wrote in the spring of 1916, '. . . wise concessions which served to please and hearten the British public.' He also claimed to have established 'a properly constituted Press HQ' that 'became a natural rallying-point for the smoothing out of many difficulties and the avoidance of the routine and delay which are inevitable when matters of this kind are passed through purely formal channels'.

In May 1915 he acquired another official title, Canadian Record Officer, and began to run a considerably expanded operation in both London and France. He decided to build up a complete Canadian war archive by collecting the official diaries kept by every unit and copies of all documents about Canada's role. He started a newspaper for the Canadian troops, the *Canadian Daily Record*, and arranged to have photographers and film-makers attached to the Canadian forces. He set up press trips by British and American journalists to the Canadian front. Complaints began to be heard that the Canadians were receiving disproportionate publicity and acclaim; Aitken regarded these as a tribute to his efforts. Next he decided to publish a book based on his reports: he financed it himself, and gave the profits to support the war, but he was determined that the public should pay for it. 'The policy of this office', he wrote, 'has always been based on the firm belief that no propaganda reaches the hearts and minds of the people unless it is so convincing and attractive that the public is ready and anxious to pay a price to see or read it.'

If Aitken's main aim was to record and glorify the exploits of the Canadians, and to keep the public as fully informed as possible, there was a deeper purpose too, as he kept reminding Borden and Hughes. 'Publicity for Canada during this war,' he wrote crisply, 'is inseparably bound up with Canada's credit.' The more the British were reminded of their debt to Canada, the better for Canada's post-war status and for the great cause of Empire unity. His own reputation did not suffer either, as the ebullient Sam Hughes was quick to observe; in late August 1915 he wrote to Aitken: 'Canada today thanks to Bonar Law, you, Sir Robert and myself stands recognised in a hundred new ways, not as a serfdom but as a full partner . . . perhaps the most pleasing part of it is the fact that the great heart, ability and capability of a dear little Canadian boy has commanded the respect, admiration and recognition of everyone.' Although Aitken continued to have enemies in high places in Canada, and questions about his authority and whether he was paid for his services came up more than once in the Canadian Parliament, there can be no doubt that his energetic patriotism on Canada's behalf improved his reputation there greatly. After Borden visited England and France in the summer of 1915, Aitken was promoted to honorary colonel and given a more directly military role as Canadian Military Representative at the front.

He even thought of becoming a real soldier, telling Sam Hughes he would like to command a battalion, and would if necessary 'gladly go to Canada and recruit my own. . . .' Two days later he had changed his mind; sounding somewhat chastened, he cabled: 'I am not suited to command a double company and Bonar Law and Sir F. E. Smith have persuaded me to leave matters in abeyance.'

During the second year of the war Aitken met and took a liking to a man who was rather different from the serious-minded politicians and editors he had been mixing with, and who was to introduce him to a more dashing social world. Valentine Castlerosse was eleven years younger than Aitken, the son and heir of an old Anglo-Irish Roman Catholic family; his father was the 5th Earl of Kenmare, and Valentine had been brought up at Killarney in County Kerry in an enormous Victorian house near the lakes. His childhood had been unhappy; Valentine was an eccentric, odd-looking boy, who grew up unsure of himself and, according to his brother, 'starved for affection'. Lord Castlerosse joined the Irish Guards on the eve of the war and was sent to France; he was badly wounded and left with a permanently disabled arm. When he and Aitken first met, in Paris in 1915, Castlerosse was on bad terms with his family, who greatly disapproved of a romantic attachment he had formed with a famous French courtesan, Forzane, during his convalescence, and was at a loose end. He ran into F. E. Smith at the Travellers' Club and was taken to a lunch party being given by Colonel Sir Max Aitken MP, who had just returned from the front. 'I took much note of Sir Max Aitken', recalled Castlerosse:

> He was not very tall but sturdy enough. His head was large and round – eyes far apart. He was dressed in the uniform of a Canadian colonel, wearing no strap on his belt and boots that laced up the centre. Not a military figure from a Guardsman's point of view but singularly engaging from a young man's angle. The approach to youth is delicate. Some have a sensitive touch and they alone always know how to get response out of mankind . . . Max Aitken had this touch. I found myself getting on with Max Aitken in great style. Here was a man who laughed with you – who encouraged extravagance of statement, provided of course that it was in keeping with the flow of fact. I did not know then that Max Aitken had a very decided weakness for lame ducks. Later I was to discover that he was frequently unaware how lame they were.

Aitken enjoyed the meeting also: he noted in a diary that he had met 'a brave young officer in the Irish Guards' whose name was 'Lord Rosscastle'.[6]

By the end of 1915, Aitken had moved from the periphery of the war to a position of strength. His energy and generosity were all exercised to the full: in London the Canadian Record Office, still at Lombard Street and staffed by Canadians who were either medically unfit or recovering from wounds, became a meeting-place for the Canadian community and a casualty information centre. Aitken took trouble over all individual enquiries. His own family suffered, too: his brother Allan was wounded at Gallipoli and, as Christmas approached, a shadow fell over the Aitkens' circle when John Kipling was reported missing after the battle of Loos. Aitken did his utmost to discover what had happened; Carrie Kipling wrote in her diary for 3 October: 'Sir Max Aitken comes over from France to bring us what news he could about John, which is very little.'[7] Although both Aitkens pressed the Kiplings and Elsie to come to Cherkley for Christmas as usual, they felt unable to do so. Kipling wrote to Aitken on 18 December: '. . . we have only a very thin skin of bravery to cover our sorrow and find it cracks at unexpected moments so we are not fit even for – or perhaps because of – your and Gladys' kindness'.[8]

'A CHOICE OF MUD OR DEATH'

In January 1916 Aitken's first book was published by Hodder and Stoughton. *Canada in Flanders*, Volume 1, went through four printings in the first month and was strikingly well received by reviewers in London as well as in Canada, not only in papers under the Aitken influence. 'A great book by a big man', wrote *Reynolds' News*. 'A book to thrill and inspire,' said the *Sunday Times*.

For a small volume by a novice writer, the book had heavyweight support. Bonar Law, Colonial Secretary, wrote a preface, and the Prime Minister of Canada an introduction. Kipling, who had given the author much help, declined to be acknowledged, but lines from 'Our Lady of the Snows' formed the epigraph on the title page. Even when enthusiastic, Bonar Law sounded a defensive note: 'The author of this book is an intimate personal friend, and possibly for that reason I take too favourable a view of his work. . . .' But he went on to call it 'a model of lucid, picturesque and sympathetic narrative'.

Aitken's own introduction adopted a modest tone. He said he had been urged to publish his account, despite its limitations, by 'persons of much authority'. He would be content

> . . . if even one Canadian woman draws solace from this poor record . . . if even one reader recognises for the first time the right of Canadians to stand as equals in the Temple of Valour with their Australian brothers who fought and died at Anzac; if the task of consolidating our Imperial resources, which may be the one positive consequence of this orgy of destruction, counts one adherent the more among those who have honoured me by reading these records.

The book is a straightforward account of the arrival of the first Canadians in France and what happened to them; the core of the book is the dramatic story of the second battle of Ypres. In clear, if flat, prose the writer explains in detail the complex movements of troops, and describes many brave deeds. He takes every opportunity to stress the excellence of the volunteer army; the enthusiastic, patriotic Canadian amateurs are repeatedly contrasted with the Kaiser's dragooned professionals. Both by implication and directly he boosts the reputation of the Canadian soldiers, other ranks as well as officers, and proclaims them the equal of any Briton. The Canadians are seen as partners in the battle, not as colonial cannon fodder.

By the standards of the time, Aitken's account is fairly free of bombast and rhetoric; and when he does adopt a portentous tone it is tempting to detect Kipling's hand. To say of a VC's death, 'And so there went home to the God of Battles a man to whom battle had been a joy' sounds more like Kipling than Aitken. To glorify the carnage of Ypres may strike a false note now, but it was acceptable, even necessary, at the time, as the public searched for some justification of it all: 'The wave that fell on us round Ypres has baptised the Dominion into nationhood – the mere written word Canada glows now with a new meaning before all the civilised world.' Overall, however, Aitken's style is simple, with the occasional biblical touch that became his trademark: 'I give a little handful from a great harvest', for instance, and 'men fell like wheat before a scythe . . . .'

The most vivid passages evidently describe what he himself witnessed. The ghastly squalor of the trenches was little written about until after the war; Aitken is never lurid, but he is blunt. 'The men stood in mud, sat in mud and lay in mud . . . it was a choice of mud or death.' His curiosity and his courage are clear: 'The nearer the firing line the more difficult you find it to set eyes on men. . . .' Of the trenches: 'It is only the chance of death that gives them their peculiar interest over other holes excavated by men in clammy earth. The bee-like buzz of an occasional bullet overhead reminds you that death is searching for its prey.' Among captured Germans he noted one man especially, 'a Frankfurt banker, whose chief concern later was what would become of his money'. Already, Aitken shows an impulse to broaden his account to include the politics of the war; and once or twice, notably over the battle of Neuve Chapelle, he becomes directly critical of its higher direction: 'The price was too high for the result.' In general, he showed an impressive ability to grasp and distil a mass of complex material, and an even more impressive confidence in his own judgement.

MILITARY ADVISER

While his book was being published, Aitken was back in France, where early in 1916 he was witness to an absurd episode that revealed the lurking tension between the regular Army and some of the politicians who, the professionals felt, played at soldiers when it suited them. F. E. Smith, by this time Solicitor General, joined Lloyd George and Bonar Law on an official visit to the front, but omitted to acquire the correct pass from the military authorities. They arrested him in the middle of the night as he was about to visit the trenches with Churchill, with whom he was staying, and kept him under guard. Next day the matter was sorted out, but it had caused wild rumours and serious resentment. Smith had not behaved well, his natural arrogance compounded by drink, but as Aitken later summed up: 'A lot of men – quite insignificant from any national standpoint – were dressed up in authority at GHQ and thought it a duty to humiliate any

civilian of importance who happened to expose himself by some careless-
ness or error of judgement.'[9]

Aitken's own deportment was very different from F. E. Smith's. During
1915 and 1916 his powers of diplomacy and discretion were exercised to
the full. Aitken's whole position as Eye Witness, Record Officer and
Canadian Military Representative at the front depended on the volatile
Sam Hughes, who showed an alarming tendency to upset the delicate
balance of Anglo-Canadian relations by over-reacting to any slight, real
or imagined, on the part of the British High Command. Aitken had to
keep Hughes's confidence without allowing him to go too far.

One episode can stand for many. In late November some proposed
changes in the command structure sparked an hysterical cable from
Hughes to Aitken:

> You will kindly protest most emphatically against staff and other positions
> in Canadian forces being filled by British officers we have soldiers fit for the
> highest positions . . . the men who fought so well at St Julien and Festubert
> require no staff college theorists to direct them on the contrary it is the
> general opinion that scores of our officers can teach the British officers for
> many moons to come stop . . . they were no strength whatever in any of the
> big fights on the contrary in some instances they were a serious weakness to
> us stop you may make this as clear as you wish stop Better read this to Bonar
> Law.

Aitken's answer to Hughes is missing, but his prompt reassurance to
Borden survives: 'Did not show Hughes telegram to Law stop Frequently
I receive telegrams which contain unsatisfactory expressions and I consider
my duty to suppress anything which conflicts with harmonious relations. . . .'

Despite his total lack of military knowledge, Aitken soon became much
more than a go-between. He advised Hughes on military matters ranging
from the general deployment of Canada's forces to specific army
appointments. 'For this winter', he cabled Hughes in late 1915, 'I strongly
urge you to limit troops in France to two divisions plus corps troops and
to definitely refuse to send troops to Egypt. . . .' He took charge of
Hughes's relations with the Colonial Secretary: 'Bonar Law wants to visit
Canadians with me next week suggest you telegraph him direct asking him
to go also Lloyd George . . .' (26 January 1916). He sent both Hughes and
Borden coded messages about battles in progress and his opinion of the
likely outcome; during the battle of Verdun he cabled: 'Battle has
developed into ghastly slaughter of troops engaged. . . . Events will
probably determine fate of Verdun today stop I consider no reason for
optimism stop Bonar Law optimistic. . . .' A few days later, a cable
headed 'Very Secret' went to Hughes: 'Found French artillery unprepared
with guns trained on wrong side of salient. . . . General in command was
dismissed and General Pétain was placed in charge. . . .' Around this

time, he wrote to Hughes suggesting a change of code: 'As by this time I think it quite probable that the British authorities will have discovered the codes which we are using I think it desirable that we should now make a change. As you are as clever at compiling cable codes as Mr Bonar Law is at bridge, I shall be obliged if you will make a substitute. . . .' While concealing his activities from 'the British authorities' Aitken was, it should be remembered, a British MP.

In the spring of 1916 a storm blew up when the British General Alderson fell out with two of his subordinate Canadian generals and proposed to dismiss them. Hughes immediately turned to Aitken: 'Please advise me re important changes made or proposed at front or in England. . . .' Aitken's reply was unequivocal: 'I have given the closest council [sic] to all the facts and am convinced that the loss of Turner and Ketchum would affect disastrously the Second Division. . . . I came to the conclusion that General Alderson is incapable of holding the Canadian divisions together. . . . I would respectfully request that you show this dispatch to Sir Robert Borden.' Aitken went to see Sir Douglas Haig, the Allied Commander-in-Chief, and put the problem to him; later, he remarked on the extraordinary nature of the encounter: 'I was speaking on behalf of the civil power of the Dominion to a British commander in the field on a matter relating to generals directly under his command.'[10] Alderson, described by Aitken in his book as possessing 'a genius for the leadership of men', was duly transferred. In the ensuing reshuffle of top Canadian military posts, Hughes again sought Aitken's advice; Aitken made about a dozen suggestions for brigadiers and brigadier-generals, a peculiarly confident activity for an honorary colonel, and was quick to tell Hughes when he thought the War Office was outflanking him: 'Have just seen copy of cable from Carson to you stating that I concur in certain recommendations concerning which I was not consulted. Please note that my concurrence in recommendations to you will be communicated direct.'

If the professional soldiers and diplomats whom Aitken was undercutting had any idea of what he was up to – and it is likely that they had at least a shrewd suspicion – his pre-war reputation for string-pulling can only have grown. Aitken himself swung, characteristically, between confidence and anxiety. He had extraordinary influence; yet his manoeuvres were often unofficial, which made him vulnerable. As long as Hughes was secure, so was Aitken: hence his message of May 1916: 'So far I have been getting on well with the conflicting interests and have succeeded to a considerable extent in suppressing and reconciling the antagonisms which have done great injury to our service here although I am sure in this respect we do not rival imperial authorities at War Office or in France . . . I recommend you to continue to assert your authority here with a firm hand.'

TROUBLE WITH SAM HUGHES

Sometimes, Aitken felt his efforts were not sufficiently appreciated in Canada. In May he wrote to Borden, after a particularly demanding few days taking Canadian journalists to the front: 'I feel that, so far as you are concerned you understand what I am doing but it is not perhaps generally understood how much time and effort I devote to the discharge of my duties.' In June, he became more forthright when his request for funds to support the expanding Records Office was questioned. 'I exercise the most rigid economy. . . . I am far from exacting. I draw nothing for my own services, and I have given the use of these offices, their fittings and furniture, to the government. I hate to repeat this statement, and I only do so because it appears that uninformed persons are still disposed to make enquiries in regard to my expenditure in general.' As for *Canada in Flanders*, 'every expense has been born by myself' and the royalties of $5000 'donated to Canadian War funds'. Two further volumes appeared, in 1917 and 1919, with Aitken's help but largely written by others.

During the summer of 1916 Aitken's dealings on behalf of the Canadian government became yet more Byzantine; he was asked by Canadian Intelligence to place false material in his articles for the Canadian press in order to mislead the enemy. Aitken consulted his trusted aide in France, Colonel Sims, who advised him not to comply, but in the end he did. He made his position clear to Borden, recommending him at the same time not to take the responsibility on himself: 'I fully understand that the public is to be deliberately misled, and by me. The task may not be a pleasant one, but I am prepared to carry it out.' When Sims pointed out the risks, he replied: 'It would be wrong to hesitate to deceive the enemy at the risk of reputation.'

When Sam Hughes visited England and France in his capacity as Canadian Minister for War, Aitken introduced him to leading politicians and conducted him round GHQ in France. Sir Sam (knighted at Aitken's insistence in 1915) went home even more impressed by Aitken; writing to Lloyd George in September he burst out in praise of his friend (to whom he sent a copy): 'Our mutual friend Sir Max Aitken has proved himself a great patriot as well as a marvel in diplomacy. His fearless manhood, tempered with sound judgement, has proven of the greatest service to all of you . . . the Empire and the cause of human liberty owe much to Sir Max Aitken – much more than can yet be told.'

Thus enthused, Sir Sam allowed his conviction that he and Aitken should be allowed a free hand with Canadian forces in Europe to run away with him. He demanded the rank of lieutenant-general and proposed to set up a military council in England through which he would exercise direct control. When he met opposition from Borden he cabled Aitken in panic: 'Find systematic attempt in certain circles to discredit you and me all such have thus far failed you must come accredited by British government on important mission and come as soon as possible. . . .' Aitken prudently stayed put, and in the tangle that followed remained calm. Determined to curb Hughes, Borden proposed to make the Canadian High Commissioner in England, Sir George Perley, a resident Minister. Hughes instantly threatened to resign, and pointed out in a long, somewhat overstated letter to Borden how unfair any move would be that displaced Aitken: 'He is respected by everyone in the War Office, in the Canadian service, in the Colonial Office and in the Foreign Office.' Aitken meanwhile advised Hughes not to resign; Hughes then proposed that Aitken himself should be given the new job. 'It is a question of the man and not of the office,' he proclaimed to Borden (sending copies of all his missives to Sir Max).

Triumphantly he wired Aitken on 27 October: 'Have requested the Premier to appoint you and not the other stop will you accept.' Aitken would not play: 'I cannot accept as I am not qualified to fill the post . . . I strongly recommend you accept PM's proposal and on no account resign.' Undeterred, Hughes wired back on the 31st: 'My proposal is to make you Privy Councillor for Canada you could thus act as you do now with the dignity of recognition. . . .' But Aitken, with the political scene in England fluid, had no wish to be pinned officially into his Canadian role. On 8 November he was able to wire Hughes conclusively: 'I have accepted Chairmanship of War Office Committee for Propaganda. . . .'

On 12 November Hughes resigned. Aitken urged him to be careful with his public statements, but discretion was not Hughes's way. Soon he was gleefully writing to Aitken, 'There is a tremendous upheaval brewing. The Borden cabinet is doomed. . . .' But Aitken knew that Hughes had lost, and his main concern was to put paid to rumours that he had conspired for the job that Hughes had tried to thrust upon him. He asked him to publish their exchanges 'on account of my position in my constituency and elsewhere . . . .' 'Elsewhere' included Bonar Law's office, as a letter from J. C. C. Davidson, Law's private secretary at the Colonial Office, shows; he wrote on 17 November:

> In fairness to Sir Max Aitken . . . the construction which one would naturally put upon the telegrams from Canada viz that Sam would not carry on without Max and that Max had probably pressed strongly for the post of overseas Minister here is wrong. . . . I think you ought to know this because, whatever one's private opinion may be of Sir Max, he was not out in this particular instance for gain and never for one moment entertained the suggestion.[11]

Hughes had over-reached himself. Borden appointed a Minister of Overseas Forces, and Aitken ceased to be Military Representative. But this change in his Canadian position coincided with a powerful intensification of his political activities in London.

TAKING OVER THE *DAILY EXPRESS*

Even as this burst of political activity started, Aitken was given the opportunity of adding a new, and permanent, weapon to his armoury. It would be even more effective in helping him to make his mark than the investment tips, hospitality and jokes on which he had hitherto relied.

The triangular dance round the *Daily Express* was reaching its last stage. In 1915 the paper had run into yet another financial crisis. Once again Conservative Central Office agreed to put in money; and once again renewed its demand that the business management must be under party control. Steel-Maitland agreed to put in £10,000 from party funds. Then, when Aitken used the power of his stake to support Blumenfeld's insistence on remaining the paper's financial manager, he withdrew the offer. That was a mistake. Aitken and Blumenfeld drew up a memorandum accusing Steel-Maitland of breach of promise, and Aitken threatened to send it to the two most influential Conservative editors of the day, Garvin of the *Observer* and Gwynne of the *Morning Post*. Steel-Maitland, furious, appealed to Bonar Law, describing the threat to circulate the memorandum as 'quite indefensible'. But Aitken was a move ahead. He had already seen Bonar Law and secured his backing.[12]

Again the company was reorganized, this time by Aitken. Blumenfeld was left at least formally in control of the business side as well as the editorial one and given a new contract: £3000 a year, and a quarter of any net profits, in return for 'support of the Conservative Party as defined and led by Mr Bonar Law'.[13] Not surprisingly, Bonar Law thought these arrangements very reasonable. Once more, Blumenfeld seemed to have kept his grip on the paper; as a friend and ally of both Bonar Law and Aitken, he saw no reason to jib at his political commitment to the former or his financial dependence on the latter. He soon had a faint taste of the future. In April 1916, while still commanding the Canadian Corps in France, General Alderson complained about a *Daily Express* headline, and Aitken gave Blumenfeld, Aitken assured the general, 'a real good talking to'.[14] Late in November 1916 Aitken took the final step. Johnston of Bovril, a principal shareholder of the new company, was tiring at last of his unproductive investment and told Blumenfeld he was ready to sell. Blumenfeld told Aitken. Aitken, in confidence, consulted Northcliffe. ' "How much are you worth?" Northcliffe asked. I gave him a frank answer. He then went on: "Well, you will lose it all in Fleet Street." '[15]

Nevertheless Aitken paid Johnston £17,500 for his shares and bought the paper. He kept his purchase quiet, though, since he was by now caught up in a massive political upheaval, and thought it best if the exact extent of his control of the *Express* remained obscure.

CHAPTER 8

THE OUSTING OF ASQUITH
1916

DURING THE FIRST six or eight months of the war, Aitken showed little interest in British politics. His adventures with the Canadians in France kept him busy; and in London there was a political truce, uneasy though it was, while Bonar Law as Conservative Party leader did his patriotic best to dissuade his followers from attacking the Liberal government. By the spring of 1915, however, concern about Asquith's conduct of the war and the difficulty of restraining his colleagues led Bonar Law in the direction of a coalition. Aitken's interest in British politics now revived. Although he pursued his Canadian duties, he was increasingly preoccupied with two clear and in his view complementary aims: to manoeuvre Bonar Law into a position of power, and to replace Asquith with a leader more likely to win the war.

The Prime Minister was under pressure. An anxious public had begun to realize that there would be no quick victory; and the press had begun to report the mounting tension between the generals and the politicians. Aitken's view of Asquith was not flattering. He saw him as past his prime (he was sixty-two and had been Prime Minister for six years), full of an exaggerated sense of his own superiority, and fatally slow to take decisions. 'Mr Asquith is hard to describe because within his own limited sphere, the management of Parliament in quiet times, he was perfection, and he was a failure because outside those limitations and yet within his own range of time, lay a world of battle, murder and sudden death.' Aitken acknowledged his 'immense capacities', but bracketed them with 'intense intellectual laziness'. At a time of national crisis it appeared to many people, including Aitken (himself always a compulsive worker), that Asquith was too wedded to a leisurely routine and too preoccupied with his pleasures: golf, bridge, drinking and the friendship of pretty younger women.

Asquith's two most dynamic and restless colleagues, Churchill at the Admiralty and Lloyd George at the Exchequer, made moves in the direction of a coalition. A curious proposal by Lloyd George to nationalize the drink trade in order to control alcohol consumption by munitions workers led to consultations between the party leaders; but the proposal lapsed, partly because it was leaked to the *Daily Express*. Aitken was suspected of causing the leak, which he denied; Blumenfeld corroborated Aitken's denial, and stated that he was sent an anonymous document so detailed and circumstantial that he had no possible reason to doubt it. Bad news from France in May 1915 and a press campaign by Northcliffe attacking the government over shell shortages increased the demand for change; meanwhile at the Admiralty Churchill was on the verge of rupture with the First Sea Lord, the eccentric Admiral Fisher, over Churchill's insistence on concentrating naval forces in the Dardanelles. When Fisher abruptly resigned on 15 May, the evident disarray in the war leadership made reconstruction inevitable. Bonar Law went to Lloyd George and proposed a coalition, which Asquith immediately accepted.

It was a telegram to France from Blumenfeld that alerted Aitken to the crisis brewing at the Admiralty. Aitken hurried back to England, hoping that Bonar Law might perhaps become Prime Minister, but by the time he reached London Bonar Law had already agreed to serve under Asquith in a coalition. Aitken made every effort to galvanize Bonar Law into insisting on a dominant role for himself in the new government, either as Chancellor of the Exchequer or as Minister of Munitions. 'When Bonar Law went out that morning,' wrote Aitken, 'he promised his friends that, whatever happened, he would not give way; he returned to inform them that he had done so.' Aitken claimed that Law agreed to take the less important post of Colonial Secretary out of patriotic disinclination to make demands in wartime, and to demonstrate a spirit of generosity appropriate to a coalition; but he allowed his exasperation to show: 'The truth of the matter is that over and over again in his career Bonar Law would have given rein to this passion for self-abnegation if others had not held up his hands.'

While the new government was being put together, Aitken at Bonar Law's elbow had a close view of the allocation of offices, and some influence on them; a grateful letter from F. E. Smith's wife shows that it was partly through Aitken's support that Smith got the job of Solicitor General he desperately wanted.[1] There was, apparently, a chance that Aitken himself might get a post, but nothing came of it. He wrote later: 'The lions roaring after their prey were many, and the provender pitiably small. I thought perchance if I snatch the meat from them, they will make a meal of me.' Aitken also claimed that he tried to persuade Bonar Law that Churchill should be retained at the Admiralty, but to no avail. Bonar Law was always suspicious of Churchill, whom he regarded as unreliable and self-seeking. As Aitken summed it up: 'Churchill never did justice to Bonar Law's intellect and Bonar Law always underrated Churchill's character – by which I mean the power of holding resolutely to those things in politics which one believes to be true.' Aitken had the awkward task of telling Churchill that Bonar Law would not back him; his verdict on

Churchill at this point is enlightening – about both men. Churchill's single-minded concentration on the strategy of the war, though patriotic, seemed to Aitken foolhardy. 'He failed to remember that he was a politician and as such treading a slippery path; he forgot his political tactics . . . as he worked devotedly at his own job, the currents of political opinion slipped by him unnoticed.' As with Bonar Law, Aitken was drawn to a man whose character was very different from his own. 'He possesses another virtue – exceptionally rare in politics – or, for that matter, almost anywhere. He is strictly honest and truthful to other people, down to the smallest details of his life. He will not even tell what is usually known as a "dinner lie" to get out of a distasteful engagement. Yet he frequently deceives himself.'

Around this time, the question came up of a further honour for Aitken. A letter in the Bonar Law Papers exposes an awkward episode. Bonar Law, as Colonial Secretary, tried to persuade the Canadian Prime Minister, Borden, to nominate Aitken for a KCMG on the colonial list. Borden demurred. When Bonar Law himself then put Aitken up for a baronetcy, Asquith protested so vigorously that he felt compelled to withdraw. To save face all round, Bonar Law asked Aitken to decline the honour. His letter is full of guilt:

> I really feel that I have acted like a fool and a weak fool throughout this business and that it has ended in sacrificing you to make things easier for myself. I can only say that I honestly believe, if my judgment is worth anything, that so far as the opinion of all your friends here is concerned you will gain by what you have done and understanding your nature a little I feel that your liking for me must be very strong indeed to have stood the test of what I am sure has seemed to you and probably rightly my unnecessary timidity.[2]

On the same day, 2 June 1915, Aitken wrote as requested to Bonar Law: 'I need not say how much obliged I am to you for the proposal made in your letter today but, as I feel certain that the honour would be criticized on the ground that it was given to me on account of personal friendship, I must definitely decline it, because I think even a small thing like this might weaken your position at the present time.'[3] This episode no doubt put Bonar Law, with his scrupulous nature, still further in Aitken's debt.

Attempts by Aitken to strengthen Bonar Law's hand in 1915 failed time and again. He later forcefully expressed his irritation about Bonar Law's tendency to vacillate under pressure; the passage, muted before publication, reads:

> This tendency points to a very real defect and a very dangerous weakness in character. It makes him undependable and incalculable at moments of crisis to his friends, for if you are going into action under a man, the one thing you want to be sure of is what he is going to do. What must be the morale of a garrison if it suspects that its commander may suddenly be convinced

that self-surrender is a Christian virtue? Again, a statesman ought not to be content to take up his duty and shoulder his responsibilities when men or events simply thrust them upon him; he ought to go out boldly and take them up of his own courage and volition. . . .

This weakness was particularly dangerous, Aitken went on, because of its effect on Bonar Law's opponents. Certainly Asquith's supporters have depicted Bonar Law as uncertain of himself, overawed by Asquith and unable to stand up to him.[4]

There was another reason, never cited by Aitken, why Bonar Law should have been uneasy when the coalition was formed. His brother John, who had remained with the Glasgow steel merchants William Jacks and Co., was caught up in a scandal: the company had been accused of trading with the enemy. Bonar Law, who had no part in running the company but retained a financial stake, was both distressed and embarrassed when the case came to trial. His brother was exonerated, but two other partners were found guilty and sent to prison. Bonar Law was playing bridge at his club when the verdict was announced, and it was Aitken who took him the news; he was so upset by what he considered the unfair treatment of two old friends that he was in tears.[5] This episode, it has been suggested, may well provide a clue as to why Bonar Law did not fight harder for a leading role in the coalition.[6]

THE BRIDGE GAME

For both Aitken and Bonar Law, 1916 proved momentous. Between them they took steps that altered the direction of the war, destroyed one great Liberal Prime Minister and elevated another. Early in the year they were together in Paris, where Aitken accompanied Bonar Law at the War Council of the Allied leaders. For the next few months the political pot continued to boil, and Aitken took every opportunity to stir it. At home, a bitter debate over conscription and the resurgence of the Irish problem placed the coalition under great strain; in France, the successful resolution of the war seemed further away than ever.

As unease over Asquith's conduct of the war mounted still higher, Aitken was on the alert for an opportunity to push Bonar Law forward. Law himself was reluctant to join any plots against Asquith; loyalty and diffidence combined to make him deeply reluctant to take any initiative. Thus there was plenty of scope for his self-appointed alter ego.

Bonar Law was not the only politician whom Aitken tried to activate; he was also encouraging Churchill, who since his resignation from the government had been commanding a battalion on the Western Front, but was now considering a return to active politics. This was the lowest point in Churchill's career, and Aitken's friendship and confidence greatly sustained him. The foundation of their vital if stormy relationship was laid at this time. Two days after the unhappy departure from the Admiralty in May 1915 Aitken had written an article for Northcliffe, proclaiming Churchill's merits and predicting a great future for him; it was never published, but Churchill kept a copy.[7] In the winter of 1915 Churchill used Aitken's house at St Omer as his base, and wrote to his wife describing it as 'a sort of Canadian war office – where I am very comfortable and well-looked after'.[8]

In January 1916 Aitken found himself the host at an unplanned but momentous meeting in France between Bonar Law, Lloyd George, Smith and Churchill, at which it was agreed that Asquith would have to go.[9] In March, when Churchill was home on leave, Aitken, among others, urged him to exploit the weakness of the Asquith government and put himself forward as part of a vigorous new approach to the war. Churchill's wife, Clementine, was always extremely anxious lest her husband be unduly influenced by the wrong people; her view in 1916 was that he should wait to be called back to public office, and not be drawn into intrigues that would look self-serving. Clementine never really liked Max Aitken; she suspected him, and F. E. Smith, of leading Winston astray, encouraging him to drink and gamble and keep louche company. She was especially wary of Aitken's political influence on her husband, and wrote to Winston at this juncture: '. . . everyone who really loves you and has your interest at heart wants you to go step by step . . . .'[10] After Churchill returned to the Front, still undecided, he wrote gratefully to Aitken:

> In the Field,
> 28.3.1916;
>
> My Dear Max,
> . . . I did not feel able after all to take your advice; for though my instinct agreed with yours I had small but insistent obligations here wh cd not be hastily discarded for the sake of a personal opportunity. . . . I was touched at the kindness wh led you to take an interest in my affairs, and I shd be vy delighted to hear from you. I have really throughout this war tried only to do the right thing at whatever cost. But the problem wh now faces me is vy difficult. My work out here with all its risk and its honour wh I greatly value: on the other hand the increasingly grave situation of the war and the feeling of knowledge and of power to help in mending matters wh is strong within me. . . . I did not feel in me the other night the virtue necessary for the tremendous task you indicated. My interests were too evident and one cannot tell how much they sway one's judgment.[11]

Churchill remained desperate to know what was going on in political circles; his letters to his wife are full of instructions to keep her ears and eyes open on his behalf. Aitken was a good source for him; he may also have wanted his own position conveyed to Bonar Law. By the middle of April he had decided to return, and by the beginning of May he was back.

Events were already conspiring to bring Bonar Law and Lloyd George closer. They had long been on unusually friendly terms for political opponents, playing golf together. There was no real hostility between them, although Bonar Law disapproved of what he regarded as Lloyd George's backstairs intrigues against the Prime Minister. Then on 5 June 1916 Lord Kitchener, the Secretary for War, and all his staff were drowned after their ship struck a mine off the Orkneys. This event changed everything, and gave Asquith's critics the chance they had been waiting for to move against him.

It was clear that the two main contenders for the crucial post left open by Kitchener's death were Bonar Law and Lloyd George. Bonar Law was prepared to take the job, without being especially keen to do so; as Aitken later wrote, 'Lloyd George was anxious, Bonar Law willing, to take it.' On Sunday, 11 June the two men went down to lunch at Cherkley. As Aitken recalled, the occasion was not easy. 'The conversation between them began extraordinarily badly. . . . Bonar Law stated his complaints against Lloyd George as a colleague quite frankly. . . . Lloyd George met, or rather avoided, these accusations, with great tact.' He even went so far as to say that he would support Law's claim to the War Office, 'yet even to this gesture Bonar Law did not respond very readily'. After lunch, things improved; after more lengthy discussion, it was agreed that Bonar Law would after all back Lloyd George.

Bonar Law was due to leave for France the next day with Aitken; but when he tried to reach Asquith to settle the matter he learned that the Prime Minister had gone to his country house, The Wharf, at Sutton Courtenay on the Thames near Abingdon, for the long Whitsun holiday weekend. They had to postpone their journey. Next morning, Whit Monday, they drove over from Leatherhead; Aitken, as he recalled, waited in the car while Bonar Law, already critical of Asquith's relaxed attitude to a major government crisis at the height of the war, found Asquith playing bridge with some female guests and was asked to wait till the game was finished. (The detail about the bridge game only surfaced forty years later, when Aitken told it to Bonar Law's biographer.[12] Uproar then broke out among Asquith's family and supporters, led by his daughter Lady Violet Bonham Carter, who maintained that the suddenly famous bridge game never could have taken place. Scrupulous later research is inconclusive, but indicates that, if not literally true, Aitken's story was an accurate reflection of Asquith's patterns of behaviour and of the disquiet his habits provoked – among colleagues as well as opponents.)[13]

At all events, Asquith and Bonar Law met and talked. Asquith did not want his energetic rival Lloyd George at the War Office; so he immediately offered Bonar Law the job. Bonar Law told him he was too late; his support was promised to the other man. Asquith therefore had little choice but to submit. Such was the version of events from the Aitken–Law camp; and although Asquith supporters have raised questions about the timing of the appointment, and demonstrated that it was by no means a foregone conclusion after the Whit Monday meeting that Lloyd George would succeed, the matter was settled by 28 June. To one contemporary at least, Asquith's outspoken wife Margot, the episode was ominous. 'We are out,' she wrote in her diary. 'It can only be a question of time now when we shall have to leave Downing Street.'[14]

Aitken and Bonar Law proceeded to France as planned; Law stayed overnight with Aitken: 'He told me to let Lloyd George know the upshot of the Sutton Courtenay interview,' wrote Aitken later.

> I sent Lloyd George a telegram, vague in form but clear enough in meaning. It was intercepted for a time by the military censorship. This used to happen quite frequently, although I was at that time the representative of the Canadian Government. Messages to my own Canadian Prime Minister were sometimes intercepted. The desire was, I fear, only to show a little brief authority, for the telegrams were always despatched in the end.

It is hardly surprising that the censor or the intelligence authorities were trying to keep track of Aitken; his intrigues, after all, were affecting the fate of political leaders, generals and lesser soldiers on two continents.

Aitken's own position was improved by these events. Lloyd George moved to the War Office, from which Aitken's office as Canadian Representative was not far away – well placed for both casual and official encounters. The matter of his baronetcy now came up again. At first, all seemed plain sailing; at Bonar Law's request the Canadian Prime Minister Borden this time expressed his warm support of Aitken. However, all Canadian recommendations for honours had to be conveyed to the King via the Governor General, the Duke of Connaught, who had quarrelled with Sam Hughes over military ceremonies which they both felt entitled to head. Aitken's connection with Hughes led the Duke to take the unusual step of sending a private letter with the official recommendation, in which he claimed that Borden himself 'regretted an honour being conferred on a man with a Canadian reputation such as the particular individual possessed'. This naturally alarmed the King, who was already suspicious of Aitken; Bonar Law therefore found himself responsible after all for putting Aitken's name on the Prime Minister's list. After further protests from the King the baronetcy went ahead, awarded 'for wartime services to Canada'; if, as is likely, Aitken realized something of all this, he must have been first offended and then triumphant. It cannot, however, have encouraged warm and loyal feeling in him towards the monarchy.[15]

THE 'HONEST INTRIGUE'

All his life Beaverbrook harked back to the events of late 1916. In 1934, asked to name 'the biggest thing you have ever done', he answered: '. . . the destruction of the Asquith Government which was brought about by an honest intrigue. If the Asquith government had gone on, the country would have gone down.'[16] The 'honest intrigue' is regarded as one of the most important changes of Prime Minister in British history. The successful outcome of the war was in question; the future of the Liberal Party was drastically altered; and so was the face of British politics.

In the autumn of 1916 Lloyd George began to press hard for a reconstruction of the War Cabinet, which he and others considered too large and too slow to act. He proposed a War Council of three members, including himself. Many Conservatives also were concerned about the way Asquith was running the war, but remained hostile to the dangerous radical Lloyd George and any extension of his power. Bonar Law continued to regard Asquith as indispensable. Aitken had his doubts, for he was becoming more and more impressed by the effectiveness of Lloyd George.

Now began a month of high drama. On 8 November a close vote in the Commons showed Bonar Law that his support among Conservatives was being eroded by his loyalty to Asquith. A week later Lloyd George wired Aitken from Paris, asking him to set up a meeting with Bonar Law as soon as possible; Aitken wired back urging him to return to London at once. Various attempts to bring the two men together failed. On 18 November Aitken lunched with Bonar Law and put Lloyd George's case for reform.

Aitken's aim was the enhancement of Bonar Law's power and status. No doubt at first he hoped that Bonar Law might emerge from the crisis as the new Prime Minister; after all, he was the leader of the other party in the coalition. The trouble was that Lloyd George, although a radical Liberal and regarded with deep suspicion by most Tories, was the more magnetic character. Although Aitken was completely committed to Bonar Law, and would have been nowhere in British politics without him, he was also fascinated by Lloyd George and full of admiration for his qualities, which were very much in contrast to Bonar Law's. In many ways Aitken and Lloyd George were alike. Both were full of vitality and exciting to be with; both were interested in other people's characters and weaknesses; both liked women. Above all, they shared a genius for manipulation. Compared to Lloyd George, who was like quicksilver, Law was inert material, waiting to be galvanized. Lloyd George never needed galvanizing.

Describing how Lloyd George changed after the war began, Aitken wrote:

> As the compass turns to the north, so Lloyd George's instinct always turned in the direction of the menace. . . . Once he had taken up war as his metier he seemed to breathe its true spirit; all other thoughts and schemes were abandoned, and he lived for, thought of and talked of nothing but the war. Ruthless to inefficiency and muddle-headedness in his conduct, sometimes devious, if you like, in the means employed when indirect methods would serve him in his aim, he yet exhibited in his country's death-grapple a kind of splendid sincerity.

143

This is stirring stuff, especially when compared with Aitken's account of Bonar Law's nature, in which respect and admiration are tempered by frustration and incomprehension. 'I had an almost unlimited belief in Bonar Law's powers,' he wrote. 'His one weak point was that he had not this belief in himself.' Sometimes, he sounds almost puzzled.

> Disinterested beyond his contemporaries and colleagues to an almost abnormal degree, he was capable of occasional flashes of personal ambition. . . . Then the fire died away, and he resumed an attitude of passive philosophy beyond and outside that of passion and strife. He was not really bored with life, but the original affectation that he was so had by long habit almost superseded the reality. . . . But his distinguishing mark was undoubtedly his freedom from self-interest. The idea of whether he stood to gain or lose from a particular decision in politics never entered his head. He was therefore in this sense a great patriot, but he fell short of greatness in that he did not possess that supreme passion of patriotism which enables a man to be ruthless for the public good.

As for Asquith, there is savagery, and some satisfaction, in Aitken's description of the Liberal grandee who had looked down on him as a shady Canadian outsider: 'His colleagues would observe him in the midst of the transaction of affairs laboriously writing, in his own hand, long letters to private correspondents. He was violating one of the first canons of politics – that no man can afford to neglect business.' By 1916 Aitken had probably got wind of Asquith's obsession during the earlier part of the war with Venetia Stanley, his daughter Violet's great friend, who had dealt him a heavy blow in May 1915 by marrying his colleague and protégé Edwin Montagu. Aitken was before long to make friends with the Montagus, and thus to gain private access to much of Venetia's remarkable correspondence with Asquith.[17] Can he have been referring to the letters written to Venetia during Cabinet meetings (the identity of the recipient at that time was known only to a very few) when he wrote of the Prime Minister 'dreaming of his Peace in War'?

In late 1916, then, Aitken's main role was to forge the link between Lloyd George and Bonar Law. This was a vital task, because each needed the other's support if Asquith, who for all the mutterings against him appeared unshakeable, was to be persuaded to do something he did not wish to do: allow Lloyd George to take over the conduct of the war.

Frances Stevenson, Lloyd George's young and intelligent secretary who was also his mistress, mentions Aitken in her diary several times in late 1916, and draws a clear picture of him as Bonar Law's henchman, bent on drawing Bonar Law and Lloyd George together. She was not especially impressed by Law under pressure. On 18 November she wrote that Bonar Law

> . . . is evidently in a wobbly state of mind . . . he is very jealous of his position as leader of the Unionist Party and does not want to play second

fiddle to anyone, even D [David Lloyd George]. Max Aitken acts as the go-between between these two. He is a very good friend to D though he confesses quite frankly that he is first, second and always a Bonar Law man. . . . I think he is quite loyal and very patriotic, and simply wants an arrangement whereby we may obtain victory by the surest and quickest means. He is very anxious for D and BL to join forces and get on with the war.[18]

Bonar Law's caution, and loyalty to Asquith, were evidently frustrating to Lloyd George.

On 20 November Aitken arranged a meeting between Bonar Law and Lloyd George; it did not go well. Lloyd George's dismissive attitude to Asquith shocked Law, whose mistrust of his ambitions deepened. After much toing and froing, on Saturday, 25 November, over lunch at Pembroke Lodge, Bonar Law, Lloyd George and Carson drew up with Aitken's help a draft statement addressed to Asquith, proposing a war council triumvirate with the Prime Minister as overlord. That same day Bonar Law took the proposal to Asquith, who agreed to think it over. The next day he rejected it.

Aitken brought Lloyd George and Bonar Law together for a second time on the 25th, in his rooms at the Hyde Park Hotel. In the taxi on the way to the meeting Aitken warned Lloyd George about Bonar Law's reservations; as a result, the encounter went better. Two days later, on 27 November, while Lloyd George was dining at the Berkeley Hotel in Piccadilly (the Montagus were in the party), Aitken had Bonar Law with him at the Hyde Park Hotel, where Bonar Law indicated that he was ready to proceed. 'I had the means of finding Lloyd George at any hour,' writes Aitken, tellingly. He took a taxi to the Berkeley, kept it waiting, and attracted Lloyd George's attention across the dining room; Lloyd George immediately made his excuses, left the table and the taxi sped back to the Hyde Park Hotel.

On 1 December Lloyd George presented his renewed demands for reform of the War Cabinet to Asquith, who played for time. Meanwhile Aitken was in touch with Blumenfeld, stimulating a public campaign of open support for Lloyd George in the press. 'Max Aitken is doing his best to persuade Bonar to come out,' wrote Frances Stevenson, 'but has told Bonar that he [Max Aitken] is going to put his money on Lloyd George and will give him the backing of the *Express*. This will be a great asset to D even if Bonar refuses to come out.'[19]

Sunday, 3 December was the crux. Senior Conservatives met at Bonar Law's house to determine their response to the Lloyd George démarche. They arrived incensed by a dramatically pro-Lloyd George article in that day's *Reynolds' News*. Lord Robert Cecil had already accused Bonar Law of dragging the Conservative Party at the coat tails of Lloyd George. Aitken waited, on tenterhooks, in another room.

The meeting drew up a statement addressed to Asquith which said:

We share the view expressed to you by Mr Bonar Law some time ago that the government cannot continue as it is.

It is evident that a change must be made, and, in our opinion, the publicity given to the intention of Mr Lloyd George makes reconstruction from within no longer possible.

We therefore urge the Prime Minister to tender the resignation of the Government.

If he feels unable to take that step, we authorise Mr Bonar Law to tender our resignation.

After the meeting dispersed, Aitken stayed to lunch and Bonar Law showed him the statement. It is plain from his published account, and even plainer from his draft, that when Aitken read the lines referring to Lloyd George's publicity campaign he fell into a great panic. Ostensibly he was alarmed because he feared that Asquith would immediately deduce from the wording of the message that the Unionists were disgusted with Lloyd George and still potentially loyal to himself; he was also embarrassed because he knew that he was himself to some extent responsible for the pro-Lloyd George press campaign. He was in complete control of the *Express* by this time, a fact he later tried to conceal: 'My immediate medium was the *Daily Express*. I did not at that time own the controlling shares of this newspaper but I was on intimate terms with the editor. . . . I must confess that the responsibility for the disclosure to the *Chronicle* and the *Express* was entirely mine . . . whatever was done with these newspapers was done by me.'

Over lunch, Aitken tried desperately to persuade Bonar Law that the references to Lloyd George and the press must be dropped or changed. In his published account, his main motive purports to be to protect Lloyd George and prevent the extent of the Unionists' dislike of him from offering Asquith a way out of his difficulties; but the draft shows that he was even more concerned with protecting himself, and shielding Bonar Law from the consequences of his actions. Aitken suddenly realized at lunch, when he looked hard at the resolution, that he might have over-reached himself and stirred up trouble that would vitiate all his efforts. He had thought that by manipulating the press he would help the alliance between Bonar Law and Lloyd George and damage Asquith; the ghastly possibility now loomed that he might have achieved the opposite. Moreover, he himself was in an invidious position, and so by implication was Bonar Law. In his draft, one can almost hear him trying to put things right.

Now as a matter of fact the publicity campaign had been launched not by George but by me – eg the articles in my own paper [no pretence here that he did not control it] the *Express* and to a minor extent in the *Chronicle* on the day before. Bonar Law had a vague idea from being with me that I had put something into the *Express* but he had no idea of the extent to which I had carried on the Press campaign. He was much startled and perturbed by my news. I pointed out to him that it was an odious task to take to the Prime Minister, in a document very likely to become public, a charge which he now knew to be largely untrue.

Furthermore I was much opposed to this clause ever going out for another reason. It was practically certain to come to George's knowledge, and if it did it might lead to a misunderstanding between Bonar Law and George considering that George knew I had launched the publicity campaign. . . .

When F. E. Smith was called in to help settle the matter, he was no help to Aitken at all. 'He said that the resolution was definitely intended to be offensive to George and to reflect upon his press activities and that to modify it would alter the whole intention of the resolution.' Smith must have known that it was Aitken himself who was in the really uncomfortable position; he had already warned him, according to another sentence deleted in the published version: 'He [Smith] warned me that I had a lot on my conscience. . . .'

Thus when Bonar Law went off to see Asquith with the crucial Unionist message unchanged, he went with the unwelcome knowledge that it was his own trusted aide who had stimulated much of the press clamour for Lloyd George. In his draft, Aitken makes this much crystal-clear. 'I have dwelt on this point at some length because it explains Bonar Law's state of mind during the interview with the Prime Minister. He felt responsible in some sense for my action, and in consequence it was the publicity question, and not the general problem, which was uppermost in his mind during the interview.'[20]

At the interview Bonar Law told Asquith what the message said, but omitted to give him the document itself; Asquith was left with the false impression that the Unionist ministers were solidly with Lloyd George and against him. Soon afterwards, at a meeting with Lloyd George which Bonar Law joined, Asquith yielded to the demand for a small War Committee chaired by Lloyd George and to a general reconstruction of the government.

Next day Asquith's attitude changed again. A *Times* leader gave the impression that he had been persuaded of his weakness as a war leader and had therefore handed over power to Lloyd George; Asquith was so incensed that he decided to fight back. He was also made aware how strongly some principal Conservatives – Curzon, Cecil, Chamberlain and Long – disapproved of Lloyd George and preferred him. Asquith then wrote to Lloyd George reasserting his determination to retain 'supreme and effective control of war policy'. On 4 December, Frances Stevenson wrote of the crucial Sunday meeting: 'We are now given to understand that the Tory meeting yesterday was hostile to D and that the reason for their demanding the resignation of the PM was that they thought it would cut the ground from under D's feet.'[21] The chances are that they were 'given to understand' as much by Aitken himself.

On 5 December 1916 Lloyd George resigned; on the same day Asquith followed suit, in the hope that Lloyd George would after all fail to form a government and that he would be called back. But Asquith's support melted away, and on the 7th Lloyd George became Prime Minister with Bonar Law at his side. On 9 December Aitken accepted a peerage.

'LORD BUNTY PULLS THE STRINGS'

When Lloyd George came to form his government, the new Lord Beaverbrook did not get a job. In later years, he proclaimed that he had made a grave mistake in becoming a peer because he thereby deprived himself of a serious political career. He also liked to maintain that the status and privileges of the House of Lords went against the grain of a Canadian democrat. So he told a rueful tale of how Lloyd George had promised him the important post of President of the Board of Trade; how he, foolishly presuming the post to be a *fait accompli*, instructed his agent in Ashton-under-Lyne to prepare for a by-election (then required when an MP took office); how he despatched his wife to get the campaign rolling; and how in the end, when the job went to someone else, he had no alternative but to save face by accepting the peerage. As a crowning irony, he concluded, when he tried to resist elevation he was informed that his seat in Parliament was needed for the new President of the Board of Trade, Albert Stanley.

However, the facts appear to be that Stanley was always intended for the Board of Trade and that Aitken was never a serious contender for such a major job; as Lloyd George later informed him, 'I knew nothing of your desire to go to the board of trade. Bonar never suggested it to me.' At the time, it appears, he was not unwilling to take the peerage. On 9 December, the day that Lloyd George wrote making the offer, Aitken replied expressing gratitude and received an encouraging letter from Bonar Law: 'I hope you will accept L.Gs offer . . . it would be a delight to me if I felt that this would give you pleasure.'[22] Once again the King objected, as it did not appear to him that the public services of Sir Max Aitken called for such special recognition. Lloyd George and Bonar Law stepped in, pointing out that both the recipient and his constituency had been informed; the Palace, reluctantly, gave way.

'Generally speaking the Tories who had supported Carson and George received inadequate recognition,' Beaverbrook wrote in an unpublished note. 'The two middle-aged Tories who were overpaid for their services were Derby and myself. Derby stormed at my getting a peerage and I laughed at the idea of his being at the War Office and the world laughed with me.' He also left a more detailed account than he eventually published of Churchill's disappointment at not getting a government post, which throws light on the relationship and expectations of both men. 'That evening,' Beaverbrook wrote about Tuesday, 5 December,

I was dining at Smith's with George and Winston. George was in good spirits and we had a pleasant evening, till George left to attend a meeting. . . . Winston then turned to me and said that on the principle of the spoils to the Victors I ought to have the Post Office. Rather with the idea of returning the compliment than anything else I said I hoped he would get an offer. 'What,' said Winston, '*Aren't* I to be in the Government?' I replied faithfully enough that I did not know – the thing was absurd as we didn't even know who was to be Prime Minister yet – 'Smith,' said Winston with great emphasis, 'This man knows that I am not to be in the Government.' An almost ludicrous scene followed – Churchill changing from complete optimism to violent anger and depression. He abused me most violently, and when I got tired of it and replied in kind he picked up his hat and coat and without even putting them on dashed into the street. Smith ran out after him and tried to calm him but in vain – a curious end to the day.[23]

Christmas 1916 was spent by Beaverbrook and his family at Cherkley, with Bonar Law and his children. He was already starting to compile his own record of the crisis; he jotted down in pencil on Cherkley writing paper brief notes of his own activities between 13 November and 6 December, and asked Bonar Law to compose his own account. Law complied and wrote about four thousand words, dated 30 December 1916. Around the same time Beaverbrook also extracted their version of events from Edwin Montagu (Minister of Munitions), Robert Donald (editor of the *Daily Chronicle*) and Sir Reginald Brade (Permanent Secretary at the War Office).[24] Thus when it was barely over Beaverbrook made preparations to present his inside view of the crisis to posterity, as if he knew instinctively that to control the record is to control history.

During the Christmas holidays the Kiplings, despite their grief at the loss of their son, managed a visit to Cherkley. Kipling engaged in discussion with Beaverbrook about the coat of arms for his peerage, and urged him to make the beavers regardant more ferocious. The title itself is said to derive from a stream the young Max Aitken fished in as a boy, where he watched the beavers at work; this story is picturesque but unlikely. Beaver Brook, as it was spelt in 1916, is a French lumber settlement without much of a stream several miles outside Newcastle, and Newcastle children have better places to fish nearer to home. Probably he found the name on a map. It was widely assumed that he was being elevated as a reward for his machinations during the crisis. The *Morning Post* proposed that he should call himself Lord Bunty, after a popular play called *Bunty Pulls the Strings*. Lord Northcliffe sent the new peer an amiable letter on 30 December: 'My dear Aitken, I have received a telegram from you signed Titkin. I trust that is not going to be your new title.'[25]

CHAPTER 9
THE PROPAGANDA PERIOD
1917–1919

'IN 1917,' WROTE Beaverbrook, 'my position in public life was that of a frustrated and disappointed seeker after employment.'[1] It was to be over a year before he finally acquired office; in the meantime he played his familiar role of adviser and supporter to Bonar Law, now Chancellor of the Exchequer and Leader of the House. Beaverbrook soon realized that Lloyd George as Prime Minister was going to have an uphill struggle to assert his authority over the generals and the feuding politicians. Beaverbrook found Sir Reginald Brade at the War Office an excellent source of news about the tensions between the soldiers and the civilians, and enlisted him in his network of well-placed informants. On 6 January Brade wrote conspiratorially to 'My Dear Max' from Paris about tensions between Northcliffe (the great supporter of the generals) and Lloyd George: 'You ought to know, but not from *me*, that LLG and Northcliffe quarrelled in Paris when they met during this week and the latter threatened to break the former!!'[2] From the start of Lloyd George's premiership, his relations with newspaper proprietors were a source of speculation and criticism.

During the early summer Beaverbrook was active on Bonar Law's behalf in a battle with the Governor of the Bank of England, Lord Cunliffe. Bonar Law wanted to float a new War Loan, and believed, rightly as it turned out, that the country was in the mood to accept, for patriotic reasons, a longer-term loan carrying lower interest than ever before. Cunliffe disagreed; Law called in Beaverbrook to back him up. 'Bonar Law thought I could convince most persons,' Beaverbrook recalled wryly, 'particularly on financial issues. He was wrong about Lord Cunliffe.'[3] Later that year Beaverbrook got his own back when he helped Bonar Law rally support in the banking community against Cunliffe in a successful test of the Chancellor's authority over the Bank.

With Bonar Law installed at No. 11 Downing Street, where Lloyd George would walk through from No. 10 to call on him each morning, Beaverbrook was not needed as go-between, especially as the two men established a harmonious working relationship. His offices were required, however, in June, when Lloyd George decided that it would be better to risk the fury of the Conservatives by bringing Churchill back into the government than to leave him outside, frustrated and a potential threat. Knowing that Bonar Law was hostile to Churchill as a colleague – asked once whether it would not be preferable to have Churchill working for rather than against him, he said he would much prefer the latter – Lloyd George offered Churchill the Ministry of Munitions, and made the announcement without consulting Bonar Law; he deputed Beaverbrook to convey the news. Beaverbrook recalled walking down Whitehall to Downing Street to see the Prime Minister and wondering if he might be offered a job himself. In a rare flash of aggression towards his hero Beaverbrook entered Law's famously stuffy, smoke-filled room at No. 11 thinking to himself: 'This will put his pipe out' – and, he goes on, 'it did.'[4] That Lloyd George chose Beaverbrook to sugar the pill is testimony to a subtle operator's appreciation of Bonar Law's fondness for his protégé.

Beaverbrook was of little political use to Bonar Law at this period. As Leader of the House, Bonar Law had to focus his time and energies on Westminster, and Beaverbrook was not even an MP. As for the Lords, he did not attend once during his first twelve months as a peer, after he was introduced on 14 February by Lord St Audries (the former Acland Hood) and Lord Rothermere. Bonar Law relied increasingly on his Parliamentary Private Secretary, J. C. C. Davidson, and his political underling at the Treasury, Kipling's cousin Stanley Baldwin.

Beaverbrook was needed more as a friend to Bonar Law than as a political aide during 1917, the year when Bonar Law, the devoted family man, lost his two elder sons on active service. His second son, Charlie, was reported missing in April. Then in September his eldest son, James, was shot down in France; the body was never found. The grief and shock almost destroyed Bonar Law; he could not work, and sat brooding, submerged in despair. Always at his best when those he cared about were in trouble, Beaverbrook took his stricken friend to France to try to find out what had happened and to seek comfort in talking to James's brother officers. Bonar Law asked to see a plane his son had flown, and climbed into the cockpit. Beaverbrook and the others left him alone; after two or three hours he climbed out, and afterwards seemed to manage his sorrow rather better.[5] Although they escaped the terrible bereavements that the Kiplings and Bonar Law endured, Beaverbrook's family were all, by 1917, 'doing their bit', as a story in a Canadian newspaper pointed out. Of his four sisters, two were working with the Red Cross and two, including the eldest, Rahno, were matrons of hospitals in America 'and have volunteered for war service'. Of his four brothers, one was in Calgary, a major in charge of recruiting, one was with the Canadian 208th battalion, one with the Royal Army Medical Corps, and the youngest, Allan, after recovering at Cherkley from his wounds, had joined Haig's staff. 'This five brothers and five sisters in one family are all busy – quite a record.'[6]

Beaverbrook himself had a brush with death during 1917, when a businessman of his acquaintance turned out to be a religious maniac and threatened him with a revolver, asserting that God had told him Beaverbrook could be a great power either for good or for evil. 'On your knees, Beaverbrook,' he commanded. Beaverbrook escaped and told the story to F. E. Smith, who irritated him by regarding it as a great joke and spreading it all over London.[7]

Beaverbrook may have been dormant politically in 1917, but he promoted one fruitful new idea: the recording of the war through painting and film. He became head of the Pictorial Propaganda Committee under the Department of Information, and set up the Canadian War Memorials organization, which commissioned British and Canadian artists to go to France. Beaverbrook never knew much about art and greatly preferred naturalism to modernism, but he sought expert advice and the artists commissioned under him included Wyndham Lewis, Muirhead Bone, C. R. W. Nevinson, William Orpen and Augustus John. He also became chairman of the War Office Cinematograph Committee, where he encouraged a number of film-makers including the American D. W. Griffith, who asked for forty thousand troops 'with full equipment for a period of thirty days', French and German uniforms, half a dozen aeroplanes, and 'the official endorsement of the British Government on my production'. Despite the collapse of Griffith's project he and Beaverbrook remained friends, and Beaverbrook's interest in the fledgling film industry continued for ten years after the war.

ARNOLD BENNETT

In November 1917 Beaverbrook first met the renowned writer and journalist Arnold Bennett, who became one of the few men in his whole life who dealt with him on equal terms and took part in most aspects of it. Bennett was fifty, twelve years older than Beaverbrook, and like several of the men whom Beaverbrook instinctively liked he was self-made, from a modest provincial background.

Bennett had worked hard for his success. The son of a pawnbroker turned solicitor, in 1889 he left Stoke-on-Trent in the industrial midlands for London, where he took a job as a solicitor's clerk and gradually built up a reputation as a freelance journalist. His first novel was published in 1898. Over the next twenty years he produced, as well as a stream of books (notably *Anna of the Five Towns, The Old Wives' Tale* and *Clayhanger*), many stories, plays, pamphlets and articles. Bennett also became an influential critic. He acquired a yacht and a country house, enjoyed spending money on good wine and expensive (some said flashy) clothes, and stayed in the best hotels; but there remained something artless about him. Partly it was his slightly absurd appearance: his teeth stuck out and he had a receding chin. Virginia Woolf thought him: '. . . a loveable sea lion, with chocolate eyes, drooping lids, and a protruding tusk . . . he has an odd accent; a queer manner; is provincial; very much a character'.[8] Bennett was vulnerable to women, despite a veneer of sophistication acquired in his thirties after he lived for a time in France. Unlike his friend H. G. Wells, Bennett was not a seducer; in 1907, after a humiliating broken engagement, he married an ambitious Frenchwoman with whom he had an increasingly difficult relationship. He was a great worrier about his health, and suffered for a while from a terrible stammer. By the time he met Beaverbrook, Bennett had become greatly respected and widely liked.

Their first meeting was at Beaverbrook's instigation; Bennett insisted, before he would sit down and talk, on reading out to Beaverbrook an article he had written criticizing him. Such plain dealing appealed to Beaverbrook; it would also have made him all the more set on capturing Bennett's allegiance. Within a few days, after lunching together, Beaverbrook impulsively bought his new friend a present, as Bennett described in his journal. 'At this second meeting he asked me to take him to Leicester Gallery, where I had mentioned there was a good etching of Rops. I did so. . . . He asked which was the etching, bought it (20 guineas) and gave it me on the spot. This was at only our 2nd meeting. Un peu brusque.' Rops was known for his erotic drawings. Soon the two were meeting regularly. Beaverbrook invited Bennett, who was knowledgeable about painting (he owned a Modigliani), to sit on the Imperial War Memorial Committee, where Beaverbrook represented Canada; Bennett regarded this as an opportunity to get commissions for promising young painters. Although never an avant garde figure himself, Bennett was always generous and encouraging to new talent in all the arts, and Beaverbrook often asked his advice.

Bennett found in Beaverbrook a younger man of great influence who valued his company and his opinions, and showed him not only generous hospitality but the world of politics and public affairs. Slightly against his better judgement, Bennett succumbed to his new friend's charm. 'I have become such firm friends with that other bête noire of the public, Beaverbrook, that I can't attack him,' he wrote. Although interested in the issues of the day and sympathetic to social reform, Bennett was never really political; but his intense interest in character and behaviour and his need for settings for his novels and plays made him eager for vicarious experience. Before long they exchanged confidences about their families; 'Max gave me the history of the last 15 years of his father's life, beginning with the old man's phrase when he retired from the pastorate at the age of 70: "The evening mists are gathering" – meaning that doubts had come to him about the reality of the doctrines he had been preaching. He died at 85, and in his last years he spent 55,000 dollars of Max's money. It is a great subject for a novel.' With Bennett, as with Kipling, Beaverbrook could not resist turning his father's old age into a good story. It was in fact the son who urged the minister to travel in comfort and stay at the best hotels; but anyone who accepted Beaverbrook's largesse usually paid a price in the end.

'I WANT HIM ANCHORED'

On 23 January 1918 the government chief whip, Frederick Guest, wrote to the Prime Minister: 'I do hope you will consider Max for Controller of Propaganda. He is bitten with it, knows it, and I want him anchored.'[9] On 10 February Beaverbrook became the first-ever Minister of Information, and Chancellor of the Duchy of Lancaster, with a seat in the Cabinet. The next ten months saw him attempting, at the height of the war, to create an entirely new ministry and deploy against the enemy a comparatively recent and still mysterious new weapon: propaganda. 'I had tumbled into office, and into trouble,' he wrote. 'Politicians were my enemies, strengthened by high-born voices.'[10]

Although Beaverbrook himself barely acknowledged it, there had been much activity, albeit of a somewhat ill-coordinated kind, on the propaganda front since early in the war. At the beginning of September 1914 C. F. G. Masterman, the new head of the War Propaganda Bureau and a former literary journalist and MP, called a secret meeting of twenty-five leading writers to discuss how they could help to win the war. They included Arnold Bennett, James Barrie, G. K. Chesterton, Sir Arthur Conan Doyle, Thomas Hardy, H. G. Wells, John Galsworthy, John Masefield and John Buchan. Kipling sent a message of support. Masterman also used film, and created a big photographic syndication service which was influential in neutral countries. But his propaganda effort was mainly literary: Bennett, Wells and Kipling were sent to France and encouraged to produce books, pamphlets, articles and lectures on patriotic themes. Secret deals were struck with commercial publishers whereby suitable books were subsidized and large orders for them placed. Sir Gilbert Parker, a Canadian-born Conservative MP and successful romantic novelist, was put in charge of propaganda in America; in a report to the Cabinet in 1917, Masterman claimed that Parker had a network of thirteen thousand influential people in the United States – editors, journalists, academics.

From the beginning, however, the Bureau came under attack. Because it was largely covert, it was frequently criticized for not doing enough. The great departments of state, especially the War Office and the Foreign Office, were determined to continue to run their own propaganda, and remained hostile to the new outfit. Money was a constant source of tension. The Bureau was financed by secret service money supplied through the Prime Minister's Office, and there was strong competition for it. When Masterman was not under attack for doing too little, he was accused of extravagance. He was also in charge of censorship. As the war dragged on and the early glow of patriotic heroism sank, like the Army, into the Flanders mud, the press became less inclined to accept the censor's rulings. While Asquith remained in power Masterman was able to weather the storm, but after Lloyd George took over his days were numbered. In February 1917 Lloyd George made John Buchan head of a new Department of Information; Masterman stayed on in charge of books, pamphlets, photographs and war artists. Two new sections were created: one for wireless, press and cinema and another for political intelligence.

These changes reflected wartime developments in the technique and scope of propaganda. Reporting, despite censorship, was a far faster, more dramatic and flexible medium than book-writing; and the impact of photography and film had been immense. But Buchan, although responsible directly to the Prime Minister, found it increasingly hard to reach him. Eventually Buchan concluded that only a full Ministry could do the job properly.[11]

Beaverbrook nearly never became Minister at all. Knowing the background, he was determined to take over only if he was given ministerial rank, and it was agreed that the new job should be coupled with the handy post of Chancellor of the Duchy of Lancaster; but when this proposal was put before the King for approval, the royal distaste for Lord Beaverbrook surfaced yet again. Previous Chancellors had not all been Anglicans, but the Palace had not objected. Now the King pointed out that the Chancellor of the Duchy had to deal personally with the monarch over ecclesiastical preferments in the Church of England, which, George V argued, was inappropriate since Beaverbrook was a Presbyterian. An ominous pause ensued; press rumours burgeoned; Beaverbrook worried.

Two draft letters to Lloyd George of 7 February 1918 demonstrate Beaverbrook's anxiety and touchiness. In one he declines the Prime Minister's offer with regret: '. . . the main work, the co-ordination of the activities of several separate departments with a common object but separate offices into a single whole, would, I think, have lain within my competence'; but the 'prolonged delay' between 'the intimation given to the Press about the job and official confirmation' had meant that 'my own merits and demerits for the task were widely canvassed and discussed', and, as a result, 'I feel that I should not have a clear start or a fair field. . . .'

The other draft letter gives as his main reason for refusal 'the extremely invidious position in which I have been placed . . .' as a result of 'the apparent withdrawal of the promise of ministerial rank'. Meanwhile Lloyd George wrote firmly to Lord Stamfordham, the King's Private Secretary, stressing the vital need for better propaganda and saying that Beaverbrook was widely thought to be 'the best available man. . . . I cannot get him without offering him Ministerial rank. He is a first-rate business-man and will administer the Duchy well. I wish you to assure His Majesty that I

155

attach great importance to the appointment of Lord Beaverbrook to this post.'[12] Three days later, the appointment was confirmed. Beaverbrook never took a government post without similar complaints, hesitations and demands for reassurance about the powers he would exercise.

Although the miscellaneous duties of the Chancellor of the Duchy of Lancaster were mainly left to civil servants while the new Ministry fought for its life, Beaverbrook did his best. An early contretemps over the living of Rothbury was settled after the intervention of the Bishop of Newcastle; Beaverbrook noted, '. . . ecclesiastical patronage is something which is outside my line and quite strange to me'. Equally strange, but less contentious, were his duties relating to the appointment of magistrates and justices of the peace and the affairs of 'bastards intestate'. The most unlikely letter Beaverbrook ever signed derived from the Duchy office. It reads: 'I return you herewith the Royal Sign Manual Warrant for the formal appointment of Commissioners of Sewers in Lincolnshire.'

FORMING PUBLIC OPINION

Beaverbrook liked to claim that his new role was created by public demand: 'The public clamoured for a British Ministry devoted to the development of propaganda instruments able to raise morale at home, convince the allies and Dominions of the vast strength of the British effort, and persuade the neutrals to believe that the victorious armies of the Empire would bring peace to a war-weary world.'[13] There were two more cogent reasons; as Lloyd George told the House of Commons, Beaverbrook had organized 'a Canadian propaganda which is acknowledged to be amongst the most successful, perhaps the most successful, piece of work of its kind on the Allied side'; and, as Guest candidly said, it was important to keep Beaverbrook, with his press influence, 'anchored'. Beaverbrook maintained that he persuaded Northcliffe to take charge of propaganda to enemy countries for the same reason. But when Bonar Law heard of Northcliffe's appointment he feared the worst: 'One of you newspaper barons was too much,' he said to Beaverbrook. 'Well, you'll hear of this.'[14]

Beaverbrook turned for help once more to Kipling. 'He came to Cherkley continually through the war,' Beaverbrook recalled. 'He stayed with me in town at a flat in Knightsbridge, and also at the Savoy Hotel. He liked visiting me in town, where he was free to do as he wished without any ties at all. . . . When I became Minister of Information I tried to get Kipling to join me. We were at that time on the very best of terms. . . . He refused, but he wrote me many letters of advice, and I should think that I adopted everything he recommended.'[15] According to Carrie Kipling, her husband and Beaverbrook met on 5 February 'about his new role as propaganda chief'. On 19 February she noted: 'Rud declines a post in the propaganda service (but offers them lots of advice).'[16] The use of Kipling as an official propaganda spokesman had been firmly vetoed in

156

the early days of the war by the Foreign Secretary, Sir Edward Grey; it was feared that Kipling was too extreme in his views, certainly for America where it was proposed that he should lecture. Kipling was indeed unbridled in his expressions of hatred for the Hun, and wrote constantly to journalist friends like Blumenfeld and Gwynne with suggestions for whipping up popular feeling against the enemy.

Beaverbrook's political troubles began at once, as Bonar Law had feared. There was already, in the wake of Asquith's fall, much disquiet in political circles about what was seen as the sinister advance of the power of the press and the influence of press lords; now disquiet became loud hostility and alarm, especially on the Conservative side. In the House of Commons, Austen Chamberlain led a fierce attack on Lloyd George's appointments. The government, he said, 'have surrounded themselves quite unnecessarily with an atmosphere of suspicion and distrust because they have allowed themselves to become too intimately associated with these great newspaper proprietors . . . .' He urged the Prime Minister to 'make things quite clear, open and plain to all the world and sever this connection with the newspapers'.[17] On the same day, the Unionist War Committee (the Conservative and Unionist Party's war policy group) passed a resolution stating that 'no one who controls a newspaper should be allowed to be a member of the Government or to hold a responsible post under it so long as he retains control of that newspaper'.[18] Lloyd George came under considerable pressure; Lord Milner wrote to him saying: '. . . there really is more stir about this than I have yet known in any of these purely domestic rows. . . . The less people hear or see of Northcliffe, Beaverbrook (certainly the most unpopular name of all) etc. for the next few weeks the better.'[19] On the other hand Guest, along with F. E. Smith and Churchill, advised the Prime Minister that he would be in worse trouble if he changed his appointments than if he stuck by them.

In a second debate, on 11 March, Lloyd George made a spirited defence of his appointments; but Lord Hugh Cecil renewed the attack.

It sounds to me quite reasonable to say that Lord Beaverbrook is a great expert in propaganda, and should be entrusted therefore, with the work he so well understands. But is he also so ideally well fitted to be a Peer of the Realm? Is he also so ideally well fitted to be Chancellor of the Duchy of Lancaster? . . . I am a little suspicious, when I find that these various distinctions have been bestowed upon him, that there is probably some other motive at work leading the Government to honour him besides his fitness for the work of propaganda.

At this point, Bonar Law decided that duty required him to advise his friend to resign. Beaverbrook kept a draft, in Bonar Law's hand on No. 11 Downing Street writing paper, of a letter of resignation they drew up together. But it was never sent; he decided to fight it out. Tim Healy said to him: 'Don't resign; wait until you're sacked,' which became one of Beaverbrook's own favourite pieces of advice. His account is jaunty and pugnacious: 'If I was to be wrecked along with the office which I had only that moment taken on, then I would sink to the bottom with my flag at the top of the mast.'[20] After Austen Chamberlain himself accepted a post from Lloyd George the fuss died down. But it was hardly a good start.

Beaverbrook was never tentative. A series of confident memorandums set out his general view of his new job. 'The function of propaganda is the formation of public opinion. The method is to tell the truth but to present it in an acceptable form.' He noted that the British were reluctant to blow their own trumpet; 'It was not our way to explain to the world at large our own efforts or our own virtues.' He pointed out, too, that it is hard to discuss propaganda in the abstract: '. . . the principle of propaganda is the story of its practice'. He saw a clear difference between public opinion, which to him was essentially informal, and formal or diplomatic opinion. The Ministry of Information 'has a diplomacy of its own. Its object is to get into touch not with the official but with the unofficial powers – those forces which though not always marked with titles and ribbons sway and mould the thoughts of their fellow countrymen.' The man in the street is the target: 'He gets up and reads his paper, cables and articles, he talks it over in the club or the pub. . . .' In conclusion, Beaverbrook stated grandly: 'From the point of view of the Minister the proper study of the propagandist is man.'

His approach was that of a newspaperman, not a diplomat or a politician. In a memorandum requesting more newsprint he described newspapers as 'a necessity, without which the modern state cannot properly govern itself or direct its full energies to the war. The mind misses news and comment quite as much as the body misses food, and lack of proper news produces a morbid and unhealthy state of mind inimical to the fighting spirit.' Partly because of his experience in reporting the war and influencing public opinion thereby in Canada, partly because he was already drawn more towards newspapers than to politics, Beaverbrook concentrated the propaganda effort much more deliberately than before on journalism and the press: 'The Ministry of Information is the Ministry of publicity abroad. Its business is to study popular opinion abroad and influence it through all possible channels, of which the chief is the overseas press. Its object is to state the British case to the world.' Such views may seem obvious now that press and public relations are an integral part of national and political life. But to Beaverbrook's contemporaries it was not so simple.

WAR WITH THE CECILS

'Beaverbrook has an astonishingly candid mind,' wrote John Buchan soon after his successor took over, 'and is so willing to learn.'[21] The new

Minister kept Buchan on as Director of Intelligence, and Masterman as Director of Publications. Under Buchan worked a motley collection of 'nationals', in charge of propaganda in different countries. A handful of Beaverbrook's appointments were literary, notably Arnold Bennett – who became 'national' for France, allegedly because of the insight into the French mentality displayed in his recently published novel about a courtesan, *The Pretty Lady*, regarded as scandalously frank and much admired by Beaverbrook. Bennett made a success of the job and Beaverbrook came to rely on his support. Another leading author, Hugh Walpole, was 'national' for Russia.

Beaverbrook also looked to his business acquaintances, on the grounds that men who had long-standing commercial connections with a foreign country would at least know the ropes. Thus he made C. E. Hambro, of the bankers Hambro and Sons, whose firm had done substantial business with Sweden, Director of Information in Scandinavia, and Hugo Cunliffe-Owen, of British American Tobacco, Director for Asia and the Far East. His Director of Finance was formerly manager of the Colonial Bank. Canadians were well represented. Sims, who had done so much to help him in France and was now a brigadier general, was made Director of Personal Propaganda, in charge of foreign correspondents, press visits and the cultivation of influential people, a branch of propaganda that Beaverbrook rated highly: unusual then, commonplace now. The Ministry started the first Overseas Press Centre, where journalists could meet for briefings and send cables. Beaverbrook was photographed at the opening, with the wide grin and gleeful air of a boy at a fancy dress party, wearing a top hat, stiff collar, tail coat and striped trousers. He launched an ambitious programme for overseas journalists, especially those from the United States and Canada, with special tours of the front, interviews with leading British politicians and audiences with the King. He sought out his new friend Lord Castlerosse and gave him a job taking groups of influential Americans to France. Castlerosse was well suited to this public relations work: he had an Irishman's charm, an impressive title and a gallant war record. He wrote: 'I came to know by instinct which of my flock was dedicated to the enshrinement of virtue and which to the furtive pursuit of sin, and sent them to Notre Dame or the Moulin Rouge accordingly.'[22]

The job gave Beaverbrook wider scope than ever before to pursue curious schemes and stir up trouble, which he frequently did. He approached the Ministry of Works with a proposal for a club for Canadians in part of Buckingham Palace, which not surprisingly drew a testy letter of refusal. He tried to gain control of the distribution of newsprint for his Ministry; the Board of Trade pointed out that the suggestion 'is open to the strongest objections'. As overlord of the Pictorial Propaganda Committee that ran the War Artists scheme, he intervened vigorously on behalf of Jacob Epstein, who wanted to contribute to the War Memorial project but was rejected because of his foreign birth. When the unruly

William Orpen, however, appealed to him for support when the authorities wanted him removed from France – 'Let me remain here Lordship please. To my mind the things done on the spot here will be of far more value than all the huge decorations which can be done afterwards' – he backed him, and won. Beaverbrook's interest in films continued, and during 1918 rumours spread about his close relationship with a pretty, dark-haired young singer and actress, José Collins.

Showing his readiness to take risks, Beaverbrook was from the outset determined to prune the tangled ministerial finances that he had inherited. He called in, without telling the Treasury, an outside firm of chartered accountants, and instructed his recruits from the business world to exercise strict control of expenditure in foreign countries. Such individual and decisive methods were bound to cause trouble, and indeed they did. The most damaging disagreement, which undermined much of what Beaver-brook hoped to do, arose not from his appointments or his financial interference but from his clash with the Foreign Office and other departments of state over the delicate matter of intelligence.

He argued that, to do its job effectively, his Ministry must not only set up its own network of information gatherers and propagandists, covert as well as open, but also be allowed to use the networks of other ministries. His request, in February 1918, for 'direct access to the entire political intelligence of the Admiralty, War Office and the FO' was remarkable in its nerve and naïve in its presumption. The Foreign Office was already suspicious; Beaverbrook must have known that his demands were liable to cause alarm, especially as the Foreign Office was being run by his old antagonists from the Cecil family, Balfour and Lord Robert Cecil. He protested that he did not want to cause trouble: 'I do not wish to roll the Apple of Discord among the various Departments of State concerned,' he wrote plaintively to Lloyd George. Balfour was a subtle and fearless opponent: 'The creation of a new Department,' he wrote crisply three weeks after Beaverbrook took over, 'which regards it as one of its functions to co-ordinate all the most confidential information which three other departments have collected for their own purposes is not only indefensible from the point of view of organisation but would render secrecy even more difficult to maintain than it is at present.'

Balfour thus threw down the gauntlet. During the next four months the battle raged, as letters, memorandums and appeals to the Prime Minister winged to and fro. Beaverbrook complained, with some justice, that he could scarcely operate at all if information was withheld from him. Balfour would concede only that the Ministry of Information might be allowed limited access to intelligence after it had been sifted by the Foreign Office. Beaverbrook complained that, because the scope of his Ministry had not been clearly defined at the beginning, he was forced into the contentious role of establishing its powers after it had been set up. Balfour had a strong hand and played it with skill – an experienced cat dealing with an increasingly frantic mouse. Balfour combined fundamental hostility – 'I disapproved of the creation of the Department of the Ministry of Information. I believed, and believe, that propaganda in foreign countries must be controlled by this office . . .' – with immaculate politeness and patience. On paper, he appeared to make concessions; Beaverbrook, thinking he had won his point, would then drop his complaints. When the point was tested in practice, Balfour blocked Beaverbrook's initiatives by ignoring them, thus forcing Beaverbrook again on to the offensive, making him appear repetitive, querulous and a nuisance to the hard-pressed Prime Minister.

Balfour's side had the best of the battle. They even managed to scoop up the experts in the old political intelligence division of the Information Department – Arnold Toynbee and L. B. Namier among them – who, when offered the choice of joining the Foreign Office or staying to take their chances under Beaverbrook, decided to move. Beaverbrook felt humiliated by what he saw as poaching.

Even in less sensitive areas than intelligence Beaverbrook was repeatedly frustrated. He found himself in conflict again with the censors, this time over photographs. The Ministry had its own photographers working in France, where their pictures were subject to censorship. The same photographs were then again censored in London by the War Office. 'It is the Ministry of Information,' Beaverbrook claimed, 'which should decide whether their publication is or is not good propaganda, for publicity is its sphere.'

Then there was the vexed question of the mission to Japan. The War Cabinet agreed in March 1918 that Beaverbrook's Ministry should send representatives on a military mission organized by the Foreign Office. After Beaverbrook had asked various important people to go, the Foreign Office changed its mind about including them. Oddly enough a Cecil, Lord Salisbury, was to head the mission. 'I was placed in a position of great embarrassment and almost humiliation by this démarche,' Beaverbrook complained.

In the middle of June Beaverbrook sent Lloyd George a monstrously long memorandum – twelve typed foolscap pages – detailing the difficulties and frustrations he had suffered. Trying to sound accommodating, he appealed to the Prime Minister to resolve the arguments: 'I am desirous of working in all these matters in the closest co-operation with the Foreign Office, whose knowledge and experience I appreciate in the fullest degree.' He returned to the issue of 'secret political intelligence':

If the Ministry of Information represents the democratic and the popular side of the Foreign Policy then it seems to me that it should be precisely in the same position as regards secret political intelligence as the Foreign Office. . . . All political intelligence concerns us, and it is impossible for another department to decide what is or is not of propaganda value. As to the argument that the F.O. should be the clearing house for all confidential

161

political intelligence in the first instance, I cannot agree. . . . My work cannot be performed with the efficiency toward which I insist on striving if any filter is to be interposed between my department and the supply of full political information.

When thwarted, Beaverbrook responded by over-reaching himself. His demands grew more and more sweeping; it was hardly reasonable to expect Lloyd George, with his immense responsibilities, to take the field on behalf of Beaverbrook against the Foreign Office. The logic of Beaverbrook's position was clear: the existing system caused 'endless delay and friction'; therefore, either he got the powers he wanted, or the Ministry should be reduced to a department of the Foreign Office.

In response to this mingled threat and plea, Lloyd George played for time and did nothing. After ten days, Beaverbrook could not take any more; he offered his resignation. Another week went by; he wrote again, asking for his resignation to take effect immediately. At this, Lloyd George finally responded, promising to intervene and try to get Balfour to make concessions. Things went on much as before; but Beaverbrook, not entirely fairly, emerged as the importunate troublemaker.

DIANA AND VENETIA

During the war, Beaverbrook began to move in a smarter, younger milieu than he had known previously – not one frequented by Kipling, Goulding or Bonar Law. Among the well-off, well-connected young, whose lives were likely to be cut short or ruined by the slaughter in the trenches, social life was frenetic. The pressures of the war loosened restraints and conventions; ways of behaviour inherited from Victorian forebears seemed stuffy and irrelevant. As the patterns of upper-class social behaviour shifted, an outsider like Beaverbrook, with his wealth and influence, puckishness and curiosity about people, could more easily than ever before become the friend and confidant of the younger generation, especially of young women.

When Beaverbrook first came to know Lady Diana Manners, the youngest daughter of the Duke and Duchess of Rutland, she was in her mid-twenties and already much admired, not only for her beauty but for what her granddaughter has described as 'an adventurous spirit, an appetite for life and a capacity for friendship that animated her beauty, increased it tenfold and left the beholders dazzled'.[23] Her hero, Raymond Asquith, son of the former Prime Minister, had been killed in 1916; her preferred suitor was Alfred Duff Cooper, clever, ambitious and with a well-earned reputation for drinking, gambling and romance. One of her closest women friends was Venetia Stanley, Lord Sheffield's daughter, Asquith's beloved at the height of the war and married since 1915 to Edwin Montagu, the second son of a wealthy Jewish merchant banker, Lord

Swaythling. Montagu was a moody, sensitive man; thirty-five when the war began, he was older and more serious than most of the group. He had been a Liberal MP since 1906 and one of Asquith's private secretaries for ten years; in 1917 he became Secretary of State for India.

The Montagus' London house in Queen Anne's Gate was a favoured meeting-place for powerful politicians and the younger set, as Lady Diana recalled: 'At his house we saw . . . the Prime Minister and Margot, Winston and Clemmie, Augustine Birrell and most of the government, politicians, new bloods of the town. . . .'[24] It was hardly surprising that Beaverbrook was attracted by this potent combination of glamour, class and influence, nor that young women like Diana and Venetia should enjoy the attentions of a different kind of admirer – one, moreover, who was not about to be brutally snatched away by the war.

It was during 1918 that Lady Diana Manners 'saw almost daily this strange attractive gnome with an odour of genius about him. He was an impact and a great excitement to me, with his humour, his accent, his James the First language, his fantastic stories of his Canadian past, his poetry and his power to excoriate or heal.'[25] Her letters to Duff Cooper in France frequently refer to Beaverbrook; she was intrigued by him, his money, and the rumours of his shady past. She and Duff nicknamed him 'Crooks', short for 'Beavercrook' (Rosa Lewis who ran the notorious Cavendish Hotel is said to have christened him Beenacrook);[26] she occasionally wrote to him herself as 'Dear Lord Crooks'.

She observed with fascination how he exercised his power. After one dinner party in May 1918 she wrote: 'Beaverbrook talked of the *Daily Express* and of how much of his interest he gave to it. Every night, he said, he rang up and told them to insert and omit so and so, and put in the fact that Lady D Manners has a new giant mastiff with a diamond collar on the front page, not the inside one. . . .' A few days later:

> Great success and fun at Max Beaverbrook's last night. He lives at the Hyde Park and we had an amazing meal in a sitting room, Edwin [Montagu], Nellie [Romilly, a cousin of Churchill's], Mr Means the Canadian representative at the Conference, host and self. Edwin really stimulated with argument and Beaverbrook terribly attractive. Lloyd George's name was brought up as knowing some small point which he could not remember. He rang the bell for a confidential servant and ordered him to find out where Mr Lloyd George was dining and ask him to come round. After an hour's work on the servant's part, he appeared again pale and exhausted and said: 'Mr Lloyd George is on his way, my Lord.'[27]

Lloyd George was then Prime Minister, and Beaverbrook his beleaguered Minister of Information. Another evening, over dinner at the Savoy, Diana met Arnold Bennett and discussed whether or not she had been the model for the society girl Queenie in *The Pretty Lady*; after dinner Beaverbrook took the party back to his suite at the Hyde Park Hotel, where he retired to bed wearing, Bennett noted with surprise, 'second-rate pyjamas'. Diana and Bennett sat together on the window-sill looking out over the park and talked about life and love; afterwards, Beaverbrook asked Bennett what he thought of her. 'I told him I thought she was unhappy, through idleness. He said he liked her greatly.'[28]

One of the obstacles to Diana's plan to marry Duff Cooper was shortage of money. All her life, Lady Diana was inclined to use her many rich admirers as a source of funds. Beaverbrook was one of her first financial backers; and the game was played with gusto on both sides. 'I have been thinking,' wrote Diana to Duff in August from Breckles Hall, the Montagus' country house in Norfolk, 'that journalism, with Max's backing, might be a lucrative and honourable livelihood. Could you not write an article or so about the beauty others have missed at the war?'[29] Around the same time she tried her own hand: 'My dear Lord B, here is an article – it's incredibly bad. . . . I haven't cashed the cheque, so no harm is done. Perhaps an experienced "grub" of yours can pick it up.'[30] Again, Diana wrote to Duff:

> I dined with Beavercrook and found the Edwins, Nellie and McEvoy my fellow guests. . . . Money and one's needs was the dinner talk – Edwin wanted 60,000 for his debts, Nellie 8 for a new bath – I asked and hoped for 1000 for the brave boys in hospital, at which Max rose and walking to the telephone rang up the *Daily Express*, ordering the sub-editor to make an appeal for the said 1000 tomorrow morning. Does he pay a man to receive such messages between eight and twelve as fudge – or is it true? I am bamfusled – it was a genuine call, for he took House of Commons news off him too.[31]

A bit later she is wondering how to pull strings to get to France to see Duff; Beaverbrook, along with Balfour and Cowans, is the best bet, and as for the money required, it was 'easily asked of Crooks'. Whenever she had a new wheeze about how to make her fortune, Beaverbrook leaped to mind. Perhaps he would back her and Katherine Asquith in setting up a lucrative private nursing home? Or how about a passenger aircraft company?

Over the years Beaverbrook was generous in many ways, not least financially, to Lady Diana and she was often spoilt with lavish presents, but though he gave her advice on investments he was too sensible to become embroiled in any of her moneymaking projects. He always addressed Lady Diana in fulsome terms ('my beloved of all women' . . . 'dear beloved' . . . 'my best loved' . . .). One early letter has survived which gives the impression that at the beginning at least he was hoping to get closer to her.

> Dearest Lady,
> How unhappy you make me. Why did you send me a message over the telephone to say you would not hold communication with me? Now you write

me a letter I'm glad to get but it's so difficult to understand. You know I'm most anxious to do anything for you – but I'm so sensitive to rebuff. You see I've had to go through a life so different from the usual sort of experience of the average Englishman. Won't you take pity. Yours ever Max.[32]

When in June 1919 she married Duff Cooper at St Margaret's, Westminster, Beaverbrook was among the guests, with tears pouring down his face. He gave them a motor car as a wedding present.[33]

If Beaverbrook's relationship with Diana Cooper was comparatively light-hearted, that with Venetia Montagu was more intense, at least in its early stages. Diana was in love with her husband, whereas the Montagu marriage was apparently uneasy from the start. Venetia lacked Diana's radiant beauty, but she was dark and striking, with a reputation as an intellectual and wit. She was a favourite of Churchill's, and Clementine's first cousin. Above all, as a consequence of Asquith's infatuation with her and her marriage to a member of the government, she had access to the kind of inside information and gossip that Beaverbrook most relished.

It is striking that Gladys Beaverbrook is nowhere mentioned in Lady Diana Cooper's account of her early friendship with Beaverbrook. According to the Cherkley visitors' book, Diana and Duff Cooper and the Montagus were entertained there several times during 1918, so it was not that Beaverbrook kept his new friends and his wife strictly apart; but his expanding new social life in London was led independently of her.

'NO MAN IN ANY PARTY TRUSTS MAX'

By the summer of 1918, Beaverbrook's relations with Lloyd George were under considerable strain. Apart from the departmental in-fighting, Lloyd George had grown restive under the continual requests from the Ministry of Information for the Prime Minister to give interviews to visiting pressmen. In April, a row blew up over a *Daily Express* scoop revealing that Lord Derby was to go to Paris as Ambassador, relinquishing the post of Secretary of State for War to Lord Milner. The King's secretary, Lord Stamfordham, rang Lloyd George to complain that His Majesty was not at all pleased that the *Express* had published the story before the official announcement, and to ask how the leak had occurred. On 22 April Beaverbrook sent the Prime Minister a long letter of justification and argument. He denied, with much circumstantial detail, that Blumenfeld had got the story from him; he described himself, in a phrase he was to make much use of in the years ahead, merely as the *Express*'s 'principal shareholder'. The editor had come by the news 'in his professional capacity', wrote Beaverbrook firmly, 'and he was absolutely right in publishing, and he would be justified in doing the same thing again under similar circumstances'. He then went on to raise the whole question of his position in the government, again trying to place the ball in Lloyd George's court. 'I am still strongly of opinion that newspaper proprietors ought not to be debarred from office . . . such incidents as the *Daily Express* announcements are certain to recur from time to time, and I am anxious to obtain from you your opinion as to whether I am embarrassing the Government by remaining in office under these circumstances. . . .' Beaverbrook's constant need for reassurance must have begun to seem wearing.

Further political trouble was brewing. Beaverbrook's ambitions for the Ministry, his unusual appointments and battles with other departments, had inevitably become public knowledge, and now formed the grounds for a full-scale debate in Parliament and an attack on the government. A savage leading article in the *Westminster Gazette* at the end of July summarized the hostile line.

> What is the Ministry of Information, of whom does it consist, and what is it doing? Its chief, Lord Beaverbrook, we know or are getting to know. He has many irons in the fire, financial and political, his friends say he has boundless energy, and ambition to match . . . he was given a peerage by special creation before his services to the nation had been known or explained to the public, and during the subsequent fifteen months the noise of his approach to the seats of the mighty has become rapidly louder. . . .

Of his job as Minister of Information, the *Westminster Gazette* went on, '. . . outside the War Cabinet hardly any position could be more important. Upon the right charge of its responsibilities depends in large part whether our cause is kept high or falls low in the world . . . the Director of Information is thus in a measure the keeper of our conscience, the trustee of the moral and spiritual causes for which we stand. . . .' The journal then proceeded to cast doubt on the fitness of Lord Beaverbrook to hold so great a trust. It listed, in sardonic tones, all the businessmen Beaverbrook had employed, with their commercial links and interests. 'It is, as the reader will perceive, a grand enterprise and a unique department. Lord Beaverbrook and his missionaries are a veritable pageant of British commerce. Ships, railways, rubber, tobacco, high finance in all its branches are spread out before us. How exactly they spread information is not yet understood, but will no doubt be explained to Parliament this week.'

Faced with this onslaught, Beaverbrook looked round for support. Bonar Law felt he could not defend his friend in Parliament; Baldwin was deputed to do so. Not much reassured, Beaverbrook called in Tim Healy, regarded as a master of parliamentary tactics, and summoned him over from Dublin. In one of the most characteristic passages of his memoirs, Beaverbrook described how he awaited his counsellor anxiously at Cherkley. When Healy arrived, he insisted on having a good lunch. Afterwards he declined to look at the paperwork Beaverbrook had prepared for him or to listen to suggestions about how to counter the attack. 'I shall watch the House and decide,' he said.

The radical MP Leif Jones led the attack, making special play with Beaverbrook's business connections. He also suggested that sinister aims lay behind Beaverbrook's use of films, and raised grave doubts about a new project of the Ministry's, the establishment of an Imperial News Service based on a chain of Imperial Wireless Stations. The spectre raised was of a ruthless press tycoon bent on acquiring the implements for mass brainwashing of the public. Baldwin defended his colleague ably, if not with enthusiasm: 'The Minister of Information is a man of very strong personality. Men with strong personalities have this in common, that the magnetism which comes with that personality either attracts or repels . . . Lord Beaverbrook has taken on a most difficult, delicate and thankless task. . . . Give him a fair chance and let him be judged by results.' Then, at a crucial moment in the debate, Healy mentioned Ireland; the House was distracted, and the attack on Beaverbrook died away. Later that evening Healy joined Beaverbrook, who was waiting nervously at the Hyde Park Hotel. 'Get me some pea soup and a steak and a bottle of beer, and I will tell you the fun,' said Healy, triumphant.[34]

Beaverbrook survived, but the allegations made against him cast a shadow, as a letter he soon received from Baldwin shows. He advised Beaverbrook that, if his department persisted with a plan to send a man previously tainted by the Marconi scandal on an official mission, the House of Commons would be outraged. 'The House has for the time being swallowed your businessmen,' wrote Baldwin, 'but they would throw this particular appointment up. I know the feelings of the silent men as well as of the vocal.' He went on to warn Beaverbrook of another danger: 'My chief concern is that any error of judgment you make reacts on Bonar pretty quickly, and I am sure that any result of that kind would be as unwelcome to you as it would be to me.' Beaverbrook's reply was frigid. He thanked Baldwin politely for his advice, and continued:

It would be absurd that my action should affect Bonar's position. I did not owe my appointment as Minister to him: when the trouble about newspaper proprietors started immediately afterwards, he wanted me to resign; and he does not support my minutes in the War Cabinet. When there is any conflict between this Ministry and the Treasury he supports the Treasury, so that it is not so much a question of my actions reflecting on him as of the actions of the Chancellor of the Exchequer reflecting on this Ministry. So I really think that it ought to be admitted that I am on my own.

The whole exchange between Baldwin and Beaverbrook radiates mutual dislike and suspicion.

Beaverbrook's political position was increasingly uneasy. During the summer Balfour accused him of interfering with foreign policy over the vexed question of a national home for the Jews, as promised in the Balfour Declaration of November 1917. Beaverbrook had been lobbied by Jewish anti-Zionists, including Edwin Montagu, and had raised their concern with

Lloyd George. Before the end of August a bitter row broke out with Lloyd George over a *Daily Express* leader which implied that, in an election, the paper could not support Lloyd George unless he gave pledges about Tariff Reform and Imperial Preference. As Lloyd George was planning an election to confirm the coalition in power before the war came to an end, he was furious, and expostulated to Bonar Law: 'That is Max. Having regard to the risks I ran for him and the way I stood up for him when he was attacked by his own party I regard this as a mean piece of treachery. It explains why no man in any Party trusts Max. . . . I am sorry, for I have sincerely tried to work with him.' A little later, Churchill wrote to Bonar Law: 'Look after Max, or he will make a great mistake which all of us and he most of all will have cause to regret.'[35]

By the early autumn of 1918 Beaverbrook was tired of bureaucratic battles, at odds with Lloyd George, and smarting from the kind of public exposure and criticism he most detested. Not surprisingly, he began to feel ill. This time, although many of his circle assumed that strain had had its usual effect, he was suffering from a glandular disorder that turned out to be serious. In October, with the war almost over, he resigned once and for all. On 19 October Arnold Bennett wrote him a blunt letter with the ring of truth about it that summed up the ten previous months:

> If you resign, I do. I came into the show through you originally. . . . I would stick to the show, if I thought the Ministry would be given a fair chance of being an efficient machine. But I don't think so. I know perfectly well, and all the responsible heads of departments know, that the hand of every other Ministry is against it. This of course is notorious. . . . The explanation of this general hostility is plain. That there ought to be a Ministry of Information is certain; there ought to have been one much earlier. But the belief widely exists that the Ministry was brought into being for the sake of the Minister, and not vice versa. It may be quite wrong, but it is the origin of the hostility which does and must impair the efficiency of the machine. . . .

'I am sorry in a way that it is over,' wrote Beaverbrook to Bennett in reply. '. . . I feel sure that our personal friendship will survive the mere dissolution of office ties.' Their work in the Ministry of Information brought them closer, and is perpetuated in the realistic political novel Bennett wrote some years later, *Lord Raingo*, a study of an outsider suddenly given high political office in the middle of the war.[36]

Arnold Bennett's *Lord Raingo* is a middle-aged self-made millionaire. He has a country house, a dull wife who conveniently dies in a car accident, and a young mistress in a flat near Leicester Square. He frequents the Savoy. The novel opens with a doctor telling him that he has a weak heart and must avoid all strain; but soon he is being offered, to his astonishment, the new post of Minister of Records in charge of propaganda in the wartime government. At first he refuses, on health grounds; but is persuaded to accept by being offered a peerage. He then exhausts himself battling against the Foreign Office, the War Office, envious colleagues and hostile opponents, as he attempts to bring an energetic, centralized propaganda policy into effect. In the end Raingo's health gives way and he retreats to the country to die.

Sam Raingo's experiences and emotions are strikingly evocative of Beaverbrook's. As he walks down Whitehall to see the Prime Minister, Raingo is exhilarated: 'He had not felt so creative and so intensely alert since the morning of the day, years earlier, when, after terrible suspense, he had made a million and a quarter in one interview. . . .' When he is offered the Portfolio of Records, he remains impassive: 'In a hundred financial deals, in some of which millions of money and triumph and ruin had hung in the balance for days of protracted and intricate negotiations, Sam had learned how to wear a mask falsifying all his wishes and emotions.' He is worried by his 'extremely mediocre talent for public speaking' and by the prospect of the political manoeuvring ahead of him: '. . . he perfectly understood that politics and intrigue are the inevitable accompaniment, as well as in part the cause, of war'.

Bennett gives Raingo a sensitivity amounting almost to paranoia about his background and his colleagues' attitude towards him. 'But after all he was only a millionaire and a man of business, whereas the others had the incomparable prestige which in Britain attaches to politics alone.' When his request for funds from the War Office is blocked, he reflects that 'the order was probably a hit at himself – rascally company-promoting millionaire with no father, no public school, no style'. His best weapons are his access to his old friend the Prime Minister, who as a provincial himself is also a comparative outsider – '. . . he comprehended that political power sprang as much from intimacy as from anything' – and his skill with the press. 'He had the knack of winning over journalists; he had always had it – was born with it.'

Gradually Raingo loses his illusions, both about what his new Ministry can achieve in the face of implacable and skilful opposition, and about politics in general. When he takes his seat as a peer, 'Sam felt at once an ass, a cynic and a conqueror.' His son comes home with shell shock; 'Politics! Titles! Propaganda! What odious, contemptible tinsel and mockery. Here was the war itself, tragedy, utterly distracted fatherhood.' He comes to realize, by the end, that 'The only real war was in Whitehall'; and when the Prime Minister lets him down, he walks home reflecting: 'I had a silly, footling idea that a world war would change human nature. For all human nature cares a world war is just like company promoting.'

Beaverbrook had learnt very similar lessons from his experiences as a Minister in wartime, and was to make good use of them both in his writing and in another war.

CHAPTER 10

'BRING BONAR BACK'
1919–1922

DURING THE WINTER of 1918 and into the spring of 1919, Beaver-brook was suffering from the recurrent and unpleasant illness that had given him the excuse to resign from the government. He developed a fungal infection of the jaw and neck, actinomycosis, and had to be operated on twice; for a time it was thought he might have cancer, and the condition was not finally cured until he had been treated by a Swiss doctor who poured iodine in large quantities down his throat. For a while Beaverbrook grew a beard to hide his scars. He recovered at Cherkley, nursed by Gladys. Visitors found him restless but exhausted, swathed in bandages. 'It had not been my intention to die,' he remarked afterwards.[1]

Despite his bad health Beaverbrook was able to launch the *Sunday Express* and plan the expansion of the *Daily Express*. Nor was he too ill to visit Paris during the Peace Conference, where, with the help of his new friend and spy Venetia Montagu, he contrived to be particularly well-informed about the negotiations.

Beaverbrook's relationship with her was a mixture of flirtation and intrigue. There is some suggestion that he and Venetia did more than flirt. In January 1919 Diana Manners went to Paris with her mother, the Duchess of Rutland. They arrived on the eve of the opening of the Peace Conference, when the city was full of statesmen, diplomats, civil servants and journalists. Edwin Montagu was there with his wife and so – without his wife – was Lord Beaverbrook. On 14 January 1919 Diana wrote to Duff: 'Crooks and Venetia turned up just as we were turning out. It's a disgusting case – her face lights up when that animated little deformity so much as turns to her. They are living in open sin at the Ritz in a tall silk suite with a common bath, and unlocked doors between while poor Ted is sardined into the Majestic, unknown and uncared for.' (Edwin Montagu was obliged to stay with the British delegation at the Hotel Majestic.) After this unflattering account of her two friends, Diana went on: 'I dined with Crooks and the Montagus at the Ritz Grill. The shocking, shocking Crooks said to me, "Don't you think she's very attentive to Edwin

170

nowadays?" Sure enough she was – ridiculously so – a bad bad sign. . . . I've just left Crooks and V in their luxurious nest, and expedited Ted. . . .'[2]

Diana did not doubt that Venetia was Beaverbrook's mistress; from the surviving letters it is not possible to say so with certainty. However, during 1919 Venetia was writing to Beaverbrook frequently, feeding him what titbits she could about what was going on at the Peace Conference after he left, and helping him with his account of the fall of Asquith in 1916. Thus in April 1919 she wrote a long letter in pencil from the Ritz in Paris, describing a dinner attended by Lloyd George and Balfour. She told Beaverbrook in some detail that the dinner conversation was distinctly hostile to President Woodrow Wilson and 'what they choose to call his Sermon on the Mount manner (which apparently is intensely irritating not only to all the English but also to Clemenceau [the French Premier])'. She then reported on a party at the Hotel Majestic for the British delegation and staff, caustically entitled by Venetia 'the typists' ball'. 'The PM is obviously the idol of all of them . . . I think he adores the role.' On the whole, however '. . . scoops are remarkable by their absence. I've not seen the hind leg of one.' She told Beaverbrook her husband was being treated somewhat cavalierly by Lloyd George – 'Edwin . . . no longer the Pearl of the Harem' – and described ominous confusions and misunderstandings between the Americans, French and Italians over indemnities. At the same time she worried that her letter would not satisfy Beaverbrook's curiosity. 'I can't think why I write you these endlessly long, dull letters, when I have no illusion as to them being read or welcome.' Or again: 'No other news for you. I fear I shall get the sack as a scavenger unless I do better.'

Later in the year Venetia was in touch with Beaverbrook from Norfolk. Beaverbrook knew that her contribution to his account of the fall of Asquith could be invaluable. He was doing his best to acquire original documents; by January 1917 he had managed to get hold of the whole crucial correspondence between Law and Asquith and the letters between Asquith and Lloyd George.

Venetia was a hidden resource. During 1919 he sent her drafts, and consulted her about possible publication. She wrote to him: 'I thought your account of the fall of the first Asquith Ministry quite brilliant . . .' but went on, 'I think on the whole I would not publish it in serial form in the *Express*.' The people involved would, she thought, be 'displeased', and while those close to the centre of events would find it 'enthralling, enlightening and full of real insight', she felt the ordinary reader would not find it simple or dramatic enough. She was flattered that he wanted her opinion; ' . . . thank you a million times for letting me see your work. I enjoyed every word of it'. Her reaction must have pleased him, for he also sent her a more general account of the former Prime Minister, and when she wrote thanking him for the 'character sketch of Mr Asquith', she congratulated him again on his perceptiveness. 'Yours . . . has much more of him in it than any . . . .' The letter surveys her relationship with Beaverbrook: 'Our lunch remains with me as one of the most delightful I can remember. Out of my friendship with you there are three or four outstanding talks . . . one or two at Cherkley during those walks after tea, one in Paris on a cold wet windy afternoon when we walked to Notre Dame, one lunch at the Hyde Park Hotel, another walk up the Champs Elysées, but this last ranks high with the best.'

Was Venetia, at this time, showing Beaverbrook material from Asquith's love letters to her? It seems highly likely that she did. In October 1919 she was writing again to Beaverbrook from Norfolk, expressing disappointment at 'not getting any more proofs' and going on, temptingly: 'I've one or two amusing accounts of Winston's Antwerp activities, and I think I should come across some Gallipoli documents . . .', and just before Christmas, in a letter sending him a humorous poem by someone 'who has an even lower opinion of women than you have', she wrote: 'If you care to I would like you to keep the Winston telegram and I would also send you the Cabinet papers for your archives.'

The strange story of the Winston telegram illustrates the peculiar network of relationships between Asquith, the Montagus and Beaverbrook. At the beginning of October 1914, with the German Army poised to take Belgium, Winston Churchill, then First Lord of the Admiralty, made a dramatic dash to Antwerp in order, as Asquith wrote to Venetia, to 'beard the King and his Ministers, and try to infuse into their backbones the necessary quantity of starch. . . . I cannot but think that he will stiffen them up to the sticking point. Don't say anything of Winston's mission, at any rate at present; it is one of the many unconventional incidents of the war.' On 5 October he wrote telling her that Winston was having some success in 'bucking up the Belges' and then continued: 'I found when I arrived here this morning the enclosed telegram from Winston, who, as you will see, proposes to resign his office, in order to take command in the field of this great military force. . . . I regret to say it was received with a Homeric laugh. . . . I send you the original, which I know you won't show to anybody, to add to your collection of *mémoires pour servir*, with K's marginal pencil annotation.'[3] K was Kitchener.

Beaverbrook acquired this telegram from Venetia, and kept it quiet. In 1927, when Beaverbrook sent Churchill proofs of his book, Churchill was greatly surprised to read in it the text of the telegram he had sent from Antwerp thirteen years earlier. He had no copy of it himself. He wrote to ask Beaverbrook how he had acquired the document. Beaverbrook replied: 'I have the original message annotated in Kitchener's own writing. It would bother me greatly to explain how the telegram reached me under the Official Secrets Act. But I fear it would bother other people more. And this is a world of bother.'[4] Churchill did not pursue the matter, but he may well have guessed the source, as Asquith's letters to Venetia were by this time no secret in his circle and Venetia herself was close to the

Churchills all her life. But it was no wonder that Beaverbrook acquired a growing reputation for intrigue and omniscience.

The matter of money – Beaverbrook's ample supply of it and his friends' frequent need for it – recurs in his dealings with Venetia and Edwin Montagu. The Montagus, unlike the Coopers, were considered rich; nevertheless, both of them called on Beaverbrook for financial help, Venetia indirectly and her husband, somewhat surprisingly, directly. In 1919, when he was Secretary of State for India, he wrote to Beaverbrook (on India Office writing paper): 'I am most frightfully busy and Barclays are worrying me. . . .' Could 'My Dear Max . . . guarantee me for say £7,000 for six months . . . . I shall love you no less if you say no and no more if you say yes, for that is impossible.' All went well; on 6 May he wrote again: 'Max my dear . . . I am so grateful. . . .' The six months was extended over a number of years. Meanwhile in 1920 Venetia was writing to Beaverbrook for advice: 'A little time ago you told me that it was unwise of me to speculate in my own name and at the same time you said that if I sent you the money I was speculating with you would do it for me. Was this a joke or would you do it for me?' He did: he bought Associated Provincial Picture shares for her on 26 February. Over the years he did the same kind of thing again for her and for many of his other friends, men as well as women. Partly this was indeed generosity – the deployment of a skill which he possessed and they did not; but it was also calculated to establish gratitude, and to strengthen the structure of obligations he had begun to build up from his earliest days in England.

In 1919 and 1920 Beaverbrook invested some £700,000 in two companies controlling cinemas, Provincial Cinematograph Theatres and Associated Provincial Picture Houses; later he bought a large holding in the French company Pathé. It did not take him long to realize that the film industry was chaotic; in 1921 he tried to reorganize it, without success. At one acrimonious meeting the inventor William Friese Greene collapsed and died while speaking in Beaverbrook's support.[5] Thereafter Beaverbrook avoided film industry infighting, although he kept a close eye on his investment and enjoyed the fringe benefits appropriate to a film tycoon; he held private film shows, met aspiring stars, and from time to time arranged screen tests for young women of his acquaintance.

With his wife and children living at Cherkley, after the war Beaverbrook more than ever led his own life in London, except for weekends. He continued to make use of the Hyde Park Hotel, and frequently entertained there or at the Savoy, which was more convenient for Fleet Street; he kept a flat in the Temple. In 1920 he bought another house, The Vineyard in Fulham, a remote and unfashionable suburb conveniently placed on the way down to Surrey. The Vineyard was an agreeable but modest house for a rich man: a medium-sized, three-storey, seventeenth-century farmhouse with two acres of garden and fine trees. Beaverbrook improved and extended it and added a tennis court – tennis was immensely popular among his circle in the early 1920s and he liked to include a game in the working day whenever possible. He installed the latest American shower on the ground floor and put in a projection room so that he could show films after dinner. Gladys and the children rarely went to The Vineyard, but it was used a great deal by Beaverbrook during the 1920s for political consultations, tennis parties, lunches, dinners and assignations. He never spent more than a night or two there at a time, but kept it permanently staffed and set up a private office in a house at the bottom of the garden. It was not until 1924, when Gladys insisted that she wanted a base in town for herself and the growing children, that he bought a lease on a much more imposing and formal town establishment, Stornoway House, off St James's and overlooking Green Park. It had fourteen bedrooms, six reception rooms and a ballroom, and it was, the estate agent's advertisement said, 'almost within the precincts of the Palace'.

'ENGINEERING FOR A COUP'

Whenever the political scene was tranquil, as it was after Lloyd George's overwhelming victory in the election of 1918, Beaverbrook would turn for action and amusement to his newspapers and to his own writing. His reliving and rewriting of recent events, the acquisition of documents, public and private, and the consultations with others were a substitute for and perhaps a stimulus to political intrigue and action. He was always to maintain that he never stopped pursuing his one true goal of Tariff Reform, even hoping that Lloyd George might see the light; but in the immediate aftermath of the war, with the Peace Conference in trouble over reparations, and the people longing for the rewards of their wartime sacrifices, the Prime Minister had other preoccupations.

Now that Beaverbrook was for the first time openly in control of the *Daily Express* he soon found himself in serious disagreement with Churchill over support for the White Russian generals in the civil war that followed the Revolution of 1917. During 1919 Churchill, then Secretary of State for War, wanted to fight on in Russia, believing that the Bolsheviks would menace all Europe if not stopped; Beaverbrook took the view that the Revolution could not be reversed and that the British people were sick of war. He and Churchill quarrelled fiercely; Churchill was reported to be saying that the press must be either 'squared or squashed'.[6] Eventually they were reconciled at dinner with the Coopers in November. 'They were both obviously nervous,' Duff Cooper recorded, 'Max more so than Winston . . . [who] was at his very best, witty, courteous, eloquent. Max was less at his ease. He is never at his best elsewhere than in his own house. . . . I several times feared disaster but it was always avoided. . . .'[7]

During 1920 and early 1921 the warm glow of victory that had surrounded Lloyd George gradually faded, as his government failed to deliver its promises. His reputation began to sag amid rumours of corruption and the sale of honours. Scenting blood his Tory partners became increasingly restive. Seeking a way out, Lloyd George thought of creating a centre party by a merger between coalition Liberals and Tories, but failed to convince either; he visited Cherkley to consult Beaverbrook, who began to sense that Lloyd George, in his desperation to hold on to power, was in danger of losing his grip.

Romantic as well as political intrigue flourished at Cherkley in the spring of 1920. A regular guest of Beaverbrook's, General Sir Frederick Sykes, formerly Chief of Air Staff and now Controller of Civil Aviation, was paying court to Isabel Law. Beaverbrook, who noticed such things, informed Bonar Law, who did not; when Isabel confirmed the news of her engagement, her father rang Beaverbrook and said mournfully: 'Max, a dreadful thing has happened. . . .'[8] But he was soon reconciled to the inevitable, and the marriage took place in June.

In March 1921 Bonar Law resigned, on grounds of illness; he was replaced by Austen Chamberlain. His health was indeed poor, but his withdrawal also indicated a growing distaste for Lloyd George's style of government. As always, however, Bonar Law was too decent, or too indecisive, to make trouble. He went abroad to recover, declaring his continuing loyalty.

His withdrawal, by putting the future of the coalition in doubt, changed the political landscape and gave Beaverbrook, among others, renewed opportunities to seek change. Bonar Law knew that Beaverbrook was likely to cause trouble, as a letter he wrote to Lloyd George from Dover on his way across the Channel indicates; Beaverbrook did not know about the letter at the time.

> I think it would be worth your while, if you can do it, to send for Max just to have a talk with him for I think that he could now be easily influenced by you to support you.
> He must be doing something but I really believe he has more sympathy with you than with anyone else and the feeling he has had that I prevented him from having a free hand (of which I admit there was no sign in his action) perhaps made him more difficult than if I had been out of it altogether. He is certain to take a strong line one way or the other.

During 1921, Beaverbrook wrote a series of articles for the *Sunday Express* that were also published as a short book, *Success*. He set out to explain to the readers how to make a fortune, and what to do next; but his advice was disappointingly imprecise. He could hardly explain the complex and ingenious manipulations by which he had himself become rich fifteen years earlier. He fell back on virtuous exhortations: 'The Temple of Success is based on the three pillars of Health, Industry and Judgment . . . nothing but work and brains counts . . . I would urge on ambitious youth the absolute necessity of moderation in alcohol.' (No doubt by coincidence at the beginning of 1921 he had bet F. E. Smith, Earl of Birkenhead since becoming Lord Chancellor in January 1919, £1000 that he could not give up spirits for a whole year.) *Success* was an apologia for himself. The ideal career, he proclaimed, was to make money when young and then move on, preferably into politics. 'Success is not a process which can reproduce itself indefinitely in the same field. The dominant mind loses its elasticity. . . .' He deplored consistency. 'The man who is consistent must be out of touch with reality.' Politicians especially should avoid the consistency trap. 'They practise an art which, above all others, depends for success on opportunism.'

Beaverbrook could not turn Bonar Law into an opportunist, but he did his best to create opportunities for him none the less. During the spring and early summer, he tried hard to lure Bonar Law back into play. He wrote to him offering The Vineyard as a base and retailing the latest political gossip; but Bonar Law declined to be drawn. When he did return briefly in June, he saw Beaverbrook and Lloyd George but remained evasive about his plans; Frances Stevenson feared that Beaverbrook was up to no good. 'Beaverbrook is clearly engineering for a coup. Bonar Law came home for the weekend not for any ostensible reason, but I think it looks a little suspicious – he is so entirely in Beaverbrook's hands.' She also noted a revealing exchange reported by Birkenhead to Lloyd George; when told that he could not succeed in his efforts to displace the Prime Minister, 'No,' Beaverbrook had replied, 'but I can try.'

Beaverbrook summed up the position with relish: 'The raw ingredients of a real crisis were within reach. But how to make use of these materials had not yet been worked out.'

IRELAND AND TIM HEALY

During 1921 Beaverbrook was drawn back into Irish affairs, where he found himself seriously at odds with Bonar Law and openly active in support of Lloyd George. His interest was more personal than political. It is unlikely that he would have played much part without his continuing close friendship with Tim Healy, who for ten years had helped him in Parliament, advised him on legal matters, while always refusing offers of money, dined with him in London and visited him at Cherkley; he was a real family friend, devoted to Gladys and a favourite with the children because of his fund of jokes and songs. Janet always remembered his neatly trimmed silver beard, and the way he smelled of violets; he made up a tale of a talking football called a Leatherhead to amuse Peter, and brought Gladys presents of her beloved Waterford glass.

Healy left Parliament in 1918 after the election in which the moderate Irish Nationalist Party was displaced by Sinn Fein. He was regarded in England as a man of goodwill who wanted to see Ireland free yet was utterly opposed to violence; to some in Ireland he was compromised by his thirty-eight years at Westminster but he was in touch with the younger, fiercer generation of Irish leaders, including Michael Collins and Eamon de Valera. As the situation in Ireland deteriorated after the First World War, with ugly violence on both sides, Healy sought Beaverbrook's good offices not just as a link with government circles but over the *Daily Express*, which was by tradition an anti-Home Rule paper. At first, Beaverbrook tried not to get involved; at the end of 1919 Healy wrote to him in protest: 'When I spoke about my country to you you truly say it does not interest you. Why then interest yourself against us? Can't you leave us alone? . . . Now I read with regret the stuff in the *Express* about Ireland. It is all warped and untrue. . . .'

During 1920 Lloyd George tried to solve the Irish problem by force. Any suggestion of negotiating with Sinn Fein was greeted with horror, and dubbed 'shaking hands with murderers'. Anti-Irish feelings in government circles were profound; Bonar Law told Tom Jones, Lloyd George's secretary and right-hand man, that he considered the Irish an inferior race.[9] Tim Healy, meanwhile, bombarded Beaverbrook with impassioned accounts of the disastrous effects that the policy of repression was having in Ireland. In November he wrote in answer to an invitation: 'I will run over and see you next weekend but am too sad to go to your dinner or talk. Every morning nothing but murders, every night nothing but lies and folly. . . .' The local police were being replaced by 'a nest of Black and Tans . . . installed in their place, to rob the locality, loot the pubs, insult the women and assault the men. . . . The Germans in Belgium were under discipline. These creatures are mere thieves and cut-throats, commissioned to rob and slay in the King's name. . . . Put us down, you never will, except in coffins.'

In early 1921 the Irish crisis deepened. 'Why is every step taken in Ireland by government a false step? Can they do nothing right?' wrote Healy on 27 April. 'I am steadily advancing in the direction of your views on the government's administration in Ireland,' Beaverbrook wrote back on 2 May. During May and June Healy stepped up the pressure, sending Beaverbrook information, suggestions and copies of the Sinn Fein *Irish Bulletin* with its relentless listings of violent incidents and outrages perpetrated by the British. Opinion in England began to swing towards negotiations; all but the most fanatical Unionists had become sickened by the violence, and when both the Archbishop of Canterbury and the King appealed for peace, the politicians knew they had to act. In July, a truce was declared and the series of meetings began that were to lead, after four months of arduous and confused negotiation, to a treaty.

Although Healy was not directly involved in the negotiations he played a useful advisory role and was frequently in London during that crucial summer and autumn, usually staying at The Vineyard. Beaverbrook was thus in a position that suited him – close to a good source, and able to keep up with and even influence events behind the scenes. By this time

Lloyd George was deploying all his wiles to achieve a solution; his greatest problem lay with his Conservative colleagues. Bonar Law, from his self-imposed exile in France, remained in play, a potential rallying-point for Unionists. He was adamantly opposed to any 'coercion' of Ulster, which remained determined to stay British. Beaverbrook never claimed to have made any headway with Bonar Law on Ireland although at the time it was generally believed that he might be able' to do so. Lloyd George decided to call a peace conference with the Sinn Fein leaders in London in September; he cannily persuaded both Churchill and Birkenhead, hard-liners on Ireland, to take part.

The conference opened in London in October. When, within three weeks, it threatened to break up over the British claim to control Irish coastal defence, Beaverbrook, through Healy, helped the Irish formulate a reply to a Lloyd George ultimatum. As Beaverbrook wrote not long afterwards: 'These delegates undoubtedly wanted and needed such advice. They were threatened all the time by the extreme Republicans in their rear, and they had no ideas whatever about British public opinion, or how to address themselves to it. . . . I therefore agreed to help, and naturally saw the correspondence.'[10] Healy saved the day by diverting the argument to the precise area of Irish coastline under discussion. When Beaverbrook drove down that evening to spend the weekend with Goulding at Wargrave, along with Bonar Law, who had recently returned from France, Churchill and Birkenhead, they were all astonished to discover that he knew exactly what had been going on. The rest of the evening was spent in heated discussion over Ireland, with Bonar Law and Churchill hostile to the negotiations, and Birkenhead beginning to shift towards compromise; only Beaverbrook and Goulding (whose origins lay in Ireland) were in favour: 'We believed that there would never be harmony within the Empire while trouble in Ireland was unsolved.' Beaverbrook drew a memorable picture of Churchill infuriated by what he saw as the inconsistency between Beaverbrook's belief in a strong united Empire and his readiness to let Ireland go; even after Goulding drove them to bed, saying 'in his Irish intonation to roost, to roost', Churchill followed Beaverbrook into his bedroom to continue the argument. 'As our voices were raised in controversy, our host appeared in his long nightshirt, carrying a lighted candle, and ordered us with some show of asperity to give over forthwith. "Silence!" he cried. "Silence!" '

Beaverbrook was soon, by his own account, drawn more closely into the inner circle trying to achieve a settlement. There is evidence confirming this in the two diarists closest to Lloyd George – Frances Stevenson again, and Tom Jones. Jones records how, a few days after the Wargrave weekend, Lloyd George

. . . had attacked Winston for a leakage in the *Daily Express* of yesterday, or rather he had attacked Beaverbrook, knowing that Winston and FE and

Winter days in Newcastle, New Brunswick: Max Aitken (second from left); Dr R.B. Yorston, Aitken's headmaster (second from right)

Max (right) and his brother Arthur

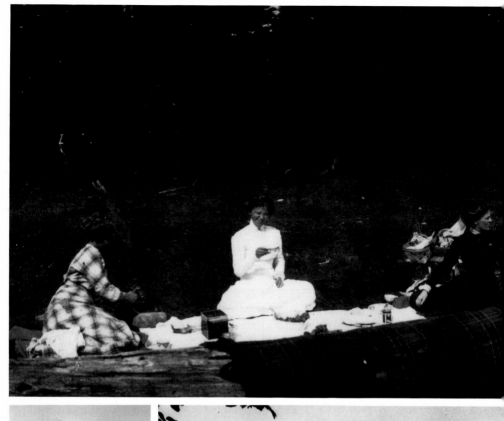

Above: Family picnic: in the centre, the Reverend William Aitken, Max's father

Opposite page, left and right: St James Presbyterian Church, Newcastle and the Aitken family at The Manse, Newcastle

This page, left and right: Jane Aitken, Max's mother and Max (centre back) at Harkins Academy

Sir Max Aitken, MP, in Ashton-under-Lyne, October 1912. Rudyard Kipling (standing left); Lady Aitken (second from right); Mrs J. Neild (far right)

Sir Max Aitken's wife Gladys (née Drury)

Opposite page:
Above: (from left to right) J.C. Buckley, Conservative agent for Ashton-under-Lyne; R.B. Bennett, later Prime Minister of Canada; Aitken; Izaak Walton Killam, future millionaire

Below: Aix-les-Bains, 1923: Bonar Law (right) with his 'intimate friend' and his son Richard (left)

France, March 1916: Aitken (left) with Sir Sam
Hughes
Lord Beaverbrook, Minister of Information, 1918

Opposite page:
Above: Canadian teachers visit England, 1926:
Gladys Beaverbrook (seated centre) with Lloyd
George on her right and Beaverbrook behind him

Below: Hyde Park, 1919: Beaverbrook recuperating
with nurse

French Riviera, 1920

Above: Deauville, 1922: Beaverbrook with his
wife (left) and her sister, Helen Drury

Right: Seville, 1924: Arnold Bennett with
Gladys Beaverbrook (left) and Janet Aitken

Left: Beaverbrook with his sons: Max (at the back) and Peter

Below: Daily Express canteen, General Strike 1926: Lady Beaverbrook pouring tea

Foot: Madrid, 1924: Bearded Tim Healey between the Beaverbrooks; Arnold Bennett is behind Healey's right shoulder

Left: Harriet Cohen

Below: Rebecca West

Above: Barbara Cartland

Right: José Collins

Doris Castlerosse

Daphne Fielding
(with Major
Bradford Atkinson)

ove: Moscow, 1929: Beaverbrook and Arnold
nnett with Lady Louis Mountbatten (left) and
Hon. Mrs Richard Norton
ove left: The Dolly Sisters
t: Tallulah Bankhead (left) and Toto
pman at the première of *The Private Life of*
Juan, 1934

Beaverbrook and Lady Diana Cooper,
Nice, 1935
Lady Diana Cooper

Beaverbrook and
Jean Norton at
Biarritz, 1934

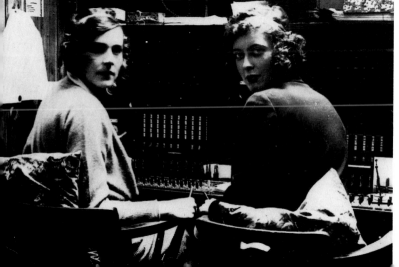

Jean Norton (right)
and Edwina
Mountbatten on the
Daily Express
switchboard during
the General Strike

Empire Crusade, Norwich, 1931

Bonar Law had spent last weekend in a country house with Beaverbrook. Winston and FE denied the impeachment saying that they had been scrupulously careful to give away nothing and that during their official life Max never asked them for information but that what struck them was the amount of information he already possessed. Beaverbrook told Winston that one of his men was in very close touch with Collins.[11]

Beaverbrook was important to Lloyd George at this juncture for three reasons: the Prime Minister wanted the support of the *Express*; he hoped to influence Bonar Law; and he needed Beaverbrook's cooperation in his scheme to use Birkenhead and Churchill to bring the Conservatives into line. In Beaverbrook's account, it was within a week of the Wargrave weekend that he was told by Birkenhead that Lloyd George wanted to talk to him. 'He knew my views on Ireland and the treaty proposals, which were much in evidence in the leader columns of the *Daily Express*, but he wanted to have a clearer understanding of my future conduct in view of Bonar Law's hostility to the Irish negotiations.' They met over dinner at Birkenhead's house; Churchill was also present.

Lloyd George asked me whether the opinions of the *Daily Express* on the Irish issue were also my own. I replied in the affirmative. He then asked whether I was prepared to fight for them and I said I was. But supposing a settlement with Ireland involved a defeat in the House of Commons and a dissolution, meaning thereby a Conservative revolt, was I still prepared to stand by the policy of settlement? Again I replied that I should stick to my opinion.

Over the next few weeks, while the official delegations struggled to reach agreement, Beaverbrook once again was the go-between and stage manager for Bonar Law and Lloyd George, although Tom Jones's detailed account of these weeks hardly confirms the claim made by Beaverbrook that the Prime Minister would not talk to Bonar Law unless he was present. Over lunches and dinners at The Vineyard Lloyd George, Churchill, Birkenhead and Beaverbrook met repeatedly to plan the next step in the campaign; meanwhile the two *Express* newspapers moved into high gear, combining scoops on the latest twists in the story with fervent support for Lloyd George. To Frances Stevenson, Beaverbrook's loyalty in the face of Bonar Law's opposition was astonishing; Lloyd George was seriously threatening to resign if his policy was rejected, and there would then have been a clear opportunity for Bonar Law. She wrote on 6 November: 'Bonar is influenced by Carson and also by the hope that this may be his chance of becoming Prime Minister. The extraordinary thing is that Beaverbrook is all out for D [Lloyd George], supporting him most vigorously in his papers. D says he will only be for him for a short run, but over a thing like this it is worth

179

while taking all the support you can get. Beaverbrook is trying to influence Bonar Law. . . .' Three days later: 'D is frightfully hurt about Bonar Law and the attitude he is taking. This is all the more extraordinary as Beaverbrook is fighting for D and a settlement for all he is worth. . . . D is seeing F.E. and Winston and Beaverbrook almost every night, so as to keep them on his side.'

As for the newspapers, Beaverbrook used Tim Healy as his adviser, for his aim was not merely to support Lloyd George but to put across to the British people the moderate Irish case. 'When the Conference, or rather the successive Conferences, began to meet, I intensified the propaganda in favour of agreement. I felt it was vital that Ministers should not feel that they had no backing in the country, and that their signatures on a settlement might spell their ruin.'[12] Meanwhile on 15 November a letter went off to Tim Healy from an aide at the *Express*:

> On request of Lord Beaverbrook I enclose herewith all the articles on Ireland which have appeared in the *Sunday* and *Daily Express* since you came to The Vineyard on October 22. They have been written by Mr Maurice Woods and Major Hore-Belisha, who are the political correspondents of the *Express*, on the instruction of Lord Beaverbrook, who would like you to read them. If you have any views on their general policy Lord Beaverbrook would be glad to hear from you.

Two days later Healy wrote back to Beaverbrook directly: 'I am indeed grateful for all you are doing for Ireland. You have more than kept your word to me. The articles are splendid and much cleverer than anything I could have suggested because they have an English appeal. They are copied extensively here and carry the greatest weight.'

During the first week of December the negotiations moved into the final tense stage. On 1 December Healy sent another emotional letter of thanks to Beaverbrook, with a special message for Gladys – the only reference in the surviving papers to her political opinions. 'Tell Gladys I asked about her, and wished her well. Say also to her (who stood by me against Bonar for Ireland) that you helped the good old cause in dire straits.'

In the early hours of the morning of 7 December, the treaty was signed. Although the troubles of Ireland were hardly over, peace was established; the Free State, forerunner of the Republic of Ireland, set up; and the separate existence and rights of Ulster guaranteed. It was a formidable achievement against immense odds by Lloyd George and his supporters, and Beaverbrook certainly played his part, if only on the sidelines. Later that day, he and Healy were in touch over an *Express* reporter who was hoping to obtain an exclusive series of interviews with Michael Collins. Cables went backwards and forwards: 'Will you please see Collins', Beaverbrook wired Healy, 'and assure him that I will do anything in my power to make series successful and will spend thousands of pounds in advertising. . . .' While Beaverbrook pursued a scoop, Birkenhead celebrated his key role in the treaty negotiation by abandoning his bet with Beaverbrook and taking up spirits again.[13]

As the year drew to an end, Healy was writing to Beaverbrook of his conviction that despite the bitter arguments in Ireland over the treaty, which were to end in civil war, the Irish Parliament would ratify it. He ended his letter: 'Whatever happens, I am, gratefully for Ireland, your obliged friend. . . .' A year later, when the Irish Free State was formally constituted, Tim Healy became its first Governor General – despite objections raised by Bonar Law, who, according to Jones, said that 'he was impulsive and he drank too much whisky at night. I said there were precedents for the latter defect and that now he was old and less impulsive and his appointment would have a great effect on moderate opinion in Ireland.'[14] Beaverbrook was naturally delighted at Healy's elevation, and gave the new Governor General a banquet at the Hyde Park Hotel.

But if his contribution to the Irish treaty brought Beaverbrook closer to Tim Healy, it ended his friendship with Kipling, who regarded it, and Lloyd George, with contempt. Beaverbrook tried to moderate Kipling's violent antagonism, but failed. The last of the many Kipling signatures in the Cherkley visitors' book appears in December 1920. He and Beaverbrook hardly met again, although their wives remained friendly. Over the ten years they had known each other, Beaverbrook had learnt the political ropes too well for Kipling's liking.

THE UNDERSTANDING WIFE

Tim Healy's regular references to Gladys are almost the only traces that survive of her presence, let alone of her opinions, during this hectic period of Beaverbrook's life; otherwise she is almost invisible. Evidently she had little choice but to play the invidious part of the understanding wife, which she seems to have played exceptionally well. Beaverbrook made certain that very little survived in the archives by or about Gladys. Among the fragments were a handful of notes apparently left for him to read when he came in late after she had gone to bed. They were always loving and sometimes apologetic; one clearly referred to an argument about money.

> My Lord dear Lord
> I enclose the P. S. S. saying what you desire. I greatly regret that such a mistake entered my head, perhaps I wasn't thinking clearly (or too clearly) what say you.
> Till three when we meet.
> Your sleepy
> Wifie

The enclosure read: 'I Gladys Beaverbrook agree to pay super tax on my private income which is to come in on June 1st' and was signed 'Gladys Beaverbrook' with 'Gladys Drury' and 'Gladys Aitken' as witnesses.

An affectionate, if offhand, note (undated) from him had a characteristic impersonal jauntiness:

> Sweet and beautiful
> Dear and only
> I am off & wishing so much that you were with me.
> My love to you for ever and a day,
> M.[15]

Those who recall Gladys at this time are full of praise for her, but she remains a shadowy, idealized figure. Did she have any life of her own? Her niece by marriage, Jean Aitken, came to England in the early 1920s and remembered that Aunt Gladys had, if not an admirer, at least a 'regular escort', a handsome man who would appear in evening dress to take her to the opera; a rumour flickers in the family that at one stage Beaverbrook's brother Allan, also a tall and handsome man, was a little in love with Gladys.[16] Certainly she presented the bravest possible face. The young actress Gwen Ffrangçon-Davies, who was taken up for a while by Beaverbrook after she had her first big stage success in *The Immortal Hour* in 1922, recalled a visit to Cherkley where she met Lloyd George, and also Gladys Beaverbrook. 'She was so charming . . . at the end of the evening I was sitting by the fire, looking into it and he was sitting there too, she came up and put her arms around his shoulders from behind and just said, "Oh Max, hasn't it been a lovely evening?" It was very touching. Of course he was consistently unfaithful to her but she must have been a very wise lady. He was devoted to her. She knew I was no threat.' Beaverbrook's interest in Gwen Ffrangçon-Davies waned, but not before he had arranged for her to be unusually prominently reviewed in the *Evening Standard* and given her a piano.[17]

Another young woman in a good position to observe the relationship between Max and Gladys Beaverbrook was Margaret Guthrie (later Mrs Ince), a secretary at the *Express*, who was asked by Beaverbrook to work for his wife in the early 1920s. She felt that she was expected to spy on Gladys, but found she wanted to protect her. Beaverbrook, she remembers, sought to control his wife's expenditure by giving her a fixed allowance, negotiated by a lawyer, even though she was not extravagant; for such a rich man this seemed surprisingly mean. Gladys was made nervous by her husband's scrutiny, and Margaret Guthrie did her best to get bills paid without calling undue attention to them. She recalls Gladys as a warm, titian-haired woman in a cloud of delicious scent, friendly to everyone, a devoted mother who despite immense provocation always behaved with dignity and restraint. 'She knew it all, but she never put a foot wrong.'[18] Her daughter Janet wrote: 'Her gentleness and understanding were irresistible and would remain so as long as she lived. . . . I never saw her angry or bitter, even though . . . she was driven to the brink of despair. . . .'[19]

People who loved Gladys were angry on her behalf, and among descendants of the Drury family in Canada to this day a sense of resentment lingers. Matters were further complicated by the presence in England from 1920 of Gladys's younger sister Helen, also a beauty but a very different type – smaller, more elegant, dark-haired, with a face like a pekinese and a distinctive husky voice. Unlike Gladys, Helen had a touch of the *femme fatale*. She quickly became a social success.[20] There were, and are, many rumours about Beaverbrook's relationship with her and a great many appointments with her, alone as well as with others, in his 1920s engagement books. In 1923 she married a much older man, Evelyn Fitzgerald, from a distinguished Catholic family, but carried on breaking hearts. She became what Gladys never was nor seemed to want to be, a prominent society beauty. In the early 1920s she was much in evidence at Cherkley, among the politicians who were regular guests; a photograph of 1921 shows her standing between Churchill and Lloyd George, with Beaverbrook looking admiringly in her direction.

'THESE MEN MEAN WAR'

At the end of 1921 and into the spring of 1922 Lloyd George contemplated calling a general election to strengthen his hand before his Irish success turned sour. In late December 1921 Birkenhead arranged a dinner party for the Prime Minister to sound out Chamberlain, Churchill and other influential figures; but the Conservative response was lukewarm. Beaverbrook was present, as was the brewer and prominent Liverpool Conservative Sir Archibald Salvidge, who recorded his advice in his diary. 'I said that "Bring Bonar Back" was the best watchword I could give them. . . . Beaverbrook followed me out as I was leaving and, gripping my arm, announced: "You've said it. 'Bring Bonar Back'. They can't see it, but that was the best thing of the evening." ' So moved was Beaverbrook by Salvidge's slogan that when Salvidge seized the opportunity to register a complaint about a *Daily Express* campaign against the high cost of beer, he instantly replied: 'Say no more. What's the campaign? The price of beer? I'll stop it.' When Salvidge offered to send him evidence that beer was remarkably cheap, Beaverbrook went on: 'I never hit my friends. . . . Say no more. I won't listen. Goodnight.' Thereafter, Salvidge recalled, not another line appeared in the *Express* about the exorbitant cost of beer.[21]

Within days of this dinner, Beaverbrook joined an unusual Christmas party of politicians – Birkenhead was again the organizer – in St Moritz.

The plan was to move in the New Year to the south of France, where Lloyd George was to attend a meeting of European leaders in Cannes, and where Bonar Law was also, by coincidence, enjoying the winter sunshine. Telegrams flew between Beaverbrook, Birkenhead and Churchill as they tried to bring their principals together. Churchill cabled eagerly from London: ' . . . Wire conditions with you weather and painting possibilities PM goes Cannes Tuesday expecting you and Fred [Birkenhead] early there what are your plans for moving south wire reply urgent.' Beaverbrook, who always disliked being at the mercy of other people's arrangements, had already had enough; he wired back, 'No sun, no snow, no ice, no train until Monday when I leave for the Riviera'.

In Cannes, where Lloyd George took up residence at the Villa Valetta, Beaverbrook took part in further tactical arguments. 'The decision in favour of election was my goal,' wrote Beaverbrook many years later. 'Then I could say – support from the *Daily Express* and enthusiasm on my part with the possibility of interesting Bonar Law too. But only if the Empire banner was put in the forefront of the battle line. Lloyd George was giving me reason to hope.' The presence at the villa of a talking parrot produced one of Beaverbrook's favourite political anecdotes: after one impassioned speech in favour of an election the parrot intervened. ' "You bloody fool! You bloody fool!" cried the parrot. The company was shaken. The Ministers departed. I went off with Churchill. We drove into the night, and along the way we laughed over the parrot.' Beaverbrook always amused Churchill. Once again the go-between, Beaverbrook brought Lloyd George and Bonar Law together in his rooms at the Carlton Hotel: but Bonar Law would not be tempted, even when offered the post of Foreign Secretary.

Back in England, Beaverbrook wrote to a leading Canadian MP in February: 'Life is very exciting in politics here. Ll G may resign at any moment . . . it is clear that he suffers too from the fault of indecision. It is always an early sign of declining powers. Bonar Law is very strong. He has immense power and no responsibility. I think he is the only possibility if Chamberlain sticks to Lloyd George.'[22] But in March Beaverbrook was in close touch with Lloyd George, hoping that he would come out in favour of 'the Empire Programme', and advising him on tactics: ' . . . the main object of attack should be the opposing newspapers. The Press is always unpopular with members of the Commons and you would rally a lot of sympathy. If you want some stuff on this line I will give it to you.' But Lloyd George, preoccupied with his role at the forthcoming Genoa conference on European security and hoping that a triumph abroad might restore his position at home, let the moment for the election pass.

By the summer, the coalition was floundering. Civil war was raging in Ireland and the Genoa conference had collapsed. Scandals were brewing over the sale of honours. Nevertheless, by his own account Beaverbrook remained on excellent terms with Lloyd George, although it is unlikely that either really trusted the other. In late June, during dinner at The Vineyard, they discussed the future of *The Times*; Northcliffe was ill, known to be out of his mind and approaching death, and Lloyd George suspected that Beaverbrook might have plans to acquire the paper. According to Frances Stevenson: 'D would like to get *The Times* and if it is to be sold will try and get it bought by a friendly syndicate. He is very afraid that Beaverbrook may try and get control as B is trying very hard to get at Northcliffe and pretends not to believe that the latter is mad.' At weekends, Lloyd George would often visit the Beaverbrooks at Cherkley. Janet Aitken, then fourteen, remembered his flowing silver hair and mellifluous voice; she nicknamed him 'The Loved One'.[23] 'In mixed company he dominated the table talk,' Beaverbrook wrote. 'His Welsh nationality always shone forth. Describing the great men of Wales, he declared that Cromwell was a Welshman and his real name was Williams. H. G. Wells, sitting quietly under the spell of the magician, interrupted the monologue, adding "Williams the Conqueror" to the list of Welsh worthies.'

Throughout the spring of 1922 Beaverbrook was playing a devious game. Churchill, furious with the Prime Minister over his decision at Genoa to recognize the Bolsheviks, was hoping that Austen Chamberlain might take over the government from Lloyd George and that he himself might become the leader of the coalition Liberals. Perhaps because such a move would not be to Bonar Law's advantage, Beaverbrook moved quickly to put Lloyd George in the picture. He suggested that Lloyd George might do well to isolate Churchill by fusing his Liberal and Conservative supporters: 'Not that I write this in any unkindly spirit towards him,' he wrote unconvincingly. 'Churchill's tendency is all to the right, and his principles are becoming more Tory,' he went on. 'I am sure he would not fancy being shut up in a coop with you, even for a short time . . . because such close collocation within a narrow circle would cloud his own brilliance in the light of your own superiority. . . .' Two days later he wrote again to urge Lloyd George to outflank Churchill. 'I put the probability of Conservative opposition to Winston's retention of office to him the other day. He was obviously immensely surprised and had not thought of it. . . . As you know he is subject to periods when the intensity of his imagination quite overbalances his judgment. . . .'[24]

In the end, the crisis that destroyed the Lloyd George coalition arose not from domestic political intrigue but over foreign policy, as the government, and with it Beaverbrook, was swept up into the Chanak crisis. Early in August 1922 Beaverbrook and Churchill decided to travel together to Deauville, then at the height of fashion, with several grand hotels and a casino, for a short holiday. Beaverbrook remembered how after lunching in Boulogne they drove on singing hymns, with Churchill giving a 'dramatic rendering' of 'Splendid are thy courts below. In this world of sin and woe.' At their hotel in Deauville they encountered the Aga Khan, and discussed with him the ominous situation in the Near East where war had broken out between Greece and Turkey. The Turks had never accepted the post-war transfer of territory to Greece, and under Mustafa Kemal were bent on taking it back by force. Lloyd George's policy was strongly pro-Greek, and the Aga Khan – naturally, as a Moslem leader, pro-Turk – impressed on Beaverbrook the dangers of Britain drifting into war with Turkey. He urged Beaverbrook to go to Istanbul, meet Kemal and act as mediator.

Back in England, in late August Beaverbrook brought together Lloyd George, Churchill and Birkenhead for a weekend at Cherkley during which he tried to persuade the Prime Minister to back his Turkish venture. Lloyd George was non-committal; the other two appeared favourable. So Beaverbrook set off for Istanbul, planning to send back articles to his newspapers and play the international peacemaker.

By the time he arrived the Turks had gone too far to be interested in mediation, and he was denied any support by the British Embassy; in London, Curzon, the Foreign Secretary, had raised awkward questions about his journey and stirred up hostile press comment about the 'mysterious mission'. Beaverbrook hurried back to England, pausing in Athens to file a dramatic account of the routed Greek Army. On his return he found war fever spreading, along with news of the brutal sacking of Smyrna; Birkenhead was now fervently pro-Greek, and there was a serious prospect of British forces attempting to stop the Turkish Army at Chanak. Messages had been sent to the Dominions, including Canada, requesting support.

Over more meetings at The Vineyard Beaverbrook tried to calm Birkenhead and Churchill, but without success. Lloyd George joined them and the arguments continued. But Lloyd George was alarmingly determined; as Beaverbrook saw it: 'Being by this time a weak man, he had decided to be strong.' Churchill accused Beaverbrook of wanting to 'scuttle' and of being incapable, as an outsider, of appreciating that England's honour was at stake.

Beaverbrook also, to his frustration, found Bonar Law unresponsive. He did not feel able to undermine Lloyd George at a time of crisis. 'When three or four days' discussion had proved unavailing,' wrote Beaverbrook, 'I went to Bonar Law in his retirement and said to him "These men mean war." '[25] The following evening, 6 October 1922, 'when I had almost despaired of Bonar Law's intervention, he came to my house at Fulham just at dusk. We sat in semi-darkness. . . . He said that he had made up his mind. He would send a letter to *The Times*.' He told Beaverbrook what he intended to say. 'To my mind the dominating sentence in the letter was to the effect that we could not police

186

the world alone. . . . I recommended him to send his letter to other newspapers as well as *The Times*.' The next day, the 7th, it appeared in *The Times* and, not surprisingly, the *Express*. The first sentence of the *Express* story accompanying the text was: 'There will be NO WAR.'

Although Bonar Law refrained from directly attacking the government's policy, and indeed wrote that it was 'undoubtedly right' that Britain should try to prevent 'war and massacre', he went on to say: ' . . . it is not however right that the burden of taking action should fall on the British government alone . . .' and, in a telling phrase that has remained a text for isolationists, he concluded: 'We cannot alone act as the policemen of the world.'[26] On the evening before publication, Birkenhead dined with Beaverbrook at The Vineyard and learned what Bonar Law was to say. He was, Beaverbrook recalled, 'greatly put out'; and also observed, 'with his usual shrewdness, that it was a new political situation. It implied the re-emergence of Bonar Law from retirement.'

Bonar Law's letter ruled out war with Turkey and threatened the survival of the coalition. His next moves were crucial. Birkenhead asked Beaverbrook to find out whether Bonar Law would rejoin Lloyd George – perhaps, again, as Foreign Secretary; the answer was no. On 9 October their seconds arranged for Lloyd George and Bonar Law to meet at The Vineyard.

Bonar Law arrived first, and told Beaverbrook that he regarded the prospect of an election with great alarm, not least for the party, which he feared would be split. As for himself, '"Office under Lloyd George would be intolerable," he said, "leading straight to war. . . ." Bonar Law then spoke sharply to me. He asked: "What do you want? Are you just playing the fascinating game of political intrigue?" He asked me what object I sought in arranging the lunch with Lloyd George . . . "What are you trying to do?" he asked. "Maintain the coalition? Or do you wish to break it down?" '

Evidently Bonar Law recognized that Beaverbrook was enjoying himself, but Beaverbrook's answer was that all he really wanted was 'An Empire programme, with Free Trade' and that he could only see this happening under a Conservative administration with Bonar Law as Prime Minister; 'Bonar Law remarked that he would not accept responsibility. . . . He would not be Prime Minister. I must make my representations elsewhere.' Nevertheless, Beaverbrook realized that at last Bonar Law had decided, faced with a possible war, that he could no longer back Lloyd George and that therefore 'the two leaders would meet for the first time as rivals for public approval – their differences might turn a quiet lunch party into a very lively event'.

Beaverbrook's account reads like a novel.

It was a moment of high drama when Lloyd George entered the little room at The Vineyard. He came with his swaggering step – one foot thrown forward and leg slightly outward. His greeting was gay without any sign of patronage. Bonar Law responded with little enthusiasm but much dignity. He was no longer the courtier. He had a better understanding of the temper of the dominating Tory Party in the House of Commons – and Lloyd George knew it. From that moment Bonar Law was the master of the scene.

As for Beaverbrook, he describes himself as playing an almost unnaturally modest and self-effacing role.

> I had nothing to say. Lloyd George turned to me with friendly though distant courtesy. I was not 'Max' to him that day. He called me 'Beaverbrook', a sure sign of disfavour. The drawing room at The Vineyard is small. It gives a feeling of intimacy when men sit and converse in it. When the first feeling of stiffness was over we got down to a more sympathetic basis. I was not in a hurry to go into the dining room. I preferred that the conversation should develop a bit. . . .

Although Lloyd George tried his hardest, he could win no promises from Bonar Law. Beaverbrook was impressed by Bonar Law's air of authority: 'I had never heard him to such advantage.' Afterwards, Birkenhead stayed on to confer with the host. They agreed that each would keep the other informed of any new move. However on 11 October Beaverbrook learned from Bonar Law that the government had just decided on an immediate election; Birkenhead's excuse was that he had promised Austen Chamberlain to say nothing. Bonar Law was still refusing to throw his hat in the ring; Austen Chamberlain and Birkenhead were resolved to support the coalition, but the party was in turmoil. 'I returned to Bonar Law,' says Beaverbrook, 'and received his approval to set out on a campaign of propaganda against Lloyd George and his Conservative colleagues.' Suddenly he and Birkenhead were on opposite sides.

On the same day Beaverbrook summed up the new situation in a letter to Dwight Morrow, the American banker-ambassador.

> We are now in the throes of a political crisis. The failure of the PM's Greek policy has resulted in the collapse of his prestige with the Conservatives . . . the immediate future will decide whether the Conservative Party is to remain intact, or whether the PM is strong enough to split it. It will be a great achievement to have smashed two parties in one short administration. . . . Bonar is the obvious choice for the Conservative leadership. He alone can lead the quarrelling groups. With extraordinary artfulness and much mental agility, he has offended none of them, and at the same time, yielded nothing.
>
> The only doubt lies in his own personality. At the critical moment a desire to walk humbly before the men of his own generation may destroy his opportunity for a place with posterity.
>
> I have not been so intrigued for a long time. It is like the beginning of

the drug-taking habit. What we shall do for excitement when this crisis is over, I do not know.[27]

On 15 October Austen Chamberlain decided to call a meeting of the Conservatives on Thursday, 19 October at the Carlton Club, where the party would decide whether or not to follow him in supporting Lloyd George.

CHAPTER 11

PRIME MINISTER'S FRIEND
1922–1924

FACED WITH THE opportunity of his political life, Bonar Law characteristically hesitated. Beaverbrook was aware that it could be dangerous for him to swing into action. Although Bonar Law had support in the party hierarchy and among backbenchers, all the Cabinet heavy-weights – including Balfour and Birkenhead – were committed to Chamberlain.

Beaverbrook remembered Bonar Law as prey to 'internal struggle. On the one side stood a sense of duty of which Bonar Law had boundless store. On the other was a fund of natural modesty, a love of well-earned ease, laziness and kindly feeling towards Lloyd George.' Hoping to be told that his health was not up to it, Bonar Law consulted Sir Thomas Horder, only to learn that he was considered perfectly fit. (Later, Beaverbrook learned from Horder that another of his patients at this time, Churchill, who was suffering from appendicitis, was keenly interested in Bonar Law's health. 'How's our ambitious invalid? What about our gilded tradesman?' he would ask. Bonar Law would inquire after Churchill too.[1] Beaverbrook found Sir Thomas a useful source on such matters.)

Meanwhile Beaverbrook discovered that some of the coalition suppor-ters, especially – and most damagingly – the well-informed Birkenhead, were trying to weaken Bonar Law by spreading the idea that once again he was Beaverbrook's puppet. Birkenhead 'subjected Bonar Law to ridicule. He told a story that Bonar Law was really abroad playing golf. That I had been dressed up in Bonar Law's clothes and disguised to look like him . . . that the Party meeting would be addressed by me masquer-ading as the real Bonar Law. . . .' Other, dirtier rumours were spread too. Salvidge informed Bonar Law that

> . . . one of the things being said was that much of the demand for a change
> of government had been engineered by Lord Beaverbrook because, though

he had till recently been a Coalition supporter, he had failed to exercise over the present Cabinet the influence he desired on behalf of certain oil interests in the East. To Bonar's retort that surely I neither believed such a tale nor suggested that he should for a moment consider it, I answered that I happened to know Beaverbrook did not possess any oil interests in the East.[2]

The same rumour surfaced in a Paris newspaper. Beaverbrook started legal action against the newspaper concerned and was furious with Salvidge for spreading the story; he did not speak to Birkenhead again for some time. Even in his later account, anxiety emerges through the bravado. 'I should have been a simpleton if I had allowed myself to be overcome by any such tactics. I resolved to do everything in my power to dispel the suspicions which others were trying to sow in Bonar Law's mind. When I was summoned to his house I would sit for ever so long discussing every conceivable subject except politics.'

On Wednesday, 18 October, the day before the Carlton Club meeting, Bonar Law sat at home in Onslow Gardens brooding over his decision. Beaverbrook, after a long talk on the telephone in the morning, awaited a summons.

> The hesitation of Bonar Law drove me to extreme anxiety. He knew I wanted him to go to the Carlton Club. If he did not send for me or give me news of his intention, surely he was rejecting the contest and refusing the Party conflict, and perhaps deciding upon retirement from public life and departure from the scene. . . . It was such a long day. . . . Impossible to turn my mind to any pursuit. Conversations with my newspaper colleagues failed to hold my attention. It was almost as though I had become obsessed by a single thought.

By eight that evening, when the summons came, Beaverbrook was literally in a fever – he had a cold and a temperature. He hurried off to Onslow Gardens and was taken into the small, stuffy library where Bonar Law told him that he feared no good could come from his attendance at the Party meeting. He then talked of retiring altogether from politics, and produced a letter to his constituency chairman declaring that he would not be standing at the next election. Beaverbrook maintains that he kept calm and 'continued to dodge the issue', reminding Bonar Law of how annoyed he had been when Beaverbrook had destroyed his letter of withdrawal to Chamberlain in 1911. 'So I said, I am not going to make such a mistake again. Your letter is your own affair.'

Finally, when he saw that he was beginning to irritate Bonar Law, 'I at once plunged into the arguments which I thought would be most effective in support of our cause. . . . I needed no notes, for I had prepared myself all day long for this critical quarter of an hour. I came to the end of my plea, concluding on a high Imperial note. He calmly refilled his pipe and said quite simply: "I am going to the meeting." ' Hot and cold with excitement and fever, Beaverbrook asked if he could make a statement to that effect to the Press Association. 'He concurred. I fled. . . . Then I returned home and to bed with two hot water bottles and one of rum with a bowl of sugar. One last word of warning on the telephone to the *Daily Express* to make the most and the best of the great news. And then a night of sleep.'

At eight next morning, Bonar Law was on the telephone wanting to reconsider. 'I replied: Have you seen the morning newspapers? which was a conclusive answer. . . .' When Sir George Younger, the party chairman, arrived at Onslow Gardens he found Bonar Law still dithering, sitting in his slippers in front of the fire; but Younger managed to persuade him to get ready and carried him off.

The result of the meeting at the Carlton Club was a resounding defeat for Austen Chamberlain; the MPs present voted by 187 votes to 87 to end the coalition. The way was clear for Bonar Law to become leader of the Conservative Party and, after the resignation of Lloyd George that evening, Prime Minister.

Beaverbrook gives the impression that his intervention, when it came, was conclusive. He was not, however, the only or even the last person consulted on the critical night of 18 October. Wickham Steed, the editor of *The Times*, visited Bonar Law between 8 and 9 p.m. and left with the clear impression that he had decided to act; and he was telephoned soon after midnight. 'He asked me if there were any news . . . when I told him that *The Times* of 19 October would announce his intention to attend the meeting he did not demur beyond saying, characteristically, that his mind was not fully made up.'[3] Bonar Law himself, in a letter a few days later, said: 'Up to the last moment I was very undecided and if my own family – my sister and children – had not been so strong against my giving up, I believe that is the course I should have adopted.'[4]

Beaverbrook was not offered a job when Bonar Law formed his administration, and there is no evidence that he either expected or wanted one. His published account merely says, with uncharacteristic vagueness, that Bonar Law's victory 'brought the joy of new opportunities to secure the political objectives to which I had dedicated my public life', and pays generous tribute to the defeated Lloyd George: 'I valued his friendship. I admired his strength, his courage, his high endurance.' Bonar Law retained Curzon, a late but important supporter, as Foreign Secretary, and less predictably made Stanley Baldwin, who had made a telling speech on his behalf at the Carlton Club, Chancellor of the Exchequer, after Reginald McKenna turned the post down. A general election was called for 15 November and Bonar Law's triumph was overshadowed by anxiety about the fierce fight ahead. Not that Bonar Law was especially triumphant; Beaverbrook recalls him 'plunged in gloom . . . there was neither confidence nor joy at future prospects in Bonar Law's house. . . .'

'TRICKY POLITICS'

It is abundantly clear that, especially with an election imminent, Beaverbrook's friendship with Bonar Law was not regarded as an asset to the Conservative Party. Several of Bonar Law's other advisers and supporters had long been suspicious of his influence. J. C. C. Davidson left an account of the relationship rather different from Beaverbrook's own. 'Although Bonar appreciated and liked Max very much, he never let him into any state secrets, and I think he knew his Max extremely well. . . . I could talk with great openness to Bonar about Max and his little foibles, which Bonar appreciated just as much as anybody else.' Like Baldwin, Davidson was protective of Bonar Law and anxious lest too close an association with Beaverbrook should tarnish him. He had not been happy about Beaverbrook's peerage in 1916 ('. . . Of course Max very much wanted to be a peer') and was well aware that there were people, including MPs, who suspected that Bonar Law must be on Beaverbrook's payroll. Davidson regarded Beaverbrook as 'amoral', and always refused to spend a night at Cherkley: 'I didn't like the house or the way it was run.' At the same time he knew that Bonar Law's career and reputation owed a great deal to Beaverbrook, and grudgingly recognized his 'very bright attractive mind'. To a respectable Conservative insider like Davidson there was something unnerving about the emotional allegiance Beaverbrook showed to Bonar Law. 'Max's devotion to Bonar had a very feminine aspect.'[5]

Beaverbrook recalled that Sir George Younger warned him that

> . . . only harm would result if I took any apparent share in guiding Bonar Law personally through the campaign. . . . Bonar Law himself denied that any direct representation was made to him on this score, but he was conscious of a movement of public opinion against the idea that the new Government should be a Beaverbrook government. Considerable precautions were therefore taken, during and after the formation of the government, as to methods of communication between the new Premier and myself. These methods were telephone, notes and a trusted intermediary.

He went on to claim that 'in some ways this lack of free and direct access was probably unfortunate'. If he had been asked to approach McKenna, he could have persuaded him to take the job; as it was, despite receiving 'countless letters' asking for his help he took 'almost no part' in Bonar Law's choice of ministers, apart from recommending Samuel Hoare, who became Secretary for Air and henceforward a friend and protégé. He wrote to Bonar Law on 21 October: 'I think it would be better if I remained outside, doing everything in my power to secure your election through the columns of the *Express* only. . . . I am convinced that you must look after your propaganda.'[6]

The election campaign was short and acrimonious, fought more on

personalities than on policies. Beaverbrook tried hard to persuade Bonar
Law to include a promise of Tariff Reform and Imperial Preference in his
programme, but without success; Lord Derby raised the old bugbear of
food taxes and threatened to resign, and Salisbury supported him. Bonar
Law played safe. His platform was tranquillity at home and abroad,
although he undertook to call a conference of Empire Prime Ministers to
consider how best to promote imperial trade and economic development.
On foreign policy, Beaverbrook tried to push Bonar Law into promising
to withdraw British forces from Mesopotamia and Palestine. He wrote to
him on 25 October: 'You must not imagine for a moment that this means
that I, as (about the only) rare newspaper proprietor who does not want
or won't take anything from you in the way of honours or office, mean to
declare hostility to your administration. On the contrary I am going to help
you all I can in the circumstances. But I feel so strongly on the Middle
East question that I am going to bring public pressure to bear. . . .' Bonar
Law replied on the same day: 'It would be a strange thing indeed if you
added to my troubles and worries in the position into which I have fallen
and I am sure you will not do that. You yourself said on Sunday that
although you wanted a bag and baggage policy you realised that I might
find it impossible. There is nothing more that I can say.'[7]

Both Lloyd George and Birkenhead were scathing about Bonar Law
and his team, calling them 'the Second Eleven'. Bonar Law found the
prospect of retaliating against his former colleagues distasteful, but
Beaverbrook did not. When Sir George Younger did a deal with the
coalition and agreed not to oppose them in a number of constituencies,
Beaverbrook swung into action. Determined to disassociate Bonar Law
entirely from the old coalition gang, whether he liked it or not, he funded
and supported in the *Express* a number of independent Conservative
candidates. Not surprisingly, this infuriated his opponents. One victim was
Frederick Guest, Churchill's cousin and formerly Lloyd George's chief
whip, who had pushed Beaverbrook as a minister in 1918. He represented
East Dorset, where the son of an old associate of Beaverbrook's during
the war, Hall Caine, was suddenly inserted as an anti-coalition Tory.

'In tricky politics I am quite a novice compared with you,' wrote Guest,

> . . . but I had however thought my knowledge of human nature was fairly
> wide and accurate.
>   Guided by my instincts I have for now nearly nine years consistently
> defended you, in the world in which we both live, from misinterpretation
> and attack.
>   The world has said that you were an adventurer with a closed past, that
> you were subtle, ambitious, unscrupulous and unreliable and that the word
> friendship was an unknown word to you.
>   . . . Can it be that the world was right in its diagnosis and advice and that
> I have been wrong in adhering to my belief that you had a sometimes hidden
> heart of gold!

I remember towards the end of the war helping you over the stile into the government, so that having once faced the music of public opinion you could lay your foundations in British public life for all time.

Have you forgotten your hesitancy? . . . It is not too late for you to reassure me. . . .

Two days later, on 5 November, Beaverbrook hit back. His letter was a prime example of his brilliance in epistolary counter-attack.

I have no desire to disturb the friendship to which you refer. I therefore overlook your observation about 'tricky politics'. . . .

I also appreciate the personal defence you have made of me against charges, which never had behind them the slightest foundation in fact. But I will remind you that we have both lived in a stormy atmosphere, and that I have often pleaded your cause in your own society. . . .

I really do not feel inclined to go into a kind of balance sheet of the past services we may have done each other in politics – except to deny the suggestion that I desired office, or accepted it at your hands. . . .

I pass on to the issue of public policy which is, after all, really the thing that matters. Your proposal appears to be that I should withdraw opposition on account of friendship.

This argument did not move me when Churchill insisted on fighting the Russians, and it does not move me now when you and your friends are turned out for trying to fight the Turks. . . . I cannot put you in a category apart in response to an appeal based on friendship.

As to East Dorset I am not responsible for Hall Caine though I shall support him. . . .[8]

He had in truth encouraged Hall Caine to stand against Guest and had offered to pay his election expenses. During the campaign he sent down extra reporters, produced a special edition of the *Daily Express* and spoke himself in the constituency three times. Beaverbrook was not popular in coalition circles. Churchill 'went about calling me Machiavelli' (and later sent him a copy of *The Prince*).[9] Beaverbrook did not seem to care. As he later wrote with some satisfaction: 'Under the changed attitude of asperity the situation improved greatly and our prospects of victory at the polls were enhanced every day.'

Nevertheless on election day, 15 November, Bonar Law was full of trepidation and Beaverbrook extremely tense. He spent the day taking voters to the polls. That evening, while the Prime Minister waited in Downing Street, Beaverbrook dined with Gladys and the McKennas, '. . . beset by fears, distressed by foreboding and filled with anxieties'. 'Bonar Law wanted me to go to Downing Street but I declined,' he wrote. 'My wife and McKenna however went there and found Bonar Law in a curious state of mind. . . .' He was depressed and convinced he was going to lose his own seat at Glasgow. Beaverbrook went to the *Express* office to get the latest news: 'My wife and McKenna . . . urged me to go to Downing Street but I did not care to go, knowing it would be full of reporters who would draw some kind of insidious conclusions.'[10]

The first returns were not especially encouraging; the next day, however, when the rural results came in, the picture brightened; and Bonar Law won the election with a convincing majority of 77 over all other parties combined. In his later account Beaverbrook wrote simply: 'And we rejoiced.' An unpublished fragment relates that when it was all over he fell ill and went to bed.

For all his efforts to keep out of the way, to at least one onlooker it was plain who should reap the praise, or blame, for the election's outcome. William Orpen, the painter and Beaverbrook's protégé from the war, attended a party given by Sir Philip Sassoon at his house in Park Lane for Lloyd George, Birkenhead and other coalition supporters. A tickertape machine reported the results as they came in. Orpen wrote a wry verse on the occasion.

> Gee, it was late – that raw black night
> And we were almost all quite tight
> Mid Beauty and the flowing wine
> And clouds of nicotine divine
> We sat
> And watched
> And waited
> Till LO the small machine began
> To tic tic. . . .
> 'Twas like the writing on the wall
> That told of old King Nibs sad fall
> When in the dawn we learnt it all
> Old England's choice, we clearly saw
> Was Max!
> I beg pardon! Mr. B. Law.

Frederick Guest MP was defeated in East Dorset by five thousand votes.

'YOU ARE A CURIOUS FELLOW'

During the campaign Bonar Law had more than once lost his voice. This misfortune was ascribed to exhaustion; officially he was fit (and Horder had privately told Beaverbrook as much) although Law himself, pessimistic as ever, continued to have doubts and had with difficulty been dissuaded from announcing that he would lead the government for a year only. Between the election and the end of the year, however, he dominated Parliament with no signs of strain.

Once again Bonar Law spent Christmas at Cherkley, with his son Richard. Beaverbrook's joy at having his friend under his roof as Prime Minister was muted by Bonar Law's low spirits. Once again his voice failed. Beaverbrook noticed that he ate little, and as soon as he could he would light a cigar. 'This haste to be finished with eating, and desire to begin smoking was an invariable sign with him of nervous tension. . . . He was not happy. His tasks were bearing heavily on him. . . .' Nevertheless, Beaverbrook was hoping that by the time of the Imperial Conference, planned for the autumn, Bonar Law would be more confident and prepared to commit himself to Tariff Reform and Imperial Preference.

But at the end of January an unforeseen crisis very nearly brought Bonar Law down, and all Beaverbrook's hopes to nothing. The new Chancellor, Stanley Baldwin, was in the United States to negotiate a settlement of British war debts. Bonar Law believed strongly that it would be disastrous for Britain to repay its debt to the United States before arranging to be repaid by France and other allies. Baldwin was supposed to play for time. Instead, under pressure from the Americans, he decided to settle at once. Summoned home for discussions, he made a statement on arrival at Southampton explaining his decision and outlining his provisional settlement, thus forcing the Prime Minister's hand. Bonar Law objected so strongly to the terms that when a majority of his Cabinet supported the Chancellor he contemplated resignation.

Beaverbrook left a long unpublished account of this crisis, which stresses his closeness to Bonar Law, his own objections to Baldwin's devious conduct, and the effect of the crisis on Bonar Law's health.[11]

It appeared to me that his spirits were damaged by a setback on what he considered a most important issue of policy and that loss of spirits reacted on his health. In any case his self-confidence did receive a severe shock by his absolute failure to carry his cabinet. He had seen [Lloyd] George wangle a cabinet so often, that he had not perhaps realised that George never undertook the task without calculating well in advance, that the effort would be successful. The blow to his prestige and influence hit him hard.

He began to fall soon afterwards into moods of depression. I used to find him sitting in a state of dejection, smoking his pipe continually, and sitting with all his windows closed in an overheated room. Near him on the floor lay a dog called Farmer, which was, as it turned out, suffering from cancer of the snout. The dog was obviously ill, but Bonar Law would not be separated from it, nor would he have it destroyed. . . .

During the spring, three by-elections went against the government, which depressed Bonar Law still further. By the Easter recess his voice had almost gone, and he had to ask Baldwin to speak for him in the Commons. His doctors assured him that they could find no trace of organic disease, and advised him to go to the seaside and rest; he went to Torquay. Beaverbrook was away on a trip to Palestine and Rome (where he took Gladys and her sister Helen to an audience with the Pope and had a rosary blessed for Mrs Tim Healy)[12], but 'the accounts I received were of such a character as to bring me back quickly. . . . On the Sunday he stayed with me at Cherkley, and then resumed his place in the Commons on the

Monday. . . . But he was unable to address the House, as I had feared from my observation during the weekend.'

Still Beaverbrook continued to hope. Rumours about the Prime Minister's health began to appear in the press: the *Observer* forecast that he would have to resign. Beaverbrook and the *Express* worked hard to ascribe these rumours to political hostility. Bonar Law continued to go to the House, but when he tried to speak he was inaudible. According to Beaverbrook, Bonar Law consulted him and McKenna about Baldwin's first budget: they strongly recommended lowering income tax. 'In fact I brought a message from McKenna on his bed of sickness to the Premier, that to leave Income Tax at its current height would be disastrous. . . . Bonar Law put the case to the Chancellor, and he agreed to the change of plan quite easily, except that he halved the proposed reduction of the Income Tax to 6d.' Beaverbrook did his best to ensure that the budget received favourable press coverage. On 22 April the *Sunday Express* proclaimed: 'This is the best government which the present generation has seen', and likened Bonar Law to Disraeli, 'the keystone of the arch'. On 26 April when Bonar Law, in gold braid and feathered hat, attended the wedding of the Duke of York to Lady Elizabeth Bowes-Lyon in Westminster Abbey, the *Daily Express* enthused: 'He walked like an athlete.'

But Bonar Law was a sick man. On 28 April it was announced that he was going to try sea air and a warm climate for a month. According to Beaverbrook, he had been most reluctant to leave London. 'I asked him to see Sir Thomas Horder again which he was unwilling to do, as he said that Horder had already made up his mind that nothing but time would effect a cure. The whole of this business of inducing the Premier to hand over command and go abroad for a time was an absolute death grapple with his unwillingness to do anything of the kind, and cost hours of time.'

Bonar Law set off for the Mediterranean by boat with his son. He wrote to Beaverbrook from Algiers and Genoa, and asked him to meet him in Aix-les-Bains. 'It was one of the most alarming letters I have ever received and brought me out posthaste to see him. On arrival the situation was unfortunately plain enough . . . if anything he was worse rather than better.' Bonar Law was in great pain, and taking large doses of aspirin that were making him still more depressed. His voice was almost inaudible. 'But the whole question of resignation still remained undecided,' wrote Beaverbrook, adding with a note of desperation: 'I hoping against hope that with companionship, and talk and encouragement, in an ideal scene, his gloom would drift away from him and he would begin to make real progress. For I still thought that the trouble was mainly neurasthenic.'

With Bonar Law declining, and his own fears rising, Beaverbrook cabled Horder to meet them in Paris, where Bonar Law stayed at the Crillon and Beaverbrook at the Ritz. 'The result of the new judgment would be of such importance to the political world that I did not wish to embarrass the

Premier by being in too close attendance on him. Ever since Bonar Law had been in power I had done everything to avoid giving any grounds for the suggestion that he was being guided by undue influence on my part – which, as a matter of fact, he never was.' After Horder had examined Bonar Law, on 17 May, he telephoned Beaverbrook and asked him to come at once. They walked in the spring sunshine on the Champs Elysées and Horder told Beaverbrook he was virtually certain that Bonar Law had terminal throat cancer. They went back to Bonar Law; Horder simply told the Prime Minister that, as his throat was not responding to treatment, he would be justified in resigning. 'Bonar Law was immensely cheered by this verdict,' Beaverbrook wrote. '. . . He was almost lighthearted in his relief at the idea of laying down a burden which had been crushing his failing vitality. . . . I was left in a terrible state of uncertainty by Horder's judgment and thought I could see that the great doctor entertained little or no hope. . . .'

Immediately, Bonar Law's relief was overtaken by a fresh anxiety: the question of his successor. 'This was obviously an issue which was liable to cause Bonar Law great worry – which he was by no means in a physical condition to sustain.' The sequence of events has been much debated whereby the man whom most people, including himself, expected to succeed, Lord Curzon, was displaced by Baldwin. Beaverbrook's view, according to his unpublished narrative, was that Bonar Law was undecided, as he so often was, which was why he dreaded having to commit himself. 'Privately, I have no doubt that he intended to nominate Curzon if he had to nominate anybody, and that he wanted . . . in his heart, to nominate Stanley Baldwin. His entourage undoubtedly favoured Baldwin.' As for Beaverbrook's own view: 'From start to finish I absolutely declined to take any side in this matter.' His main concern was to spare Bonar Law from all strain. He learned from the British Ambassador to Paris, Lord Crewe, that there were precedents for a serving Prime Minister to decline to advise the sovereign on his successor. Beaverbrook was close to neither candidate and did not care much for either of them. There is, however, evidence that Bonar Law was more involved with the eventual choice of Baldwin than he allowed Beaverbrook to realize.[13]

Soon after Beaverbrook had left Paris, the First Lord of the Admiralty, Leo Amery, arrived to plead with the Prime Minister to remain in office, officially on holiday, for three months, to strengthen Baldwin's position. When Beaverbrook was asked to support this plan, he wrote: 'I could not disclose to them the terrible knowledge which was in my possession, which made the whole thing futile. All I could say was I would think about it.' Soon after Bonar Law returned to London he was examined by more doctors, and Horder's fears were confirmed, though they were kept from the patient.

On 20 May Bonar Law resigned, and two days later George V sent for

Baldwin. Beaverbrook ensured that the press gave sympathetic coverage to Bonar Law's decision, and received a grateful letter from Mary Law. After expressing her thanks she went on: 'But it was not to say this that I am writing to you. It is from the bottom of my heart to thank you for having gone to Bonar, to have yielded to his overwhelming desire to escape. . . . I know you have a real love for Bonar and that love brings you to his rescue when he is in despair.'[14]

Bonar Law had five months more to live, and by all accounts Beaverbrook, who left no account of this terrible time, was magnificent. He devoted himself to distracting his friend, who went to Brighton for radiation treatment and spent most of the summer there; then improved enough to pay a short visit to Le Touquet for some golf. Beaverbrook spent much time with him, playing cards or chess, bringing him all the news and maintaining a cheerful front. In September he arranged a lunch at The Vineyard, so that Lloyd George and Bonar Law could be reconciled. He later wrote movingly of how the two old colleagues and opponents, one heading towards the grave, one starting a long decline, talked quietly and affectionately together and 'parted in an atmosphere of comradeship'. The story got about that Beaverbrook bought shares in the same concerns as Bonar Law so that he could bring him good news of rising prices.[15]

By mid-autumn Bonar Law was desperately ill. He was brought back to Onslow Gardens where, on 30 October, he died. His last words to Beaverbrook were, apparently, 'You are a curious fellow.'[16] On 5 November he was buried in Westminster Abbey; the pall bearers included the Prince of Wales, Asquith, Baldwin and Beaverbrook. Kipling was in the congregation, and 'Recessional' was the final hymn.

REBECCA WEST

During the grim period of Bonar Law's last illness and its aftermath Beaverbrook engaged in a romantic episode which, unlike others, has left clear traces behind. No doubt most of his amours of the period were taken lightly on both sides – regarded as an exciting, if risky, game. But when Beaverbrook gave the young writer Rebecca West grounds for believing he was attracted to her, even that he might marry her, he provoked serious consequences, at least for her.

She had known Beaverbrook since the last year of the war, when he was Minister of Information and she was a young journalist and critic who had already, through talent and nerve, made a name for herself. Beaverbrook would undoubtedly have known that since 1913 she had been H. G. Wells's mistress, with a son by him, born the day the war began. She and Wells dined at The Vineyard, and she was also connected with the Bonar Law circle; one of her great friends was Sara Tugander, Law's confidential secretary, who in 1915 had married James Melville, a lawyer who later became chief legal adviser to the Beaverbrook Press. Mrs Melville was in Rebecca's confidence, and knew all about her problems with Wells, who had no intention of leaving his wife. West, for all her fierce intelligence and contempt for conventional domesticity, felt humiliated by her uncertain status. Dark, handsome rather than beautiful, she seemed sexually liberated, but was more vulnerable than she appeared. As she fell out of love with Wells in the early 1920s she became fascinated by Beaverbrook, who, as her biographer says, was, like Wells, older and a figure in the world, and 'like Wells in other ways – in his smallness, his male energy, his driving egotism and his anxieties about his health'. In 1922 she wrote to Sara Melville: 'I found him one of the most fascinating talkers I've ever met, and full of the real vitality – the genius kind that exists mystically apart from all physical conditions, just as it does in HG.'

During the summer of 1923, when Beaverbrook was watching over Bonar Law as cancer crept up on him, Rebecca West was making plans to leave Wells and go on a lecture tour in America that winter. One evening she dined with Max and Gladys Beaverbrook; afterwards she wrote to Mrs Melville: 'It was so funny – I must tell you about it.' But what happened that evening remains a mystery. Fifty years later Rebecca West, who increasingly rewrote episodes to suit her prevailing image of herself, claimed that the wife of the man she was then in love with had told her that she and her husband were going to be divorced and that he was going to ask Rebecca to marry him. It is possible that she invented the story, perhaps out of guilt – she claimed later that she had 'deeply liked' Gladys. But something happened between her and Beaverbrook during that summer, because at Christmas 1923, after she reached New York, he tracked her down at her hotel on Central Park West and they spent Christmas together, 'on the understanding that they were in love'.

The love affair was short-lived, and Rebecca West was left with a deep sense of humiliation and the fear that she was unattractive. As West put it fifty years later, '. . . they were completely unsuited to be man and wife'. By this she presumably meant that their sexual relationship was a failure. Over the scattered, enigmatic references she made to the debacle that have survived in her papers – there are no traces whatsoever in Beaverbrook's – hovers the suggestion that with West he was impotent.

While they were still in New York, she tried to make light of things. She wrote to an American friend, the writer Fannie Hurst, who had invited them both to visit her: 'M called up and said he thought we wouldn't go tomorrow because we ought both to reconcile ourselves to the fact that life together in London is impossible and that it was torturing for him to see me . . .'; she had 'no hope' and wished 'the poor old donkey' had never come. When he left New York, sending her armfuls of red roses, she collapsed and became ill; the next stage of her lecture tour had to be put off.

Back in England in the summer of 1924 she saw Beaverbrook again; he took her to The Vineyard for lunch. Soon afterwards she wrote once more to Fannie Hurst, a painfully honest letter:

> We were alone. That was a queer thing, for nearly always he had a crowd around him. We had lunch, and we walked round the garden for a time. He then talked quite lightly of our past infatuation as if it were a tremendous joke. He laughed about it. I suddenly realised that he was physically quite indifferent to me. Fannie, I'm not telling you the truth, I'm leaving out the point. He casually implied in a phrase that when he had made love to me in London first he was drunk, and that it had been very awkward for him when he found I took it seriously. New York he didn't explain at all. Then we went back to town in the car, and he dropped me on his way. Later that afternoon I heard he is making ardent love to Gwen Ffrangçon-Davies, the young actress who is playing Juliet very successfully.

Why, she wondered, had he bothered to find her in New York at all, going to some trouble to discover her whereabouts? 'Or was that only because he wanted to see me as a friend and never told me he was making enquiries in case he revived the hopes he had raised in me when he was drunk?' West admitted the depth of her unhappiness; she realized that she had loved him for years. 'It's over but I'm over too. . . . I thought at Christmas I'd got something to give Max – that there was something worth while to be got out of it. But why was he so stricken when I told him that I couldn't have a child? I shall go mad wondering.' In the end she had to accept that 'the New York business was I suppose a panic-stricken response to what he realised was my clinging to the idea he loved me'.

Not long after their talk in the garden at The Vineyard Beaverbrook, apparently quite recovered from the episode, asked Rebecca West to a dinner party. She sent him a spirited telegram: 'If you put me next Wells at dinner I will wring your neck. Many of your friends are deadly but at least I have not lived with them for ten years.' Nevertheless she remained obsessed and tormented; she confided in several friends, and wrote to one of them: 'I feel that I shall never get out of the black magic of this relationship and get on with my life.' In 1926, when she spent the summer in the south of France, she worked on a novel based on the end of her affair with Wells and her passion for Beaverbrook. She called it *Sunflower*, and never finished it; it was published only after her death.

Sunflower, a study of a woman gripped by a bewildering sexual passion, is full of traces of Beaverbrook – his appearance, his background, his friends, his houses, his political connections, his preoccupations, his emotions. He is represented as Francis Pitt, an Australian-born millionaire who has made his fortune in California. Pitt's father was a Wesleyan minister; he is unmarried, and lives with his sister, Etta, in a house in London with the geography of The Vineyard and the appearance, unflatteringly described, of Cherkley: '. . . a villa of the sort that edge

Wimbledon Common or Putney Heath, faced with a grey mixture of cement and sand the colour of cold porridge, and surmounted with a useless Italianate tower'. Pitt, like Beaverbrook, has been an MP and has his Bonar Law, a much admired best friend called Hurrell, a leading politician, who is fatally ill and whom he cares for with devotion. Rebecca West turns herself into Sunflower, a lovely, blonde, successful actress from a modest background. Sunflower has lived for ten years with Essington, older than she is and, like H. G. Wells, married, neurotically demanding and jealous. The relationship is in difficulties. Sunflower and Francis Pitt are drawn to each other, and over walks in the garden and lunches together they come to the brink of a love affair. The novel breaks off when they are about to become lovers.

In making Sunflower her protagonist, Rebecca West created a woman as different from herself as she could imagine – perhaps the kind of woman whom she feared that Beaverbrook, and most other men, preferred: glamorous, blonde, physically perfect, not clever, instinctively womanly. Pitt, on the other hand, is given not only Beaverbrook's physical appearance but also his voice and turns of phrase ('Goodbye to you'). The main difference between Pitt and Beaverbrook is that Pitt is a bachelor. Even in fiction, Rebecca West could not allow her Sunflower self to be in love once again with a married man.

Sunflower and Pitt first meet, like Rebecca West and Beaverbrook, during the First World War. She calls at the office of a war charity of which he is chairman.

> . . . a little man with hair the colour of a fox and a very big mouth ran very quickly downstairs from the floor above. He paused and looked at her out of queer grey eyes which were the colour of bad weather, with extreme appreciation and utter lack of interest. It was plain that he cared for women, for he looked at her as a sailor looks at a ship, but everything in him was absorbed in anticipation of something he was going to do.

When they meet again, at dinner with Essington, she notices his voice, 'very deep for such a little man', and his hands, 'tiny, but very broad and strong'.

In her descriptions of Beaverbrook/Pitt, Rebecca West strives to evoke a primitive masculinity in a far from conventionally handsome form.

> With his ape's mouth, his overlarge head, and his overbroad shoulders he had an air of having been created before the human structure had added to itself such refinements as beauty and shapeliness. Yet he had as much of a body as a man needs. He looked enormously strong, and as if he could go through anything. . . . The only modern thing in his face, the only thing which would have been surprising in the death's head of a mummy found crouching in a grave dug in a place now desert but not so a million years ago, was a certain whimsicality, a certain puckishness, which spoke of an intention to break up life whenever it seems to be settling down. . . .

She refers repeatedly in the novel to Pitt's top-heavy body, huge head, great mouth, short legs, little paw hands; there is an undercurrent of astonishment that such a small, ugly person should yet be strong, charming and sexually vital. Pitt also evokes in Sunflower a series of peculiar fantasies about primeval family life, in which she is the submissive, fertile woman and he the aggressive hunter and protector. One of the novel's themes, reflecting the analysis she was undertaking while working on the book, was that the pace of modern life, especially for ambitious men, inevitably damaged 'natural' relationships between the sexes. Nevertheless, for all the theorizing, there is a basic simplicity about Pitt's attraction for Sunflower: 'He was the most self-possessed and male person she had ever met.'

Gradually, and half against her will, she falls passionately in love with him.

> She marvelled once again at the wrongness of every bit of him; at the glazed, earth-coloured skin, stretched so tightly over the queer broad forehead which, because of something bulging in the contours that made one think of bad engineering, one suspected of being no thicker than an eggshell; at his straggling hair; at the sly setting of his eyes and his great pale and shapeless lips; at his nose, which might have been pinched in wet clay by a savage; at his head which was so badly set on his neck, at his neck which was so badly set on his shoulders that round the collar he had the look of a badly packed parcel. She had never seen him more hideous, more unborn. Yet she had never known him to give out so powerfully his peculiar emanation of warmth and impish sweetness. Suddenly and keenly she wanted him to be immediately her lover.

Essington's jealous remarks about Pitt echo Beaverbrook's detractors: 'Yes, the little creature has real charm. But a wicked little creature. They say his financial record in California is shady beyond description. I remember we had qualms of letting him have a seat.' As Essington starts to be jealous, he informs Sunflower about Pitt and women. 'I've been hearing things about our little host. . . . He's evidently apt to be tiresome with women. Mechanically and promiscuously attentive. There have been several great affairs.' A musical comedy actress is mentioned, and one of the 'Nelly sisters' (gossip had linked Beaverbrook with the glamorous actress twins, the Dolly sisters). So was a 'Lady Juliet Lynn'; 'Nobody knows quite what happened but for some years a good deal of money passed. . . . She did a lot of war work posing as the Madonna. She's very lovely – for a titled person', adds Sunflower. Clearly Rebecca West has Lady Diana Cooper in mind, none too charitably.

Among Pitt's entourage is a rough diamond from his past, Sir John Murphy, 'Jack Murphy to my friends', who is evidently based on Sir James Dunn. Despite financial ups and downs, Dunn had been made a baronet by Lloyd George in 1921 and was seeing much of his old boyhood friend.

He too was unfaithful to his long-suffering Canadian wife, Gertrude, a good friend of Gladys Beaverbrook's; he and Beaverbrook sometimes pursued the same women; and his eldest daughter, Mona, was being pursued by Lord Birkenhead, with Beaverbrook's connivance. Murphy plays a part in the central scene of the novel, an intense encounter between Pitt and Sunflower during which Pitt castigates himself for his bad behaviour with women and reveals that Murphy has a hold over him from the past. 'Sex causes a great deal of trouble in this world, Sunflower,' says Pitt. 'It has caused a lot of trouble in my life . . . I have not been all that I should have been in the past. . . .' He tells her a story of how during the war he met a woman at a luncheon party, made an assignation with her for that afternoon, had arrived to find her waiting 'and had then and there . . . why did it hurt her so to hear that?' More such stories follow; 'And the stories themselves made her see ridiculous pictures of him, running after women taller than himself through immense rooms furnished like hotels so that his little legs looked comically short . . . she felt degraded and ashamed and contaminated. It was shameful, it was disgusting, but she would rather have been any of the women Francis Pitt had done that thing with than be herself.'

Pitt tells Sunflower that a man's body 'goes on making certain demands. And women have always been kind to me, too kind to me. . . .' Suddenly Sunflower realizes that Pitt's mood has changed. 'Without lifting the arm which shielded his face he muttered: "What can I do to be saved? . . . That's how my old father would have put it in the pulpit." Then awe and terror flooded his tone and he asked in deadly earnest and despair, "How am I to live so that people will think me a great man?" ' Sunflower tries to soothe him as he mutters brokenly: ' "What's the way to live? Essington and Hurrell, I thought they'd got the trick. Hard thinking and public service . . . ." '

At the mention of Jack Murphy's name, Pitt tells Sunflower why he has to keep on the right side of him: 'It's something I've never told anyone else in the whole world.' He relates how Murphy had helped him out of serious trouble in their wild youth in California, when he had feared ' "I'd never have any woman but a bought one. . . . If I were to go back on him for one moment he'd be at my throat, he'd be spilling the story all round London and I should be done." ' When Sunflower asks whether he cannot blackmail Murphy in return, Pitt insists that Murphy does not need to bother about his reputation. ' "But I'm different. If I'm to get on in politics I must be respected." '

As he is interrupted by a footman, Pitt's mood suddenly changes again. Someone has come to see him, a woman known for her intelligence, to tell him her troubles. 'Ah, clever women get into the same jams as stupid ones,' remarks Pitt, a statement that may stand as an epitaph to Rebecca West's infatuation with Beaverbrook.

Until the end of her long life Rebecca West fretted over her brief, inconclusive romance with Beaverbrook. He used her as a journalist when it suited him, and dined out on a disobliging story about how she had once bitten Wells and the wound had turned septic. But with the insight of a novelist, she has left a flawed, incomplete but convincing description of him, a mixture of self-pity, wily seductiveness and guilt.

CHAPTER 12

NORTHCLIFFE'S SUCCESSOR, BALDWIN'S FOE
1918–1929

THOSE WHO EXPRESSED alarm about the growing power of the press when Beaverbrook joined the Cabinet, in the spring of 1918, would have been still more exercised had they known the full scope of his ambitions. Like Little Red Riding Hood, they felt unease but had not yet spotted the teeth. James Gordon Bennett Jr of the *New York Herald* died that spring, having spent on himself some $30,000,000 extracted from the profits of the paper founded by his father; the result was that the terms of his will, which grandly decreed that the *Herald* should be published in perpetuity by his estate, could not be met, and the paper was put up for sale. Beaverbrook got in touch with his banker friend, Otto Kahn, secured his backing, and sent Blumenfeld to New York with $1,000,000 in his pocket to buy his old paper. Their grandiose scheme was to set up a joint Anglo-American newspaper enterprise, but they were outbid by a real estate and grocery chain tycoon, Frank Munsey. For once, Beaverbrook was under-informed about a business he wanted to buy; he did not know that the bank account of the Paris *Herald* contained a million dollars in cash.[1]

Had Beaverbrook bought the *Herald* – or the *Sunday Times*, for which he also negotiated – he might not have started the *Sunday Express*, as he did on 29 December 1918, with Lady Diana Manners pressing the button. It was an enterprise, wrote Beverley Baxter, 'launched with immense fervour by Beaverbrook and grave doubts by Blumenfeld'.[2] Beaverbrook's motive was commercial: the *Daily Express* was still losing money, though not much, and 'we believed that 7-day journalism would relieve our loss', Beaverbrook recalled. He thought, as other newspaper proprietors have thought since, that he could produce economies of scale by exploiting the resources of the daily paper and making everyone work harder – including Blumenfeld, whom he expected to edit or at least to supervise the new offshoot. He took on a staff of only six people and wedged them into two poky rooms divided by a glass partition on the second floor of the ramshackle *Express* building in Shoe Lane. Blumenfeld refused to work a seven-day week, however, and the paper's first issue, dominated by the results of the recent general election, excited nobody.

The feeble start of the *Sunday Express*, and the £500,000 of Beaverbrook's money that the new paper soon absorbed, made it still more vital to build on the wartime advance of the *Daily Express*. Back in 1902, when Blumenfeld left the *Daily Mail* for the *Express*, the future Lord Northcliffe, the man best qualified to judge, adopted his Napoleonic look, leaned back in his chair and told Blumenfeld that he was an idiot: the *Express* had no hope of prospering. The *Daily Mail* had a circulation of 1,200,000, and that was the limit of any paper's sales. In 1919, when Beaverbrook took over day-to-day control, the circulation of the *Express* was under 400,000. By 1929 it had risen by over a million copies to 1,590,336, and was poised to overtake the *Daily Mail*.

How was it done? The *Express* had not been a bad paper in 1911, when Aitken wrote a cheque for Blumenfeld in Monte Carlo. In those days, even an avowedly popular paper looked more serious than a 'serious' paper does now. The *Express* carried news on its front page – as it had from its first issue – but all the stories were single-column, and page one rarely carried a picture. For a halfpenny, the reader usually got ten pages. A news summary ran down column one, and society news of a formal kind – debutantes, comings and goings of titled persons, etc. – down column seven. Despite the single-column straitjacket Blumenfeld managed to give his front page a lively look, partly by using American typographical methods but mainly by exploiting the convention of the multi-storey headline. On 22 February 1912, for instance, with a coal strike in the offing, the *Express* carried this front-page story:

EGGED ON BY SOCIALISTS
PREACHING REVOLT TO THE WELSH MINERS
WILD WORDS
WHY SOUTH WALES IS A MENACE TO PEACE

Underneath, an *Express* man in Cardiff reported that a 'revolutionist' calling himself Captain Tupper who had made a 'sensational' speech to the local miners was not a captain at all. The phoney captain issued a writ, which Blumenfeld would have anticipated, thus giving the *Express* another front-page story five days later: 'THREATS FROM TUPPER'. To be egged on by socialists was the worst fate that Blumenfeld could imagine. He himself in 1908 had founded an Anti-Socialist Union, which organized meetings 'to counteract the fallacious statements so persistently put about by Socialist writers and speakers, particularly those who speak in parks and open spaces'. The word 'socialist', used as an offensive weapon, survived in the *Express* armoury for over half a century; after the Second World War Labour MPs were invariably called 'Socialist MPs'. But Blumenfeld was not unsympathetic to the miners, and the *Express* implored the coalmine owners as well as the miners to mend their ways.

Blumenfeld was proud of his headlines. As the 'wild words' example shows, telling the readers what to think before they read the story was a common *Express* practice even before Beaverbrook got hold of the paper. Sometimes the headlines read like abbreviated leading articles. When a play by Eden Phillpotts called *The Secret Woman* was censored by the Lord Chamberlain, exciting vigorous protests from actors and theatre managers, the front-page story in the *Express* was headlined:

THE *SCARLET* WOMAN

BANNED PLAY FULLY JUSTIFIES THE CENSOR

DULL AND COARSE

On the inside pages, the departments were much the same as in any paper today: more news – including a whole page entitled 'Tragedy, Pathos and Humour in the Courts' – a women's section ('Home Made Under Bodices'), leader page, Money Matters and plenty of sport. Blumenfeld was the first editor to recognize that sport sells papers, despite his own indifference to any sport except shooting (he was a good shot). The *Express* gave the Football Association Cup quarter finals of 1912 far more space than any paper would give the same event now, though public interest has increased. The soggy part of the paper was the leisure section. Blumenfeld scorned *The Times* for refusing to accept that readers wanted entertainment as well as news; he had learnt that lesson in his first job in New York. He learned it again from Northcliffe; on the *Express* leisure pages the influence of the *Daily Mail* was obvious. 'Popular Phrases: What They Mean' (for example, Ultima Thule) had the Northcliffeian ring. So did the competitions: £1.1s for a picture constructed from old postage stamps. But here the *Express* seemed to be aimed at quite different readers from those who read the politics. 'Telling a person's character from a handshake', with drawings, and interpreting the lines on a person's foot were not likely to attract someone who had pondered a Blumenfeld leader criticizing Asquith's Home Rule bill or the expansion of the German Fleet. The fact was that Blumenfeld had not quite got the measure of the new mass audience; he gave them what he imagined might amuse them, not what amused him. Nobody in his circle was likely to enter a '£5 Weekend Contest: What can you do with a match?'

In 1919, with Beaverbrook at the helm, the *Express* abruptly acquired a new bite. It still looked more or less the same, though the lead story often had a double-column headline and the crossheads were larger, breaking up the grey columns. But the paper had acquired a new, aggressive tone. The first of Beaverbrook's many manifestos was published over the leader columns, unsigned and in italics, on 20 March 1919:

The *Daily Express* is an independent paper attached to the interests of no party. It is opposed to privilege in any class of the community. It stands for freedom and equality of opportunity for all men. It believes in the abolition in peacetime of the Government's controls brought in by the war. It will uphold the right of the people to advance their own interests and shape their own lives, and will oppose all attempts to interfere with the simple and healthy pleasures of the nation.

The leaders became much more outspoken and confident. 'How dare Mr Austen Chamberlain lecture the public on economy? His own administration is up to its neck in a policy of public extravagance.' That was on the day of the manifesto. 'HUSH!' said the leader headline on 31 March. The country was being 'kept in the dark' about government actions in Egypt and Ireland. The leader ended: 'Any war censorship in a time of national reconstruction is a grave mistake. It resembles the other controls which strangle the birth of a new national life. Sweep them all away!' The Beaverbrookian leader was settling into the classic form initiated by Beaverbrook himself: short declaratory sentences, no qualifications, final exhortation. It was a style that scores of *Express* leader writers learned without difficulty to copy in the decades ahead.

In the same month Beaverbrook launched the first of his populist campaigns. The main story on page one was headlined, 'MONEY MADE OUT OF THE WAR' and gave examples, though it wisely named no names – one or two friends of Beaverbrook, such as James Dunn and Kipling, might have been among them. Inside, the leader conceded that the government needed money. But 'the *Daily Express* does not believe that it is possible to raise direct taxation in income tax'. Instead, why not take some of the war profits? Come to think of it, 'Why not take the whole hundred per cent? No man ought to make money out of a national calamity.' On the same day – the *Express* by this time often needed five short leaders to accommodate the flood of Beaverbrook opinions released by the peace – the paper attacked the hereditary principle whereby the sometimes inadequate sons of dead peers could automatically sit in the House of Lords.

There were other signs of a new vigour. On 26 March ('SPECTRE OF LENIN ALARMS PARIS') page one carried stories from named correspondents in Paris, Copenhagen, Geneva, Berlin and Helsingfors (Helsinki), and from unnamed special correspondents in Paris, Madrid and St John, Newfoundland. Perceval Phillips, later to appear as 'Sir Jocelyn Hitchcock' in Evelyn Waugh's *Scoop*, was in Cologne, with the British Army of the Rhine. From Warsaw, Mrs Cecil Chesterton filed on 'The Horrors of Bolshevism'. But, horrors or not, 'the *Daily Express* has always opposed a campaign in Russia'.

Before the month was out, the paper had a victory in another populist cause: it won a court case against a confidence trickster who had been selling non-existent plots of land near Brighton, in a district he called 'Anzac-on-Sea' (during the trial the authorities rechristened it Peacehaven, its present name). The *Express* congratulated itself. 'In our view it was the proper function of a great newspaper to protect the public, by the weapon of publicity, from an attempt to victimise the guileless.'

The features, too, were showing new life. Beachcomber had made his first appearance with his By The Way column – written first by D. B. Wyndham-Lewis and then, from 1924 for the next fifty years, by J. B. Morton – though to begin with it was a light commentary on current affairs, not farce. The paper had found a lasting asset in the cartoonist Strube and his Little Man, who was as nervous about socialism as Beaverbrook was. (Strube's oppressed Little Man was still oppressed a quarter of a century later, when his creator was perhaps the best-paid cartoonist in Fleet Street.) Strube, bringing in baskets of fruit for colleagues, Wyndham-Lewis with his stutter and delight in bad poetry, Morton, covered in mud from the country, and the prolific man of letters S. P. B. Mais, all at one time or another housed on a noisy upper floor of the *Express*, had started to give the paper a sense of knockabout enjoyment. The Court Gossip had moved off the front page into the women's pages, where it had been joined by Tea Table Talk – the dismal forerunner of the William Hickey gossip column: 'The Queen of Rumania's Desires', said one enticing headline, but what she desired was friendship between Rumania and England. More promising was 'The Supreme Test: Can the Dead have communication with the Living?' – a proposal for a spiritualist experiment launched by Sir Arthur Conan Doyle. 'Ready to Make the Tunnel. How Channel borings will be carried out' was a premature scoop.

Year by year, the outlines of the all-conquering *Express* increasingly emerged. The paper made its first profit in 1922, the year that Northcliffe died mad: it was selling 793,000 copies a day. Halfway through the decade, in 1925, with the price now a penny, the main outward change was in the layout. The seven-column headline had made its bow, and the body type was larger and varied, with a much jazzier impact. The paper looked sharp and confident. Innovations on the entertainment front since 1919 included aristocratic-sounding by-lines – Lady Kitty Vincent on fashion, and Lady Abdy; the adventures of Rupert the Bear; a serialized novel (the year started with Philip Gibbs); Beachcomber hitting his stride with a new method of bleaching hearse-plumes; a sports cartoon; a full page of photographs; and Shorts From the Courts (Policeman at Willesden: 'When charged he said, "I am drunk".' Magistrate: 'He was sober enough to know that. ') There was also the great new crossword craze, first introduced from the United States by the *Sunday Express* in 1924. 'The crossword,' said the *Express*, 'has conquered England . . . a great educational force.' The gossip column was still feeble, however; Tea Table Talk had been renamed The Talk of the Town, but the copy was still the same. The lead story on New Year's Day 1929 reported that the chief whip was going to Switzerland for a week's holiday; a photograph of the pretty Viscountess Ednam illustrated the news that she would be hunting regularly (she died the following year).

The paper was presenting itself more than ever as the tribune of the people, attacking the 'wholly inadequate service' of the railways, the incompetence and 'Christmas chaos' of the Post Office, and housing: 'The people need many things, but they need homes more than anything else. The *Daily Express* has denounced the London slums as the greatest scandal of our day. . . .'

Beaverbrook never had a conscious marketing strategy, and never needed one. With his 'never-ending thrust', as his fellow press baron Lord Camrose called it, he produced a newspaper that would interest him; and discovered that his interests were those of the masses. By the end of the decade the paper looked unstoppable, as it gave away a year's free insurance with 'extended protection' to all 'registered readers'. The whole paper now held together, with as much attention given to the back pages as to the front.

One of Beaverbrook's tricks was to build up writers in the same way that he built up politicians, including himself. His stars in 1929 were Beachcomber (' "I think he shows the greatest comic fertility of any Englishman" – Evelyn Waugh; "One, if not more than one, of England's greatest men" – P. G. Wodehouse'), H. V. Morton, Hannen Swaffer on the theatre, Strube, St John Ervine on books, and Trevor Wignall, paid a huge salary, on sport. The paper was wholesome. Sex was confined to the corset advertisements; and there was still no real gossip – the 1930 New Year's Day lead to what was now called The Talk of London reported that Sidney Webb, the Colonial Secretary, was giving a dinner party to his staff 'to establish friendly relations with them', which sounded like the caption to a Beerbohm cartoon but was recorded by 'The Dragoman' without irony. Politics, handed out in ever shorter and punchier leaders, was not tediously obtrusive – at least until the launch of the Empire Crusade. The *Daily Mail* found it hard to shake off the air of a lower middle-class paper addressed to junior clerks. The *Express*, spurred on by a proprietor who could simultaneously entertain the Bright Young People and deplore the London slums, was much more worldly, optimistic and classless.

RUNNING THE *DAILY EXPRESS*

There was nothing predestined about the success of London Daily Express Newspaper Ltd, or, as the group was commonly known, Express Newspapers. As Beaverbrook once said of another inventive proprietor, 'It's not all done by luck.' His first decision when he took over day-to-day control of his papers was to move into the *Express* building in Shoe Lane, where he worked in a vast room with windows on three sides that he had constructed for himself on the top floor, with views across the chimney pots to St Paul's and the Thames. Perhaps he was following Northcliffe's dictum about big rooms being the birthplace of big ideas. The room contained bookshelves stocked with the classics, a grand piano, a large divan, chairs with blue covers, a dining table, a desk surrounded by four electric heaters, and a telephone on the floor. 'Every night of his life Lord Beaverbrook dines here like a workman lunching on his job,' wrote an American reporter. 'Other newspaper owners have kept in touch with affairs by assiduous dining out. Lord Beaverbrook reverses the process and lets the mountain come to Mahomet by dining at home.'[3] His original motive for investing in newspapers may have been, as he said, political – to support Bonar Law. He may have put more money into the *Express* and *Sunday Express*, as he said, to protect his original investment. As he told a Northern Ireland journalist and MP, Sir Robert Lynn, he had come 'quite fresh' to the business, rather late in life, as a third career after finance and politics; but he never regretted it.[4] He became an addict. He did not, however, become an office fixture. Even when he was learning the business, months went by when he never went near Shoe Lane. Before and during the war he had his office in Lombard Street, in the City of London. Immediately after the war he made more use of his other office, in the Temple, between the Thames and Fleet Street: a sign of a shift of interest. In 1927 he abandoned his *Express* office altogether, likening himself to a shipbuilder 'who has built a ship but will not be her captain'; thereafter he rarely went near the building.[5] The telephone and the dictated memorandum were his preferred methods of stimulus and control. They saved time. It was the product, not the means of production, that concerned him. Besides, by using his home – whichever one he happened to be in – as an office, he could operate equally effectively in politics, finance and newspapers; any distractions were of his own choosing. Blumenfeld said of him in 1933 that, although he had learnt a lot since the early days and had become one of the world's foremost journalists, he was 'without a knowledge of the details'.[6]

To operate this method of day-to-day control without going to the office, he needed someone in the *Express* building on whom he could absolutely rely; and he found the ideal person in E. J. Robertson, who, in the opinion of impartial witnesses, was almost as important in the success of Beaverbrook newspapers as Beaverbrook himself. Robertson, another Canadian, was a student at the University of Toronto who had a vacation job as a desk clerk in a Toronto hotel when Beaverbrook first encountered him. He carried Beaverbrook's bags to his room; hence his later nickname, the Bell Hop. Beaverbrook came across him again during the war, when Robertson was in the Canadian Army records office. After the war he gave him a lowly job in the *Express* management, but rapidly promoted him to be general manager. Robertson was an austere figure; he worked for Beaverbrook for thirty-six years, ending up as chairman of Beaverbrook Newspapers, but maintained a strictly business relationship with him, always beginning his letters, 'Dear Lord Beaverbrook'. He never interfered with the editors, who in return came to trust and rely on him, a rocklike shelter in the office when a Beaverbrook hurricane was blowing outside. Like his proprietor, 'Robbie was a devil for saving the pence.' He thought it needlessly extravagant for foreign correspondents to include the word 'comma' in their filed copy, and once worked out that two hundred cabled commas cost more than £3. His shrewdness and parsimony allowed Beaverbrook to play the benefactor. 'We mustn't let that fellow Raarbertson make too much money,' Beaverbrook used to say as he handed out arbitrary bonuses to the staff.[7]

This teasing remark was characteristic of Beaverbrook's attitude to the business side of the paper. He wanted circulation, because he wanted influence; and he was ready to spend heavily to that end. In the early days after the war, when newsprint prices were very high, he paid a premium for better-quality paper. He certainly did not believe in wasting money, however. In 1926 the entire staff of the *Sunday Express* still consisted of four or five people crammed into one office, plus the editor in a room of his own; on Saturdays, they were supplemented by 'Saturday casuals'. But he did not see his papers as moneymaking machines. Through his substantial Canadian investments he had enough for his own needs, and if he needed more he made it outside the *Express* – for instance, by buying and selling a cinema chain. Early on, he stated the financial policy that he adhered to for forty years.

> I take a view of my own as to the responsibilities of newspapers. I think that when a newspaper shareholder has received a good return on his investment, any additional profits should not go to increased dividends, but should be devoted to improving the newspaper for the benefit of the reader and of the advertiser who uses it. It follows that I believe the *Daily Express* should not pay its maximum possible dividend until it is a perfect newspaper. Anyone who does not agree with that conception should not invest in the *Daily Express*.[8]

This attitude made him unique among the press proprietors who flourished between the wars. The fortunes of the two Astor brothers, Waldorf and Colonel J. J., came from outside newspapers, and they were not interested in making more money from the papers they owned, the *Observer* and *The Times*; but they knew nothing about journalism. The Berry brothers (Lord Camrose and Lord Kemsley) made their money from newspapers and continued to do so. So did Lord Northcliffe and his brother and successor Lord Rothermere. So did Lord Southwood, of Odhams and the *Daily Herald*. Of these, only Camrose and Northcliffe were journalists. Beaverbrook alone made his money outside newspapers and was also a journalist. One consequence was that he had more confidence than his rivals that vast circulations could be achieved by words alone. The ruinously expensive circulation wars of the twenties and thirties were launched most notably by J. S. Elias (later Lord Southwood) and the *Daily Herald*, with prize coupons and gifts and free insurance schemes; but Southwood was a manager, never a journalist, and his methods very nearly bankrupted his organization.

Beaverbrook had another advantage. He used his rivals' money to build up his own paper. After Northcliffe died in 1922, Rothermere set up the Daily Mail Trust as a public company. Beaverbrook had always been friendly with Rothermere, who had indeed encouraged him to take over the *Express* – when it seemed inconceivable that it would ever challenge the *Mail*. To ensure that the two proprietors thought twice about cutting one another's throats, Beaverbrook took a large stake in the Daily Mail Trust, and the Trust acquired a considerable holding in the *Express*. But since the Trust, which greatly prospered, paid substantial dividends, whereas the *Express* did not, the effect of the arrangement was that the Trust helped to finance the expansion of the *Express*. Beaverbrook became the second largest shareholder in the Trust, and refused offers to buy him out. 'I suppose in time the shares will become very valuable,' he wrote to a business friend in 1925, with prescience. He learned with satisfaction that the mineral deposits on a subsidiary company's land in Newfoundland were 'extremely valuable'.[9]

Thus it was an odd sort of competition. Beaverbrook pursued it with more energy than Rothermere. Even before Northcliffe's death the *Mail* had been coasting along, its stunts reflecting the proprietor's growing eccentricity, as in the case of the *Daily Mail* hat campaign, when Northcliffe gave a prize of £100 for a newly designed men's hat; the competition was won by a clerk in the Ministry of Health who suggested a shortened top hat with a dome, an absurd invention that Northcliffe strove in vain to popularize. And Northcliffe's death certainly helped Beaverbrook. Rothermere was a difficult, gloomy man, a devoted capitalist and unreconstructed conservative with a misplaced belief in his own power and importance. Before long, the two stalwarts who had done most to build up the *Mail*'s dominance, apart from Northcliffe himself, resigned – Thomas Marlowe, the editor since 1896, and Sir Andrew Caird, the managing director. With no one to restrain him, Rothermere took up the cause of Hungary and campaigned for the revision of its post-war boundaries; no one knew why; Hungarian monarchists wanted him as king, a successor to the Habsburgs. Combined with his welcome for Mussolini, all this was of great benefit to the *Express*, making Beaverbrook's excesses seem mild by comparison.

Rothermere remained curiously unconcerned as the threat from the *Express* developed. Outwardly, the *Mail* appeared to be competing full blast, with free gifts and cheap insurance policies for readers. Behind the scenes, Rothermere was slashing the paper's expenses and reducing the editorial columns to make room for more advertising. His social life was quite remote from the paper, as he spent his profits on Rolls Royces and mistresses. Beaverbrook's social life by contrast produced gossip and articles for the *Express*. He dramatized the contest. 'I am locked in a life and death struggle with the *Daily Mail*', he wrote in 1928 to the American manufacturers of a new way of transmitting photographs.[10] Meanwhile Rothermere, always the single-minded capitalist, was saying that even if

215

the *Express* went ahead of the *Mail* it would not be so bad for his shareholders because they had a foot in both camps.[11]

The two men had quite different attitudes to expansion, which again worked to Beaverbrook's advantage. Rothermere liked to be the biggest proprietor as well as the richest. When, on a visit to New York, he read reports that the Berry brothers owned more newspapers than he did, he at once announced that he proposed to start new papers in Manchester, Sheffield, Cardiff, Glasgow, Bristol and Newcastle to challenge them: a disastrously expensive, and doomed, enterprise. Beaverbrook concentrated his fire. Having started the *Sunday Express*, he extended his empire only once more, in 1923. Sir Edward Hulton lay dying. The Berry brothers wanted to buy his papers, but were short of cash. J. B. Joel, the South African millionaire, offered to lend them what they needed. But they failed to realize the need for haste. While they delayed, Beaverbrook walked from Cherkley to Hulton's bedside nearby with a cheque book, and bought the papers for Rothermere and himself. From the division, he emerged with the *Evening Standard*. Thereafter he never seriously sought to extend his group, though he had a controlling interest in the *Glasgow Evening Citizen*, installed machinery so that he could print the *Express* in Manchester, and in 1928 started a satellite of the *Daily Express* in Scotland, the *Scottish Daily Express*. Three papers – a morning, an evening and a Sunday, one or other of them always just published or about to be published – were enough even for someone of his phenomenal energy.

OWNERS AND EDITORS

To succeed with the *Daily Express* Beaverbrook naturally depended on good editors, and he must have chosen astutely since there were only three in forty years: Blumenfeld, Beverley Baxter and Arthur Christiansen, who retired in 1956. But none of them was an editor in the nineteenth-century sense. Blumenfeld thought that the subordination of editors to proprietors was one of the principal changes in the newspaper business during the twentieth century. 'Gone are the days when the Editor was the oracle whom no one in or out of the office denied the right to print or omit what seemed best to him,' he wrote in 1933. He instanced Delane of *The Times*, Greenwood of the *St James's Gazette*, E. T. Cook of the *Pall Mall Gazette* and William Mudford who 'reigned like an Eastern potentate' over the *Standard*. He recalled how one of Mudford's predecessors, H. A. Gwynne, had informed Lord Dalziel, when he took financial control of the paper in 1910, that his place was in the board room, not the editorial department. Tell a newspaper owner these days that his influence should be confined to the board room, said Blumenfeld, 'and you'll take an indefinite holiday with, of course, a large but final cheque to compensate you for your enforced departure'.[12]

Blumenfeld wrote from experience. Nightly in Shoe Lane he barked out his abrupt orders and laid down rules: no sentence should begin with the word 'and'; 'commence' was banned. But it was not long before he found his independence slipping away. His son summed up the role he came to occupy: Blumenfeld supplied the professional techniques, and Beaverbrook supplied the controversy – the political 'punch'.[13]

No doubt fissures were inevitable, given Beaverbrook's confidence in his own often unorthodox political views and Blumenfeld's relative orthodoxy. There were deeper reasons as well. If Northcliffe's *Daily Mail* started the rise of the mass-circulation papers, it was the First World War that saw the true beginnings of the modern newspaper industry. In the nineteenth and early twentieth centuries the press had often relied, secretly, on party favours or subsidies; Northcliffe was the exception to the rule. During the war, the press acquired unprecedented influence as the public's only source of information. After the war, the number of newspapers decreased as the serious evening papers with strong party affiliations, the *Westminster Gazette* and its fellows, slowly died, while prospects for mass-circulation papers, which relied much less on political coverage to attract readers, improved; and mass-circulation papers did not depend on party subsidies. So party control over the press sharply declined; now it was the politicians who became much more dependent on the newspapers. The private political correspondence of the time shows a new anxiety and watchfulness about 'newspaper agitation'; Lloyd George went out of his way to build newspapers into his personal system of support; he was the first Prime Minister to do so. Proprietors acquired extra influence and importance, while editors sank down the scale. All these tendencies were exemplified in the way Beaverbrook ran his papers. It was he, not Blumenfeld, who entertained and talked politics and plotted at Cherkley with Lloyd George or Churchill. It was he who supplied the bread and butter, as Christiansen put it, and his editors – since readers cannot live by bread alone – who were required to supply the cakes and ale.

As his public platform Beaverbrook mainly used the *Sunday Express*, writing signed columns there regularly to help circulation. He expected the *Daily Express* to echo his views silently, as it did. Blumenfeld had been accustomed to publicize the policies of the Conservative Party, with occasional slight deviations; but he soon found himself 'obliged more and more to publicise only those favoured by Beaverbrook'.[14] In 1919, when Beaverbrook made his first breach with the coalition government by attacking Churchill's policy of military intervention against the Bolsheviks, the *Daily Express* also attacked Churchill; yet in private Blumenfeld was as anti-Communist as Churchill and as fearful of the spread of Communism. On Ireland, after Beaverbrook had become a Home Ruler, Blumenfeld privately remained on the side of the Unionists, supporting his friend Carson, opposing compromise, and even approving of the Black and Tans. But it was the view of the proprietor, not the editor, that was reflected by the *Daily Express*.

Proprietor and editor differed most seriously over Baldwin. Long before Beaverbrook took over the *Express*, Blumenfeld and Baldwin had become close friends. Baldwin spent weekends with Blumenfeld at his home in Essex, dropped in at the *Daily Express* 'to gossip', and dined with him at the Carlton Club, of which Blumenfeld had become the first journalist member in 1911 – a sign of his closeness to the Conservative Party stalwarts. Blumenfeld helped to get Baldwin his first political post. In 1916 he suggested to Bonar Law, when he became Chancellor of the Exchequer, that Baldwin would make him a good parliamentary private secretary, an office of more importance, and greater opportunities, than its title implied, since the Financial Secretary to the Treasury was a member of the House of Lords and Baldwin spoke in the Commons in his stead.[15] Six years later, when the dying Bonar Law resigned, Baldwin was Prime Minister – one of the quickest ascents of the greasy pole in British history. The *Daily Express* welcomed his appointment in a leader headed 'The Right Choice'. But the attacks and criticisms soon started, and they were directed not by Blumenfeld but by Beaverbrook.

THE THREE-LEGGED STOOL

Apart from the grief Beaverbrook felt at Bonar Law's death, the disappearance of a Prime Minister and party leader who trusted him and used his talents made him henceforward an erratic force in politics. Churchill said that Beaverbrook as a political figure was like a three-legged stool, the legs being himself, his newspapers and Bonar Law. The implication was that Beaverbrook without Bonar Law lacked stability, and there was something in it. He himself wrote soon afterwards: '. . . his death broke with me a vital connection with Downing Street. Something was severed for ever in my political associations. I had never cared much for the purely political life, but Bonar Law's charm, his urbanity, his wisdom, his firm and reasonable attitude towards all problems, held me like a silken chain.'[16]

It did not take long for Beaverbrook to realize that he had no influence with Baldwin. Within two weeks of Bonar Law's death Baldwin, after a mere six months as Prime Minister and with a secure majority, suddenly in the autumn of 1923 called an election. Beaverbrook was outraged. He wrote: 'I saw Mr Baldwin once at the time this decision was being taken . . . he was determined not to listen to an outside and contrary opinion. In consequence the Conservative forces, painfully accumulated by Bonar Law, marched straight to dissolution.' He also maintained that Baldwin deliberately ignored the dying Bonar Law's advice: 'It is quite untrue that Bonar Law approved of the "rushed" election. He disapproved of it profoundly. Those who for interested political motives declared the contrary at the time were saying something which was not in accordance with fact.'[17]

Baldwin decided to fight the election – called for early December – on protection, but without special terms for the Empire. This to Beaverbrook was a travesty of the policy he had been urging on Bonar Law; and when he learned what Baldwin was proposing he made another attempt to convince Lloyd George, then on a lecture tour of America, that if he would only espouse Tariff Reform he could once more become Prime Minister. Lloyd George was tempted; and on his return there was a gathering at Cherkley.

Over the weekend of 12 November Beaverbrook brought together the core of the old coalition government: Lloyd George, Birkenhead, Churchill and Austen Chamberlain. Also present were Lord Wargrave (the former Edward Goulding), Evelyn Fitzgerald – then engaged to Helen Drury, Gladys's sister – and Arnold Bennett, who wrote unflatteringly to his nephew about the conclave: 'I never heard principles or the welfare of the country mentioned. Still I had a great lark. "Arnold," said Max to me this morning, while I sat in his bathroom as he laved his limbs, "You've seen Hell with the lid off". Well, I had.'[18]

Later, Beaverbrook maintained piously that the only purpose of the conclave had been to keep the imperialist movement alive and to try to persuade Austen Chamberlain to fight for his father's great cause, but the very fact that such powerful former allies were meeting under his roof implied an attempt to outmanoeuvre Baldwin. If that was Beaverbrook's aim, it failed. Austen Chamberlain's sense of party loyalty made him decline to lead any anti-Baldwin movement, and when on his return to London Arnold Bennett let slip to a journalist the news about the house party, uproar broke out in the Tory press. Beaverbrook was depicted once again as master manipulator and intriguer. In the end, although in his newspapers he attacked Baldwin's decision to hold the election and his failure to pursue the imperial cause, he did, somewhat half-heartedly, back him; 'Making the best of a bad election' was the *Sunday Express* headline, and readers were sternly warned against voting Labour. Beaverbrook declined, however, to contribute to Conservative election funds, although he did pay the expenses for two 'needy candidates who are sound Imperialists'. Shortly before the polls, Beaverbrook dined with Churchill and bet him that Labour would form a government. He won. Baldwin was defeated, and the first Labour government, headed by Ramsay MacDonald, came into power with Liberal support.

In the spring of 1924 Beaverbrook began to question Baldwin's competence in public. In the *Sunday Express* in February he wrote: 'Mr Baldwin is in the descending scale of values. Now that he is stripped of power and patronage he must rely on his own capabilities. His qualifications have so far proved of second rank . . . far below the level of a Prime Minister or a Leader of the Opposition.' Meanwhile Blumenfeld – a sign of growing differences with his employer – was still expressing admiration for Baldwin, though not in the *Daily Express*. In an American magazine, *Town and Country*, he praised Baldwin as the representative of 'a new spirit in English public life'. Dissatisfied, Beaverbrook swung this way and that. But for all his tinkering with party realignments, his lingering hopes for a Lloyd George comeback, and his readiness in his newspapers to give the new Labour government a chance, he knew that a Conservative revival was his best hope. The obstacle was Baldwin. He summed up his views in the spring of 1924 in a letter to his American newspaperman correspondent, Arthur Brisbane: 'All parties tend to be fissiparous – but the underlying reality is this: England (free of the Irish vote) wants by its nature, and wants now, a conservative government. It only casts off such a government because of follies and idiocies like those of Baldwin.'[19]

Meanwhile the image of Baldwin as a straightforward innocent under threat from malign press barons was spreading. The brilliant New Zealand cartoonist David Low had started to depict Baldwin as a babe lost in Tariff Reform Woods, knees knocking, with two sinister figures, one stout and bloated, one small and gnome-like, lurking behind him, daggers out: Rothermere and Beaverbrook. As Baldwin struggled to recover his lost authority and regain his ground, the menace of the press lords gave him a promising theme. Like Bonar Law he was determined, on principle as well as for sound tactical reasons, to make a clean break with what was widely regarded as the murky and discredited coalition network of favours and to provide, or seem to provide, open honest politics, with no hidden deals.

Beaverbrook always maintained that Baldwin was much less straightforward than he seemed. In May 1924 the *People* published what purported to be an exclusive interview with Baldwin. It contained a savage attack on what he called the Trust Press and was headlined: 'Baldwin turns and rends his critics.' First he attacked socialism and promised sound Tory social reform, then he attacked 'the sinister and cynical combination' of Lloyd George, Churchill and Birkenhead' – with a special cut at Birkenhead's renowned over-indulgence: 'If his health does not give way he will be a liability to the Party' – and then turned to Beaverbrook and Rothermere. 'For myself I do not mind. I care not what they say or think,' he was quoted as saying. 'They are both men that I would not have in my house. I do not respect them.'

The references to Beaverbrook were contemptuous.

> . . . The last time I spoke to Lord Beaverbrook was at Bonar's funeral. He had contracted a curious friendship with Bonar and had got his finger into the pie, where it had no business to be. He got hold of much information which he used in ways it was not intended [*sic*].
>
> When I came in that stopped. I know I could get his support if I were to send for him and talk things over with him. But I prefer not. That sort of thing does not appeal to me. . . .
>
> . . . What do these intriguers want? Simply to go back to the old dirty kind of politics! Not while I'm leader of the Party.[20]

Although within twenty-four hours Baldwin denied that he had said any of this, the damage was done. Moreover the *People* (then edited by Hannen Swaffer, who went to work for Beaverbrook eighteen months later) stood by its story, and other papers commented on how like the Conservative leader the remarks sounded. The *Morning Post* said in an editorial: 'There were some things which we should not wish unsaid, whether they were said by Mr Baldwin or came from the fertile brain of the journalist.' Outwardly, Beaverbrook was to accept Baldwin's claims that he had been misrepresented, calling the alleged interview 'incredible and absurd'.[21] But as a newspaperman he must have known that the chances of the *People* having fabricated such remarks were not strong. Either inadvertently or on purpose, Baldwin let his guard down and was then obliged to limit the damage in the usual way.

In the autumn of 1924 the Ramsay MacDonald government was defeated in the Commons when the Liberals withdrew their support. The election that followed was marked by allegations of Communist infiltration, the Zinoviev letter purporting to bring instructions from Moscow, and the general cry of Red Peril, especially in the Rothermere press. Beaverbrook was not convinced by the Red Peril campaign and continued to hope that the Liberals under Lloyd George might have a part to play, or that another leader than Baldwin might somehow emerge; again, he declined to contribute to the Conservative funds, and wrote to Younger, the party chairman, on 29 October: 'If you can conceive any plan by which I would contribute to the expenses of Conservative candidates who are definitely and publicly opposed to the Baldwin leadership, I would do my best to fall in with it. They would have to be pledged to work hard to obtain a new leader.'[22] Nevertheless, once again he backed the Conservatives in his newspapers.

The Conservative victory was conclusive; Baldwin, despite all his mistakes, was triumphant. On 30 October Beaverbrook sent a sour message to Rothermere: 'I congratulate you on your magnificent victory. You have made the new Baldwin ministry now control it if you can.'[23]

Baldwin wisely decided to consolidate his position by offering posts in the new government to former coalition supporters. Beaverbrook left a comic account of how Churchill returned to office. Although he was hoping for a job, Churchill knew that he was still regarded with deep suspicion by many Conservatives – he had, after all, not so long ago been a Liberal – and feared that he might be offered only a minor post. He decided to go down to Chartwell, his country house in Kent, to await developments; on the way he called on Beaverbrook.

. . . the sole subject was his prospects. . . . His last words to me on parting were to this effect – unless he was offered such a first rate post that hesitation would be absurd, he would not accept anything at all without consulting me first . . . .

On the day that the big Cabinet appointments were settled, it so happened that I was giving a dinner party, arranged long before anyone could have had any notice that this would be a day of fate. The guests were Churchill and Birkenhead and Freddie Guest. All the day had been agog with Cabinet making. Winston was the first guest to arrive. 'Well,' I said 'Are you in?' Meaning of course have you really got something worth while. 'Oh yes, I'm in all right' – with satisfaction! 'What have you got?' 'I am sorry' replied Churchill, 'But I would prefer not to disclose that just now.'

When Birkenhead arrived, he told Beaverbrook at once that he was the new Secretary of State for India, and on hearing that Churchill's lips were sealed he protested vigorously.

'You've been consulting with Max for weeks past in the most intimate way, you've been taking his help and advice and support. You were ready enough to appeal to him in your despair and now you neglect him in your hour of triumph.' . . .

Churchill was rather abashed and said, 'Well, I will tell you.' I said 'No, no – if you tell me I will publish it tomorrow in the *Daily Express* – I won't hear it.' . . . Dinner was not very happy.

Eventually Churchill did divulge the great news. ' "I am Chancellor of the Exchequer", he cried out. I replied, "You have told me against my will – and if I hear it from any other source but you tonight I shall publish it." ' Soon afterwards, Beaverbrook was telephoned by another new Cabinet member – very likely Sam Hoare – and was able to tease Churchill further by first announcing that now he felt free to inform the *Express*, and then relenting.

Then came the parting scene – the climax of the evening's drama. Birkenhead renewed his upbraidings of Churchill's conduct in refusing me the original information. . . . He pictured Churchill clinging to me, seeking and accepting my support and then throwing me over in the hour of victory.
   Suddenly a kind of flash of intuition came to me and I made a wild but shrewd guess. 'I don't believe Churchill is really to blame. He promised somebody he wouldn't tell me before he came – yes – he promised his wife.' Churchill said, 'You are right. She drove me to the door of your house.'[24]

THE WOLF AND THE LAMB

For all the camaraderie of this exchange, it represented a turning point not just in the friendship between Beaverbrook and Churchill but in Beaverbrook's relationship to mainstream Tory politics. For fourteen years he had been inside the magic circle. Now, he was increasingly on the outside.

Within weeks of the election Beaverbrook and Churchill were at odds again, over the government's first budget. Churchill put the country back on the Gold Standard, which Beaverbrook considered a disaster; he forecast that exports would decline and unemployment rise. This was a genuine policy disagreement, but it also brought home to Beaverbrook his exclusion from the inner ring. Although he reckoned, with good reason, that he knew more about financial matters than Churchill, his advice was not sought – and, when proffered, it was ignored. Despite all the support he had given Churchill in his attempts to get back into politics, he was evidently not to have any special leverage in return. The *Express* attacked the budget fiercely.

Churchill was well aware that Beaverbrook resented his decision not to take him into his confidence. When Beaverbrook was putting together *Politicians and the Press*, his first attempt at contemporary political history, he sent drafts and proofs to the people concerned. Churchill tried to explain why he had been kept in the dark.

> You then advised me to tell Rothermere and Burnham [proprietor of the *Daily Telegraph*] and presumably yourself, the outline of the Budget some time before it was announced to Parliament. You said – and I do not doubt it – that strict secrecy would have been preserved and that a friendly reception would in all probability have been assured. You told me that Bonar had disclosed Baldwin's budget to you and Rothermere, and that you had backed it up and secured it a favourable reception, with much else of an intimate and private character. I weighed carefully all you said, but I could not feel that my position was in any way the same as Bonar Law's. He was Prime Minister and Party leader, and therefore free to use his judgment in the communication of secrets as he thought best for the interests of the Government and of the country. An ordinary Chancellor of the Exchequer has no such latitude and would be bound to obtain the assent of the Prime Minister before adopting any such course. You and Bonar lived not only on friendly, but fraternal terms; and you were devoted to his political interests, which in turn were identical with those of the Government. Very different indeed was, and is, your attitude towards the Chief it is my duty to serve. I therefore made up my mind definitely not to impart my plans to anyone outside the indispensable official circle.[25]

Churchill went on to say that perhaps, as Joseph Chamberlain used to maintain, it was better for friends to suspend personal relations when they were politically at odds.

In the aftermath of these arguments, Churchill and Beaverbrook summed up in two remarkable letters how each saw the other. Churchill's letter was the more relaxed; he used a biblical analogy well chosen to appeal to Beaverbrook.

> The whole of our relations during the present year have been those of the Wolf and the Lamb. The Wolf has made repeated and extremely spiteful attacks upon the Lamb and has avowedly compassed his destruction. The Lamb, on the other hand, conscious not only of his own innocence but of the strength of the fold, and sustained by the sympathy of the Shepherd and

the other Sheep, has preserved a moody silence not, however, unaccompanied by some complacency.

Rather stiffly, Beaverbrook wrote back:

I will tell you my exact attitude – though I expect you will think that I deceive myself.

I have no personal ill-feeling against Baldwin whatsoever. I have never felt the slightest rancour. I simply think of him in exactly the same terms that you and I did (this is not a debating score) in 1923. You take a 1925 view of him, whereas I remain fixed in my 1923 and 1924 opinion. It is quite possible or probable that you are right and I am wrong; but my judgment then and my judgment now has nothing to do with personal feelings. It is based on a cold analysis of public qualities.

And my opposition to you, you know very well that it is not a personal matter at all. I felt very strongly about the return to the Gold Standard and fought you for that reason.

As for his attitude towards the government in general:

Believe me I would far rather be in harmony with than opposed to a Conservative executive. But if I am expected to conform blindly to anything that executive may choose to do, however wrong I may think it, I would rather go back to my own little village in Canada – where there is good fishing.

I admired your bit of imagery about the shepherd, his sheep and the wolf. Do not believe too much in some of the sheep that are in the pasture with you. The wolf does not bite – just howls. . . .[26]

In the later 1920s, Beaverbrook had little choice but to content himself with howling – in his newspapers, his first two political books and his correspondence. As his political life dwindled, his journalistic and personal life became ever busier. And as always in times of frustration, he fretted about his health; early in 1926 he declined an invitation to stay with Churchill on health grounds, although he received a full account of the weekend from Sam Hoare. There was usually someone well placed to keep him informed. In May 1926, during the nine-day General Strike that paralysed the normal life of the country, Beaverbrook, though blaming the strike directly on the government's economic policy, none the less helped Churchill bring out his *British Gazette* by lending him workers from the *Daily Express*. But they fell out badly when Churchill tried to commandeer the Beaverbrook press's supply of newsprint. By the end of the year they were back on easy terms, and Churchill was delighted with Beaverbrook's Christmas present of an American refrigerator. At the beginning of 1927 he sent Beaverbrook a warm and prescient letter:

I have a vy deep regard for you and feel the full attraction of yr vivid, genial, loyal and dominating personality. I always enjoy myself in yr company and look forward to all our meetings. The difficulty of my being in the centre of a government to which you have every right to be opposed, has I rejoice to think ceased to be any obstacle to our personal intimacy. . . . As life flows on, one does not make new friends, or meet many people from whose society real pleasure is to be gained. . . . Some day the wheel may turn – it surely will – and political action may superimpose itself on bright companionship. In the main and on the greatest issues I expect we shd be together.[27]

BLUMENFELD REMOVED

Beaverbrook was not the only person cut off from Downing Street by Baldwin. As the mutual hostility grew, Blumenfeld found that he too was kept at a distance by his old friend. Besides, he was forced to explain his paper's heterodox policies to his fellow members of the Carlton Club. His stock response was that the policies were not his but Beaverbrook's. Urged to break with him, he replied that he could do more good by staying than by resigning. Baldwin thought he had 'sold his soul' to Beaverbrook.[28]

Having turned Blumenfeld into a 'paid apologist', as he was later described by a student of his career, Beaverbrook began to wonder whether he was still the right man to be running the *Daily Express*. Beaverbrook no longer needed a politically sophisticated editor with good connections. Possessed by what Blumenfeld called 'demonic industry', Beaverbrook felt the paper needed new zest. Quite apart from his political unadventurousness, Blumenfeld was too serious-minded to throw himself with any enthusiasm into the new cut-throat circulation wars. Beaverbrook did not start them, but he relished them; when he failed to persuade Elias of the *Daily Herald* to call a truce, he drew an imaginary sword, ran it at Elias's chest and told him with glee, 'Very well, Elias, this means wa-ar!'[29]

Beaverbrook also began to have doubts about Blumenfeld's stamina, and mentioned his reasons in a conversation with Lloyd George, which Bruce Lockhart, a new Beaverbrook recruit, recorded in his diary: 'Max, referring to Snowden and Carson, both of whom have had prostate gland operations, declared that after this operation a man was no good either mentally or physically. He instanced R. D. Blumenfeld.' Blumenfeld had a prostate operation in the autumn of 1922, and when complications followed spent two months in a nursing home.[30]

In 1924, Beaverbrook in effect replaced Blumenfeld. He had already deprived him of financial control by putting in Robertson as general manager. Now he deprived him of editorial control, replacing him with the Canadian Beverley Baxter, called 'The Piano-tuner' because he, a would-be musician, was playing the piano on a transatlantic liner when Beaverbrook met and hired him in 1920 for the *Sunday Express*. Blumenfeld was kicked upstairs and became editor-in-chief of the *Express* and *Sunday Express*, but Baxter was required merely to listen to his advice, not to obey his directions. Blumenfeld retained 'an advisory capacity only', Robertson assured Beaverbrook.[31]

More unpleasantness followed when Blumenfeld quarrelled with Beaverbrook about money. Although he owned 1000 *Express* preference shares, and was supposed to be entitled to a quarter of the *Express* profits, he had never received a penny beyond his salary. Beaverbrook countered by arguing that the *Express* policy of ploughing any profits back into the business was to the advantage of all. When Blumenfeld continued to complain Beaverbrook bought his shares, which gave Blumenfeld several thousand pounds but left him with a continuing feeling of resentment towards Beaverbrook that grew in tandem with the paper's profits. Nevertheless he hung on. In 1926 Lord Camrose offered to put him in charge of a chain of London papers, and his wife urged him to accept; she thought, like many wives of Beaverbrook employees, that Beaverbrook was too demanding; but Blumenfeld decided, at the age of sixty-two, to stay with the devil he knew.

Worse was to come. In August 1929 Blumenfeld returned from holiday to find Baxter installed in his office, exercising his powers. Bitterly 'hurt and angry', he wrote to Beaverbrook saying he found it hard to believe that after twenty-seven years at the *Express* there should be, overnight, such an 'attempt at humiliating one who bore the brunt of the battle for so many years almost alone'. Beaverbrook did not relent. He pretended that the decision was not his but Robertson's. To preserve Blumenfeld's dignity Beaverbrook retained him as chairman of the Express Newspapers board, so that he appeared still to be at the heart of the expanding empire. But he went to the paper less and less, and instead consoled himself by writing books.

He stayed on the board for many years, remained on terms with Robertson, and never entirely lost touch with Beaverbrook. On special occasions he would write Beaverbrook a note, sometimes of commiseration, as when a member of the family died, and sometimes of congratulation; and Beaverbrook always sent a note back, in warm terms. But Blumenfeld did not think of the long association with unalloyed pleasure. According to his son, Blumenfeld came to regret that he had asked his young friend Max Aitken to save the *Express* from folding, even though he recognized that he had had little other choice. He had realized that his fate was tied to a whirlwind, but thought his age and experience would enable him to ride it. Instead, though readier than most to stand up to Beaverbrook, he found he was never able to influence him. At the end of his life, his son said, he looked back with 'pain but no bitterness'.[32]

Blumenfeld suffered, but the hard fact was that once he was moved aside, and Robertson was running the business side of the *Express* and Baxter the editorial, Beaverbrook had the sort of arrangement that suited him. He owed Blumenfeld a great deal and had to treat him with some circumspection, whereas he owed Robertson and Baxter nothing: on the contrary, they owed everything to him. Beaverbrook liked dependants.

Baxter made no bones about his status. He was a good popular journalist who took the trade more lightly than his predecessor, and enjoyed the social rewards of editing more than the editing itself (he liked to bring his theatre guests into the office, all of them in evening dress). Interviewed by the *World's Press News* about Beaverbrook, he said flippantly, 'He is Allah, and the rest of us are his prophets.'[33] Baxter's successor positively boasted about his subordination to Beaverbrook. 'I am in many ways his creation,' Arthur Christiansen wrote. 'Beaverbrook used newspapers to further his own beliefs and [I] made the policy attractive to the people by presentation.' He did more than that: he was a highly successful, and, within his limits, creative editor, a genuine romantic who loved newspapers and the company of journalists, and he understood how to keep his staff contented. But his relations with Beaverbrook were essentially as he candidly described them. He called Beaverbrook 'sir'.

Of all modern proprietors, Beaverbrook kept his editors on the shortest rein. He had a telephone at his side wherever he went and used it constantly, ringing the office with ideas, praise, blame and gossip paragraphs. He wrote as he spoke, and could dictate a coherent leader, or at any rate a leader that could quickly be made coherent, at four hundred words a minute. When crossing the Atlantic, once the ship had sailed out of telephone range of England he telephoned the *Express* office in New York. In London, he would summon his editors and take them for walks: in the early days of the *Sunday Express*, he and Blumenfeld would patrol Hyde Park looking for women readers. Christiansen used to try to take notes on the walks. All senior members of Beaverbrook's staff lived on the end of a thread that, when twitched, drew them into line. Usually he made his wishes extremely plain. Christiansen, when editor of the northern edition of the *Express*, was summoned to Stornoway House, where he found Beaverbrook sitting on a narrow veranda overlooking Green Park in the spring sunshine. He wanted Christiansen to be assistant editor of the *Express* in London. The *Express* already had one assistant editor, Vaughan Wilkins.

Beaverbrook: 'You will be the junior.'

Christiansen: 'In that case I would prefer to stay in Manchester. Wilkins and I do not see eye to eye.'

Beaverbrook: 'I am sorry to hear this. I hope you will change your mind. I would like you to do so.'

Christiansen, feeling the twitch, yielded. Then Beaverbrook broke the news to Baxter.

Beaverbrook: 'I want you to know that Christiansen is coming to London as assistant editor of the *Daily Express*.'

Baxter: 'If that is so, then I resign as editor.'

Beaverbrook: 'Just the same, Christiansen is coming to London as assistant editor.'

Baxter: 'In that case I withdraw my resignation.'[34]

Why did they put up with it? Part of the answer is money. Christiansen, the son of a Liverpool shipwright, joined the *Express* and at once moved into a four-storey house in St John's Wood with parquet floors and a double drawing room. As editor, he received unexpected windfalls – cash to take his wife on holiday; or £1000 out of the blue. Beaverbrook took trouble with presents, handing out cheques, or first editions, or holidays. 'He knew what you wanted before you knew it yourself. That was one of his methods of man-management,' said George Malcolm Thomson, who worked closely with him for thirty-five years.[35] But money and presents were only half the story. No other proprietor, Christiansen thought, would have given him the same freedom to practise his journalistic skills.

The excitement of working for a paper with a quickly rising circulation was another part of it. Besides, Beaverbrook generated his own excitement: a royal command to dine with fashionable women and celebrated men; a message of extravagant praise; a veiled threat; above all his capacity to make his staff, particularly its younger members, feel that each of them was engaged with him in an adventure of high importance: '. . . these cubs are sharpening their claws on the world's news; taking on jobs which used only to be given to men full of years and timidity,' he announced in his own paper, to the great satisfaction of the cubs. The *Express*, he constantly proclaimed, was the paper of youth. Like Lloyd George, he had the gift of making anyone he wished to impress feel that he or she was about to occupy a special role in Beaverbrook's life, as he asked brief, direct questions and listened with every appearance of close attention to the answers – provided they were equally brief. Consulting people was one of the ways he lured flies into his web. 'Magnetism' was a word often applied to him. If he was disappointed or thwarted in getting his own way, he would lapse into self-pity. 'This is where it hurts,' he would repeat wearily, clutching his small round belly. 'This is where it hurts.'[36]

Christiansen's first sight of him was during the General Strike of 1926, when Beaverbrook and his 'top men', as he liked to call them, walked unannounced into the *Express* composing room. Beaverbrook, then forty-seven, was seen by the young Christiansen as

> . . . a little man with a large head who seemed to me a bit lost in the crowd. . . . I got a firm, dry handshake and a meaningful stare, but no word passed between us. I remember that stare perfectly well; I have seen it on countless occasions since. It is an all-embracing probe by the world's most inquisitive, penetrating, curious eyes. It sizes up the characters of newcomers. It diagnoses the 'what-mood-is-he-in?' attitude of his cronies and his colleagues in business. It invariably governs his conduct of the subsequent proceedings.

Christiansen thought Beaverbrook changed not at all over a quarter of a century, either in character or in appearance. Soon after he settled in England he ceased to fuss about his clothes; and from then until the end of his life he wore the same blue serge suits, the same white shirts (sometimes with frayed collars) with buttoned sleeves, not cuff-links, the same brown shoes, the same loose and careless knot in his tie, the same black trilby hat and drab black overcoat.

Dictatorial though he was, he knew he had to allow his editors and journalists a certain scope. 'Like every good journalist he has to be given plenty of latitude to get good work out of him,' he wrote of the *Express* cinema correspondent. 'It is impossible,' he told his friend Jimmy Rothschild, who was irritated by an *Express* story about his betting on horses, 'for me to issue an absolute instruction about the publication of news which leaves the editor no discretion whatsoever. No good man would stay on such conditions – unless I went down to the office and edited the paper personally every day. Short of that the Editor-in-Charge cannot be absolutely tied down by orders.'[37]

News was one thing; policy was quite another, especially on the *Daily Express*, where Beaverbrook was not only in full control but wished to be seen as being in full control. Those present at a dinner at Stornoway House guessed that the writing was on the wall for Beverley Baxter when Beaverbrook overheard him, in conversation with a pretty woman, claiming credit for inventing the phrase 'Empire Free Trade'. Beaverbrook's 'face went black' and he was so angry that the table fell silent in embarrassment.[38]

'DRIVE-DRIVE-DRIVE'

One of the results of running the politics himself was that he was largely indifferent to the politics of those whom he hired. The journalists he privately most respected were those who, like himself, moved in the great world and whose views were taken seriously: men like J. L. Garvin or J. A. Spender. But there was no room for such powerful opinion-formers on publications whose opinions were formed by the proprietor alone. That did not mean that Beaverbrook did not seek to hire, and succeed in hiring, men of political experience and sophistication. They did not need to be journalists already; he had started late himself. Robert Bruce Lockhart, who joined the *Evening Standard* as Diary Editor in 1928 at the age of forty-one, and Harold Nicolson, who signed up in 1929, aged forty-three, both of them former diplomats, were two prime examples. Nicolson first asked Beaverbrook for an undertaking that never required him to write anything that conflicted with his political principles; he described himself as a 'left-Liberal or a right-Labour', and he privately regarded Beaverbrook as a disruptive and unscrupulous Tory.[39] Beaverbrook reassured him. His beliefs did not worry Beaverbrook, who wanted lively journalists much more than he wanted good Conservatives. St John Ervine and Hannen Swaffer, two of Beaverbrook's stars in the twenties, were both passionate socialists. It was not politics but distaste for the job that drove Nicolson to escape after eighteen months. Although he reviewed books for the *Express* and produced articles on political subjects, his daily task was to write paragraphs for, and sometimes to edit, the *Evening Standard* gossip column; and that his own interests were not those of his proprietor was borne in on him after he reproduced in the Londoner's Diary a nude drawing by Nina Hamnett of the sculptor Gaudier-Brezska which even Bruce Lockhart found 'crude, rude and rather suggestive of a man on the cabinet or presenting his backside as an invitation' and which produced a storm at Cherkley.[40] Besides, Nicolson hated the atmosphere of the *Standard*. He was repelled by his colleagues' 'lack of any moral or intellectual values' and found it 'very soiling to live among people so extremely empirical, quotidian, shallow and mean.'[41]

Beaverbrook lost Nicolson, but deprived the Foreign Office of a possible future permanent under-secretary and started him off in the journalism he practised for the rest of his life. It was Beaverbrook, in a rather different field, who spotted the humorist Nat Gubbins and encouraged him to produce his Sitting on the Fence column. Probably no one but Beaverbrook would have imagined that a disorganized socialite like Castlerosse had the makings of a successful gossip columnist; and no one else could have kept him in harness for so long. He also made mistakes. He appointed inadequate editors to the *Sunday Express*, and it was not until he appointed John Gordon in 1928 that the paper, then with a circulation of only 440,000, started to make money. Gordon was a Scotsman with a granite exterior who had left school at the age of fourteen and in 1924 joined the *Express*, where Beaverbrook spotted his talent. He told Gordon one day, soon after his promotion, that if the paper did not show a profit that very week he would shut it down on the following Monday. He meant it; or Gordon thought he did.[42] That week the tide turned, permanently. In twenty-four years as editor, Gordon raised the circulation to 3,200,000.

All three papers flourished; but their advance could not be fairly attributed to their pursuit of sensationalism in the modern sense. In 1926 Jimmy White, a very well known and flamboyant London impresario, wrote a long, sad letter to Beaverbrook asking for money. Immediately afterwards he committed suicide. The *Express* was thus in possession of a scoop, but instead of exploiting its luck it carried the story on an inside page and quoted only briefly from the letter. Normally, it was one of Beaverbrook's strengths to want to print everything he picked up that did not affect his own interests. When an Australian senator sent him a well-informed article exposing in detail the folly and extravagance of allegedly distinguished Britons sent out as governors of the Australian states, he showed much more enthusiasm for publishing it than Blumenfeld did. He kept a notebook beside his plate at dinner parties and scribbled notes for stories; if people complained, he would ask plaintively why they told him things they did not want him to print. Bruce Lockhart called him a one-man news agency because he supplied his papers with so much copy. He recruited the big literary names of the day: Arnold Bennett, Philip Gibbs,

Hall Caine, George Moore. Unlike most newspaper proprietors, then and since, he was at home with writers and knew how to cultivate them; after all, he was a writer himself. When the economist John Maynard Keynes sent him in 1928 an article on the causes of unemployment, he personally negotiated the fee (£60 for English serial rights).

He used his papers without inhibition to pursue his enemies and to cement relations with friends and allies. He told John St Loe Strachey to send him a message 'if on special occasions you wish me to refer to the *Spectator* in the columns of the *Express*'.[43] When Lord Robert Cecil, during the general election of October 1924, asked if the *Express* could 'lend a hand' to his niece in her constituency – Beatrice Ormsby Gore, whose six-year-old son David later became British Ambassador in Washington – Beaverbrook could not have been more accommodating: 'Please tell me exactly what you want me to do. I could send down a special man to report meetings and events for the *Daily Express* and give him space for his reports'; he could 'arrange' for the same help to be given by the *Evening Standard*.[44] Lady Milbanke (on the eve of the 1929 crash) wanted 'some slight press propaganda' for the Derby Ball: 'Sweetest Sheila,' Beaverbrook replied, 'I will speak to the man on the bridge.' At the request of the well-connected bursar of Trinity College, Oxford, Philip Landon, he instructed the *Standard* to publicize protests against the City Council's plans for a car park in the middle of the Broad – to no avail. He told Malcolm Sargent that if his forthcoming staging of *Hiawatha* in the Albert Hall ran into trouble, he would give him 'press support'.

He was frequently asked by more or less prominent persons to suppress news of scandals. Lady Orr-Lewis wanted him to 'control the press in regard to Duncan's affair with Lady Gibbons' – Sir Duncan Orr-Lewis Bart. being her son; Beaverbrook said he wished he could help her, 'but I know so well nothing can be done for I have often considered the question in relation to other people'. However, when two months later the actress Fay Compton asked him to say as little as possible about her citation as a co-respondent in a divorce suit – '. . . please Max, if you *can* do anything about this, will you?' – the reply was much more favourable.[45] In 1931, at Nancy Astor's request, he helped to ensure that no mention of her son Bobby Shaw's prosecution for homosexual activities appeared in the press.

He adopted early on the pretence, used as required, that he had no power or influence over his papers, which gave him an alibi when criticized. An elderly viscount, Lord Knutsford, got more than he bargained for in 1919. The *Express* reported that Princess Mary was engaged to the Earl of Dalkeith. Knutsford wrote to the editor saying that the story 'has given *such* pain. . . . It is said in the Marlborough Club that Beaverbrook is responsible for having sent you the news.' Knutsford ended by asking the editor to accept his letter 'in a friendly spirit'. In reply, Beaverbrook unmuzzled his full firepower. Knutsford's charges were

. . . extremely unjust. . . . The first I heard or saw of the matter was in the columns of the *Daily Express* . . . in the nature of things I would not know anything about such an item of news. I am the principal shareholder in the *Daily Express* but I am not the Editor or the Manager or even a Director of it. I practically never go to the office – indeed had not been there for three months until I looked in yesterday and was shown your letter – and I leave the staff to carry on their duties in their own way. Of course on a large and important issue of policy I should put my foot down if I thought the *Daily Express* was going wrong. But attempts to saddle me personally with what appears in the newspaper in the ordinary way of journalism are simply ignorant where they are not malevolent.[46]

He responded with equal vigour after the *Express* attacked waste at the Ministry of Pensions in 1921, and proposed that pensions should be paid through the banks to save costs. The minister, Ian Macpherson, angrily complained that the 'so-called administrative costs' were in fact incurred by 'hospitals, artificial limbs etc to deal with a million shattered lives'. Beaverbrook would not dare to repeat his charges in either House of Parliament, or at any public meeting of fellow countrymen. He played his usual card, saying he knew nothing of the attack until he read it in the paper; but then struck back, as he invariably did when he felt challenged: he noted Macpherson's 'suggestion that I would not dare in either of the Houses of Parliament to recommend the transfer of your responsibilities to a Joint Stock Bank. I will do so at an early opportunity. I will also make enquiries about your administrative costs.'[47]

Sometimes he amused himself by appearing to take his critics seriously. When Lord Leverhulme made a trivial complaint about a front-page story in the *Express* to do with a postcard he had sent Augustus John, Beaverbrook solemnly replied that he had visited the *Express* and found the 'responsible authority' there 'dismayed' by the distress caused. Then he piled on the exaggerations and the flattery. 'In the *Express* office, where is a distinct trace of Communism and a considerable degree of Bolshevism, I find that all Capitalists are subject to criticism, save only yourself. It would really astonish you to know how highly you are esteemed by the turbulent troop of pressmen. I believe there is no parallel in the history of the industry.'[48]

He seemed to feel it necessary to minimize the fun his papers gave him, as if to emphasize his remoteness. 'My life is one long struggle with the editors,' he said in 1922. He claimed to have 'practically retired from the *Daily Express*'; 'I personally take no part in the management or direction of the *Express*,' he asserted in 1928. He was, he was wont to explain, merely the principal shareholder and would soon lay down even that burden. 'I have not been near Fleet Street for a long time now,' he told Sir William Jury, who wanted to sell him the *Reading Standard*, 'and when my son Max has finished his University career, I intend to turn over to him my controlling interest in the *Daily Express*.' He told Lady Milbanke in

April 1929: 'I've deserted the ship and live in a peaceful harbour vowing never to sail the seas of journalism again.'[49] A month later, in the *Daily Express*, he fired the opening salvo of his Empire Crusade.

The notion that Beaverbrook, as he constantly claimed, left his staff to carry on their duties in their own way was always fanciful. Former employees, writing about him after they retired but before he died, almost invariably praised him as an employer – Blumenfeld and Christiansen are examples. The diaries of Bruce Lockhart, published when Beaverbrook was safely dead, tell another story. Bruce Lockhart – highly educated, travelled, well connected but self-indulgent – envied Harold Nicolson for having escaped from the triviality and daily humiliations of journalism; he envied him still more for having escaped from Beaverbrook. All Beaverbrook's senior employees, Bruce Lockhart said, were 'terrified of offending' him. When the *Evening Standard* was 'seething with discontent' in 1931 Edward Shanks, a literary journalist on the paper, laid the blame squarely on Beaverbrook 'for interfering and messing people about until all confidence is destroyed'. Bruce Lockhart became a regular member of Beaverbrook's entourage, and was often amused by him, but he found him as an employer arbitrary, demanding and sometimes ruthless in sacking people. Working conditions in the crowded *Standard* office were lamentable; and he despised himself for submitting his articles to Beaverbrook's censorship. He should have been warned from the beginning about the pressures that working for Beaverbrook would entail when, before their first meeting, Beaverbrook's secretary telephoned seven times in an hour before finally reaching him and putting him through to Beaverbrook, who asked him to lunch next day. As he was leaving Cherkley, after 'a machine-gun fusillade of questions', Beaverbrook took him aside and said, 'Ever thought of journalism?'[50] Constantly thereafter Bruce Lockhart dreamed of the emancipation from Beaverbrook's 'slavery' that his extravagance and debts did not allow. 'Max makes no effort to understand his staff,' he wrote in his diary in 1930. 'He is kind in his way, but so self-centred that he can appreciate none of the finer feelings in others. His one method is to drive-drive-drive, and in the end the willing horse goes to the slaughter-house.' He may have been thinking of Blumenfeld.

CHAPTER 13

WRITERS AND WOMEN
1924–1928

THE DEATH OF Bonar Law was above all a watershed in Beaverbrook's public activities; but it also affected his emotional life. Attitudes were changing: discreet liaisons conducted in love-nests between men of the world and semi-professionals from a different class were fading out, and open liaisons conducted in nightclubs or at country house weekends between social equals were becoming accepted, even fashionable, as long as the conventions were observed. Divorce was frowned on; married women had a certain latitude; the unmarried had to be more cautious. Above all, nobody must make a public fuss. Newspapers, including Beaverbrook's, did not dig up scandal as long as people behaved with discretion.

Bonar Law was a natural puritan, and he had been linked by affection and gratitude to Gladys Beaverbrook. With his death, a restraining influence on Beaverbrook's behaviour was removed. Possibly he also needed to reaffirm the self-esteem he had gained during thirteen years of friendship with Bonar Law – the knowledge that he was genuinely liked and trusted – by becoming the centre of a group of younger admirers, men as well as women.

In these years a pattern emerged of Beaverbrook's attraction to younger people who caught his eye or were brought to his attention by a member of his circle. His newspapers played an important part: the press, always avid for stories and new faces, had a keen appetite for young talent. Beaverbrook could, and did, exploit this need in all sorts of ways at different stages of a relationship. An actress or a singer needed good reviews and flattering pictures, young writers needed a shop window, and, as always, most protégés appreciated financial windfalls, hospitality, introductions and travel. Beaverbrook and the *Express* could provide attention and funds; few people building a career can resist either.

Among the young men whom Beaverbrook took up for a while were two novelists, Michael Arlen and William Gerhardie – or Gerhardi, as he originally called himself. Arlen, born Dikran Kouyoumdjian in Bradford in 1895, was from the outset dedicated as much to social as to literary success. Today he is remembered as the author of wildly melodramatic, affected romances set among the upper classes, like his best-seller of 1924, *The Green Hat*. In his heyday he was treated as a serious and important writer, an observer of modern morals and manners. He was invited everywhere, and epitomized sophisticated success. Arlen remained irredeemably foreign and socially insecure; Rebecca West called him, unforgettably, every other inch a gentleman. His huge successes of the early twenties proved fleeting, but while on the crest of the wave he was on easy terms with Beaverbrook. In 1927 he dedicated a novel, *Young Men in Love*, to 'Max'.[1] The book, not one of his best, revolves around a desperate heroine called Venetia and a group of politicians, industrialists and a self-made press lord, with obvious reference to Beaverbrook.

Gerhardie's involvement with Beaverbrook was more intimate and more consequential than Arlen's. Born into an expatriate English millowner's family in St Petersburg, Gerhardie spoke fluent Russian and, despite an Oxford education and service in the Scots Guards, retained an aura of cosmopolitanism. After the war he returned to Russia with the British Embassy and observed the Revolution from close quarters. Back in England he published two novels, *Futility* (1922) and *The Polyglots* (1925), subtle books about people adrift in the post-revolutionary confusion of Russia and the Far East, that won him a critical reputation but little money. A womanizer and fantasist, he cultivated a worldly cynicism and louche attitude that amused and appealed to Beaverbrook, who summoned him from Vienna in October 1925, with results that he described in an excited twelve-page letter to his mother.

When I was ushered into his office last Monday, he got up and shook hands in a very friendly way and asked me to be seated; then went on going through his papers with his girl-secretary, who seemed scared to death of him. He treats them like dogs, and when he wants his secretary he simply whistles – and she appears. I am glad I am not his subordinate. When he had finished with his secretary, he leaned back and said: 'Well, Mr Gerhardi, I have read your *Polyglots* and I think it is the greatest book of our time,' etc. etc. He said he thought I was a man with a beard and never thought I could be 'a boy!' He asked me what sale it had in England, what reviews, whether his paper had printed good reviews of it, etc., and when I said that his paper the *Daily Express* had in fact done worse than any other, he telephoned and demanded: 'Bring in the *Daily Express* review of *The Polyglots*' and on reading it said: 'Just like him', and telephoned again: 'I want you to send up a man – a bright fellow – to write up a novelist I have with me in my office,' and when the man – a very subdued creature – appeared, he asked: 'Have you read *The Polyglots*?' – 'No, Sir'. 'Have you ever heard of Mr Gerhardi before?' – 'No, Sir' – 'A damned shame!' he said. 'Here is a man who has written the most brilliant book of the age and it has only sold 2,000 copies. Only the intelligentsia has heard of it – the big public has never heard of him. And here we're boosting a football player as though he were God

Almighty. Everybody is agreed that Mr Gerhardi's book is brilliant – a brilliant book, a <u>brilliant</u> book, and for all the difference it makes to him he might have never written it. I want,' he said, 'to present Mr Gerhardi as the great new literary figure,' and he ordered the subdued critic to read the book at once and praise it for all he's worth. 'If you haven't time to read it all tonight, just read the bedroom chapter,' his lordship ordered. . . . I thanked him, and he said, 'Not a bit, I can't tell you how glad I am to do it. I am one of your greatest admirers. I have actually bought 200 copies of your book and sent it round to friends.' And in my presence a copy was despatched to Lady Diana Cooper. The same day he left for Newmarket, – having bought new horses: he also wants to win the Derby – previously arranging for me to meet the critic who is to write about me, and next day I had a letter from his secretary to say that before leaving town Lord B had expressed the wish to see me again on his return on Thursday.

On the Friday Gerhardie presented himself at Stornoway House, which he found impressively grand. Over tea he met a Canadian millionaire, a motor manufacturer, who was 'chaffed' by Beaverbrook over the contrast between the young writer, living on a pittance but producing a master-piece, and himself: ' "Here are you, a parasite, with more money than you know what to do with, producing 3,000 cars a day." I wanted to go,' Gerhardie continued,

. . . but he ordered me to stay, and I remained alone with him (it was the day of the return of the Prince of Wales and outside we could hear the cheers of the crowd) and the telephone kept ringing up occasionally and the editors of his various papers would be asking him for advice and Lord B would say: 'No, I am going to support the Admiralty against the Air Force', and that sort of thing; and I had scarcely finished tea when he said: 'Have a drink?' I said I couldn't stand whisky. 'Have wine', he said. I suggested red wine, but he said: 'Wd you like champagne?' I said yes. He whistled and told the butler to bring the wine list and ordered half a bottle of champagne for me alone, but I could only drink one glass as I didn't want to get dizzy.

Not sure if he was expected to stay for dinner, Gerhardie tentatively asked if he was expected. 'Of course. I'll be very grieved if you don't come, I can't tell you how I like doing this. I want you to know that I admire you intensely and quite sincerely.' At dinner, to his intense gratification, Gerhardie met and was praised by H. G. Wells. Even so, he was not completely bowled over. 'The fact of the matter is, as I have now discovered,' he told his mother, 'that Lord Beaverbrook, who is only 43 & at the height of his power and wealth, wants to be <u>the</u> man in everything and he is lionising me because he wants to say afterwards that it was he who discovered me. I don't mind, of course. But he has really read my books. . . .'

The next night Gerhardie went to a party at The Vineyard, where Beaverbrook informed the guests: ' "Wells is not a bit nice to anyone, especially to other writers. But this was wonderful – to see the older writer paying homage to the younger one." ' Gerhardie told his mother:

> Last night Lord B said: 'I am trying to persuade Mr Gerhardi to take to journalism' but I told him I had not sufficient interest in that direction, that I was chiefly interested in the novel and short story. He then said he'd take short stories from me, or in fact anything I chose to write. And now he keeps worrying me about this short story – whereas I can hardly gather my wits together after all this continuous excitement and entertainment.

Even so, he agreed that he would try to write a novel in instalments, as a serial.

The *Express* assigned H. V. Morton, one of its leading reporters, to interview him. Morton noted his shabby suit and exaggerated his poverty, which pleased D. H. Lawrence's miner father when he realized that here was a writer doing even worse than his son. Lawrence himself warned Gerhardie to steer clear of Beaverbrook: 'He hates you,' he said. 'I don't say he hates you personally . . . but these men, they're like vampires. When they see an immortal soul they hate it instinctively.' Gerhardie took no notice.

Beaverbrook's campaign to 'boom' the sales of *The Polyglots* was a failure. Nevertheless he continued to promote Gerhardie, inviting him to dinners in London at The Vineyard or Stornoway House and to weekends at Cherkley where he met the famous. Within weeks of their first encounter he had introduced Gerhardie to the Aga Khan, Admiral Beatty, John Middleton Murry, Maurice Baring, Arnold Bennett, Lloyd George, Bertrand Russell and Lord Castlerosse, who later tried to make a match between Gerhardie and the Maharanee of Cooch Behar. In his memoirs, Gerhardie reflected on Beaverbrook's extraordinary charm.

> He discussed willingly his work in the world and somehow invited you to share the glamour of it. . . . I would go to see him almost daily, and then he would take me to dine at his house, or his office at the top of the *Daily Express*, or some night club. He would say: 'I will provide the champagne, and you the conversation.' I would reply: 'You will provide both.' . . . If you asked him whether Max was not an abbreviation of Maximilian, he would say 'Maximultimillion.' . . . He cannot be shocked, he is uncontaminated by moral indignation, and is open to argument at any hour of the day or night on any subject in the world. I have myself, at two o'clock in the morning, when everyone was fagged out and longed to go home, opened a conversation concerning the illusory nature of time, and Lord Beaverbrook, who was helping himself to a whisky and soda in the corner of the room, swiftly turned round, took up the question and argued ably till half past three.

The clue to Beaverbrook's magnetism, Gerhardie decided, was above all

> . . . his faculty of giving everybody he meets his individual attention. The impression is assisted by his habit of conducting his business by telephone

while entertaining his guests, as if his friends were his real preoccupation, and business an agreeable irrelevance. There is something irresistible when, behind all this solid success, behind the solemn outposts of editors, you penetrate to the signalbox and find the man who pulls the strings a youngish little man with the face of a mischievous urchin. You cannot resist the fascination of being there with him in the signalbox.

Gerhardie noticed that, of the group surrounding Beaverbrook, Arnold Bennett seemed to be the only one ever able to reprove him, 'to shake him, so to speak, by the collar'. Most of his friends would prepare their stories and wait for his approval. As for Lady Beaverbrook, Gerhardie tells a story against himself that brings her briefly into focus; while dancing with her one evening, 'I said to her: what a charming man your husband is – just to get her to say "He says you're a genius." "Yes," she replied. "He's a genius." ' But for all the mutual admiration and hospitality, Beaverbrook was not under any illusions either. When Gerhardie, who was often compared with Chekhov, told Beaverbrook of that writer's relations with Suvorin, the Russian newspaper tycoon of his day, Beaverbrook asked if Chekhov was grateful, and added: 'You know, many young men would have given anything for the chance you've had.'

Beaverbrook often played the confidant in his young friends' romantic lives. He liked to spring surprises. When Gerhardie was encouraged to hurry straight round to The Vineyard with a problem, he found a dinner party in progress that included Lloyd George, and guests waiting to hear the latecomer's troubles. The next night he attended a rather different kind of party, consisting of 'young lords and chorus girls'; he opened a bedroom door to find Beaverbrook busy with two young women.[2]

Sometimes, Beaverbrook liked to bring his protégés and his friends together and await developments. He was amused by matchmaking, and it was a convenient way of breaking with a girl he had tired of. In the mid-1920s both The Vineyard and Stornoway House were the setting for lunches and dinners at which Beaverbrook's men friends, his age or older, usually though not invariably without their wives, dined in the company of one or other of the attractive, ambitious young women who were in favour. One of these was Barbara Cartland, then in her early twenties, well connected but short of money. A young man at a cocktail party had told her that the *Express* paid well, so she began to send in stories; and it was not long before she caught Beaverbrook's eye. One day the phone rang, a car arrived, and she was taken to see him at The Vineyard. There ensued a period, Miss Cartland has recalled (and his engagement book confirms), when almost every day she was summoned; he would ask to see her copy, which she took round to him at the Hyde Park Hotel. Several times she dined at The Vineyard with Churchill, Birkenhead or Tim Healy; to her, these legendary political figures were enthralling but old; she longed for the evenings to break up so that she could go dancing with an admirer her own age.

Barbara Cartland thinks that Beaverbrook was for a time in love with her, and that his feelings were connected with the death of Bonar Law.

Max said to me once almost savagely, as though the words were torn from his lips: 'Do you know what it's like to watch someone you know dying slowly, day by day, to know that you cannot help them, that you can do nothing for them? . . . I watched a man die.' He was to say it over and over again because it had happened just a few months before I came into his life. His thoughts still dwelt on it, he was still deeply and emotionally involved.

He also told her stories, somewhat exaggerated, about his impoverished youth and early struggles. To Barbara Cartland, a social insider, it was obvious that Beaverbrook would always feel an outsider. 'Max must have endured in England many personal rebuffs and snubs more wounding than anything he had encountered in his boyhood. He was ugly, short and brash – a defiant cover for his shyness – and because he was a Canadian he was all the more ready to resent the aristocratic indifference of those whom he met . . . in society.' What was attractive about him, she has said, was his energy; 'He was the vibrating type.'[3]

In due course, Barbara Cartland was invited to Cherkley where she met Lady Beaverbrook. 'He was very fond of her, in a funny sort of way. She was awfully good with him; she let him do whatever he wanted to do. She was very sweet indeed, but you didn't feel she was of any great importance. She was charming to everybody. I never heard her make a strong statement about anything.'

Through Beaverbrook Barbara Cartland met Sir James Dunn, who pursued her for a time before marrying her great friend Irene Queensberry. At this period Beaverbrook and Dunn saw much of each other. Dunn had rented Templeton, a grand house at Roehampton, not far from The Vineyard, where he gave lavish parties. Cartland saw Dunn and Beaverbrook as very different types – Dunn far more attractive, Beaverbrook, 'a complex, twisted person', far more complicated. She was driven home after one Dunn party with Beaverbrook and Tim Healy, who sang hymns together loudly and urged her to join in. Beaverbrook once said to her: 'I can't ask you to marry me but I'll make you the most important journalist in the world.' She remarked sixty years later, 'Of course there was an if to that. I said No.'

At least one of the flirtations between the middle-aged men and young girls of the Beaverbrook circle led to semi-suppressed scandal and tragedy. Birkenhead, long married, fell in love with James Dunn's daughter. Mona Dunn was a fair-haired beauty, a friend of Birkenhead's eldest daughter Eleanor Smith; the two girls, aged seventeen, went to finishing school in Paris together in 1919. By the early 1920s Birkenhead and Mona were deep in a serious love affair. To Eleanor's fury, Beaverbrook provided them with opportunities to meet. In 1925 Mona married a suitable young man, Lieutenant-Colonel E. H. Tattersall, perhaps in an attempt to end the affair, perhaps because as a married woman she would have more freedom. She gave birth to a daughter, and then died in Paris in December 1928, aged only twenty-six, after an operation whispered to be an abortion.[4] Birkenhead wrote an intense, melodramatic poem to her memory, which Beaverbrook declined to publish in the *Express* (though he included it many years later in a biography of James Dunn). Beaverbrook himself wrote an appreciation of Mona calling her a genius that was printed on the front page of the *Sunday Express*, to the distaste of people in the know. Duff Cooper wrote to Diana:

> I think the whole thing very disgusting. Poor Mona was a person not only utterly unimportant but also very disreputable. Because Max knew her he thinks it right to give a leading column on the front page of the *Sunday Express* to writing up her death. The fact that he is still further degrading his dirty newspaper doesn't matter very much; nor does it matter much more that he is insulting his public by thrusting down their throats his own sentimental twaddle about a dead friend; but what does matter is that he is doing it from the best motives, and honestly thinks that Mona can have no prouder monument than a leading column in the *Sunday Express*.[5]

Beaverbrook had a professional as well as a personal impact on Barbara Cartland and many other young women protégés over the next forty years. He genuinely tried to help them become proficient journalists; he told Barbara Cartland to work out first what she wanted to say and then to put it on paper clearly and concisely, without unnecessary words. Then she married, and his interest in her waned. She continued to contribute to his newspapers, but he issued instructions that she was not to be mentioned in the social columns. 'He thought that would hurt me. Typical Max.'

BENNETT'S BEST FRIEND

Throughout the 1920s Beaverbrook was in constant touch with Arnold Bennett. Beaverbrook trusted Bennett, especially about writing. Before the end of 1918 he had shown him passages of his account of the 1916 crisis: ' . . . the secret book really does you very high credit,'[6] Bennett wrote. After the war he roped in Beaverbrook as an investor in his theatrical ventures, although he found his rich friend hard to pin down and his interest limited; but Beaverbrook and Bennett attended first nights, dined at the Savoy and went out dancing.

Frequently Bennett advised Beaverbrook on his newspapers and proposed contributors on literary or theatrical topics. In 1923, when Beaverbrook acquired the *Evening Standard*, he wrote to Bennett: 'I want so much to talk over the new situation in journalism and to get the advantage of your cynical viewpoint.' This led to a three-page letter from Bennett in which he urged Beaverbrook to raise the intellectual level of the paper. 'This is the only evening paper that appeals even a little to educated people, and it ought to be made to appeal a great deal more to them than it does. You can't, in my opinion, get much prestige out of a yellow paper. Hence I wouldn't let it be yellow.' This excellent advice was followed. Bennett spoke his mind; he took Beaverbrook to task for the *Express* policy on Europe, already in the twenties distinctly isolationist: 'Your policy about retiring from Europe may be sound, but I don't think you'll get any Government to adopt it. There is a moral side to this matter that counts heavily. You might, and would, argue me to a standstill, but I should continue to think that to clear out of Europe was not right.' He assumes that Beaverbrook is after 'moral prestige. If you think only of circulation you won't get prestige, and if you think only of prestige you won't get circulation. . . .'

Beaverbrook and Bennett regularly played tennis, went yachting – Bennett introduced his friend to his favourite pastime – dined out and discussed wine merchants. They shared a taste for good champagne (Krug 1911 was supplied to Bennett, he told Beaverbrook, at 240 shillings per case). Beaverbrook sent Bennett a copy of 'the best English Bible'. Bennett visited Cherkley and became an admirer of Gladys Beaverbrook. In the spring of 1924 Bennett, with Tim Healy and Dr Horder, joined Beaverbrook, Gladys and their daughter Janet, aged sixteen, on a three-week journey to Spain; a photograph shows Gladys and Janet, both looking rather plump, smiling self-consciously in Spanish dress with mantillas, while Bennett clowns between them in matador costume. In his thank you letter Bennett called it 'the royal progress', praised his host's 'finest munificence', and only regretted that he had not 'rivalled Tim in the vast business of putting champagne out of sight'.

Beaverbrook kept Bennett informed on politics. In early 1924, Bennett wrote in his diary, 'Max B lunched with me yesterday. Asked "what about the Tory Party" he said: "A is an idiot, B has sciatica, C is whoremongering and D is taking dancing lessons." ' At the same lunch, Bennett received a bulletin on Beaverbrook's state of health, a subject of keen mutual interest. 'He said he had been cured of his illnesses (whatever they were) by cutting off all fleshmeat and all wine and that he felt perfectly well. At lunch he had nothing but an omelette fines herbes, boiled potatoes and carrots and very little even of those. He kept his jacket buttoned all the time, and it was not very well cut.' This lunch represented a minor triumph for Bennett; for some time he had been trying to get Beaverbrook to be his guest. Diet was one of many excuses Beaverbrook used to ward off those who pressed him to attend social events; increasingly he liked to be in control, to choose the company and the food and in general to arrange his extremely busy social life to suit himself.

Influenced by Arnold Bennett, Beaverbrook went through a musical phase. He became a patron of the young cellist Eugene Goossens and of the rising conductor Malcolm Sargent, and took to hiring a quartet to entertain him and his guests at Stornoway House or The Vineyard. But his disinclination to listen in silence and his abrupt changes of plan led to frequent tiffs, and he soon lost patience with the musical temperament. Meanwhile Bennett also kept Beaverbrook up to date with new writing; he particularly praised D. H. Lawrence; 'He is the best of the younger novelists. In fact he is a genius.' Beaverbrook duly wrote off to Lawrence asking for an unexpurgated copy of *The Rainbow*. Beaverbrook amused Bennett by his attitude to writing.

> Beaverbrook on the phone the other day after seeing Shaw's *St Joan*. 'Arnold, what do you think of *St Joan*? I haven't seen many plays; my experience is limited, but it is the greatest play I ever saw . . . Arnold, I've come to the conclusion that there's a technique for play writing. There's a trick in it, a technique and I've worked it all out. My theory may be wrong but it deserves consideration because I've thought it all out very carefully.'

Here, Bennett comments,

> . . . was a perfect example of the working of that masterly and yet often crude brain. He didn't see the ridiculous side of suggesting that a dramatic technique existed. But I have no doubt that his own independent theory of dramatic technique will be very interesting and well worth listening to. I remember he once told me that he wanted to write some narrative (I think it was the life of Christ) in the form of a novel. But he found he couldn't do the dialogue. So he read in the *Old Wives Tale* to 'see how it was done'. But even then he couldn't do dialogue. So he gave it up. He told me all this quite simply and naturally, without noticing the comical ingenuousness of it.

In 1921 Bennett's marriage finally broke down; he wrote to Beaverbrook announcing, 'Henceforth I shall be decidedly more free.' By 1923 he had fallen in love with an appealing blonde actress, Dorothy Cheston, who in due course changed her name by deed poll and in 1926 gave Bennett his only child. Bennett's wife would not divorce him, extracted a huge financial settlement, and in 1924 wrote a book about him which she offered to the *Daily Express* as a serial. Both Beaverbrook and Bennett handled this embarrassing episode well. Bennett's journal gives an account of it.

> Max Beaverbrook rang me up last night, and said: Arnold, I want to tell you, the *Daily Express* has been offered a biography of you written by Mrs AB. They want to make it a condition that we should treat the offer as confidential, secret; but I absolutely refused to do any such thing. So I'm telling you. Our man has read it all through and likes it. Says he wouldn't mind anyone saying of him in his lifetime what is said of you in the book. If you have any objection I won't buy it; but if you haven't, I'd like to. . . .

Bennett's response was shrewd: '. . . if it is to be published I would sooner it be published by someone who is very friendly and who will take care that nothing offensive appears in it'. On 19 November 1924 the first instalment appeared in the *Express*, preceded by a large front-page explanation which Beaverbrook and Bennett had agreed was needed: Mrs Bennett had written the memoir without anywhere making it plain that she and her husband were separated. 'And now, in her position of remembered intimacy,' said the *Express*, 'Mrs Arnold Bennett . . . has written the story of her married life. . . . Should this private life be told in public? The *Daily Express*, without expressing approval or disapproval of Mrs Bennett's departure from tradition, has decided to publish it. . . .' The story ran for ten days and created much interest; as Beaverbrook had said, it was 'unadulterated praise'.

The culmination of Beaverbrook's friendship with Bennett was the collaboration of 1925 and 1926 that resulted in Bennett's political novel *Lord Raingo*. On 11 May 1925,

> . . . at lunch at the Vineyard I had my first long serious detailed talk with Max Beaver [*sic*] about political material for my novel *Lord Raingo*. It lasted just 1½ hours. He was marvellously effective and efficient. He didn't need to be told what sort of stuff I wanted. And he gave way at once when he was on the wrong tack – for me. He has exactly the right sort of imagination, and a very powerful and accurate one. He can invent pieces of plots to fit certain incidents, and is just as interested and as effectual in the matter of women as in the matter of politics. I got an immense amount of stuff.

Sometimes Beaverbrook tried too hard. In September, Bennett caught his adviser out in a bit of invention. Beaverbrook told him about a speech in 1918 which, he said, had routed his critics in the House of Lords. Bennett intended to put a version of the speech into Lord Raingo's mouth, and he looked back at *The Times* to check it. Puzzled, he wrote to Beaverbrook to say he could find no record of such a speech. Bennett could not find a report of the speech because Beaverbrook never made it. No answer from Beaverbrook survives.

Beaverbrook was working on a book of his own. In October 1925 he sent Bennett his first published attempt at contemporary history, a brisk and self-congratulatory collection of episodes involving his newspapers entitled *Politicians and the Press*. Bennett did not think much of it, and did not hesitate to say so. Calling it 'Barefaced propaganda on behalf of the two *Expresses*', he went on:

> If you intend it to be this . . . well and good. . . . The mere writing (phrasing) is a bit loose, and needs careful revision throughout. . . . Do not mistake my meaning: the fundamental quality of the style is excellent. But many details of expression are in a literary sense maladroit. . . . I doubt whether the book has the sort of interestingness that will appeal to a very wide public. . . . You will be accused of self-advertising and cannot rebut the charge. All you can say in reply will be: Churchill has advertised himself at much greater length.

Beaverbrook wrote back the next day expressing deep gratitude and acknowledging that the 'sole purpose' was indeed to advertise his papers. The book was published before the end of the year and sold a hundred thousand copies. Beaverbrook was encouraged to press on with his chronicle of the war.

At the beginning of November Bennett sent Beaverbrook the first half of *Lord Raingo* and anxiously awaited his response. Within a few days Beaverbrook rang him up. Bennett's letter resounds with pleasure. 'I can't tell you how relieved I was. . . . I was *tremendously* afraid that you might have found the political stuff all wrong in the "feel" of it. I trembled when I was told you were on the phone. . . . Of course without you I could not have *begun* to do the book.' For Christmas 1925 Beaverbrook sent Bennett two dozen bottles of champagne (Montebello 1906), accompanied by the message that he hoped to be given it when he came to dine.

Sometimes Bennett was able to do Beaverbrook a favour. A bizarre little episode in 1925, when G. K. Chesterton attacked Beaverbrook in print using a suggestive metaphor, led Bennett to write a private letter in protest, perhaps somewhat overstated.

> . . . you had some comments upon Lord Beaverbrook's social policy. Lord Beaverbrook has got hold of the idea that these comments were meant to have a personal application to himself – which would mean that he was practising miscellaneous fornication on the one hand and on the other opposing birth control, etc. Certain Canadian papers have already interpreted your remarks in this sense. Beaverbrook is a close friend of mine; he is an absolutely clean living man. . . .

At last, in November 1926, *Lord Raingo* was published, preceded by much tantalizing publicity in the *Express* and the *Standard* stressing that the novel was based on real people and real events. Interest in any political insight provided by the novel was muted; curiosity focused on the affair between Lord Raingo and his mistress. Soon, thanks to the trumpetings of Lord Birkenhead (who was apparently afraid that the adulterer in the novel was himself), a dispute broke out over the identity of Raingo, much to the delight of Bennett and Beaverbrook, who foresaw increased sales. Once again Beaverbrook sent Bennett some very special champagne for Christmas; this time it was, he wrote, 'the last bottle of 1906 champagne out of my own cellar. . . .' They were closer than ever, for during the autumn it had been agreed that Arnold Bennett would contribute a weekly article on books to the *Evening Standard*. His first piece appeared on 18 November, and the column, which rapidly became a great success and established the *Standard* as an authoritative literary voice, was to continue until his death. It was regarded as a column that actually sold books.

Beaverbrook even managed to put a book about God on his crowded agenda, along with his newspapers, his protégés and his girlfriends.

Just before Christmas 1925 he wrote to Tim Healy: 'Here is a secret. I am working on the *Life of Jesus*'. His visit to the Holy Land in 1923 had started him thinking, he later claimed, about the historical basis for the gospels; and during 1925 he had prompted a series of articles in the *Express* entitled 'My Religion' in which contributors wrote about their beliefs. Much controversy and correspondence ensued, and Beaverbrook found himself provoked by a letter from a Minister of the Gospel. 'He said in effect, "I value the articles you have published highly, but I disapprove of the personality which has been the instrument of publication. Your pursuit in life is an accumulation of money." ' Beaverbrook then decided to write his own account of what the Christian faith meant to him. At first Healy was encouraging, although he pointed out that 'our old Monks kept a separate pen to write the name of God and did so always on their knees'. He sent him a long list of scholarly books to be consulted, including *The Popular History of the Jews* in five volumes, adding, 'I shall read anything you send me but it is not a subject to be rushed.'

However before the end of February 1926 Beaverbrook sent Healy four draft articles, the first chapters of *Jesus: The Viewpoint of a Worldly Man*, which he proposed to publish in the *Daily Express*. Healy was appalled. He pointed out to Beaverbrook that what he had written was largely about himself, and in his view theologically unsound, likely to cause outrage among scholars and to upset believing readers. In deference to Healy, or so he always maintained, Beaverbrook abandoned the *Life of Jesus* for the time being.

The draft sent to Healy contains details about Beaverbrook's early attitude to religion that appear nowhere else. '*The Life of Jesus* and all that it implies is a subject which has interested me beyond all others from my very earliest days,' he proclaimed. 'I have always felt that the topic might absorb me to an extent which would eliminate most of my other interests.' As a child, he went on, he at first accepted the obvious discrepancy between 'Gentle Jesus', 'a being utterly incapable of any kind of aggressive action', and the 'avenging God' of the Old Testament; until one day on his way back from school he saw something which led him to question everything he had been taught. 'My whole faith in the doctrine and wisdom of my elders crumbled at a touch.' A stallion had been brought to the town to serve the local mares; hanging around with his schoolfriends, Beaverbrook saw enough to realize that all the stories he had been told about reproduction – 'that children were brought down from heaven and deposited with their parents by storks' – were not true. 'My whole intellectual and religious world was shattered by this discovery,' he wrote, 'and though it may appear a laughable matter in these days, it did not appear so in childhood. I went through days of torturing doubt.' Christianity and all its doctrines, he decided, was a myth. 'The keystone had fallen out of the theological arch.'

Nevertheless, as the Minister's son he still had to go to church. 'I sat under my father with a growing contempt for his intellectual narrowness.' He remained fascinated by the Old Testament, partly as great writing and partly as a source of worldly wisdom – 'I studied every incident of David's adventurous career upward to a throne' – and he continued to pump the organ: 'I wanted the twenty-five cents.' But secretly, he decided, he was an atheist.

As he grew older, Beaverbrook went on, he realized that he was not really an atheist after all. Like many others, he found the faith of his forebears tenacious. 'You begin by accepting Jesus out of prescriptive authority – you reject him when the claim of authority fails – and then you come back to Him again by some path of your own devising.' In his own case, his renewed faith was based on 'the fear or mystery of death' and an instinctive desire for 'personal immortality'. Healy was right in protesting to Beaverbrook that it was himself he was writing about rather than Jesus; what the abandoned fragment reveals is that in middle age Beaverbrook connected his loss of faith with his discovery of sex, and its recovery with his fear of extinction.[7]

HARRIET COHEN

Through Arnold Bennett, Beaverbrook took an interest for a time in another talented young woman, the pianist Harriet Cohen, also a friend of Rebecca West, who based her novel *Harriet Hume* (1929) upon her.[8] Harriet, then in her late twenties, was of Russian-Jewish extraction, dark, spirited, emotional, dedicated to her work but susceptible to the famous. She was also pursued by Gerhardie, who took her to Cherkley, and she always remembered

> Max's extraordinary performance at the dinner table as we sat over coffee and cigars. This son of the Manse began to declaim from a book of the Old Testament . . . he chanted the whole book: it was an awesome and moving occasion. Afterwards he turned and looked me deep in the eye and said: 'You are Esther – Esther from the Bible.' Shortly afterwards Max gave a special dinner in the restaurant of the Savoy to which AB was asked to bring me. Winston Churchill was there too and the first thing he said to me was: 'So you are Esther.'

Harriet Cohen was evidently fascinated by Beaverbrook and wanted to see more of him. Arnold Bennett kept her in touch; he wrote to her from Spain in 1924:

> Max is a most generous host, but he is not a good host owing to megalomania; he is not conceited or vain; he is extraordinarily interesting; his

grasp of things is marvellous. But as a host I can give him quite a lot of points. His wife humours him the whole time, but then she adores him. I think I am the only person of whom he is a little afraid. He is not in the least afraid of Sir T Horder, the Kings fizissian [*sic*], nor of the Governor General of the Irish Free State. I get on admirably with both these persons, and I adore Lady Beaverbrook.

Bennett was not, however, prepared to invite Beaverbrook to join a party including Harriet on his yacht. 'As for Max, my dear child you are approaching madness. In the first place he wouldn't come at any price, and in the second place if he came he would explode like dynamite and burst up the party in 24 hours. He is excruciatingly restless, and he is bored with terrifying facility, and when he is bored the whole world knows it. I wouldn't be at sea with Max in anything less than the Leviathan.'

Soon, Harriet Cohen was being invited to dinners at The Vineyard, where she met Rothermere and Lloyd George. Once, she was able to inform the company of how many mules the Yugoslav Army could put into the field; her father had had a passion for military matters. 'The next time I met Churchill at the Savoy,' she added, 'he remarked: "Ha, Young Clausewitz, I hear." ' After this she dined often with Beaverbrook, who took to sending her 'once a week, mostly on Saturdays, "a little nosegay" of a hundred or more roses . . .' and apparently spent a long evening 'trying to talk me out of continuing my career. . . . With a ruthless persistence he pointed out the hardships, remarked on my thinness, predicted that I would starve or die.' She does not say what, if any, alternative he had in mind for her; he was observant, for she was soon found to be consumptive, and was confined for some months in a sanatorium in Switzerland.

Throughout the 1920s Harriet Cohen kept up a busy and increasingly celebrated life as a concert pianist. Her circle of admirers came to include Ramsay MacDonald and the composer Arnold Bax; and she continued her flirtations with both Bennett and Beaverbrook. Letters that she later wrote to Beaverbrook demonstrate her attempts to advance their relationship, and his elusiveness.[9]

'Do you remember' she wrote,

> . . . I wrote to you from Scotland and you didn't answer, and I met you later at a party, and you said: 'You write the most wonderful letters – I never answer 'em, but will you write to me sometimes, when you feel like it'?? That is why sometimes I write to you . . . dear Max, it keeps alight the flame of our most marvellous friendship. Gerhardie can't understand such a spiritual relationship. He can't understand a girl not wanting anything from a rich man – or a man not just coveting a girl's beautiful body! I told him he didn't understand you – he was furious, and said he did.

She had recorded a piano piece called 'Beloved Jesus': Beaverbrook told her he played the record again and again. 'He [Gerhardie] can't believe that you should love Beloved Jesus . . . jazz is right for you, he says.' A fervent, if confused, religiosity seems to have linked Harriet Cohen to Beaverbrook, at least in her mind. She associates him with the prophet Isaiah, and tells him that reading Revelations reminds her of him.

Gerhardie teased Harriet about Beaverbrook: 'He won't believe that I like you better than him – but I do!' There was at least one visit to Cherkley when Harriet had a romantic interlude with her host. 'Darling Max,' one letter opens,

> This is my bread and butter letter . . . but rather it should be called my Cypress Tree one. I have only to shut my eyes to see those two sentinels, dark against the sky. I felt strangely protected, and cared for beneath your roof last night – in more ways than one! ! ! . . . I always feel when I am with you, that we just adore each other. . . . Not good for either of us to let each other go completely again!

She pressed him to attend her concerts ('I would play ten times better if I knew you were in the audience') or to dine with her at her 'appartement'. 'The simplest food. Not even any salt in the cooking if you don't want it darling. . . . If you'll come here of course I shan't ask William. . . . I shall want you to myself. . . . William is still trying! ! ! ! ! ! ahem! ! ! ! When will you come, Angel Face?'

The only sign of a letter – a secretary's copy – from Beaverbrook to Cohen is brief, thanking her politely for a record. 'I am most grateful to you . . . your records always give me so much pleasure and I am sure I shall play this one over and over again. With many thanks, I remain, Yours sincerely. . . .' This communication, and some mischief of Gerhardie's, made Harriet furious: 'Thank you for your prim little letter. Don't thank me for records that you will probably often find on your doorstep to show you that your friend often thinks of you. I am very angry with you. William G says you told him I was in love with him! ! You to be so psychologically wrong about me. . . .' Not for her, she goes on, are 'oversexed young men'. She was not angry for long; but Beaverbrook continued to elude her. He was, she said, 'the one man I feel I can say anything to, that is your genius . . . and the one man who apparently doesn't want to see me, and perhaps doesn't like me.' Nevertheless, she sends him 'a big hug and all these baisers' – and writes Max in large capital letters made up of little xxx's.

When, years later, Gerhardie attempted to write a biography of Beaverbrook, he made some random notes on Beaverbrook's appeal to women. 'The language of love', as Beaverbrook called it, was a topic of keen mutual interest; Harriet Cohen was not the only woman they both pursued. Even love could be turned into journalism, as Gerhardie recalled: 'Max bawls into the telephone at Cherkley my contribution to a series of love-letters to be edited by a well-known young beauty for the *Sunday Express*; the cows stop chewing the cud, the gardener stops work, the birds stop singing in astonishment at the sound of unbridled passion rolling out of his bedroom window on a beautiful summer's morning.' Like many others, Gerhardie was puzzled that a man as odd-looking as Beaverbrook, with his warts and hairy arms, could have such notable sexual success – 'he was built like a pair of scissors' – but perhaps that was the secret? 'There was something touching in this disproportion that appealed to women; the confident long stride joined to a boy's undeveloped frame, crowned by Caesar's massive head.' Gerhardie tried to evoke what it was like for a girl to meet Beaverbrook at Stornoway House for the first time. 'She was lifted by high spirits before her lips were moistened by champagne. The moment he came up, with hand outstretched, in his long, slow stride, admiration kindling in his eyes, an answering sympathy and warmth and delight in his concentration on herself welled up in the sparkling beauty's breast.' Gerhardie gave up at this point; and the secrets of Beaverbrook's love life remain unrevealed.

Gossip around the *Express* indicated that his capacities were admired and that he was not secretive about them. One actress, so the story went, described him as her best lover since the music-hall star Little Tich, her first; she liked to describe his habit of giving a great shout of laughter every time. It seemed that Beaverbrook took special delight in tumbling the pride of society women. One of his editors was disconcerted to find a society lady sitting on his lap, caressing his face with her hand the whole time Beaverbrook talked. Another editor complained that what annoyed him most, on being woken in the morning by Beaverbrook shouting criticism down the phone, was to hear feminine laughter, and to realize that the performance was designed to amuse some girl with him.[10] What is quite clear is that Beaverbrook in middle age had numerous love affairs and that some of his ex-mistresses remained his friends for life.

JAZZ AND JASPER

Soon after he was taken up by Beaverbrook, Gerhardie started a novel about his patron. Beaverbrook was not only pleased, and keen to discuss the themes of the book, but offered Gerhardie the £250 advance agreed with the *Express* for serial rights in weekly instalments. Gerhardie quickly found himself in difficulties. Thanks to Beaverbrook, his social life was exhausting; and he was constantly being asked for progress reports. Eventually he left London and went to the south of France, where during 1926 he made better progress with the book, despite Beaverbrook's interruptions. In France he encountered Rebecca

West: ' . . . you were the theme of our discussion,' he wrote to Beaver-brook. 'Curiously enough she is also writing a novel about you. . . .' Beaverbrook was not best pleased by this news, and sent West 'a dis-agreeable message'. Gerhardie seems to have picked up the story of Beaverbrook's alleged inability to perform sexually with Rebecca. He later wrote, in the context of their meeting: 'I define an impotent man as one deemed unable to seduce a woman who, lacking attraction to him, has really failed to seduce him. . . .'[11]

In June 1927 Gerhardie published *Pretty Creatures*, a book of short stories, which he dedicated to Beaverbrook, offering him the choice of two phrases: 'In the absence of Napoleon Buonaparte to William Max-well Baron Beaverbrook', or 'To Lord Beaverbrook'. The former was preferred. When in 1928 the new novel, *Jazz and Jasper*, was ready, he dedicated it to H. G. Wells; but although Beaverbrook told him it was brilliant it was not accepted for serialization in the *Express* after all, though Gerhardie was paid the promised sum.

Jazz and Jasper, a complex, fantastical novel of great originality, would have puzzled *Daily Express* readers.[12] It starts simply, with the eager, impoverished young writer Frank Dickin being summoned by the press magnate Lord Ottercove to the *Daily Runner* office in Fleet Street. Handed on from acolyte to acolyte, Frank ascends to the heart of the shrine: 'In a vast radiant space of yellow and blue, at an octago-nal table surrounded by chairs, sat a slim middle-sized figure in a dark blue suit, a negligent lock over the brow. It rose promptly, shook hands, gave the visitor one searching look with its penetrating grey eye . . . . From time to time Lord Ottercove would take up the receiver and say "Give me the Prime Minister" or "Give me the Duke of Liverpool." ' Ottercove instructs Frank to read his latest novel aloud and plies him with champagne; he also tells him he can draw as much money as he needs on account. Ottercove has Beaverbrook's turns of phrase – 'I am a man of the people. And my sympathies are with the people' – know-ledge of the Bible, and abrupt phrases for dismissal: 'Goodbye to you'. He also has some of Beaverbrook's friends, notably Vernon Sprott, 'the foreman of British fiction', and an eccentric Irish peer, Lord de Jones. Soon Frank finds himself joining the Ottercove entourage and starting to write a novel about him. He visits his town house overlooking the park, Stonedge Lodge, where Ottercove proclaims his passion for his newspapers ('I am amazed, with a sweet amazement, when I suddenly look into my heart and discover the depth of my love for these journals of mine') and also his 'unofficial home' in the leafy suburbs, 'whither he retired whenever he felt like swinging a loose leg', and where Frank encounters lovely, twittering actresses and is encouraged by Ottercove to make advances to a society beauty. Gerhardie captures the comedy and the menace of Beaverbrook's personality, his erratic generosity, and the electrifying impact he could make on a new admirer: 'To be alone with a man who has wrecked more than one Ministry . . . to feel the contact of power!' Like Beaverbrook, Ottercove moves in a whirlwind of secretaries, editors, maharajas, ministers and pretty women. He launches bizarre political campaigns – an increased crop-growing scheme, an anti-dog crusade. Gerhardie makes him godlike, but childlike too: 'He is Hannibal playing quoits with the world. Not, I regret to say, because he loves the world but because he loves playing quoits.'

A brilliant and convincing evocation of Beaverbrook and his milieu, *Jazz and Jasper* soon abandons realism and plot altogether and takes off, like Lord Ottercove's magic flying motorcar, into wilder and wilder fantasy, ending with the apocalyptic disintegration of the planet, the founding of a new race, and Ottercove himself, along with Vernon Sprott, transformed into stars twinkling in the night sky.

Gerhardie's novel was much admired by other young writers, especially Evelyn Waugh, and by Rebecca West, who read it 'with the greatest possible amusement'. Arnold Bennett went further, finding Ottercove described 'with a ruthlessness which yet somehow shows both appreciation and affection'. But like Gerhardie's previous books, it failed to sell. Ottercove reappeared in a later novel, *Of Mutual Love*, after Beaverbrook had taken on as a secretary, and very likely seduced, Gerhardie's great love Vera Boys. Beaverbrook's impact on his protégé was a mixed blessing: he made him famous more as a personality than as a writer, and distracted as much as he stimulated him by introducing him to smart society and profitable journalism. Beaverbrook's sudden enthusiasms cooled fast, and within a year or two his flying chariot had moved on, leaving Gerhardie, and his real but fragile talent, behind.

LORD CASTLEROSSE EXPANDS

Throughout the 1920s, wherever and whoever Beaverbrook was entertaining Viscount Castlerosse was likely to be present. After the war, Castlerosse had tried to settle down in his uncle Lord Revelstoke's Baring's Bank. He proved spectacularly unsuited to it. Rebuked for coming in late, he replied: 'But think how early I leave.'[13] Beaverbrook found Castlerosse an amusing and congenial companion, with useful social connections; and Castlerosse's increasingly dramatic indulgence of his appetite for food, drink and women provided Beaverbrook with a fascinating spectacle, at once titillating and shocking. 'Max has become my never ending lord of appeal,' Castlerosse wrote. 'He is always there, and always indulgent when I have made a fool of myself.' Already a big man, Castlerosse started to swell in an alarming manner; soon he was an imposing and instantly recognizable figure, with an egg-shaped, balding head, and a huge, billowing stomach that tapered down to elegantly shod feet. His shirts and suits were made for him by the best tailors; he patronized London's leading wine merchants, tobacconists, florists and barbers. His expenses were colossal.

Beaverbrook subsidized his friend's tastes. If they dined together, Beaverbrook naturally paid; if they went abroad together, as they began to do regularly, Beaverbrook took care of travelling and hotel expenses. They made frequent visits to Paris, and to the fashionable French coastal resorts – Deauville, Biarritz, Cannes and Monte Carlo. Sometimes Gladys and the children were in the party; more often they were not. In 1923 Castlerosse and Beaverbrook made rather a different journey together, to the Middle East; Beaverbrook, who was strongly anti-Zionist, was interested in seeing the region for himself. Castlerosse does not appear ever to have been seriously interested in either national or international politics, and was still mourning the loss of his French mistress. The curiously contrasting pair climbed the Mount of Olives together: 'Max was thinking of his maker and I was thinking of my Forzane,' Castlerosse observed.

Soon Castlerosse began to dabble in journalism. In 1922, on holiday in the south of France, he and Beaverbrook each wrote a story about Monte Carlo for the *Sunday Express*; Beaverbrook decided that his friend's was the better, and it was duly printed. 'I was proud as a Killarney peacock. It was then that Max asked me why I didn't go in for the newspaper business – why didn't I buy the *People*, for instance, which was then on the market? I laughed and told him the facts about the Kenmares, saying I had no money and didn't know anything about journalism. He said: I have money and I know about journalism. So we started negotiations.'

It was not until 1926 that Beaverbrook had the idea that gave Castlerosse his chance, and led both to his apotheosis and his self-destruction. Beaverbrook decided that the struggling *Sunday Express* should have a new kind of gossip columnist, a real insider, a social figure in his own right, someone who could produce not merely snippets of social news but a witty, reflective weekly account of high society. He offered Castlerosse the job of writing the Londoner's Log every Sunday, and announced him as 'the most brilliant diarist in London journalism'. From the outset, the column was a success: Castlerosse became a national figure and a power in social circles. As he himself conceded, his patron had a lot to do with the metamorphosis. 'Almost daily I would arrive with an article and he would correct it and criticise it. . . . I was beaten, bullied and badgered until I became a semblance of a journalist.' To Beaverbrook's delight, Castlerosse's column stirred up trouble. Influential people put pressure on Beaverbrook to control him. At the end of his first year, Beaverbrook wrote: 'He would be surprised to learn what some who are supposed to be his closest friends say about his work – while trying, often enough, at the very same time to get their names into his next article at any cost.' All of which provided Beaverbrook with the kind of game that he most relished. Castlerosse enjoyed himself too: ' . . . I am finding the only way I can express myself is in journalism. There is nothing that enthralls me quite so much as the written word – particularly at the bottom of a cheque.' He earned a fortune and claimed another in expenses, but still found he needed other sources of income, as his colleague Bruce Lockhart later discovered. A friend in the film business informed him 'that Castlerosse was the most expensive of all the London journalists. I asked him what he meant. He said he wants the most and insists on getting it for everything he puts in his Log about a show or an actress. I told Bell that if this were true Beaverbrook would be furious.'[14]

THE CHILDREN, GLADYS AND MRS NORTON

While his children were still small, Beaverbrook's frenetic life and increasingly public philandering scarcely affected them. They were secure at Cherkley with their mother's constant love and attention, and a series of nannies, governesses and tutors. Their father and his friends would descend in an exciting flurry of large cars, perhaps for a weekend of tennis, or for a party with music and dancing where a star like Noël Coward or Paul Robeson might appear; then they would all vanish again. Beaverbrook swung between indulgence and sudden moods of puritanical disapproval; the boys were often in trouble over pocket money, and Janet was infuriated by being ordered to leave the Cherkley cinema whenever a love scene began. She discovered the facts of life from a groom.

As they entered their teens, it began to be clear that none of the children was likely to be academically outstanding, and Max and Peter, both of whom were sent to Westminster School in London, began to concentrate on sport, to their father's alarm. Although he was proud when Max did well at cricket, and Peter proved to be an excellent tennis player, he increasingly thought they took games, and later cars and boats, too seriously. Once in the summer holidays he refused to let Max join a school cricket tour, insisting that he pack papers at the *Express* instead.

Max was taller and better-looking than his father, resembling his mother's father and brothers; as the elder son he bore the main weight of his father's expectations, and struggled to please him. Peter, the youngest, was quieter, very close to Gladys, and his relationship with his father was never easy. It appeared to the Cherkley staff and his teachers that he was frightened of Beaverbrook, and so retreated into silence. As a small child, Peter had been injured by a car in the drive at Cherkley; some members of the family believe the head injuries he received affected him for the rest of his life. Janet was strikingly like her mother in appearance, but her temperament came from her father. 'At her age I was much more wayward and gave plenty of trouble to those about me,' Beaverbrook wrote to Gladys as Janet grew up. 'As to Max and Peter. They are taking after you, just as Janet takes after me. And you have a much better personality than I have.'[15]

By the time she was in her mid-teens, Janet had begun to realize the distress her father's behaviour was causing her mother.[16] She fought with him frequently, especially when she started to acquire admirers of her own. He was not at all pleased when Michael Arlen courted her after she went to finishing school in Paris in 1925 at the age of seventeen. One contemporary has never forgotten a row between Janet and Beaverbrook at Stornoway House, when he snatched a large Chinese vase from the mantelpiece and smashed it on the floor. Beaverbrook used Castlerosse to keep track of his daughter's social life. He made her ride with him in Hyde Park in the early mornings, when he would accuse her of deception. 'Time you stopped gadding about. Develop a sense of responsibility.' 'Responsibility! To whom! Mother? What about you!' She accused him of hypocrisy in disapproving of her behaviour when his own was far worse. They had their worst row, she recalled, over Tallulah Bankhead, the extravagantly glamorous American actress who arrived in London in 1923 and became a theatrical sensation in the stage version of Arlen's *The Green Hat*. 'Father seemed to be getting too fond of Tallulah and I couldn't bear the thought of him hurting my beloved mother,' she wrote. 'When I told him so, a very bad argument followed. Father was defiant, telling me to shut up and mind my own business.'

Eventually, though, it was not an actress nor a writer nor any of his young protégés who caused serious trouble between Beaverbrook and Gladys, but a well-connected young married woman with two children, the Hon. Mrs Richard Norton.

In 1925 Jean Norton was twenty-seven and had been married for six years to her first love, Richard Norton, heir to Lord Grantley, from a landed Yorkshire family. Jean's father was Brigadier-General Sir David Kinloch, a Scottish baronet. The Nortons led a busy social life in London; she was strikingly good-looking, with blue eyes, wavy golden-brown hair, a glowing complexion and slender figure; he was easy going and witty, with a tendency to gamble and flirt. From the start the friendship with Beaverbrook included them both and their children, John and Sarah. Richard Norton remained on amicable terms with his wife's lover, no doubt because he had adventures of his own and because, although the relationship was no secret, the proprieties of the time were observed. Norton worked in the City and later in films, drove racing cars and was always short of money. Long before his marriage he had forfeited most of his inheritance as a result of rash borrowings. Nevertheless the Nortons lived in some style in a large London house with a ballroom, employed a butler, entertained and dined out, were seen at fashionable nightclubs and parties and formed part of a celebrated young married set that revolved around the Mountbattens. Michael Arlen used Jean Norton as a prototype for the elegant socialite women who fill his novels. Edwina Mountbatten and Jean were close friends; Lord Mountbatten was Sarah Norton's godfather. Richard Norton was a friend of Lord Birkenhead; another link to Beaverbrook's circle was Evelyn Fitzgerald, described by Norton as his second father.

By the end of 1925 Beaverbrook was seeing Jean Norton, known to her friends as 'Jeannie', frequently both in London and at Cherkley, sometimes with her husband, more often without. This time Gladys Beaverbrook's tolerance wore thin; perhaps the humiliation was too public, or perhaps she sensed that this time her husband was seriously in love with someone else. Janet thought her mother liked Jean, recognized her intelligence and character and was in a way relieved that Beaverbrook had taken up with someone of her quality; ' . . . she and Father fell genuinely in love,' wrote Janet. 'Gone were the actresses and the crazy times. . . . Mother's reaction was typical; relief on the one hand, for Father's own sake as much as hers, and on the other hand sadness and a profound sense of loss. . . . She tried her best to explain her feelings to me, asking me again not to be angry on her behalf. But I could see how hurt she really was.'

She had good reason. After nearly twenty years of marriage, Beaverbrook brought Mrs Norton into the centre of his life in a way he had not brought his other women. In 1925 he arranged for her to run a cinema he owned in Regent Street; he was still deeply involved in the film industry through Provincial Cinematograph Theatres, which by the mid-1920s controlled some eighty cinemas, and through his holding in Pathé, which led him for a time to consider linking newsreels with his newspapers. In May 1926, during the General Strike, Jean Norton and Edwina Mountbatten took over the switchboard at the *Express*, while Gladys Beaverbrook ran the canteen. Old friends of the Beaverbrooks began to invite Mrs Norton and Beaverbrook together; Arnold Bennett and Dorothy did so, as did Winston Churchill, to Clementine Churchill's alarm. She wrote to him, on hearing that in her absence Churchill was giving a lunch party at Chartwell: 'Please do not allow any very low conversation before the children . . . and I hope the relationship between him and Mrs Norton will not be apparent to Randolph and Diana's inquisitive marmoset-like eyes and ears. . . .'[17] Gladys Beaverbrook, according to Janet, even bought a separate house in London for herself and the children, but Beaverbrook made sure they never moved into it. Rumours persist among family and friends that she seriously threatened to leave him around this time, perhaps to go back to Canada for good; his brother Allan, who was devoted to Gladys, was said to be ready to marry her.[18]

The summer of 1926 was especially demanding for Lady Beaverbrook. Janet Aitken came out in the grand style: in May she was presented at court, wearing a Chanel dress in silver lamé with a lace train and the traditional feathers in her hair, and on 18 June a lavish ball was given for her at Stornoway House. On top of organizing her daughter's first season, Gladys had a prominent public part to play in a three-week tour of Great Britain, funded by her husband, by a group of high school teachers from New Brunswick.[19] The teachers arrived in Glasgow on 9 July, and on the 13th were given dinner by Lady Beaverbrook in Edinburgh, complete with 'haggis and nips', followed by speeches including 'A Welcome to the Mother Country' by Lady Beaverbrook. After touring through the Lake District, Warwick and Stratford they were given lunch at Stornoway House on 19 July and an eight-course formal banquet that evening at the Hyde Park Hotel. A quartet played, Beaverbrook's favourite New Brunswick song 'The Jones Boys' was sung, and both Lady Beaverbrook and the guest of honour, Lord Birkenhead (then Secretary of State for India) made speeches. Next day she entertained them to tea on the terrace of the House of Lords; two days later, after being received by the Vice Chancellor in Oxford, they were at Cherkley, where they met Lloyd George. In a group photograph taken on the terrace a genial Lloyd George sits on Lady Beaverbrook's right, a small dog scrabbling at his knee. Leaning over Lloyd George's shoulder is a smiling Beaverbrook; the ranks of Canadian teachers are ranged behind Gladys. She wears a becoming wide-brimmed hat and pearls, and looks wistful.

As in Ashton-under-Lyne fifteen years before, Gladys Beaverbrook was always a success on public occasions; but to one observer, her secretary Margaret Guthrie, it appeared that Beaverbrook was not pleased when his wife made an impression on an audience. She recalls an occasion when, after Gladys spoke,

> . . . they were clapping and cheering and standing on tables, she was so marvellous. He didn't like that at all, and ordered the car and sent her home. He had Lady Mountbatten and Mrs Norton there too, of course. He sent her back to Cherkley alone. Miss Evans, the housekeeper, who was devoted to her rang me up and said: 'What's he doing to her now? I think it's driving her to drink'. Apparently she got out of the car weeping and asked Miss Evans for a whisky and soda, which was very unusual for her.[20]

One weekend at Cherkley in the late summer of 1926, when Jean Norton was again one of the guests, Gladys Beaverbrook, according to Janet, decided she had had enough. 'Late one night, she came to my room and sat on my bed. Impulsively she grabbed my hand, then smiled. "Let's go to Canada," she said.'

Mother and daughter spent several months in Canada during the winter of 1926 and the spring of 1927. For much of the time, Gladys was mysteriously ill; she was in hospital in Montreal for several weeks, had two minor operations and a long convalescence during which her brother Chipman Drury kept Beaverbrook informed of her progress and supplied her with flowers on her brother-in-law's behalf. Janet herself suddenly got appendicitis and was also in hospital, but Beaverbrook did not visit them. In November 1926 the Dean of the Medical School at McGill University wrote to Beaverbrook about his wife's condition. He reported no 'organic disease' but went on,

> Lady Beaverbrook suffered from a very obvious and marked nervous exhaustion; she has apparently been living up to the limit of her nervous strength now for a good long while. . . . We have all discussed the question of her going back to England and we feel it would be well for her to wait here until after Christmas in order to avoid the many duties which her position naturally involves, and I hope you will not object to this decision.[21]

A few letters have survived from Gladys to her husband from Canada; they call him 'My Darling One', and suggest that she still loved him and wanted to be back with him. He preserved one long letter he wrote to her while she was ill.

> How I wish you well again. There is so much happiness in life for you and me if you will get strong. . . . For myself, I have many faults. But I love you. If the expression of that love is full of faults the defects spring from a wilful and wayward past. But so far as my love is constant and fixed you are the object of it. . . . You must show me how to bring back the happy and joyous days of our youth . . . if you don't get well quickly you know in your heart I shall get into a state of apprehension and anxiety. And when you are doubtful think of how much I've improved in such a short time. Heaven knows there was room for it. And I declare that you are the only permanent love in my bad and wicked life. So come back soon and strong too.[22]

Fond though this letter is, it also carries the strong suggestion that she could get well if she really wanted to and that it is her duty to him to do so. Meanwhile the visitors' book at Cherkley for Christmas that year has four signatures: Beaverbrook, his two sons Max and Peter, and Jean Norton.

In April 1927 Gladys returned to England, apparently better, but still inclined to complain of headaches and exhaustion. Doctors, principally Sir Thomas Horder, ascribed her malaise to emotional and nervous troubles, and recommended rest; and so while Beaverbrook spent much of the summer cruising round the resorts of northern France in chartered yachts with parties of fashionable people including the Nortons, Castlerosse and the Fitzgeralds, Gladys stayed quietly at a hotel in Le Touquet. Janet remained with her, but was distracted by her first ious love affair: she was set on marrying Ian Campbell, the future ike of Argyll. Suddenly Gladys Beaverbrook's condition worsened; doctors were brought from England to take her home. Janet remembered a rough crossing and her mother in terrible pain.

During the summer of Gladys's illness, Beaverbrook's mother died suddenly at the age of seventy-eight. In the years since the First World War she had travelled a great deal, usually with one of her daughters, at Beaverbrook's expense; she visited Europe several times, and especially enjoyed the south of France. It was on her way to visit her daughter Laura, now married and living in a large house in Scotland, that she died; she had a heart attack while trying to open a window at Newcastle station. William Gerhardie, who met her in Cannes in 1926, recorded in a notebook that he found her 'an old lady of formidable strength of character. She looked as though she had been hewn out of granite.' He also thought Beaverbrook seemed 'ill at ease' in her company, 'even though he had just nipped round to settle her hotel bill'. She was buried in Scotland.

On 9 September Beaverbrook set off for a short visit to Germany, taking with him Diana Cooper, Venetia Montagu, Castlerosse and Arnold Bennett. In Berlin there were meetings in connection with a film to be financed by Beaverbrook, written by Bennett and to star Lady Diana – alas, never made. Castlerosse took the party round the transvestite nightclubs; the young Sefton Delmer, in Berlin for the *Express*, was sent out to buy 'homosexual and nudist magazines' for the party's amusement. In London, Gladys continued to be ill; old friends like Carrie Kipling came to see her;[23] everyone was concerned, but the doctors, including Horder, still reported that they could find nothing physically wrong with her and that her troubles were emotional. Beaverbrook believed them; when invited to stay at Waddesdon with James de Rothschild, along with Venetia Montagu, Diana Cooper and the Birkenheads 'and Gladys if she is well enough', he wrote on 30 November declining on grounds of Gladys's illness, but added: 'Gladys' condition is not dangerous but she has sudden attacks of great stress and I am useful when things go wrong.' But later the same day he cabled to her brother Chip in Montreal: 'Gladys seriously ill and we are anxious.'[24]

In the early hours of 1 December, at Stornoway House, with a frantic Beaverbrook still being told by Horder that she would recover, she died. She was thirty-nine, and was found to have had a brain tumour.

Beaverbrook's grief, compounded by guilt, was intense. 'My father looked stunned, as if for the first time in his life something had affected him too deeply for him to comprehend it,' Janet wrote. ' "My harbour has gone," he said. The tragedy of it seemed to mystify him. Then, "I loved her so much but she was too good for me." He kept saying it, over and over again.' Margaret Guthrie recalls that Beaverbrook was 'devastated. For the moment, he was a broken man.' He exhibited what struck her as clear signs of a guilty conscience. He made a point of destroying all his wife's papers, including almost all her letters to him; then he took her secretary out in his car and questioned her, 'to find out what I knew; but he had got the wrong person'.[25] He also, it is said, approached the nurse who was with his wife at the end and offered her money to remain silent: he was afraid that she might have let slip something damaging to him.[26] The family felt a lasting sense of anger against her doctors, especially Horder, but he continued to be on excellent terms with Beaverbrook.

Gladys Beaverbrook was buried on 4 December 1927 in the churchyard at Mickleham, the village close to Cherkley. The Fitzgeralds were present, as were Sir James Dunn, Castlerosse, Blumenfeld, Arnold Bennett and Ian Campbell. Janet Aitken laid posies of violets, her mother's favourite flowers, in the grave. Bennett wrote in his diary:

> The entrance of the coffin, covered with really magnificent wreaths, was moving. Max was leaning on young Max's arm and looked quite old. Chopin's funeral march at the end – not equal to Handel's. 'Abide with me' at the end. . . . Then the coffin goes out again, and a scene of terrible damp cold at the graveside, and our hats off . . . these funeral rites in an English winter are absolutely barbaric. I met Max at the gate, and was so moved, unknown to myself till the moment came, that I could not speak to him.

The editor of the *Sunday Express* wrote a tribute to Gladys Beaverbrook, praising her ' . . . warm sincerity and radiant spontaneity of feeling. . . . The little world of Shoe Lane adored her. . . .' In the *Express*, Lord Birkenhead wrote: 'She had great humour and great humanity. . . . She was essentially womanly and being womanly she was incredibly understanding. . . . She made allowances easily and generously. . . .'

Two days after the funeral Beaverbrook asked the Church of Scotland minister of St Columba's, Pont Street, to make the arrangements for Janet's wedding to Ian Campbell. The wedding was to be strictly private, with no music except the wedding march. Janet decided to marry immediately because Campbell pressed her and because she wanted to escape her misery. Friends remember that her father never quite forgave her; she remembered him saying: 'If you think it will make you happy, darling. But never forget that I disapprove.' Thus it happened that, nine days after her mother's death, Janet Aitken was married; she wore a traditional white dress with veil and train and carried violets. Both the rector of Mickleham who had taken the funeral service and the minister who conducted the wedding received handsome cheques from Beaverbrook. On 14 December Beaverbrook left for New York and Canada with his sons.

In his letter of thanks, the minister sent Beaverbrook his deep sympathy and added that he must be undergoing 'a profoundly strange mixture of feelings at this time'.[27] The minister was right; by the end of 1927 Beaverbrook was in a curious state of mind. It was hardly surprising. In the space of six months he had lost not only his wife, who for all his neglect he relied on and in his selfish fashion cared for, and who was his strongest link with the high hopes of his earlier self; he had also lost his mother; and finally his eldest child and only daughter, through marriage to a man about whom he had misgivings from the start, a man from the heart of the aristocratic society that Beaverbrook always partly envied, partly despised. For once, as he distributed Gladys's jewellery and Waterford glass among her relations and friends, he looked back and reflected; in a letter to a friend of hers in Canada he wrote: 'How I wish we might turn time back to twenty years ago. It was such fun and we didn't know what to make of our opportunities. We have done well . . . but we have lived too swiftly to know the joy of it.'[28]

Around the same time he told a new political acquaintance, Frank Wise, 'Unhappily I am a ruined man in the world of politics. I cannot take any interest in current events . . . the real truth is that I am no longer of any use in the world.'[29]

CHAPTER 14

THE GREAT CAMPAIGN
1928-1929

SIX WEEKS AFTER Gladys's death, on his return from the United States and Canada on the *Aquitania* with Max and Peter on 13 January 1928, Beaverbrook resumed his love affair with Jean Norton. She was to play a large part in his life for the next seventeen years, although his love for her was neither exclusive nor consistent. While undoubtedly in love with Beaverbrook, Jean Norton – by all accounts a sweet-natured woman – remained devoted to her family and on good terms with her husband. Her relationship with Beaverbrook was stormy; and although the general view at the time and since was that he treated her badly, wanting her complete attention and devotion while allowing himself the freedom to conduct other affairs, she too wanted things both ways – to hold on to him while at the same time remaining respectably married, looking after her children and keeping up a busy, glamorous social life. She was often torn by divided loyalties.

Four of Jean Norton's diaries covering the years 1928–31 are still among Beaverbrook's papers. Although the entries are brief, they record emotions as well as engagements and give clear, if fragmentary, glimpses of the relationship. On the day that Beaverbrook arrived back in London she wrote: 'Had tea in the nursery with the children and waited till 7.30 to telephone. . . . M came to see me at 10 and we talked till 12.' Next day he went down to Cherkley with his sons; according to the visitors' book, the only people staying there for the first weekend party since Gladys's death were Evelyn and Helen Fitzgerald. During the next few weeks Cherkley saw a stream of Beaverbrook's oldest and closest friends: Castlerosse, Blumenfeld, Sir James and Lady Dunn, Mrs Montagu (to whom he had sent an emotional telegram on sailing from New York, one of the very few scraps of evidence of distress that survived his removal of the traces of Gladys's death from his files: 'I turned to you in my despair and you gave me comfort: Max'), the McKennas, the Coopers, Tim Healy, Lord Wargrave, Arnold Bennett and Birkenhead.[1] Jean Norton's name does not appear; but her diary tells a different story. Every few days during the spring and early summer she and Beaverbrook would meet. Sometimes he called on her; more often she went to Stornoway House or they walked or rode in Green Park. She was often at Cherkley, for a night or two during the week as well as at weekends. In London they met frequently at The Vineyard; sometimes she dined there and then returned home; sometimes she dined elsewhere, often at the Embassy Club, and joined him later. He was not always alone: 'Went to V late Winston Churchill there,' one diary entry notes.

Occasionally Richard Norton was also present; but he travelled abroad a good deal and pursued his own love affairs. The conventions were observed, but no one close to either establishment could have had any doubt as to what was going on – apart from the Nortons' two children, who were too young to regard Beaverbrook as anything other than a family friend. Indeed, Beaverbrook took trouble to be precisely that. He discussed banking business with Norton, who in 1927 secured a well-paid job with Kuhn, Loeb, where Beaverbrook's old friend Otto Kahn was a partner. He cultivated Jean's father, Sir David Kinloch; he was warm and flattering to Norton's sister Kay, who ran a dress shop, and to Jean's sister Kitty. He sent the Norton children presents and gave them treats. For her part, Jean took trouble with Beaverbrook's children, with some success where Janet was concerned; the boys were less easy, but everyone behaved well.

Every week or two, there would be 'trouble' or 'a row with M'. Trouble always arose from the same sources; her plans conflicting with his; his interest in other women; and money. Over the years Beaverbrook gave Mrs Norton substantial sums in cash and shares, some of them in his newspapers. He made her an allowance, provided her with a car through the *Evening Standard*, and helped her to buy and furnish a house.[2] Apparently he paid Richard Norton's debts more than once.[3] Her friends at the time all recall that Jean Norton was extremely jealous of the various women to whom Beaverbrook paid court. Her diary shows that between 1928 and 1931 she was particularly wary of Diana Cooper, Helen Fitzgerald and Bridget Paget; there would be rows over 'my making a fuss', after which she would try to be 'sensible' when he announced that he was having dinner with one or the other.

In the summer of 1928 Beaverbrook was not easy to be with. He was unsettled and moody and talking of changing his way of life entirely – of expanding the horse-racing interests he had started in a small way in 1925, of abandoning his newspapers, leaving London and giving up Cherkley, as if he needed to get away from the places where Gladys's presence lingered. Instead, some time after her death he put up a huge cross in the garden, which was floodlit at night. He planned to spend more time at Newmarket, where Jean Norton helped him buy furniture and plan the decorations for a new house which he decided, with bravado, to rename Calvin Lodge. Much energy was spent on a plan for an enormous mural in the dining room by a briefly fashionable painter, Mary Adshead. She was commissioned to paint a group of Beaverbrook's friends, including Jean Norton, Diana Cooper, Venetia Montagu and the Lords Castlerosse, Derby and Birkenhead. Lord Beaverbrook's horse Restigouche in his colours (beaver brown, with maple leaf green cross belts and cap), his dog Tasso, and two of his menservants, Albert and Chambers, were also to be featured, and photographs of them all were supplied. The whole scene was to have the paddocks at Newmarket for background and to be entitled *Going to the Races*. Alas, by August Beaverbrook had changed his mind and withdrew the commission, contriving to pay the artist barely half what she asked for her work to date.[4]

Neither Beaverbrook's preference for Newmarket nor his interest in racing lasted much longer, although he had his biggest success at Epsom in 1928 when one of his horses, Alacrity, won the Great Metropolitan Stakes. But he found the unpredictability and the rumours of fixing intolerable. Beaverbrook hated to feel that he was an amateur in the hands of experts, whom he assumed would trick him. Racing, he decided, was a mugs' game. A gossip columnist observed him frequently at the races 'wearing a soft black hat which makes him look like an artist, and sadly watching his horses come in last'. Arnold Bennett visited Calvin Lodge and left a poignant picture of Beaverbrook's reaction when one of his best colts was injured: 'The host was considerably upset. "Dear, dear! This is very grave!". He kept on muttering to himself. "The colt was only six months old and worth £3,000." Deep gloom.' Beaverbrook made Bennett accompany him on 'a muddy tour of the vast field to find traces of equine hair and blood on the wire. . . . The host suddenly remarked, "All possessions are a mistake! All possessions are a mistake." We returned to the house and had a melancholy tea.'[5]

In the aftermath of Gladys's death Beaverbrook relied upon his old cronies and companions, and was less than ever inclined to share them. He was thus greatly put out by the secret marriage, in May 1928, of Valentine Castlerosse to the society adventuress Doris Delavigne. He, along with Castlerosse's elderly parents, the Earl and Countess of Kenmare, and most other observers, could see only trouble ahead: Doris was beautiful, ruthless and unlikely to be faithful. By the time she captivated Castlerosse she had already been the mistress of a series of rich men and was renowned for extravagance, quick temper and bad language.[6] It was widely assumed that she was after Castlerosse's title and social influence; their rows, both public and private, were soon famous; and the Kenmares came over to London to ask Beaverbrook to dissuade his friend and protégé from such a disastrous match. The story goes that Beaverbrook, hearing rumours of marriage, at once invited Castlerosse on an irresistible jaunt to Cannes, where the fact that Doris soon joined him only came to light after Beaverbrook noticed that he was being charged for a large quantity of champagne and an extra room. Beaverbrook failed to stop the marriage and was given the task of breaking the news to the Kenmares; Lady Kenmare was already in such a state that Beaverbrook told her doctor to stand by, but she rallied when he informed her that the ceremony had been performed in a registry office. 'Thank God. That means they're not really married,' she gasped. Beaverbrook then brought mother and son together to decide on an announcement, and would later recount with much amusement how they argued over the wording.[7] However, at the time he took the capture of Castlerosse hard: 'M got bad news about Valentine. Gloomy evening,' wrote Jean Norton, on 25 May.

MEMBERS OF THE CIRCLE

Perhaps because of his wife's death and his need for distraction, or perhaps because Jean Norton and her circle were playing the central part in his life, in the late 1920s and early 1930s Beaverbrook was more involved in high society than ever before. At Stornoway House and at Cherkley – The Vineyard was used for quiet rendezvous – he was host to fashionable and titled society women like Sylvia Ashley, Maureen Stanley, Bridget Paget, Sheila Milbanke and June Inverclyde; his correspondence is sprinkled with affectionate, wheedling notes from hostesses asking him to support their charity balls; his brief replies are frequently flirtatious. He was on amiable terms with the leading hostesses of the day, Sibyl Colefax and Emerald Cunard – although he greatly disliked Lady Cunard's passion, the opera, and usually managed to dodge it.

Apart from Castlerosse, who was out of favour for a while following his marriage to Doris, at the end of the 1920s Beaverbrook was much in the company of two well-connected younger men whom he had added to his payroll: Robert Bruce Lockhart and Michael Wardell.

Bruce Lockhart possessed many advantages. He was clever, handsome in a dark, saturnine manner, highly regarded for his knowledge of foreign countries, especially Russia, and a good writer. His weaknesses were for high life, drink and women. Partly on that account, leading to constant worries about money, he was – as his voluminous diary shows – in thrall to Beaverbrook both personally and professionally, in a way that he recognized but could not easily break. He was married with a small son, but his marriage was under strain and he was always involved with at least one other woman; in the later 1920s it was Lady Rosslyn, known as Tommy, wife of the 5th Earl. Through her he met the Prince of Wales. Although Beaverbrook and the Prince hardly knew each other, they were connected in various ways from the mid-1920s onwards, not least through Jean Norton, whose husband had known the Prince since Cambridge and whose sister, Kitty Kinloch, married in 1927 Peregrine Cust, the heir to Lord Brownlow and another of the Prince's contemporaries. Beaverbrook was about to give Cust a job on the *Standard* when his father died and he inherited the title; instead, Beaverbrook lent him a large sum to tide him over.[8] At first, the heir to the throne was wary of the press lord; in 1928, shortly before he took up his new job, Bruce Lockhart played golf with the Prince and his then mistress, Freda Dudley Ward, and wrote afterwards in his diary: 'The Prince does not like Beaverbrook, says he wants to get everyone under his thumb and, if he cannot get them, he tries to down them.'

Michael Wardell was another member of the smart young set surrounding the Prince of Wales. He was a tall, dashing ex-cavalry officer with a passion for hunting, who had lost an eye in a riding accident and wore a black patch that increased his considerable success with women. For a time Wardell was a lover of Edwina Mountbatten, still Jean Norton's closest friend. As he later recalled, one day in 1926 after a weekend with the Mountbattens and the Prince he received a sudden telephone call from Beaverbrook and instructions to report next day to the *Evening Standard* office, where he would be offered a job. After a tricky moment when it was realized that the job in question was already taken, a space was made in the circulation department; he soon rose to be managing director and remained part of Beaverbrook's team and on close terms with Beaverbrook for the next thirty years.[9]

The Mountbattens, unlike most of Beaverbrook's stylish but impecunious upper-class friends, had no need of his money; but sometimes other favours were required. Lord Mountbatten would ask for a job for someone leaving the Navy, or favourable press coverage for a naval event, and early in 1928 Beaverbrook stepped in to protect Edwina, who was about to be named as co-respondent in an American divorce case. Beaverbrook cabled a friend, the leading New York lawyer Paul Cravath, to ask if the threat was serious. If so, 'Our money resources are sufficient or if money no use we will offer immense social influence in support of plaintiff. . . .' He offered to do 'anything at any time . . . even to go to America'. Evidently Cravath persuaded the plaintiff that it would be unwise to name Lady Mountbatten; the lawyer received Beaverbrook's lavish praise and thanks 'for taking such effective steps . . . so deeply am I attached to Lady Louis that I felt bound to approach the best lawyer in America.'[10]

More and more, Beaverbrook's entourage resembled a court, with favourites, both men and women, jostling for position. Jean Norton and Castlerosse (who was back in favour before long, spreading a tale about how boring Beaverbrook had been finding Wardell's company) were queen and court jester respectively, but even they were kept on the alert – by the whims of the sovereign as much as by the wiles of the competition. Both, after all, were financially dependent on Beaverbrook – indeed, could not have led the life they liked without him. Castlerosse especially struck Bruce Lockhart as knowing how to handle Beaverbrook, and what was expected of him:

No man plays up to Max better than Valentine who is the prince of toadies and 'bum-suckers'. Valentine, however, is not the fool people take him for. He has an amazing belief in his own journalistic genius, believes that he can sway millions of people, and that he is an immense power in Fleet Street. He does not write with his tongue in his cheek. Hence his success. To do him justice he is very loyal to Max and fights his battles for him with a lack of finesse and subtlety which would drive Max frantic if he could hear him.'[11]

Beaverbrook always kept a soft spot for his old favourites, especially Venetia Montagu, and above all remained devoted to Diana Cooper, although he and her husband, Duff Cooper, never liked each other and were increasingly at odds politically. He sent her presents and cheques, bought champagne for her parties and still wrote to her (though she was not the only one) as 'My first and last love'. During the mid-1920s she was in the United States for much of the time, appearing in the religious spectacular *The Miracle*; Beaverbrook's banker friend Otto Kahn was one of its major backers. Her earnings financed her husband's entry into politics, as Conservative MP for Oldham, in 1924. By 1928 she was back in England and often saw Beaverbrook; the favours and expressions of mutual affection continued, but sometimes even she could not make him do what she wanted. In 1928, when he sold his cinema interests for over £1 million to the Ostrer brothers, the deal took precedence over an arrangement with her and he sent her a mock grovelling telegram: 'Dear and good Diana . . . I returned to Stornoway House at half past eleven greatly excited and forgetting everything except the aftermath of financial battle. . . . Men of affairs are unreliable in social appointments and deserve nothing but contempt and derision from the world of society and politics. But I plead for and seek after forgiveness confidently from one who understands everything. I would ask in person but must spend all this day counting the money we get from our sale.'[12]

When Duff Cooper needed Beaverbrook's support at the general election in 1929, Diana did not hesitate to ask for it and believed she had it. However, when the *Daily Express* ignored his campaign, she wrote Beaverbrook a scorching letter. ' . . . you . . . repeatedly and emphatically declared that for my sake you would do all that you could for Duff in this election . . . the *Daily Express* up here should give his speeches more reports than the speeches of those unblessed by your friendship. . . . There is neither trouble nor discomfort in what you appeared so ready to do for me, and yet. . . .' He wrote coolly in reply: 'Your letter is an interesting exposure of the many defects in the conduct and character of the *Express* newspaper', and continued, 'I am sending instruction through Robertson to the Editor of the Manchester edition to support Duff and give space to some of his speeches.'[13] Even so, Duff Cooper lost. In general, the Beaverbrook papers gave him an easy time even when his views were diametrically opposed to the proprietor's. 'Do you love your wife?' he was said to have asked an *Express* journalist who produced some anti-Duff copy: 'Well I love Cooper's wife, so lay off him.'[14]

Later in 1929, when Diana was anxiously awaiting the birth of her child, Beaverbrook wrote from the Ritz in Paris a particularly affectionate and concerned letter of, for him, unusual length: 'I am longing to hear news of you and I am just now waiting for a call to the D.E. office.' He offered her advice, should she feel any nervous strain, 'based on experience' – presumably Gladys's, rather than his. He tells her how he longs to see more of her; '. . . my race is nearly run [he was just fifty] as we say in our church. So you should see me sometimes during my last lap. . . .' To amuse her, he describes the Castlerosses' fights. 'This woman Lady Castlerosse is at the hotel. I had no idea until I arrived with her hubby. Believe me truly the civil war is the worst I've ever known in my wide experience of married life. . . .' Doris was staying two floors above Beaverbrook and Castlerrosse. 'The telephone is going by night and by day and the shouting and the turmoil never dies but the Captain (that's me) is about to depart. . . . It is beyond my power to get to the bottom of the well or cess pool . . . here is the end of the paper and I'm still waiting for the telephone. How I hate suspense. For ever and ever, Max.'[15]

When Diana Cooper's son John Julius was born, on 15 September, she soon sent Beaverbrook a telegram: 'Poor Baby a Repliqua [sic] of you' and asked him to be godfather 'in case the Presbiterians [sic] are right'.

For all his close involvement with Jean Norton and his enduring, if erratic, devotion to his old flames, Beaverbrook remained susceptible to young women, and in the late 1920s he took up one in particular: Daphne Weymouth, a tall, exceptionally attractive and eager girl who in 1927 had married Lord Weymouth, heir to the Marquess of Bath. Like Diana Cooper, Daphne was drawn to Beaverbrook at first by the enticing prospect of making money writing for his newspapers; the young couple were having trouble living on their allowances from their respective parents. It was Castlerosse who, as Daphne (later Fielding) has described, took her to Stornoway House after lunch one day in 1928:

> As we entered the sitting room downstairs, which was approached through an anteroom bristling with telephones, typists and secretaries, I was faced by a little man with an enormous head spreading himself in a big armchair, with one leg cocked over the other and a grin on his impish face stretching from ear to ear. Valentine explained that I wanted to be a journalist, and Lord Beaverbrook asked me if I would like to write an article for one of his papers. Nothing could have delighted me more.

He asked her a lot of questions about herself and then said: 'How would you and your husband like to come on a trip to the West Indies with me?' When Daphne said she would love to if her husband agreed, Beaverbrook asked them both to dinner. He then gave her a subject for an article – the art of conversation; she soon produced a rough draft. 'My effort was rotten,' she says, '. . . and my choice of conversationalists was not at all representative. He told me it was no good and began describing those figures in modern society who he thought were the best talkers. I went home and wrote another article, airing his opinions as my own. . . . "Good stuff", said Lord Beaverbrook when I handed it in.'[16]

Jean Norton, meanwhile, spent much of the summer of 1928 with Beaverbrook, although there was terrible 'trouble' over her refusal to agree to go on the visit he was proposing to make to Russia. Beaverbrook left for Deauville with his sons; after a few days Jean Norton joined him, travelling out with Edwina Mountbatten. Later in August she spent ten days at Cherkley, and then they went to Scotland to see his daughter Janet, who, pregnant and unwell, was staying with her aunt.

Janet's marriage to Ian Campbell was already in difficulties.[17] By her own account, it was during their honeymoon that she first realized that he was a compulsive gambler: he had taken some of her jewellery and sold it. She had to ask her father to pay their return fares from Jamaica; she was already pregnant. When she saw him again, '. . . a wide grin spread from ear to ear. It spread even wider when I told him he was to be a grandfather.' Nevertheless, 'I sensed he knew more about my husband than either of us was prepared to admit.' He probably did; he liked to know people's weaknesses, and it would not have been hard to discover Ian Campbell's. But he did his best; he proposed Campbell as a candidate for Ashton-under-Lyne, and fixed him up with a job on the *Evening Standard*; neither came to anything. He rented the young couple a house near Cherkley. When Ian Campbell again needed money, Janet appealed once more to her father. He wrote back:

> My little lamb,
>   I have received your letters. Don't bother any more. Your husband's complicated financial affairs should not concern you in any case. Look after your own money and keep it safe for your middle life. In old age, the poor-house is just as agreeable as a palace. Some other day, when you are in London and well and strong, I will talk with you about your baby boy or girl. But I think it would be better if I, too, avoided any dealings with your husband in money matters. It would make for better relations all round. So we will agree not to discuss money with him – or to discuss his money or the want of it with each other. Your loving Father.

Janet took this evasive, if loving, letter as a rejection. 'So I was going to have to make it on my own. I hid my mother's jewellery and waited, trying not to panic.'

Towards the first anniversary of Gladys Beaverbrook's death, in November of 1928, the birth of Beaverbrook's first grandchild was imminent. At the end of November he received a letter from Gladys's sister, Arabella Languedoc – a letter full of affection and concern, with not a hint of reproach. She thanked him for the generous present, apparently of money, that he had given her when she was in England that year, and signed herself 'your devoted Arabella'.[18]

On 10 December 1928, after a difficult birth, Beaverbrook's first grandchild, Jeanne Louise Campbell (later known as Jean or Jeannie), who was to become his favourite and, as she grew up, an increasingly important presence in his life, was born. Christmas that year was spent at Cherkley; on 28 December, driving up to London with Maurice Woods, a talented member of his personal staff for ten years, the car was involved in a serious accident in which Woods was badly hurt, though Beaverbrook was only bruised and shaken. Jean Norton rushed to Stornoway House to look after him: 'M slept very badly stayed up most of the time.' The next day, however, found her playing bridge to cheer him up, along with Castlerosse, Max and Peter; but to Beaverbrook it must have seemed an ominous end to the year.

To Baldwin, it appeared that Beaverbrook had been changed for the better by his recent experiences. In the aftermath of his accident he decided to give £25,000 to charity, and he chose Baldwin to organize the distribution of the bulk of the money. Baldwin told the deputy secretary to the Cabinet, Tom Jones: 'He is an extraordinary mixture and I think that since the death of his wife the better elements of him have been coming to the surface. He had a really narrow escape from death and I found him very earnest about things. . . . He told me that after Bonar's death he had played a low mean game and that he was sorry. Whereupon I said I wished to bear no malice towards any man, and I shook hands with him.'[19] The money for charity was not the only financial negotiation between Beaverbrook and Baldwin at this time. Correspondence with J. C. C. Davidson, by now chairman of the Conservative Party, shows that between late 1928 and mid-1929 Beaverbrook tried to buy a knighthood for Andrew Holt, the businessman son of Sir Herbert Holt, the Montreal banker. The sum of £10,000 was apparently sent to Davidson for the purpose; after the arrangement came to nothing, the money was returned.[20]

In a difficult year, there had been one constructive achievement. In the autumn of 1928, Beaverbrook published the first volume of *Politicians and the War*, covering 1914–16 and dedicated 'To Mary Law and the memory of the past'. It had been more than ten years in the making, and he had done his utmost to ensure, by sending proofs to those concerned, that his version of events would not be accused of inaccuracy or cause offence. To Churchill he wrote flatteringly at some length: 'You will reap the harvest of history owing to the importance of the period in which you have taken a leading part. . . . My view is that you should not object to a just and impartial contemporary sketch written by no unfriendly hand.' Churchill produced no serious objections, although he did wonder where Beaverbrook had acquired some of his material, and Beaverbrook wrote again to assure him he was safe. 'Nowhere in the book is there the slightest charge of intrigue brought against you – which is more than can be said of other figures in these pages.' Churchill wrote back: 'I think it vy valuable and sincere, recalling the earliest Max I knew – when he still had worlds to conquer, and kings to captivate . . . it has given me gt pleasure to read it. Candour and faithful keeping of confidences are not easy to combine. But you have succeeded.' After deploring the 'ghastly muddle' that the war became, despite the best efforts of decent men, Churchill added a postscript that reads ironically today: 'No More War'.[21]

Beaverbrook had summed up his approach, unaware of any inconsistency, in a revealing letter to another of his subjects, Birkenhead: 'My one desire is to be honest in my narrative, and at the same time to praise and glorify the good deeds of the friends I believe in. I am sincerely concerned to exalt the reputation of the public men who carried the responsibilities of office during the war.'[22] In the published introduction to the book, he went further: '. . . the idea that statesmen have little or nothing to do with the winning or losing of war is a dangerous delusion. The politician in war-time has a sufficiently bad time anyhow. War certainly does nothing to exalt him above his due. He is not a popular figure, and the soldiers and sailors get all the worship and glory.' He presented the book with uncharacteristic diffidence, calling it 'not history in the strict sense. It is merely a contribution to history. . . .' The book was serialized in the *Standard*.

The reception of *Politicians and the War* was warmer in private than in public, although it sold 9000 copies. Beaverbrook's book was compared unfavourably to Asquith's memoirs, which also appeared in 1928, and the best reviews appeared in his own papers. The *Daily Express* called it 'a work of great historical importance' and A. G. Gardiner in the *Sunday Express* acknowledged it as 'a real contribution to the resources of the historian'. The *New Statesman*, however, was contemptuous: 'A great deal of it is sheer unhistorical nonsense.'

Publication of the second part of the story, dealing with the crisis of 1916, was put off by Beaverbrook's renewed political activities and by an altercation with the publishers over terms. Eventually, when Beaverbrook decided to publish it himself, it appeared early in 1932. After repeating that his purpose remained to do justice to the contribution made by politicians, as well as 'military – and in a few cases naval – . . . personages who naturally tend to exalt their own professions at the expense of the civilian', he made the central theme of Vol II crystal-clear. 'I know that Bonar Law was the greatest figure on the political stage . . . from 1915 to 1922. And I can prove it.' The book received less praise, and sold worse (under 3000 copies), than the first.

LOVE AND MONEY

To mark his recovery from his car crash, Beaverbrook took a party of friends for a cruise; the place to go for sun in the winter had become, instead of the south of France, the West Indies. In January 1929 his party for a month on the *Laconia* included Jean Norton, her sister and brother-in-law Kitty and Perry Brownlow, his new friends Daphne and Henry Weymouth, and a friend of Daphne's, Lady Lettice Lygon, daughter of Earl Beauchamp. The women brought their maids. As the departure date approached Jean Norton was anxious and unwell. She had annoyed Beaverbrook by asking if she could leave him while he was convalescing to go to Scotland to fetch her children. 'Very stupid of me,' she wrote. She developed a bad cold and went to bed, feeling miserable. 'Can't think why I am such a fool when I do mean so well.' But then Beaverbrook, evidently recovered, came to visit her and they made up their quarrel: 'M came round, lovely time. Life is so good again,' she recorded on 7 January.

She was still unwell when she joined the group at Southampton, and so went straight to bed. Next day she heard from her sister Kitty that Beaverbrook was flirting with one of the other women: 'Can't believe it really but wish I was up and about and able to be with him.' Then things looked up, but within a day or two trouble struck again: '. . . very unhappy night tried hard to be wise because I shall drive him away if I go on being foolish. . . .' By the end of the month they have reached the West Indies and all is bliss. St Vincent, 31 January: 'Lovely lovely night I am so happy.'

Daphne Weymouth, in her account of the same trip, described how Beaverbrook challenged his young courtiers to amuse him. 'Max acts like a spur on the company he rides,' she remembered. 'A splendid talker himself, he fires others, and the prize of his great burst of giant's laughter encouraged us all to show off. To see him lying back in his chair, holding his shaking sides, weeping with merriment and murmuring "Dear God" made us all try to outdo each other in jumping through his hoops.' In Jamaica, as they lunched by the sea, a woman went by with a huge water jar on her head. 'Max bet Henry and Perry Brownlow five pounds that they could not carry it in the same way; and with the confidence born of rum punch they accepted the challenge. Max then stood at the top of a short path holding a five pound note.' Naturally, every time they failed to reach him they were soaked as the water spilled; the audience was amused, and Beaverbrook kept his five pound note.[23] In Havana they were joined by Allan Aitken, and Beaverbrook reminisced about the Cuba he had known twenty-five years before; in Nassau, where Jean Norton wrote ecstatically '. . . wish this trip would last for ever', they received the sad news that Maurice Woods had died from his injuries.

Back in England in the spring, Beaverbrook evidently got hold of Jean Norton's diary; pencil notes in his hand are scrawled over a few pages, protesting against her assertion that he had had too much to drink. 'Bunk', he wrote; and again across her entry 'M was drunk' he scrawled 'M was ill'; and then, firmly, 'M was recovering slowly but still sorry for himself and angry with the rest of the world.' On a short trip to Paris in April, again with the Weymouths, there is 'trouble over my bills on Ms account';

Jean Norton's tenth wedding anniversary fell while they were in Paris and she felt miserable. 'Everything wrong and I don't know how to put it right.'

Beaverbrook's closest relationships were all affected by money; money and love were, as always, an explosive mixture. He was often more generous with outsiders than with his intimates, whose behaviour he frequently wanted to control through the giving or withholding of financial favours. Mutual resentment was the usual result. Apart from Jean Norton's dependence, and his daughter Janet's continuing troubles with her gambler husband, Castlerosse's debts were threatening to swamp him, and in the summer of 1929 Beaverbrook put a considerable amount of time and energy into trying to sort out the mess.[24] Marriage to Doris had, predictably, made thing worse; Castlerosse's creditors were losing patience and he was threatened with bankruptcy. Again his parents, the Kenmares, appealed to Beaverbrook for help.

For weeks letters flowed between Beaverbrook, the Kenmares, Lord and Lady Castlerosse and their respective accountants, lawyers and creditors. In April, a dramatic rescue plan was proposed. 'When Valentine married he was in the hands of moneylenders,' Beaverbrook wrote to the Kenmares, 'and I paid certain liabilities on the ground that I was to be repaid when his affairs were settled. Since then his situation has become desperate and he came to me asking my advice.' The idea was to mortgage Castlerosse's Irish inheritance in return for Beaverbrook's ready money. A Canadian property company was to be formed to take over the whole of the family trust investments and the Killarney estate; Castlerosse was to have shares in the company; Beaverbrook was to guarantee Lord Kenmare his present income; £20,000 was to be released to pay Lord and Lady Castlerosse's debts. In return for all this 'Lord Beaverbrook will have complete control of the Company'. Despite this assurance – or perhaps because of it – the Kenmares, while expressing the deepest gratitude, hesitated. They wanted any help for Castlerosse to be conditional on his getting rid of Doris. Lady Kenmare tried to reason with Valentine, but found him abusive and impossible. Beaverbrook wrote back trying to soothe her: 'I am so sorry that Valentine distresses you. On the same day I dined with him. He was almost out of his head and he carried on with me in much the same way. . . . I really wondered if I could stick it to the end of dinner. So you see he cannot have been responsible for his conduct at the time. Since then he has improved greatly. . . . I am well aware of the necessity for a separation of Valentine and his wife.'

Beaverbrook was playing a delicate game. He wanted to detach Castlerosse from Doris without his purposes being obvious to either party; so he continued to invite her to Stornoway House and Cherkley and exchanged amiable notes with her. While wanting to please the Kenmares and to help his friend out of his difficulties, he wanted it done in a businesslike fashion – a takeover bid rather than a rescue operation. He informed all concerned that the deal had to be done within two months, instructed Mr Millar, his confidential accountant at the *Express*, to extract a full statement of Lord Castlerosse's debts, and castigated Castlerosse for his 'dilatory habits'. He reminded him that he also owed £1625 to the *Daily Express*. Castlerosse was wriggling. He proposed that Killarney – the most desirable part of the estate – should be excluded from the deal and mortgaged to his uncle Lord Revelstoke. Beaverbrook became impatient. Castlerosse wrote him a plaintive letter: 'I wanted to come to you with everything ready. . . . It is not that I am ungrateful – it is that I feel ashamed which makes me sometimes hide my head.'

Meanwhile Doris was making trouble. Castlerosse wrote again to Beaverbrook, complaining that he had tried to see him without success. 'Then apparently you saw Doris and told her that you now found me a nuisance and a bore – whereas you used to find me amusing – so I thought I had best go ahead as best I could on my own. . . . ' Beaverbrook sent a chilly reply saying that it was best if they dropped the whole matter, and adding, 'You have always known that it would not be right of you to take your news of my opinion of you from Lady Castlerosse.'

With the bankruptcy case approaching fast, Castlerosse told Beaverbrook he was going to have one more try at settling his affairs himself, within the family. 'That I am a fool I need not tell you. . . .' Beaverbrook sent him a humorous response: 'You have six days and nights. The world was made in a period of six days. But God didn't rest until the seventh day.' Castlerosse's reply was no less apt: 'You must remember it was God the Father who made the world in six days – if the idea had emanated from God the Son, and God the Father had been unable to make up his mind without constant references to God the Holy Ghost (here represented by Messrs Peacock [the family lawyer] and Revelstoke) I doubt whether to this day that they would have achieved anything more interesting than the moon.' Eventually, the Kenmares caved in and paid their son's debts, which had by now risen to £30,000. 'We cannot endure the thought of leaving him to bankruptcy,' Lord Kenmare wrote to Beaverbrook. Castlerosse wrote to thank him for all his trouble: 'This letter is very insufficient – I would like to tell you how sorry I am for many things, and how grateful I am for many more.' Beaverbrook wrote kindly back: 'I am very glad you have escaped the trials and worries which confronted you . . .' and Mr Millar received a letter from the lawyers: 'We understand that there will be no further necessity for the formation of the property company.'

But Castlerosse quickly reverted to form. He could no more alter his spending habits than he could control his eating and drinking. Mr Millar continued to collect Lord Castlerosse's bills; by the middle of 1931 he was again several thousands of pounds in debt to Cartier, Floris, the Ritz, wine merchants, cigar shops and shirtmakers; six writs were outstanding from Ladbroke's. Bargains were made and, inevitably, broken. Castlerosse's salary from the *Express* was being paid back almost as fast as he earned it. Beaverbrook had his court jester entirely under his control; whether he knew it or not, he was dealing with a man addicted to spending and consuming. Perhaps he thought he was being kind – he was certainly making it possible for Castlerosse to live like a lord.

As for Janet, by the middle of 1929 her marriage to Ian Campbell was near collapse. She realized during the summer that her father was indeed more closely involved with their financial affairs than he had told her. Her mother-in-law showed her a letter from Beaverbrook: 'I will do everything I can [for Janet] except give her more money than would be good for her! . . . She can have the tiara back, and all her mother's jewellery if she wishes. I give her £4,000 a year less tax which brings it to about £3,000 per year.' He had somehow recovered the pieces that Campbell had purloined and sold on his honeymoon.

'So he had been watching in the wings,' Janet wrote over fifty years later. 'He had bought back the jewellery, all of it, and said nothing. He had welcomed Ian into his house, laughed and joked with him, without ever once giving either of us the slightest inkling that he knew. Did he do it for my sake? For Ian's? Or did he do it because he enjoyed his secret knowledge, knowing the power it gave him over my husband?' The Campbells went to live in the south of France, 'banished', as Janet put it, 'in an effort to put distance between Ian and Whites.' When she discovered that he was gambling at the casino in Cannes and becoming involved with a rich American girl, Janet rang her father and caught the Blue Train for Paris with her daughter. But her husband had a French mother and, Beaverbrook pointed out, could therefore invoke French law to stop his child leaving the country. Janet wrote:

> So when after hours of hiding Jeanne under rugs and trying not to look anyone in the face we arrived at the Gare de Lyons, I was little more than a nervous wreck . . . . Then I saw him; the small figure in the black hat, blue suit and brown shoes, grinning at me across the platform. My father. I hugged and kissed him. 'Get in this car,' he said gruffly. 'It'll take you to Calais. Then get on the steamer. You'll be met. . . . If you come with me, you'll be caught. They're watching the airport. Goodbye, darling'. . . . Everything went as he had planned it . . . and when at last I carried Jeanne through the doorway of Stornoway House, Father was there to meet us. 'They searched my plane,' he said angrily. The next day I made Jeanne Louise a ward of court.[25]

It was on his fiftieth birthday, 25 May 1929, that Beaverbrook began a custom he kept up for the rest of his life; he would throw a party, invite his favourite women friends, and give them all a large present, usually a cheque. Jean Norton, Daphne Weymouth, Kitty Brownlow and Helen Fitzgerald all received £250. Edwina Mountbatten, who hardly needed cash, was given an emerald and diamond brooch. According to Bruce Bruce Lockhart, that first year 'There was also a lottery with numerous prizes amounting to £500 for the servants.' Two days later, an American journalist called Viereck came to interview Beaverbrook, who was, Bruce Lockhart tells us, in great form – 'real Puckish'. When Viereck asked him that his motto in life was, Beaverbrook adapted the biblical exhortation he had chosen for the gravestone of John F. Stairs a quarter of a century earlier. 'Act justly, love money, and walk humbly,' he proclaimed.[26] The substitution of 'money' for 'mercy' was a joke, but a joke with a point.

THE EMPIRE CRUSADE

The year 1929 was disastrous for the world, but not for Beaverbrook. During its first five months, he still lacked all sense of direction. By the end of the year, he had not only survived the Great Crash by selling shares before it struck, but was engaged in the most single-minded and prolonged campaign that any British newspaper proprietor – Northcliffe notwithstanding – had ever conducted to change the policy and leadership of a great political party.[27]

At one level, the Empire Crusade of 1929–31 was about economic doctrine and imperial ideology; at another, it was one man's test of the power of the popular press. Beaverbrook first met Northcliffe in 1910, when mass-circulation press campaigns in Britain were still a novelty; and was soon worsted by him over food taxes. Thereafter, as he once told Rothermere, 'I definitely set out to compete with that overwhelming personality, and all the power it stood for.'[28]

He first publicly addressed the subject of press power in 1925, in *Politicians and the Press*. In April 1926, just before the General Strike, he produced a much more interesting document. This was a lecture, to be delivered in Liverpool, that identified Northcliffe 'as the supreme instance in the first two decades of the century of the use of the power of the independent popular press'.[29] There was nothing original about that judgement. What was striking was the enthusiasm and force of Beaverbrook's analysis, and endorsement, of the way Northcliffe used this power 'to coerce the politicians'. As his main example, Beaverbrook took Northcliffe's 'great popular press campaign' against food taxes in 1911. Northcliffe had learned that Bonar Law, the Conservative leader, encouraged by Beaverbrook, was likely to make a speech backing a 'whole hog' food tax policy, which Northcliffe opposed.

What did Northcliffe do? First, Beaverbrook explained, he aroused public interest by creating an air of mystery about Bonar Law's intentions.

We were informed that the whole political world was talking about no other question. And by all these mysterious hints and allurements the prophecy fulfilled itself and the boast became true. . . . At last when the public was really excited – then, and not till then – Lord Northcliffe unmasked his batteries and aimed a shower of journalistic shot and shell on the hostile

275

position. He demanded the abandonment of food taxes by the Conservative Party on the ground of its unpopularity in the constituencies. No Conservative seat would be safe unless they were abandoned. He succeeded in frightening the Conservative members of the House of Commons. They became terrified, quite unreasonably, of their own constituents. They were called on to deliver the goods of apostasy to Carmelite House [Northcliffe's headquarters] and they did so. The Conservative leadership was informed that sitting members would not face the Food Tax issue at the next election – and this decision Bonar Law accepted.

The politicians panicked and fled, and their leader led the retreat. 'The press had beaten the politicians.'

Beaverbrook cited two further examples of 'the efficacy of the weapon of the press'. The first was the passage through the House of Lords of the Parliament Act in 1911, an event that 'changed the face of history', which was engineered by 'Lord Rothermere acting through his brother Lord Northcliffe'. This statement was a typical Beaverbrook exaggeration. The second was Northcliffe's undermining of Kitchener in 1915.

Beaverbrook's conclusion about press power was as follows:

When skilfully employed at the psychological moment no politician of any party can resist it. It is a flaming sword which will cut through any political armour. . . . That is not to say that any great newspaper or group of newspapers can enforce policies or make or unmake governments at will, just because it is a great newspaper. Many such newspapers are harmless because they do not know how to strike or when to strike. They are in themselves unloaded guns. But teach the man behind them how to load and what to shoot at, and they became deadly. It is only genius which can so load and point. The risks of its control are therefore limited, seeing that genius is rare. And this is as well, for so great is the potency of the weapon that if it ever fell into the hands of a thoroughly unscrupulous man of genius, there is no limit to the harm it might do.

At this point, Beaverbrook evidently realized that his audience might be wondering about the scruples of Northcliffe, Rothermere and the lecturer himself. To all three he gave excellent character references. Britain, he said, was lucky that Northcliffe, the creator of the popular press, had been 'a scrupulous, high-minded, sincere and patriotic man'. As for Rothermere, his whole character was noted – here Beaverbrook, perhaps tongue-in-cheek, stated the exact opposite of the truth – for 'modesty, toleration and self-effacement'. True, Conservative 'party hacks', resentful of attacks on Baldwin, had accused Rothermere and himself of a 'personal vendetta' against the Prime Minister. The idea was absurd. Were that the case, 'the campaign against certain aspects of government policy would be something far more deadly sinister and effective. . . . Was it not Clive, who when he looked back on his opportunities for corruption in India stood astonished at his own moderation? Something of that same feeling is in my own mind when I regard my own strict adherence to journalistic scruple.'

Beaverbrook spoke disparagingly of the humiliations of political life, of the way that politicians' judgement was sapped by the desire for office, and of their 'pride and vainglory'. The original text of his lecture continues: 'It is time perhaps that they were stripped bare of their pretensions. And I believe I could do this if I had a mind to.' But he crossed out the last sentence.

At no point does Beaverbrook attempt to justify the use of popular press power by unelected newspaper proprietors to coerce elected politicians. He implicitly approves it, because whereas politicians compromise and 'modify their convictions from day to day to remain in the swim with their colleagues . . . journalism can afford to be uncompromising'. He uses the word 'compromise' pejoratively. Political journalists 'can generally be trusted to fight for what they think is right'.

Before he delivered the lecture Beaverbrook sent the text to Rothermere, whose annotations show a low opinion of journalists but a deep respect for proprietors. Beaverbrook mentioned the eminent editor of *The Times*, Delane; Rothermere wrote in the margin: 'He was really a cap in hand journalist never refusing a meal in the houses of prominent politicians.' Of another editor he noted: 'St Loe Strachey practically ruined the *Spectator*. He is not only an egoist but also a prig.' Most revealing is his note on his brother, Northcliffe: 'He was in England the first of the great journalist proprietors in quite a different category to any mere journalist however distinguished. The journalist qua journalist must always express more or less the views of the proprietor. Northcliffe myself and yourself express our own view untramelled [*sic*] by any one.'

The two press barons had never been better placed, or more confident. A month later, during the General Strike, they easily defied Churchill when he tried to commandeer their newsprint stocks. Radio began to show its importance in the General Strike, but was still in its infancy. The mass-circulation papers dominated and reflected the middle-class market, and continued to do so. 'You are incomparably the biggest figure in current journalism,' Beaverbrook told Rothermere in 1928.[30] The circulation of the *Mail* was rising towards two million, that of the *Express* towards a million and a half.

Yet Beaverbrook was bored by his papers. 'I am practically retired,' he told Rothermere. 'I do not take any interest in my newspapers. I have tried to take an interest in the Cinema, but not with any success.'[31] In the spring of 1929 he talked again about giving up newspapers entirely, and 'passing my interests to my son'. H. G. Wells noticed Beaverbrook's need for a cause. During 1929 he wrote a novel, *The Autocracy of Mr Parham*, containing a tycoon with some traces of Beaverbrook who 'had acquired a colossal power of ordering people about' but 'had not the slightest idea what on the whole he wanted them to do'.[32]

Relief from boredom was at hand, however: Baldwin called a general election. Conservative Central Office, having consulted Benson's advertising agency, decided to go into battle with the most uninspiring banner in British political history – 'Safety First' – and, to their surprise, lost. Harold Macmillan, who was voted out in Stockton, was not surprised, or indeed resentful: 'Safety meant the dole. They wanted work.'[33] Thus on 5 June Ramsay MacDonald became Prime Minister for the second time; and on the same day Beaverbrook wrote to Sir Edmund Vestey of the shipping and meat empire: 'In my opinion the Conservative Party will have no success in the future unless there is a change of leadership. Mr Baldwin is a stubborn man, and like all stubborn men, he is weak and vacillating and quite unable to take decisions in most matters.'[34]

Beaverbrook was back in business. Whatever loyalty he had felt in the past towards the Conservative Party, as distinct from his loyalty to Bonar Law, had faded by 1929; between 1924 and 1929, he said, the Conservative government had 'nearly ruined the country'.[35] On election night he gave a huge party at Stornoway House attended by, among others, Birkenhead ('very drunk and bad-tempered'), the Nortons, Lady Milbanke, Castlerosse, the Brownlows and Venetia Montagu, and was observed to be 'clearly elated at Baldwin's failure'. He had a butler called Stanley; at once he began calling him Oliver – the name of Baldwin's son, who had been returned as a Labour member.[36]

To Beaverbrook, the remedy for the Conservative sickness was obvious: to end the party argument about Tariff Reform that had threatened party unity since 1903 by the adoption of 'whole-hog' protectionism. Either Baldwin must swallow protection whole-heartedly, or he must go – and in particular he must swallow food taxes. 'The keynote of the whole project is the tax on foreign wheat and meat coming into England,' Beaverbrook wrote to Lord Elibank, a former MP now active in business in the City of London.[37] 'Without the tax, there is little hope of winning the farmers to our side.' This was the idea that scared Baldwin most: a revival of the old Tory nightmare that support for any tax on food, when 'cheap food' was the strongest Labour and Liberal card, would bring the party down in ruins.

The election over, Beaverbrook soon went to work. At first, he tried to achieve his ends by his old backstairs methods – working inside the party, seeking to bring pressure to bear on Baldwin by winning over former Cabinet ministers, none of whom, Beaverbrook thought, was a sincere Baldwin supporter. But, having talked to almost all of them, he abandoned this approach: '. . . there is a list of "Untouchables",' he told Rothermere on 3 July. 'Both you and I are on this list.' Rothermere thought it scarcely worth bothering about personal persuasion. Did not he and Beaverbrook have the whip hand? 'Without our active support,' he told Beaverbrook, 'there is not the remotest chance of the ex-Premier and his group of intimates returning to office.'[38]

278

Besides, there was an increasingly disaffected and pro-protectionist body of opinion in the country that Beaverbrook believed he could tap and deploy in his own support. Sir Edmund Vestey, despite his wealth, was by no means alone when he told Beaverbrook that in his experience British manufacturers and British workmen were being crippled by the politicians' reluctance to impose tariffs. Vestey's Union Cold Storage Company employed 35,000 people. His company also owned a knitting mill in Chorley, Lancashire, which used to export to Argentina 'stockinettes' in which the Argentines wrapped the meat they sold to Vestey. Now the Argentines had slapped a 50 per cent tariff on imported stockinettes, which had thrown the knitting mill employees out of work: '. . . they are mostly on the dole and doubtless mostly Socialists – you and I certainly would be under their conditions'.[39] Foreigners profited while the British suffered.

Churchill, a Free Trader, wondered in 1930 whether Beaverbrook might have embraced protection from motives of 'vanity or boredom'.[40] Beaverbrook, however, could rightly claim to have been fervent for many years in the cause of what he came to call Empire Free Trade. His first mentor, John F. Stairs, had strongly supported the Imperial Preference ideas of Joseph Chamberlain. New Brunswick was the home of a very special kind of imperial enthusiasm. Sir George Parkin from New Brunswick, forgotten now, was in his day, both on the platform and in print, the most persuasive, rational and respected of all advocates of Empire unity; a source of Churchill's boyhood inspiration; a friend of Alfred Milner, the mentor of the younger English imperialists; and the first secretary of the Rhodes Trust scholarship fund. The Maritimes were full of loyalist families whose ancestors had left the United States in order to remain under the British flag – Beaverbrook's Macquarrie forebears among them. The weaker the Maritimes' imperial links, the stronger the chance that they would be crushed by the industrial power of the United States. Protection, in Beaverbrook's thinking, was the only way to defend Canadian independence – political as well as economic – against its mighty neighbour.

In his Northcliffe lecture, Beaverbrook had stressed the importance of timing in the conduct of a newspaper campaign. Now in the summer of 1929 the timing seemed exactly right. Baldwin dared not launch an all-out attack on the Labour government, whose supporters in any case he wished to see assimilated into the parliamentary system, lest a new election consolidated Labour's power and allowed them, freed from their dependence on Liberal votes, to introduce a genuinely socialist programme. Nor could he bring himself to do a deal with the Liberals under the detested Lloyd George. At the same time, he had no clear policy with which to rally his own troops and to repulse Conservative critics, some of them vociferous, of his inaction. His one source of strength was that there was no agreed alternative leader – and no mechanism for finding one. On 2 July, the Conservative Central Council gave him a unanimous vote of support.

Beaverbrook launched the Empire Crusade on 8 July. After the election result was known, the *Daily Express* had criticized Baldwin for not having beaten the Empire drum. The *Morning Post* protested that the *Daily Express* had been equally remiss. On 30 June, in the *Sunday Express*, Beaverbrook had written a penitential article taking some blame for the defeat; he had not, he admitted, backed the cause of 'fiscal union of the empire' with sufficient zeal, and promised to make amends. On 1 July Leo Amery, Colonial Secretary and then Dominions Secretary between 1924 and 1929, the most prominent advocate of the Imperial and Commonwealth ideal and a long-standing advocate of Tariff Reform and Empire preference, had asked to see him; he suspected that Beaverbrook's article represented a whim of the 'stunt press'. 'I asked him if he really meant business and meant to go on with it and he assured me he would. He is undoubtedly keen but rather sketchy; inclines to think that mutual free trade between Canada and Great Britain could be arranged at once. . . .' On 2 July, also reacting to Beaverbrook's article, Sir Herbert Morgan had said in a letter to the *Express* that the movement talked about by Beaverbrook needed a name, and referred to 'crusaders'. Then on 8 July, on the front page, the *Express* proclaimed the birth of 'a new and powerful minority movement . . . a party of Empire Crusaders'.

On the 11th Beaverbrook wrote the *Express* splash: 'I have combined with the *Daily Express*,' he announced, 'to launch the Imperial Crusade.' He expressed his admiration for Joseph Chamberlain's Tariff Reform movement of twenty-five years before, but explained that the Empire Crusade was entirely different. Chamberlain had wanted a tax on all foodstuffs, with a preferential rebate for the dominions; the Crusade stood for completely free trade within the Empire, in agriculture as well as manufacturing. In Chamberlain's day America was bidding for Empire markets, and was actually proposing reciprocity with Canada. Today, the United States was spurning the dominions and erecting an 'impenetrable tariff wall'. 'There is only one reply to the rich free trade unit within the borders of the United States – that is of a far more vast and a far more powerful free trade unit within the borders of the British Empire.' Had Chamberlain been alive, Beaverbrook added, he would have asked him to lead the crusade: 'I neither intend or desire leadership.'

On 15 July, in the news columns on page 2, the *Express* captured its first big name when it printed a letter from Conan Doyle in favour of Empire Free Trade. Years later, Beaverbrook was asked by the historian Robert Blake why he used this slogan. 'Beaverbrook's reply was that the British public was addicted to free trade and fond of the Empire; they would only swallow protection if suitably disguised.'

On the 17th the *Express* fired its first political shot across Baldwin's bows. A by-election was in the offing and the paper came out with a headline all across the front page: 'EMPIRE ISSUE TO BE FOUGHT AT TWICKENHAM: SIR JOHN FERGUSON'S GREAT SPEECH'.

Telling the readers what to think before they read the story was part of the campaign technique. Sir John had made a great speech because he had spoken in favour of Empire Free Trade. Things were warming up. On 23 July, Conservative Central Office handed Beaverbrook a valuable bonus: they repudiated Sir John, a decision endorsed by Baldwin. On 24 July, an *Express* leader duly attacked Baldwin; and on the same day Lord Waring, chairman of the Waring and Gillow store, wrote an article saying, 'I am all for this Empire Crusade.' Gathering the support of big business was an important part of the strategy. The chairman of Imperial Chemical Industries, Lord Melchett, was an early, though not unqualified, supporter. So, much more wholeheartedly, was Sir Hugo Cunliffe-Owen, chairman of the British American Tobacco Company, who had worked with Beaverbrook in 1918 at the Ministry of Information and had later been advised by him about Canadian shares. They were soon joined by the industrialist Sir Harry McGowan (later Lord McGowan), also of ICI.

Beaverbrook showed some skill in exploiting McGowan's recruitment, using one article by his new man to beat up three days of Crusade news and comment. The front page of Saturday's *Daily Express* carried a news story announcing that a 'great executive supports the new Crusade' and prefiguring the article. Next day in the *Sunday Express* came the article. Then Monday's *Daily Express* ran a comment by Cunliffe-Owen in praise of the article by McGowan, together with a leader saying that 'against the strong school of obstructionist thought which sees risk in all change – forgetting that the very law of life is change – we place the testimony of Sir Hugo Cunliffe-Owen, Lord Beaverbrook, Sir Harry McGowan, and Lord Melchett'.

Throughout the campaign, Beaverbrook was always treated by his newspapers as if he and they were entirely unconnected: the *Express* leader writers often wrote as if the paper and its proprietor had arrived independently at the same conclusion. In the McGowan leader, Beaverbrook was citing his own testimony in support of himself.

As polling day in Twickenham approached, the *Express* stepped up the excitement. On 26 July, the paper announced that two blocs were bound to emerge in the world – Europe and the United States – and asked: 'Are we to become a hanger-on of the European system, a satellite of America?' The choices were: Europe and deterioration; America and subservience; or 'the British Empire made one and everlastingly prosperous by the unbreakable link of Free Trade between all its parts'.

On 30 July P. J. Hannon, Conservative MP for Birmingham and the chairman of Birmingham Small Arms, joined the chorus. In a long article headlined 'EMPIRE SHIRKERS' he argued that the Empire could be 'completely independent' of foreign markets. Why should foreign nations have the 'free run of these vast areas of the British Empire which have been explored, pioneered, peopled and civilised by British

281

flesh and blood?' He also put in a word for the proprietor. Lord Beaverbrook's scheme, he said, 'may stagger some people by its boldness, its comprehensiveness and its magnitude'; however, it did not stagger Hannon.

Three days before the vote, the *Express* produced more evidence of the Crusade's gathering strength. 'CANADA JOINS THE EMPIRE CRUSADE,' it announced on the front page. 'DOMINION SUPPORT FOR THE NEW MOVEMENT. GREAT CANADIAN JOURNAL SPEAKS OUT.' The word 'Canada' was an exaggeration. What the story revealed was merely that the *Alberta Farmer* favoured the new movement. Possibly impressed by this evidence of transatlantic support, or by an eve-of-the-poll letter to the *Express* from the co-operative Sir Hugo Cunliffe-Owen, on 8 August the Twickenham voters elected Sir John Ferguson as their new MP. 'Sir John, the Crusader,' said a triumphant *Express* leader next day, 'won without the help of a party machine.' So he did, but he was fighting a safe Conservative seat that he nearly managed to lose. Nevertheless Beaverbrook had tasted blood, barely a month after he had unmasked his batteries.

THE RUSSIAN JOURNEY, 1929

Two days later, Beaverbrook sailed away on his much-discussed trip to Russia. He took with him on the *Arcadian* his brother Allan, Arnold Bennett, Michael Wardell, Venetia Montagu, Edwina Mountbatten and Jean Norton. Harriet Cohen longed to go, too, and suggested to Beaverbrook that he might get the Russians to invite her to play in Moscow; he did not. Although the expedition was private, it had a certain significance: the *Arcadian* was the first British passenger ship to sail to Russia since the Revolution, and Beaverbrook's the first visit by a former Cabinet minister. The Russians must have been conscious that their private visitor was a special case, someone well worth cultivating, a wartime propaganda minister and now a leading newspaper tycoon; they were also no doubt aware that Beaverbrook was accompanied by one of the leading British writers of the day, and the millionairess wife of a close relative of the murdered Tsar.

'Edwina and I sharing v nice cabin but chaos for the maids with clothes,' wrote Jean Norton in her diary. The group passed the time on board agreeably enough, sitting in the sun reading. Beaverbrook had all the newspapers delivered to him at each port of call. In the evenings they danced, or more often played cards. Beaverbrook played pingpong with Wardell; he liked to win. They arrived in Leningrad on Sunday, 18 August, drove round the deserted city, visited the Winter Palace and dined at the Hotel Europa. At midnight they took the train to Moscow. Two special cars had been booked for them.

The next morning, in Moscow, they were treated more like a special delegation than like tourists. 'Found we are staying as guests of the Foreign Office,' wrote Jean Norton, 'at a house overlooking the Kremlin which once belonged to a sugar king – sumptuous breakfast and vast rooms.' The party spent only two days in the city, and it seems that Beaverbrook skipped some of the sightseeing and conferred with officials. After seeing St Basil's Cathedral, driving in official cars to the Moscow hills and doing a little shopping, Jean, Edwina and Wardell had dinner at their residence: 'After dinner we went to the floor above and met Mme. and M. Litvinoff [*sic*], the Foreign Secretary.' Litvinov was married to an Englishwoman, Ivy, who wrote to her sister describing the visitors. She was not taken with Beaverbrook, whom she described as having 'bad tempered lines from nose to mouth, maniacal eyes, terrifying changes of mood'. She also noted his attentiveness to Lady Mountbatten: '. . . purring around her all the time'.[41]

The following day the party visited the Kremlin, and in the afternoon Beaverbrook went with the others to the Garden of Rest and Culture, described by Jean Norton as 'a sort of Coney Island, full of young pioneers or Soviet boy and girl scouts'. In the evening they went with Madame Litvinov and her two children to see a 'propoganda [*sic*] film' and after dinner caught the train back to Leningrad.

On their final day in Russia, Arnold Bennett and the women visited the royal palaces at Tsarskoe Selo outside Leningrad, while Beaverbrook, his brother and Wardell stayed behind in the city. On 22 August they sailed away again on the *Arcadian*. The weather on the return journey was poor, and Beaverbrook felt ill; his mood and his childish behaviour cast a gloom on the party. 'M not speaking to me all day. Fancy dress ball after dinner. M refused to play baccarat and went to bed and Edwina, Venetia and I played rummy.' Perhaps Beaverbrook was annoyed about Jean Norton's plans: they docked on 31 August at Southampton, where she transferred immediately to the *Aquitania* to join her parents in New York. Beaverbrook drove back to London with Edwina Mountbatten and her husband, who had come to meet them.

Beaverbrook himself said little, then or later, about his first short trip to Russia, even though he met Stalin. On the day after his return he had Bruce Lockhart to dinner at Cherkley. 'He has returned from Russia with no good impressions,' Bruce Lockhart wrote in his diary.

The whole thing seems to have depressed him. Mike Wardell says it is because the Bolshies did not make enough of him, but he saw Stalin, and Litvinov lived in his pocket, and he was given special cars, etc. He seems to have been more impressed by the religious revival than by anything else. Told me a very good story about the office for marriage and divorce, which costs nil. In the office there is anti-religious and anti-syphilitic propaganda.[42]

Beaverbrook also told Jean Norton that he and Arnold Bennett had both seen Stalin, but neither of them wrote about the encounter – perhaps the dictator made that a condition.

Edwina Mountbatten told her husband the visit had been interesting but depressing;[43] Venetia Montagu, in a fulsome letter of thanks, referred to 'the horror of Moscow and Leningrad' and cited 'the four or five meals on the ship when you were at your very best' as the high spot of the trip. 'I sometimes think after listening to you it's a pity you made so much money,' she wrote, 'for had you been reduced to becoming a professor of history or literature your lectures would have been the most inspiriting that anyone could have listened to!'[44] Arnold Bennett, who wrote to André Gide from Leningrad, describing the scene in a memorable phrase as 'half desolation and half hope',[45] contributed four long articles to the *Daily Express* early in September. It is likely that his thoughts and reactions would have been akin to Beaverbrook's, although Beaverbrook's presence as host on the visit was nowhere mentioned in the series. Bennett was struck by the dreariness and shabbiness of the cities, the poverty of the people and the endless queues for food. He was not unsympathetic to what he called 'the biggest, the most arduous, most daring political experiment in all history'; but he was well aware of the tyrannical nature of the regime. In Moscow, he was surprised by the number of churches and the fervour of the worshippers. His party, he remarked, received special treatment and was 'encouraged to obtain the most enormous and splendid meals . . . and rarely have I tasted better champagne and never – save in London – have I tasted finer vodka'.

One passage might possibly derive from Beaverbrook's encounter with Stalin. Pondering the illusions that had led to the downfall of the Tsar, Bennett went on: 'I could not help wondering whether a similar condition of affairs was not developing now in the mysterious apartments of the Kremlin, where the touchingly arrogant Stalin, secretary of the Communist Party, sits as the head of the Government today.' The two main illusions from which Stalin suffered, he went on, were 'that members of the last British Tory Cabinet were corrupt' and took bribes in return for working against Russia; and that only Ramsay MacDonald was preventing the British masses from demonstrating full support for the Russian regime. 'People who would believe these things would believe anything,' was Bennett's somewhat Beaverbrookian comment. As for propaganda, Bennett, an old propaganda hand himself, was amazed at its clumsiness. Why, if the Russians had so much to be proud of, did they not let visitors see for themselves? Why did they send a spokesman aboard the ship to lecture the crew on Communism, rather than allowing them ashore? Above all why, since the authorities were no doubt aware that the 'marked group' of which he was a member were not naïve, was the Russians' approach so crude? 'They seemed often to imagine that they were talking to the innocent,' wrote Bennett. 'Incidentally they committed the singular folly of attempting to proselytise for Communism among British personal servants.'

CHAPTER 15

FRUSTRATIONS OF
A CRUSADER
1929–1935

BACK FROM RUSSIA, Beaverbrook threw himself with extra energy into his Crusade, concentrating at first on putting together a campaign organization. This was financed entirely from his own resources, and revolved entirely around himself. At its heart was ornate Stornoway House: essentially Beaverbrook surrounded by long-suffering secretaries. When he applied to a secretarial agency for a shorthand typist, it was explained that the hours would be 'somewhat irregular' and applicants must be prepared to work eleven and a half hours a day, starting at 9 a.m. and finishing 'at various times' up until 8.30 p.m.; at weekends they must be willing to transfer to Cherkley.'[1] Just before he went to Russia he had persuaded Bruce Lockhart to become his chief campaign lieutenant; thereafter Bruce Lockhart drafted important letters, acted as a go-between, ghosted articles and wrote innumerable leaders for all three Beaverbrook papers, whose editors published them without comment; the day after the Twickenham result, his salary was raised by £1000 to £3000 a year.[2] Beaverbrook made it a rule never to go out to lunch, and rarely to dinner. His days were spent telephoning, dictating and seeing visitors at half-hour intervals; in the evenings, Jean Norton and his cronies came to dine.

At the *Daily Express*, the manager, Robertson, the accountant, Millar, and the editor, Baxter, screened approaches from people and organizations that Beaverbrook did not know and advised him how to respond. He housed the campaign's administrative headquarters in Grand Buildings, Trafalgar Square under Fred Doidge, an efficient, smooth-talking New Zealander seconded from the management of the *Express* (he later became the New Zealand High Commissioner in London); Doidge hired campaign workers, put out literature and supervised the funds.

All the principal Crusade workers were thus in Beaverbrook's personal employment. When he set up an Empire Crusade Committee of prominent people, at least two of them were in his pay, too. One was Sir James Parr, the New Zealand High Commissioner, who after nearly four years in

London decided that he needed a retirement job. He wanted £3500 a year, which included £500 for tax; he also pointed out that New Zealand gave him a car and driver, and asked for a fare to New Zealand and back (£100). Beaverbrook's method in such cases was simple: he did not negotiate, he stated his terms. He offered Parr £3000 a year, without making any reference to tax, car or fare. Parr accepted, stressing that his 'honorarium' must be kept 'private'.[3] Thus public spirit alone seemed to have inspired Sir James to march with the Crusaders. A much more important and active committee member was the Rt. Hon. Charles A. McCurdy, a former coalition Liberal whip: ' . . . when a dyed-in-the-wool Liberal becomes a whole-hearted Empire Crusader,' said the *Express*, 'something has happened which cannot possibly be ignored by his quondam leader [Lloyd George]'. In February 1930 Beaverbrook put McCurdy on his payroll: 'I will undertake to provide you with Directorships representing not less than £1500, dating from 1st March next, and running for a period of not less than three years'; one of the directorships was of the *Daily Express*.[4] The other members of the Crusade Committee were Elibank; Lord Lovat, who had served in the Baldwin government as Under Secretary of State for the Dominions; Lord Chaplin, who was the son of a Cabinet minister under Salisbury; Sir Hugo Cunliffe-Owen, who was in charge of fund-raising; P. J. Hannon MP; and Beaverbrook. Randolph Churchill told Bruce Lockhart that Beaverbrook paid Hannon £2000 a year.[5]

Beaverbrook was right in expecting the Crusade to strike a chord. Soldiers, farmers, local newspaper editors, cotton manufacturers, Conservative candidates disappointed at the last election, working men and aristocrats wrote to Beaverbrook pledging their support. The secretaries produced typed summaries of the longer letters, and all correspondents except the obvious lunatics – 'This man is crazy', Beaverbrook scrawled – received an appropriate and beautifully courteous reply, usually signed by Beaverbrook himself. The burden of many letters was that the 'dumping' of foreign goods was making life impossible for farmers and manufacturers alike, and doing British workers out of jobs. A Harrow salesman with twelve years on the road said he was 'astounded' by the 'enormous amount of foreign foodstuffs consumed in this country'. An egg producer asked how anyone in his business could compete against cheap foreign eggs. A man wrote in about 'sausage casings, many thousands of pounds of which are imported every year from Denmark, Chicago, and China'. 'Free Trade', wrote Lord Carnock, Harold Nicolson's elder brother, 'was invented, not to benefit the working classes, but the manufacturers, who wanted to keep wages down as low as possible'; Empire Free Trade, he went on, 'will solve the problems of unemployment and poverty'. Lieutenant Commander Sir Warden Chilcott, a former MP, suggested that defeated Conservative candidates should be sent to preach the Crusade gospel in the colonies: Beaverbrook told his staff to write a 'pleasant end to letter and avoid the issue he raises'. Younger Conservatives, bored by

Baldwin, were delighted that Beaverbrook was stirring up the party: greatly preferable, said J. T. C. Moore-Brabazon, who had lost his seat at the last election, to a man with a pipe in his mouth peering through a red safety first triangle.[6] The promising young Conservative MP for East Aberdeenshire, Bob Boothby, was briefly captured for the cause; Beaverbrook had a soft spot for him thereafter throughout his chequered career.

With Twickenham behind him, Beaverbrook set to work to try to dismantle the main obstacle to his campaign. Empire Free Trade, said the doubters, meant taxing foreign food imports; therefore the price of food must go up, which nobody wanted. In early October Beaverbrook contributed to the *Express* three articles about farming which were designed to allay this fear. If farmers had a guaranteed market, they would 'produce abundantly', and there would be no need to increase the retail price of food. A. P. McDougall CBE, managing director of a firm of land agents and livestock salesmen in Banbury, wrote: 'You say, there will be no food taxes until cheap and abundant supplies are available from Imperial sources. How then will it ever be possible for the output of British agriculture to be increased to enable us to dispense with supplies from foreign nations?' For instance, the Argentine supplied Britain 'with almost illimitable quantities of meat at prices far below the cost of production in this country and indeed in Australia. England is the only customer for Argentine meat . . . '; therefore, 'unless there is an immediate tax on Argentine meat, increased production cannot be expected in England'. To this argument, Beaverbrook offered no reply.[7]

The farming articles annoyed the High Commissioner for Australia, Major-General the Hon. Sir Granville Ryrie. Beaverbrook had said that 'beef cannot be successfully transported in frozen conditions. I would like to point out that frozen beef has been successfully transported from Australia since 1872.' Beaverbrook ignored Sir Granville's request for space to reply in the *Express*, and said that informed opinion agreed with him, Beaverbrook, about frozen beef: 'I have discussed it with butchers and consumers frequently'.[8] Less easily outflanked were the critics who pointed out that the dominions, much as they might want free access to the UK for their primary products, could not sweep away all tariffs on manufactures from Great Britain without grave damage to their own infant industries.

As always, Beaverbrook's motives were under constant scrutiny. 'Beaverbrook is probably sincere in his Imperial aspirations,' Neville Chamberlain concluded in July 1929, 'but mixes with them a desire to "down" S. B. [Baldwin]'.[9] Baldwin in the autumn described him, according to Bruce Lockhart, as 'one of the most corrupting influences in the country'. The rich young Victor Cazalet was one of the seven Conservative MPs who had appeared on Sir John Ferguson's platform in Twickenham; he received a sharp rebuke from Asquith's wife Margot:

. . . Joining the Beaverbrook bunkum of taxes on food is the most foolish thing any MP who values his future can do. You have not seen all this before, but it is precisely the same folly that I saw from 1903 to 1906; but that folly was led by a much greater man than Beaverbrook [Joseph Chamberlain] and backed by more distinguished men than the candidate for Twickenham. I don't suppose you realise the donkeys you will have to associate with. To cripple our shipping and increase the cost of food would keep the Party out for at least 10 years . . . I am very fond of Beaverbrook but he is a *profoundly* ignorant man.[10]

(Margot Asquith had been less fond of Beaverbrook in 1916; but since then Beaverbrook had contributed to a pension for her husband.)

Beaverbrook's campaign technique involved pulling a series of new rabbits from his hat. On 24 October 1929 the speculative bubble in the United States burst and Wall Street crashed. On the same day, the *Daily Express* announced: 'MANIFESTO OUT TODAY: THE NEW POLICY FOR PROSPERITY: MUST BE READ BY EVERY OPEN-MINDED MAN AND WOMAN'. He had rushed out the pamphlet to spike the guns of Melchett and Amery, who were on the eve of producing an economic policy statement of their own that Beaverbrook thought would not go far enough on food taxes. *Empire Free Trade by Lord Beaverbrook* was the title, and the price was one penny. As in the First World War, Beaverbrook worked on the principle that propaganda bit deeper if people had paid to read it. The pamphlet's coloured cover, a striking design by J. Hoch, showed a helmsman at sea, bare-chested, gripping a wheel beneath a high curling wave: an image made more powerful by the news from Wall Street. Round the rim of the wheel ran the words 'The British Empire', and, on the visible spokes, 'Canada', 'Australia' and 'Ind . . .', which fairly represented Beaverbrook's order of interests. As ever, he was concerned to counter the fear that Empire Free Trade must mean more expensive food: 'The cry of dearer food does not apply.' Ample food was available; millions of acres in the Empire lay idle. Five days later Beaverbrook addressed Sussex farmers in Lewes town hall; '. . . the largest gathering of its kind ever held in Lewes,' said the *Express*. Copies of the pamphlet were sent round the country. A puzzled Bishop of Lichfield said he had no knowledge of the subject, but promised to consider it with care.

In November, a compromise between Beaverbrook and Baldwin seemed briefly possible. If Baldwin adopted the Leo Amery policy of declaring himself free of all limiting pledges pending the negotiation of treaties with the dominions and colonies, would Beaverbrook drop his agitation? Beaverbrook at first seemed to accept the deal. When on 22 November Baldwin told the annual Conservative Party conference in the Albert Hall that 'our progress depends on our capacity to visualise the Empire, the Dominions and the Colonies alike, as one eternal and indestructible unit for production, for consumption, for distribution . . .'

the *Express* hailed MR BALDWIN'S GREAT EMPIRE SPEECH: NEW CONSERVATIVE POLICY' – even though Baldwin had spoken only of the 'framing of such a policy'. Amery, who wanted to go further down the protectionist road than Baldwin but not so far, or so fast, as Beaverbrook, counselled patience; after all, he told Beaverbrook, 'even the most sanguine can hardly expect internal free Trade in the Empire to come about except as the result of a process covering a good many years'.

Patience, however, was not a prominent Beaverbrook characteristic; nor did he trust Baldwin. Besides, and most important, his courtship of Rothermere was showing signs of success. Beaverbrook disliked Baldwin's false humility and thought him slippery, but he was enough of a politician to be prepared to come to terms with him under certain circumstances. But Rothermere's feelings amounted to hatred. He had backed Baldwin strongly in 1924, and his subsequent disenchantment was thought to be connected with Baldwin's unaccountable failure to reward him with an earldom and his son Esmond, an MP, with a post in the government. By 1929 Rothermere, a man of pessimistic temperament, had come to believe that with the socialists in power the world was nearing its end; and Baldwin was doing nothing to save it. He was especially disturbed by the independence movement in India, to which he thought both the government and Baldwin were almost criminally indulgent. Thus the way seemed clear for a Beaverbrook–Rothermere alliance to remove Baldwin. The difficulty was that Rothermere was as opposed to food taxes as Northcliffe had been. Beaverbrook approached him gently. He told him on 24 October: 'I know perfectly well that support for the campaign cannot be expected in the columns of the *Daily Mail*.' On 2 November he told him he was 'most grateful for your decision to give the Empire Free Trade a hearing in public'. On 19 November he sent Rothermere an article for the *Mail*. On the 29th they dined together. Evidently Beaverbrook at this stage had not quite decided whether to run Crusade candidates against official Conservative candidates at by-elections or not. Rothermere sent him a telegram on 1 December saying: '. . . unless you definitely decide to run candidates at by-elections movement cannot possibly succeed'. Beaverbrook thought he saw the makings of a close alliance and quickly replied: 'You can be quite certain of candidates at by-elections', adding that if Rothermere could be persuaded to join the Crusade 'our committee would like to make you chairman'. Rothermere was not quite ready to be landed, but he did say, '. . . will help you in every possible way in your campaign but cannot take any official position'.[11]

The campaign now resumed, Beaverbrook having decided that a press alliance with Rothermere was much more likely to help his cause than any agreement with the devious Baldwin. Canada, the *Express* editor announced on the front page of 5 December, was moving rapidly towards the adoption of Empire Free Trade, and he quoted Canadian newspapers to prove it. On 6 December, readers were advised: 'EMPIRE SHOPPING THIS CHRISTMAS: BUY IMPERIALLY'.

On 7 December, as the depression deepened, Beaverbrook made a 'prosperity speech' in Eastbourne, his young protégé Edward Marjoribanks's constituency. On 10 December, in what amounted to a clear breach with the Conservative Party, the *Express*, under a front page headline 'JOIN THE EMPIRE CRUSADE TODAY', proclaimed that 'the great body of feeling in the country which is behind the new movement must be crystallised in effective form'. A register of supporters was to be opened, and Crusade 'officers' selected. The *Express* appeal for 'recruits' was repeated in the *Sunday Express* and *Evening Standard*. Next day: 'FIRST CRUSADERS JOIN UP: TREMENDOUS RESPONSE BEGINS'. P. J. Hannon MP enrolled as one of the first members. A campaign fund opened with Sir Hugo Cunliffe-Owen in charge. The following day: 'FIRST MARCHING ORDERS TO CRUSADERS: YOUR TASK TO ENROL YOUR FRIENDS'; '. . . we are an army with a great task before us . . .' Rothermere warned Beaverbrook to bar the politicians from his organization: 'They will capture it and it will become a mere annexe of the Central Conservative Association. You should be very careful.'

Behind the scenes, Beaverbrook wrote round his acquaintances in the House of Lords to drum up an audience for a coming speech by Lord Elibank; '. . . during the last debate', he wrote to Elibank, 'you sat below the gangway on the Government side. If you mean to sit there again, perhaps our friends would like to gather round you.'[12] The day after Elibank's speech, an *Express* leader-writer said that it 'drove nail after nail into the coffin of outworn Cobdenism'. McCurdy was extolled for taking the Crusade to the north. The last burst of the year, on 28 December, reported on the front page some encouraging remarks about Beaverbrook made to the Canadian press by his old friend R. B. Bennett, now leader of the Conservative opposition in the federal parliament; he said, after a visit to England, that he was 'really amazed' to discover 'greater interest in Empire Trade in Britain today than even in the time of Chamberlain'. Careful *Express* readers at this point might have been forgiven for thinking that the Crusaders were a stage army.

While masterminding every detail of his Empire campaign, Beaverbrook kept busy elsewhere. He engaged in a long correspondence with the manager of the W. H. Smith newsagent at Leatherhead railway station about the money they charged for delivering newspapers to Cherkley (thirty-six papers on a Sunday); after the dispute was referred to head office, Smith's discovered that they were in fact subsidizing Beaverbrook, since a boy on a 'special bicycle' was covering thirty miles a week for a delivery charge of 3d. Beaverbrook nevertheless changed newsagents. He complained to Waygood-Otis about their bill for inspecting the lift at Stornoway

House. Whether it was Smith's or Waygood-Otis or Baldwin, he could not abide the suspicion that someone might be getting the better of him.

Religion, as usual, hovered in the background. He read Edwin Muir's biography of John Knox, concluded that Muir 'disapproves of our spiritual leader', and tried to persuade another writer, Duncan Carswell, to produce a counter-biography: 'I think a tale could be told of courage and endurance, coupled with intellectual rascality, which would be a permanent addition to English biography.'[13] He answered a questionnaire from the Salvation Army's *Life-saving Scout and Guard* magazine: the hero or heroine of his youth? John Knox. The books that had helped him most? Samuel I and II. His motto? Do justly, love mercy and walk humbly. The qualities needed for a successful career? Judgement, health and industry.

His philanthropy continued. He helped to fund a new medical school for St Mary's Hospital, Paddington. At the University of New Brunswick he financed twenty scholarships and commemorated his late wife by building the Lady Beaverbrook Residence for students and furnishing it with a peal of bells that played 'The Jones Boys'. Bruce Lockhart worried that the hyper-activity was affecting his master's health. Leo Amery had more serious anxieties: at a packed meeting of the 1900 Club on 13 November he found Beaverbrook 'holding forth with passionate earnestness. He really is tremendously worked up and there was something in the glint of his eye that made me wonder whether he is not really near the edge of his balance. Curiously enough a man came up to me afterward and said "B. will be following Northcliffe before very long."'[14]

The year ended well for Jean Norton. Two months after Wall Street crashed, she noted: 'Given lovely present of £1000 *Daily Express* shares for Christmas.'

'GLORY, HALLELUJAH!'

In 1930 Beaverbrook became more and more convinced that he, and he alone, knew how to solve the nation's, and indeed the Empire's, problems. 'Beaverbrook will not take advice,' Bruce Lockhart noted in February. Gerhardie noticed 'an air of "What I say, goes" about his utterances which robbed them of their former charm'.[15] The state of politics was propitious for a single-minded newspaper proprietor. The Labour government struggled on ineffectually in the face of world depression and rising unemployment. The Liberals under Lloyd George were immobilized in a tactical cul-de-sac: unwilling to put Labour out, unwilling to put Baldwin in. The Conservatives were equally confused, divided by Empire policy, the question of dominion status for India, and above all by Baldwin's halting leadership.

Beaverbrook, an early practitioner of single-issue politics, kept proclaiming that he was interested only in Empire Free Trade, but kept behaving as if his true ambition was to destroy Baldwin. Intermediaries – Neville Chamberlain, who became the new Conservative Party chairman

291

in June; Amery, the imperialist who did not quite agree with either Baldwin or Beaverbrook – occasionally damped down his pyrotechnics and stirred up the 'molluscuous inertia' of Baldwin, achieving brief truces; but the conflict soon flared up again.[16]

Beaverbrook began the year by trying to drive more wedges into the Conservative Party. He tried to recruit Churchill to the Empire Free Trade cause: 'Winston drunk but unconvinced,' Bruce Lockhart recorded.[17] Churchill, increasingly restless about Baldwin's support for dominion status for India, was not interested in the Crusade, and Beaverbrook was not interested in India. He wooed Amery, who, though in sympathy with his ends, remained wary of his headstrong means. He tried to persuade Amery's brother-in-law, Lord Greenwood, to take over the chairmanship of the Crusade Committee. None of these approaches succeeded.

Beaverbrook's general strategy, however, was now in place. At the turn of the year he corresponded with Rothermere about historical parallels. Rothermere asked to be sent details of the Anti-Corn Law League and how it had forced Peel to change. Rothermere's factotum, Ernest Outhwaite, told Beaverbrook the details of Rothermere's Anti-Waste League, founded in 1919; the national budget was then £1000 million a year. Rothermere accused the government of 'squandermania' and said the country could be run for no more than £800 million; to set an example, he moved into a small flat and served his guests water instead of wine at dinner. Three years later, the budget was actually reduced to £800 million and the League was disbanded.

All this had been achieved, said Outhwaite, when Rothermere only had two papers, the *Daily Mirror* and the *Sunday Pictorial*. 'Had we also had the *Daily Mail, Evening News, Daily Express, Evening Standard, Sunday Dispatch* and *Sunday Express* we could quite easily have made it the predominant party, with its own Prime Minister. . . . And those were the days of Lloyd George and Bonar Law.'[18] The secret of success was to build up pressure on the politicians indirectly.

On 4 January Beaverbrook dined with Rothermere and his editors; on the 5th in the *Sunday Dispatch* G. Ward Price, a faithful Rothermere mouthpiece, said there was 'no man living in this country today with more likelihood of succeeding to the Premiership of Great Britain than Lord Beaverbrook'. In case the point had been missed, the *Daily Mail* added that Beaverbrook ought to replace Baldwin as Conservative leader. Beaverbrook responded by describing Rothermere as 'the greatest trustee of public opinion we have seen in the history of journalism'.[19] On 13 January, asked by Baldwin what he thought lay behind the Beaverbrook–Rothermere manoeuvres, John Buchan commented: 'Lord B . . ., as I know well, has no admiration for the other fatted calf. I fancy it is Lord B's restless ambition temporarily combined with Lord R's detestation of you.'[20] No better explanation has since emerged. On 12 February Baldwin and Beaverbrook met. Beaverbrook made three demands: the right to put up Empire Free Trade Conservative candidates; the right to try to get Empire Free Trade candidates selected as official Conservative candidates; and the right to persuade Baldwin's front-bench colleagues to declare for Empire Free Trade. Baldwin rejected these impossible terms. 'Baldwin said, "I am a simple and straightforward man". "Believe me," said Beaverbrook, "I am neither simple nor straightforward, but I am more so than you!" '[21]

For the rest of January, the *Express* continued the Crusade campaign with undiminished energy and ingenuity: printing letters of support on the front page, urging readers to become 'founder members' of the Crusade, producing an 'Empire Manifesto by five Liberals', publishing articles by Beaverbrook – 'Lord Beaverbrook Tables His Plans' – and attacking an anti-Beaverbrook speech by Lloyd George in the Commons as 'buffoonery'. On 14 February Bruce Lockhart noted in his diary: 'In evening saw Lord Beaverbrook who will announce his New Party on Monday, provided Rothermere comes out in favour of food taxes. It is a big venture.' Beaverbrook's strategy was now settled. If he ran Crusade candidates at by-elections and general elections, too, '. . . we would wreck the prospects of many Tory candidates, thus destroying Baldwin's hopes of a majority in the next Parliament'. Under such pressure, Beaverbrook calculated, Baldwin would have to retreat and adopt Beaverbrook's policy. 'NEW PARTY FORMED, THE UNITED EMPIRE PARTY', the *Express* announced on 18 February. '. . . No one of the existing parties is big enough to embrace the doctrine of Empire Free Trade in its entirety. . . .' The announcement took Conservatives by surprise; they had not expected Beaverbrook to start a real party. On 19 February the *Express* reported: 'LORD ROTHERMERE SUPPORTS THE NEW PARTY'. So he did, though he did not support food taxes. A leader appealed to women to support the party, too. On 20 February: '£100,000 FIGHTING FUND OPENED', accompanied by a Beaverbrook article appealing for funds. On the 21st: '£18,500 the first day. . . . Every subscription will be acknowledged in these columns.' Daily the fund rose higher – not surprisingly, since before it opened £40,000 had been promised or paid in by half a dozen very rich men: Beaverbrook, Rothermere, Cunliffe-Owen and Dreyfus of British Celanese, who were soon joined by Sir James Dunn and by Andrew Holt of the Royal Bank of Canada. Signing himself 'Always, Harold', Rothermere told Beaverbrook with dangerous arrogance in mid-February: 'No two men ever had the ball more completely at their feet than you and I have today.'[22]

On 26 February, the *Express* presented Conservative MPs with an implied ultimatum: 'No MP espousing the cause of Empire Free Trade will be opposed by a United Empire candidate. Instead, he shall have, if he desires it, our full support. If the Conservatives split, they will do so because at last the true spirit of Conservatism has a chance to find expression. . . .' In the *Daily Mail* Rothermere ran stories about the new party on the front page for ten days in succession. With their combined total of eight national papers, and Rothermere's chain of provincial papers, the press barons were laying down a joint barrage scarcely paralleled in newspaper history. This was the combined operation that Beaverbrook had sought. On 28 February the *Express* reported on page one, 'Lord Beaverbrook opens the campaign'; his speech in Gloucester 'was the greatest meeting the city has ever witnessed'. Rothermere told him the same day: 'This movement is like a prairie fire.' On 2 March, Amery found Beaverbrook 'bubbling over with excitement and triumph'.

For the next few months, *Express* readers were taken on a mystery tour. They had subscribed to a brand-new political party and were told that the Conservative Party under Baldwin did not reflect the spirit of true conservatism. Suddenly on 5 March they learned that the greatest advance in the history of the Empire Crusade had occurred the previous day at the Hotel Cecil; and the person responsible for the advance was, not Lord Beaverbrook for once, but Baldwin. He had pledged himself, if returned to power, to hold a national referendum on food taxes. Three days later, they had another surprise. Beaverbrook had withdrawn from the United Empire Party, and all donations to the new party were being sent back. Lord Rothermere, they were told, was enlarging the scope of the party – he wanted to add to its objectives 'ruthless economy', no more surrender on India and no diplomatic relations with Moscow – while Beaverbrook was interested only in Empire Free Trade. Bruce Lockhart, 'very tired and run down', wrote in his diary on 14 March 1930: 'The little man will have us all in our graves before he is finished.'

The readers must have felt the same. They had scarcely got back the money they had subscribed to the United Empire Party when on 3 April they were told that the Empire Crusade fund had reopened and that Beaverbrook was appealing for £250,000. On 5 April H. V. Morton announced the formation of a League of Young Crusaders. Next came a by-election in West Fulham. 'Will West Fulham cast its vote for the Empire or for a Little England? That, and nothing else, is the issue.' Beaverbrook was 'violently restless', Bruce Lockhart noted, and so was the *Daily Express*. On 1 May Beaverbrook made his thirty-eighth speech since the Empire Free Trade campaign began, and gave himself a boost in an *Express* leader: '. . . because he seeks no reward of office or wealth he goes into the fight with unencumbered hands'. On 3 May, with the West Fulham by-election three days away, he once again sought to give the voters the feeling that the tide was flowing strongly in his direction. The *Daily News*, the *Star*, the *Daily Chronicle* and the *Herald* (all anti-Conservative papers) 'have mocked and derided the efforts of the crusaders . . . Canada is stretching out her hand to us. Australia is saying, "we are ready, we have been ready for years." New Zealand, as always, is declaring "the Empire first". South Africa is giving the policy more and more support.' On 5 May, at an eve-of-poll meeting, Amery noted that

Beaverbrook had 'come on immensely as a speaker, full of rhetorical artifice even if his economic inferences and facts were rather sketchy'. But he also noted that 'Max is completely tired out and overwrought and if Cobb [Beaverbrook's candidate] is badly beaten will be pretty unhappy.'[23]

Cobb, however, won; and after midnight at The Vineyard 'Beaverbrook was in the seventh heaven of delight. The Press Association rang up to ask for a message, '"Glory, Hallelujah!" said the chief, and "Glory, Halle- lujah!" it was,' wrote Bruce Lockhart in his diary. 'Big triumph for M,' wrote Jean Norton in hers. Although Cobb was in favour of food taxes he had had the support of Conservative Central Office, who had not repeated their mistake with Ferguson. The *Express* presented his win as a victory for Beaverbrook: 'CRUSADER CAPTURES SOCIALIST SEAT'. Beaverbrook told his associates, talking about Baldwin: 'The man must go. We shall get rid of him.' Bruce Lockhart wondered if he was wise to make these 'indiscreet boasts', and how many of his 'so-called friends' could be relied on.

Five days after the West Fulham triumph the *Express*, announcing a 20,000 lift in its circulation to 1,689,432 copies, led with: 'EMPIRE LOAF DEMAND: FINEST BREAD IN THE WORLD'. Intense nationwide interest, the paper said, had been aroused by the birth of the Empire loaf: '"Empire wheat, British milled in British bread" is fast becoming the country's slogan.' 'NEW TRIUMPH OF THE EMPIRE LOAF', said the paper three days later: 'Harrods have made the Empire loaf the outstanding feature of their Bakery Week which starts this morning.' Perhaps munching their Empire loaves at breakfast a week later, having told their retailer, as urged by the *Express*, 'We want the Empire loaf', readers learned that Beaverbrook had changed tack once more; he now wanted to scrap the proposal for a referendum on food taxes because Conservative Central Office was using it 'not as a spear with which to fight for Empire Free Trade, but as a shield behind which to shelter from the issue of a tax on foreign foodstuffs'. In a leader, the *Express* endorsed the proprietor's recommendation.

Senior Conservatives thought that Beaverbrook was running wild; after all, the referendum had been his idea, privately put forward, and he had welcomed Baldwin's public acceptance of it. At a dinner on 19 June, designed to persuade Beaverbrook that the party was more likely to adopt his way of thinking if he, instead of beating it over the head, used kindlier tactics, Amery observed that Beaverbrook became vehement, passionately exaggerated the differences between himself and the party, and 'stupefied us by saying that unfit as he was for the job, he might be compelled to be Prime Minister!'[24]

Why was Beaverbrook so erratic? Hitherto, when he had taken part in critical political events, he had been working on the inside, as the ally of, or the intermediary for, men in office. Now, he was by himself on the outside. True, the Empire Crusade had long since ceased to be the 'stunt' that some critics had thought it to be at its launch. Beaverbrook had the backing of influential businessmen, of a significant section of national opinion, particularly in agricultural regions, and of some aspiring politicians; but he was not fully supported by a single senior politician of weight. When he felt threatened by isolation Beaverbrook invariably fed on his grievances, becoming aggressive and often unpredictable. He continued to maintain friendly relations with Rothermere, but Rothermere did not always agree with him – he had been against the referendum as well as food taxes – and in any case was rarely in London, as he toured about from grand hotel to grand hotel with his entourage of secretaries and girlfriends.

In the last week of June, however, Beaverbrook finally hauled Rothermere aboard: Rothermere had made very careful enquiries, and concluded that 'taxes on foreign foodstuffs are not only economically desirable but electorally possible'. Twenty years after Beaverbrook had been opposed by Northcliffe on food taxes, he had won over his brother. On 23 June the *Express* outlined the history of Beaverbrook, Baldwin and Empire Free Trade, and said it was 'inconceivable that the break can now be mended'. To the outrage of many Conservatives, Beaverbrook proposed that subscribers to Conservative Party funds should divert their subscriptions to him. On 24 June the *Express* proclaimed: 'LORD ROTHERMERE'S BOMBSHELL', giving the news about Rothermere's switch on food taxes.

In 1930 Beaverbrook was leading an extraordinary life from three bases: Stornoway House, The Vineyard and Cherkley. Conservative politics revolved round the agenda he had largely set – the referendum, Empire policy and Baldwin's leadership. Senior Conservatives – Chamberlain, Amery and Sir Robert Horne (a former Chancellor of the Exchequer whose Presbyterian father had recommended Beaverbrook's father for his first job in Canada) – tried to calm him down. Up-and-coming younger Conservatives, such as Edward Marjoribanks on the right and Harold Macmillan on the left, sought his advice (he told Marjoribanks that 'the only prize worth anything is the Premiership. A man in any other post is only wearing the Prime Minister's livery').[25]

His alliance with Rothermere grew so close that at one stage Rothermere even told him he could give orders about the Crusade directly to the *Daily Mail*. The smart young set approached him for work: John Heygate, who had run off with Evelyn Waugh's wife and had to leave the BBC; Peter Rodd, the 'very superior con man'[26] who was courting Nancy Mitford; and Waugh's undesirable friend the 'satanic' Basil Murray.[27] He had a finger in every political pie. When Oswald Mosley resigned from the Labour government in May, he and Beaverbrook briefly flirted. Prominent left-wingers – Frank Wise, Jennie Lee and James Maxton – dined at Stornoway House. So did Churchill, Lloyd George and another former Chancellor, Reginald McKenna. Beaverbrook gave a Commonwealth

Press party for 1500 people at the Albert Hall, addressed the annual *Express* Empire Day concert and procession in Hyde Park ('massed bands and hymns of Empire: world broadcast of the great festival'), and spoke at a banquet for Sir Abe Bailey, the South African magnate, at the Savoy Hotel. He also sold his stud, disregarding the pleas of his racing manager, Lord Adare, who assured him that he had 'such a very valuable collection of young mares and such a number of good nominations that it could not help being a great financial success if you sell the yearlings', and cancelled his nominations to Phalaris and Sansovino; racing had served its turn as a diversion.[28] In August he took the usual crowd – Jean Norton, the Weymouths, Bruce Lockhart – on a cruise to France and came back with paratyphoid; even that did not incapacitate him for long.

He was once disconcerted. An Australian, Gibson Young, whose writing paper described him as a 'Vocalist, Lecturer, and Community Singing Conductor', had been invited to conduct community singing at a Crusade gathering in the ballroom at Stornoway House and took with him his fourteen-year-old son Michael to see the great man in action. Beaverbrook spoke, and then announced that he was going to ask the youngest person in the room of some two hundred people to say why he or she was supporting the Crusade. Sixty years later Michael Young, by then Lord Young of Dartington, remembered his alarm.

I froze in my chair and pretended not to be there but to no avail. I was hauled out of the back row and marched up to the little platform at one end. I said that I was not at all a supporter of the Crusade. I thought it was a strange old-fashioned idea not at all in tune with the times and anyway I didn't think it was ever going to arouse any support. I knew something about Australia where I had been brought up and I thought there'd be hardly a soul in Australia would be a supporter. If I'd been more confident I might not have been so truthful. There was a deathly hush and I could feel Beaverbrook standing at my side fidgeting. He at once realised he couldn't possibly reply to a child of my age. So, I thought rather to his credit, he just closed the meeting – rather a disaster for a rally of his supporters from all over the country.[29]

In the next room, champagne and sandwiches had been laid out. They remained untouched. Afterwards, Beaverbrook congratulated Gibson Young on having so bold a son.

As the year drew on, talk in Conservative circles centred round possible successors to Baldwin. Beaverbrook, not alone, judged that both Baldwin and Chamberlain would be out in six months; he told Amery he would 'serve' under him. Publicly and privately, the tide was running in favour of protection, if not altogether in favour of Beaverbrook's 'whole hog' version. Bankers endorsed it; so did *The Times*; so did the Trades Union Congress.

Baldwin alone dithered. Buchan and Amery came to the extraordinary conclusion that he was not really interested in politics; his one adviser seemed to be his protective wife Lucy (Beaverbrook thought it a great joke that she called her husband 'Tiger'). Only once in 1930 did he show any of the fight and oratorical power of which he was sometimes capable. Rothermere had written a typically clumsy letter to Hannon, saying he would not support Baldwin or any other leader 'unless I am acquainted with the names of at least eight, or ten, of his most prominent colleagues in the next Ministry'. He allowed Hannon to make the letter public. At a special party meeting, in June, Baldwin let fly: there was nothing more curious in modern evolution, he said, than the 'effect of an enormous fortune rapidly made and the control of newspapers of your own'. Such power, he said, 'goes to the head like wine, and in all these cases' – he named Beaverbrook, Rothermere and the American William Randolph Hearst – 'attempts have been made outside journalism to dictate, to domineer, to blackmail . . . you cannot take your politics from men like that'. Then he turned to the Rothermere letter: '. . . a more preposterous and insolent demand was never made on the leader of any political party. I repudiate it with contempt and I will fight that attempt at domination to the end.'[30] Rothermere had enabled Baldwin to turn the question of the leadership into a question of constitutionalism.

Two by-elections in early and mid-summer, North Norfolk (a Labour seat) and Bromley, where both the official candidates were Empire Free Traders, produced an uneasy, off–on alliance between the party and Beaverbrook, and sent Rothermere veering away from both, like one of his Rolls Royces with defective steering. Beaverbrook made ten speeches in Norfolk and used an aeroplane, creating excitement and linking modernity to what was in truth an antique cause. The seat was not, however, won: '. . . fearful gloom,' wrote Jean Norton. In Bromley, Rothermere had the idea of putting up his son Esmond, and refused to support the Conservative candidate because of his proclaimed loyalty to Baldwin.

Beaverbrook now went off to Canada, angry that Jean Norton could not go with him because of her children; and blundered. He gave an interview to the *Toronto Globe* seeming to back the incumbent Liberals under Mackenzie King against his old friend the Conservative leader R. B. Bennett. The *Globe* held back the interview and published it on the eve of a general election, which, unfortunately for Beaverbrook, Bennett won. At an Imperial Conference in London in early October 1930, convened mainly to discuss trade, Bennett announced that Empire Free Trade was 'neither desirable nor possible' – a body blow to Beaverbrook and to the *Express*, which had been telling its readers for a year that Canada endorsed it. Instead, Bennett said that Canada was ready to do deals with Britain on preferential tariffs; and Baldwin picked up the offer. At the next election the Conservative Party would seek a free hand to impose the necessary duties – in other words, it no longer ruled out food taxes.

Beaverbrook tried to make it up with Bennett, but Bennett – 'he was not free from rancour', Beaverbrook wrote – ignored his approaches.[31] With others, it was Beaverbrook who failed to respond, even when the moves came from those who, unlike Baldwin, were not ill-disposed to him personally, such as Amery. Blumenfeld, technically the *Express* editor-in-chief, complained that Beaverbrook never consulted him. Churchill told Harold Nicolson that Beaverbrook was 'a neurotic' and in September told Beaverbrook that he could do great things for the nation if only he would stop behaving to the Conservative Party like an old-fashioned dancing master.[32] Bruce Lockhart thought he was insane to break with Baldwin and set off into the wilderness. Even Elibank, Beaverbrook's close supporter, told him he was more likely to achieve his aims if he modified his methods and did deals with the Conservative leadership over its new policy. Beaverbrook paid little attention: Baldwin had still not swallowed food taxes, and he believed he could win the fight, Amery noted, by relying simply on himself and his newspapers.

He threw himself with glee into the South Paddington by-election, due on 31 October. The local Conservative association produced Sir Herbert Lidiard as its candidate. Beaverbrook wrote him a tough letter telling him he had to choose between Baldwin and himself. Lidiard chose Baldwin. Beaverbrook then put up Vice-Admiral Taylor as the first fully fledged Empire Crusade candidate. 'Conservative Imperialist v. Conservative Wobbler,' said the *Express*. Gerhardie watched him speaking in support of the Admiral at Paddington Baths; he noted 'a strange mystic look in his eye' as he mounted the platform amid cheers 'and immediately began to rage and weep and implore, looking at a distance like a sublime frog'.[33]

Baldwin too seemed to be wobbling dangerously when, alarmed by the way Conservative support was crumbling in the constituencies, over forty Conservative MPs told the chief whip that 'a change of leadership is essential to the national interest'. On 30 October, the day before the poll, Conservative peers, MPs and candidates attended a crucial evening meeting at Caxton Hall, in effect to vote on the leadership crisis. Beaverbrook went, and 'got in my few sentences entirely on policy and returned to my place amidst a little ripple of applause from the anti-Baldwin section'.[34] Another account said he was 'greeted with hoots'.[35] But he was isolated. Lord Hailsham – a leading if not the leading candidate to replace Baldwin if Baldwin went – was thought to have made the decisive speech: if the vote went against Baldwin, he said, every future party leader 'would have to dance to the tune of the Press Plutocrats'.[36] 'Mr Baldwin wins – and loses,' said the *Express*. '116 votes for his resignation. Vote of confidence carried. Majority of 346.'

Next day 'THE EMPIRE WINS SOUTH PADDINGTON', said the *Express*. Beaverbrook, after the 'depression' of the Baldwin defeat, felt 'exaltation'. But Baldwin was equally pleased; Admiral Taylor had beaten the official Conservative by less than a thousand votes, and for Baldwin in any case the vote at Caxton Hall had been far more important. 'The Beaver is now trying to climb back!', he wrote. 'He is beat fair and square.' On 17 November he noted: 'The foul press is lying very quiet.'[37]

It was at this moment that Beaverbrook was annoyed by a Scottish aristocrat. Another by-election was coming up in East Renfrewshire. Hitherto, Crusade strategy had been to contest by-elections only where support for the cause was strongest: middle-class London residential districts and suburbs; southern English farming seats. By-elections were much more common then than they later became, and Beaverbrook entirely ignored those in the industrial Midlands and the north, in Wales or in Scotland. But in East Renfrewshire the Conservative candidate was the Marquess of Douglas and Clydesdale, the young heir to the dukedom of Hamilton and a former Scottish middleweight boxing champion; Beaverbrook thought he spotted an opening. He sent emissaries to persuade the Marquess to come out for the Empire Crusade. Clydesdale refused and indeed supported the official Conservative policy.[38] When on 1 December he quintupled the Conservative majority, the *Express* gave him five lines on page 9. Beaverbrook did not forget the rebuff.

'SMASHING UP THE CONSERVATIVE PARTY'

The 'foul press' did not lie quiet for long. 'We are on the verge of war to the knife with Baldwin again and are to contest East Islington,' Bruce Lockhart recorded on 23 January 1931. This decision, soon made public, not only infuriated the Conservative Party managers but also alienated the old anti-Baldwin dissidents, who had promised to abide by the result of the vote at Caxton Hall. East Islington was held by Labour, but since unemployment was soaring and the Labour government floundering when its MP died, the Conservatives were thought virtually certain to win the by-election. Besides, in Thelma Cazalet they had a personable and strong-minded young candidate who seemed exceptionally well equipped to attract the important new 'flapper vote' – the women enfranchised in 1928 by the lowering of the age limit to twenty-one. When Beaverbrook announced that an Empire Crusade candidate, Paul Springman, a barrister, was taking the field, these hopes were shattered, since the Conservative vote was now bound to split. Nobody was angrier than Thelma Cazalet's brother, Victor Cazalet MP. After appearing on Sir John Ferguson's Crusade platform he had publicly recanted, and since then had been consistently denigrated by the Beaverbrook press; he was sure that 'personal elements were involved' in Beaverbrook's decision, seeing it as the 'deliberate political assassination' of his sister.[39]

She seemed to be suddenly reprieved when the assassin's instrument, Springman, pointedly described by Thelma Cazalet as 'a decent and honest person', realized that his views were almost identical with hers and withdrew. Beaverbrook helped to draft the letter of withdrawal. Then he changed tack. He wrote to Thelma Cazalet inviting her to come out in full support of his policies, with the implied but unmistakable threat that, if she declined, he would put up another Crusade candidate against her. He also sent her a pro-Crusade letter to sign. She issued a furious statement: of Beaverbrook's letter she said that 'no Conservative or other candidate could have put his signature to it without losing every sense of independence and honour – naturally I refused . . . his primary object and interest lies no longer in Empire matters but rather – as he has told us in two of his recent speeches – "in smashing up the Conservative Party"'.[40]

In the background, Rothermere urged on Beaverbrook against the official Conservatives. 'If you, with my assistance, can overthrow the Central Conservative organisation, the Conservative Party is ours,' he wrote on 2 February. He included a suggestion: to make it worthwhile for Crusade members and candidates to 'stay put' by paying them, if necessary. 'For ten or fifteen thousand a year in directorships you can certainly get twenty "trustys".'[41] Beaverbrook had had the same idea long since.

His new Crusade candidate was Brigadier-General A. C. Critchley DSO, a forty-one-year-old Canadian who had started the first greyhound racing track in England and was regarded in fashionable circles as a cad. Harold Nicolson thought Beaverbrook had 'made a complete fool of himself'[42] by his dithering, and Bruce Lockhart thought he would confirm his reputation as a 'twister'.[43] Thelma Cazalet attracted much sympathy: Springman spoke for her during the campaign; so did Amery, a sign of Beaverbrook's isolation from his old dissident allies; Lord Hailsham called Beaverbrook a 'mad dog' (the *Express* put the insult in a box on page one). Beaverbrook wrote later to Henry Weymouth: 'Old Baldy would not come down to Islington, but he sent his wife, who was headlined as "Mrs Baldwin Smites Beaverbrook". I was a fool not to put my daughter Janet up to smite her. I will next time.'[44]

The *Express*, now carrying daily on its masthead a drawing of a crusader with sword, helmet and shield, reported the campaign as if Critchley was the sole candidate and Beaverbrook the hero. As the Critchley campaign made 'whirlwind progress', Beaverbrook 'stood bareheaded in the cold night wind with one hand extended to General Critchley. "This is your man – Empire Free Trade is your policy".' Beaverbrook, said the paper, 'turns his back on Europe' and instead reaches out to 'six Dominions, 43 Colonies, nine Protectorates, and seven Mandated Territories'. These statistics must have surprised the readers, since hitherto Beaverbrook had reached out principally to Canada, and his papers had made no attempt to report the effect that Empire Free Trade might have on particular colonies, let alone on the protectorates and mandated territories.

As the poll approached, the *Express* came dangerously close to presenting Beaverbrook as a demagogue, laying out one speech like verses from the Bible:

301

'I have given you an unanswerable case for my policy.

'So I make my point

'The faith of the Empire Free Trader is not in the old markets but in the new markets

'Not in old measure, but in new measures

'And –

'Not in the old politicians but the new politicians . . .'

He stepped back and caught General Critchley by the arm –

'The Young Man!'

The rolling thunder of cheers shook the hall.

A. J. Cummings of the Liberal *News Chronicle* described Beaverbrook's 'all-embracing look of contemptuous fury' as he attacked Baldwin. 'The other night I heard him in East Islington,' wrote C. Lionel Harrington in a feature. 'To me it was almost uncanny. His voice, his gestures, his language – where had I heard it all before? And then it came back to me, in a rush of memory. His father, the fiery, soul-saving Presbyterian minister of Newcastle, New Brunswick, lives again in his son.'

On the eve of the poll, across the top of page one the *Express* published a row of portraits headlined: 'WHY THEY WILL VOTE FOR GEN-ERAL CRITCHLEY'. The accompanying news story summarized the choice before the voters: 'It is a decision between higher and lower wages; between depression and prosperity. . . .' The story reported that Beaver-brook, at a meeting the previous evening, had entered the hall to a 'storm of cheering and applause'. It added that cars were needed to take Crusade voters to the polls and told them where to report. There was no word about any other meeting or any other candidate.

The Conservative vote was split, as everyone expected and Beaverbrook intended, and the Labour candidate duly won with 10,591 votes; Critchley came second and Cazalet third, with a total of 15,496 votes. 'So much for the Crusade party!' wrote Victor Cazalet bitterly; and his anger was widely shared.[45] Beaverbrook had split not only the vote but the upper classes: 'M quite pleased to beat the Tories,' Jean Norton put in her diary, as she and Castlerosse were whisked off to Paris by their benefactor. In many Conservative eyes, Beaverbrook now seemed to be not so much a true Conservative seeking to change party policy as a destructive force giving aid to the socialists. The banker Sir Henry Strakosch told him: 'It is more important than ever to avoid any internecine strife amongst those who believe in the maintenance of the established social order.'[46]

East Islington was immediately followed by one of the most celebrated by-elections of British political history, in St George's Westminster, about the safest Conservative seat in the country. Since the Caxton Hall vote in the autumn, the Conservative Party had sunk back into frustration and grumbling, and Baldwin's standing had sunk with it. On 28 February the *Express* named its candidate: Sir Ernest Petter, a Conservative industrial-ist, 'who will stand in opposition to Mr Baldwin's leadership and policy'.

On the same day the prospective official Conservative candidate, J. T. C. Moore-Brabazon, withdrew, saying he could not defend Baldwin. Meanwhile the party's chief political agent had been taking soundings and now reported 'a very definite feeling' that Baldwin was 'not strong enough to carry the party to victory'. This should have been Beaverbrook's moment of triumph, and nearly was, for Baldwin read the memorandum on the morning of 1 March and at 3 p.m. the same day summoned Chamberlain and told him he was going to resign at once. Beaverbrook had won: using 'press power' he had ousted the leader of a great political party – an unprecedented act. His victory lasted some six hours. After dinner, Baldwin was persuaded to defer any resignation until the by-election was over; and before the evening was out, moving from gloom to euphoria, he was talking about fighting St George's himself.[47] He was dissuaded from that course also. But still no other candidate came forward. Finally, when it was beginning to look as if nobody was willing to risk going into the ring against Beaverbrook seconded by Rothermere, on 6 March Duff Cooper, who had lost his seat at Oldham in 1929, stepped forward and was adopted: 'Mr A Cooper,' the *Express* called him. When Duff Cooper protested, the *Express* said that 'the rejected member for Oldham took exception to the *Daily Express* referring to him as Mr A. Cooper'. Next day, he was punished with a headline reading: 'Mr Duff Cooper's 44 Listeners: A Meeting Fizzles out at St George's.'

It was an odd election for Beaverbrook. Not only was Duff Cooper's wife, Lady Diana, a woman whom he ardently pursued and occasionally employed, but Duff Cooper's career had been helped by the *Express*, which extravagantly praised his maiden speech in 1924, and by sage advice from Beaverbrook in 1928 about how to improve his humourless platform style – though he had been less helpful in the election of 1929. By rights it should have been Duff Cooper, who liked to think of himself as a latter-day Charles James Fox, and Lady Diana who campaigned for their patron Beaverbrook, godfather to their infant son, and Petter, a dull manufacturer of diesel engines from the West Country, who supported Baldwin. Class was important in St George's, where there was a large 'deference vote' among the domestic staffs of Mayfair and Belgravia, which was why Duff Cooper tried to insist on the use of his full name: Mr Cooper v. Sir Ernest Petter gave quite the wrong impression. Pursuing the flapper vote and impressing the deferential, Lady Diana took to the hustings, a white camellia pinned in her cap, with her sister-in-law, the Duchess of Rutland, and other society women. Beaverbrook countered with the only slightly less grand Lord and Lady Weymouth and the Hon. Mrs Richard Norton, and with a popular hero, Sir Malcolm Campbell, the famous racing driver – a move that provoked Duff Cooper to a violent outburst. 'MR DUFF COOPER ATTACKS SIR MALCOLM CAMPBELL'S HONOUR. "BOUGHT BY THE EXPRESS"', reported the *Express*. Duff Cooper had said it was 'the vilest, dirtiest, and most disgusting thing that they should get a man who does one thing well and to the admiration of his fellow countrymen to pronounce his views on politics . . .'. But the fact was that Sir Malcolm had approached Beaverbrook, in writing, to offer help, and Duff Cooper was forced to back down.[48]

Rothermere and the *Daily Mail* joined in with crude and abusive support. The *Mail* called Duff Cooper a 'softy' and 'Mickey Mouse', and accused him of having made a speech in Germany 'apologising' for the British Empire: a misunderstanding, either wilful or ignorant, of the title of his lecture – 'An Apologia for the British Empire'. Rothermere's obsession with India produced a warning to the voters that became famous: 'Gandhi is watching St George's.' Beaverbrook and his allies were trying to fight the election on Baldwin's leadership, but were hampered by the way Rothermere and his newspapers, with the connivance of Petter, kept harping on India. Baldwin, having recovered his nerve, fought on the issue of press dictatorship. He was assisted by a statement signed by prominent Liberals, including Lords Crewe, Grey and Reading, who said that 'the power which the multiple-newspaper gives to irresponsible amateur politicians to mislead their readers by the weapons of distortion and suppression constitutes a menace to our treasured political institutions, the gravity of which it would be impossible to overstate'.

However, the non-multiple newspapers were not unwilling to use their own power. Geoffrey Dawson of *The Times* instructed his staff always to give Duff Cooper his full name and his DSO, and invited Duff Cooper to let him know if 'I can do anything . . . to correct misstatements which the "stunt" papers decline to admit.' Fred Lawson (later Lord Burnham), general manager of the *Telegraph*, recently acquired by the Berry brothers, went further: he told Duff Cooper that ' . . . you will find all our people, editorial, circulation, and everybody doing their damndest for you . . . .'[49]

The *Express* discussed the dictatorship question in a leader on 16 March:

> The *Daily Express* and the *Daily Mail* are trying to persuade Mr Baldwin to retire and make way for his successor.
> Q. Is that dictatorship?
> A. The Baldwinites say so.
> Q. But *The Times, Telegraph,* and *Morning Post* say that Mr Baldwin should not resign. Is that dictatorship?
> A. No. That is loyalty.

The leader writer was making a reasonable point. The distinction between the *Mail* and *Express* and other newspapers was not that the former wished to use their power and the latter did not, but that the *Express* and *Mail* made more noise and their proprietors seemed more wilful; other proprietors controlled their editors with more discretion.

Still, by this stage Beaverbrook and Rothermere, far from increasing the pressure on Baldwin, were solving his problems for him. If their candidate lost, he was safe. If their candidate won, he was equally safe, because his party could scarcely oust him in such circumstances without appearing to truckle to the unelected press barons. All Baldwin had to do, therefore, was to ensure that 'press dictatorship', not his leadership, was perceived as the dominant election issue. His opportunity came on 17 March in the Queen's Hall, and he took it with unusual eloquence. The newspapers of Beaverbrook and Rothermere, he said,

> . . . are not newspapers in the ordinary acceptance of the term. They are engines of propaganda for the constantly changing policies, desires, personal wishes, personal likes and dislikes of two men. What are their methods? Their methods are direct falsehood, misrepresentation, half-truths, the alteration of the speaker's meaning by putting sentences apart from the context, suppression, and editorial criticism of speeches which are not reported in the paper. . . . What the proprietorship of these papers is aiming at is power, but power without responsibility – the prerogative of the harlot throughout the ages.[50]

This devastating sentence is thought to have been written by Beaverbrook's former adviser, Kipling.

Next morning, the *Express* led the paper with 'SIR ERNEST PETTER'S TRIUMPH' in a speech to '2,000 at the Victoria Palace Theatre'. Lower down, across two columns, ran the headline: 'Mr Baldwin Denounces His Enemies.' The paper's editor, Beverley Baxter, had assigned himself to cover the meeting, but his story was less a report of Baldwin's denunciation than a commentary on it. Baldwin, the editor wrote, had said that the press distorted and exaggerated. 'That was legitimate fighting. The political platform allows for over-statement and Mr Baldwin knew what was expected of him.' The next section of the story was printed in bold type. 'But suddenly he lost his head. . . . Mr Baldwin swung to the *Daily Mail* and harangued Lord Rothermere and that journal in language that knew no restraint. He made one smear at Lord Rothermere, however, that simply is not done. When he had made it, he looked furtively at his audience and licked his lips.' By the end of the speech, which, Baxter claimed, he had determined to listen to with 'a mind unprejudiced', the audience was 'restless' and the hall like a 'public morgue'. Thus readers of the *Express* were deprived of the heart of perhaps the most effective speech that Baldwin ever delivered, and the editor himself proved the justice of Baldwin's charge of suppression.

Beaverbrook spoke three times a night for ten days. Pamela Chichester, Bruce Lockhart's girlfriend, wrote to him: 'All London, whatever their political convictions, are united on one point, and that is that you are far away the finest speaker we've got in the country.'[51] Beaverbrook sent her money. He did not lose his gaiety. He wrote to Tom Clarke at the *News Chronicle*: 'It breaks my heart to see you giving a column to Lady Diana Cooper, when you could be giving a column of news. You can do more damage to Petter in a column of news.'[52] He told a correspondent: 'Duff Cooper is the bad-tempered fellow, I am the little ray of Canadian sunshine.'[53]

The sun went behind the clouds on 20 March, when Duff Cooper won the election by 17,242 votes to Petter's 11,532. 'Terrible debacle,' Jean Norton wrote. 'Fearful gloom. Crept round to Stornoway . . . went in by basement owing to hostile crowd outside . . . stayed with M.' Next morning the *Express* reported the result as if the chief sub was a Baldwinite: 'BALDWINITES' BIG MAJORITY AT ST GEORGE'S: COMPLETE TRIUMPH FOR THE CONS'.

Three weeks earlier, Baldwin had believed he was finished. Now he was secure, his leadership of the party impregnable. He had been saved by the press lords. Beaverbrook struggled to come to terms with the result. 'I am horribly disappointed at the failure,' he wrote privately. 'It is much worse than I expected. I cannot believe that Press dictatorship was the reason for it.'[54] He told a supporter the day after the vote: 'We lost St George's because of the strong cross-currents. It was a baffling contest and we were driven off course. We cannot take the result as a rejection of Empire Free Trade.'[55] He concluded that he had been misguided to fight on the leadership, when the electorate was more concerned about the 2,600,000 unemployed.

The Crusade was over. It had lasted nineteen months. Only the helmeted crusader, his sword drawn on the *Express* masthead, remained as a memorial to a lost campaign. At the end of March Beaverbrook and Chamberlain, who was representing the Conservative Party and Baldwin, agreed a truce, called by Beaverbrook the Stornoway Pact. Baldwin agreed to employ quotas, prohibitions and duties to help agricultural production, and Beaverbrook recognized that these measures had 'advantages'. Elibank assured him: 'The main planks in your programme have been won.'[56] Beaverbrook was not so sure. Jean Norton wrote on 30 March: '. . . reconciliation between Max and Conservatives – but not too satisfactory. M not very well pleased with it.' Beaverbrook invented an ecclesiastical image of Baldwin appearing to accept Empire Free Trade, entering church and coming to the mercy seat in propitiation for his sins – and then, lo and behold, as the congregation sang 'We shall come rejoicing,/Bringing in the sheaves!', crawling away down the aisle. On the day the pact was published Beaverbrook wrote to Duncan Fitzwilliams, consulting surgeon at St Mary's Hospital: 'Secretly . . . I do not think the fight is over. . . . There is room for Baldwin to crawl down the aisle again. As you and I will be in the choir on that occasion, Baldwin can get through the door before we can catch him.'

A DEMANDING PERIOD

During this particularly demanding period, Beaverbrook lost three old friends who meant much to him: Birkenhead, Tim Healy and Arnold Bennett. He had latterly been reconciled to Birkenhead after another quarrelsome patch over politics and what Birkenhead described as Low's 'filthy and disgusting' cartoons of him in the *Express*. Undermined by years of hard drinking, Birkenhead died, aged fifty-nine, in September 1930, leaving his family in low water financially. Beaverbrook immediately came to the rescue, offering to pay for the new Lord Birkenhead's education and making Pamela and Eleanor Smith an allowance of £325 a year apiece.[57]

Tim Healy, who was seventy-six and had been ill for some time, died in Ireland in the spring of 1931. Beaverbrook had been kept informed of his decline by a mutual friend, who wrote to tell him that on his deathbed Healy had whispered, when told of Beaverbrook's concern, 'Dear old Max . . . .' He made enquiries as to whether Healy's family needed money (he had seven children) but was told they did not: 'I am missing him very, very much,'[58] he wrote.

Arnold Bennett's death at sixty-three was unexpected. He had become ill in January 1931 with typhoid contracted from bad water in France; Beaverbrook visited him several times and was observed, when Bennett was delirious, watching silently in the doorway.[59] Bennett's lingering illness was reported widely and received much space in the *Express* and the *Standard*. The last of his many letters to Beaverbrook had to be written for him, on 14 February. He regretted that his doctor had forbidden all visitors, and sent his love. Five weeks later, he died. Obituaries and eulogies poured out, including one in the *Daily Telegraph* by Rebecca West, who wrote: 'All London will miss him . . . some of his closest friends were men who had no other friends. His rich understanding of human nature enabled him to bridge gulfs that others could not.' Perhaps she was thinking of Beaverbrook. His much-quoted remark about Bennett – 'How I loved my Arnold, and how he loved my champagne' – distorts the nature of their friendship, or perhaps reflects Beaverbrook's deep-seated fear that no one, except perhaps Tim Healy, ever really loved him for himself.

The summer of 1931 was no better than the spring. Beaverbrook had become obsessed with the idea that he had a stone in his kidney, and made the long-suffering Bruce Lockhart visit a 'stone quack' alleged to be able to cure the condition without an operation, and feign his master's symptoms.[60] He was worried about his children: Janet and Ian Campbell were on the verge of divorce, and Max, who had just come down from Cambridge, seemed to his father to be too interested in enjoying himself and not eager to get down to work. He had a large twenty-first birthday party at Stornoway House and, being handsome and eligible, was soon beginning to attract young women considered unsuitable by his father, not least because his father was frequently attracted to them himself. Relations with Peter continued to be awkward. Wardell wanted to get married, to Beaverbrook's displeasure, and the Castlerosse marriage was once again noisily on the rocks. In June, Bruce Lockhart found Beaverbrook 'pessimistic about himself, says his life's work is done, and wants to pull out of England altogether'.[61] Against this background more serious 'trouble' than usual blew up between Beaverbrook and Jean Norton, and looked as if it might bring their relationship to an end.

The crisis began as usual over Jean Norton's social life, which took her attention and energy away from Beaverbrook in a manner that he ignored when he was himself busy and confident, and found infuriating when he was low and anxious. That her social activities were subsidized by his money added fuel to the flames. She was particularly caught up that summer with the Mountbattens, partly because Edwina roped her in to help entertain the recently deposed King of Spain, and partly because they were themselves having trouble with their marriage and calling on her for advice and help. For some time Edwina had been restless; now she planned a long trip to Mexico, and rumours of divorce were spreading. Jean Norton was much involved in consultations with Mountbatten, over dinners and weekends at the Mountbattens' country house in Hampshire.[62] Beaverbrook became curious and intensely jealous. At the same time he was planning his usual summer journey to the USA and Canada, and wanted Mrs Norton to go with him.

By early July they were arguing almost every day; on 11 July she went down to Cherkley for the weekend. 'Long talk with M and after deciding to part and leave next day he came into my room and God knows what is to happen,' she wrote. During the next week the tension mounted; Beaverbrook took her to Southampton to look at a yacht. 'What in God's name does this mean?' she wrote frantically. He seems to have been keeping her in suspense about his plans, and she was trying to conceal her own. By the following weekend she was calmer: 'Fairly satisfactory talk with M, rather more hopeful that he may go to Canada and let me go south with the children . . . I feel there is some hope but you never know. I dare not talk of going south.' Plainly she did not want to lose him, but equally plainly she had no intention of joining him in Canada. Finally, to her relief, he went. Beaverbrook took with him Castlerosse, who had wanted to go as badly as Jean Norton had not. 'Max has been playing hurt feelings,' Bruce Lockhart noted. He had certainly been playing games, telling Castlerosse that his reputation was so bad that he could not take him, and only relenting when Castlerosse, amid promises of reform, began to cry. 'I could not resist the tears,' Beaverbrook said.[63]

RAMSAY MACDONALD IS GRATEFUL

One of Beaverbrook's strengths was his ability to be active simultaneously on many fronts. His private life, however complex and demanding, rarely for long took precedence over his wish to be involved with people in power. He had been defeated by Baldwin, the Conservative leader, at St George's, and had no hope of coming to terms with him; so he courted instead the Labour Prime Minister. In the summer of 1931, despite the raging economic blizzard, Ramsay MacDonald found the time to invite former ministers to join him in starting a library at Downing Street, which did not possess a single standard work of English literature or work of reference. Beaverbrook sent eight volumes of Burke and took out his oil can.

> May I say that my admiration for your direction of the Socialist Party in office gives me great satisfaction. This may be the sort of thing you would expect from a 'Press Peer'. But it is not. Bonar Law told me that you were the only possible person who could establish and maintain a Socialist Ministry. I believed him. I have said so ever so often, and I therefore feel very much like the backer, who put money on the Derby winner. Of course, I am so much opposed to you on Imperial Preference – or, as I prefer to call it, Empire Free Trade – that I must be marked by you as a Hittite.

MacDonald wrote back in his own hand: '. . . Hittite or not Hittite (that's your good Presbyterian origin!) I am very weary of disagreements at this terrible time, when the country needs understandings.' Beaverbrook sent more books, including *Torquemada and the Spanish Inquisition*: 'I do not recommend it for your reading, but it may be useful for another Prime Minister.'[64]

Beset by bitter internal Labour disputes, economic alarm and unemployment, in August 1931 MacDonald formed the coalition known as the National Government; afterwards, Beaverbrook asked him to dinner. Had he accepted, he might have found himself sitting next to Beaverbrook's latest mistress, Mrs Dorothy Hall. By September, MacDonald was seeking his views on the financial crisis. Almost alone among Conservatives, Beaverbrook and Amery were outraged by the deflationary policy of the orthodox financiers and economists, perforce accepted by most politicians including the Prime Minister. Beaverbrook was firmly on the side of the so-called 'economic radicals' of the period – Mosley, Lloyd George, Keynes, Macmillan – and against the 'economic conservatives' of all parties, in industry and in the banks.

Beaverbrook had disapproved of a National Government; he preferred battle lines to be clearly drawn. But when MacDonald called a general election in October to confirm the National Government's legitimacy Beaverbrook, both through his papers and on the platform, played an active and important role. The vote produced the rout of Labour, the virtual obliteration of the independent Liberals and a triumph for the Conservatives. The victorious Conservative candidate in Frome, Somerset was Henry Weymouth, who loyally stood by Empire Free Trade and made his maiden speech on Tariff Reform. Beaverbrook sent MacDonald a telegram of congratulations for leading the National Government to victory, and three days after the result MacDonald replied. 'How grateful I am to you for all you have done,' he wrote, adding the extraordinary statement for a man who had remained Prime Minister only by abandoning most of his former Labour colleagues: 'It has been a wonderful time.'[65]

Others, not socialists, thought the same; expressions of gratitude and compliments flowed in to Beaverbrook from those who since 1929 had been listening for the socialist tumbrils. The Duke of Westminster, a heavy contributor to the Empire Crusade, told him he had saved the country. So did Sir David Kinloch, Jean Norton's father.[66]

With the Conservatives dominant in the government, the tide was running in favour of the Tory nostrum of tariffs; and the imperialists, Beaverbrook among them, had high hopes of the great imperial gathering held in Ottawa in July and August 1932. 'It was our conviction that the day of Empire Economic Unity had dawned,' Beaverbrook wrote. R. B. Bennett was in the chair. 'But we had forgotten the cunning of Stanley Baldwin.' Baldwin was the leader of the British delegation, and it was he who wrecked the ambitions of the imperialists by stampeding his ministerial colleagues into refusing the dominions' request for a duty on foreign meat, and for the admission of Empire meat free, by playing on the old Tory fear of food taxes. Bogged down by meat, the conference degenerated into the negotiation of a dozen bilateral trade agreements. 'Baldwin had triumphed.' That was Beaverbrook's view. True, the conference was a failure. It did nothing to advance the wide imperial unity of which others besides Beaverbrook had dreamed. But the cause lay deeper than the twists and turns and 'false scents' of the 'fox' Baldwin. In a depression, the British were bound to protect the British farmer; and the dominions could not offer any concessions to British manufacturers without hurting their own industries. Characteristically, Beaverbrook thought that things might have been different if he had been invited to Ottawa by Bennett as an adviser. 'How I longed for such an invitation!' As it was, after the conference ended in mutual recriminations, 'The banners of Joshua were trailing in the mire.'[67]

'NEVER SAY NO TO YOUR LOVER'

On his way back from New York aboard the *Bremen* in late August 1931 Beaverbrook had met a twenty-eight-year-old American woman, Dorothy Hall, and started an affair with her.[68] Mrs Hall was a different kind of woman from the society beauties Beaverbrook collected in London. She was an outsider, she was observant, and, above all, she was not dependent on him. She neither wanted nor needed his money. Dorothy Hall was the daughter of a millionaire banker, and granddaughter of one of the founding partners of Kuhn Loeb. Her father, Mortimer Schiff, an acquaintance of Beaverbrook's and colleague of his old friend Otto Kahn, had recently died. When she met Beaverbrook, Dorothy was restless; her marriage was unsatisfactory, and she was taking her two children on a short holiday to Paris. Later on, as Dorothy Schiff, she was to become owner and publisher of the liberal daily newspaper the *New York Post*, and an influential figure in American politics and journalism.

Sitting at dinner with some friends in the first-class restaurant on the first night out, wearing a black lace dress, Dorothy noticed 'two unusual-looking men – one, a big fat man with a red complexion, and the other was a little man with a huge head'. The fat man came over, introduced himself as Lord Castlerosse and said: 'The big boss over there wants to meet you.' She knew who Beaverbrook was from New York society columns; when her friends protested that it would be more appropriate if Beaverbrook joined them, Castlerosse said: 'Well, he won't do that. Just join him for coffee and a liqueur; then I'll come and bring you back. He's very easily bored.' Dorothy went over to Beaverbrook's table. Next, '. . . we went down to his cabin, which turned out to be a suite, and made a few moves – backgammon ones.' Beaverbrook's approach was wily. First he asked her if she was Schiff's daughter; then he told her a moving tale of how during his early days, after Morgans had refused to lend him money, '. . . he went to my grandfather, who gave him the loan on his personality, or so he said. Anyway, he repaid it and became very rich. The memory meant a lot to him.' The next move was even more ingenious. 'Presently, he surprised me by saying that he had always wished he had been born a Jew. I asked "My God, why?" He said he was fascinated by them, they were brilliant, knew more than other people, and so on. The next morning three dozen roses arrived at my cabin with a note saying I was to sit at his table for the rest of the voyage.' Castlerosse, his job done, sat elsewhere.

Dorothy was captivated by Beaverbrook and his aura of energy and importance. The whole way across the Atlantic cables kept arriving for him; she even wondered at first if he was having them delivered to impress her. He appeared to fall for her too, and urged her to go with him to London; when she refused he joined her in Paris, wooed her with champagne and lobster at the Ritz, and charmed her suspicious mother, who afterwards told Dorothy that he was the most dynamic man she'd ever met. Beaverbrook was interested in whether Mrs Schiff felt guilt over her husband's death; she had been away in Europe at the time. Dorothy related this to his own evident feelings of guilt about Gladys. In Paris, they went to an exhibition of Indo-Chinese art; Beaverbrook suggested she write an article about it; he then corrected it for her and gave it back. He also took her to a restaurant where he pretended he did not have money to pay the bill, which she found a curious idea of a joke. She thought him odd-looking – 'He really did resemble a bullfrog,' she said, 'and in spite of the little valet he was rather unkempt, almost seedy. He would wear brown shoes with a blue suit. He was not what we used to call the Arrow type' – but she could not resist going back to London with him. She was flattered by his interest in her and at the same time he made her feel protective, almost maternal.

In London in September she stayed at Stornoway House, where she was given Janet's room on the fourth floor looking over the park. She found herself acting as Beaverbrook's hostess, listening to the political conspiracies being hatched over dinner. The financial crisis of 1931 was at its height. 'He held a sort of men's salon every night – just these very bright young men and me with a few older established names thrown in.' She met Churchill, Sir John Simon, Bruce Lockhart, Edward Marjoribanks and Leslie Hore-Belisha, then a young Conservative MP, who told her he would never come to the USA because Jews there were not admitted to the best clubs. She also encountered Gerhardie and Arlen and H. G. Wells, and Sir Thomas Horder, who felt obliged to apologize to her when over dinner one evening Beaverbrook asked her loudly how rich she was and called for a cutting giving details of her father's will. He struck her as fascinated by money; when she declined his offer to finance her in London he was incredulous, saying: 'You're the only woman I've ever met who won't accept money from me.'

Beaverbrook's concentration on Dorothy was intense, while it lasted.

> Max told me he would make me the toast of London; I guess I was already the talk of it. But it wasn't a cheap affair; I thought it was terrific and I was very proud of him. He talked about me a lot, as usual always asking questions. . . . We used to walk endlessly in St James's Park, and he'd tell me all kinds of fascinating things, he loved gossip and knew exactly how many mistresses and lovers people had had . . . he wasn't really witty, just terribly cruel – and he knew everything about everything and was extremely sophisticated. He was a full-time job.

She felt that he enjoyed spotting young talent and developing it, and also that it amused him to introduce her to young men and await developments. 'They didn't interest me one tiny bit, the young writers; only Max did.' He even talked of a possible future: 'Max used to discuss marriage a lot, arguing with himself about whether it could work. He said I was too young at 28 and that after a couple of years I would be taking on a young lover. He was terribly jealous. . . .' Towards the end of September Dorothy had to leave London to collect her children in Paris and take them back to school in America; to her surprise, he took her departure badly. 'I had no choice,' she recalls,

> . . . and besides, I thought things would keep on ice until he came to New York in November. When the morning for the boat train came – they left at some unearthly hour – he had gone down to his room and was in bed when I came to say goodbye. He couldn't believe I was really leaving and was terribly upset, saying 'Never say no to your lover'. As I tried to explain once more that I had to, he said: 'But you can't do this.' Then he turned to the wall, his back to me, and I heard my maid in the hall. . . . And Marjoribanks, to my surprise, was downstairs to take us to the train.

Jean Norton, meanwhile, had returned to London. The day after her arrival she dined at Stornoway House, along with Dorothy, Castlerosse,

Bruce Lockhart and Marjoribanks; Beaverbrook seems to have made no attempt to keep the two women apart. Before long Jean realized something was going on, but still he said nothing. When she learned that he had taken Mrs Hall to hear him speak at a meeting in Norfolk, she rebelled. At the end of the month there was a showdown: 'Hell of a row . . . decided to leave tomorrow.' She went to Paris and comforted herself with shopping at Schiaparelli and teas at the Ritz; but after a series of telephone calls and wires she went back to London. At first she was unsure where she stood; but Mrs Hall had gone, and after a day or two the relationship resumed.

Whether it was Jean Norton's return, or resentment at Dorothy Hall's departure, or just that his mood had changed, it was immediately clear to Mrs Hall when she saw Beaverbrook again in New York in November, shortly after the British general election, that the affair was over. She was hurt, and full of regrets: '. . . here was this interesting stimulating almost primitive man, and so wicked, and I had literally thrown it all away.' Later, she heard that he had gone back to an old flame. To her considerable irritation, he at once set about trying to promote a match between her and Hore-Belisha, telling her that he was sure they were made for each other, both being Jewish. They remained friends, however, and he would always send her flowers in London and call on her in New York. Although Dorothy Hall was not heartbroken and went on to make two more marriages, and to form a romantic friendship with President Roosevelt, she always remained interested in Beaverbrook. As her infatuation faded, she became more critical; when she saw him again in New York a year or two later, she remarked: 'Max arrived with his entourage in high spirits and filled with his political importance. He acts all the time, and now that I know him better, he has ceased to impress me. He seems to be making a great noise about nothing, has fascinated himself and appears to get much pleasure from his synthetic life. Yet he has courage . . . I suppose the reason is he likes to fight.' Decades later, she reflected further: 'Max was extremely neurotic, with I think a subconsciously low opinion of himself . . . Max was a very sad man, and I see now that I was right to leave when I did.'

There is no sign that the affair with Mrs Hall affected Beaverbrook for long, and his relationship with Jean Norton lasted, despite quarrels and reconciliations, for many more years. She continued to be jealous when his eye wandered, and he continued to be irritated by her social and family ties. His suspicions about her closeness to Lord Mountbatten lingered on. When the anniversary of Gladys's death came round again in December, Bruce Lockhart found him in low spirits.

Today was the anniversary of Lady Beaverbrook's death, and Max was mournful and lugubrious. He is very observant of all anniversaries. I sat alone with him after dinner. He was silent for long intervals. His only reference to Lady Beaverbrook was at dinner when he said: 'Four years ago today I was sitting in this chair listening to very satisfactory reports from the doctors about my wife's health. The same evening she died. All doctors are frauds anyway.'[69]

Two days later, to Jean Norton's distress, Beaverbrook dined with Gladys's sister, Helen Fitzgerald.

COMPLICATIONS WITH CHILDREN

His children's romantic entanglements gave Beaverbrook more trouble than his own. It is generally agreed that he handled them exceptionally badly. Like many men who have become rich by their own efforts, he resented his children's advantages and something in him despised them for being what his wealth had made them. His worst fault was inconsistency. Just as in her childhood Janet never knew when her beloved ponies would suddenly disappear, so as a young woman she was never certain whether he would give her the house, or the dress, or the loan she needed. After her marriage to Ian Campbell finally ended (they were divorced in 1934) she moved back into Stornoway House with her daughter Jean and lived with her father; but they fought so badly, usually about money, that she had to move out. For a while he stopped her allowance, but then she sent all her bills straight to him. Janet was headstrong, not a model of consistency herself, but resilient; she had violent rows with her father, but was never crushed by him.

With his elder son, Max, matters were more complicated. To his father, Max was altogether too much of a playboy. 'Little Max', as he was sometimes called, was devoted to his father, and longed to please him, but was incapable of turning himself into what his father would have liked – an heir-apparent with a passion for newspapers and politics. His son's lack of aptitude for such matters provoked Beaverbrook, and he would berate him in public for his dullness – sometimes in front of his contemporaries and friends – in the most savage and humiliating way.[70]

At the same time he was demanding. When in 1931, soon after his twenty-first birthday, Max began a romance with Margaret Whigham, the most celebrated debutante of the year, his father was greatly put out. 'Daddy had a long long talk with me this morning,' Max wrote to Margaret.

He started off about my work and how we've got to make the newspaper the greatest in all the world and how absolutely essential it is for me to be in absolute and complete partnership with him. Darling, he is frightfully jealous of you because he used to be the only person I would go to the end of the earth for. . . . He went on and on and said that I would be God's biggest fool to get married. . . . He is the loneliest man I know. Everyone is frightened of him because he has such unlimited power. And I seem to be the only person he will confide in and who he enjoys having around.

Max Aitken and Margaret considered themselves engaged; she soon changed her mind, but not before she had become, she recalled, a favourite of Beaverbrook's herself, after a private interview when she told him to stop being so unkind to his son.[71] Beaverbrook was indeed jealous; the old lion was being supplanted by the young in the most fundamental way of all.

Castlerosse, too, was having trouble with the younger generation. In the early 1930s Doris had a flagrant affair with Randolph Churchill, who was a year younger than Max Aitken, just as good-looking and much more troublesome and badly behaved. When Randolph turned twenty-one in 1932, Winston Churchill gave a dinner for him at Claridge's at which many of his contemporaries were accompanied by their fathers. Beaverbrook accompanied Max Aitken, Rothermere brought Esmond Harmsworth, Lord Hailsham came with Quintin Hogg, Lord Camrose with Seymour Berry. The late Lord Birkenhead's son Freddie made a speech, as did Randolph himself, to much praise from the gossip writers, including the *Evening Standard*'s.[72]

Castlerosse and Beaverbrook between them arranged a small exercise in deflation. The *Daily Express* ran an article headlined 'Pity These Great Men's Sons' and included in the survey of the 'young pigeons . . . aping the habits and fine feathers of peacocks' both Max Aitken and Randolph Churchill. 'Wherever I go I am confronted by the son of some magnate on whom the son of some other magnate passes favourable comment,' Castlerosse wrote. 'These bantams, by their own confession, expect to step straight into their father's shoes . . . they seem to think that fate and fathership have ordained them to immediate importance and command. . . . History proves almost indisputably that major fathers as a rule breed minor sons, so our little London peacocks had better tone down their fine feathers and start trying to make a name of their own.' When Randolph, never one to suffer in silence, claimed the right of reply, Beaverbrook asked him to dinner and agreed. 'You can't attack God in the *Daily Express*,' he said. 'But you may attack Castlerosse.'[73] It was the kind of mischief Beaverbrook greatly enjoyed, and it amused the readers, but there was a sour note beneath the fun.

Another young woman taken up by Beaverbrook in the 1930s was Lady Sibell Lygon, who met him through her sister Lettice. All the Lygon children were great friends of Evelyn Waugh, through his Oxford friendship with Hugh Lygon; their family home, Madresfield, and the painful scandal that ensued when their father, Lord Beauchamp, was accused of homosexuality by his brother-in-law, the explosive Bendor, Duke of Westminster, inspired Waugh's *Brideshead Revisited*. The novel contains a backward glance at Beaverbrook: '. . . the unmistakeable chic

– the flavour of "Max" and "F.E." and the Prince of Wales, of the big table in the Sporting Club, the second magnum and the fourth cigar . . .' Lady Sibell, who became a favourite with Beaverbrook and a lifelong friend of his daughter Janet, remembers Mrs Norton's jealousy of any pretty young newcomer to the inner circle: 'She was simply madly in love with him. She would have burned her grandmother to keep him.' She also remembers the storms between Beaverbrook and his children. 'Janet was always doing something awful. Beaverbrook said one day to Jeannie, who was then about 3 or 4, "What shall I do about your mother?", and Jeannie said, "Cut off all her money granpa."' Years later, Beaverbrook said to Lady Sibell: 'For all the awful things I've done in my life, I am paid back by my children's behaviour.'[74]

Beaverbrook was often nicer and more generous to his children's friends, or to his favourites among their contemporaries, than to them. Lady Mary Pakenham caught his eye after she started working on the *Evening Standard* social and fashion columns in 1934, and he would invite her to Stornoway House for tea and gossip; when one day Janet appeared, he growled: 'This is m'daughter. She der-rinks.'[75] But 'he was simply wonderful to all of us,' says Lady Sibell. 'He gave me two hunters which was sweet of him because he didn't like one hunting, he thought it was too dangerous.' Most of all, she remembers his help during the family crisis. Driven abroad in 1931 to escape arrest, Lord Beauchamp wanted to return to England when his wife and son died within three weeks of each other in 1936. Bendor put pressure on the Home Secretary, Sir John Simon, to take action. 'Max always took our side, always stood up for us,' Lady Sibell has said. 'Bendor said father would be arrested if he so much as put a foot ashore. I appealed to Max and he intervened. He spoke to the Home Secretary, and then he rang up and said, "It's all right, he can come home, nothing will happen."' Beauchamp came back for his son's funeral, although an aeroplane was kept waiting nearby in case the authorities changed their minds.

Even the favourites, however, sometimes became Beaverbrook's victims. Daphne and Henry Weymouth were alarmed when a film they had made of themselves cavorting naked in a boat off the Lido at Venice was retained by Kodak. They appealed to Beaverbrook, who recaptured the film and entertained his cronies by showing them tantalizing glimpses of it.[76] The Weymouths realized that their secret had become an after-dinner joke among the Beaverbrook circle and that they had no choice but to laugh at it themselves; and they continued to accept his invitations.

Beaverbrook was especially wary when he thought unsuitable young women were after his sons for their money – or rather Beaverbrook's. Another girl who started a romance with Max in the early 1930s was still married, and Beaverbrook was furious at the thought of his son being caught up in a divorce case. Lady d'Avigdor-Goldsmid remembered that neither her father, a conventional ex-soldier, nor Beaverbrook was at all happy with the prospect of her divorcing her then husband and marrying Max Aitken. 'Divorce was a disgrace still and anyway my father thought the Aitkens were common. I think the old man was impressed that my father didn't want to nail him.' She nevertheless came to be very fond of Beaverbrook herself, and when, after four years of waiting for the divorce, Max Aitken went off with someone else his father 'was wonderful to me, took my side and held my hand.'[77] Max Aitken's next involvement was, from Beaverbrook's point of view, in every way disastrous, and it caused a prolonged estrangement.

In 1933 or 1934 Beaverbrook had met and himself had an affair with a delicately exotic half-Dutch, half-Javanese girl in her mid-twenties called Catherina Koopman, always known as Toto. She was already a leading fashion model, a favourite with Chanel and such photographers as Steichen and Hoyningen Huene, and had started a film career; in 1934 she appeared opposite Douglas Fairbanks in Korda's *The Private Life of Don Juan*. Toto was also pursued by Castlerosse, whose wife proposed to cite her in their often threatened divorce case; when in 1935 she started to be seen everywhere with Max Aitken, who was infatuated and soon determined to marry her, Beaverbrook was outraged. 'Then he turned very nasty,' said Toto Koopman, nearly sixty years later. 'He called me "that black woman" and ordered no one to mention me in the papers ever again.' He also put pressure of the crudest kind on his son, first trying to bribe him with a new car, then telling him that if he would give Toto up he could have unlimited money and an important job, and finally banishing him to work in Scotland and threatening to cut him off completely.

Max and Toto ran away to Spain; when they returned, Beaverbrook tried again. 'He told Max: "I'll give you a lot of money if you promise not to marry that girl." I said, "Take it!" So he did, and we had a wonderful time.' They lived together in a splendid penthouse flat in Portman Square for the next four years. Looking back, Toto remembered being struck by Beaverbrook's ugliness – 'like a little monkey' – and also by his complicated attitude towards women. 'He had great charm, but he was not lovable, and he wasn't really sure of himself.' Sexual jealousy and fear of looking foolish, coupled with distaste at the prospect of a half-Javanese daughter-in-law, led Beaverbrook to handle the affair between his son and Toto very badly; nevertheless, as Toto herself recalled, 'he really loved Max'.[78]

When he was at odds with his sons, Beaverbrook would cast around for young men to act as substitutes, or threats. Usually they were his employees; but the most dramatic example was his nephew William Aitken, son of his brother Mauns. In the early 1930s Beaverbrook summoned Bill, as he was usually called, from Toronto, where he was working as a journalist, telling him he was needed in London. When Bill, who was a few years older than his cousin Max, arrived, he found that Beaverbrook had told his sons that as they were so useless he had decided to groom Bill to take over the newspaper empire. Bill lived at first with his aunts, Beaverbrook's sisters Gyp and Nan, who moved into The Vineyard in 1933, and was given a job on the *Standard*; not surprisingly, his cousins and his colleagues regarded him with suspicion. Before long, Beaverbrook changed his plans; thereafter, although Bill continued to work for the *Standard*, where he did well and was soon much liked, he saw little of his uncle who appeared almost to resent his success. He became friends with all three of his cousins, especially with Janet, as always the child most likely to cross her father.[79]

In 1935 Janet remarried. Once again her choice was a handsome, unreliable, impecunious son of an aristocratic family: Drogo Montagu, younger son of the Earl of Sandwich, who had already been divorced by a friend of hers, Tanis Guinness. Montagu's passions in life were flying, skiing and philandering. Janet told a story of how they went to Switzerland for their honeymoon, accompanied by Max and Toto; both men disappeared on the first evening and were later discovered with other women. Beaverbrook made the best of things, helped the Montagus generously with money and a house, and paid for a new plane for Drogo; at first all went well, and his first grandson, William, was born in February 1936.[80] Peter Aitken had married in 1934, to his father's displeasure. He had followed his brother to Cambridge, but left after a year; Beaverbrook then sent him to Canada where his Uncle Allan found him a job. He married a Canadian girl, Janet MacNeill, and they had a daughter, Caroline, but the marriage was soon in trouble.

By the middle 1930s, then, although Jean Norton was still very much present, Beaverbrook's personal and family life was tangled and not very satisfactory. He was travelling a great deal, especially in winter seeking the sun, and in January 1935 set off for South America taking with him Jean Norton, Castlerosse, the young journalist Frank Owen, his secretary 'Tich' Whelan – a former secretary to Lord d'Abernon, British Ambassador in Berlin – and Lady Diana Cooper, who in letters home to her husband left a close-up glimpse of her host.

In the train from Victoria to Dover she sat opposite Beaverbrook, who used the time to go through his household bills.

'What's this? 3 doz eggs, 1 doz eggs, a further 2 doz eggs. Will you tell me what the hell I keep a chicken farm for? Tell the staff for the hundredth time that they are not to take Mrs Campbell's orders. Tell the Leatherhead Gas people I'm not going to pay 10d a therm for my gas – the gas is not worth that money. Tell them Lord Beaverbrook is very unsatisfied with their rates. Mrs Campbell's telephone calls are not to be charged to me, and Max is not to charge me up with calls to that black bastard bitch.'

Walen [*sic*] has to shorthand every word. It gives you no idea how funny it was, and the tinyness of the items queried. 'What are Canadian Tabs, Walen? I'm not going to be charged 1/3 for Canadian Tabs, whatever they are.' They were calendar refills. 'I will *not* have the bidets repaired until they have been estimated for.' The joy of it all was that the books are always 'up' every month just like mine. . . .

After dinner Beaverbrook, who had learnt that Castlerosse was writing an autobiography, insisted against the victim's will that it be read aloud to the group. 'Well it was done – in the open bar. Walen spluttered through it to us jeerers. It was pretty bad too. "Not worth a damn, is it." – Val never winced.'

In Beaverbrook's presence, Diana Cooper noticed that his guests (apart from her) deferred to him: 'Jean Norton's grovel is alarming. . . .' Later, without him, talking the day over in Castlerosse's cabin, they agreed that their host was not enjoying himself. 'Jean said to Val, "Do you know that I'm almost beginning to believe that Max when he's not trying is capable of being almost a bore." Val shook and laughed till the tears ran down his cheeks.'[81]

Partly through his children and their friends, partly through his young women protégées, and partly out of journalistic instinct, in the early 1930s Beaverbrook gave exposure and much-needed income to many of the more talented of the Bright Young People of the period. Some, like Tom Driberg, became stars; others, like John Betjeman, who was briefly film critic for the *Standard*, or the aesthete Edward James, had brief moments of employment before moving on. Well-connected young men wanting to travel, like Robert Byron (who got him to pay for a journey by air to India), would give Beaverbrook newspapers a try, and sometimes win an invitation to Cherkley. Evelyn Waugh, who had worked for the *Express* as a reporter for all of seven weeks in 1927 ('. . . papers are full of lies,' he wrote in his diary), found after he became instantly celebrated with *Decline and Fall* in 1928 that the Beaverbrook papers were among the most lucrative outlets for the stream of articles he wrote to make a living; his first signed newspaper article, on censorship, appeared in the *Express* in October 1928.[82] Waugh quickly became a social as well as a literary success, and two of the women he liked most, Daphne Weymouth and Diana Cooper, were, to his displeasure, Beaverbrook admirers. In the early 1930s, when *The Miracle* was revived and toured England, Waugh often kept Diana company in the provinces. When his 'novel about journalists', *Scoop*, came out in 1938, 'Mrs Stitch' was immediately identified as Diana Cooper, and the newspaper magnate 'Lord Copper' has an equally recognizable connection with Beaverbrook. Moreover the lobby of the *Daily Beast* in Fleet Street reads like a parody of the *Daily Express* building, a black glass palace opened in 1931.

The gleaming new palazzo in the middle of Fleet Street opened a new stage in the Beaverbrook advance, ultra-modern and confident beside the almost contemporaneous stolid pillars of the *Daily Telegraph* or the hidden muddle of Northcliffe House in a back street. Circulation in the thirties roared onwards and upwards. By 1938 Beaverbrook was producing more newspapers than anyone else, and the *Express*, at 2,329,000 copies a day, was 300,000 ahead of the *Herald*, 740,000 ahead of the *Mail* and a million ahead of the *News Chronicle* and *Daily Mirror*. At the *Sunday Express*, John Gordon had trebled the circulation to 1,337,000 in ten years.

The phenomenon of the press baron was at its height, though not all of them had been made peers because of their newspapers, and one of them, Lord Astor, had inherited his title. Northcliffe had been created the first press baron in 1905. It was said that he bought the honour, directly or indirectly, but the truth seems to be that he was rewarded merely as someone who had been useful to the Conservative Party. Beaverbrook told Stanley Morison that Northcliffe had been offered a peerage for £110,000 and had refused to pay.[83] After the First World War, almost anyone who owned an important paper could take it for granted that they would be rewarded with a peerage from one party or the other: Lord Rothermere of the *Mail* and Lord Burnham of the *Daily Telegraph* in 1919, Lord Camrose of the *Daily Telegraph* in 1929, Lord Iliffe of the *Birmingham Post* in 1933, Lord Kemsley of the *Daily Sketch* and *Sunday Times* in 1936, Lord Southwood of the *Daily Herald* in 1937. Beaverbrook was by far the best known, and, among the mass-circulation press, the *Daily Express* was the paper that most journalists wanted to work for. Christiansen claimed that in the entire 1930s his approaches were only twice refused.

The successes were achieved by the creation of an air of optimism, a daily surprise (sometimes created through a pronouncement by Beaverbrook himself), the projection of every story throughout the paper, a no-expense-spared policy on news gathering (in 1960 the *Express* still owned a camel and caravan it had bought in the thirties to cover some forgotten story), short sentences and typographical drama. But success did not come from prurience or scandal. The word 'rape' was barred; it was reduced to 'criminal assault'. 'Abortion' was 'an illegal operation'. Adultery was unmentionable; it was disguised as 'misconduct'. The gossip columns – Castlerosse in the *Sunday Express*, the Londoner's Diary in the *Evening Standard* – eschewed sexual innuendo or scandal. Broken marriages and liaisons, while commonplace in Beaverbrook's circle, had no place in Beaverbrook papers – one reason why the *Express*, like other British papers, cut Mrs Simpson out of photographs of Edward VIII on holiday. Stunts, on the other hand, were encouraged: for instance offering a title to Edgar Wallace, the most popular and highest-paid thriller writer in the world, to see if he could construct a full-length, 80,000 word *Express* serial round it within a given time limit. Wallace delivered the first 12,000 words of *The Man at the Carlton* in four days.

A consolidated list of people who wrote or drew for Beaverbrook in the late twenties and thirties shows the range: James Agate, Michael Arlen, Arnold Bennett, Bruce Lockhart, Robert Byron, Barbara Cartland, Churchill, Geoffrey Cox, Sefton Delmer, Tom Driberg, Trevor Evans, Michael Foot, C. B. Fry, Lloyd George, William Gerhardie, Nat Gubbins,

Hore-Belisha, Keynes, David Low, Hilde Marchant, Alan Moorehead, J. B. Morton (Beachcomber), Malcolm Muggeridge, Harold Nicolson, Frank Owen, Strube, Hannen Swaffer, Edgar Wallace, Evelyn Waugh, H. G. Wells and Rebecca West. Beaverbrook made Sefton Delmer change his name from David Sefton Delmer, as he also made Jack Gourlay change to Logan Gourlay, and, later, Harry Chapman Pincher to Chapman Pincher; he advised Blumenfeld's son John to change to John Elliot.

Apart from the politics, what did the rest of the excitement – 'Give them stardust,' said Christiansen – amount to? Lord Deedes, who spent much of his long journalistic career working almost next door to the *Express* at the *Daily Telegraph*, of which he became editor, concluded that Beaverbrook brought about nothing less than a 'social revolution. . . . During the 1930s he introduced through his newspapers a transatlantic philosophy to our still highly class-conscious and stratified society. I am not one of his admirers; but he did more through his newspapers to emancipate our society than any of the pre-war political leaders. A cat may look at a king, he constantly reminded his readers.'[84]

CHAPTER 16

APPEASEMENT AND
ABDICATION
1931-1939

THE ROOTS OF Beaverbrook's attitude to the great international drama of the 1930s, the growing power of Nazi Germany, can be traced back at least ten years. The legacy of the Chanak crisis of 1922, when Britain nearly went to war over Turkey, was never forgotten. Beaverbrook's one rule for foreign policy remained Bonar Law's: that Britain should not play policeman to the world. The same rule underpinned his relentless hostility to the League of Nations and all manifestations of the doctrine of collective security from the Locarno Pact of 1925 onwards. There was never any question about Beaverbrook's isolationism; but what about his attitude to Fascism, especially as Hitler began to gather strength in Germany in the early 1930s?

VISITS TO GERMANY

Although he had never taken much interest in European culture or politics, from the time he settled in Britain in 1910 Beaverbrook regularly made visits to the continent for holidays or for his health. He went mainly to France, to the grand hotels of the Riviera, the Normandy coast, Biarritz or Paris, but he also went to Germany – to Berlin, Munich or one of the spas. In the spring of 1931, in a renewed fit of hypochondria, he paid another visit to Germany, accompanied by Jean Norton and Daphne and Henry Weymouth. In Munich he consulted a Dr Muller about his irritable bladder; the doctor scrutinized his urine, diagnosed phosphaturia and a danger of kidney stones, and prescribed the familiar treatment: simple meals, not too much red wine or champagne, plenty of Vichy water, a regular life and rest. He summed up the patient easily enough: 'Phosphaturia is to be found in the nervous, the overworked and those of quickly changing moods', and added for good measure that public speaking exacerbated the complaint by causing so much of the body's water to evaporate as steam.[1] Beaverbrook was not too ill to take an interest in the dramatic rise of National Socialism. He wrote from Munich: 'I have just seen Hitler's headquarters. His supporters are all in uniforms and the establishment is conducted on military lines. I should think the government will have to take repressive measures, or suffer repression at the hands of Hitler.' Dr Muller told him that more than two-thirds of the students at the University 'are enlisted in the Hitler ranks'.[2] On his return, he struck Bruce Lockhart as 'in a very pleasant mood . . . liked his German trip and the Germans, thinks that Hitler will do well . . . .'[3]

Beaverbrook was right, both about the menace of Hitler to the German government and Hitler's likely progress; but he himself, and therefore his newspapers, was not particularly pro-Nazi or pro-Hitler, unlike the *Daily Mail* under Lord Rothermere. Beaverbrook was too subversive by nature to endorse the hero-worship of a dictator; he instinctively disliked regimentation. By March 1933, when the first elections after Hitler became Chancellor took place, Beaverbrook had taken against him.

'6 March. Max has been in Berlin,' wrote Bruce Lockhart.

> He went, as usual, without telling anyone. When I was writing my paragraphs on the German elections, he came through with his own. They were very derogatory to the Nazis – and to the Jews. The stories of Jewish persecution are exaggerated. It is true that the Nazis say, when asked what they are collecting money for, 'to build a new Jerusalem', but they are not really worse to Jews than to others – unless they are Communists. Max saw the storm troopers and did not think much of them. He said, or made me say, that the cavalry leader could not sit on his horse, that the bands were bad, and that the men, mostly ill-formed lads and dissipated old boys, gave no appearance of a disciplined body.[4]

On this visit to Berlin Beaverbrook was accompanied by his daughter Janet and Castlerosse; Janet remembered the 'squalid' night life and the way Castlerosse lured her into a brothel by pretending it was a nightclub.[5]

As well as attacking the Jews, the Nazis were hostile to the Protestant churches in Germany; Beaverbrook, who was proud of being a son of the manse, no matter how renegade, and who seldom, throughout his life, rejected an appeal for help from a clergyman, found this hard to swallow. Nevertheless he was quite capable of making a joke of it. In July he had an exchange with the young Prince Louis Ferdinand, a grandson of the Kaiser, who was on a visit to London. The Prince informed him that while Hitler's popularity lasted he would be 'God, Pope and Kaiser . . . .'

> Max: 'I am pro-German. I had hoped for much from Hitler. But he's a persecutor.'
>
> Prince, nervously: 'I think there has been some exaggeration about the Jewish affair.'
>
> 'To hell with the Jews!' says Max. 'He's persecuting the Lutheran Church.'[6]

Not only was Beaverbrook's opinion of Hitler mixed, but it varied. In the summer of 1934, in the wake of the Roehm purge, when Hitler allowed his former ally to be murdered and the crude violence of Nazism was blatantly displayed, he suddenly issued instructions that Hitler's obituary should be revised: '. . . he is convinced that Hitler will be assassinated,' noted Bruce Lockhart. 'He has now turned solidly, fanatically, anti-Hitler, refers to him as Al Capone and to the Nazis as gangsters!' The old obituary, written within the previous year, 'was fairly favourable, Max then being not very anti! So this time I had to do the whole thing all over again, – of course very anti, according to instructions and denying him any spark of genius.' Beaverbrook had, however, learnt a trick or two from Bruce Lockhart's account of some of Hitler's platform methods – 'notably walking straight on to the stage without an introduction and without a chairman!' No doubt, Bruce Lockhart added wearily, he would be writing more Hitler obituaries in due course.[7]

During 1935 Beaverbrook met both Mussolini and Hitler. He had recently discovered the speed and convenience of flying, and over the next few years often chartered his own plane for quick visits to Europe; all his life he remained a slightly nervous passenger, given to singing the 23rd Psalm as the aircraft prepared to land. His favourite pilot in the pre-war years was a reliable Swiss, a senior pilot with the new Swissair company, called Walter Mittelholzer.[8] It was from Mittelholzer, who had contacts with the German military, that he learned in September 1935 that the Germans would like to meet him and had suggested that Mittelholzer fly him to Germany 'in order to inspect their airforce armaments'. Beaverbrook wrote back: 'As for going to Germany to see their Air Force, I will go like a shot, providing it is definitely understood I am going for that purpose. . . . I would pay my own expenses, there and back.' He was, however, wary: 'Before having me over there, Hitler and the propaganda system should be asked. For I am opposed to the Germans on account of the Calvinists and the Jews. Particularly the Calvinists for I am a Calvinist myself.' Mittelholzer went ahead, first through the Secretary of the German Air Ministry and then through Ribbentrop, whom he described to Beaverbrook on 23 October as 'Herr Hitler's proxy' who would be in charge of all the arrangements. Mittelholzer met Ribbentrop, who questioned him closely about his client. By the middle of November, after repeating that he would pay his own expenses and insisting on a formal invitation from the German government, Beaverbrook was ready to proceed.

Meanwhile in July he had made a quick tour of Italy and central Europe, stopping in Rome and Budapest. According to Wardell, who was present, Mussolini amused Beaverbrook and impressed him. In late November Beaverbrook and Wardell flew to Berlin. Ribbentrop was then Hitler's foreign affairs adviser, assiduously working to improve his own reputation and Germany's by cultivating influential people, preferably outside normal diplomatic channels. Wardell observed that the Nazis made a considerable fuss of Beaverbrook. '. . . A wonderful reception . . . no crowned head could have been better received.' Beaverbrook dined with Ribbentrop, who had German Foreign Office experts standing by in case he wanted information. Wardell recalled Ribbentrop's 'passionate protestations of Germany's desire for friendship with England'; Hitler, he told them, had expressed a strong desire to meet Beaverbrook, and he had arranged it. Indeed, all the Germans seemed very friendly and eager to show off their achievements; but Wardell noted that they were 'conscious of their own strength – and threat behind the pride'.[9]

When Beaverbrook met Hitler, in the last week of November 1935, they conversed with the help of his principal interpreter, Paul Schmidt. Hitler too emphasized how much he wanted England and Germany to be friends; but according to Wardell, to whom Beaverbrook described the meeting immediately afterwards, it was the style rather than the content of Hitler's conversation that struck Beaverbrook most.

> While he [Schmidt] was speaking Hitler followed his words with animation, his eyes bright with intelligence, nodding his head and moving his lips, touching them with his fingers as though he were understanding and bursting to speak. Beaverbrook was unquestionably impressed with him, finding him stimulating and magnetic. I had been with him in Rome when he talked to Mussolini, and in Moscow when he talked with Stalin, and he was certainly more struck with Hitler. . . .[10]

Although nothing in praise of Hitler appeared in Beaverbrook's papers on his return, four days after he got back Beaverbrook sent Ribbentrop a wire: 'I have been trying to reach you by telephone to say that I disapprove of leader in *Express* of Friday which I did not see before publication.'[11] The leader appeared on 29 November, and concerned a forthcoming Anglo–German football match. Headed 'Nazi Footballers', it advised the readers to keep politics out of sport. The lines Beaverbrook wanted to disown read: 'Probably you take the view of the *Daily Express* against Jew-baiting and Christian-beating dictatorship. But is it necessary to take your politics with you down to White Hart Lane on Wednesday afternoon?' Ribbentrop must have felt that he was making progress.

THE ANTI-LEAGUE CAMPAIGN

Although he never wholly abandoned the Empire Crusade, by the mid-1930s Beaverbrook's campaigning energies were concentrated elsewhere. His dislike of the League of Nations and the doctrine of collective security grew stronger and louder as the supporters of the policy, alarmed by Germany's behaviour, began to intensify their efforts. When in October 1933 Baldwin confirmed Britain's adherence to the Locarno Pact (whereby, in 1925, Britain had guaranteed a non-aggression treaty between Germany, France and Belgium) as necessary for national security, Beaverbrook used Empire Crusade funds to campaign against the Pact on the ingenious grounds that the dominions would be lost if Britain tried to involve them in a war over Franco–German territorial disputes.[12] As he wrote in the *Sunday Express* on 15 July 1934: 'We must join in the gang-war raging in the streets for fear the gangsters unite to attack us in our own house. Oh! The folly of it! The British Empire minding its own business is safe.'

In the autumn of 1934 the League of Nations Union launched a massive national questionnaire known as the Peace Ballot, asking people whether they were in favour of Britain remaining in the League, reducing armaments by international agreement and applying sanctions to aggressors. Beaverbrook returned to the fight with gusto. The ballot, far from promoting peace, would in his view greatly increase the danger of war. To the disgust of the organizers he christened it the Ballot of Blood, and wrote a series of dire warnings in his newspapers: 'The plebiscite will drag you and your children into a war on behalf of the League of Nations, a moribund institution which is a convenient instrument of ambitious and unscrupulous powers in Europe' (25 October); and on 17 November: 'The League of Nations is now a greater danger to peace than the armament makers. . . . Tear up the ballot paper. Throw the pieces in the waste paper basket. Turn away from Europe. Stand by the Empire and Splendid Isolation.' After much preliminary negotiation he broadcast on the BBC on 19 October, preaching the isolationist gospel as part of a series on the causes of war.

In the spring of 1935, before the Peace Ballot results were assembled, Beaverbrook received a letter supporting his views from his American newspaper friend Joseph Patterson, the proprietor and editor of the *New York Daily News*. Beaverbrook made maximum use of Patterson's few paragraphs of pro-isolationism, quoting them on the front page and in leaders. He then turned them into a pamphlet entitled *From Across the Atlantic* and told Patterson he had sent 400,000 copies to teachers, doctors, solicitors and clergymen. He also told him that he and the *Express* were asking for volunteers to distribute ten million more. On 18 April he reported further progress: 'We are now sending a bus round London almost every night. In it we carry 22 voluntary workers, ardent young people who devote a great deal of their spare time to furthering the cause of companionship in isolation with the United States.'

The ardent young isolationists, he claimed, found that the pamphlet 'makes a considerable impression . . . and leads to a great deal of discussion'. Beaverbrook also organized and funded meetings: 'Tonight a meeting is being held in Ealing . . . a Member of Parliament will be in the chair and two other Members will speak. The *Daily Express* pays (privately) for this meeting, the whole object of which will be your message.'[13]

326

Beaverbrook even wondered whether there might be a musical dimension to the isolation crusade; he was thinking, he told Patterson and, later, D. W. Griffith, his old friend from the Ministry of Information days, that he might improve Anglo–American links still further by bringing over a regimental band from the American Army to tour the country.

Even after the Peace Ballot showed that opinion in the country was massively in favour of collective security, Beaverbrook did not give up. 'The *Daily Express* will undertake to obtain a similar result for the policy of Isolation in any area, by putting in similar machinery to get the answer to framed questions. By the way are you in favour (1) of fine weather (2) more money (3) a better time all round?' In October 1935 he set up an *Express* survey of 80,000 'professional men' – 30,000 clergymen, 10,000 solicitors and 40,000 doctors. He cannot have been best pleased with the clerical response: six to one in favour of the League. 'God has given us a special responsibility,' he admonished the readers. 'In our charge there are the countless races of the British Empire. That is where our immediate duty lies. . . . By our conduct we must not impose terrible misfortunes on countless people who have no responsibility for the present situation.' It is impossible not to connect Beaverbrook's wish to keep Britain and the dominions out of any future European war with his memories of the Canadians he had seen dying in Flanders.

THE HOARE–LAVAL PACT

The *Express* ballot was held against the background of a severe national and international crisis, revolving around the question of support for the League and the application of sanctions even if war might follow. Since the summer it had been plain that Mussolini was planning to take over Abyssinia; the question was how the League would respond. Public opinion was increasingly on the side of the Emperor Haile Selassie, who travelled to Geneva to put his case; and after the overwhelming pro-League results of the Peace Ballot it became politically very difficult for the government to ditch collective security, especially as Baldwin, who had become Prime Minister in 1935 when Ramsay MacDonald retired, was planning a general election. Sir Samuel Hoare had been promoted to Foreign Secretary in June 1935; in September he spoke in support of collective action against Mussolini at Geneva. Mussolini invaded Abyssinia on 2 October; Baldwin called the election for 14 November and campaigned on a platform of collective security combined with rearmament, using the slogan 'All Sanctions Short of War'. He won convincingly.

Throughout the 1930s Beaverbrook had kept Sam Hoare warm.[14] Never an inspiring political figure, Hoare – from a rich banking family – was small and prim, 'descended', Birkenhead remarked, 'from a long line of maiden aunts'. He was, however, clever and ambitious, and backed by a formidable wife: Lady Maud, daughter of the 6th Earl Beauchamp and hence a cousin of Beaverbrook's young friend Sibell Lygon. The relationship worked along familiar lines. Beaverbrook boosted Hoare, flattered him and – as early as 1928 – invested money for his wife. In return, Hoare kept him in touch and sought his advice. Whenever Hoare felt he could do with some friendly publicity he had no hesitation in asking Beaverbrook to arrange it. During the Empire Crusade, and afterwards, Hoare acted as intermediary and fence-mender between Beaverbrook and Neville Chamberlain.

When Hoare was rewarded for his loyalty to Baldwin with the job of Secretary of State for India in 1931, Beaverbrook sent fervent congratulations and supported Hoare against Churchill over India. In 1934 Hoare brought Chamberlain and Beaverbrook together during Beaverbrook's campaign for an imperial customs union, and consulted him on how to present Indian policy: '. . . both he [Chamberlain] and I will try to do what we can in our speeches to further Empire development . . . if by chance you would like to suggest to me the way in which it would suit you best for me to talk about Indian trade, send me a line and I will focus my remarks, if I can, upon any suggestion that you may make.' But these overtures came to nothing, and Beaverbrook withdrew in a huff: 'I have come to the conclusion . . . that I can do no good by continuing the conversation with Chamberlain. The case wearies him and I weary him.' Hoare wrote back soothingly: 'I will not at all give up hope of finding a broad movement of Empire development that we can all support. I wish that I myself had more time to work at it.' When Hoare's wife wrote to Beaverbrook to thank him for a flattering cartoon of her husband, Beaverbrook wrote back in fulsome terms.

> I think he will be Prime Minister one day. I have been thinking it ever since 1922. That is twelve years ago so it is time my thoughts came true. I used to think the same of Bonar Law and he did business within twelve years.
>
> I am bound to say there is another reason why I am devoted to Sam. He is the last friend I have got in the old gang of Tory rulers. All the rest of them have written me off and, I suppose, with good cause.

If ever anything appeared in a Beaverbrook paper that Hoare did not like, he was quick to protest. An undated answer from Beaverbrook to one such letter shows how he responded:

> On my return to town I raised a great storm about the paragraph referred to. I have received a memo which does not satisfy me at all . . . any paragraph you send me in the form of a correction will be inserted in the paper. On the other hand if you think it not worth correction I will give an instruction to Blumenfeld to see that the balance is redressed.
>
> I hope you will not feel unduly annoyed. These difficulties arise in newspapers constantly. You know that I believe in your administration and that I am prepared to support you. Short of giving an order that your name is not to be mentioned in my absence I cannot give a guarantee against

another such incident in the future. But I can and do control the general policy of the paper in relation to your Ministry.

No wonder that when Hoare became Foreign Secretary in June 1935 he wrote a grateful letter to Beaverbrook: 'I am certain that without your help and advice in the Bonar Law days I should have had much less chance of reaching these giddy heights.' Beaverbrook's reply was resounding: 'You have been raised on high by capacity and character. I am convinced that you will be raised higher still, maybe to the highest place of all. . . . Your stay at the Foreign Office will be memorable. Your problems are great. Your opportunities are greater.'

Hoare's tenure at the Foreign Office was in fact brief and ended in disaster. He was exhausted by his efforts over the India Bill, and not well; but he applied himself with his usual diligence to the pressing task of defusing the Abyssinian crisis. He wrote to Beaverbrook on 16 October to complain about an *Express* headline: 'Baldwin refuses pledge for peace'; 'I should be very grateful if you could avoid a heading of this kind. As you know I am doing everything I can to ensure peace. A heading of this kind does stir up all the most bitter feelings in Italy and makes the position much more dangerous.' A week later he was able to write a letter of thanks for 'a very friendly act' – a glowing report in the *Evening Standard*.

Early in December, on his way to Switzerland for a badly needed holiday, Hoare arranged to meet the French Foreign Minister, Pierre Laval, in Paris, and pursue the long-planned joint deal with Mussolini whereby the price of peace would be the sacrifice of much of Abyssinia. According to an account written in 1960 Beaverbrook too travelled to Paris, with Sir Robert Vansittart, head of the Foreign Office.[15] On the evening of 7 December, while Hoare was meeting Laval, Beaverbrook dined with his French contact, the newspaper proprietor Jean Prouvost, whose papers had the highest circulation in France and whose premises housed the *Express* Paris office. This could hardly have been coincidence, and was presumably intended to secure favourable coverage for the Anglo–French proposals. But no sooner had Hoare left for Switzerland, confident that he had achieved a diplomatic coup and carried out the policy agreed by the Cabinet, than the secret deal to dismember Abyssinia was leaked to the press, causing an outcry. All the British press apart from the Beaverbrook and Rothermere papers attacked the pact as hypocritical and treacherous. In Switzerland the unfortunate Hoare, who late in life had taken up skating as healthy exercise, fell and broke his nose and was unable to return to defend himself for several days. Beaverbrook wrote, enigmatically, to encourage him:

My desire is to back you up, to support and sustain you in the present difficulty.

I have no views as to the course you take or as to the manner in which you deal with your problems.

But it is my intention to stand unswervingly in support of you in this crisis.

329

At first on Hoare's return he intended to fight back, and Beaverbrook helped him draft a speech accordingly. But when it became clear that Baldwin and the Cabinet were not behind him he agreed to resign, and did so on 19 December, after Baldwin had promised that he would be reinstated in the Cabinet as soon as possible. Beaverbrook regarded the episode as a typical piece of Baldwinian hypocrisy. The next day the *Express* declared firmly: 'The peace plan was sound and should have been pressed as a basis for negotiation. The Government should never have given way and never allowed Sir Samuel Hoare to be sacrificed.' Both Hoare and Beaverbrook were in Switzerland for Christmas; but they considered it politic not to meet.

ENTERTAINING RIBBENTROP

Beaverbrook was an obvious target for the Nazi propaganda effort of the mid-1930s, and Ribbentrop, who made a point of cultivating possible sympathizers in high places in Britain, singled him out for attention.[16] The two shared a preference for avoiding official channels and working behind the scenes; unlike Beaverbrook, Ribbentrop was clumsy, but nevertheless he had a certain success, especially during 1936, and Beaverbrook was among those who played along with him. Compared to a good many others, notably Lord Rothermere among the press lords and Chips Channon among MPs, Beaverbrook kept his distance from the Nazis, but his contacts with Ribbentrop after his visit to Germany in 1935 were nevertheless distinctly amiable.

Ribbentrop redoubled his efforts to woo opinion in England in the early summer of 1936, after the alarm caused by the German militarization of the Rhineland in March had abated. With the Olympic Games planned for later that summer in Berlin, the Nazis were determined to impress the world with their achievements and to improve their image by lavish hospitality. They especially wanted to remind the British that Germany and Britain were natural allies against Bolshevik Russia. Ribbentrop had been trying for two years to set up a private meeting between Hitler and Baldwin, and had been cultivating Baldwin's secretary, Tom Jones, as intermediary; he came to England at the end of May for a short visit in the hope of pulling off this coup, but Baldwin cannily evaded him. Ribbentrop's visit, however, was socially if not politically successful; he spent a weekend with Lord Londonderry, a noted pro-German; was feted in London by two leading hostesses, Mrs Corrigan and Lady Cunard; went to a nightclub with the Channons – Chips described him as 'looking like a jolly commercial traveller' – and invited them to the Olympic Games; visited the Astors, where he had a long talk with Lord Lothian; and lunched with Geoffrey Dawson, editor of *The Times*.

He also scored Lord Beaverbrook:[17] on 5 June he dined at Cherkley, accompanied by his wife. According to the letter of thanks he sent from

Berlin for 'the little dinner party at your charming country home', she and Beaverbrook compared notes about their health. Ribbentrop praised the famous view 'from the terrace of your delightful home in Surrey over the woods and valleys, which I shall not forget' and asked for details of a new American treatment for sinusitis. Beaverbrook promptly wired back that he had sent to America for the information, and relayed it in his own hand. Meanwhile Ribbentrop had written to invite Beaverbrook 'and any of your friends' to the Olympic Games, adding that 'it might interest you also to see some of our mass meetings, which I could not show you when you were over last time'.

On 17 July Beaverbrook cabled his acceptance, saying he would like to bring his daughter Janet, his son-in-law Drogo Montagu, his elder son Max, Wardell, a secretary and two menservants. A few days later he wired again, sending a carefully worded request:

> There is a colleague of Winston Churchill named Brendan Bracken member for North Paddington belonging to Churchill political school. Bracken has always been intimate friend of mine and I am indebted to him for much support. He controls daily newspaper called *Financial News* and several weekly publications. If I invite him to go I feel sure he will accept. Please let me know your views on this. Anything you say will be treated secretly.

Ribbentrop must have been delighted at this conspiratorial communication with its promise of netting an influential guest from the Churchill camp; he cabled back: 'All your friends are welcome to me'.

This building up of social connections had a purpose, as an exchange between Beaverbrook and Ribbentrop's chief assistant, Von Durkheim-Montmartin, made very plain. He wrote stiffly to Beaverbrook on 23 June complaining about a mildly critical paragraph in the Londoner's Diary, which asserted that Ribbentrop was trying to influence a diplomatic appointment. 'You will understand that we did not think the article nice. Not only are the alleged facts far from the truth, but the article contains personal attacks against a man whose whole work is devoted to promoting Anglo–German understanding. I was the more astonished to find such making [*sic*] in one of your papers considering the very friendly personal contact with you.' He had sent Wardell a statement of correction, but it had not appeared: 'May I suggest that you kindly find out some way or other to re-arrange the matter?'

Two days later Beaverbrook, an old hand with such complaints, wrote cheerfully back. 'The writer of the paragraph was a catspaw. And catspaws are always troublesome in newspapers.' He had seen the correction sent to Wardell: 'It will be published if Herr von Ribbentrop wants it. But my own advice would be to let the subject rest. On the next occasion we deal with Herr von Ribbentrop I hope we will be able to show our appreciation of him in his personal capacity. But if he has other views, let me know.'

The party that went to Berlin for the Olympics on 31 August 1936 included young Max, Janet, Wardell, and a young newcomer to the inner circle, Arthur Forbes (later Lord Granard), who had started work for the *Daily Express*. According to Janet, they flew from Croydon in her father's plane; at Berlin airport the reception was 'impressive. Obviously the word had gone out that the British press lord and his entourage were to be treated like visiting royalty'.[18] Gleaming black Mercedes cars whisked them to the Adlon Hotel. Ribbentrop called at the hotel, bringing flowers for her and an invitation to lunch at his country house the next day. She thought she noticed a change from 'the charming person I had danced and laughed with' in London to a 'vain, arrogant man surrounded by posturing sycophants'. Her father soon showed signs of boredom and unease. At lunch, when Beaverbrook announced that he did not intend to go to the Games except for the opening ceremony, Ribbentrop pressed her to stay with them and go with their party. Despite her father's displeasure she accepted, and was duly driven through cheering crowds into the stadium and seated with the Ribbentrop group. Taken up to shake Hitler's hand, she remembered that she towered over him and that his hand was 'clammy and soft'. After three days her father 'insisted' she leave the Ribbentrops and rejoin him at the Adlon; he then announced that they were going home. Later she learned he had discovered that his rooms were bugged.

Beaverbrook wrote politely to Ribbentrop on his return. 'I had a grand time. And my friends enjoyed themselves more even than I did. . . . I was very grateful for the invitation to dine at your house and I liked very much the company you allowed me to keep.'

Beaverbrook himself published nothing about his visit or the Olympics. In the *Standard*, the Londoner's Diary noted the 'pro-German propaganda' emanating from 'the expedition of friendly British citizens' attending the Games and listed a dozen, mostly with titles; Lord Beaverbrook's party was not mentioned. Coverage in the *Sunday Express* was sparse, and the *Daily Express* concentrated on the sporting results, commenting on the fracas over Hitler's failure to congratulate the black American Jesse Owens: 'The bloom is off the peach at the Olympic Games. Mr Jesse Owens . . . shows that it is not necessary to have had a Nordic grandmother in order to run faster than any other coon on earth . . . . ' Beaverbrook did not take kindly to the pressure exerted by his German hosts: he knew too much about manipulation to enjoy being the subject of it. Two months later he wrote to Lloyd George, whose enthusiastic account of his own visit to Hitler had just been published in the *Daily Express*.

> I have been very interested in your German experiences, and the viewpoints you brought back from that country. I went there too. But I hated so much the regimentation of opinion that I could not bear it.
> I was in Berlin at the opening of the Olympic Games. On that occasion privilege and class had a run the like of which has not existed in this country since the aristocracy began to marry chorus girls.[19]

Nevertheless Ribbentrop had reason to feel that his efforts to woo Beaverbrook had not been wasted. When it was announced later in August that Ribbentrop had been appointed Ambassador to Britain, Beaverbrook sent him the most fulsome possible letter.

> Never, never, never was any appointment to an Ambassadorial post in London as well received as your own.
>
> You have praise from the press and from the people.
>
> You may save the peace of Europe, I truly believe, by your conduct here.
>
> Do not bother to reply to this letter, I shall see you when you come to London.

Ribbentrop arrived to take up his post on 27 October 1936 to a chorus of approval and welcome in the British press. The *Daily Express* praised his champagne parties and called Frau von Ribbentrop 'the most famous hostess in Berlin'. The *Standard* quoted Ribbentrop in a front-page headline: 'Germany wants the friendship of Britain.' The Londoner's Diary in the *Standard* bathed him in flattery: Ribbentrop

> . . . is an excellent host. He has a frank and genial manner. He speaks English both fluently and accurately.
>
> But he has one virtue which commends him especially to English people. He is sincere in his goodwill to this country. Ever since he became associated with Herr Hitler he has been a diligent and persistent advocate of a better understanding between Britain and Germany.
>
> He will find Anglo–German relations considerably improved since he paid his first visit to London. He has already friends here. He will make many more.

THE ABDICATION CRISIS

During the last months of 1936 Beaverbrook's attention, like the government's and the entire country's, was distracted from international affairs by the King's love affair. The part played by Beaverbrook in the abdication crisis of 1936 owed more to his private connections and qualities than to any public or political motive. Although he pretended later that he knew no more than any other member of the public about what was going on before the crisis broke, few people in England were better placed to know the truth about the new King's relationship with Mrs Simpson. Beaverbrook and Edward VIII had many mutual friends – Wardell, the Brownlows, the Mountbattens, Lady Diana Cooper and the Nortons among them. Partly because the King, when Prince of Wales, had moved away from court circles and had chosen to spend his leisure among nightclubbing Londoners rather than old-fashioned country aristocrats, he and Beaverbrook moved in much the same milieu. Edward VIII had his suspicions of Beaverbrook, but he knew how helpful a friendly press lord could be; in 1929, on the way from London to Walton Heath to play golf,

Bruce Lockhart had conversed with him about his troubles with journalists: 'He drove me down in his new super-Rolls . . . all the way down he discussed the Press; begged me to use my influence with Beaverbrook to have his name kept out of the papers. He described to me what he had to endure . . .,' he wrote in his diary on 30 November.[20]

Beaverbrook, like everyone in his circle, would have known all about the Prince of Wales's sixteen-year love affair with Freda Dudley Ward, which ruled his life during the 1920s and early 1930s and was conducted in accordance with the upper-class conventions of the time, rather like Beaverbrook's own relationship with Mrs Norton. Mrs Dudley Ward stayed married and behaved with discretion; Mrs Simpson, a twice married American outsider, did not. When in 1934 the Prince fell in love with her and abruptly broke with Freda Dudley Ward, Beaverbrook would soon have heard; and when his set re-formed around Mrs Simpson it included Beaverbrook's sister-in-law, Helen Fitzgerald, who was herself conducting a love affair with one of the Prince's cronies, the sporting Earl of Sefton. In the summer of 1935 Helen and Sefton were in the party ('all tres chic', according to Mrs Simpson) entertained by the Prince in a rented villa at Cannes; they were also invited on the Mediterranean cruise on the *Nahlin* during the summer of 1936, after the Prince had become King. The *Nahlin* was described by John Aird, the King's equerry, as 'furnished rather like a Calais whore-shop'; others in the party at different times included the Coopers and the King's secretary, Tommy Lascelles, who wrote in his diary: 'Outwardly as respectable as a boatload of archdeacons, but the fact remains that the two chief passengers (the King and the Earl) were cohabiting with other men's wives.'[21]

Although the press in other countries, especially in the United States, had been speculating freely for months about Mrs Simpson, no gossip had leaked into the British press. The King's movements and guests were reported, but in a purely factual manner. The *Daily Express* of 12 August carried a picture of the King with Mrs Simpson, Mrs Evelyn Fitzgerald and others on the front page, while the Londoner's Diary gave a brief account of the guests. As the holiday proceeded, photographs appeared widely in the American and European press showing the King and his friends wearing casual clothes or bathing suits, ambling round resorts; to the censorious it was undignified, even raffish. To the London gossips, the great topic after the cruise was whether the King wanted to make Mrs Simpson his wife. Those who saw them in private knew that he was dominated by her, sometimes to an embarrassing extent; his infatuation was total. Nevertheless, until the news broke in October that Mrs Simpson was divorcing her husband, reticence and the hope that the problem would solve itself prevailed.[22]

The story of the abdication crisis has been told and retold; Beaverbrook's version appeared posthumously, but was based, in his usual manner, on an account he first wrote, after consultation with others involved, within days of the events described.[23] The part played by Beaverbrook throughout was essentially and rather uncharacteristically defensive; he found that he was trying to save the King from himself. He had the same instinctive sympathy with the King as he did for anyone in personal distress, and he was always interested in other people's romantic and sexual obsessions. Beaverbrook was also flattered at being involved, once again an insider; he could not resist a chance to try out his skills as a fixer on behalf of a monarch. As someone who had felt the weight of royal disapproval in his earlier days, he was always likely to side with the new King against the old order. He disliked the stuffy, the censorious and the puritanical. As the crisis progressed he also saw a chance to embarrass Baldwin and his government. In retrospect he came to feel that Baldwin was so concerned for his own political skin that he failed to pursue a compromise that could have saved the throne for Edward VIII. But the weight of subsequent research indicates that here Beaverbrook was wrong.

On 13 October 1936 Beaverbrook received a telephone call from the King, who asked him to go to Buckingham Palace. 'When I asked him to name an hour for the appointment he replied in effect: "Name your own time". This led me to believe that the interview was greatly desired by him.' When, three days later, he met the King, the purpose of the interview was clear and hardly unexpected: 'The King asked me then to help in the suppression of the Simpson divorce case in the newspapers . . . the reasons he gave for this were that the woman, Mrs Simpson, was unfortunate, that notoriety would attach to her because she had been a member of his party at Balmoral and in the Mediterranean . . . she was ill, unhappy and distressed by the fear of publicity. And he for his part felt that he should protect her.'

Beaverbrook was, after all, familiar with such requests. His files are sprinkled with notes, usually but not exclusively from women, asking – in some cases begging – him to keep their divorces out of his newspapers. He was on the whole sympathetic to such requests, an attitude he would justify by pointing out that to Presbyterians marriage is merely a contract, not a sacrament. 'These reasons appeared satisfactory to me,' he wrote. 'And so I took part in the suppression of the news before the divorce action took place and in the limitation of the publicity when it occurred.' After consulting the King's friend and adviser, the barrister Walter Monckton, and his solicitor, Beaverbrook lobbied a series of newspaper proprietors, including Rothermere; the *News Chronicle* chief, Sir Walter Layton; and the managing directors of several provincial papers in Scotland and Ireland. Soon the King contacted him again, wanting him to intervene with French papers and American news agencies. Beaverbrook began to realize the strength of the King's obsession. 'The King was at this time having conversations with me almost every day . . . he sometimes showed strong anxiety. . . .' At first Beaverbrook felt there was no question of marriage; but he began to wonder. 'The King's attitude was too intense, as it seemed to me, to be based on the issue of the divorce alone. I was anxious to stand down.' Beaverbrook appreciated that whereas Mrs Simpson's divorce could be kept quiet, any question of the King's marriage could not.

The Simpson divorce took place on 27 October, and the British press virtually ignored it. At the beginning of November Beaverbrook accepted an invitation to dine at the Brownlows to meet the King and Mrs Simpson. Their mutual friends hoped to ensure Beaverbrook's allegiance, as Chips Channon, the socially energetic Conservative MP whose wife, Honor, was a great friend of Jean Norton's, acknowledged in his diary. 'A plot came off, instigated by me, tonight,' he wrote on 5 November. 'Last summer, I thought it would be wise if the King and Lord Beaverbrook were to meet, and I tried to bring it about but failed, but I put the idea in Wallis Simpson's clever and retentive brain. Dining here the other night, she told Perry Brownlow that she thought a meeting would be a good idea. . . .' Honor Channon balanced Beaverbrook at dinner, to make up a party of six; both she and Brownlow thought dinner went well, although 'Beaverbrook was at first a bit touchy, though obsequious . . . however conversation soon flowed, and Max ended by being charming.' Channon and a few more guests arrived after dinner and they all sat on the floor playing a game involving piling matchsticks on top of a bottle. When Channon referred to Eden as an idealist, and the King remarked, 'Heaven spare us from idealists, they cause all the trouble', Beaverbrook agreed. Two days later, Channon and his wife discussed the King's matrimonial plans in detail with Jean Norton. 'He certainly wants to marry Wallis but she is probably too canny to allow it, yet what a temptation for a Baltimore girl. . . .'[24]

Beaverbrook was not much taken with Mrs Simpson. 'She appeared to me to be a simple woman. She was plainly dressed. She had a mole on her face which I believed to be unattractive. I did not like her hairdressing and thought that she shaved the back of her neck which did not appeal to me at all. Her smile was too affable. . . .' He observed that, although the other women guests greeted her affectionately, Mrs Simpson remained passive. 'The kiss was received with appropriate dignity by Mrs Simpson. In no case did she give the kiss.' Beaverbrook was struck by how freely the King criticized government ministers: 'I too spoke freely'. For a moment he was alone with the King and expected that the divorce would be raised; but it was not. 'When we parted the King said that he wanted to see me later as there was something he had to talk about. This showed that the dinner was to lead to something. . . . I decided to do nothing more. I feared the difficulties and the dangers attendant on the negotiations. I believed that my task was at an end and left for the United States on the 14th of November.' Far from fomenting trouble at this point, Beaverbrook was trying to dodge it.

Earlier that year, Beaverbrook suffered his first serious attack of asthma.[25] Given his family's disposition to the complaint, he was lucky to have escaped it until the age of fifty-seven, but now his hypochondria had a dramatic focus. He began a long search for remedies, and decided in the winter of 1936 to visit Arizona, having heard that the dry desert air might help. He announced his departure in the *Express*, proclaiming (not for the first or last time) that he was leaving for the sake of his health, and putting his work in the hands of others. 'I am going away. I am going away for a long time . . . back again to see once more the forests and rivers of New Brunswick, colonised by our Scottish ancestors.' Accompanied once again by Lord Castlerosse, he sailed on the *Bremen* for New York.

Two days after he left, the final stage of the crisis began when the King, told by his private secretary that the story was about to break, informed Baldwin that he intended to marry Mrs Simpson and would if necessary abdicate. Beaverbrook was showered with cables to the ship.[26] 'Following message from mutual friends,' cabled Monckton, 'never realised you leaving so soon had hoped talk to you this week and outline situation feel it important you should understand my outlook.' Beaverbrook cabled back: 'If my presence is necessary I will return immediately.' He pointed out, however, that if he was to influence the American press he could best do so from New York. On 17 November his secretary, Whelan, relayed another urgent appeal from Monckton who said that 'his client placed the highest importance on your presence here to control the publicity likely to arise from a situation now developing. You alone could do it.' The next day, 18 November, the extent of the crisis was made clear: 'Friend has now declared to authorities definite decision as soon as absolute coast is clear. . . .' After Beaverbrook reached New York, he was pursued on the telephone with similar appeals: he was even, to his great concern, telephoned by the King himself in the offices of the New York *Daily News*. He decided to return. In London, Bruce Lockhart and his colleagues heard the news with alarm: 'We know his little idiosyncrasies but this time we all gave him at least two months. Hence our laughter mingled with dismay this morning when *Express* announced Lord Beaverbrook was cured and was returning to England by same boat as he went over on. . . .'[27]

Beaverbrook arrived back in England prepared to play a more substantial role than simply advising on how to deal with the press. The urgency of the messages from the King 'led me to think that I might have a considerable status when I returned and so might be an important factor in the situation'. He went straight to the King's house, Fort Belvedere in Surrey, where, knowing he was on a diet, the King had ordered him a special lunch. The King then disclosed that he was determined to marry Mrs Simpson and that he was considering a morganatic marriage whereby she would become his wife, but not Queen.

In Beaverbrook's view the morganatic marriage proposal was a serious mistake: it conceded that Mrs Simpson was an unsuitable wife, and he did not think that either the Cabinet or the country would like it. He advised the King to decline to pursue it, to choose a minister who would present

337

his case strongly in Cabinet, and to play for time while he tried to strengthen his position. Beaverbrook nominated for the task the Cabinet minister closest to himself, Sir Samuel Hoare, and went straight from the King to see him. 'I believed, throughout that time,' wrote Beaverbrook, 'that time, sympathetic treatment, patience and endurance would bring the King safely through the crisis of his love story without any marriage, without abdication and without any publicity.' Behind Beaverbrook's search for compromise was a large measure of incredulity that any woman, especially one whom he found not particularly attractive, could be worth the loss of the throne.

'A DEVOTED TIGER'

Beaverbrook found himself chasing a moving train. Hoare, he discovered, was against the marriage, and was not persuaded by Beaverbrook's argument that he need not approve of the King's conduct in order to represent him in Cabinet. The King rapidly realized that Hoare was not playing, despite Beaverbrook's attempts to evade his insistent telephone calls. Nor would he drop the morganatic marriage idea while Mrs Simpson still favoured it. Next, Beaverbrook learned from Hoare that at the King's suggestion the dominions were to be asked their view. Beaverbrook was appalled. 'Anyone with the slightest knowledge of the Dominions knew that the answer would be swift and emphatic – Abdication.' He tried to undo damage that had already been done by urging the King to stop the message to the dominions, but it was too late: '. . . it did not occur to me that the fat was already in the fire. But it was in truth. For 75 Cabinet ministers scattered all over the Empire could not be expected to keep the secret.'

Over the next few days Beaverbrook was in constant touch with Hoare, who kept him fully briefed on the deliberations in Cabinet. He was also seeing Churchill, who was emotionally on the King's side, and Rothermere. Meanwhile the King was frequently on the telephone, night and day: '. . . the conversations were very free, so free that it caused me great anxiety'. Beaverbrook showed unexpected signs of respect for the monarchy during these telephone conversations, getting to his feet to take them and addressing the King as 'Sire'.[28] He passed on to the King what he was learning from Hoare – that the Cabinet was united in opposition to any marriage to Mrs Simpson and felt that publicity could not be held back much longer. Geoffrey Dawson, editor of The Times and close to Baldwin, was poised to come out against the King. Beaverbrook saw the King again, and argued at length that the whole matter should be withdrawn from the Cabinet. 'I said that unless this was done a decision against the King would be given. This was a most unsatisfactory conversation. The King declared over and over again that he was determined to make the marriage on the throne or off it.' Monckton went to Baldwin and asked that the Cabinet drop the subject, but to no avail.

On 3 December the press finally broke silence, with reports of remarks critical of the King by the Bishop of Bradford. 'While the speech was still in the newspaper offices the King was informed of it by me . . .,' Beaverbrook wrote. That night, after the crucial confrontation with Baldwin, the King telephoned Beaverbrook at Stornoway House and

> indicated clearly that he was proposing to abdicate and retire into private life. The conversation was very long and one-sided. I made no attempt to argue. I knew the telephone as an impossible medium. I merely reiterated over and over my desire for further conversation. There were several conversations that night and the telephone was in use almost continuously, literally for several hours.

Next day, 'I went to work on the newspaper proprietors likely to support our cause.'

Even after the dam had broken, Beaverbrook let his own papers fight for information about the crisis; he was too involved as a protagonist to become a source. At the *Express*, Christiansen knew quite well that his proprietor was 'to-ing and fro-ing it to Buckingham Palace and Fort Belvedere', but 'sometimes I got this news in the most roundabout ways. "Your boss has just gone in to the Palace by the back way", was a telephone tip-off from Charlie Smith, London Manager of the American International News Service, one night. "Bless you, Charlie," I replied sardonically, "Cable it to New York and then I'll be able to quote I.N.S. that the Beaver is in with the King." '[29]

Beaverbrook refused to give up, and threw the weight of his newspapers behind the King. On 4 December an editorial in the *Evening Standard* stated firmly: 'The country unitedly deplores abdication as a solution.' On the 5th the *Express* followed up: 'We cannot afford to lose the King. We cannot let him give up the throne.' Churchill wrote to the King late the same evening, trying to cheer him and stop him throwing in the towel; he stressed the importance of recognizing Beaverbrook's loyalty. 'Max. The King brought him across the world. He is a tiger to fight. . . . I cannot see it would do harm to see him if it could be arranged. Important, however, to make contact with him. A devoted tiger – very scarce breed.'[30] Bruce Lockhart, not knowing the extent of Beaverbrook's involvement, thought he had finally seen his chance 'of using the King issue to beat Baldwin with. We are becoming more royal than the royalists.' Wardell showed him Beaverbrook's fervently pro-King instructions; but the Diary editor said sourly, 'I see Beaver and Rothermere are supporting King. That means the poor devil is sunk.'[31]

Meanwhile Walter Monckton had decided that he could not compromise himself as a negotiator with Baldwin by remaining in open touch with Beaverbrook, who wrote him an anxious letter. 'I hope the ban does not apply to telephone communications and to letters discreetly and properly framed. . . . If you prefer that communications should be cut off altogether I hope you will indicate some other person so that I may still have a medium for sending my observations to His Majesty.'

Beaverbrook was trying to save the King, but the King did not really want to be saved. Exasperating restrictions were imposed on the press campaign:

> I and others had several talks with the King on the subject but he made our situation impossible. He insisted on the suppression of the name of Mrs Simpson from our newspapers. . . . All through these days the King constantly interfered with the presentation of the case by the newspapers which he could influence. For days the papers which I control were completely influenced on that account . . . that influence was entirely directed to dampening down controversy, to avoiding conflict with the government and Mr Baldwin and to limiting as far as possible the reference to Mrs Simpson. All three seemed to be major propositions with him in moments when abdication should have been the principal consideration.

Realizing that Mrs Simpson was the only person whom the King listened to, Beaverbrook turned his attentions to her. He composed a leader designed to please her, and asked the King if he could discuss it with her. 'My idea was to get into contact with her and see if I could persuade her to withdraw from the marriage, though this was likely to disturb my influence with the King, an influence that was waning anyhow.' But the manoeuvre failed. 'I could not break through to Mrs Simpson. The King protected the Simpson front completely.'

Shortly before the storm broke in the press, Mrs Simpson had moved from London to the King's house at Fort Belvedere; a stone had been thrown through her window, and she and the King feared further attacks. The King's supporters now decided that the only hope lay in removing Mrs Simpson from the scene; they hoped that, if she could be persuaded to go abroad, it might still be possible to keep the King on his throne. The King was also talking of leaving the country while the matter was debated by the nation; but he wanted to broadcast his point of view to the people before he went. He drafted a speech and consulted Beaverbrook and Churchill about it, but Baldwin could not allow any appeal by the monarch over the head of the government, and the King's partisans felt it would be fatal were he to leave the country at such a moment. But the King and Mrs Simpson were easily persuaded that she was at risk, and Lord Brownlow agreed to accompany her to friends in the south of France.

Brownlow was briefed by Beaverbrook: 'We relied on Lord Brownlow to put the case to Mrs Simpson immediately on her departure. We hoped that the King would be influenced by her statement, that she was prepared to give up the marriage.' During the journey through France, pursued by the press and frantic telephone calls from the King (during which, apparently, Beaverbrook's codename was 'Tornado' and Baldwin's

'Crutch'),[32] Mrs Simpson made it plain to Brownlow that she had finally understood the gravity of the situation and was prepared to withdraw; but she doubted whether it would do much good. From the middle of France, Brownlow sent Beaverbrook a telegram in code: 'Janet strongly advising the James company to postpone purchase of Chester shares to next Autumn and to announce decision by verbal methods thereby increasing popularity maintaining prestige and also the right to reopen negotiations in the autumn.'[33] When on 6 December Mrs Simpson duly stated to the press that she was anxious to avoid damage to the King or the throne and was prepared to withdraw forthwith, Beaverbrook's newspapers proclaimed that the drama was over. The *Express* announced on the front page: 'END OF THE CRISIS: Mrs Simpson – I am willing to withdraw.' That evening, the *Standard* took up the refrain in an editorial: 'The crisis is over.' Next day the *Express* went further still: 'Can we rejoice? Yes, we can rejoice. The Crisis has passed into history and the King is still with us. No question of the Crown overriding the Cabinet has ever arisen, nor have the Ministers imposed surrender on the King on a highly personal issue.'

But for all Beaverbrook's bravado, the battle was lost. Mrs Simpson's offer had come too late and the King was distracted by the strain of separation from her. Moreover, to his credit, he had no wish to force a constitutional crisis. Baldwin, supported by *The Times*, the majority of the Commons and – in his own shrewd assessment – the weight of popular feeling, realized that delay would only increase the danger to the monarchy. When Churchill, much moved by the King's misery, appealed to the House of Commons for more time, he was shouted down. Beaverbrook knew the cause was hopeless; as he said to Churchill: 'Our cock won't fight.'[34] The King accepted that the choice was between his throne and Mrs Simpson, and he chose Mrs Simpson. Beaverbrook retreated to Cherkley; after the broadcast abdication speech on 11 December, which according to his daughter Janet moved him to tears, the King rang him one last time to say goodbye.

Beaverbrook concluded his draft account of the crisis with some reflections on Edward VIII's character and behaviour that were more critical than the later published version. He blamed Baldwin for forcing the issue, but he also acknowledged 'the weakness of character and the defects in conduct of the King . . . .' He described him as having 'a capacity for charm and an element of glamour . . .', but added that he was 'at his best with strangers outside his immediate circle . . . while he had great steadfastness of purpose, there was a startling want of continuity in his conversation and course of action. He was unnecessarily lifted up by events of little importance and incredibly dejected by accounts of hostile articles in newspapers and reports of conversations expressing criticisms of himself.' This emotional volatility Beaverbrook ascribed partly to the 'great irregularity' of the King's habits during the crisis. 'He smoked continuously, sometimes cigarettes, often a pipe. There was plenty to drink. Always whisky with water and a piece of ice. At times his agitation was so intense as to give the impression of a man who had lost his balance. . . .' Beaverbrook noticed how the King would put his head in his hands, wipe perspiration away with a folded handkerchief, or sometimes 'hold the handkerchief to his forehead as though trying to protect himself from some hidden pain or secret pressure'. But throughout, 'the King would declare, while he accompanied his words with a rap-tap on the table, that Mrs Simpson would not be abandoned'.

During the crisis Bruce Lockhart had remained sceptical. As it came to an end, he wrote in his diary:

> We have taken the wrong line from the beginning . . . today [Percy] Cudlipp, the editor, and I both wanted to close the ranks and welcome the new King [George VI]. Mike Wardell agreed. But not My Lord Beaverbrook. I do not think his pro-King attitude was entirely inspired by his anti-Baldwinism. I think the King 'got' him and the little man, taken up for the first time by royalty, saw himself as a crusader defending his monarch when men of better blood had ratted. Effect however has been bad. Ninety per cent of intelligent public regard the Beaverbrook–Rothermere campaign on King's behalf as mischievous and irresponsible anti-Baldwinism . . . Winston is tarred with the same brush.[35]

Beaverbrook's support for the King was more personal and whole-hearted at the time than he maintained afterwards, not least as it became clear that George VI made a far steadier and more appropriate King than his brother. At the time, Beaverbrook did his utmost to prevent the abdication; as Edward VIII's authorized biographer puts it: 'In so far as there was a motive force behind the creation of a King's party it was provided by Max Beaverbrook.'[36] Nearly twenty years later his closest ally in the abdication crisis, Churchill, startled his secretary John Colville by revealing how far he remembered Beaverbrook being prepared to go:

> His scheme, and that of Lord Beaverbrook, had been to frighten Mrs Simpson away from England . . . great measures were taken. . . . Bricks were thrown through her windows and letters written threatening her with vitriol. 'Do you mean that you did that,' I said, aghast. 'No,' he replied, 'but Max did.'
> Years afterwards I told this story to Lord Beaverbrook who said that he certainly did not, but it was possible somebody from the *Daily Express* might have. He also said that whereas it was probably true that Winston's principal motive had been loyalty to the King, his had been that it was all a lot of fun.[37]

AMBASSADOR RIBBENTROP

As German Ambassador to Britain, Ribbentrop was notably unsuccessful, and he saw little or nothing of Beaverbrook. His hostility to the Foreign

Office was well known and reciprocated, and his refusal to conform to established diplomatic conventions did not go down well with the public; it was considered bad form when he was rumoured to have given the Nazi salute to the King when he presented his credentials. He combined bad judgement with bad luck; he had tried, with some success, to cultivate Edward and Mrs Simpson and their circle in 1936, but his arrival in London coincided with her divorce hearing. Ribbentrop's alleged influence on Mrs Simpson, and hence on the King, had been a source of anxiety to the Foreign Office; it was the main reason why precautions were taken to remove sensitive documents from the boxes sent to Fort Belvedere.[38] Both the King and Mrs Simpson were indeed disposed to be sympathetic to Germany, but his pro-dictator sentiments, although much gossiped about, were certainly exaggerated by Rippentrop to Hitler. None the less Ribbentrop wrote in his memoirs that he wanted to help keep the King on his throne, and there is evidence that he used his influence to keep the story out of the German press for as long as possible.[39] Beaverbrook was engaged in much the same way at the same time, but there is no evidence that they were in touch on the matter.

After the abdication, Beaverbrook was mostly out of the country until the spring of 1937; Ribbentrop, despite his disappointment at the departure of Edward VIII, planned a series of ostentatious parties at the elaborately redecorated German Embassy to celebrate the coronation of George VI in May. He wrote to Beaverbrook to invite him to attend a reception and a dinner, adding that he was looking forward to talks on how best to achieve 'the realisation of a good understanding between your and my country'. Beaverbrook replied from the Carlton Hotel, Cannes; after recommending Arizona for Frau Ribbentrop's health, he explained that he would not be able to attend the festivities owing to his own medical problems, but certainly hoped to be able to further Ribbentrop's 'good understanding with my country'.

Much of Ribbentrop's energy as Ambassador during 1937 went into promoting Germany's demands for the restitution of the colonies lost under the Versailles settlement and administered under League of Nations mandates. This was hardly a popular cause in Britain, but Beaverbrook does not seem to have cared much one way or the other. To him, the peace of Europe was more important – and in pursuit of it he advised giving Germany, during a relatively quiet year, the benefit of the doubt, as an *Evening Standard* leader in September 1937 makes clear: 'The chief error in British policy towards Germany is a matter not so much of actions as of attitudes. For years past British politicians have spoken harshly of Nazi Germany purely because it is Nazi . . . is it not possible to sweep that atmosphere away? Germany's system of government is Germany's affair. Britain's is Britain's.'

Despite the abdication, Ribbentrop did not give up hope of using the ex-King for Nazi propaganda purposes; but when Edward and his wife, now the Duke and Duchess of Windsor, accepted an invitation to visit Germany in October 1937 Beaverbrook did his best to dissuade them. According to Wardell, he met the Duke in Paris and told him bluntly that he would be used by the Germans for propaganda purposes, criticized by the British government for meddling in foreign affairs, and make himself generally unpopular. Knowing that the Duke's other former supporter, Churchill, would oppose the Duke's plans even more vehemently, he offered to send his own plane to bring Churchill to Paris. But the Windsors' minds were made up.[40] The visit went ahead, and did great damage to what was left of the Duke of Windsor's reputation; among the crowd of reporters intent on capturing every detail (the Duke, wisely, responded to the Nazi salute merely by raising his hat) was Randolph Churchill for the *Evening Standard*, who pulled off a great scoop by getting an interview in which the Duke apparently said he had abandoned the idea of returning to live in England. Beaverbrook himself remained on amiable terms with the Windsors, and was never to be popular with the new King, George VI, whose suspicions, inherited from his father, had only been exacerbated by Beaverbrook's activities during the abdication crisis.

LILY

In 1937 Beaverbrook encountered a young woman whose background and experiences gave him a personal connection with the realities of Hitler's advance across Europe and what it meant for the Jews.[41] Lily Ernst was Jewish, Hungarian-born but with Yugoslav nationality, and she lived in Vienna. She was a dancer with an Austrian ballet company performing in the south of France when Beaverbrook and several friends, including Mike Wardell and Arthur Forbes, arrived for a short visit in the spring of 1937. One evening in Cannes they went to the ballet. 'There were all these pretty girls,' Forbes (later Lord Granard) has recalled. 'Beaverbrook took a fancy to them and sent Wardell off to invite four of them to dinner at the Carlton Hotel. Lily was one of the few who spoke any English. Max was very taken with her.' Lily Ernst was slender, dark-haired and delicate; she was also well-educated and had a mind of her own. According to a close friend who heard the story from her, she sat next to Beaverbrook, who asked her about her plans for the next day. 'She said: "I'm going to a shop down by the sea to perhaps buy a dress," and he said: "I'll go with you and if you like it I'll buy it for you." She said: "Does that mean I have to sleep with you?" Max said, "No."' Next day, Beaverbrook took Lily in his car to a restaurant to meet the others. On the way they swerved to avoid a beggar, a ragged old man. 'Max said "bloody old Jew" or something and Lily said, "What you say? I am a Jewess – I get out. Stop the car" and he refused and there was a terrible row. That was the start of it.'

Some early letters from Lily Ernst to Beaverbrook have survived. The first is from Vienna, dated 14 May 1937. She regretted not having said goodbye; she waited for his call, but her train left Cannes very early. Then she thanked him 'for your kindness. . . . I feel proud for having won a friend quite by myself. You know it was you who made the days at Cannes for a real good time for me and you must have realised how thankful I felt and so I feel still.' She asked 'whether you miss me a little. And when do you come to Vienna?' The letter ended formally: 'Repeating my thanks heartily I remain yours sincerely . . . .' She wrote her address and telephone number very clearly at the bottom.[42]

Not long after Beaverbrook and his party returned to London they were recalling the pleasures of Cannes; Beaverbrook suddenly decided to take his private plane and go to Vienna 'and find the girls again'. So they did, but it turned out that Lily Ernst had a fiancé, a young Jewish doctor. 'Of course Max was charming, but . . . ,' recalls her friend. 'He may have said if you are ever in trouble let me know.'

In March 1938 Hitler took over Austria and the Nazis arrived in Vienna. Dramatic rumours surround what happened to Lily next. It was said that the *Express* office was ordered to find her; that she was penniless and the fiancé had fled; that she was smuggled in disguise on to Beaverbrook's plane; that she was virtually kidnapped by his staff and bundled out with only the clothes she was wearing and no papers; that she said goodbye to her parents at the railway station and never saw them again. In fact, on 1 May 1938 she wrote him a cautious letter: 'Dear Lord Beaverbrook . . . Just a year ago you told me you would be always a good friend of me. If you are still of this opinion you could make me happy in giving me a few kind words. . . .' Next, it seems, he rang her up. On 5 May she wrote again:

> I cannot tell you what it meant for me when I felt yesterday that you are still interested in my life and the moments I spoke to you have been the happiest since several months. There is no instantanious [sic] trouble I am in but I can't work any more and everything is hopeless. I don't want you to feel anxious about me but every chance you could offer me would be a great help and make me deeply thankful.

Beaverbrook swung into action. On 18 May he cabled the British Consulate in Vienna, requesting help in arranging a visa. On 25 May a letter went off to the Chief Immigration Officer at Dover. 'A Miss Lily Ernst is leaving Vienna today on a visit here at the invitation of Lord Beaverbrook.' She travelled on a Yugoslav passport, and Beaverbrook undertook that during her stay, which would not exceed six months, 'Miss Ernst will not become a public charge.'

When Lily Ernst arrived in England Beaverbrook did not know what to do next. One of his secretaries recalls that Lily made her way to Stornoway House, found it in the dark and asked for Lord Beaverbrook, who was not there and had not told the staff to expect her.[43] According to Lady d'Avigdor-Goldsmid: 'When she arrived, penniless, knowing nobody, passionately grateful to him, he wouldn't see her. He didn't know what to do with her. By this time she was so grateful she was madly in love. He didn't want the responsibility.'

Michael Foot met Lily Ernst on his first visit to Cherkley in September 1938. By this time, the visitors' book shows, she was a regular visitor; and she made a great impression on him. Observers thought that Beaverbrook hoped for a time that one of his young protégés might take Lily off his hands: Frank Owen was another possibility. Foot visited Lily in Ashtead near Leatherhead, where Beaverbrook found her somewhere to live, and later in London where he rented her a flat in George Street. 'I was really in love with her,' Foot has said; but she was in love with Beaverbrook.

Another interested observer at the time was Sibell Lygon: when Mrs Norton inevitably became suspicious of Beaverbrook and Lily Ernst, he asked Sibell to help. 'He told me Lily was there to translate Hitler's broadcasts,' she remembered. 'He did have a row with Jean about her, and he made me go to see Jean and explain that he loved her, not Lily. He got upset at Jeannie making such a fuss. "Tell Mrs Norton I love her the best, and that Lily Ernst is just there to do the translations."' It may at the time have been true; but before long Lily and Beaverbrook did start an affair. His daughter Janet found herself in the curious position of comforting Jean Norton, who had to tolerate the new favourite rather as Gladys Beaverbrook had tolerated her. Beaverbrook's relationship with Lily Ernst was, for a while, more serious than his normal casual adventures, although a friend of hers from Vienna who came to London in 1939 recalls with anger how he tried to keep the relationship quiet. 'He treated her very shabbily.'

As Michael Foot records, the arrival of Lily prompted him to present the plight of the Jews under Hitler in the *Standard* and the *Express* with extra fervour. Whether she had any great effect on Beaverbrook's attitudes is harder to judge. Certainly she made sure that he realized the plight of the Jews under Nazism; Foot remembers that she had many friends among the growing number of refugees arriving in London and that she arranged help from Beaverbrook for some of them. At his expense she travelled to Switzerland during 1939 to see her parents; she never saw them again. At her urging he arranged for a distinguished ear, nose and throat specialist, Dr Alexander, to be brought to London from Vienna, and helped him by employing him to buy paintings for Cherkley while he qualified to practise in England. Dr Alexander was amazed at Beaverbrook's charm and skill at getting people to do what he wanted. He would say: 'The man, woman or child was never born who can resist the Lord.'

Beaverbrook was not himself anti-Semitic, although he was quite capable of making the kind of reference to typically Jewish looks or behaviour that rings unpleasantly today but was commonplace in England between the wars. He was both affectionate and admiring towards Jewish American financiers like Otto Kahn or Mortimer Schiff; he had been friendly with the English Rothschilds since the early 1920s. During the

346

1930s he received a number of letters from Jewish correspondents protesting about what they saw as anti-Semitic references in his papers; in October 1933 Montague Gluckstein, of Lyons the caterers, wrote to him about a reference to Jews in the *Daily Express*, adding that he had been told by an uncle that Beaverbrook was the cleverest man he had ever met. Beaverbrook wrote back warmly but firmly: he saw nothing wrong with the item. 'It is really too much to complain of a statement that a man dislikes Jews, or Frenchmen or Presbyterians, or Canadians, and I could not be expected to suppress a statement of fact in the paper.'[44] In 1935 one of his German doctors, Professor Thannhauser, was, as Beaverbrook put it in a letter introducing him to an American friend, 'kicked out' by the Germans and was taking up a position at Tufts University in Boston. 'He is a Jew, though he does not look it,' he wrote, adding: 'He is a brilliant physician for whom I have the highest esteem.'[45]

But in the later 1930s his letters, especially to his American correspondents, reveal suspicion of Jewish-led agitation for action against Hitler. He saw the Jews as trying to provoke the war he was determined to avoid. At the beginning of March 1938, in a letter to the American journalist Herbert Bayard Swope, he blamed 'the 20,000 German Jews in England' for working against the accord he would like to see between Britain and Germany[46]; later that year a letter to another Jewish friend, Lionel Montague, shows that he felt the arrival of more Jews would be undesirable. 'You can rely on me to use what influence I have to prevent the growth of anti-Semitism in this country. That is a task in which Jews can help, by discouraging the entry of refugees from Germany.'[47] In December 1938 he went much further in a letter to the American newspaperman Frank Gannett:

> The Jews have got a big position in the press here. I estimate that one third of the circulation of the *Daily Telegraph* is Jewish. The *Daily Mirror* may be owned by Jews. The *Daily Herald* is owned by Jews. And the *News Chronicle* should really be the *Jews Chronicle*. Not because of ownership but because of sympathy. . . .
> . . . The Jews may drive us into war. I do not mean with any conscious purpose of doing so. They do not mean to do it. But unconsciously they are drawing us into war. Their political influence is moving us in that direction.[48]

Ribbentrop would have heartily agreed with that letter. Whatever he may have thought in private about Hitler's persecutions, Beaverbrook's public stance and the position of his newspapers during 1938 and 1939 remained conciliatory towards Nazi Germany.

'BE CAREFUL OF YOUR ATTACKS . . .'

In March 1938, on the eve of the Austrian Anschluss, Ribbentrop, his dream of subverting Britain's rulers by his social charms unrealized, eturned to Hitler's side as Foreign Minister. It has since been argued that Ribbentrop's failure to bring the British establishment round left him humiliated, aggressive and bent on war; at the time, however, he was still proclaiming his desire for Anglo–German friendship and Beaverbrook was still prepared to support him. When Ribbentrop's appointment was announced, Beaverbrook wrote him another fawning letter:

> It is with real pleasure that I hear today of your appointment to the highest office in the gift of your leader.
>
> I know full well that you will take full advantage of your great authority and immense power to develop still further the policy of peace and tranquillity. And you will have the loyal support of my newspapers in this pursuit.[49]

That last sentence could be regarded as the single most ill-advised and damaging line Beaverbrook ever wrote. Ribbentrop's mistaken idea that he could win the friendship of Britain for Nazi Germany was succeeded by an even more dangerous conviction: that the British were too divided and spineless to fight Hitler no matter what he did. To have Beaverbrook's statement that he could count on the support of his papers can only have fed Ribbentrop's illusions. In June 1938 a note to Frank Owen, who became acting editor of the *Evening Standard* three months later, shows that Beaverbrook was prepared to fulfil his undertaking:

> Frank, be careful of your attacks on Ribbentrop. If you get making attacks on Ribbentrop, you are going to disturb the immense efforts that are now being made for an accommodation with Germany.
>
> And we want it for the sake of our people, and we can't put any impediment in the way of it, no matter how much we may feel like doing it. . . . We have got to give over criticism of those foreign powers for the time being. . . .[50]

It was already known to the circle around them that although Owen was a radical and held different views on Europe from his proprietor, Beaverbrook had the upper hand. 'Article by Frank Owen in *Evening Standard*,' noted Bruce Lockhart on 12 April 1938. '"No War in Europe". Obviously written by Lord Beaverbrook.'[51]

In fact, although the *Standard* was regarded at the time as the most intelligent and least predictable of Beaverbrook's three papers, and certainly the paper where young left-wingers felt happiest, it was, according to a summary of its leading articles prepared for Beaverbrook soon after the war, consistent in its support for isolation and 'gave unqualified support to the Chamberlain policy of appeasement . . . the *Standard*'s attitude to Germany was as far as possible conciliatory, and when the Germans gave it the chance, actively friendly . . . .' The writer also remarked on 'a marked lack of adverse comment on Germany's internal affairs'.[52] But it was never Beaverbrook's way to exclude differing opinions from his papers completely, as both he and the readers would have found such consistency bland; moreover, both his liking for provocation and his instinct for keeping options open required a certain unpredictability.

Thus during the mid-1930s, although Beaverbrook and Churchill's friendship was at a low ebb and their views on foreign policy diametrically opposed, Churchill contributed a regular article to the *Evening Standard* every fortnight, and pursued his anti-German warnings relentlessly.

But as the European situation darkened during 1938, the divide between Churchill's fears and Beaverbrook's determined optimism became too extreme for the arrangement to survive. In February the *Express* attacked Churchill for his 'violent, foolish and dangerous campaign'; and after the Anschluss, in mid-March, Churchill's efforts to rally public and political support for Czechoslovakia led to him being sacked by the *Evening Standard*. As the editor, R. J. Thompson, wrote: '. . . your views on foreign affairs and the part which this country should play are entirely opposed to those held by us'. Churchill wrote back: 'I rather thought that Lord Beaverbrook prided himself upon forming a platform in the *Evening Standard* for various opinions including of course his own.'[53] He began to write regularly for the *Daily Telegraph* instead. It can hardly have been a coincidence, and shows Beaverbrook at his least attractive, that in April the *Daily Express* ran a story saying that Churchill's funds were so low that he was thinking of putting Chartwell up for sale, which annoyed and distressed the Churchills – not least because it was true.

Beaverbrook's disapproval of Churchill's stance on Germany intensified. One day he summoned the young Irish writer Patrick Campbell, later Lord Glenavy, who in 1938 was working on the *Express*: '. . . in the small garden of Stornoway House he said, without warning, "This man Churchill is the enemy of the British Empire." I was so astonished, and alarmed, that I stepped backwards into a wet flowerbed, covering my shoe with mud.'

'"This man Churchill," Beaverbrook went on, in fine oratorical vein, "is a warmonger. He is turning the thoughts of the peoples of the British Empire to war. He must be stopped. Go get him."' Campbell asked how he should proceed with this task.

'"We shall record his sayings," said Beaverbrook. "We shall make a dossier of his public trumpetings about war. Do it now."' For several weeks Campbell compiled the dossier and delivered it regularly to Stornoway House. He never knew what use it was to Beaverbrook.[54]

There is no doubt that Beaverbrook in the later 1930s was prepared to intervene in favour of Germany if a writer or cartoonist went too far, or if he was approached personally by a highly placed politician. In the autumn of 1937 Lord Halifax, then Lord President of the Council, was invited by Goebbels to visit Germany for a hunting exhibition. The trip was to include talks with Hitler. The Nazi leaders made it plain to Halifax that one of the chief obstacles to better relations between the two countries was the rude personal attacks on the leadership, especially on Hitler himself, in the British press. One of the worst offenders was the *Standard*'s cartoonist, David Low. When Halifax returned, a lunch was arranged by Wardell at Beaverbrook's behest at which Halifax put pressure on Low. The cartoonist agreed to moderate his contemptuous depictions of Hitler and Mussolini, and invented an only slightly less offensive composite, named Muzzler; but he afterwards regretted that he had made any concessions at all.[55]

Although the Beaverbrook papers, along with the rest of the press, condemned with vigour Hitler's annexation of Austria in March 1938, it was the method rather than the deed that aroused indignation. As an *Evening Standard* leader said, it was 'no part of this country's duty to block the peaceful expansion of German influence over people of German race'. When, after Austria, it became apparent that Czechoslovakia was next, Beaverbrook stuck firmly to his familiar line: European problems, especially eastern European, were nothing to do with Britain.

HOARE AND MUNICH

Beaverbrook was closer than ever during 1938 to Hoare, who was a member of the Cabinet's Foreign Policy Committee and who became, along with Halifax and Simon, Chamberlain's close adviser during the mounting Czechoslovak crisis. Ever since Hoare, as promised, returned to Baldwin's Cabinet in May 1936 as First Lord of the Admiralty, Beaverbrook had supported and boosted him in public and in private more vigorously than ever. After he was promoted to Home Secretary by Chamberlain in 1937, it looked as if he still had a great political future; certainly Beaverbrook persisted in telling him so. He relished having a senior Cabinet minister once again tied to him by past history and assorted obligations.

It was also a great advantage to Hoare that he could deliver Beaverbrook's support to Chamberlain; Beaverbrook began to praise Chamberlain's qualities, even going so far as to compare him with Bonar Law. Chamberlain needed Beaverbrook, especially as he was determined to pursue friendship with Germany and to achieve peace in Europe. To do so, he needed to cultivate the press. Under Chamberlain, Downing Street began to take a much more direct interest in the deployment of news, much to the annoyance of the Foreign Office, but with the active co-operation of Beaverbrook and Hoare.[56]

After the Anschluss, Beaverbrook began to use the phrase that was to become infamously synonymous with appeasement: 'There will be no war.' The phrase itself dated back to 1922, but the prominence and repetition of the slogan was new. On 1 September 1938, with tension over

Czechoslovakia rising, the *Daily Express* printed it again; and as Chamberlain began his series of flights to Germany to negotiate with Hitler and sell out the Czechs, Beaverbrook offered Halifax advice on how to coordinate press support. On the day after Chamberlain met Hitler at Berchtesgaden he wrote that the newspapers were 'all anxious to help the Prime Minister and to help you. But they are greatly in need of guidance.' He proposed the selection of a minister 'authorised to have direct contact with the newspaper proprietors individually and personally . . . great benefits would flow from the decision'. The aim would be 'to guide the newspapers in their policy, to strike out errors and to crush rumours'.[57] His choice of minister was not surprising; on the same day he wrote to Chamberlain, proposing Hoare and praising his 'balance, judgment and prestige'. Beaverbrook assured the Prime Minister that, if the necessary guidance was given, 'the newspapers of the right and left will go with you in your decisions'.[58]

Hoare began to hold daily meetings with editors and proprietors. At Beaverbrook's instigation and with his full support, he orchestrated the all but unanimous support of Chamberlain's Munich policy. On 22 September the *Express* headline announced, in huge letters:

This is the Truth.
    Britain never gave any pledge to protect the frontiers of Czechoslovakia. . . . There is no duty or responsibility whatsoever on this country to defend that Central European power. . . .
    It is wicked and untrue to accuse Great Britain, your own country, of selling Czechoslovakia or of deserting France.
    (signed) Beaverbrook.

On 29 September, when Chamberlain flew back to Germany for the third time to meet Hitler, Mussolini and Daladier, the front page shouted: 'It's all Right'. Next day, reporting the Munich agreement, the front page read: 'The *Daily Express* declares that Britain will not be involved in a European war this year, or next year either.' On 1 October, Chamberlain took over the front page: 'You may sleep quietly. It is peace for our time.' Britain and France had averted war by giving in to Hitler's demands on Czechoslovakia. Relief swept the country, mixed with shame. Two of Beaverbrook's friends were notably demonstrative: Beverley Baxter was prominent among MPs waving their order papers to welcome Chamberlain back to the Commons, and Perry Brownlow gave him a cigarette case 'on which was engraved a map of Europe with three sapphires marking Berchtesgaden, Godesberg and Munich'.[59] Only one newspaper – *Reynolds' News* – protested, and only one Cabinet minister, Duff Cooper, resigned. Beaverbrook wrote Chamberlain a fervent letter of admiration.[60]

It was against this background of Hoare and Beaverbrook's closest and most effective collaboration in nearly thirty years, at a moment when the

foreign policy of appeasement that they both advocated seemed triumphant, and when Hoare's stock within the government had never been
higher, that Beaverbrook received a remarkable letter from Lady Maud
Hoare.

> Sam must make up his mind whether he goes on in active politics after the
> next election, or whether he tries to make a new career. . . . Sam is
> convinced and I believe rightly so – that we can hardly afford to go on in
> office. . . . We grow poorer every year and that is worrying all enjoyment
> of life out of him.
>
> If he is not to retire at this election he must be relieved of financial
> anxiety. . . . If he goes, I believe it will be a great loss to the country . . .
> but unless my view is shared by those who can and will help, go he must.
> Do you share this view? . . . What is your advice? . . . I believe Sam has
> mentioned his troubles to you and your long friendship must be my excuse.

The message could not have been clearer; if you believe in Sam Hoare's
political future, and want it to continue, will you subsidize him?
Beaverbrook was quick to respond. Within four days Hoare himself was
thanking him for a 'most kind and helpful talk', and on 22 November
Beaverbrook wrote his reply – not to Lady Maud, but to Hoare.

> My dear Sam,
> My long experience in public life has given me a very brilliant picture of
> the financial misfortunes of the man who takes office.
> He not only loses his income from directorships and other employments
> but he invariably neglects his investments and loses his capital.
> A very superficial enquiry has disclosed to me that you conform in every
> respect to this picture of the man who takes office.
> It is on this account that I send you out of a full pocket a very small sum
> which I would like you to put into your purse.
> And this time next year and for the rest of this Parliament and for next
> Parliament, if you still decide to stay in office, and if I still have the necessary
> money, I will send you another dribble of the same size.
> Yours ever. . . .

On 24 November 1938 Hoare wrote to Beaverbrook twice. The first was
a personal note of thanks. The other was on Home Secretary's writing
paper, referring to a speech he was about to give in Cambridge and
promising to stress the Empire theme.

Beaverbrook's first payment to Hoare was £2000, hardly 'a very small
sum'; his annual salary, as Home Secretary, was £5000 a year. The same
amount was sent on 1 September 1939, and again in November 1939. In
the letter accompanying the second cheque Beaverbrook wrote: 'I have
always opened my pocket book to my friends. . . . I am not taking any
special or particular place in your life that might single you out from
others.'[61]

There is some evidence that Hoare, who in the aftermath of Chamberlain's Munich triumph urged the Prime Minister to strengthen his position by calling an immediate election, also advising him to broaden the base of his Cabinet, pressed Beaverbrook's claims to a Cabinet post, perhaps as Minister of Agriculture. Hoare himself referred in 1943 to his attempts in the months leading up to the war 'to push Neville into more resolute action and particularly, if you remember, to take you into the government'.[62] Hoare was a creature of Beaverbrook's long before he asked him for a subsidy; but there can be no doubt that the financial arrangement between them in 1938 and 1939 would have caused outrage and ended Hoare's career in public life had it come to light at the time.

NO WAR

During the last year of peace Beaverbrook was one of the most whole-hearted, industrious and effective promoters of appeasement, the policy 'conceived as the alleviation of international tension by diplomacy' which became the means of 'purchasing peace by dishonourably sacrificing the interests of other smaller countries'.[63] Beaverbrook's support for Chamberlain was unwavering. After nearly ten years on the sidelines, he found his return to the mainstream exhilarating. Early in November 1938, Robertson of the *Express* told Bruce Lockhart ruefully that he doubted whether Beaverbrook would be making his usual extended winter journey abroad 'because he was enjoying himself too much here. In Baldwin's time people [ministers] were afraid to go and see him. Now he has Sam Hoare, Belisha, etc on his doorstep, and Chamberlain's speeches read like *Daily Express* leaders.'[64]

There can be no doubt either that Beaverbrook, in his determination to promote the idea that war was unthinkable, encouraged the belief that in the end Britain would yield to virtually any demand Hitler might make. The Foreign Office recognized Beaverbrook's power: Charles Peake of the beleaguered Foreign Office News Department, struggling to counter-balance the Downing Street line, noted of the post-Munich *Daily Express* that editorial optimism about the danger of war having lifted went 'considerably further than we have been authorised to go' and bore 'all the marks of official inspiration from Number 10'. 'What a pathetic state of affairs,' wrote a senior official on Peake's minute.[65]

Moreover, during late 1938 and early 1939 Beaverbrook was still prepared to placate Ribbentrop. When the German Foreign Minister arrived in Paris in early December 1938 to sign the Franco–German side of the Munich pact, Bruce Lockhart prepared some mocking paragraphs for the Diary recalling Ribbentrop's humble origins and early visits to Paris as a champagne salesman, and noting that he, Goebbels and Hitler were known among Eton schoolboys as Rib, Hit and Gob: 'Paragraphs were sent over to Max, who turned them down as too cruel,' he wrote in his diary.[66] Evidently Ribbentrop still thought it worth trying to cultivate

Beaverbrook; on 15 March, the very day that German troops took over Bohemia and Moravia, thus ending the independence of Czechoslovakia in brutal proof of the worthlessness of the Munich pledges, he wrote Beaverbrook an unctuous letter expressing thanks for the press lord's continued 'interest and sympathy' in his wife's health and hoping for a chance to discuss before long the attitude of the British press to 'a just solution of the colonial question'. The letter was actually written from Prague, Ribbentrop reveals, 'where I arrived with the Führer this evening, and I hope the Führer will settle the future relations between the German and Czech peoples once and for ever and to the benefit of all'. He pressed Beaverbrook to pay another visit to Berlin, and deplored the fact that there had been 'an interval of about two years' since they last met. On 28 March Beaverbrook replied that he might indeed go to Berlin, as he would like to see Ribbentrop again, and 'now that I have your charming invitation the desire is all the stronger'.

Even when at the end of March the British government finally drew the line and pledged itself to defend Poland, Beaverbrook still did what he could to undermine its resolve. He himself wrote, so the Polish Ambassador was told, a paragraph for the *Evening Standard* claiming that Chamberlain's choice of words – he referred to Poland's independence, not territorial integrity – left room for manoeuvre, and was not an absolute guarantee that any German move against Poland would mean war.[67] Although the Foreign Office issued a denial, and insisted that the guarantee meant full protection for Poland, any indication – especially from papers known to be in Chamberlain's pocket, like *The Times*, which took a similar line, and Beaverbrook's – could only feed Ribbentrop and Hitler's contempt for Britain.

Beaverbrook's behind-the-scenes contribution to the last stages of appeasement can be glimpsed only in fragments. A fuller and more vivid picture emerges from the recollections of those around him, especially if they worked for his newspapers – like the *Daily Express* editor, Christiansen, and one of the outstanding young reporters covering Europe, Geoffrey Cox.

Christiansen found little or no difficulty in supporting Beaverbrook's line, although the Munich settlement caused him a rare moment of unease. 'I remember feeling sick when Neville Chamberlain over the radio described Czechoslovakia as "a far away country" and I remember expressing my revulsion to Lord Beaverbrook over the telephone. But when he said in a harsh voice, "Well, isn't Czechoslovakia a far away country?" I agreed that it was and got on with my job of producing an exciting newspaper.'[68] He was proud that the Munich headline in the *Express*, 'PEACE', was set in the biggest type ever used in an English newspaper.

Cox was a New Zealand Rhodes Scholar in his twenties, who had decided from personal experience of travelling in Nazi Germany that

Hitler was 'both dangerous and evil'. He had reported the Spanish Civil War for the *News Chronicle*, and joined the *Express* to cover Europe in the summer of 1937.[69] He saw Beaverbrook rather differently. The *Express*'s pro-German editorials and headlines caused him embarrassment and heart-searching; but his stories from Vienna and Prague were printed unchanged. Once he thought he felt Beaverbrook's disapproval when Christiansen wrote to him that his despatches had 'an undercurrent of depression' and suggested he cheer up and take a more positive line; but although after Munich he seriously thought of resigning, he had a pregnant wife, needed the job, and besides, 'If I resigned I gave up this chance to depict to millions of people events as I saw them, and would perhaps make way for someone who would present them from an appeaser's angle.'

During the months between Munich and the outbreak of war Cox was based in Paris where 'one of the hazards of the job', Cox has since written, was that Paris was on the route between London and the south of France, so that Beaverbrook and his entourage frequently passed through. 'Whilst he was in the city the Paris correspondent had to be ready to be summoned at short notice to Beaverbrook's suite at the Ritz, to answer questions about developments in France or give his views on whatever subject was uppermost in his lordship's mind at that moment.' Cox first met Beaverbrook in the Ritz, 'with its pink silk-lined walls and gilt Louis XV furnishings', his dictaphone with its small, trumpet-shaped mouthpiece on a table in front of him; and noticed the large head, huge mouth and wide-set, keen eyes: 'the tough magnate, not the puckish jester'.

On one such visit, in 1938, a subject on Beaverbrook's mind was his suggestion that Cox should return to London and become a leader writer. Cox had already informed Christiansen that he was determined not to do so: 'I did not want to work in a post where my own judgement would be swamped by that of the proprietor. Yet that was something which was inescapably part of the role of leader-writing for a Beaverbrook news-paper.' Beaverbrook appeared to concede gracefully: 'He picked up his dictaphone and said, "Memo for Mr Christiansen. Kaarx (my name was drawled out in his Canadian accent into what seemed like polysyllables) doesn't want to be a leader writer. Better let him ride."' Only eighteen months later did Cox learn that Beaverbrook added a phrase after he had left the suite: 'Sack him within a month.' It was not acceptable to Beaverbrook, Cox later thought, to have such a mark of his favour and confidence rejected. Christiansen managed to get him a reprieve.

Cox saw Beaverbrook on his last visit to Paris before the war, in July 1939. The sleek and portly Castlerosse was with him as usual; and Beaverbrook assigned the unlikely pair a task. 'He wanted a candid survey made of the attitude towards a possible war of the ordinary people of France and Germany. This, he claimed, needed a fresher eye than a resident correspondent could bring to bear.' He told Cox to go to Germany, while Castlerosse canvassed the French, to find the answer to the question: 'Will your country fight for Danzig?' They were to meet three days later at the Ritz to deliver their findings. When Cox reappeared with his verdict – that the Germans were behind Hitler – Castlerosse claimed to have done nothing. 'I haven't got much further than the bar at Fouquet's,' he told his employer. 'No one at the bar at Fouquet's is going to fight for Danzig.'

In August 1939 Beaverbrook arranged another survey; he instructed Christiansen to ask all the *Daily Express* correspondents in Europe: Will there be war in Europe this year? Fourteen reporters replied; twelve said 'no'; two, including Cox, 'hedged their bets'. He expected that 'Chamberlain would find a way to "do a Munich" on the Poles, as indeed he would have done had Hitler been prepared to accept a Polish surrender instead of yielding to the temptation to launch the first blitzkrieg. So I replied: "The odds are now in favour of there being no war this summer and autumn – but only just."'

Meanwhile in London Christiansen was at Beaverbrook's side.[70]

August 1939 . . . the nation breathes an uneasy sigh of relief as the Bank Holiday period passes, and Hitler has not emulated the Kaiser's action in 1914. But in every newspaper office in the world there is the smell of gunpowder and every man has his orders, especially the men on duty in Berlin, Vienna, Prague, Danzig and Warsaw. In the *Daily Express* office, Robertson and I are summoned repeatedly to Stornoway House, and despite Robertson's objection, we decide to run the 'No War' slogan yet again.

'We've *got* to reduce the temperature', argues the Beaver fiercely. 'If it keeps on going up there will be no hope at all. We've got to curb the war fever.' He expresses no view on the accuracy of the slogan, but he may well believe in it, for soon afterwards he leaves for Canada. Newspapermen often fall for their own propaganda.

By 31 August Beaverbrook, on Robertson's advice, was back. 'Robertson is carrying his umbrella as though it is a rifle,' he joked. Hoare called editors and proprietors to Whitehall again, but this time to explain the government's plans for mobilization. To the last, Christiansen recalled, Beaverbrook kept trying. On Friday, 1 September came the first reports that German tanks had crossed Poland's borders. The next day, having no paper to get out, he went to a football match: 'Afterwards I telephoned the office for news. The first edition of the *Sunday Express* had not yet gone to press, and I gathered that the intention was to prophesy even at that time that war would be averted.' But the British issued an ultimatum; by 11 a.m. on Sunday, 3 September, the war Beaverbrook had decided would never happen had begun.

CHAPTER 17
PATRON OF THE LEFT
1929-1939

'THE BEAVER', CHRISTIANSEN wrote, 'is fascinated by Left Wingers.'[1] Christiansen did not attempt to analyse the phenomenon, however, although the fascination lasted forty years, puzzling many outsiders. The authorized biographer of Gaitskell, Philip Williams, a Fellow of Nuffield College, Oxford, wrote of Beaverbrook's 'long flirtation with the Labour Left', and ascribed it to a shared interest in sabotaging the moderate leaders of the Labour Party.[2] This theory brought Williams a sharp rebuke from Michael Foot; there were, said Foot, 'more things in heaven and earth than the Nuffield school may include in its curriculum'.[3]

Over the years Beaverbrook employed many socialists, or at least people who claimed to be on the Left when their paths first crossed with his, starting in the twenties with St John Ervine and Hannen Swaffer, and continuing with, among others, Tom Driberg, Frank Owen, Harold Nicolson, Jennie Lee, Sydney Elliott, Michael Foot, Hector McNeil, James Cameron, Woodrow Wyatt, the cartoonists David Low and Vicky, Robert Edwards, Robert Pitman, Robert Millar, Hugh Cudlipp and A. J. P. Taylor. Of these, Owen, Foot, McNeil and Taylor joined his inner circle – in the sense that they called him Max and he sought their company. Four of them he made editors: Frank Owen, Michael Foot and Sydney Elliott edited the *Evening Standard* during the Second World War; after the war, Robert Edwards edited the *Daily Express*. Beaverbrook hired five of the left-wingers – Foot, Edwards, Pitman, Millar and Wyatt – directly from the left-wing journal *Tribune*. One of the founding members of *Tribune* in 1937, and later its editor, was Aneurin Bevan, the dominant left-wing politician of his time and, off and on, a close Beaverbrook friend, as both his biographer Michael Foot and his wife Jennie Lee have testified.

The origins of the fascination, or flirtation, must be traced back to a small dinner party in a modest London flat in December 1929. Planning his trip to Russia, Beaverbrook had turned for help and advice to the obvious person: Frank Wise, a former civil servant who had been Lloyd George's expert on the Russian economy in the First World War, and by

1929 was a Labour MP and chief economic adviser to the Soviet Trading Mission in London. He was much more of a socialist than the Labour Party's leaders, and a much better economist. Wise duly gave Beaverbrook the advice about special trains and coaches that he sought, and after Beaverbrook came back from Russia asked him, rather boldly, to dine in his 'small flat on the top floor of an office block off Holborn'.[4] The other guests were to be James Maxton and Jennie Lee – both, like Wise, on the Labour Left, and full of ideas about how the Labour government should be adopting full-blooded socialism to tackle the economic crisis. Beaverbrook for once made an exception to his rule about eating at home. Afterwards, he sent Wise 'grateful thanks for a grand dinner party', said that Maxton 'fascinates me', and added seductively, '. . . when you get tired of politics come and join my Fleet Street circus'.[5]

This was one of Jennie Lee's first visits to Frank Wise's London bolt-hole – he was separated from his wife, who lived in the country – and her first meeting with Beaverbrook. Recently elected MP for North Lanark-shire, she was twenty-five, a combative, clear-headed graduate of the University of Edinburgh, whose uncompromising socialism had been formed by the 1926 General Strike and her father's loss of his job in the pits. She particularly admired Wise because although, like her, he was an optimist about Russia, he was also a realist, as indeed he had to be since he was trying to sell Russian products to Western capitalists. Most of the people they knew were bored by his talk about the facts and figures of the business world. Beaverbrook was an exception. She was impressed that he had

> . . . found it worthwhile to clamber upstairs to Frank's top floor flat in John Street in order to inform himself on the current state of the Russian economy. Beaverbrook advocated many crazy policies in his time, but his attitude towards Russia, in season and out of season, was that instead of trying to crush the Revolution it would have been far better for us as well as for Russia if we had ceased to interfere with its internal affairs and had concentrated instead on developing sound trading relations.[6]

Three months after the Wise dinner, Beaverbrook returned the compliment – at a time when Wise, Maxton and Jennie Lee were all particularly active on the left wing of Labour Party battles – and asked the trio to Stornoway House. That autumn Jennie Lee and Wise – by this time her 'favourite parliamentary colleague' and 'the centre and base' of her life – travelled together to Moscow and Tiflis.[7] In 1931, soon after she lost her seat, Beaverbrook wrote her a beguiling letter. He said he had seen 'by the paper' that she was going to the United States to lecture on Russia, and he hoped she would include Canada. 'I would like to be of use to you in connection with your journey there. I put myself at your service.' He went on: 'You will not find any Labour Party there. You will have to consort with Capitalists altogether. And the Capitalists are not the financiers of New York. They have lost all their money. The Bankers are wallowing in the mud.'[8]

Jennie Lee wrote back to say her tour would indeed include Canada and, as it was her first visit, she would 'value any suggestions'. In reply, Beaverbrook said he had sent warning of her trip to Arthur Brisbane, the head of the Hearst organization, to Roy Howard, 'head of the Scripps-Howard group, who own all the newspapers in America that I can remember at the moment – except the *New York Times*', and to Sir Charles Gordon, the president of the Bank of Montreal.[9] Characteristically, he did not tell her everything he had arranged. Lecturing to a lunch club in Ottawa, she found herself sitting between the Leader of the Opposition, Mackenzie King, and the Prime Minister, R. B. Bennett, whose attendance was entirely unexpected; the Premier asked her to a family dinner and showed her with pride a signed photograph of Mussolini. Forty years later, she discovered that Beaverbrook had asked Bennett to look after her.[10]

When Wise was away from London Jennie Lee went out with another newly elected left-wing Labour MP, Aneurin Bevan. Beaverbrook first heard about him from Edward Marjoribanks, who had been much impressed by Bevan's ferocious attack in Parliament on Lloyd George over the Coal Mines Bill of 1930. (So was Lloyd George: he called it 'a very able speech marred by imputing mean motives to other people'.) Beaverbrook made his first approach to Bevan after the 1931 election.

The timing is significant. Beaverbrook was toying with all the economic radicals. At the height of the Empire Crusade, he and Sir Oswald Mosley sniffed at one another's heels. After Mosley resigned from the Labour government in 1930 (while in office he had taught Jennie Lee how to eat oysters), bursting with the desire to galvanize and reshape British politics, he told Harold Nicolson that '. . . if I could have £250,000 and a press I could sweep the country'; he meant Beaverbrook. Nicolson advised him to beware: Beaverbrook enjoyed a fight but 'soon gets bored and makes trouble. He lives only by opposition. If he cannot find an opposition he creates one.'[11] Beaverbrook in turn hoped to recruit Mosley to the Crusade, until he discovered he 'showed bias against food taxes'. In December 1930, as unemployment rose higher and higher, Mosley produced a sweeping programme of economic and parliamentary reform, with a strong authoritarian bent, that was signed by seventeen Labour MPs including Bevan. Most of them soon took fright, as Mosley moved to break with the Labour Party, but in March 1931, when his insurrection led him to start his New Party, Beaverbrook was still ready to give him 'as much publicity as possible'.[12] However, when the New Party lost a by-election in – by a curious chance – Ashton-under-Lyne, Beaverbrook judged that the result had 'done in Tom Mosley'.[13] He was still further done in, so far as parliamentary politics went, when his New Party was obliterated by the 1931 October election, sending him off to Mussolini and Fascism.

Having decided that Mosley had swung too far to the Right to get anywhere in British politics, Beaverbrook began to investigate the fieriest, most rebellious and most promising of Mosley's former supporters on the Left. On 2 February 1932 Beaverbrook wrote to the House of Commons: 'Dear Bevan, Will you come and stay with me at Leatherhead on Saturday and Sunday of this week? My house is called Cherkley, and it is up on the top of a high hill. If you are coming, I will arrange to transport you by motor. Yours sincerely, Beaverbrook.'[14] Next day Bevan wrote back, beginning his reply 'My Lord', and accepted.

On 26 February Beaverbrook cast another fly. From the Ritz Hotel he complained that he had heard nothing of Bevan since Cherkley. 'Will you kindly let me know about your health. If you have not yet thrown off your trouble, will you let me arrange for the St Mary's Hospital staff to look into it? I have a long connection with that hospital.'[15] On 11 March Bevan replied with a declaration of independence, clearly laying down the conditions on which their association could proceed. He thanked 'my lord' for his very kind and thoughtful letter, but he had 'recovered' and had

> . . . therefore no need to avail myself of your kind offer to consult your medical advisers.
>
> Nevertheless a warmth remains with me because of your offer and the kindness which prompted it.
>
> The circumstances in which this letter is written tempts me to say what otherwise I should lack courage to say.
>
> You hold a position of great power and consequence and this tends to falsefy [sic] your personal relationships with people. It is therefore, difficult to speak to you as one would speak to those differently situated. But as one who hates the power you hold, and the order of life which enables you to wield it, and furthermore, because I know I shall never seek that power for myself, I feel emboldened to tell you that I hold you in the most affectionate regard, and confess to a great admiration for those qualities of heart and mind which, unfortunately, do not appear to inspire your public policy.[16]

Beaverbrook was undeterred. In April, he asked Bevan in a reply-paid telegram: 'Are you going to come and stay with me at Leatherhead Saturday'. In July, he promoted a public contest that gave *Express* readers ringside seats to the verbal jousting that was commonplace round the dinner table at Cherkley. The *Express* described Bevan as 'brilliant, bitter, proud, class conscious, boastful of his ancestry and his family'. He was guilty of 'a kind of class consciousness quite as objectionable as it is in the man who boasts of his Norman blood'. He was 'a dangerous fellow . . . with every intention of tearing down the pillars of society if he can. He can hardly enter a railway train because there is no fourth class.'

Bevan replied in the paper a few days later: 'My heart is full of bitterness. For when I see the well-nourished bodies of the wealthy I see also the tired, haggard faces of my own people.' He did not mention that he saw some of these well-nourished bodies at the *Express* proprietor's dinner table while taking some nourishment there himself. His name appears seven times in the Cherkley visitors' book for 1932, in company with Castlerosse, Sir James and Lady Dunn, H. G. Wells, Brendan Bracken and the Fitzgeralds. Around this time he was much taken with Lady Sibell Lygon, one of Beaverbrook's favourite young women; they used to go for long walks together, and Bruce Lockhart heard rumours that he wanted to marry her. Yes, his article went on, he was proud of being the son of a miner. 'But there are better reasons for being proud of belonging to the working classes. It is better to have a future than a past. There is no imposing future for the present rulers of England. Too many hungry generations tread them down.' The *Express* had called him 'a menace to the capitalist system'; his ambition, he said, was to prove that charge true.

The following year, on 5 November 1933, a Sunday evening when Jennie Lee and Bevan were together in London, Frank Owen telephoned from the *Express* to tell Jennie of the sudden death of her beloved Frank Wise. Owen was another radical closely linked to Beaverbrook; he was a clever, happy-go-lucky Welshman, popular with women, who had taken a first in history at Oxford, got a job as a reporter on the *South Wales Argus*, served briefly as a Liberal MP, and had shared a mews flat over a garage in the Cromwell Road with Bevan, becoming also a friend of Jennie Lee's. Beaverbrook hired him as a leader writer for the *Express* in 1931, and made him one of his cronies.

A few weeks after Wise's death Jennie Lee wrote to a friend: 'Did I tell you that Ni [the spelling used by Nye Bevan's closest circle] wants to share a cottage with me?'[17] A year later, on 24 October 1934, they were married and, while living in Jennie's flat in Guilford Street, beginning to dream of a home in the country to escape from the London that Bevan always loathed. Beaverbrook, as usual, knew what people wanted. Why did they not, he asked on 13 May of the following year, take a cottage on the Cherkley estate?

It was a daring offer: from the backbenches Bevan was deploying his formidable eloquence against the whole face of capitalism, and beginning to expound a Marxist critique of international relations – a thorn in the flesh of the government and the Labour opposition leaders alike. From the surviving correspondence it sounds as if Bevan was ready to put his head in the lion's mouth, but was restrained by Jennie. She was always more wary than her husband of what she called the Beaverbrook 'ménage'.

'As you know,' Bevan wrote to Beaverbrook,

> Jennie springs from the same Covenanter stock as yourself, only she has sprung further, or not quite so far, according to the point of view. She takes the view, for which of course there is much to be said, that it would be improper for us to live within the shadow of your castle walls. Like Lobengula, you cast a long shadow, and it is difficult to grow under it.
>
> In plain English, we think it would be politically indiscreet for us to take

the cottage on your estate. We feel it is extremely kind of you to have offered
to have us, and we are exceedingly sorry that our views of political
expediency compel us to go elsewhere in less congenial surroundings.

He signed himself, 'Yours affectionately, Aneurin.'[18]

It was a relationship conducted with care on both sides. Bevan enjoyed
the high life, though he also used to paraphrase a verse from Ecclesiasticus
about the rich men who 'eat up the poor': 'Stand not too near the rich man
lest he destroy thee – and not too far away lest he forget thee.' He was
interested in cooking, and a good cook himself; he went to the best
restaurants when he could. One night when they were drinking Beaverbrook's champagne Brendan Bracken MP, waving his arms 'like a partly
domesticated orang-outang', jeered at Bevan: 'You're just a *Bollinger*
Bolshevik!'

'Why shouldn't I like good wine?' answered Bevan. 'The best I ever had
from you, by the way, Brendan, I'd call bottom lower-class *Bolshevik*
Bollinger.'[19]

Beaverbrook deployed champagne as a weapon. Christiansen recorded
how one night he served a 1904 Veuve Clicquot, announcing that to get
four drinkable bottles nine had been opened.

> 'How do you like it, Nye?'
> Bevan appraised the still old wine with the eye of a connoisseur.
> 'Well, since you ask me, I don't like it at all. I like champagne young,
> fizzy – and cold.'
> The Beaver is not to be outmanoeuvred. He bawls for his butler. 'Bring
> the Bollinger Bolshevik a bottle of young, fizzy, cold champagne, all to
> himself,' he orders.[20]

Bevan knew where to draw the line. Beaverbrook could tempt him to
be a regular guest and to accept his champagne, but not to use his doctors
or his cottage. He also gave Bevan space in his papers. When Bevan was
suspended from the House of Commons during an all-night sitting about
South Wales and other distressed areas, Beaverbrook gave him a platform
to state his case in the *Daily Express*.

Christiansen noted that the two men fascinated one another and had
'many, many things in common', without specifying what these things
were. He could have mentioned that both had been brought up in homes
where money was tight, dominated by the Bible, with a bookish father and
a strong mother who was the organizer and disciplinarian; both had been
middle children in a family of ten; neither was good at school, and both
were rebellious; both started work in their teens. Both of them boasted
about their modest origins. Jennie Lee said that Bevan always struck her,
when he was among English people, as an alien; people thought the same
about Beaverbrook. She explained the relationship, of which she did not
wholly approve, by saying that Bevan was 'exploring enemy territory'.[21]

To Michael Foot – sometimes Bevan's ally, sometimes his opponent, always his admirer – there was nothing to explain.

> When the rumour spread that Bevan frequently dined with Beelzebub in person, many grave eyebrows were raised and many whisperers were ready to mock him as a hypocrite. But there was no real mystery. Beaverbrook's household bore little enough resemblance to what the outside world thought of as West End society; it was rather a private Hyde Park Corner, with many of the best debaters and arguers in the land proclaiming their contradictory creeds from well-upholstered soapboxes. . . . Neither Beaverbrook nor Bevan was ever foolish enough to suppose that he could deflect the political faith of the other.[22]

Nevertheless, it is hard to believe that the association between these two exceptional men was based entirely on a shared taste for argument. Bevan certainly acquired a politically useful sense of his opponents' characters that he could not easily have acquired elsewhere; he learned to test and match himself against other heavyweights. Beaverbrook, too, was 'exploring enemy territory', meeting in Bevan a more formidable – and angrier – left-winger than any he had previously known. Bevan was convinced that his own time would come; Beaverbrook liked to know the young lions. Perhaps they both sensed, as frustrated outsiders seeking to influence public policy in a time of turmoil, that at some stage they might combine to mutual advantage. If so, their instinct was correct.

TOM DRIBERG

Beaverbrook's relations with some of the left-wingers he employed require little explanation. He took on Hannen Swaffer and St John Ervine simply as theatre critics; and when Swaffer, an old-fashioned, self-promoting Fleet Street stereotype who spilled cigarette ash down his tie and laid into all comers, went off elsewhere – having finally wondered why he, a socialist, was working for an unreconstructed capitalist – Beaverbrook bore him no ill-will, intermittently stayed in touch, and in his old age wrote him letters of comfort. Infinitely more complicated were his dealings with Tom Driberg, who joined the *Daily Express* as a sallow young man with curly hair and a centre parting in 1928. Driberg, later Lord Bradwell, was, as all the world now knows, a homosexual – though it is not true, as was later said to amuse, that he engaged in left-wing politics to gain access to working-class men. He was an active member of the Communist Party when he joined the *Express* through an introduction from Edith Sitwell, who mistakenly regarded him as a promising poet, and he was virtually down and out, living and working in a Soho café whose upper floors housed a brothel specializing in fat women. On his paternal ancestry Driberg was vague, though he knew he was not Jewish, as some supposed, and his mother's family was old and Scottish. He had been educated at

Lancing, where he and Evelyn Waugh were altar boys together, and at Christ Church, Oxford, where he became friends with W. H. Auden.

By 1935 Driberg had been on the *Express* for more than seven years, at first with a niche on the Dragoman gossip column and then, very much under Beaverbrook's guidance, with a column of his own published under the pseudonym of William Hickey, the name of a gossipy eighteenth-century diarist that the editor of the *Sunday Express* and Beaverbrook picked out of the *Dictionary of National Biography*.[23] In the autumn of 1935 Driberg was accused of indecent assault by two unemployed Scottish miners whom he had met by chance late one night in London and, since they had nowhere to sleep, taken them home to his flat, where all three slept in Driberg's bed. Next morning the miners went to the police. Driberg told Christiansen, and went to see Beaverbrook. 'I was in the bath when I saw him,' Beaverbrook said later. 'It was buggery, you know. I noticed that he had developed quite a large belly. "You're not so beautiful as you were, Tom", I thought, as he pleaded with me to kill the story.'[24] Beaverbrook did so, sending messages to other newspaper proprietors; no report of the case, or of the trial by jury in the Central Criminal Court, appeared anywhere. Beaverbrook gave Driberg 500 guineas to hire a front-rank defence lawyer, charged to 'general expenses' in the *Express* accounts, not to 'editorial expenses', in order to maintain secrecy 'regarding the real purpose of the arrangement'.[25] In addition, according to Driberg, Beaverbrook discussed the case with the Lord Chief Justice, Lord Hewart; Hewart told him he understood that 'it had all been a mistake' – a disclosure whose implications Driberg found 'disturbing' when Beaverbrook told him about it. At the trial, Driberg was acquitted.[26]

For the next seven years he often enjoyed loans or bonuses from the *Express*, paid by order of Beaverbrook. In 1940 he wrote to Beaverbrook and told him that, since he regarded him, because of his many past kindnesses, as being 'in a sense, in loco parentis', he needed a loan of £2000; it was not profligacy that had caused his debts, he claimed; indeed, they could be said to have been incurred to some extent for the public good, since they had arisen from the repairs to a fine old house, virtually a public monument, that he had bought on the east coast at Bradwell-juxta-Mare. Beaverbrook made him a present of £1000, and lent him the rest.[27]

Driberg was a member of the Communist Party from the time he joined as a youth until he was abruptly expelled in 1941. He never knew the reason for his expulsion, and was taken aback when it happened. He was thus a party member for virtually the entire ten years when he was writing the William Hickey column. Since he was also a practising Christian, a high Anglican, it may be thought that he cannot have been a serious Communist; but he certainly said he was. At the beginning of the Second World War, when the Nazi–Soviet Pact was still in place, he did his bit for the party by doing his best to interrupt the production of the *Express*, which he thought would weaken the war effort.[28]

What bound the parties in these incongruous alliances? In Driberg, Beaverbrook was employing a talented journalist; Christiansen said that out of twenty-three William Hickeys between 1933 and 1957 only three were any good, and Driberg was by far the best. Michael Foot thought so highly of Driberg's prose that in the 1960s he asked him to edit both volumes of his life of Bevan. But on Beaverbrook's side there seems to have been more than admiration for Driberg's journalism. There was often something fatherly in Beaverbrook's relations with the young whom he took up; in 1956, when Beaverbrook was enraged by Driberg's biography of him, his then secretary, Josephine Rosenberg, remarked that he had been particularly upset by the book because he regarded Driberg as 'a surrogate son'.

Driberg was fully aware of the anomalies in his own position as a Communist on the most joyfully capitalist of all British newspapers. Yet he made no attempt to get a job elsewhere. In his early days, as an underling on the Dragoman gossip column, he persuaded himself that by writing in semi-satirical tones about the extravagances of the idle rich he was advancing the revolution; later, when he had established the Hickey column, his reporting became more personal and politically opinionated. He wrote scornfully in 1938 (before the Nazi–Soviet Pact) about Unity Mitford's admiration for Hitler and her 'swastika badge specially designed for her on Hitler's orders'; he visited Palestine in March 1938 and wrote in strong opposition to partition; and he managed an occasional column sympathizing with the plight of the downtrodden working classes – though he was also capable of referring loftily to the 'obsequious hat-liftings from loyal herds who gather in Downing Street and such places'.[29] To some slight extent his claim that his column was secretly subversive, exposing the rottenness of British society, was justified; the tone of the column is tongue-in-cheek rather than sycophantic. Sometimes he felt uneasy. He told his fellow-Communist John Strachey how 'awful' it was to work for a paper in which one could not criticize Ribbentrop, the German Ambassador. Strachey advised him to stay on as Hickey, 'partly because I was part of the open underground resistance within the *Express* office, partly because the space which I filled daily might otherwise have been filled by more positively objectionable material'.[30] How this alleged 'resistance', for which no other evidence exists, could be both open and underground simultaneously Driberg, despite his pride in his own exact prose, did not explain.

He was deceiving himself. From the beginning Beaverbrook kept him on a rein, and Driberg was less independent than he later claimed. Was it a coincidence that his very first solo column contained both a story about Sir Algernon Aspinall of the West India Committee and an attack on one of the Cecils? On Beaverbrook's fifty-fourth birthday Driberg wrote a paragraph about him, too, having first asked permission to do so: 'He reads a good deal, especially the Bible.' Beaverbrook gave Driberg just enough scope to satisfy his elastic conscience. Disputing a claim made by Hannen Swaffer in 1956 that on the *Express* he did as he was told, Driberg wrote to Swaffer: 'Untrue. I had *some* freedom – e.g. to back the Spanish Republicans, to attack Mosley.'[31] But Beaverbrook did not care which side won in Spain, and attacks on Mosley were not going to damage the circulation of the *Daily Express*, since the *Daily Mail* was losing circulation by supporting him. As for the idle rich, Beaverbrook despised them as much as Driberg did, and probably more; he was certainly less of a snob. Sometimes, Driberg thought discretion the better part of valour. He concealed the shock of the Nazi–Soviet Pact by writing a frivolous piece saying that 'it is extremely unfair of foreigners to spring news like the Soviet–German pact on us at 11.20 p.m.', because 'not only does it inconvenience morning newspapers', but catches 'clubmen, stockbrokers, politicians while they are considering their nightcaps . . . upsetting their digestions'. Then he quoted the alleged muttering of old buffers in a 'West End club at 2 a.m.', including 'Hmph, end of the British Empire.' On the central issue of war and peace, Beaverbrook and Driberg saw eye to eye. Driberg flew with Chamberlain to Berchtesgaden on 15 September 1938, but expressed no hint of public opposition to Chamberlain's (and Beaverbrook's) policy of appeasement; then he went on holiday just at the time when a show of 'resistance' in the *Express* office, whether open or underground, might have seemed most urgent to someone of his professed beliefs. In the following year, he faithfully reflected Beaverbrook's policy of trying to lower the temperature and to persuade *Express* readers that they stood in no danger from Germany. William Hickey's 'tip' nine days before war broke out, an endorsement of what the paper itself was proclaiming, was that there would be 'no war'.

AT THE DINNER TABLE

One lasting benefit to Beaverbrook that sprang from his link with Bevan was his long, close friendship with Michael Foot. Foot came from a plain-living and high-thinking Liberal family in the West Country; at Oxford he was President of the Union; in 1935, he was the unsuccessful Labour candidate for Monmouth; and in 1937 he joined the infant *Tribune* as an assistant editor. *Tribune* had been started as a left-wing but not a fellow-travelling weekly journal, financed by two rich Labour MPs, Stafford Cripps and George Strauss, with Bevan, Ellen Wilkinson, Harold Laski and H. N. Brailsford on the Controlling Board. The editor, William Mellor, was good at his job (he persuaded Bevan to write a regular column) and well respected, but in 1938 the board decided that *Tribune* must co-operate much more closely with the Left Book Club, a highly successful venture launched shortly before *Tribune* and dominated by Victor Gollancz and his Communist allies. Mellor, who had no intention of editing a paper that followed the Communist line, objected, and was brusquely fired by Cripps. Foot then resigned: a young man of twenty-five with a forceful pamphleteering prose style and a burning interest in politics but no job.[32] Bevan, sympathizing with the reasons for Foot's resignation, came to the rescue. Would he like to meet Beaverbrook to see if he had anything to offer? 'Of course I would,' Foot replied.[33] Given the identification of Beaverbrook with Beelzebub current at the time in most left-wing circles, this was a surprisingly enthusiastic answer.

That autumn, three weeks before Munich, Beaverbrook invited Foot to Cherkley over a weekend. He often asked young journalists whom he might employ what was in the day's papers, presumably to discover whether they were genuinely interested in journalism as a whole. Usually, when he asked the question, he already knew the answer. During the 1930s the *Sunday Express* political columnist, Peter Howard, was required on Saturday nights, after he had finished work for his own paper, to read all the other papers and telephone a digest to Beaverbrook next morning at six o'clock.[34] On Foot's first Sunday morning at Cherkley Beaverbrook asked his guest to read the papers and tell him their contents when he came back from his ride. He came back, had a bath, and Foot recited his findings – without written notes. Beaverbrook assembled his other guests – twenty or so. 'Now Mr Foot will tell you what is in today's papers.' The task did not daunt the former President of the Oxford Union. Beaverbrook was impressed. He hired Foot for the *Evening Standard*, where his first job was to write a column about other newspapers. He was often at Cherkley thereafter.

Beaverbrook paid him double what he had been getting at *Tribune*. He also introduced him to a new world. Foot was used to argument; what struck and fascinated him about the arguments round Beaverbrook was their 'ferocity'. Beaverbrook sat in the middle of one side of the table, not at its head, conducting the conversation like the leader of an orchestra, seeking to show off not himself but his guests, whom he chose and seated with some care. Foot was surprised to find him such an attentive listener, with much more than a good host's flattery of his guests; he was, Foot soon concluded, insatiably and almost indiscriminately curious, which was one of the characteristics that made him 'a very great journalist'. Here was one of the secrets of Beaverbrook's attraction for journalists of Left or Right: he made them feel that he and they were in the same line of work, regardless of political (or financial) differences – as to some extent they were. At the Beaverbrook dinner table, 'Municheers' and 'anti-Municheers' met and clashed. Michael Foot surmised that Sir Robert Vansittart, the Permanent Under-Secretary at the Foreign Office, a strong opponent of appeasement who privately compared Chamberlain's journey to Munich with Henry IV's humiliation at Canossa, was able to unburden himself of his true feelings at Beaverbrook's dinner table more freely than he could anywhere else, even though his host's views were more or less diametrically opposed to his own. Brendan Bracken, friend of both Churchill and Beaverbrook, and Randolph Churchill were often present; Beaverbrook actively encouraged Randolph to attack the Municheers, Foot observed, even though he might himself get 'an occasional blast'.

On these occasions Beaverbrook made Foot as a journalist feel that he was in the right place, perhaps the best place in the kingdom, to learn what was going on. There were other attractions. Beaverbrook's champagne was the best that Foot had ever tasted, then or since, though the food he thought less remarkable. On his first visit he met the most beautiful woman he had ever seen: Lily Ernst. Before long, Beaverbrook introduced him to his childhood hero, H. G. Wells. Foot inherited a passion for books from his father, Isaac Foot, who had built up a huge and exceptional library – a letter from Coleridge might fall out of a volume of Wordsworth's poems – and he soon decided that Beaverbrook's own library, largely collected by himself, contained a lot of interesting books. He was impressed to discover that all the Wells books were signed by the author, and that Beaverbrook was 'pretty familiar' with their contents.[35]

Nor did Beaverbrook's politics seem, to Foot, as outlandish or outrageous from the inside as they did to some readers of his newspapers. Beaverbrook could sound quite radical in the presence of radicals – in his consistent advocacy of normal relations with Russia, his support for high wages, his claim to have been a Keynesian before Keynes, his opposition to bankers, his dislike of aristocratic privilege and his proclaimed lack of respect for the monarchy. Foot was a romantic at heart, given to larger-than-life heroes, whether in literature, history or real life. He was drawn to giant-killers, and he put not only Bevan but Beaverbrook in that class – regardless of the number of giants they actually slew. Foot shared with Beaverbrook a tendency to see the world in black and white, a characteristic that gave force to their journalism. Beaverbrook liked the opinion-givers on his newspapers to write with passion, and Foot scarcely knew how to write in any other way. Swift and Junius were the writers he had sought to emulate from his earliest youth; Beaverbrook taught him much about modern newspapers, but it was Foot the polemicist, unrivalled when on form, who was prized by his employer.

In the early summer of 1938 Beaverbrook took under his wing another up-and-coming man of the Left. He visited the offices of the *Scottish Daily Express* and asked Sandy Trotter if he had any bright young men on his staff. Trotter recommended Hector McNeil. Beaverbrook invited him to dinner and asked if he would like to try leader-writing in London. McNeil said he would, and arrived in London shortly before Munich.

Thus on the eve of the Second World War Beaverbrook had close ties, either friendly or fiduciary, and in some cases both, with the politician whom Attlee hoped would succeed him as leader of the Labour Party (Bevan); a journalist who did become leader of the Labour Party (Foot); a journalist who became a Labour Minister of State at the Foreign Office and was expected by his contemporaries to rise to great heights before his premature death (McNeil); a future chairman of the Labour Party (Driberg); the journalist who was to be almost sanctified by the Left (James Cameron, who moved from the *Scottish Daily Express* to the *Daily Express* in 1939); and the best left-wing cartoonist (Low). Of these men one was a Communist and all the rest were convinced socialists.

The more that Beaverbrook's contacts and affiliations of the 1930s are examined, the less consistency or seriousness they show. He was able to publicize Bevan and employ Foot while simultaneously praising Ribbentrop and subsidizing Hoare. He was swayed as much by love of controversy and an addiction to being on the inside as by any abstract idea. His personal links, to old associates and new, always played a strong part in determining his course of action.

CHAPTER 18
'THIS WAS HIS HOUR'
1940

BEAVERBROOK WAS ONE of the few people in Britain who had thought until the last minute that war would not come, and who ever afterwards believed that it might have been prevented. He personally, he maintained in 1962, might have stopped it had he been in the right place: 'Unhappily I was in Canada through August 1939, and I did not come back until the die was cast. But I firmly believe that had I been here I might have been able to strengthen the hands of Chamberlain and Hoare.'[1] After war was declared, while the rest of the nation stirred, Beaverbrook, in Michael Foot's words, remained 'sulking in his appeaser's tent' (Foot used those words after Beaverbrook was safely dead).[2]

That Beaverbrook sulked is an inadequate description of his activities and attitude during the 'phoney war'. Joseph Kennedy, the American Ambassador in London, was a notorious isolationist and defeatist who believed that for Britain to have declared war on Germany was 'folly'. Two weeks after the war started, on 19 September 1939 Robertson wrote to assure Beaverbrook that his orders had been carried out: ' . . . a written instruction has been given to Christiansen, Gordon and Frank Owen making it clear that Mr Kennedy is not to be criticised in the columns of our papers, but that he is to receive favourable comment'.[3] On 8 October the *Sunday Express* published an article by Lloyd George that was, in Leo Amery's view, 'miserably defeatist'.[4] Its publication coincided with the first serious rumours to reach the Cabinet about German moves towards a negotiated peace; the Cabinet discussed the article and took the unprecedented decision to raise such a matter with a newspaper proprietor; Churchill was deputed to complain. On 1 November a senior Foreign Office official, Oliver Harvey, recorded that 'Ambassador Kennedy is engaged in defeatist propaganda with Beaverbrook.'[5] When Lord Perth, a former Ambassador to Italy, complained to Beaverbrook in December that articles about the Italian Army had 'caused great indignation to Mussolini', Beaverbrook replied that 'anything that could offend Italy was completely contrary to the policy of the newspaper', and referred to a leading article in the *Evening Standard* written a day or two earlier under his direction.[6]

In the south of France Beaverbrook's 'appeaser's tent' was at Cap d'Ail, two miles west of Monte Carlo – La Capponcina, a beautiful villa on a promontory overlooking the Mediterranean, protected by a high wall, bought shortly before the war from Captain Edward Molyneux, the dress designer. Beaverbrook was at La Capponcina when the Russians invaded Finland in November 1939. Here was the first issue of the war on which he and the Left agreed, though for different reasons. Most ordinary Britons were appalled by the brutality of the Russian action and wanted the British government to help the Finns. Neither Beaverbrook nor the Left took this view. Bevan condemned the invasion, but did not want the government to do anything about it. Nor did Beaverbrook. 'Do not let us wantonly assume fresh responsibilities,' said the *Evening Standard*. Instead Beaverbrook advanced a far-fetched scheme whereby the British would incite Scandinavians living in the United States to agitate for their government to send the Finns financial aid, and thus somehow draw the Americans into the European war. 'The Pharisee might have intervened before the Good Samaritan if he had recognised the victim at the side of the road as his cousin,' the *Standard* wrote.

Having thought the war could bave been prevented by giving Hitler a free hand in Europe, Beaverbrook thought after it started that it could and should be stopped. An extraordinary episode in January 1940 would be scarcely credible if less well attested. Beaverbrook went to see the Duke of Windsor, who was visiting London from his insubstantial military liaison job in France, at the house of Walter Monckton, the Duke's adviser. Charles Peake of the Foreign Office heard about the meeting from Monckton:

> W. M. tells me that he was present at a frightful interview between the D of W & the Beaver two days ago. Both found themselves in agreement that the war should be ended at once by a peace offer to Germany. The Beaver suggested that the Duke should get out of uniform, come home & after enlisting powerful City support, stump the country in which case he predicted that the Duke would have a tremendous success. W. M. contented himself with reminding the Duke that if he did this he would be liable to UK income tax. This made the little man blench & he declared with great determination that the whole thing was off.

After Beaverbrook left, Monckton told the Duke he had been 'speaking high treason', a point that had apparently escaped his, and Beaverbrook's, attention.[7] The Duke notoriously lacked judgement. That Beaverbrook, the master of popular journalism, should have been so ill informed about popular opinion (not to mention the nature of Nazi Germany) as to imagine that it would rally behind the Duke, of all people, is more surprising. Chamberlain heard about this fantastic exchange.[8]

Fantasies about a negotiated peace produced strange dealings not only between Beaverbrook and the Duke but between Beaverbrook and left-wingers. On 5 March 1940, Beaverbrook invited Jimmy Maxton and one or two other leaders of the Independent Labour Party to dinner at Stornoway House to discuss their anti-war campaign. Whether he offered to finance the campaign is not clear: later the ILP said he did, and he said he did not. But some sort of flirtation occurred. A day or two afterwards Beaverbrook heard about Nazi peace feelers communicated through Dublin to the ineffectual pacifist Lord Tavistock (later the Duke of Bedford), who relayed them both to the government and to Richard Stokes, a well-to-do Catholic Labour MP and businessman, who in turn passed them on to Beaverbrook. Captain Basil Liddell Hart, the well-known but disaffected military commentator, called at Stornoway House on 7 March. He had been writing for Beaverbrook's papers, advocating 'a policy of restraint in regard to taking the offensive' until Germany showed herself willing to reach 'an agreed settlement'. Beaverbrook shared these views, but told Liddell Hart he was being attacked for publishing them. He was worried about pressure to bomb the industrial Ruhr coming from the father of the Royal Air Force, Lord Trenchard. Then Stokes arrived to talk about Tavistock and the Nazi peace terms. Beaverbrook 'showed scepticism at anything arriving via Tavistock', but Stokes, while agreeing that Tavistock did not amount to much, insisted that the terms were authentic. Then Stokes said he was about to make a speech on the subject. 'Beaverbrook jumped up, strode to the dictaphone and dictated instructions that it was to be promptly reported.'[9] Stokes wanted 'a negotiated peace now'.

Stokes was on the Labour Left and an ally of Bevan's. Only one exchange between Beaverbrook and Bevan survives from the phoney war, but it shows them on friendly terms. Bevan wrote to Beaverbrook in April 1940 to say he was going to Paris and seeking the names of people who could give him inside political information. Beaverbrook asked for more details, so that he could target his French contacts more precisely.[10]

At the *Evening Standard*, Frank Owen as editor and Michael Foot as a leader writer (classified C4 for war service because of his asthma, an affliction that formed a bond with his proprietor) threw themselves with enthusiasm into the exciting task of making the *Standard* into 'the voice of wartime London', even if they were ordered to make 'favourable comment' about Joseph Kennedy. They were too enthusiastic for Robertson. He reported to Beaverbrook that the paper was 'inclined to be too much of a propaganda sheet, and I am urging Frank to avoid that tendency, and give more and more space to news, particularly to strive after news of a human character, as a relief from war news'.[11] At the same time the business head of the *Standard*, Michael Wardell, was a lukewarm anti-Fascist and trying, according to Foot, 'to influence the paper's policy in that direction'.

Not only was Beaverbrook half-hearted about the war; his celebrated *Express* columnist, William Hickey, was equally lukewarm. True, Tom Driberg's column written on the day war broke out ended with the words 'We're all in it'; but he was exaggerating. The Communist Party of which he was a member was not really in it, and was at sixes and sevens because of the Nazi–Soviet Pact. Driberg did his best to sabotage the paper's production – the paper in which his own column was appearing, and which had just lent him money to do up his house – at the behest of the Communists. He explained later in his autobiography how the Communists lobbied intensively to get him elected chairman of the federated union chapels at the *Daily Express*; and how he then, from this position of strength, compelled Robertson to negotiate conditions of work during air raids that, Driberg wrote, 'tended to obstruct the newspaper's contribution to the war effort'.

Throughout the phoney war, the *Express* too was obstructing the war effort. It criticized the blackout, and ran a campaign against food rationing that Hugh Cudlipp, then editor of the *Sunday Pictorial* (and later a Beaverbrook employee), thought 'bordered on sedition'.[12]

The single constructive contribution that Beaverbrook made to the war's efficient prosecution in its first nine months was to do with the Ministry of Information. Four weeks after the war started, his American newspaper friend Roy Howard wrote to tell him that Britain was getting a poor press in the United States thanks to the 'inexcusably inept' censorship system. The Germans were getting a good press. Beaverbrook printed this letter as the *Sunday Express* splash headed 'STOP THIS STUPID SECRECY', preceded by a blast from the editor saying that the ineptitude of the Ministry's propaganda departments had done 'our country much more injury than the whole fighting force of Germany combined'. Robertson, who organized the story, wanted Beaverbrook to take over the Ministry.[13] So did Leslie Hore-Belisha, the Secretary of State for War, who thought the country needed 'a man of his calibre to outmatch Goebbels'.[14] Beaverbrook, remembering 1918, half felt he was entitled to the job – 'I have the experience . . . and in character am just the type to have made a success,' he told Hoare – but said he did not want it.[15] The *Express* – among others – railed against successive ministers, including Duff Cooper, and promoted Brendan Bracken until he was given the job (in which he was a success). He told Beaverbrook he would neither have been offered the Ministry nor taken it without his backing.[16]

Beaverbrook's attitude to the war was changed not by second thoughts on his part but by Hitler. In early April 1940 Hitler invaded neutral Norway, forestalling the British but not reckoning with the British determination to drive him out. The phoney war was over and the real war had begun: British troops, as well as Poles and Canadians, were now fighting Germans. But the Norwegian campaign, with Churchill at the Admiralty closely involved, did not go well. On 1 May, in an attempt to soothe rising public disquiet, Chamberlain changed the upper direction of the war and gave Churchill new authority and control over the Military Co-Ordination Committee and the Chiefs of Staff.

That was the turning-point for Beaverbrook. He must at once have written Churchill a letter of strong encouragement and support, though it has vanished, because on 2 May Churchill wrote back on Admiralty paper in his own hand: 'My dear Max, I am vy grateful for yr letter. It is a real help & spur. Yours ever W'. On 3 May Lord Davies, who had been parliamentary private secretary to Lloyd George in the First World War, sent Beaverbrook a call to action: 'Dear Kingmaker, Why have you given up your job? You did the trick in 1916 and, by getting rid of old Squiff [Asquith] you enabled us to win the war. Now, even more than in 1916 we are up against it. . . . Throw your weight into the scales', Davies went on, 'and replace Chamberlain with Churchill.'[17] On 6 May Beaverbrook wrote vigorously in the *Express*, on the tense eve of a Commons debate on the conduct of the war, playing down the Norwegian failures, recognizing that 'the war must now be fought out', and saying that the outlook was bright. He stated with 'some confidence' that British cities would not be bombed; and the Germans, unless 'desperate', would not attack the Maginot Line. This was an implicit defence of Churchill, as well as of Chamberlain, who thanked Beaverbrook for his backing. Next day Beaverbrook told Davies that Asquith's First Government, Asquith's Coalition Government and Lloyd George's government in 1922 had all been broken by a revolt 'from within. The same applies this time. Those who try to do it from without are simply wasting their time.'[18] He was not prescient. That day the Commons began its assault on the government, especially on Chamberlain, inflicting fatal wounds.

MINISTER OF AIRCRAFT PRODUCTION

Shortly before midnight on 8 May, while the government tottered, Ambassador Joseph Kennedy called on Beaverbrook and told him that American sources in Germany were predicting that Hitler would attack the Low Countries in the morning. 'He was a day too soon.'[19] Beaverbrook was back in business: communications between Stornoway House and Admiralty House were at once fully restored. Beaverbrook passed Kennedy's news to Churchill, who informed Chamberlain. Next morning, Beaverbrook saw Churchill and advised him that, with Chamberlain now certain to resign, he must on no account agree to serve under Chamberlain's preferred successor, Lord Halifax. 'He was immoveable. He would not stake his own claim.' After Beaverbrook left, Bracken talked to Churchill, saying that Chamberlain would certainly ask him if he would agree to serve under Halifax. How would he answer that question? 'With reluctance Churchill at last accepted Bracken's advice that he should not answer. What would he say? Nothing!'[20]

That afternoon, Halifax, Chamberlain and Churchill met to discuss the formation of a National Government including the Labour Party. In his memoirs, Churchill describes how Chamberlain implied that Churchill could not succeed him because he would not get the backing of the Labour leaders. 'As I remained silent, a very long pause ensued.' The silence lasted perhaps two minutes. Then Halifax spoke, and 'by the time he had finished it was clear that the duty would fall upon me – had in fact fallen upon me'. This was, said Beaverbrook, 'the great silence that saved Britain'. However, a note dictated by Halifax that day – Churchill's account was written more than six years after the event – indicates that Halifax realized without prompting that his position, partly because he was in the Lords, would be 'hopeless' and that 'Winston was a better choice'.[21]

That evening Churchill told his son Randolph, 'I think I shall be Prime Minister tomorrow.' Early next morning, the German armies invaded Holland and Belgium: the blitzkreig had begun. That day, 10 May, Churchill lunched with Beaverbrook.[22] Summoned to Buckingham Palace that evening and asked to form a government, Churchill gave the King the names of a few of those whom he hoped to include in senior posts, Beaverbrook among them. Soon after he returned to Admiralty House he received a letter in the King's own hand, his first to his new Prime Minister:

My dear Prime Minister,

I have been thinking over the names you suggested to me this evening in forming your government, which I think are very good, but I would like to warn you of the repercussions, which I am sure will occur, especially in Canada, at the inclusion of the name of Lord Beaverbrook for air production in the Air Ministry. You are no doubt aware that the Canadians do not appreciate him, & I feel that as the Air Training Scheme for pilots & aircraft is in Canada, I must tell you this fact. I wonder if you would not reconsider your intention of selecting Lord Beaverbrook for this post. I am sending this round to you at once, as I fear that this appointment might be misconstrued.

I hope you will understand why I am doing this, as I want to be a help to you in the very important & onerous office which you have just accepted at my hands.

Believe me, Yours very sincerely
George RI.[23]

The King had personal reasons for disapproving of Beaverbrook, given his role in the abdication crisis; and he and the Queen had toured Canada only a year earlier, when he sat up late having 'very confidential talks about general politics' with the Governor-General, Lord Tweedsmuir, who as John Buchan had served under Beaverbrook at the Ministry of Information in 1918.[24] Successive Governor-Generals, including Tweedsmuir's predecessor, Lord Bessborough, were fully aware of the distrust of Beaverbrook that persisted in the upper reaches of Canadian society.

Churchill ignored the King's advice; Beaverbrook was exactly the man he needed. Remembering the vital role of the Ministry of Munitions in the

First World War, both under Lloyd George and under himself, Churchill was determined to remove Aircraft Production from the Air Ministry; this drastic surgery had to be performed at speed and without regard to the resentment and resistance it would inevitably stir up in the Air Ministry, since the division implied criticism of their performance. 'The Ministry of Aircraft Production was torn from their very body,' Beaverbrook said later. 'They saw the power and the authority passing elsewhere. . . . [They were] utterly distressed and completely hostile.'[25]

It may seem surprising that Churchill should have been so intent on calling to his side a man who had done his utmost to neutralize Churchill's warnings about the dangers of Nazi Germany, and who only two months earlier had flirted with the idea of a negotiated peace. Twice before in 1940, however, Churchill had urged Chamberlain to employ Beaverbrook's energies in the prosecution of the war, approaches that Chamberlain dismissed as one of Churchill's 'pet suggestions'.[26] When Churchill formed his own ministry, he kept on some of the Men of Munich – Chamberlain, Halifax, Kingsley Wood – and, though urged to chop off all their heads, sacked only one of them, Hoare, the Air Minister, who was appointed Ambassador in Spain. 'No one', Churchill wrote, 'had more right than I to pass a sponge across the past. I therefore resisted these disruptive tendencies.' In any case Beaverbrook, by backing Churchill's extra powers of 1 May and by choosing to defend the government's conduct of the Norwegian campaign, had shown how far he had moved: a real war had started, and the bellicose Churchill was the leader best fitted to wage it.

Beaverbrook, aged sixty-one, and Churchill, sixty-five, were the only survivors of Lloyd George's wartime Cabinet of two decades earlier, apart from the seventy-seven-year-old Lloyd George himself. Their association was as much personal and informal as it was political: at dinner, after dinner, at weekends, on holidays abroad. Churchill had been aware of Beaverbrook's capacities for a quarter of a century: his power to inspire and drive, his ability to get at the heart of a problem at speed, his refusal to despair or admit defeat. Their relationship had never depended on shared political convictions; it had survived in spite of politics, not because of them. Like others who befriended Beaverbrook, such as Michael Foot, Churchill chose not to regard Beaverbrook's somewhat oversimplified general political views as of prime significance; they were fads, or prejudices, part of his nature, like hypochondria. In war, Churchill knew, Beaverbrook's sustaining strengths would outweigh his weaknesses; in a context of supreme national danger his previous views and conduct, however deplorable and ill-advised, did not matter. 'I needed his vital and vibrant energy,' Churchill wrote.[27] On the various alternative lists that Churchill drew up as he formed his ministry, Beaverbrook's appointment was the only one never in doubt. As usual when faced with the prospect of becoming part of a team, Beaverbrook hesitated; but as Churchill later wrote, 'I persisted in my view', and on 14 May the appointment was announced.[28]

Twelve days had passed since Beaverbrook decided to join the war. Having done so, he waged it from home. Overnight, Stornoway House turned into the Ministry of Aircraft Production. From Whitehall came three outstanding civil servants, whose task was to produce orderly administration from near-chaos: Eaton Griffiths (who later ran Wimbledon as secretary of the Lawn Tennis Association) and Edmund Compton (later the first Ombudsman) to run the minister's private office; and Sir Archibald Rowlands from the Treasury as Permanent Under-Secretary. The Air Ministry transferred to him the two joint heads of the Department of Development and Production, Sir Charles Craven, formerly managing director of Vickers Armstrong, the armaments firm, and Air Chief Marshal Sir Wilfred Freeman; it was this department, severed from the Air Ministry, that formed the core of the new MAP.

Round this professional core buzzed the amateurs. In a top-floor bedroom Beaverbrook installed two personal secretaries, the wily George Malcolm Thomson from the *Express*, and David Farrer, aged thirty-three, who had been working for him as a 'political secretary' – that is, newspaper summarizer and ghost-writer – though only for six weeks. Another *Express* journalist, the news editor J. B. Wilson, was brought in as propaganda and public relations man – an unusual post in those days, though not now. Lord Brownlow became his Parliamentary Private Secretary. Then came the hit-men, the industrialists, who knew more about factories and production lines than Beaverbrook did, prominent among them the forty-one-year-old general manager of the Ford Motor Company at Dagenham, Patrick Hennessy; he was put in charge of getting materials, especially aluminium and magnesium, and told to increase production. Of equal importance was Trevor Westbrook, who had been general manager of Vickers Armstrong for some nine years until – hot-tempered, difficult and proud ('there was no one in the MAP or in the industry with my record of *results*') – he had a row with his employers and was fired.[29]

Beaverbrook realized very quickly the importance of repairs to damaged aircraft and engines. In October 1939 Lord Nuffield, the motor-car magnate, had challenged the whole Air Ministry plan for repairs, and distributed the salvage jobs among industry. Beaverbrook's 'settled policy', which proved of signal importance, was to make the MAP responsible not only for this Civilian Repair Organization but also for the repair work carried out by the RAF; he achieved his aim in six weeks, which his supporters thought nobody else could have done, worsting both Nuffield and the Air Ministry. He put Westbrook in charge of all repairs to aircraft and engines.

The MAP was by no means Beaverbrook's only concern after he joined the war. Churchill's personal staff recognized Beaverbrook's ability to sustain and encourage his old companion in times of melancholy or doubt – a role he had first played in 1915 when Churchill, 'a lost soul', was removed from the Admiralty. 'I was glad to be able sometimes to lean on him,' Churchill wrote.[30] Characteristically, soon after Churchill became Prime Minister Beaverbrook, concerned about how a man of sixty-five might stand up to the immense tasks ahead, arranged with other friends for Sir Charles Wilson, later Lord Moran, to become Churchill's doctor.

Attlee, asked after the war about the Churchill–Beaverbrook relationship, said that Churchill listened to Beaverbrook's advice but was too sensible to take it.[31] This was not entirely true. On 12 June, after the worst news from France thus far about the Germans' rapid advance on Paris, Churchill's private secretary, John Colville, noted in his diary that Beaverbrook was at Admiralty House in the evening, making 'a lot of noise, presumably hoping to cheer people up thereby'.[32] Next morning, Churchill included him in the eight-strong British mission that flew at short notice to Tours in an attempt to stiffen French resistance. The airfield where the British landed, in a thunderstorm, was pitted with bomb craters from an attack the night before; no one at the aerodrome knew who they were, or cared; no one waited at the prefecture to greet them. Eventually Paul Reynaud, the French Prime Minister, arrived, and the grim possibility emerged that France, unless given an immediate pledge of help from President Roosevelt, would make a separate peace, leaving Britain alone. Appalled by the collapse of French resolve, Churchill asked for an interval to consult his colleagues; and they paced up and down the drab garden, dodging the puddles and the dripping branches of laurel, discussing uncertainly what to do.

'Then suddenly Beaverbrook spoke,' General Sir Edward Spears, Churchill's liaison officer with the French government, recorded.

> His dynamism was immediately felt. 'There is nothing to do but to repeat what you have already said, Winston. Telegraph to Roosevelt and await the answer. Tell Reynaud that we have nothing to say or discuss until Roosevelt's answer is received. Don't commit yourself to anything. We shall gain a little time and see how those Frenchmen sort themselves out. We are doing no good here. In fact, listening to these declarations of Reynaud's only does harm. Let's get along home.'[33]

These words were felt by the others to be 'the voice of common sense', Spears said, and they were soon on their way back to London, making a wide detour to avoid the battle zone north of Paris.

Beaverbrook's intervention illustrates part of his usefulness to Churchill. The Prime Minister thought in sweeping historical terms, of national honour and disgrace, and of the long-range consequences of his decisions. In Tours, as he recorded in his memoirs, he 'lay under the impression of twenty years of history – the United States withdrawal from the League of Nations; the MacDonald efforts to reduce the French army to equality with Germany; our inadequate contribution to the awful battle'. Beaverbrook was a realist – and at heart an isolationist, too. He wrote at this time to

Samuel Hoare in Madrid, noting that Churchill's 'outlook was always very closely bound up with the French alliance' – unlike Beaverbrook's.[34] He himself when in a crisis thought of immediate advantage; the future must take care of itself. Churchill searched for gestures to keep France in the war, or at least to ease their humiliation in defeat; Beaverbrook did not share this concern. France had collapsed, and that was that. He was an optimist: the United States, he was confident, was about to enter the war.

The fall of France was the blackest moment of the war, not only for France but for Britain too, and Beaverbrook was close to Churchill while its implications were being assessed. British strategy, based on the Anglo–French alliance, was in ruins. On 14 June German troops entered Paris; Churchill, in the process of moving from Admiralty House to No. 10, spent that night with Beaverbrook at Stornoway House. This was a remarkable act, given that Churchill had waited all his life to occupy No. 10 – a clear sign of his need for Beaverbrook's staunchness. On the 16th France asked Germany for an armistice. The following weekend, 21–22 June, Beaverbrook was at Chequers, with Churchill and others, when the terms of the armistice came through, making it clear how total the French surrender was to be. Article 8 required all French warships to be demobilized and disarmed under German or Italian control; thus the immediate danger was that the powerful French Fleet would fall into the hands of the Germans or Italians and transform the balance of power in the Mediterranean.

Beaverbrook was summoned on 2 July to the Cabinet Room, where he found Churchill with the First Lord of the Admiralty, A. V. Alexander, and the First Sea Lord, Admiral Sir Dudley Pound. Once again Churchill brought in Beaverbrook when he had to make a desperately hard decision. The principal warships of the French Fleet lay in Oran and Alexandria. According to Beaverbrook's account, he said that the French must be attacked. 'The Germans will force the French fleet to join the Italians, thus taking command of the Mediterranean. The Germans will force this by threatening to burn Bordeaux the first day the French refuse, the next day Marseilles, and the third day Paris.' Churchill seized Beaverbrook's arm and rushed into the garden. 'There was a high wind blowing. He raced along. I had trouble keeping up with him. And I began to have an attack of asthma. Churchill declared that there was no other decision possible. Then he wept.'[35] The attack at Oran cost 1250 French lives. Informing Parliament of the action, Churchill said he left judgement of the battle 'to the world and to history'.

GUILTY MEN

The success of the blitzkrieg not only galvanized Beaverbrook, transforming his whole 'sulky' attitude to the war, but changed his attitude to the pro-appeasement politicians with whom he had been allied. The peculiarity of this change emerged most fully, though, not in anything

379

he did or wrote himself, but in what was written by three of his employees.

He kept in touch with his journalists. On the day of his appointment, 14 May, he found time to write gaily to Michael Foot at the *Evening Standard*, referring to capitalists (in a tone reminiscent of the letter he wrote to Jennie Lee in 1931 before she went to the United States) as if to reassure Foot that their adherence to opposed political beliefs was not to be taken seriously. 'Here is a magnificent and splendid private fortune,' he wrote, 'which you may invest in war loan, or some other security, thus establishing yourself for all time in the ranks of the capitalists.'[36] Foot replied that the unexpected bonus had left him 'breathless' and went on: 'I am sorry I was not able to say exactly what I wanted in the paper today about the most important new appointment in the government. . . . Gibbon wrote of the Emperor Theodosius that "the public safety seemed to depend on the life and abilities of a single man". As we read the news of the air battles it seems the same today.' In a subsequent letter of thanks, undated, for a 'much enlarged cheque', Foot said: 'I will keep quiet about the way in which such Bolshevik propaganda as we are able to purvey is so generously recompensed.'[37]

On 26 May, the British Expeditionary Force in France began to withdraw towards Dunkirk. On the 28th Belgium surrendered. By Friday, 31 May, it was clear that a miracle had happened, and that 338,000 Allied troops – not 50,000 or 100,000, the most that Churchill had dared to hope for – had been rescued from the beaches. That night, after the *Evening Standard* had been put to bed, Foot, Frank Owen and Peter Howard discussed in privacy on the roof of the building the news they had heard from reporters with the troops. They agreed, Foot wrote, that 'even the wartime *Evening Standard*, in the liberal and inspired hands of Frank Owen, could not say everything he wanted to say. Something more was needed to touch the ferment of the times.' They decided to produce jointly a short polemical book designed 'to drive the Chamberlainites from the Churchill cabinet', and to publish it under a pseudonym – to deceive Beaverbrook, they claimed, among others.[38]

Part of their collective strength, besides their journalistic talents, was that they represented all three political parties. Foot was a full-blooded socialist, Owen an erratic Liberal who admired Trotsky, and Howard a former would-be Tory candidate. Howard was a strikingly handsome young man who had captained Oxford and England at rugby, married a Greek-born Wimbledon doubles champion, and started on the Beaverbrook papers as a sports writer before becoming a political commentator on the *Sunday Express*; by 1939 both Beaverbrook, who had taught Howard his trade, and Robertson regarded him as 'one of our very best journalists'.[39] Behind his good looks and affability lay 'the unspoken hatred he felt for men in positions of power' – always excepting Beaverbrook.[40]

The book was written at feverish speed, partly at Howard's house in the Suffolk countryside. It was finished, some forty thousand words, by 4 June. On the 5th it was accepted for publication by Victor Gollancz, whose pre-war Communist leanings had now been replaced by a fierce patriotism; a few possible libels, all from the pen of Howard, were swiftly adjusted to meet the anxieties of Gollancz, and in July it was published. The title page read: 'Guilty Men by "Cato" ' – the title was supplied by Michael Foot from an episode in the French Revolution. The joint authorship was concealed by the occasional use of the pro-noun 'I'.

It was a devastating document, marked by humorous contempt, and as effective in its way as anything written by Foot's heroes and exem-plars, Swift and Junius. The book opened with a description of British soldiers limping home from the shambles of Dunkirk, their spirits high, but conquered by German steel. Why had our men been asked to resist the most powerful mechanized assault in history with inferior armoured power? How had such a thing been allowed to happen? 'This war broke out in 1939. But the genesis of our military misfortunes must be dated at 1929.' Then followed the sorry tale of appeasement and the nation's fail-ure to rearm adequately, and an informed analysis of what had gone wrong in France written by Frank Owen, an amateur military strategist who cultivated students of war such as General Wavell, J. F. C. Fuller and Liddell Hart. The principal guilty men were the prime ministers of the thirties, Baldwin, MacDonald and Chamberlain, but twelve others – of whom Lord Halifax, Sir Samuel Hoare, Sir John Simon and Sir Kingsley Wood still held office – were lashed with equal vigour.

One of those given a contemptuous cut in passing was Beverley Baxter:

> The blitzkrieg. It means lightning-war. This was that blitzkrieg which Mr Beverley Baxter M.P., in his role of Government soothsayer, had assured his Sunday-dinner public in April, 'threatened to become a comic epitaph'. 'It is extremely unlikely that Germany will attack France', wrote Mr Bax-ter three days before the greatest war in the West. This Mr Baxter is at present officially haranguing the British factory workers on the need for output to hold up the blitzkrieg which has laid mighty France, mangled and bleeding, by the roadside.

What *Guilty Men* did not say was that Baxter's optimistic views had been published by, and had been a regular feature of, the *Sunday Express*. Nor did the book refer to Beaverbrook's support for the appeasers. The Hoare–Laval policy of helping Mussolini to consolidate his gains in Abyssinia was noted and scorned, but the book did not say that the Beaverbrook press and the Rothermere press had been among its few supporters.

The book traced the events leading to the abandonment of Czecho-slovakia. Hitler had been able to swallow Czechoslovakia, it argued, because Chamberlain, after he became Prime Minister in the spring of 1937, had done no more to rearm Britain than Baldwin. Again, *Guilty Men* omitted pertinent information. In 1937 Churchill was writing his fortnightly articles for the *Evening Standard*. In October he had invited Frank Owen to Chartwell. Owen wrote to Beaverbrook: 'I think that Winston asked me to come to Chartwell primarily to pump his armaments propaganda into me. . . .' Churchill's articles harped on the need for Britain to rearm and to rally support for Czechoslovakia in the face of Hitler's threats, and Frank Owen was about to become the *Standard* editor when Churchill early in 1938 was dropped because his views were not those of the paper. But *Guilty Men* did not suggest that guilt over Czechoslovakia's fate should be shared by others besides Chamberlain and his government.

Again, the writers quoted and mocked those who, after Munich, 'spent their time telling us that all was well' – Chamberlain, Sir John Simon, Sir Samuel Hoare – without referring to the equally well-advertised confidence of the *Daily Express* that there would be no war. The book described the aftermath of Munich, and the 'mood of hysterical approbation' it engendered. One of the authors, Peter Howard, had shared that mood, writing in the *Evening Standard*: 'Today we walk in the sunlight: from our path has been lifted the shadow of the clouds which so long darkened our journeying. . . . By his air journey to Herr Hitler, the British Prime Minister reinforces and establishes the high position which he has already gained for himself in the heart and affections of the people.'

Beaverbrook was mentioned three times, all favourably: twice for his anti-Baldwin 'Grow More Food' campaigns designed to stop the drift from the land; and most prominently in the book's conclusion, which celebrated, in capital letters, the replacement of Chamberlain by Churchill: 'In Mr Churchill as premier, and in his three service supply chiefs, Ernest Bevin, Herbert Morrison and Lord Beaverbrook (to name only four) we have an assurance that all that is within the range of human achievement will be done to make this island "a fortress".'

There was an irony here. Unknown to his employees, just as this peroration was about to be published Beaverbrook on 30 June resigned, telling Churchill that six weeks earlier there had been 45 aircraft ready for service, and now there were 1040: ' . . . my work is finished and my task is over'.[41] Churchill replied saying that 'at a moment like this when an invasion is reported to be imminent there can be no question of any Ministerial resignations being accepted'.[42]

There was something else the writers did not know. Nobody in the book was attacked more trenchantly than Sir Samuel Hoare, both for his pusillanimity as Foreign Secretary and for the responsibility he bore, as Air Minister for three separate periods, for the 'criminal' delay in building up the RAF. The writers did not know, and Beaverbrook never

382

told them, of Beaverbrook's private subsidy to Hoare to keep him in the government.

W. H. Smith and Wyman's refused to sell *Guilty Men*, which gave the book valuable notoriety. Helped further by speculation about its author, it went through six impressions in a month. 'Who is this Cato?' asked Michael Foot, reviewing his own 'searing, savage' work in the *Evening Standard*. Peter Howard reviewed the book in the *Daily Express*, referring to 'the mysterious author'. All three authors spread rumours about the 'real' author: it must be some notorious anti-Municheer; perhaps Duff Cooper, perhaps Randolph Churchill. Before long, *Guilty Men* had sold 200,000 copies.

When the identity of Cato finally became known, the 'exposure', Foot wrote, 'was not fatal'.[43] Neither he nor his colleagues can have expected that it would be. Here was a book published by a left-wing publisher that laid the blame for Dunkirk and Britain's peril squarely on the isolationists and appeasers of the previous decade; its indulgence towards Beaverbrook in effect found him not guilty. It went further: it gave him a seal of approval as one of Britain's potential saviours, placing him with the Churchillites, not with the pro-Munich 'deadheads'. From the first, Beaverbrook looked with favour on the book – 'he loved it', according to his secretary, David Farrer – though it is not clear how long he remained in ignorance about its authorship.[44] Being a 'very skilful old man', Foot wrote, he never directly questioned the trio and did not, after they knew that he knew, sack them; instead, he was content to allow his newspaper employees to undermine his government colleagues.[45] Sometimes he half-pretended that 'Cato' was himself; when Halifax asked him mockingly how he managed on his ministerial salary, Beaverbrook replied, 'Ah yes, but I've still got my royalties from *Guilty Men*, haven't I?'[46] There were indeed similarities of style: Peter Howard's descriptions of some of the cast – short sentences, lively detail – showed clear traces of his mentor.

The spirit and attitudes of the writers were Beaverbrookian, too, conveniently forgetting the policies advocated by their newspapers in the past, lining up four-square behind Churchill and reviling those politicians, Churchill's opponents, whom Beaverbrook not long before had whole-heartedly backed. *Guilty Men* was a classic indictment, and the charges undoubtedly stuck; but the jury had not been told the truth, the whole truth and nothing but the truth. 'We let him off extremely lightly,' said Foot fifty years later.[47] That was an understatement. *Guilty Men*, it has been said, 'was to fix the demonology of appeasement in the public mind for a generation'. Beaverbrook escaped the dock; and for once he had not had to lift a finger to adjust the record. In 1944, asked by the future Senator Fulbright to name those responsible for appeasement, he replied: 'Everybody knows that. Halifax, Hoare, Simon and the dead Chamberlain.'[48]

RUNNING THE MINISTRY

At the core of 'Dante's Inferno', as Patrick Hennessy called the MAP, were exceptionally competent professionals, but Beaverbrook put to work anyone who was to hand.[49] His old friend and business partner from New Brunswick, R. B. Bennett, had retired to England in 1939 after a bruising period as Prime Minister of Canada. He bought a mansion next to Cherkley, where he pottered about in wing-collar and morning coat. Beaverbrook sent him off to address factory workers and open new airfields, a task he performed 'rather as if he was at a charity bazaar' (he was rewarded with a viscountcy in 1941).[50]

Jennie Lee, eager to find war work, was 'more grateful than I can say when Lord Beaverbrook's gruff voice on the telephone told me there was a job he wanted me to do'. Beaverbrook was obsessed by the way aircraft factories shut down as soon as there was an air raid warning. Jennie Lee's job was to visit factories and persuade them to carry on until enemy planes arrived – 'a reversal of the heavily-publicized government instructions asking everyone to seek cover as soon as the sirens sounded'. She also became one of the 'glorified messengers' whom Beaverbrook sent round the country to find out why deliveries had failed to arrive on time: was it men, management or lack of material? The messengers reported directly to Beaverbrook. 'The great point was that we were not paid, not slotted into any civil service grading scheme and so could move fast and cut through a great deal of red tape.' At a factory in Reading, when the siren sounded the men rushed home across the fields to be with their families, who had no air raid shelters; Jennie Lee promised to build them shelters. ' "Hell!", said Beaverbrook. . . . "Where are we going to get the cement?" There was an acute shortage at the time; but he got it for me. This was just one of the many times when he nipped in quickly and had supplies intended for the Army and Navy diverted in his direction.'[51]

He appointed Stephen King-Hall MP, a political commentator and ex-naval officer, to advice him on the defence of aircraft factories. One factory suggested that a few naval ratings would be useful as spotters of enemy planes, and King-Hall conveyed the suggestion to Beaverbrook. Next, the First Lord of the Admiralty, A. V. Alexander, rang up King-Hall to ask why 'fifty admirals' were needed. King-Hall went to see Beaverbrook to correct the mistake. No, said Beaverbrook, he wanted admirals. King-Hall told Alexander that five admirals would do. Beaverbrook tackled King-Hall about countermanding his instructions; King-Hall quickly said the five were an instalment. The first to arrive was Admiral Sir Michael Hodges, a former C-in-C of the Atlantic Fleet who had returned to duty with the rank of commander. He wanted to know his duties, so King-Hall took him to Beaverbrook who was 'equally vague', but 'suggested he should go round aircraft factories to buck up morale and also keep an eye on the managers'. Beaverbrook insisted that he must wear

384

his admiral's uniform, which delighted Hodges since it followed that he would be paid as an admiral. His reports led to the dismissal of several managers during the brief term of his engagement. As for the other admirals ordered, the Admiralty provided a dozen, of whom three were dipsomaniacs. The scheme lapsed.[52]

Beaverbrook followed no routine, and treated his senior staff as he treated his editors. Craven complained of being telephoned with orders at half past two in the morning, and again at eight to see what he had done. About to fly off somewhere, Freeman was told that his aircraft had been grounded. Why? Enemy aircraft were approaching. 'Oh, My God, is that all? I thought it was a telephone call from Lord Beaverbrook.'[53] Farrer and Thomson worked for three months without a day off; when they showed signs of collapse, Beaverbrook gave them every other Sunday free. The Minister's Council – Craven, Freeman, Rowlands, Hennessy – met in the ornate ballroom of Stornoway House at strange hours, or not at all. There was always a queue outside his office; inside, he transacted two or three different items of business with different people simultaneously; his visitors, including senior officers, were not offered chairs. It was like the old days at Royal Securities in Montreal. 'Often the most important decisions were taken across the dinner table – cold chicken and Alsatian wine.' After dinner, presided over by his gentlemanly new bi-sexual valet, Nockels – formerly in the employ of Prince Arthur of Connaught, as he often mentioned – managers of assembly plants or engine factories rang Beaverbrook direct; at midnight or later, out would go individual messages of praise or blame. 'Night after night,' Hennessy recalled, 'and into the small hours of every morning, seven days each week, Westbrook and I were with the Minister, going over any and every way of increasing production . . . all the big endeavours were born during these discussions which so often became fierce arguments.'[54] Every day after lunch Beaverbrook took a twenty-minute nap; ' . . . he didn't need waking up; he had an alarm clock in his head,' one of his secretaries remembers.[55] He toured factories and blitzed cities, preaching urgency. Saturday afternoon was the key moment, when the Minister was shown the weekly production charts.

After the aircraft production department returned from its wartime home in Harrogate to London, at Beaverbrook's insistence, Stornoway House became too small; so everyone moved to an ICI building on the Thames near Lambeth Bridge. Beaverbrook put up two slogans in his office there: 'Committees take the punch out of war' and 'Organization is the enemy of improvisation'. To avoid the committees he continued to work at Stornoway House as much as he could, until it was bombed during the blitz. According to Farrer, Beaverbrook was nervous about the bombing, though he expected his staff to work while it was going on. A secretary remembers that during a raid she and the Minister assured one another that they did not want to take shelter; a moment later, they dived simultaneously to the floor. Already Beaverbrook was constructing his own myth, as in the First World War; on 15 September, the day commemorated as 'Battle of Britain Day', Beaverbrook was at Cherkley during the battle's crucial phase, but browbeat Farrer, despite the support of George Malcolm Thomson, into recording as fact his presence in London.[56]

As usual, he drove his subordinates by a mixture of bullying and flattery. When Rowlands resigned after a disagreement, Beaverbrook sent Thomson to collect a case of whisky and champagne and deliver it to him as a humble peace-offering, which worked. Beaverbrook even tried to flatter Ernest Bevin, the Minister of Labour – which did not work.

He proceeded by rows, many of them with Bevin over manpower. He fought and won a battle with Lord Nuffield for control of the large aircraft factory he had started at Castle Bromwich; Nuffield thought that Spitfires could be mass-produced like Morris cars, with the result that it was nine months before Castle Bromwich produced a single plane. After Beaverbrook took charge, women were drafted in from all over the UK (a Westbrook idea), and worked two shifts, from 8 p.m. to 8 a.m. at night and 8 a.m. to 6 p.m. in the day: a fifty-six-hour week for £2 11s (men worked a sixty-hour week). It was 'a lovely atmosphere,' said one woman. A male factory worker said: 'It was only when we were retreating from Dunkirk that we really felt we wouldn't survive unless we got on with it. I always felt Beaverbrook was the right man.'[57] The new post-Dunkirk sense of urgency in the workforce was one important reason why production went up. Between June 1940 and November 1945, Castle Bromwich turned out 11,500 Spitfires.

Beaverbrook boasted later about one characteristic exploit. Aluminium extrusions were essential for building aeroplanes. In England there was only one designer of extrusion presses, a Jewish refugee named Loewy who had fled with his staff from Germany to England, where he was interned by the Military Police. 'I used my ministerial authority to send two German-speaking Jews to all of the internment camps to seek my extrusion engineers and any other trained aircraft workers willing to join our service. The extrusion engineers were restored to Bournemouth. Other technicians were directed to various centres.' Then the storm broke. Everyone, including the Military Police, protested about the release of 'enemy aliens'.

> In this emergency I devised a method of defence against my police pursuers. Bennett would be asked to hold an investigation. He would at any rate clear my extrusion engineers of any evil intent! The pressing need for extrusions of aluminium was explained to him. The insistent demand for more extrusion presses he understood. He would, I felt sure, report in support of the release from internment of these refugees, and his high reputation in judicial circles would be my shield.
>
> Disaster! Bennett came down in favour of internment of the German Jews,

and I rejected his report!

Again the tumult broke out, this time more fiercely than before. The Military Police protested violently. Appeals to Churchill against me and my outrageous conduct in ignoring my own referee met with no reply from him.

Bennett's wrath against me was slow to burn out. For many days he was difficult; he was deeply hurt by what he termed my disregard for protocol.[58]

It was easy to see why Beaverbrook's own wrath was aroused by the stately procedures of Whitehall. In early June, while France was falling, he proposed urgently to the Air Ministry that the MAP should take over the 'ferry pools' – the pilots who flew aircraft from factories to Aircraft Storage Units where they awaited transfer to squadrons. Sir Archibald Sinclair, the Air Minister, wrote to him on Monday, 10 June, while Rouen fell to the Germans and the French clamoured for more air support:

> You were kind enough to make a suggestion on Saturday that you would be willing to take over the Ferry Pools, to staff them with civilian pilots and to release any operational pilots who are working in them. I told you that I could not give you an immediate answer without finding out more than I already knew about the Ferry Pools and consulting AMSO [the ministry's supply organization], but in response to your suggestion I readily agreed that you should yourself consult AMSO about it in order to see whether your proposal was workable. I have since been into it with AMSO who tells me. . . .

There followed another five hundred words, setting out the difficulties. Beaverbrook replied by hand the same day:

> Dear Secretary of State,
>   Thank you for your letter of today,
>   I consider that the Ferry Pools belong to this Ministry.
>   I am referring the matter to the Prime Minister.
>   Yours sincerely, Beaverbrook.[59]

Churchill almost on that very day was lamenting the 'feeble and weary departmentalism' that impeded the war effort. The MAP did not fall into that category. Even so, it was six and a half weeks before the ferry pools were transferred. As the Battle of Britain intensified, the need for trained pilots became more urgent than the need for aircraft. Jim Bailey (later Wing Commander Bailey DFC) joined a new squadron and found he had two Hurricanes to himself.[60]

Most of Beaverbrook's messages to Sinclair were staccato. Like his journalists, his private secretaries learned to reproduce his style; and they found that lengthy communications from other departments could usually be summarized in two or three sentences, saving the Minister's time and patience. In August, Sinclair asked him to stop paying civilian pilots £3000 a year to fly aircraft from North America to Britain; the high salaries, Sinclair explained in detail, were undermining the RAF's recruitment system. Beaverbrook replied: 'It is too late to consider such a course.' The British Overseas Airways Corporation annoyed him by transferring a flying boat from the transatlantic route, where it was useful to Beaverbrook, to West Africa, where it was not. 'The MAP should take over the BOAC without further delay,' he told Sinclair on 26 September. On 4 October he wrote again: 'Please consent at once. It will save such a lot of trouble.' Sinclair complained that Beaverbrook's proposals came out of the blue, unresearched and without regard to anyone's 'priorities' except his own; he also complained that Beaverbrook sometimes sought to circumvent the Cabinet.[61]

The most senior RAF officer in the MAP was Freeman; through his earlier job at the Air Ministry in charge of long-range research and development, he, as much as any other man, had given the RAF aircraft of superior quality. On 23 May Beaverbrook pressed the Air Ministry to promote Freeman from air marshal to air chief marshal. Then he harried him. On the production of trainer aircraft (30 June): 'I wish to point out that this programme will be no use. It has got to be enlarged.' On 13 July: 'You promised me a copy of a letter that you had written to Mr Tedder [Air Vice-Marshal A. W. Tedder]. It has not been received. You promised me news of Botha and Beaufort [two types of aircraft]. I have not heard. Have you forgotten?' On 10 August, after complaining about the disappointing output of Pegasus aircraft engines: 'The motto of this Ministry is "Production is the Ark of the Covenant".'

Freeman, deeply frustrated, told Beaverbrook the same day that 'it was obvious that when the MAP was formed that many of my former duties would be taken over by the Minister . . . as things are at present there is considerable overlap and consequent waste of energy'. He added that 'the time has come when I can be better employed than in this Ministry'.

Again on 6 September he asked to be released. His position was 'unbearable'. Beaverbrook's paper to the Prime Minister urging the formation of an Army Air Force was 'fundamentally opposed to what I believe is right. . . . I disagree with you on so many other points of policy.' He was 'gravely disturbed at the quarrels which seem to take place incessantly between the MAP and the AM [Air Ministry], many of which I feel are provoked by this Ministry rather than by the Air Ministry. I do not understand your policy of non-cooperation with the AM . . . these quarrels and lack of co-operation are doing great harm and may seriously prejudice the proper conduct of the war'.

'Dear Air Chief Marshal,' Beaverbrook replied,

> You make a very curious mistake about the relations between this Ministry and the Air Ministry. These relations are very good. We get on quite

happily. It is true that I have had to oppose the Air Ministry on several issues. But on most of these occasions I have had your approval. An example of minor issues. The Air Ministry has been in the habit of refusing my applications for promotion, with the exception of your own elevation.

On 20 October Freeman's house was bombed. Beaverbrook told him that his flat at the *Evening Standard* in St Bride's Street was 'on the roof and the guns make a lot of noise'; and Stornoway House was uninhabitable as the windows were boarded up and there was a hole in the roof; but he and Lady Freeman would be welcome to stay at Cherkley. Freeman decided, rather than leave London, to sleep in the office.

In November Freeman was recalled to the Air Ministry, where Sir Charles Portal, the Chief of Air Staff, was pressing for him to be his second-in-command. By then, Freeman did not want to go; he had genuinely changed his mind about his tormentor. 'Had it been left with me I should have elected to continue to serve in your ministry . . . ,' he told Beaverbrook.

> Your kindness to someone who must have appeared slow to understand and appreciate your methods I shall ever remember with gratitude. Nor shall I forget the energy, courage and decision with which you tackled the difficult problem of aircraft production. Without the ever-increasing flow of aircraft from the ASUs for which you have been entirely responsible, our pilots could never have won such resounding victories . . . if at any future date I can serve you in any capacity, I shall be grateful indeed for the opportunity.

Beaverbrook wrote back, recognizing Freeman's earlier work in aircraft production: 'To your vision, more than to any other factor, we owe the victories that saved our country. . . . And deep is my regret that I can no longer avail myself of talents so various and valuable or enjoy a working relationship of so much charm.' The master-flatterer, when he decided to press the button on what he called 'the oil can', was not to be out-flattered. Later on, the RAF thought that much of the credit lavished on Beaverbrook for producing the aircraft that won the Battle of Britain properly belonged to the unsung Freeman. They did not know that Beaverbrook had been the first to make their point.[62]

Freeman had objected strongly when Beaverbrook wanted to create an Army Air Force. In November 1940, when Coastal Command was in urgent need of more aircraft to meet the strain of the battle of the Atlantic, Beaverbrook suddenly tried once more to clip the RAF's wings. He proposed in the Defence Committee that Coastal Command should be transferred from the RAF to the Navy; the Navy, he thought, should have its own training establishments, pilots and maintenance staff. He asserted that, although it was the task of the RAF to supplement the surface craft of the Fleet, 'it has failed to do so'.[63] Churchill instituted an inquiry. It concluded that excellent co-operation between Coastal Command and the Navy already existed, and it would be a wasteful duplication of effort and resources to change the system. Churchill came down against Beaverbrook, and Beaverbrook let his idea die; but not before the Air Force chiefs had been confirmed in their view that the Minister of Aircraft Production, when he stepped outside his own ministry, was a time-waster and troublemaker.

They also thought they had caught him committing the barely forgivable sin of using his newspapers to support positions he was taking in Cabinet. Three leaders on three successive days advocating the transfer appeared in the *Evening Standard*; Lord Trenchard, the father of the RAF, who was retired but still powerful, wrote to Churchill saying that any such dismemberment would greatly weaken the RAF.[64] Churchill sent Trenchard's letter to Beaverbrook, together with a warning note. Defending himself, Beaverbrook said he was not directing the *Evening Standard* and that the paper was a supporter of the government and all its members (*Guilty Men* was still selling briskly); this reply left open the possibility, if not the certainty, that he was nevertheless making the occasional 'suggestion' to its editor.

His raids on other departments' supplies, whether for manpower, cement or spare parts, were the most frequent cause of complaint; but here, in contrast to his démarche over Coastal Command, he had serious reasons for behaving as he did. Colonel (later Lieutenant-General Sir Ian) Jacob, one of the three military secretaries to the War Cabinet, shared a lift with him after a particularly stormy meeting when his piracy had been under attack. Beaverbrook told Jacob he did not approve of the orthodox way of dealing with shortages. Orthodoxy decreed that scarce men and materials were allocated among claimants, who took what they were given. The result, said Beaverbrook, was that everyone then sat back and did nothing to increase supplies. Under his system, or non-system, if he collared materials intended for someone else then the someone else was forced to go out and scavenge to get what he wanted, thus increasing supplies. Jacob was closely concerned with Allied supply problems in London and Washington during the war; reflecting later on the theory that inspired Beaverbrook's piracy, he concluded that 'there was something in it'; from Jacob, not an unqualified Beaverbrook admirer, this cautious verdict amounted to an accolade.[65]

Sir Arthur Salter, then at the Ministry of Shipping, observed Beaverbrook's theory in action shortly after the fall of France. As he and Beaverbrook sat in an ante-room in Downing Street waiting to see Churchill, they overheard a discussion about a consignment of goods originally destined for France but now held at a British port. Beaverbrook vanished. He telephoned the port; and the consignment became the property of the Ministry of Aircraft Production. Salter suspected that Beaverbrook invoked the authority of the Prime Minister.[66]

Beaverbrook used Churchill as he used everyone else – appealing for support against rivals, complaining in tones of self-pity when he did not get it. Every now and again, he resigned. Between May 1940 and the end of the year he resigned four times. His task was over; he was not appreciated; he could better serve the cause outside the government by running his papers; he was exhausted and laid low by asthma. Considering the peril of the nation and Churchill's own burden, the Prime Minister treated these time-wasting resignations and their petulant, childish quality with astonishing forbearance. He continued to need Beaverbrook in a crisis: he again depended on his support in December 1940 when the Americans threatened to stop supplying munitions unless Britain handed over her gold reserves.

Beaverbrook claimed later, to Churchill, that the resignations were

> . . . a deliberate act of promotion. The object was 'urgency and speed'. It was in storm over delays, protests on account of procrastination, hostility and opposition to government by committee, fortified and strengthened by threats of resignations, that I tried to accomplish all the many tasks that you entrusted to me.
>
> I was always under the impression that, in your support for my methods, you wished me to stay on in office, to storm, to threaten resignation and withdraw again.[67]

The notion that the resignations were Churchill's idea was far-fetched. Asthma was part of their cause; but the asthma often seems to have coincided with frustration. Beaverbrook had been his own master since the death of J. F. Stairs in 1904, and was used to getting his own way without difficulty. Outside government he never sat regularly on a committee in his life, not even on the boards of his own newspapers.

To Battle of Britain pilots, factory workers and particularly to readers of the *Daily Express* and *Evening Standard*, Beaverbrook came to seem second in importance only to Churchill as a leader who could win the war. On the 'home front' the government made constant appeals for salvage, and the earliest of them was Beaverbrook's Pots and Pans Appeal: 'We will turn your pots and pans into Spitfires and Hurricanes,' the message ran. Lady Reading, chief of the Women's Voluntary Service, broadcast in July 1940: 'We can all have the tiny thrill of thinking, as we hear the news of an epic battle in the air, perhaps it was my saucepan that made part of that Hurricane!' Pots and pans poured in; photographs were taken of saucepan mountains; Lord Harrowby presented the aluminium body of his Rolls Royce. The campaign was hardly necessary, since plenty of scrap aluminium was available, and in any case 'the amount of aluminium produced as a result of the sacrifice of the housewives of this country was negligible (one day's supply),' Rowlands told Liddell Hart in 1943.[68] Still, the appeal was a great popular success, and so was Beaverbrook's Spitfire Fund, which was soon bringing in £1,000,000 a month; the contributors never quite realized that money could not put Spitfires in the sky. Air Marshal Sir Hugh Dowding, who was in charge of Fighter Command throughout the Battle of Britain and a Beaverbrook admirer, said that Beaverbrook's morality was 'not the ordinary code of morality. He was certainly dishonest about the Spitfire Fund.' Visiting Canada, Dowding was besieged by enquiries about what machines had been built and by requests for photographs for local ceremonies. People told him they had written to Beaverbrook, 'but Beaverbrook had not troubled to send them any answers'; his reputation in Canada, never high, had 'suffered all the more', Dowding concluded.[69] It did not suffer in Britain. Both campaigns, run by Wilson of the *Daily Express*, confirmed the picture of Beaverbrook as a grinning, buoyant little dynamo in perpetual motion, as drawn by Low in the *Evening Standard*. Enemies said the campaigns boosted Beaverbrook more than the war effort. Perhaps they did; but their contribution to morale as the bombs rained down – to the sense that this was a people's war in which everyone, from the seventy-five-year-old Earl of Harrowby to the dustman, could help to win the Battle of Britain – was incalculable. 'It is Winston and Beaverbrook who have really galvanised the country and the Government departments,' Colville wrote in his diary on 13 June, and the same remained true for much of 1940.*

HIS CONTRIBUTION

Beaverbrook was appointed a member of the War Cabinet on 2 August, and there his conduct came under the measured scrutiny of the intellectual soldier Ian Jacob, a professional judged by Colville to be 'far above the average in both intelligence and common sense'. Jacob noticed that Beaverbrook

> . . . would never read anything if he could avoid it. He particularly disliked long papers, and if he was going to read anything, he liked it to be very short. In Cabinet, he would state his views very crudely and definitely, though he was quite prepared to argue. He didn't approve of, and

---

* Whether it was Beaverbrook, under cover of another campaign – to salvage scrap iron – who gave the order to commandeer Baldwin's gates has been much discussed. A footnote to *Friends*, Beaverbrook's memoir of R. B. Bennett published in 1959, says: 'At the height of the War effort park railings and gates everywhere were seized for scrap. But Baldwin wanted to keep his gates. In the House of Commons, which he once dominated, it was said by a Tory member who had served under him: "It is necessary to leave Earl Baldwin these gates to protect him from the just indignation of the mob".'
Part of the original draft of this footnote reads, in Beaverbrook's own handwriting: 'While the gates of others were taken for Munitions, he appealed against the order of removal signed by me as Minister of Supply and Churchill directed me to rescind it.'

had a pretty good contempt for, the Chiefs of Staff; he thought they were stuffy, with no go; they didn't have the drive he had. There was no doubt about it; he did have drive.

Jacob thought 'he loved the aircraft production job: a sort of blitz'.

The only female member of Beaverbrook's immediate MAP staff, Betty Bower, was very young when she joined it through an agency. She sat at a desk outside the door of a large ante-room that led to Beaverbrook's spacious office overlooking the Thames: a watchdog. 'One day the door opened and in came Lloyd George in his black hat and coat; obviously I couldn't keep him out. Beaverbrook was alone and asleep on the settee. "Oh, hullo David. I have to go out. My secretary will entertain you until I come back." ' On another occasion, when Beaverbrook could not at once see the Chinese Ambassador, Wellington Koo, her employer told her: 'Take him round the park for twenty minutes and talk to him.' He knew how to entertain elderly and middle-aged men. He interested himself in Miss Bower's emotions; driving down to Cherkley he asked: 'Who is the most attractive man to you in the Ministry of Aircraft Production?'

'Air Vice-Marshal Tedder.'

'Good God. Do you mean it?'

'Yes.'

'I can't stand him.'

In the suite he kept at the Savoy, he said: 'Get me Perry' – Lord Brownlow, his Parliamentary Private Secretary. Miss Bower gave the hotel exchange Brownlow's number in Grantham.

'How do you know the number?'

'I've got a good memory.'

Beaverbrook pointed his finger at her: 'You're having an affair with Perry.'

A. V. Alexander, the First Lord, pursued Miss Bower strenuously, with Beaverbrook's encouragement – though not Miss Bower's. The green scrambler telephone for conversations between ministers rang at Cherkley: the First Lord was calling the Minister. Beaverbrook picked up the receiver and passed it to Miss Bower: 'It's for you. It's the First Lord.'

She spent the Christmas of 1940 at Cherkley; Beaverbrook gave her £100 to spend on clothes, and seemed anxious to see how she would behave. The other guests were Randolph Churchill's wife, Pamela; Jean Norton (who had driven a mobile canteen for the Women's Voluntary Service throughout the London blitz); Helen Fitzgerald; Frank Owen's wife, Grace; Alexander; R. B. Bennett; and President Roosevelt's envoy, Averell Harriman. Miss Bower slept in the 'Asthma Room', which was equipped with every medicine and breathing apparatus; here Beaverbrook went, 'kettles going', when attacked. On the Sunday after

Christmas Miss Bower overslept, and was awakened by the sound of cars setting off for church. Fearing she had blotted her copybook, she asked a maid if her host had gone to church; no, he was at breakfast with Mr Harriman. She went down.

'Whaddya want?'

Could she have a car to church?

'Waal, it all depends. Are you a Presbyterian or an Episcopalian?'

'I am an Episcopalian.'

'Waal, you bloody well walk' – and walk Miss Bower did. She recalled: 'It was not really a joke. It was frightful weather and a long walk. He didn't often swear. There was a touch of sadism.'

Bower, as Beaverbrook always called her, was taught how to assemble and fire a Sten gun, to defend her Minister in the event of a German invasion. The gun, disassembled, was housed in a kind of briefcase, which she carried; Nockels the valet was similarly equipped for the same emergency, and so was the Minister's Air Force chauffeur. Beaverbrook had his Rolls Royce armoured against bombs; a taxi banged into it, which seriously damaged the Rolls but left the taxi unscathed. So Beaverbrook acquired an armoured car. On the night the Germans bombed the House of Commons – 'That was close,' said Beaverbrook – the armoured car was due to make its first journey from the Embankment to Cherkley. 'Well now, Bower, as you're a woman you had better sit in front.' Slits in the windscreen for the driver supplied the only external view. It was bitterly cold. Beaverbrook sat hunched and cross-legged in the back. At 1.30 a.m. they reached Cherkley, hungry and frozen stiff. Would Bower like something to eat? A sandwich. But Beaverbrook – 'typically', in Bower's experience – roused the whole staff, cook and maids, and they sat down to a full-scale supper. Beaverbrook ordered an electric fire to be fitted into the armoured car overnight. It could not be turned off; Beaverbrook arrived back in London next morning roasting and furious. The following evening, the RAF driver slammed the door and cut off two of his own fingers. That was the end of the armoured car. Farce, produced by the conflict between Beaverbrook's unreasonable expectations and the ways of the world, was never far away, whether during the Battle of Britain or at other times.

Miss Bower 'didn't like him as a person', or some of his friends, such as Castlerosse and Brendan Bracken, but ' . . . we wouldn't perhaps have won the war without him. I was there and I know he did it.'

That was a view from the bottom. It was no different from the view from the top. Churchill wrote: 'All his remarkable qualities fitted the need. . . . He did not fail. This was his hour. His personal force and genius, combined with so much persuasion and contrivance, swept aside many obstacles. Everything in the supply line was drawn forward to the battle. . . .'[70]

In 1943 Dowding described Beaverbrook's impact on aircraft production as 'magical'. He wrote in 1945: 'We had the organisation, we had the men, and we had the spirit which could bring us victory in the air, but we had not the supply of machines necessary to withstand the drain of continuous battle. Lord Beaverbrook gave us those machines, and I do not believe that I exaggerate when I say that no other man in England could have done so.' Beaverbrook, he said, 'saved England by the dynamism he had shown in the early summer of 1940'.[71] Rowlands took the same view: 'The Royal Air Force won the Battle of Britain. . . . It would never have had the chance to do so but for the activities of one man – and that man was Lord Beaverbrook.'[72] Recent historians of the Battle of Britain, however, have modified these verdicts, and 'the myth that Lord Beaverbrook waved a magic wand and lo! there were aircraft where none had existed before'.

One of Churchill's first demands as Prime Minister was that the numbers of aircraft produced must be increased. On 3 June he told Sinclair, the new Air Minister, that Beaverbrook, who had then been in office for three weeks, had already effected a surprising improvement. On the 4th Beaverbrook gave the War Cabinet the figures. Fighters were being manufactured at a rate of 15 a day. For all types of aircraft, the figure was 400 a week. Between 19 May and 1 June, 453 aircraft of all types had been produced. Of these, 151 were Hurricanes and 39 Spitfires. On 8 June, the War Cabinet 'recorded their appreciation of the success achieved by the Minister of Aircraft Production in increasing the output of fully equipped aircraft of operational types'.[73] On 18 June, Beaverbrook reported that new aircraft were up from 245 a week to 363 a week.

Little sense can be made of these figures. Beaverbrook's own reports show the numbers of aircraft produced per week going down, not up, in June: 400 a week (report of 4 June) down to 363 a week (report of 18 June). On 30 June, he said there had been 45 operational aircraft when he took over in mid-May; on 2 September, he said there had been 884.

The matter is put in clearer perspective by a table published in 1974 in the official three-volume history of the Royal Air Force 1939–45.[74] The relevant columns of figures for 1940 are as follows:

	Prodn all types	Prodn fighters
Feb	719	141
Mar	860	177
Apr	1081	256
May	1279	325
June	1591	446
July	1665	496
Aug	1601	476

John Terraine comments in *The Right of the Line*, published in 1985: 'It is quite clear from this table that the turning-point of production was in April, before Beaverbrook's appointment, and in that month fighter production, in particular, made its first dramatic progress, well maintained in May, before even Beaverbrook's great energies could bear fruit.'[75] The percentage increase between March and April was far higher than in any other month in the table. Thus, if the table is to be believed, Beaverbrook was not responsible for turning the corner on fighter production. None of this is to deny, as can also be seen from the table, the achievements of the Minister, the Ministry and its factory workers during June, July and August – and August was the crucial month, when the Luftwaffe was supposed to win the Battle of Britain and failed.

One man well placed to make a calm judgement about Beaverbrook's contribution was Sir Maurice Dean. He got a first in both parts of the mathematical tripos at Cambridge; he then won first place in the Home Civil Service examination, becoming head of the air staff secretariat in the Air Ministry in 1940 and the Assistant Under-Secretary in 1943. During the war he worked closely with the principal leaders of the Air Force, particularly Portal and 'Bomber' Harris, and from 1955 to 1963 was Permanent Under-Secretary in the Air Ministry. In 1979, in retirement, he gave his verdict on Beaverbrook. 'For a time, short but crucial, he was the right man in the right job.' But 'in the long run, of course, Beaverbrook's effect on aircraft production would have been disastrous'. He meant that Beaverbrook's methods, by concentrating first on fighters and then on all combat aircraft to the exclusion of everything else, resulted in a very slow increase in the number of new types of aircraft needed, particularly the heavier types needed by Bomber and Coastal Commands.[76]

There is one particularly striking example of the baleful effect of Beaverbrook's methods. The crucial importance of photographic reconnaissance for air warfare might be thought self-evident. It was plainly crucial in 1940, both to Bomber Command for assessing the results of raids on Germany, and to Coastal Command for monitoring German preparations for an invasion. In September 1939 two aircraft had been ordered for 'Photo-Recce' – so-called 'Type D' Spitfires that had to be specially constructed for the job; but the delay in producing them, despite the overwhelming urgency of the need, was inordinate. The Air Ministry eventually ordered an inquiry, which revealed that they had been taken off the priority list and no further work was being done on them. It took a month for these two machines to regain the same priority as standard Spitfires being produced by the score for Fighter Command, with the result that they only became available more than a year after they had been ordered – ' . . . another casualty', John Terraine comments, 'of Ministry of Aircraft Production methods under Beaverbrook'.[77]

396

He ran the ministry for eleven months. By then it had long been clear, as he kept telling anyone who would listen, that 'my usefulness has come to an end'.[78] Air Vice-Marshal Tedder (later Lord Tedder) agreed; he wrote when he left the MAP in November: 'I am compelled to state that . . . the present organisation and working of the Ministry are such as gravely threaten the efficiency of the Service and consequently the safety of the country.'[79] In December, Churchill wrote to Beaverbrook about the 'warfare' between Aircraft Production and the Air Ministry, saying that the Air Ministry regarded Beaverbrook almost as an 'enemy', though Churchill, with his long record of hostility to the Air Ministry, considered this 'sharp criticism and counter-criticism' greatly preferable to the exchange of 'ceremonious bouquets'.

Nevertheless the inter-departmental war was out of hand. For another four months Beaverbrook kept up his stream of complaints to Churchill about the Air Ministry's deficiencies – its use of bombers, its failure to employ civilian pilots – and his wish to resign. 'I am not now the man for the job. I will not get the necessary support. In fact, when the reservoir was empty, I was a genius. Now that the reservoir has some water in it, I am an inspired brigand. If ever the water slops over, I will be a bloody anarchist. A new man is needed. Moore-Brabazon is best.'[80] Churchill in turn kept telling Beaverbrook he must stay, sometimes using strong terms: 'Your resignation would be quite unjustified and would be regarded as desertion. . . . No Minister has ever received the support which I have given you. . . .'[81] The Australian Prime Minister Robert Menzies, visiting London, dined on 18 April 1941 with Leo Amery, who wrote in his diary: 'Max he admires but thinks it all wrong that he and not Air Ministry should decide what planes should be built.'[82] Finally, on 30 April 1941, after yet another resignation – Beaverbrook's staff counted fourteen in all – which included the gnomic statement that 'too many idols are being thrown down and too many hearthstones are being torn up', Churchill gave way.[83] As always, Beaverbrook gave asthma as a reason for resigning. His doctor, Sir Charles Wilson, was sceptical. On 18 April he wrote to Beaverbrook telling him he had made it clear to the Prime Minister that there was 'no health reason why you should not go on doing your job'. Wilson throughout the war attributed Beaverbrook's temperamental behaviour to a 'profound mistrust of himself'.[84]

Beaverbrook's own candidate, J. T. C. Moore-Brabazon (Lord Brabazon of Tara), succeeded him. Like Menzies, he was a Beaverbrook admirer, but he wrote later: 'When I arrived at the Ministry of Aircraft Production, for some reason, things were not going too well. The Air Ministry and the MAP were scarcely on speaking terms, so to speak, and as our sole reason for existing was to supply the Royal Air Force with planes, this struck me as rather ridiculous.'[85]

397

FAMILY ANXIETIES

Beaverbrook's difficulties with his elder son were forgotten during the war when Max, who had taken up flying at Cambridge and joined the RAF as a fighter pilot as soon as he could, was constantly at risk during the Battle of Britain. His relationship with Toto Koopman had ended, and in 1939 he married a suitable debutante, Cynthia Monteith. Max Aitken was an outstandingly brave and effective pilot, and Beaverbrook was at last able to be straightforwardly proud of him. He was awarded the DFC in 1940, the Czech War Cross, and the DSO in 1942; his father went with him to Buckingham Palace for the presentation. He was naturally anxious for his son's safety; those close to him remember how he would sit up and wait, at Cherkley or at Stornoway House, for the nightly telephone calls when Max was on a mission. Peter Aitken joined the Royal Fusiliers, was wounded in the leg and, having divorced his first wife, married his Australian nurse, Patricia Maguire; his father refused to attend the wedding, but gave the couple a cottage at Cherkley where their two sons, Tim (named after Tim Healy) and Peter, were born. Janet was farming in Sussex; in 1940 Drogo Montagu, from whom she had been living separately, was killed in a flying accident. She went with her father to the Montagus' family home, Hinchingbrooke, for the funeral. On the way back, seeing her distress, Beaverbrook told her it would do her good to attend the dinner he had arranged at Cherkley that night and to help him with his guests; she declined. The following year, through her Canadian cousin Chip Drury, who was with the Canadian Air Force, Janet met his brother officer Captain Edward Kidd; in the summer of 1942 they married, and during the next two years their daughter Jane and son Johnny were born. Throughout the Second World War, as in the First, Beaverbrook tried to look after any young Canadians, especially the children of friends and relations, whom the war brought to Britain; and his sister Gyp Stickney, who had been living at The Vineyard since the mid-1930s, became head of the Relief Division in London of the Canadian Red Cross, distributing clothes, blankets and provisions from Canada to victims of the blitz all over England. A Canadian newspaper described her as someone 'whose family characteristic is energy'.

CHAPTER 19

RED WOLVES
IN THE KREMLIN
1941–1942

BEAVERBROOK'S RESIGNATION WAS accepted by Churchill with qualifications: he was to leave the Ministry of Aircraft Production but to remain in the War Cabinet, with a title invented specially for him that later proliferated – Minister of State, an appointment made on 1 May. At Cherkley, Michael Foot and Beaverbrook wrote a humorous leader for the *Evening Standard*, set in type but never used, surmising that he must have been called Minister of State 'to distinguish him from his father, who was a Minister of the Gospel'.[1] The vagueness of the title was matched by the vagueness of the job; Beaverbrook became deputy chairman of the Defence Committee (Supply), where his duties would require him from time to time to conduct enquiries on behalf of the Prime Minister into supply matters of special importance, and to act as a referee 'in respect of priorities'.[2] It would have been hard to design a less suitable job, since it seemed to have no executive function. Beaverbrook expressed doubts from the beginning. Writing to Hoare in Madrid, he remarked that, although Churchill had promised to delegate, he was in truth temperamentally incapable of doing so, 'and indeed it is a comment that has sometimes been made about me'. It was Churchill's war, and that was that; even the House of Commons was fully 'under his control. . . . The Front Bench is part of the sham. There Attlee and Greenwood, a sparrow and a jackdaw, are perched on either side of the glittering bird of Paradise.'[3] Beaverbrook foresaw that his enquiries on 'behalf of the Prime Minister' would merely arouse the hostility of those in charge of the production ministries he was enquiring into: Aircraft Production, the Admiralty and the Ministry of Supply.

Nevertheless he moved into 12 Downing Street, and set to work with his customary zeal. Jacob now saw this 'most extraordinary man' in action outside the Cabinet for the first time.

I would be summoned over. With other ministers, you were shown in by a private secretary, but not with Beaverbrook. Everything was going flat out. You would arrive in his office and three or four different people would be there already. I would be writing minutes of a meeting he was conducting at the same time as he was doing other things. Not many people could do that. He was very good at editing a piece of paper. I took him something I thought was pretty good, and he edited it in a few minutes extremely well.[4]

But without power, Beaverbrook could achieve little. Churchill soon realized that he was in the wrong job, and after a month offered him the Ministry of Food. 'I do not know anything about food,' Beaverbrook replied, 'and cannot grasp the problem in a short time.' What he had, he added, was 'energy and a sense of urgency. These are at your disposal if you can use them in face of hostility from all these elements doing little and delaying much.'

Next day, 3 June, he put his grievances into a long memorandum to Churchill, listing sixteen numbered complaints.[5] 'You appointed me Deputy Chairman of the Defence Committee and I expected to exercise power and responsibility through that appointment. I get neither, and for many reasons. In my appointment as Deputy Chairman, I do not even possess the power of an Under-Secretary.' Then he lectured Churchill: 'The war calls for speed. Urgency is a state of mind difficult to attain, and we have not yet reached that condition although it should have been possible after one year of good government. We are confronted by an energetic and ruthless enemy. Regular ways are our method. Theirs are unexpected and often take us by surprise. We hold to ordinary devices. The enemy avoids them.'

Next he detailed his particular complaints, several of them aimed directly at Churchill, despite having told Hoare a month earlier that an inability to delegate was 'just one of the aspects of his [Churchill's] temperament which must be accepted'.

> You tell me that I am to fix the Haining terms of reference [General Haining was due to go to the Middle East in charge of supplies] and select a civilian colleague for him. I do both, when unexpectedly the whole negotiation is taken out of my hands by you.
>
> The Minute is prepared by you, far better than I could have done it. The nature of the organisation is settled by you.
>
> And all those about me who should be relying on my decision ignore me altogether. Some of them even complain if I show any disposition to take action. . . .
>
> You called on me to preside over the next Tank Parliament in the presence of all the members. For the two following meetings you took the chair. You are a better man for the post than I am. But by that act you ruin my situation in relation to tanks and leave me somewhat in the position of a secretary carrying out your instructions with no executive power, or responsibility. Yet I believe the tank programme to be a failure. . . .

The tank programme was 'utterly inefficient'; anti-tank weapons and ammunition were in a 'shocking condition'; gas and electricity supplies might fail next winter because of a coal shortage; '. . . agriculture is not developed to the limit of our resources. Far, far short of it.'

He ended with another tabulated list:

(1) I may have lost the qualities which made me a valuable Minister a year ago. If so, I should be informed of it.

(2) You should give me the power and the responsibility, allowing me to take decisions on my own account within my own sphere and dismissing me if I plunge you into political difficulties.

(3) Or I should recognise the existence of a difficult situation in which I am no longer necessary to your defence schemes.[6]

Rowlands told Liddell Hart that 'the relations between Winston and Beaverbrook' – of which he saw so much during the time Beaverbrook was Minister of Aircraft Production – 'reminded him of the typical man-to-woman relationship so common in marriage. And each of them embodied both aspects. They quarrel, but cannot break away from each other. They feel a sense of repulsion, combined with an equally strong sense of attraction.'[7] Within a day or two of writing his memorandum Beaverbrook sent Churchill a present of five dozen bottles of Deidesheimer Hofstück 1937. Internally 12 Downing Street was connected with No. 10, and while Beaverbrook was sending Churchill a string of written complaints and criticisms he was also seeing the Prime Minister regularly and giving his views on all topics. Colville wrote of Beaverbrook in his diary: 'Brendan says that he takes up more of the P.M.'s time than Hitler.'[8] Churchill had no small talk, Jacob observed, and liked to discourse on grand themes chosen by himself. Beaverbrook was one of the few people he sought out and was always prepared to listen to, and by whom he was reinvigorated. Churchill 'took him as a kind of stimulant or drug,' said Attlee.[9] Hoare wrote to Beaverbrook:

Whilst I have the greatest admiration of Winston's genius, I do feel that he needs someone like yourself constantly at his side to discuss with him the really big issues that are now more than ever emerging in the war. And after all Winston has the faults of his qualities, and one of them is as being a better talker than anyone else he is disinclined to listen to other people. You and he are on such intimate terms together that he will always however listen to you.[10]

Beaverbrook told Churchill what he thought about General Auchinleck as the new Commander-in-Chief in the Middle East, about Lord Halifax's lacklustre performance as Ambassador to the United States, about the need for air cover in Crete, and about the astounding arrival of Hitler's deputy, Rudolf Hess, in Scotland by parachute. How seriously Churchill took these opinions is another matter. He wanted to harness

Beaverbrook's drive and energy to the service of the government, and, like Lloyd George in the First World War, did not want him outside the government stirring up trouble with his newspapers, for Beaverbrook's general attitude to military strategy was still very different from Churchill's. Leo Amery had 'a real old heart-to-heart talk' with Garvin of the *Observer* in December 1940, about how Churchill 'surrounds himself entirely with his little set' of the scientist Lindemann, Bracken and Beaverbrook. 'Like so many just now, especially in the House of Commons', Amery recorded, 'Garvin is frightened by Max's purely defensive and Little Englander outlook as regards military operations.'[11] In the following months, that outlook did not change. In the spring of 1941, while Churchill was intent on a Mediterranean strategy and the defence of the Middle East, Beaverbrook was insisting that by far the most important issues were the transatlantic supply lines – the battle of the Atlantic – and the defence of the British Isles. As Minister of State Beaverbrook was a square peg in a round hole, but Churchill, though recognizing that he was in the wrong job, could not let him go, and Beaverbrook was unsure whether he wanted to cut adrift or not – which made him, as Colville noted, 'particularly troublesome'.[12]

The position was abruptly changed, like much else, by Hitler's attack on Russia.

MINISTER OF SUPPLY

According to Michael Foot, Beaverbrook learned of the attack when Foot, staying at Cherkley, awakened the household on 22 June with a gramophone record of the Internationale.[13] Beaverbrook's own unpublished account, ghosted by Farrer, takes the story forward:

> Two men were summoned to Mr Churchill's side at Chequers soon after the news was received: Lord Beaverbrook, at that time a member of the War Cabinet and of the Defence Committee, and Sir Stafford Cripps, on leave from his post as Ambassador in Moscow.
> It was a case of the optimist and the pessimist side by side. For by temperament Beaverbrook was ebullient, impatient of difficulties or delay, refusing to see obstacles, rejecting counsels of caution, the maker of many mistakes but the breaker time and again of the pessimist front; while Cripps was clear in his reasoning, restrained in his predictions, looking on the dark side – and on this Russian issue too pessimistic in his prophecies. . . .
> Mr Churchill listened, questioned, considered, all through the day. Occasionally he sat in the garden in the hot sunshine. Then again he would stride to his office, restless to a degree. But though he was restless he had in fact early made up his mind. He would broadcast that night his determination that Russia should be given all the aid in Britain's power.[14]

According to Colville, the Prime Minister had in fact made up his mind the night before Beaverbrook reached Chequers; he had been expecting

Salute to Russia rally, Birmingham, June 1942

Left: Beaverbrook and Lord Rothermere, 1935

Below left: Beaverbrook and Sir James Dunn at Waterloo station, February 1938

Below: Cannes, 1927: Beaverbrook with Lord Castlerosse at Cannes Golf Club

Wing Commander
Max Aitken with his
father, December
1942

Faked Stalin/
Beaverbrook photo
– *Daily Express*, 3
October 1943

41 Defence Committee: (seated) Beaverbrook, Attlee, Churchill, Eden and A.V. Alexander; (standing) Air Chief-Marshal Sir Charles Portal, Admiral of the Fleet Sir Dudley Pound, Sir Archibald Sinclair, Sir Andrew Duncan, General Sir John Dill, General Ismay, Colonel Hollis

Left: Broadcasting from 12 Downing Street to USA and Canada, 17 June 1941

Below: 11 August 1941: Beaverbrook with Churchill aboard HMS *Prince of Wales*

Janet Kidd with her father

Picture sequence: Electioneering in
West Fulham, 11 June 1945

Opposite page: Beaverbrook and
Beverley Baxter in Hyde Park's Rotten
Row, 1949

Right: With the second
Lady Beaverbrook
Below: Lily Ernst
Below right: Toto
Koopman

With Margaret Duchess of Argyll and her daughter Frances

Right: The *Express* building in the Second World War
Below: The Vineyard

Above: Children's party at Cherkley

Left: Beaverbrook with telephone and Soundscriber at Cherkley

Daily E

WORLD'S LARGEST DA

Friday, September 30,

No. 11,970

The Daily Express declares that
in a ·European war this yea

PEA

Ultimatum withdrawn at Munich

AGREEMENT SIGNE
AT 12.30 a.m. TODA

German troops may go tomorrow: Then occupat gradually: No plebiscit

DUCE DRAWS FRONTI

IT IS PEACE

A— 2.30 A.M. TODAY HITLER, MUSSOLINI, CHAMBERLAIN AND DALADI
AT MUNICH A FOUR POWER AGREEMENT WHICH SOLVES THE CZECHO-SLOVAK

When Mr. Chamberlain returned to his
hotel at 1.35 a.m., after a series of conferences which started before noon yesterday
and continued almost without interruption.
he said: "Everything is fixed up now." He is
today.

Germans and Czechs in Hitler's ma
Slovakia was drawn by Mussolini hi
The area to be surrendered
so large as was demanded by Hitler
Nazi Storm Troopers formed a cor
of Mr. Chamberlain's Munich hotel las
houts of "Heil Chamberlain" an

BEAR BRAND'S *Slimming* **Sy-metra**
TRUE FASHIONED *Stockings*

(One Penny)

will not be involved
next year either

CE!

| Cession less than Hitler plan |

The *Daily Express* reports the Munich agreement

Beaverbrook and *Express* editor Arthur Christiansen *Below:* Vicky cartoon of Beaverbrook launching himself at De Gaulle, *Evening Standard*, 30 January 1963

THE PRIME MINISTER MEETS MUSSOLINI AT MUNICH

Weather: cooler
(see page 11)

E.MAY
BE

ARE

You are fond of your family. You provide them with a good home, education — in fact, with everything they need.

Above: Beaverbrook with his last secretary, Colin Vines

Left: Beaverbrook with Mrs Emery Reves

Above: Beaverbrook's birthday, 1961, with Churchill and Macmillan; and *right:* the last party: Beaverbrook, aged 85, with Lord Thomson at the Dorchester

In the West Country, 1957

the attack.[15] But Beaverbrook certainly gave the decision his fullest backing; and Churchill almost at once offered him the Ministry of Supply which, after making his usual attempt to lay down conditions beyond those that Churchill was ready to concede – for instance that, having applied his 'immediate methods' in order to 'drive up production', he should retire on 1 January – Beaverbrook accepted. At the Ministry, in Shell-Mex House in the Strand, the appointment was greeted with some consternation. Beaverbrook's methods, the senior civil servants thought, might have been effective, and even desirable, for a few months at Aircraft Production, which had been a brand-new ministry responsible for one single item – aircraft; but Supply was fully staffed and in charge of two-thirds of Britain's entire war production, from ball-bearings to tanks. The Minister's task was to keep the whole machine moving forward on all fronts simultaneously, not to give absolute priority to one item at the expense of everything else. Under Beaverbrook's predecessor Sir Andrew Duncan, a former chairman of the Iron and Steel Federation, the machine had worked well, though the Ministry had not solved the problem of tank production.[16] A future Prime Minister serving in the Ministry, Harold Macmillan MP, who became Beaverbrook's second-in-command, was as apprehensive as the civil servants. Many years later, Michael Foot told Macmillan's biographer how, on what he thought was probably Macmillan's first visit to Cherkley, he saw the visitor waiting in a lounge outside the library: 'I remember him giving me a great eulogy of what he thought of Beaverbrook, full of flattery, and it was obviously planted to be passed on by me – so of course I did – and Beaverbrook laughed.'

Macmillan was worried that he might be somehow captured or compromised by Beaverbrook, and formulated a strategy for preserving his independence:

> I made up my mind that the only way to treat Max was to be very aloof from him. I never went into his room and talked. About 8 o'clock – I always stayed at the Ministry until about nine – he'd say, 'You haven't been to my room, come and see me there.' I'd say: 'You didn't send for me.' 'Well, come to dinner . . . .' 'I was going out with some friends.' Then he'd say, 'Will you come to stay at Cherkley with me?' I was very pompous and said, 'Of course – what are we going to discuss?' 'No, we're just going to have a party.' I'd reply, 'Usually, when I'm asked to a country house party, my wife has been asked with me.' 'Oh no, it isn't that kind of party.' 'Well, I think perhaps I won't come . . . .'
>
> He tried to trap me. . . . He couldn't resist seducing men in the way he seduced women. And once a man was seduced by him, he was finished. I've seen two or three people ruined by it.[17]

One man impervious to seduction was the young, clear-headed and austere Oliver Franks, an Oxford philosophy don who had joined the Ministry of Supply at the bottom in 1939 and risen at high speed to the top. Anticipating that Beaverbrook would arrive at Shell-Mex House very early on his first day, in order to establish his dominance by complaining about the indolence of the absent civil servants, Franks took care to arrive even earlier, so that he could appear armed with all the new Minister's problems and proposed solutions the moment he was summoned. Largely because of Franks's skill in channelling Beaverbrook's energies by the way he fed him the paperwork, the routine of the Ministry was not often disrupted, though it was quickly apparent that Beaverbrook was not temperamentally fitted to running a large department of state that offered little scope for piratical forays.

What the new job did do, coupled with the attack on Russia, was to propel Beaverbrook to the centre of the international stage. In June 1941 the United States was half in and half out of the war. President Roosevelt, constrained by the strength of isolationist sentiment in Congress, was helping Britain as much as he dared; in March he had sent to London his childhood friend Averell Harriman, a handsome, enormously rich, forty-nine-year-old polo player and Wall Street banker, to 'recommend everything that we can do, short of war, to keep the British Isles afloat'. Thus Beaverbrook's new job and Harriman's interlocked, forming the main supply link between Britain and the United States; and Harriman and his daughter, Kathleen, who had secured a job in the London bureau of the International News Service to be near her father, were soon invited to Cherkley. Kathleen wrote to her sister:

> Our host looks like a cartoon out of *Punch*: small, baldish, big stomach and from there he tapers down to two very shiny yellow shoes. His idea of sport is to surround himself with intelligent men then egg them on to argue and fight among themselves. Sitting at dinner while all this is going on makes New York very remote. Even his best friends are half-scared of him, because he's got a fearful temper and no one seems to know when it will break. On top of all this, he's kind, very kind, and is wonderful with children; for some reason he doesn't seem to scare them. . . . He and Averell got on beautifully.[18]

The two millionaires soon found themselves charged with keeping Communist Russia as well as Britain afloat, as during the summer the German armies drove deeper into the Ukraine and towards Leningrad and Moscow. Both men were present, in August 1941, at the historic first meeting between Churchill and Roosevelt aboard the American battleship *Augusta* in Placentia Bay. The main public outcome, announced on 14 August, was the Atlantic Charter, which pledged the two countries to a set of common principles. Beaverbrook claimed to have secured the alteration of a sentence that would have committed post-war Britain to the abandonment of Imperial Preference; but the evidence is against him. The main private outcome was the decision to send a joint aid mission to Stalin, with Beaverbrook leading for the British and Harriman for the Americans. (The main diversion occurred when Churchill's butler got drunk and tried on Roosevelt's hat.) Beaverbrook then flew to Washington, where he persuaded the American production chiefs to raise their targets. As a North American, a self-made millionaire, and a successful wartime production chief himself, Beaverbrook was perhaps the one member of the British government whom the American industrialists would have listened to; he successfully urged them, for instance, to produce landing craft.

One person boosting his reputation in the United States was Jean Norton's daughter, Sarah, who occasionally wrote for the *Baltimore Sun* and the Associated Press as 'Mary Fitzmaurice', since her mother forbade her to use her real name.[19] She filed a profile of Beaverbrook in August:

England's Minister of Supply, 62 year-old Lord Beaverbrook, has probably cut more yards of red tape, coupons notwithstanding, than anyone else in Britain. He works fifteen hours a day, sometimes longer.

He will not write letters when he can save time by using the telephone. A handwritten letter from Beaverbrook is almost unknown. His methods are unorthodox, violent, invigorating and inspiring. One of his editors describes him as 'our inspired anarchist'.

. . . His dinner parties are amusing and sometimes sensational. Before they go into dinner, he will stand on the terrace and shout 'Come and eat'. The guests troop in. 'Sit there', says Max, 'And you there. See what lovely women there are beside you.'

His interest besides work is work. When Beaverbrook retires at night, it is not to sleep but to listen to the world. Guests staying at his house have sometimes wondered at the sound of a radio, heard faintly through the night.

Next morning his newspapers will be rung up and his lively voice inquires: 'Why don't you get the news from Russia? Everyone knows about that except you fellows.' He goes to bed at about 2.30 a.m. and gets up at 7. He then goes to his London office and does not come back again until 8 p.m. . . . All the rooms at Cherkley Court are simply furnished with the exception of one room, which has bright red carpet and curtains. The rest of the furniture is in silver tones. In his bedroom there are complicated instruments, telephones, radiograms, sunray lamps, and (before the war) television.

. . . He cannot bear to see a woman smoke. He can be really tiresome about that. Beaverbrook professes himself utterly indifferent to criticism. Nobody loves a row better than he.

'Is the fellow truculent?' I hear him say. 'I like truculence'. But Beaverbrook is really an intensely sensitive man. If he is savagely attacked, he will hit back with redoubled fury. Let his enemy fall, and he begins to see wonderful virtues in him, especially if he fought hard. . . .

'A good man makes a good peace.' But if his critic is a friend, he will laugh and say, 'What do I care?' and then again and again he will refer to the attack saying, 'I wonder why he (or she) did it?'

His hobbies are many and always dangerous. Once it was motor cars, then Lockheed airplanes. Now Beaverbrook drives a pony and cart. It is equally terrifying. . . .

Perhaps he is best described when I tell you what we ourselves feel in England today. We say, in times of trouble and stress, when things want putting right: Where is Beaverbrook at the moment?

The departure date of the mission to Moscow was set for 22 September. On the 15th Beaverbrook called together in the big War Cabinet room a group of high British officials and the American mission, who had only just stepped off the plane from the United States; he then tried to bully Harriman into stating exactly what 'implements of war' in what quantities the Americans would send to Russia, while Beaverbrook seemed to be suggesting that he would decide the nature and scale of British supplies only after he reached Moscow. His aim in this manoeuvre, Harriman thought, was to establish himself as the principal negotiator with Stalin, since under Beaverbrook's plan Harriman would have nothing to negotiate about; and in that case, Harriman told the meeting with some annoyance, there would be no point in the Americans going to Moscow at all. Fur flew, but Beaverbrook backed down.

Kathleen Harriman wrote home: 'Lord Beaverbrook doesn't like to be contradicted, and he's inclined to be set in his ways and views about people. . . . Dinner tonight (with Beaverbrook) was in rather sharp contrast to last night – with the P.M. One's a gentleman and the other is a ruffian. Ave, luckily, can talk both languages.'[20]

With every day that passed, it became clearer that the mission to Moscow would be rough going. On 4 September Stalin told Churchill that the Russian position in the Ukraine and Leningrad had 'considerably deteriorated' and that it was essential for Britain to open a second front somewhere in the Balkans or France. On 15 September Stalin made the wholly unreasonable demand that between twenty-five and thirty British divisions should at once be sent to fight in southern Russia. Nor were the British of one mind. On the 19th, at a contentious meeting of the Defence Committee, it became plain that the only participants wholeheartedly in favour of aid to Russia were Churchill; Eden, the Foreign Secretary; and Beaverbrook. Neither the service ministers nor the chiefs of staff could see how Russia could be helped without dangerously weakening Britain. But Churchill overrode the opposition. His fear, reinforced by the view of Russia's prospects being taken by Cripps and the military attachés at the British Embassy in Moscow, was that Stalin might make a separate peace. He therefore insisted that promises already given to Stalin about numbers of tanks and aircraft must be fulfilled, even at some risk to Britain. As for other supplies, '. . . it was only by the most determined insistence . . . that the PM was persuaded to give way sufficiently to allow me sufficient latitude to deal with the Russians'.[21] That referred to immediate supplies. For the future, Churchill gave Beaverbrook full discretion to encourage Stalin's hopes about the cornucopia of supplies that he could expect in the long run – a carrot of the kind that Beaverbrook had been expertly dangling in front of people ever since he sold the 'stuff' to the sceptical sea captains of New Brunswick.

Before leaving for Moscow, Beaverbrook made two moves intended to assist his dealings with Stalin. He and Churchill agreed on a Tanks For

Russia week, whereby all tanks produced in the seven days ending 27 September – just as Beaverbrook was due to arrive in Moscow – would be sent to Russia. Characteristically, Beaverbrook drafted a message 'To all workers in the tank factories' that read like a leader from the *Daily Express* – too much so for Churchill, who cut out a sentence saying that 'the bravery of the Russians, their fortitude and courage, the endurance they have shown, stir us all to admiration and praise'. However, the workers responded even to the toned-down message: tank production figures for the week went up by 20 per cent.

Beaverbrook's other move was to visit Rudolf Hess. The unheralded arrival of the Deputy Führer in Scotland on 10 May 1941, though a matter of intense concern to the authorities in Berlin, Moscow and London, had soon acquired its own comic mythology with the British public. Stories were told of how the Duke of Hamilton's butler had discreetly informed His Grace during dinner that a Mr Hess from Berlin had arrived in the grounds by parachute and would like a word; how the Duke, having inspected Hess, had returned and asked his guests if they thought he should perhaps telephone the Prime Minister; and how Churchill had told the Duke that, Hess or no Hess, he was watching a Marx Brothers film. But if the British thought the episode funny, it was regarded in a very different light both by Hitler, who was deeply depressed by what he took to be Hess's desertion, and by Stalin, who suspected that Hess had flown to Britain to make peace as the prelude to the German assault on Russia.

Beaverbrook had met Hess in Berlin before the war. German wartime diplomatic documents said he was 'the only man who has the courage, the power and the standing to bring about a change in England even against Churchill, since Churchill has for a long time been in Beaverbrook's pay' (possibly a garbled interpretation of Churchill's work for the *Evening Standard*).[22] Soon after Hess landed, the Lord Chancellor, Lord Simon, and Ivone Kirkpatrick of the Foreign Office interviewed him. It was essential that no one should know that a minister had seen Hess, lest it be thought that the British government was negotiating for peace; and so the authorities had decided that Simon and Kirkpatrick should assume the names of 'Dr Guthrie' and 'Dr Mackenzie' and be described to the guards as two well-known psychiatrists.[23] Kirkpatrick characterized the meeting as a Mad Hatter's Tea Party, with Simon unable to extract any sense from Hess beyond the fact that he had come to make an honourable settlement between Germany and Britain, and proposed, having done so, to return to Hitler in triumph.

Beaverbrook was one of only four people circulated with the Kirkpatrick report. Four months later, on 1 September, he wrote to Hess in Aldershot:

Dear Herr Hess,
    You will recollect our last meeting in the Chancellery in Berlin. It has been my intention of late to make the suggestion to you that we should have some

further conversation. So if this is convenient to you perhaps you would tell me where and when you would like the meeting to take place.[24]

Hess thanked Beaverbrook for his 'friendly letter' and said he would like a talk of 'an unofficial character'. No interpreter would be needed, he went on, because 'my English will be good enough'. Beaverbrook assured him: 'Everything that you say will of course be private' – except, he might have added, from the British government and Stalin.

Both on the War Office permit giving him access to Hess's place of detention in Aldershot, and in the verbatim transcript covertly made of the conversation, Beaverbrook was called 'Dr Livingstone'. Evidently the authorities assumed that the guards were not *Daily Express* readers.

The meeting took place in Hess's bedroom at 7.30 p.m. on 9 September. The exchange had its surrealistic moments, with Hess telling Beaverbrook that Hitler 'likes you very much' and Beaverbrook replying that his newspapers 'always gave him a good hearing'. If the conversation can be judged to have had a theme, it was Beaverbrook's attempt to pick Hess's brains about why Hitler had attacked Russia before he had finished the war with England. 'I can't understand the campaign for 1941,' he told Hess. If Hitler was going into Russia, why did he go into Yugoslavia? Why had he gone into Greece? Since he went to Greece and had captured Crete, why had he not gone on to Cyprus and Syria? Hess, long out of favour with Hitler, was in no position to answer these questions with authority; still, the meeting did give Beaverbrook some items he could feed to Stalin. Hess had handed him a twelve-page document predicting that Germany would defeat Russia, and that England would be forced to capitulate. If, on the other hand, England's hopes were realized and Germany was defeated, then the Bolshevik giant would be well on the way to its goal of world domination. Beaverbrook took his Hess documents with him to Moscow.

His role in the Hess affair had not been quite straightforward, however, and one person who believed him to have been vindictive was the Duke of Hamilton. In 1941 it was ten years since, as the twenty-seven-year-old Marquess of Clydesdale, he had refused to support the Empire Crusade in the East Renfrewshire by-election. Having won the election, he had remained an MP until his elevation in March 1940 to be the 14th Duke of Hamilton and premier peer of Scotland. From time to time he was sniped at – for spurious reasons, he thought – in Beaverbrook newspapers.[25]

Clydesdale was no effete Scottish aristocrat. After he stopped being a boxing champion, in 1933 he became the first pilot to fly over Mount Everest. Aviation was his main interest; he became an instructor in the Auxiliary Air Force. In August 1936 he went with other MPs to Berlin for the Olympic Games, but his real aim was to see something of the Luftwaffe, which he did, passing on the information he gleaned to the British Embassy in Berlin. He also made the acquaintance of Professor

Albrecht Haushofer, an ambivalent figure who had no illusions about the Third Reich (he was shot in 1945 by the SS) and yet was a close associate of Rudolf Hess. In 1938 General Milch invited Clydesdale to Germany to address an aviation society, but Clydesdale refused. Thus he had never met Hess until, after he was captured in Scotland, the German asked to see him.

The Duke was by then a wing commander in charge of a Scottish airfield. Having concluded that the unexpected visitor was, as he claimed, the Deputy Führer, the Duke flew south and saw Churchill, who, after looking at photographs of the prisoner, did indeed say, 'Well, Hess or no Hess I am going to see the Marx Brothers' – though after the film he questioned Clydesdale for over an hour. On 12 May the government made a bare announcement saying that Hess had arrived. Colville recorded in his diary for 13 May: 'The poor Duke of Hamilton feels acutely the slur of being taken for a potential Quisling – which he certainly is not.'[26] On 14 May Churchill drafted a full statement, detailing Hess's confused ramblings to his interrogators, which he proposed to make in the Commons next day. Eden objected, saying that the Germans must be kept guessing; and so did Beaverbrook. Churchill abandoned the idea, then returned to it. Again Eden and Beaverbrook dissuaded him. Churchill raised the matter once more, in the War Cabinet; Eden recalled: 'Lord Beaverbrook told me afterwards that we might have to "strangle the infant" a third time, but fortunately it was not reborn.'[27]

Fortunate it may have been for Eden and Beaverbrook, but it was unfortunate for the Duke, since a statement by the Prime Minister would have removed the slur. As it was, he was sworn to secrecy. On 15 May the *Express* splashed the story: 'HESS: I WANTED TO SEE THE DUKE OF HAMILTON: WROTE FIRST – NO REPLY'. A picture of the Duke in uniform was captioned: 'Met Hess at Olympic Games'. No reader could have failed to conclude that the Duke was somehow implicated in Hess's 'plan for peace'. A week of intense speculation passed with no government statement, while the Duke suffered in enforced silence what he understandably construed as 'insinuations' about his patriotism, particularly in the *Sunday Express*.

On 22 May the Air Minister, Sir Archibald Sinclair – not Churchill – finally told the Commons that Hamilton had never met Hess, and 'contrary to reports which have appeared in some newspapers', had never been in correspondence with him: 'It will be seen that the conduct of the Duke of Hamilton has been in every respect honourable and proper'; the statement was published by the *Express* on an inside page. Thus armed, the Duke consulted his lawyer. He secured an apology from Harry Pollitt, the Communist leader, who had been distributing libellous pamphlets. His lawyer, Godfrey Norris, also called on John Gordon, editor-in-chief of the *Sunday Express*, and urged him to withdraw damaging statements that the Duke had met Hess before the war and had been in contact with him after the war started. Gordon agreed to do so. Arriving for a second visit, Norris was told that Gordon was with the 'management'; when he came in, his attitude had markedly changed and he now declared the Air Ministry statement 'false', and himself ready to defend the *Sunday Express* in the courts. Norris concluded that 'management' meant 'owner'; only one man had the power to over-rule Gordon.[28]

What was the explanation for Beaverbrook's hostility towards a man rarely in the news and otherwise without enemies? One possible reason for his conduct was that he wished to distract attention from his own connections. Unlike the Duke, Beaverbrook had met Hess. Beaverbrook had been in close touch with the 'pacifists' of the Independent Labour Party when an ILP candidate fought the March 1940 by-election in East Renfrewshire caused by the Duke's elevation. Rumours and allegations about Beaverbrook's peace-mongering were in the air in the early summer of 1941. Churchill told the Commons that no credence should be given to them. But Beaverbrook was still worried by what he called 'a series of rumours' about his old connections with the 'peace front' in the following year. He wrote to Brendan Bracken on 20 June 1942: 'Do you think that any part of the fault lies with me?' Bracken reassured him – 'like all lively men you are pursued by a band of snapping critics'; but the truthful answer would have been 'Yes'.[29]

SCAPA FLOW TO ARCHANGEL

As the mission to Moscow prepared to set off, the Russian Ambassador in London, Maisky, described it as 'the hope of the world', and spoke of 'a turning point in history'.[30] This last phrase was not mere rhetoric, since the theme of the Second World War was whether Hitler could achieve his stated aim of turning Germany into a world power, a greater German Reich, that would stretch from the Pyrenees to the Urals and the Caucasus, and command natural resources equalling those of the United States. The mission was the first sign that resources situated outside Europe, in the Urals and the United States, were going to be combined to thwart this aim – and, indeed, to destroy Germany as a power altogether.

Originally Beaverbrook had expected to fly to Moscow, as he told Hess, in one of the new long-range American bombers, the B24s, but the War Cabinet secretariat decided that there would be less risk of enemy attack or delay by bad weather if the mission travelled by sea. Besides preparing himself by assembling all the information he could get hold of about Russian industry, Beaverbrook took the precaution of sending on ahead a member of his staff with instructions to 'get me a quiet bedroom to sleep in'. HMS *London*, a cruiser, was the ship chosen. Beaverbrook and Harriman were allotted the admiral's and captain's day cabins; '. . . generals and other senior officers will sleep on the floor in passageways'. So on 21 September twenty-three members of the British mission, and eleven

Americans, sailed from Scapa Flow for Archangel. The British party included Harold Balfour, Under Secretary for Air; General 'Pug' Ismay, military secretary to the Cabinet and Churchill's universally trusted right-hand man; Rowlands, the civil servant; Churchill's doctor, Sir Charles Wilson; and a valet – Beaverbrook never travelled without one, even to Moscow. Churchill warned Beaverbrook and Ismay to be careful not to let slip any clue that Britain had broken German codes – Beaverbrook was one of the handful of people with access to the de-cyphered German messages known as Ultra. Orders were issued saying that 'no secret paper will be taken into Russia unless it has been approved by Lord Beaverbrook himself'. Among his papers, Beaverbrook carried a letter from Churchill to Stalin saying that 'Lord Beaverbrook has the fullest confidence of the Cabinet, and is one of my oldest and most intimate friends.'[31]

The aim of the mission, as Beaverbrook saw it, was nothing less than to keep Russia in the war; if Russia was conquered, the war would be lost. The method must be to bolster Russian morale; to encourage Russia's 'martial spirit'; and to remove all thoughts of a separate peace by confirming to Stalin that Britain and the United States would send the numbers of tanks and aircraft already stipulated, and by undertaking to supply whatever else the Russians needed, as far as possible.

All agreed that the success of the mission depended on Stalin. To amuse himself on the voyage, Beaverbrook teased his British colleagues by telling them that there would be little for them to do in Moscow as he proposed to do all the work himself, face to face with Stalin. The problem was Stalin's distrust. As soon as Beaverbrook agreed to lead the mission, he had asked his officials how much material had been sent to Russia thus far: '. . . very little,' he was told – mainly rubber; the two hundred Hurricanes promised by Churchill had not so far been sent.[32] Yet two months had passed since Churchill, immediately after the German attack, had pledged 'whatever help we can to Russia and the Russian people'. Who, Stalin might well ask, did the British want to win the war in Russia? Or were they hoping that Russia and Germany would knock one another out? Exchanges between Moscow and London had been less than friendly. Stalin had not been pleased by Britain's response to his demand of 4 September that the British must open a second front to relieve pressure on Russia. Churchill – restrained, Beaverbrook thought, by undue reliance on his cautious Chiefs of Staff – told Stalin that a second front 'must depend on unforeseeable events'; and instructed Cripps to explain to Stalin that Britain could not invade Europe in strength 'without diversion of shipping and naval strength paralysing to our supply of the Middle East'.[33]

Before Hitler attacked, Beaverbrook had been opposed to the 'exporting' of 'the implements of war' he thought should be kept for the defence of Britain. After the attack, his attitude changed. Now he was in favour of diversionary assaults to help the Russians. On 14 September he proposed a raid on the port of Cherbourg 'without delay', which would 'surprise the enemy and encourage our friends' and 'would be evidence to the Russians of our good faith'.[34] In the War Cabinet he became the champion of all-out aid for Stalin, even at the expense of Britain. On the eve of Beaverbrook's departure, Churchill felt it necessary to warn him that he must 'make sure that we are not bled white in the process and even if you find yourself affected by the Russian atmosphere I shall be quite stiff about it here'.[35] Harriman dictated a memorandum on the way to Archangel: 'When B. makes up his mind he oversimplifies to the point of disregard of other considerations. He now claims that the PM underestimates Russia. I can see no indication of this and, in fact, share the PM's views regarding the importance of Turkey and the Middle East. I am personally also less ready to strip England than either of them.'[36]

On the voyage, Beaverbrook explained his strategy to his colleagues. He was going to Moscow, he said, not 'to bargain but to give'. Cripps, frustrated by an impenetrable wall of Russian suspicion and secrecy, wanted the mission to trade supplies in exchange for information about Russian production and Russian plans. Beaverbrook maintained that the way to break down the suspicion that had led to the secrecy was 'to make clear beyond a doubt the British and American intention to satisfy Russian needs to the utmost, whether the Russians gave anything or not. It was to be a Christmas tree party, and there must be no excuse for the Russians thinking they were not getting a fair share of the gifts on the tree.' He proposed to ask Stalin what he wanted and give it to him. Military discussions, Beaverbrook told Ismay, would not be allowed to cut across negotiations about aid.[37]

On the third day out, as the *London* sailed far to the north to avoid the German Air Force based in Norway, Beaverbrook showed signs of euphoria. On Ministry of Supply writing paper, bearing a Ministry crest, he wrote an extraordinary letter to Robertson at the *Express*; it was dated 24 September, which would have put Beaverbrook somewhere off Bear Island, the nearest he ever got to the Arctic Circle. 'I have been reading the paper,' he wrote.

You should improve it. It is not nearly as valuable a paper as you could give at the present time.

You should have much better foreign correspondents, and a good deal more attention should be paid to the foreign service of the paper.

Your centre page article ought now to be more informative and it should have some valuable contribution from abroad – really valuable, written by men who are trained to see and have a reputation for doing so.

Add more – a good bit more – to your editorial charges.

Give up now the popular presentation of small events. The front page should be a document of the war. You do not want any more net sales, and you should make no popular appeal whatsoever.

Here is an opportunity for your young fellows to build up the greatest newspaper in the world – the greatest ever imagined. On your net sale you can build so soundly and so well.

    All this must be done with serious thought. And when the decision has been taken and the line settled, it will be still more difficult to sustain.[38]

This is perhaps the only example of the proprietor of a popular newspaper telling his staff to stop being popular. Was Beaverbrook thinking of the readers, or did he suddenly feel that the *Express* ought to become more internationally minded and thus keep in step with his own new role as the honest broker of future relations between Moscow, Washington and London?

    Having reached the mouth of the Dvina river, the mission transferred to a Russian destroyer for the brief journey to Archangel. On board to greet them with toasts and speeches was the Soviet Foreign Minister, Molotov, who, the mission had been warned in a letter to Ismay from General Mason-Macfarlane, the military attaché in Moscow, was 'one of the most unpleasant creatures I have ever met'.[39] From Archangel the party flew to Moscow in four Russian aircraft which were fired on by Russian anti-aircraft guns as they skimmed the autumnal trees – an event that did not increase the visitors' respect for their new ally's efficiency and caused Beaverbrook to remark that, whatever else Stalin might need, he did not need any more anti-aircraft guns.

'STALIN LIKED THE JOKE'

Beaverbrook stayed at the Hotel Nationale in Moscow, not the British Embassy. He had told Harriman on the voyage that he was always ill at ease with teetotallers, especially socialist teetotallers who were candidates for sainthood. More important, he was determined to exclude Cripps from the negotiations, to give himself a free hand. Harriman likewise excluded the American Ambassador.[40]

    No sooner had the mission arrived than Beaverbrook and Harriman learned that Stalin had agreed to see them at once: a good omen. They drove together in an Embassy Packard through blacked-out Moscow to a camouflaged Kremlin; Harriman found it 'an eerie experience'. Guards shone torches into their faces; a heavy gate swung open; and then the visitors were led to Stalin's office, a large room dominated by large portraits of Lenin, Marx and Engels, with a desk that looked unused and a big table against the wall furthest from the window. Stalin, heavy moustache flecked with grey, wearing a brown tunic without decorations, greeted them correctly but with reserve. Beside him stood Molotov, and next in line Litvinov, the Foreign Minister whom Molotov had replaced. Both Harriman and Beaverbrook had known Litvinov in his prime, when he had championed collective security at the League of Nations in Geneva; and both now were shocked by his appearance. It had been Beaverbrook's idea to make what he hoped would be seen as a friendly gesture by asking the Russians to supply an interpreter. They proposed their Ambassador to Washington, but Harriman had a low opinion of him and instead, only three hours before the meeting, Harriman and Beaverbrook asked for Litvinov. 'They dug him up from somewhere,' Beaverbrook recalled. 'He was a pathetic figure. Shabby, worn, with holes in his shoes'.[41] Nobody mentioned, apparently, Beaverbrook's meeting with Litvinov and Stalin in 1929.

'Stalin did all the talking,' Harriman recalled. When Molotov tried to say anything, Stalin brushed him aside. Cripps had predicted that Stalin would avoid any discussion of Russia's beleaguered military state, but he did not; he talked candidly about Germany's preponderance in tanks and aircraft, the superiority of the Russian infantry and the importance of holding Moscow at all costs – which both British and American embassies had doubted. Tanks, he said, were what he needed most: 2500 a month, of which 1400 could be produced in Russia. The visitors offered him 500 a month. He named other needs: anti-aircraft guns, bombers, fighter and reconnaissance planes, barbed wire. He also suggested to Beaverbrook that Britain should send troops to fight in the Ukraine. When Beaverbrook replied that perhaps some of the British troops already in the Middle East might be moved to the Caucasus, Stalin said: 'There is no war in the Caucasus. But there is in the Ukraine.'

That moment apart, the talks went far better than either Beaverbrook or Harriman had expected; Beaverbrook thought it a good sign when at 8 p.m. tea was served, with cakes placed in the middle of the big table. He told Harriman that he had been 'very hungry but as the cakes were not offered him he didn't take any but ate a lump of sugar that had been offered him instead'. By the time they left the Kremlin, it was after midnight and both visitors were 'more than pleased'. Beaverbrook, who all his life sought to tie up deals at speed, talked with a touch of euphoria of having one more session the next day and then going home. He was restrained by Harriman, who reminded him that they were due to meet Molotov next morning to set up six tripartite committees to discuss aircraft, Army, Navy, transport, raw materials and medical supplies, which would teach the Americans and British something about Russia's strengths and weaknesses; Mason-Macfarlane had been complaining to Ismay that the Russians were holding back information and technical assistance that would be of great value.

Next evening, at 7 p.m., armed with the committees' reports on the day's work, Beaverbrook and Harriman again drove to the Kremlin. Stalin had noticed Litvinov's appearance, and this time 'he came walking in dressed up to the nines – new suit, new shoes, new shirt, everything'. Otherwise everything had inexplicably gone downhill. 'Stalin was very restless,' Beaverbrook noted, 'walking about and smoking continuously, and appeared to both of us to be under an intense strain.' First he said that three-quarters of any aircraft sent him should be bombers and only

one-quarter fighters. 'We expressed surprise. . . . He made no explanation.' Then he said he would be 'entirely satisfied' with three fighters to
one bomber. He showed signs of animation when Harriman offered him
5000 jeeps; he accepted, then abruptly asked for more. Beaverbrook had
kept Churchill's personal letter in reserve; now, when he handed it to
Stalin, the Russian leader ripped open the envelope, barely glanced at the
letter and left it unread on the table throughout the meeting. His whole
demeanour expressed dissatisfaction with what he was being offered, and
at one point he openly questioned their good faith: 'The paucity of your
offers', he said, 'clearly shows that you want to see the Soviet Union
defeated.'

No tea and cakes were served on this occasion. Beaverbrook scribbled
a note to himself: 'Open door'. Someone out of sight, he guessed, in a
dark room behind the door, was checking up on Litvinov's translation. At
nine o'clock, with little settled, Stalin said he had to leave. Beaverbrook
pointed out that they had not yet even mentioned raw materials. Stalin
said they could talk to Mikoyan, the Foreign Trade Commissar. Beaverbrook said that would not be convenient, because the issue must be settled
and Stalin alone could give the final word. Stalin then offered, to
Beaverbrook's and Harriman's great relief, to meet them again the next
evening.

It had been, Harriman noted, 'very tough going'; and 'Max was rattled'.
After the meeting he talked to Harriman about the damage that would be
done to his political reputation if the mission was a failure; and the message
he sent back to London that night was less than frank about Stalin's
hostility and unpleasantness. Beaverbrook 'was constantly thinking about
his own reputation with his colleagues in the British government',
Harriman recalled. 'It was for this reason, I suppose, that he asked me to
present at the third meeting the list of weapons and materials that the
British and American governments were prepared to supply. Then, if
things did not go well, the fire would be directed at me.'

The third meeting went much better, however, though the door still
mysteriously stood open. 'We developed our tactics in the form of
cumulative effect,' Beaverbrook said later. 'That is, we built up the
concessions that we would make from time to time and followed up with
lists of articles that could not be conceded. Then a long list of materials
with which we were in agreement.' Harriman methodically went through
the numbered list until Beaverbrook, sensing a change in Stalin's mood,
passed him a scribbled note reading, 'I suggest stop at 70 and wait.'
Harriman stopped, and Beaverbrook asked Stalin if he was satisfied. Stalin
smiled and nodded. 'Shortly after, at one moment, the interpreter Litvinov
bounded out of his seat and cried with passion, "Now we shall win the
war".'

When the list was finished Beaverbrook began to add to his offers,
asking expansively whether the Russians wanted bombs, flares, instru-

ments, etc., which he said he could supply in substantial quantities. Harriman told Stalin that if necessary he would gladly come back; Beaverbrook whispered, 'I won't.' Talk became general. Stalin wanted the British to threaten Finland. How could they force Turkey into the war? He raised the question of a treaty with Britain after the war. Beaverbrook said that he personally would favour it; the Defence Committee – Churchill, Attlee, Eden and himself – 'would decide the question without consultation with anyone else'. Stalin then himself raised the subject of Hess with Beaverbrook: '. . . he said the German ambassador had told him that Hess was crazy. I expressed my view that Hess was not crazy.' Beaverbrook believed that Hess, with Hitler's knowledge, had come to Britain under the illusion that a small group of aristocrats could set up an anti-Churchill government to make a peace with Germany that would be welcomed by a majority of the British people. Germany with British help would then attack Russia. 'Stalin', Harriman noted, 'relished the amusing and detailed comments by Beaverbrook who was in his best form as a raconteur.'

Rough jokes followed. Stalin asked if Ambassador Maisky lectured Beaverbrook on Communist doctrine.

Beaverbrook: 'I don't give him a chance. What about our fellow?'

Stalin: 'Oh, he's all right.'

Beaverbrook observed that there was nothing wrong with Cripps except that he was a bore.

Stalin: 'In that respect, is he comparable to Maisky?'

Beaverbrook: 'No, to Madame Maisky.'

Beaverbrook flattered himself that 'Stalin liked the joke immensely'. The meeting ended, Harriman reported, in the 'most friendly fashion possible'.

Beaverbrook told London:

> The plan of campaign laid down by Mr Harriman and me had been carried out with precision. There had not been any hitch. The structure of it was simply this.
>
> 1. The story from Stalin of his military situation.
> 2. A niggardly and grudging account of available assistance.
> 3. A generous and bountiful list of available supplies culminating in an enthusiastic acceptance. It was sunshine after rain.

Harriman cautioned Roosevelt: 'This paragraph about our plans for the three nights is written after the event. The facts are we had hoped to be able to finish our discussions with Stalin the second evening, as we were afraid he might not be willing to continue to meet with us personally, but his attitude and mood on this evening made it quite impossible.' Whether Stalin had been worried by military news, or 'considered that he would get more if he was tough with us', or was 'just moody', he and Beaverbrook

416

did not know.

Beaverbrook, who scribbled notes to himself in Moscow as he did in London, wrote after the third meeting with Stalin: 'Drawing wolves'. Later he expanded the note: 'Draws pictures of wolves while talking and fills in background with coloured pencil.' In a memorandum that night he wrote:

> While the interpreter translated Stalin's words to us, Stalin occupied himself by drawing numberless pictures of wolves on paper and filling in the background with red pencil.
>
> Altogether at this time we had spent over eight hours with Stalin in continuous conversation. We had got to like him – a kindly man with a habit when agitated of walking about the floor with his hands behind his back. He smoked a great deal and practically never shows any impatience at all.

Next day, 1 October, Beaverbrook and Harriman reviewed the work of the committees and in the evening attended a great banquet in the Catherine the Great Hall in the Kremlin. On a previous evening Ulanova had danced *Swan Lake* in their honour; she had been summoned to Moscow from somewhere behind the Urals, where, with Leningrad under German siege, the Kirov Ballet had been evacuated. On that occasion, Beaverbrook and Harriman had had deputy Foreign Minister Vishinsky, formerly state prosecutor at the show trials that purged Stalin's rivals, sitting between them; now they had Stalin. Harriman thought the lavishness of the banquet 'disgusting'; whereas Churchill was always careful to conform to British rations, the Kremlin menu, at a time when the Russian people were hungry, started with hors d'oeuvres, various forms of caviar and fish, went on to cold suckling pig, hot soup, chicken and a game bird, and finished with ice cream and cakes for dessert; each man had in front of him a number of bottles containing pepper vodka, red and white wine, and a Russian brandy, with champagne to accompany the dessert.

Beaverbrook's attention was concentrated on Stalin, and he behaved like a journalist, scribbling notes and writing them up immediately afterwards. His notes read: 'Drank continuously during dinner from small glass (liqueur) which he replenished always. Kept a glass on top of champagne bottle which explained to preserve gas. Ate well and even heartily. Promoted toast drinking.' He observed that Stalin ate caviar with his knife and without any bread and butter. Conversation during the evening ranged widely. Stalin told Beaverbrook that Lady Astor, on her visit to Moscow, had talked to him about the Bible. He said 'he went to bed at 4 am–6 am in these troubled times. He said he slept until noon and sometimes until 2 pm.' He defended his treaty with Hitler by arguing that Munich had convinced him that the British were trying to divert German aggression to the east; and he feared standing alone.

More ominously, he asked Beaverbrook about a second front, saying, 'What's the use of having an army if it doesn't fight?', and telling Ismay

417

that Britain could not rely on sea power alone and must build up her martial spirit. Given that Russia had not lifted a finger to help Britain for two years, Harriman thought these remarks lacked tact. Beaverbrook wrote a memoir to himself describing how, after dinner, at about midnight, they went into a room 'beautifully furnished. I . . . was told that the furniture had been provided by Nicholas the First. I then said that I liked sleeping in great four-poster beds.' Shortly, Stalin led the way to a cinema:

. . . he walked through with his back bent and his hands behind his back, which is a characteristic pose.

Immediately we sat down some nuts were brought to us. Stalin had some.

Before the performance began, Stalin put his lavatory at my disposal. I did not avail myself of the privilege. He then made use of it himself. On his return, he asked if we would like some more champagne. I agreed. This time a bottle was brought. Stalin poured some for me and took a large glass himself, placing the bottle down in front of him.

All this time there was a considerable guard in the vicinity of Stalin – alert men, big of stature, possibly a Georgian bodyguard. I did not ask anything about them.

Stalin drank plenty of champagne during the picture and the moment the performance began he ceased to talk. Litvinov, who addressed him on my behalf as Comrade Stalin, could only get brief and terse answers. . . .

After a little, and while the picture was still running, Stalin went off to the lavatory for the second time.

Two pictures were shown. Stalin made no comment on either of them. But when the comedy was shown he laughed long at some of the jokes, which were quite unintelligible to us.

He said he had not seen the first, which was a war picture, for 2 years. The second picture, which was a comedy, seemed to engross him, and I came to the conclusion that he sees the cinema quite often, although a question to this effect was answered in the negative.

We left him at 1.30 when he suggested a third picture. I would like to have stayed, but I knew I could not keep awake any longer.

Beaverbrook's other notes of the evening said:

I asked if Kalinin had a mistress, as I had been told that he had an actress friend. Stalin said he was too old.

He made a joke about his Minister of Information, who was present sitting near him and constantly raising his glass to Stalin. I could not quite follow the point of it but possibly it related to the inability of that functionary to take decisions without referring his problems to higher authority.

His curiosity about Churchill was insatiable.

His hatred of Hitler appears to be real.

His confidence in the Americans and Great Britain is limited.

His power I should have thought is absolute, and the bottleneck the most effective in history.

Before leaving Moscow, Beaverbrook sent a message to the workers in the British tank factories: 'Boys! Oh, Boys! You have raised the roof and lifted the lid and beaten the band. Now let us show them that we can do the same and better for a Tanks for Britain week.' He wrote a farewell message to Stalin, saying that 'it is with confident anticipation that I review this morning the work of the last five days', expressing 'entire confidence in your higher command', and signing himself 'Yours fraternally'. He sent Molotov 'warm thanks' for his leadership 'and for the kindness you showed me'. Perhaps more genuinely, he thanked the American Ambassador for his 'beautiful present' of Aunt Jemima pancake mix, which 'has been taken to my heart and my belly'.[42]

He was on top of the world, feeling that he had 'got along well with Stalin. I made my way with him'.[43] Harriman told Roosevelt: 'Beaverbrook has been a great salesman. His personal sincerity was convincing. His genius never worked more effectively.' Ismay, freely admitting that he had been apprehensive about Beaverbrook's 'daring' plan of action, wrote to him later to say that if he, Ismay, had been 'playing the hand', he would have advised a more cautious and methodical and stereotyped line of approach. 'In the event your plan led to a glorious success; mine would have utterly failed. We would still be there – or perhaps trekking eastwards!'[44] Rowlands thought that Beaverbrook had got on 'amazingly well' with Stalin, making a stronger impression than any previous visitor from England, the reason being that they were 'both racketeers' and could understand each other.[45]

The air journey from Moscow back to Archangel was 'so rough as to be unbearable at times', and 'all suffered' – Beaverbrook told the Russian Ambassador to Washington, in thanking him for a present of gramophone records – 'except Harriman and myself'. Transferring at night in rough seas from a minesweeper to the *London*, Harriman and the others managed to scramble across a gangway between the two ships, but the sixty-two-year-old Beaverbrook had to be lifted across by breeches buoy. Harriman gave his fur gloves, scarves and galoshes to a young American Embassy official to protect him against the coming Russian winter. Beaverbrook, who had lost one of his gloves, 'peeled poor Russell [John Russell of the British Embassy] of all the fur clothing he had'.[46]

CHAPTER 20

CHAMPION OF RUSSIA
1941–1945

BEAVERBROOK RETURNED FROM Moscow in triumph. The train carrying 'the men from Russia', as the *Evening Standard* called them, arrived at Euston precisely on time at 10.12 a.m. on Friday, 10 October. 'The conference', said Harriman at a brief ceremony of greeting, 'was a great achievement on the part of Lord Beaverbrook.' At 10.15 Beaverbrook jammed his black hat on his head, ducked under a thick red rope barrier, hopped into his car, and drove off to the Ministry of Supply.

That night, Beaverbrook and Harriman dined with Churchill. In Moscow, Beaverbrook had bought 25lb of caviar for the wardroom officers of HMS *London* and friends in Britain, including Churchill. The *News Chronicle* reported that this luxurious consignment was all for Churchill, who sent off a blistering telegram to Beaverbrook. At dinner, Beaverbrook argued about the rights and wrongs of the caviar incident until Harriman changed the subject. 'Churchill seemed greatly reassured by our reports of Stalin's determination to fight on. He was not however so totally absorbed in affairs of state that he had forgotten the argument. Turning to Beaverbrook as we left the dining room, he said, ' "Now, after all the talk, where is that caviar?" '[1]

Next day Beaverbrook held a press conference, well attended by American as well as British journalists, and on Sunday night broadcast to the nation. He began with a dramatic account, staccato and vigorous, of the mission's arrival: 'It was Sunday morning. The airplanes landed smoothly on the airfield at Moscow . . . as night fell, Mr Harriman and I drove up the hill to the Kremlin.' Practically everything asked by the Russians had been agreed, he said. Aircraft and tanks, 'guns we have promised also, a few big guns, plenty of good guns and plenty of ammunition. Raw materials too, aluminium, copper, zinc, tin, cobalt, brass, rubber, jute, wool, phosphorus and diamonds, shellac . . . .'

There followed perhaps the most sympathetic portrait of Stalin ever broadcast by the BBC.

Is he an easy man to satisfy? Not so. He is an exacting man, even though he does not look it. He is short of stature. Well dressed, very well dressed. There is nothing slovenly about him.

He is always ready to laugh, quick to see a joke and willing to make one. His eyes are alert. His face quickly reflects his emotions. Gloom and joy are marked therein. His countenance lights up with pleasure when the word of assent is given.

He is a judge of values, and his knowledge of armaments is vast and wide, comparable only to that of our own Prime Minister.

Stalin 'trusts us, Harriman and me. He puts his faith in our pledges.' Beaverbrook went on to praise every aspect of the Russians' war effort: their 'genius for mechanisation', the efficiency of their production methods, the skill of their pilots, the quality of their aircraft. They would make good use of any help Britain and the United States could provide. Britain, for her part, must plan for the production of tanks and aircraft on a scale 'vaster than any yet laid down or by many even contemplated'. He ended on a high note: 'Shadows we will endure with them, and sunshine we will share with them. . . . These are the promises we made to Stalin in Moscow in your name. These are the pledges we shall carry out.'[2]

Perhaps this was the most important speech of Beaverbrook's life. As Minister of Supply, he had been made responsible for material aid to Russia; now he was taking responsibility for Britain's political relations with Russia as well. The outcome of the war, he implied, depended on the trust established between himself and Stalin on the one hand, and on an alliance between himself and British factory workers on the other. He spoke using Churchillian rhetoric, like the second man in the kingdom.

In Cabinet, he went further. On 19 October, at Shell-Mex House, George Malcolm Thomson drafted a memorandum headed 'Assistance to Russia' for Beaverbrook to submit to the Defence Committee of the War Cabinet. It read like an *Express* leader:

There is today only one military problem – how to help Russia. Yet on that issue the Chiefs of Staff content themselves with saying that nothing can be done. They point out the difficulties, but make no suggestions for overcoming them. . . .

The Chiefs of Staff would have us wait until the last button has been sewn on the last gaiter before we launch an attack. They ignore the present opportunity.

. . . If we do not help them now the Russians may collapse. And, freed at last from anxiety about the East, Hitler will concentrate all his forces against us in the West.

The Germans will not wait then until we are ready. And it is folly for us to wait now. We must strike before it is too late.[3]

The War Cabinet Defence Committee met next day at Downing Street, with Churchill in the chair and the memorandum before them. The minutes recorded:

The Prime Minister said that the paper expressed the impulse which the whole Committee felt, but he had not taken it as meant to be an attack requiring a reply in detail.

Lord Beaverbrook said that it was intended to be an attack. He found himself in disagreement with his colleagues on the Russian issue. He wished to take advantage of the rising temper in the country for helping Russia. Others didn't. He wanted to make a supreme effort to raise production so as to help Russia. Others didn't. He wanted to fulfil in every particular the agreement made in Moscow. Others didn't. He wished the Army to act in support of Russia. The Chiefs of Staff didn't. The line of cleavage between himself and his colleagues and the Chiefs of Staff was complete.[4]

Colonel Jacob was taking the minutes. When Beaverbrook went on to say that if he could not secure his colleagues' agreement he would have to 'consider his position', Jacob thought, as he later remembered: 'Hullo. This chap wants the top job. Then Churchill did what I can only describe in poker terms: he saw him. He said in that case they would *all* have to "consider their positions".'[5]

Beaverbrook did not at once raise the stakes, though he left his money on the table. He argued for an immediate attack on the Germans in Norway. Churchill said that he too would have liked to attack Norway, but such a move, which in any case could not be mounted before December, would merely perhaps cause the Germans to pull back a division from Finland or move one or two up from the Low Countries to replace those from Oslo moved up to meet the attack; they certainly would not interrupt their operations on the Eastern Front. Beaverbrook declined to back down. He said that 'the arguments in favour of the operation in Norway were convincing'; then he complained that 'we were not fulfilling what was decided upon on supplies to Russia under the Moscow Agreement', especially shipments of aircraft and spare parts for tanks. Churchill replied that he had deliberately made Beaverbrook chairman of the executive to deal with such matters, and if there were any shortcomings it was open to him to report them immediately to the War Cabinet.

Publicly, all was sweetness and light between Moscow and London. Maisky, the Russian Ambassador, was made an honorary member of the Athenaeum, and the *Evening Standard* envisaged a time when he might sit down to a rubber of bridge with his fellow members, the Archbishop of Canterbury, Mr Montagu Norman and Churchill.[6] 'All aid to Russia' was 'now established as the dominant, guiding principle of British strategy', the *Standard* said. A Low cartoon in that paper showed Beaverbrook, in magician's cloak and pointed hat, grinning and waving his magic wand outside a tank factory and saying, 'Boy, oh Boy! Now watch me do something really BIGSKY!'

Behind the scenes, on 27 October Cripps reported to the War Cabinet that relations with Stalin were getting worse. If Britain could not open a second front, the only way to improve matters was to send troops;

Churchill replied that Britain could not send troops. In November, Stalin and Churchill had a sharp exchange over a Russian request for Britain to declare war on Finland, Hungary and Rumania. Ministry of Supply civil servants found the Russians in London so suspicious that they refused to make morale-boosting tours of the British factories that were making tanks for their army.[7]

Beaverbrook's single-minded enthusiasm for pacifying and supporting Stalin disturbed others. Cripps, already angry that Beaverbrook had excluded him from the negotiations with Stalin, was incredulous when he found out, two weeks after Beaverbrook returned to London, that he had not even been fully informed of their content. He particularly complained about Beaverbrook's acceptance of a Stalin proposal for Russia and Britain to open talks about the shape of post-war Europe; the result would only be to make Stalin still more suspicious when they did not happen.[8] The Chiefs of Staff were dismayed when Beaverbrook recommended Eden, the Foreign Secretary, who was about to set off on a pacifying mission to Stalin in December, to arrive with an offer of 'a force in one hand and more supplies in the other'.

Macmillan, as Beaverbrook's second-in-command, fed his ambition. As Minister of Supply Beaverbrook controlled most of the factories but not their supply of labour, which was the responsibility of the Minister of Labour, Ernest Bevin. Beaverbrook could not work with Bevin. This was not entirely Beaverbrook's fault; even Oliver Franks was critical of Bevin's sluggish mobilization of women for factory work. Beaverbrook tried his usual methods. He sent out his own recruiting agents, which led Bevin to burst out, 'This is not government but anarchy.' He produced his own manpower figures. When, in Cabinet, Bevin said he did not trust them, Churchill asked whose figures would he trust. 'Mr Franks's,' said Bevin. Franks set an assistant secretary, Douglas Jay, and his statisticians to work. They reported that Franks could justify the Minister's figures, but only by an elaborate statistical sleight of hand. 'That', said the magisterial Franks, 'would be chicanery.'[9] Macmillan found the position as unsatisfactory as did Beaverbrook. On 13 October he wrote to Beaverbrook saying that unless changes were made the government would not last; Macmillan's proposed solution was to divide the war and home fronts, with Churchill in charge of one and Beaverbrook running the other. On 28 October he wrote again, stressing the need for a Production Ministry that would include labour.[10] Beaverbrook responded by trying to woo Bevin, telling 'my dear Ernie' that 'there is a desire on my part to serve you', and signing his letter 'yours ever, Max'.[11] But Bevin remained immune to Beaverbrook's flattery; and Churchill saw no need for a Production Ministry.

On 17 November at Pratt's club Macmillan ran into Harold Nicolson, who recorded Macmillan's view of Beaverbrook in his diary: 'He thinks him half mad and half genius. He says that he thinks only of his present work, and that all his old fortune, newspapers and women are completely forgotten. But he also says that Beaverbrook gives no man his complete confidence.' As his frustrations multiplied, Farrer found him 'at his most irascible. Nockels [the valet] was harried mercilessly.'[12] Beaverbrook wrote to Churchill: 'I am the victim of the Furies. On the rock-bound coast of New Brunswick the waves break incessantly. Every now and then comes a particularly dangerous wave that breaks viciously on the rocks. It is called "The Rage". That's me.'[13] Churchill wrote to his son Randolph: 'Things are pretty hard here now that the asthma season has come on. Max fights everybody and resigns every day.'[14] One day, in a Cabinet meeting, Beaverbrook wheezed so badly that Churchill thought it was his cat.

'EXORCISE THIS BOTTLE IMP'

On 7 December 1941 the whole course of the war was transformed for the second time in the year when the Japanese bombed Pearl Harbor – a 'supreme world event', in Churchill's phrase – and the United States declared war. Then Germany declared war on the United States. A week later, Beaverbrook was the only Cabinet minister who sailed with Churchill to Washington in the Navy's newest battleship, the *Duke of York*, for the first Anglo–American discussion on global strategy. Beaverbrook was always assured of a generous welcome in the United States, and now that Britain and the USA were allies he was greeted with extra warmth.

Letters, telegrams, invitations and Christmas messages poured in, showing the exceptional range of the North Americans he knew: family – his doctor brother Arthur at the Niagara Sanitarium in Lockport, New York; his sister Rahno in California, where she, like Beaverbrook, was suffering from asthma; newspapermen – Henry Luce of *Time-Life*, Arthur Sulzberger of the *New York Times*, Damon Runyon and his wife; film people – Jack Warner of Warner Brothers, Walter Wanger of Universal, Darryl Zanuck; millionaires like Joseph Kennedy, who had belatedly changed his tune about Germany winning the war; politicians – Mackenzie King of Canada, Henry Morgenthau of the US Treasury; showbusiness – Eddie Duchin the pianist, and Gertrude Lawrence, who pressed him to cut the red tape delaying a tour of Britain by Jack Benny, Fred Astaire, Ginger Rogers and Deanna Durbin. There were echoes of his past: A. R. Doble, his ally in the cement merger, had died in Montreal; Helen Fotheringham recalled the old days in Chatham forty years earlier and the skating rink and toboggan slide on Chapel Hill; F. B. McCurdy, the Halifax stockbroker who had helped to promote Puerto Rico railway stock in 1907, wrote to say he was still in the same line of business, 'pushing a provincial victory loan'.

All got a reply; one of them, his former *Express* protégée Molly Castle, now in New York, was sent Beaverbrookian dicta: 'You often get a good woman. You sometimes get a good journalist. But very rarely do you get the two together. All men journalists are bad.'[15] His London support system operated. George Malcolm Thomson and Farrer sent him summaries of British newspapers; Robertson at the *Express* reminded him about Blumenfeld's golden wedding.

On this visit, which lasted two weeks, with frequent meetings in the White House and at the Mayflower Hotel, Beaverbrook attended one or two sessions of the Military and Naval Group at the White House, with Churchill and Roosevelt and their advisers, but otherwise took little part in the strategic talks. The American and British Chiefs of Staff adopted a position of which he violently disapproved: they agreed that 'it does not seem likely that in 1942 any large scale land offensive against Germany, except on the Russian front, will be possible . . .' but that a landing in North Africa, later known as Torch, should be planned for as early as March 1942. On a cross-Channel invasion, they went no further than to agree that 'in 1943 the way may be clear for a return to the continent, across the Mediterranean, from Turkey into the Balkans, or by landings in Western Europe'. Beaverbrook wanted a cross-Channel invasion as soon as possible, and regarded North Africa as a diversion.

But he got his way over production, and made what Thomson judged to be his second most important contribution to winning the war. Supported by Harry Hopkins and Harriman, he argued that the American production targets set before Pearl Harbor were now far too low. 'This is the war of the machine,' he constantly proclaimed.[16] Britain, he said, had been much too slow to get moving, and America must not make the same mistake. The strategy of success was to set targets for the production people instead of allowing them to set their own. This approach appealed to Roosevelt, with his distrust of experts, and he accepted Beaverbrook's figures virtually unchanged.

When he announced the new targets, his planners were appalled. The old target for new operational aircraft in 1942 was 28,600; Roosevelt raised it to 45,000 for 1942 and 100,000 for 1943; he doubled the figure for tanks, from 20,400 in 1942 to 45,000, and to 75,000 in 1943. One result was that the mighty American motor car industry did not produce a single civilian vehicle until the war was over. The planners scornfully called the new targets FDR's 'numbers racket'; but they were almost all achieved.

Beaverbrook had one row with Churchill in Washington – the first serious row they had during the war, according to Archie Rowlands, who was well placed to judge the relative seriousness of Beaverbrook–Churchill disputes.[17] Policy towards Russia was the cause. Beaverbrook had accepted cuts in American supplies to Britain for the sake of keeping promises made to Stalin. Churchill criticized Beaverbrook directly, and Beaverbrook predictably resigned. On 12 January Churchill refused to accept his resignation.

For the journey home Beaverbrook and Churchill first flew to Bermuda, where the *Duke of York* waited at anchor. The Prime Minister decided that, instead of travelling by warship, he would prefer to save time by flying home in a BOAC flying boat. The Chief of the Air Staff, Sir Charles Portal, closely cross-questioned the aircraft's captain, Captain Kelly Rogers, about the safety of the trip, and was reassured. So, despite an instruction from the King that none of the leading members of the mission must ever fly in the same aircraft, Churchill, Beaverbrook, Portal, Sir Dudley Pound (the First Sea Lord), Sir Charles Wilson (the doctor), Colonel Hollis (the military secretary), and John Martin (the Prime Minister's principal private secretary) took off together with the air of naughty schoolboys. Captain Rogers flew over the *Duke of York* at 1500 feet, imagining the mixed feelings of those on board. They would have been justified in feeling that the Prime Minister's decision marked the beginning of the end for transatlantic shipping, since the journey took only 17 hours 55 minutes instead of a week. The evening meal was 'a festive affair', the captain reported to his superiors, with the Prime Minister, Beaverbrook and the First Sea Lord at one table and the rest at another. The menu consisted of cold consommé, shrimp cocktail, filet mignon with fresh vegetables, sweet, dessert, coffee, champagne and liqueurs. The captain wrote: 'All the passengers had gone to bed except Lord Beaverbrook, who sat up reading the whole time. If I had not known Lord Beaverbrook to be an air traveller of many years standing and the maker of several transatlantic flights, I would have thought him a nervous passenger, but I knew his anxiety was entirely on the Prime Minister's account, particularly when he said, "If we lose Churchill we lose the war".'

After touching down in rolling fog off Plymouth Hoe – Churchill in the co-pilot's seat and Beaverbrook standing beside him – the party quickly boarded a train for London, and no goodbyes were said. Later in the day Rogers had a call from Beaverbrook, 'who mentioned the oversight and stated that the Prime Minister had been very sorry about it'. Beaverbrook then asked Rogers to spend a night at Cherkley, which he did, in 'superlative comfort', his fellow guests being Portal, Sir William Rootes, Mr and Mrs Randolph Churchill and Sir Walter Layton. Beaverbrook went to Rogers's bedroom just before he turned in and expressed his appreciation of the flight.[18]

The party returned home on 18 January 1942 to crisis. On the eve of their departure for Washington they had learnt that the Japanese had sunk two Royal Navy battleships, the *Prince of Wales* and the *Repulse*, off Singapore. Now Singapore itself was on the point of being lost. The army had been defeated in the Western Desert. Hong Kong had fallen. It was the third winter of the war, and Churchill's position had never been more exposed. On 29 January he won an overwhelming vote of confidence in the House of Commons, but mutterings about the conduct of the war did not cease. Some of the criticism was directed at Beaverbrook: the War Office and Air Ministry complained that aircraft and spare parts for tanks, urgently needed by Britain, were being shipped by him to Russia.

Undeterred, Beaverbrook continued to harry everyone about Russian aid. Sometimes his tone was soft; he wrote to Harold Balfour at the Air Ministry:

> This won't do. We want the planes to get to Russia. If the Russians fight in the snow, surely we can move aeroplanes in the snow. It would be a terrible confession if we had to write to Stalin and tell him that Harold Balfour, whose cheek he had kissed [Balfour had been in Moscow with Beaverbrook], is unable to provide the planes he promised because of snow. I look to you to produce a great change, and I hope to see the word go forth that, come wind, come weather, England will send the promised planes to Russia.[19]

He was sharper with Washington: 108 fewer tanks had been shipped than promised: 'It is vital that our tanks should reach Russia for the Spring battles. And time is short.' He badgered the Minister of War Transport about lorries: '. . . we are publicly pledged to strain every nerve. . . .'[20] He discussed deficiencies in shipments to Russia with the King. Maisky sent him 'my most sincere gratitude for the understanding you have of our position'. Betty Bower went into Beaverbrook's office one day with papers and without knocking (his staff were forbidden to knock) and found Churchill in Beaverbrook's chair with her employer nearby – the Prime Minister must have entered via the communicating corridor with No. 10. Beaverbrook introduced her, and she had turned to leave when Churchill called her back and said she could help them. 'It was a question for a woman, Churchill said. Would it be good for the morale of Russian women if we sent sanitary towels? I said, Yes! So we did.'

Despite the vote of confidence, Churchill was pressed into considering a shake-up; and the biggest change was to be the creation of a Ministry of Production with Beaverbrook in charge. On 2 February Beaverbrook presented a document defining his new powers. Shipbuilding and labour were both to be under his control, a notion that Leathers at War Transport and Bevin at Labour strongly opposed.

Beaverbrook was increasingly restless and becoming increasingly isolated, for reasons all connected with Russia. In December Stalin had told Eden that the map of Europe should be redrawn to recognize Russian frontiers as they had existed on the eve of the German invasion; that is, he was claiming the Baltic states, part of Rumania, much of eastern Poland and a strip of Finland. Churchill had replied that these demands ran directly counter to the Atlantic Charter, to which Russia had subscribed. Beaverbrook was all for accepting Stalin's case. On 31 January, in a memorandum to the War Cabinet headed 'Policy Towards Russia', he argued that the Charter's principle of self-determination should apply only 'where it does not conflict with the needs of strategic security' – otherwise Gibraltar should be handed over to Spain. Stalin had also told Eden that Russia would underwrite any demands that Britain might make after the war for bases on the continent of Europe, especially on the Channel coast. Beaverbrook recommended the government to take advantage of this thoughtful suggestion. Given the uncertainty about France's future, 'those bases may after the war prove essential to our security,' he wrote.[21]

Beaverbrook kept up the pressure, as he usually did. On 7 February he addressed another memorandum to the War Cabinet in support of Stalin's demands. 'Russia asks for the 1941 frontiers with Finland, Rumania and the Baltic States. These frontiers fall short of the frontiers she possessed in Tsarist times. . . . The Baltic states are the Ireland of Russia. . . . As for Russia's claims on Finland and Rumania, these two countries have, by throwing in their lot with Germany, forfeited all right to our consideration. . . .'

Beaverbrook went on to make an extraordinary suggestion: if the Cabinet could not agree, 'may we not appeal to public opinion, so that the people may settle the deliberation on our behalf?' His colleagues could be forgiven for thinking that he must be teasing; but he was not, as a note written on 28 February shows: 'I then asked that my newspapers should be allowed to campaign in favour of meeting Stalin's wishes. I claimed that the public needed guidance. . . . This plan, however, was resented by Mr Bevin, opposed by Mr Morrison, and denounced by the Prime Minister. Mr Attlee said he would leave the government rather than yield the domination of the Baltic states to Russia.'[22]

On 9 February Beaverbrook told Harriman he was going to resign, and Harriman advised him to go ahead. Beaverbrook had exhausted Harriman and Bracken by keeping them up at night, endlessly rehashing the arguments he was having with the Prime Minister. Harriman reported to Roosevelt: 'Beaverbrook has quibbled and quarrelled with the PM to the point where the PM will not tolerate it any longer. He feels Beaverbrook has been unjust and disloyal to seize this moment of all moments to make an issue. I believe Beaverbrook over-emphasises the adverse effect on the government of his resignation. The PM is confident it will not be serious and, even if it were, there is nothing he can do about it.'[23]

Meanwhile the war went from bad to worse. The public was shocked to learn that on the night of 11 February two German battle-cruisers, the *Scharnhorst* and *Gneisenau*, had been allowed to pass through the English Channel in daylight apparently unscathed. Singapore fell four days later.

Beaverbrook, as usual, felt both that he was indispensable and that if thwarted he should resign. On 18 February he returned yet again to the attack, telling the War Cabinet that 'It is now impossible for the British government to refuse the Russian claims', and describing Lithuania, Latvia and Estonia as the 'native soil of the Russians'.[24]

By now he was totally isolated. In his Ministry, he was not regarded with either the affection or the fear he had inspired at Aircraft Production; his staff felt, Macmillan observed, 'a sort of uneasiness at not knowing what is really happening'.[25] Eden, and to a lesser extent two Labour ministers,

Dalton and Morrison, were inclined to agree with him about some of Russia's demands, and to think that the Americans should be urged to face up to them. But Attlee and Bevin were resolutely opposed. In the past, in his disputes with Churchill, Beaverbrook had usually been angling for Churchill's support in stirring up other ministers. But Churchill, with his own authority in question, could not support him against the leader of the Labour Party and his most powerful backer. Churchill wanted to retain Beaverbrook as Minister of Production; but he could not award him the powers he was demanding, particularly over manpower. Bevin was utterly opposed to any such change: one condition on which Labour had joined the coalition was that manpower would be in the hands of a trade union leader. Attlee, when consulted by Churchill, agreed with Bevin: if it turned out otherwise, there would be trouble with the party as well as with Bevin. The trade unions distrusted Beaverbrook and had done so for decades. If he was given manpower Bevin would resign and provoke a political crisis at a time when the government was already in difficulties.[26] Colonel Jacob, a detached observer, summed it up: 'Churchill could afford to lose Beaverbrook, but he couldn't afford to lose Bevin.'

So Beaverbrook's job at Production lasted only twelve days, and then went to Oliver Lyttelton, without manpower. There was another cause of strife. Churchill proposed to make Attlee deputy leader of the government. Beaverbrook vigorously opposed the decision. Nor was this all. Cripps had returned from Russia, still smouldering under Beaverbrook's high-handed treatment, and supplanted Beaverbrook as the hero of the Left, who regarded him, despite Beaverbrook's self-advertisement, as the 'symbol of our close alliance with the Soviet Union', in the words of Aneurin Bevan's *Tribune*.[27] Churchill proposed making Cripps Leader of the House and Beaverbrook opposed that decision also.

Churchill was under pressure at home, because of Beaverbrook, as well as in the office. His wife wrote to him, probably on 19 February:

> I do beg of you to reflect, whether it would not be best to leave Lord B entirely out of your Reconstruction.
>
> It is true that if you do he may (& will) work against you – at first covertly and then openly. But is not hostility without, better than intrigue & treachery & rattledom [*sic*] within? You should have peace inside your Government – for a few months at any rate – & you must have that with what you have to face and do for us all – Now that you have (as I understand) invited Sir Stafford, why not put your money on him?
>
> The temper & behaviour you describe (in Lord B) is caused I think by the prospect of a new personality equal perhaps in power to him & certainly in intellect.
>
> My darling – Try ridding yourself of this microbe which some people fear is in your blood – Exorcise this bottle Imp & see if the air is not clearer & purer – You will miss his drive and genius, but in Cripps you may have new accessions of strength.[28]

These were strong words – 'intrigue' and 'treachery'. They clearly reflect the Churchills' fear that Beaverbrook, if excluded from the inner circle, would 'work against' the Prime Minister. Nevertheless, when Churchill met the demands of his critics and announced his reconstruction, Beaverbrook was out of the War Cabinet, though still in office. Then on 23 February Stalin made a speech to the Red Army, and Bruce Lockhart, now head of the Political Warfare Executive in the Foreign Office, quickly circulated a secret memorandum analysing the speech. Stalin's mistrust of Britain, he wrote,

> reached its apogee at the time of Munich, declined slightly after the visits of Lord Beaverbrook, and recently has regained its former strength . . . we must act quickly. . . . Russia should be granted (a) her security demands (b) an equal say in the conduct of the war (c) an equal say in the pooling of supplies (d) an equal say in the peace settlement of Europe. . . . Doubtless it may be unpleasant to have the Russians sitting in our talks on strategy. But it will not be half so unpleasant as to have them walk out on us altogether.[29]

On 26 February Beaverbrook wrote a final letter of resignation to Churchill, proclaiming his continuing devotion. The Prime Minister wrote back saying he hoped that when he had recovered his strength he would again be available to serve. Macmillan thought Beaverbrook went because he was exhausted. He himself gave asthma as a principal cause. He said also that the appointments of Cripps and Attlee had inspired his withdrawal. But the underlying theme of all his disputes since his return from Moscow had been Britain's policy towards Russia. He agreed with Bruce Lockhart; and Bruce Lockhart's views were shared by nobody else in the government.

Were these fundamental differences about Russian policy, then, the cause of his withdrawal? A month later, the shrewd Archie Rowlands – who had learnt from experience that Beaverbrook often concealed his true motives behind a smokescreen – surmised that his 'real reason for refusing to stay in the War Cabinet was that he judged that the present administration was losing ground in public esteem and was likely to be short-lived – and he did not want to be associated with its collapse.'[30]

'STRIKE EVEN RECKLESSLY!'

Almost at once, Beaverbrook regretted the circumstances of his resignation. They had allowed Churchill to obscure profound differences over policy by ascribing his departure to exhaustion and asthma; and the official announcement that followed, vague as it was, saying that he was going to the United States to work on 'the pooling of resources between the United Nations', created a tie he could not very well avoid. Yet the last thing he wanted was to leave London; he told Liddell Hart, 'emphatically and repeatedly, that he did not want to go to the US – and be out of the way'. He feared that once he got to America Churchill would find some excuse for keeping him there. Suspicions that he was being tricked were reinforced by the messages sent by Churchill to Roosevelt about his coming; they were flattering, but by stressing that 'Max' was out of power by his own wish and that the two of them remained close friends and 'intimate political associates',[31] Churchill was, Beaverbrook concluded, trying to hobble him.

To make it clear that he did not intend to be hobbled, Beaverbrook wrote to Churchill on 17 March saying that he proposed to try to change government policy in three respects – all to do with Russia: Russian frontiers; increased supplies to Russia; and 'an expedition into Europe' to relieve German pressure on Russia. 'Stalin,' he said, 'has suffered many vexations.' Beaverbrook also galvanized his newspapers. 'We must decide the sea war and the land war alike in 1942 . . . ,' said an *Express* leader on 12 March. 'When the piled up weight of German attack sways against Russian attack we must turn the scales with British attack.' The *Standard* of 9 March proclaimed: 'Britain needs new inspiration. She will need it this spring to seize the initiative from our great enemies.' On 13 March Aneurin Bevan in *Tribune*, of which he had lately become editor, outlined the case for a second front. On 17 March, the *Standard* made rare use of the phrase 'second front'. Here was the beginning of the strange alliance between Beaverbrook, left-wingers, Communists and armchair strategists that became known as the 'Second Front Now' campaign. Among the foremost campaigners were two of the most brilliant polemicists in the country, Frank Owen and Michael Foot of the *Standard*; they marched in step with their mutual friend Bevan, whose writing was not much less forceful than theirs and who had now begun, in the House of Commons, to attack Churchill himself.

On the eve of his departure for the United States Beaverbrook went to Downing Street from his new flat in Park Lane, acquired after Stornoway House was bombed, to give Churchill a final lecture about the shipping shortage. On the same day, 19 March, he summoned Liddell Hart: 'Beaverbrook remarked that Winston was a great man, very difficult to deal with and impossible to control. Whatever anyone might think necessary, or wish to do, they had to remember that "this is Churchill's war". Unfortunately he thought of it in terms of fighting "the wars of Marlborough". . . .' Liddell Hart quoted Beaverbrook as saying: 'He [Churchill] cannot grasp mechanised warfare.'[32]

Beaverbrook's reluctance to leave London was increased when Attlee made slighting references to his semi-mission in the House of Commons. Farrer overheard Beaverbrook shouting at Brendan Bracken: 'I won't, I won't, I won't.'[33] But he did, taking with him Farrer, the sycophantic Senator R. D. Elliott from Australia who had originally come over to work under Beaverbrook in the Ministry of Aircraft Production, and Nockels the gentlemanly valet; they flew in an overcrowded flying boat from Poole to Ireland, to Lisbon (where there was nobody to meet them), to Bathurst in West Africa (where their arrival took the Governor by surprise), to Trinidad, to Miami, to Baltimore and finally to Washington, where the Senator, who was responsible for these unfortunate travel arrangements, was sent back to England.

Publicly, Beaverbrook was in the United States to discuss supplies; privately, he had decided to lobby Roosevelt about Russia's demand for recognition of her 1941 frontiers – or so he told Liddell Hart. In Washington, his intentions changed. He found there an invitation from the Newspaper Proprietors' Association of America to address their annual banquet in New York in a month's time: a grand event that brought together a thousand publishers, editors and business managers from all over the country. Staying a night in the White House, Beaverbrook discussed with Roosevelt and Hopkins not supplies or frontiers but his speech and a second front.[34]

The American position on a second front – taking that term to denote, as it usually though not always did, a cross-Channel invasion – was then as follows. Roosevelt and his advisers had agreed in December, much to British relief, that despite Pearl Harbor the main Allied effort should be against Germany and Italy, rather than against Japan. During March, the American Army planners in the War Plans division, led by a little-known staff officer called Dwight Eisenhower, concluded that that meant a cross-Channel assault should be launched as soon as possible. The Joint Chiefs endorsed Eisenhower's conclusions on 16 March, and their recommendations were on Roosevelt's desk during the Beaverbrook visit.

In London, Beaverbrook's journalists were adopting much the same strategic posture as the US Chiefs of Staff. On 24 March Frank Owen began a signed series in the *Standard* advocating 'attack in Europe'. Next day, Beaverbrook learned from the *New York Herald Tribune* that Owen had been called up into the Army, three days before he was due to chair a mass meeting in Trafalgar Square on 'aid to Russia and Victory this year'. The talk in Fleet Street, the *Herald Tribune* reported, was that the government was so perturbed by the *Standard*'s constant demand for the opening of a second front that it was willing to go to considerable lengths to remove Owen from his editorial chair. Owen's call-up, the paper went on, 'will cost the Russians the most consistent friend they have ever had in the British Press'. Christiansen, reporting to Beaverbrook, said the implications of the article were 'unwarranted', though Owen's case had been dealt with personally by the Minister of Labour, the Secretary of State for War, and possibly by Churchill as well. But Owen wanted to join the Army in any case.[35] On Sunday, 29 March, under a different chairman, some forty thousand people massed in a Trafalgar Square decorated with flags and large portraits of Churchill, Roosevelt, Stalin, Chiang Kai-shek and Nehru to listen to speeches, of which one of the most striking – the

Standard reported next day – was by John Gordon of the *Sunday Express*, on the theme 'Attack in Europe!', and the 'best-delivered and best-constructed' was by Ted Bramley, a Communist.

Back in Miami, where he rented an apartment in a hotel, Beaverbrook next day took up the theme himself, in a broadcast to Canada. The Allies, he said, must play their 'full part' in helping the Russians – a covert reference to the need for a second front. C. V. R. Thompson reported the broadcast on the *Express* leader pages: 'Attack – By Sea, By Air, and in the Field: Beaverbrook says the cry is now for offensive action.'

Roosevelt accepted the Eisenhower recommendations on 1 April, and on the 3rd informed Beaverbrook that he was sending General Marshall and Harry Hopkins to London to work out a schedule for an invasion. Marshall's proposition was simple and straightforward: that the build-up of American forces in Britain should start forthwith, and that in 1942, or at the latest 1943, an assault should be launched into the heart of Germany by the shortest route. Here a misunderstanding occurred that Beaverbrook exploited. The British saw the advantages of the American proposal. They saw the attractions of the short route, and of relieving the pressure on the Russians. But the active fronts in the Middle East and Far East were absorbing everything that could be shipped by the long voyage round the Cape, and it was out of the question to stop the flow. The U-boat campaign was still highly threatening, and German forces in France powerful. Marshall, to the British, seemed to think that the sheer momentum of the American build-up would carry his troops across the Atlantic and the Channel and into France, and appeared to have little idea of what he would do when he got there. After two years of war and disasters the British were less sanguine. Until the Germans had been considerably weakened, they thought it would be 'madness to try to place comparatively small and as yet untried armies ashore in France'. Thus when Marshall and Hopkins left London in mid-April they believed a firm decision had been made, whereas the British thought a decision had been made in principle only. Churchill told Harriman that an assault later that year would be 'impossible, disastrous'.[36]

On Miami Beach, and later in a borrowed villa at Sea Island on the coast of Georgia, Beaverbrook fired off demands for facts and figures to George Malcolm Thomson in London and worked obsessively on a speech that argued exactly the opposite – as he well knew. Walking the sands with Farrer, he had two refrains: 'He won't like it, will he?', referring to Churchill; and 'What am I doing here?'[37]

For the return trip to Washington, at the last minute Beaverbrook decided he would go by overnight train. Farrer telephoned the railway company; the train was full. It was Lord Beaverbrook who wished to travel; then room would of course be found. The train drew into a dark station. Farrer and Nockels settled Beaverbrook into his compartment for the night. Then they realized they were alone in a specially attached coach.

What would Beaverbrook say? He had been insisting since London that they must on no account waste taxpayers' money. Nockels kept his head. What time did the train reach Washington? At 8.30 a.m. Then at 8.15 a.m. he and Farrer would start clumping up and down the corridor outside Beaverbrook's compartment with suitcases – a stage army of passengers. After the train arrived, Nockels would suggest that His Lordship should wait briefly before alighting, to let the other passengers disperse. Farce once again hovered round Beaverbrook. The plan worked.

In Washington Beaverbrook showed his speech to Roosevelt, who approved it line by line. That one of Churchill's 'intimate political associates' should publicly advocate the policy Roosevelt was privately urging on a reluctant Churchill suited Roosevelt very well. Beaverbrook travelled on to New York in a mood of 'nervous truculence', and moved into the 39th floor of the Waldorf Towers. On 23 April, wearing a carnation with full evening dress, and looking tanned and rich, he delivered his speech, broadcast coast-to-coast, to an enthusiastic audience in the Waldorf ballroom. 'Beaverbrook Asks 2D Front in Europe to Bolster Russia. Britain Wants Action Now in Effort to Doom Hitler This Year, he tells publishers. Puts High Faith in Stalin,' said the *New York Times* page one headlines next day. Beaverbrook, said the story, wanted 'a second front opened in Western Europe while Russia is still holding the Nazis in the east, in the hope that it will bring about Hitler's defeat before the year is ended'.

It was a lengthy and powerful address. Part of it described the 'many sacrifices' of the people of Britain:

> They have adopted black bread for white. They have given up eggs. There is no more beef. Oranges and lemons have been forbidden. There is not even an apple in this 'other Eden, demi-paradise'. They have accepted a system of food rationing thorough and complete. They have sacrificed sugar to the Russians, whisky to the Americans, corn to the Egyptians, railway engines to the Persians, and railings to the tank factories. They have abandoned turn-ups on their trousers and buttons on their cuffs. And don't ask the poor man for a match or the rich man for a dime, because they have neither.

Another part of the speech lavished extravagant praise on 'our great leader, Mr Churchill', dismissing rumours that he would fall before the summer was out. But the central section consisted of extravagant praise of Communism:

> Communism under Stalin has produced the most valiant fighting army in Europe. Communism under Stalin has provided us with examples of patriotism equal to the finest annals of history. Communism under Stalin has won the applause and admiration of all the western nations. Communism under Stalin has produced the best generals in this war. . . .
> Persecution of Christianity? Not so. There is no religious persecution. The

church doors are open. And there is complete freedom to practise religion, just as there is complete freedom to reject it.

Racial persecution? Not at all. Jews live like other men. . . .

Political purges? Of course. But it is now clear that the men who were shot down would have betrayed Russia to her German enemy. . . .

This is a chance, an opportunity, to bring the war to an end here and now. . . . Strike out to help Russia! Strike out violently! Strike even recklessly! . . .

He assured his audience that the project for 'a second front in Europe' was practicable. 'How admirably Britain is now equipped in weapons of war for directing such an attack on Germany, I well know.'

Next morning, as the messages of congratulation arrived, including one from Roosevelt, Beaverbrook said to Farrer, 'I wonder what that fellow Churchill will say.' He soon found out. Churchill proposed that he should stay in Washington to coordinate American supplies to Britain. This was exactly what Beaverbrook had feared and he paid no attention, returning to London on 5 May. Churchill tried again. He sounded out Roosevelt about Beaverbrook becoming British Ambassador, which was 'of course agreeable' to Roosevelt. But nothing happened, perhaps because Beaverbrook said he would go only if Churchill promised to adopt a stronger line on a second front, or perhaps because Churchill concluded that he would appear to endorse Beaverbrook's speech if he sent him to Washington so soon afterwards.

WAITING FOR THE CALL?

The months that followed Beaverbrook's visit to the United States are the most inscrutable of his life. Did he seriously believe that he might become Prime Minister and intrigue to that end?

He returned from Washington to an anxious country frustrated by the course of the war. For nearly a year she had been allied to Russia, and for five months to the United States. Yet the British Army in Libya was stalled; the Japanese advance continued unabated in the Far East; and in Russia the Germans were besieging Stalingrad and driving deeper into the Ukraine. Churchill, Minister of Defence as well as Prime Minister, was under fire.

With his Waldorf speech Beaverbrook had put himself at the head of the movement for a second front. Nobody was more delighted than Michael Foot, editing the *Evening Standard* in succession to Frank Owen. The lead paragraph in the Londoner's Diary the day after the speech reported that 'almost everyone' was talking about it, and that General Sikorski, Commander-in-Chief of Polish exiles in Britain, agreed with Beaverbrook. Foot told his employer that the address was 'stupendous'.[38] Foot was no Communist; but he was no implacable anti-Communist either – unlike the Labour Party leaders. He suspected, as did his second front allies, that the reason why the government was not straining to open a second front was that Churchill was less interested in helping to relieve pressure on the Russians than in letting Germany and Russia destroy one another. Beaverbrook, by contrast, had never been anti-Russian; he was ready to defend Stalin and to trust him; and he was, in Foot's eyes, a realist: he thought the only way to win the war was by going all out to help the Russians, which meant subordinating all else to a cross-Channel invasion at the earliest possible date. The inspiration of Foot and his left-wing associates was to some degree ideological, but they did not doubt that Beaverbrook was on the same side.

The second front alliance included Bevan and *Tribune*. On 1 May, in *Tribune*, a pseudonymous writer using the name Thomas Rainboro', the leveller in Cromwell's army, began a series of sensational but well-informed articles attacking Churchill's conduct of the war. Was Churchill pursuing a Russian victory without reservations, the writer asked. Had he not, in 1940, when the Russians were failing to break the Mannerheim Line in the Finnish war, delivered the verdict: 'Thus does Communism rot the soul of its victims in peace and make it abject in war'? Rainboro' went on to censure Churchill's performance in Libya, Greece, the Balkans and North Africa, and over aid to Russia.

Bevan was back in touch with Beaverbrook; he stayed at Cherkley on 15 May (he climbed a ladder and helped to put out a fire). Many people made the reasonable assumption that he was Rainboro'. But he was not. Rainboro' was Frank Owen, then training with the Royal Armoured Corps. However, he was still on Beaverbrook's payroll, at a salary of £3000 a year.[39] (Michael Foot, Beaverbrook told Kingsley Martin of the *New Statesman* in November, was being paid 'nearly £4000'; in June, Foot thanked Beaverbrook for putting a room in his London flat at his disposal.[40]) This was the second time – the first was *Guilty Men* – that Owen had written anonymously in support of causes of which his employer did not disapprove; and Bevan, Foot and Beaverbrook kept his secret.

Another left-winger and Beaverbrook employee came out strongly against the conduct of the war at this time: Tom Driberg, who was still William Hickey on the *Express*. In late May, when a by-election unexpectedly cropped up in the safe Conservative seat of Maldon in Essex, where he owned the house that Beaverbrook had unwittingly helped to subsidize, he decided (though still firmly pro-Communist) to run as an Independent. Beaverbrook thought little of his chances, but did not stand in his way and even gave him some advice – to buy a hat. 'The British electors', he said, 'will not vote for a man who doesn't wear a hat.'[41] The *Express*, in a half-humorous comment, said that Driberg's opinions were his own, not those of the paper; in practice, however, on the war they were much the same: they both attacked its conduct, while refraining from direct criticism of Churchill. The Prime Minister supported Driberg's opponent.

On 21 June, Beaverbrook addressed thirty thousand people at a Salute to Russia Demonstration in Birmingham from a rostrum draped with the Hammer and Sickle and Union Jack sewn together. The speech was broadcast – Beaverbrook's sixth broadcast of the war: he proclaimed the need to cultivate a 'stern and righteous hatred' for the Germans and Japanese, but his main theme was the urgent need for a second front. That day news broke of the fall of Tobruk, the worst disaster since the loss of Singapore. 'On the morning of 21 June the second front was a near-certainty; by the evening the odds were 100 to 1 against,' said the account of the second front campaign drafted by Farrer under Beaverbrook's supervision. The cry now, Beaverbrook anticipated, would be: 'What folly to attack in Europe! We must defend the Nile Delta!'[42] On 25 June Driberg was elected by an overwhelming majority.

Beaverbrook was right about the fate of the campaign he was leading, though for the wrong reasons. It was not Tobruk, but what seemed to the British Chiefs of Staff to be ineluctable facts that ruled out a second front in 1942. At two vital meetings in June and July, the Combined Chiefs of Staff – the British and Americans sitting together – concluded that the conditions for a landing in France did not exist. They decided instead, since an attack must be made somewhere, particularly in order to take pressure off the Russian front, to land in North Africa the available British and American divisions in Britain and certain American troops from the United States. These decisions, taken with reluctance by the Americans, determined Allied strategy for the rest of the war.

But they did not end the second front agitation. On 2 July, just after Tobruk, Churchill faced what was expected to be the most serious challenge to his authority since he had become Prime Minister. In the event he won a handsome majority, 475 votes to 25, with 20 abstentions. Bevan delivered another assault on the war's direction, and again made an eloquent demand for an immediate second front.

Did Beaverbrook know about the Allied decision to land in North Africa and postpone a second front? Liddell Hart and Bruce Lockhart – who did know – discussed the point, and Bruce Lockhart said he surely must; but he talked as if he did not.[43] At all events, his newspapers – and Aneurin Bevan – continued their campaign. In July, the *Express* prominently reported a second front rally that again drew forty thousand to Trafalgar Square; it also promoted a characteristic Beaverbrook invention: a 'movement' called 'The *Daily Express* Centre of Public Opinion'. The editor wrote on 7 August:

> Meetings are held all over the country at which a speaker, stating the government's views, is provided. The purpose is to launch discussion and to let the public have their say. The function is to ascertain opinion and not to make it. There were pitfalls. There has been too much talk about the Second Front at most of the meetings. So much talk about the Second Front that it has sometimes been hard indeed to get opinion on other topics.

Beaverbrook was playing a careful hand. His papers gave little publicity to Bevan, who by this time was both widely hated by the Conservative Party and an irritant to his own Labour Party leaders in the government. But the *Express* and the *Evening Standard* were beating the same drum as Bevan, which might help to account for the fact – if true – that there was so much talk about the second front at *Daily Express* meetings. On 16 July in the *Standard* Michael Foot addressed himself to 'The Men – The Ships – The Will: Suppose the Second Front became number one priority. Perhaps then the greatest seafaring nation the world has ever seen would be able to find the ships. . . .' The theme of both papers was constant: 'Russia bleeds'; the West must give Russia all the help in its power; therefore a second front must be opened not in 1943 or 1944, but at once.

During these months Beaverbrook was seeing less of Churchill than at any time since he had joined his administration in 1940. On 11 June he talked to Liddell Hart about Churchill's 'underlying lack of confidence', saying that his 'doubt as to the security of his own position had made him fearful of taking any strong line that might bring him into conflict with the military trade union, and hence, in all probability, with the mass of the Conservative party'. Next day, he wrote to Sir Samuel Hoare in Spain saying that 'a combination of bad news from abroad with mismanagement in domestic affairs would, in my view, bring about a crisis which might well be fatal to the government as at present constituted'.[44] Churchill had his suspicions about Beaverbrook's activities. The *Express* had said it did not support Driberg's candidacy, but Churchill believed otherwise. He wrote to Beaverbrook on 14 June: '. . . the fact that Mr Driberg and Mr Frank Owen [here he was misinformed] are standing as Independent candidates in two by-elections will of course be taken by everyone as indicating that you are running election candidates against the government. This would be a great pity from many points of view.'[45] Political circles speculated. A. G. Gardiner, the old Liberal editor of the *Daily News*, wrote on 11 May: 'Beaverbrook is an intriguer first, last and always, and he is the more dangerous because his intrigues are governed by no principle that I have ever been able to discover – always by personal aims and an insane passion to pull strings.'[46] At the Foreign Office, the well-placed Oliver Harvey in his diary compared Beaverbrook to Laval, who had undermined his colleagues as a prelude to a deal with Hitler.

In July Beaverbrook was giving cross-party dinners to MPs. Leo Amery heard that Beaverbrook had

> addressed them with great vigour on the subject of the Second Front, his whole address being on the psychological necessity of preventing a Russian collapse, disregarding all other questions of possibility or another Dunkirk or of feasibility. If ever there was a one-track mind it is Max's, though sometimes it is that sort of mind which leads to victory. . . . He seems to have been friendly to Winston and avoided all attack upon the Government as such. All the same I think he means mischief. . . .[47]

Did the mischief encompass the idea of becoming Prime Minister? It was not a wholly new idea. It had been a youthful ambition. Rothermere had floated the possibility during the Empire Free Trade campaign. In the Second World War, Colonel Jacob seems to have been the first person to believe that Beaverbrook really was 'after the top job', in October 1941. According to David Farrer, soon after he resigned Beaverbrook invited Sir Arthur Salter to dinner alone at Cherkley: '. . . after two cocktails Beaverbrook came to the point. Would Sir Arthur join him in forming an anti-Churchill party? Sir Arthur's answer was brief and to the point. No. The rest of the evening passed in considerable embarrassment.' Farrer adds: 'This story was told to the author by Sir Arthur.' He concludes: '. . . from my own observation at very close quarters I am convinced that he never did more than flirt with the idea' of becoming Prime Minister, though 'some of his cronies in high places – the General Manager of the *Daily Express* among them – encouraged him to go further.'[48]

On 2 May Liddell Hart recorded a talk with David Owen, a member of Cripps's staff; Cripps was in the War Cabinet and himself had an eye on the premiership.

> Owen had gathered from certain sources that Beaverbrook had given directions for a campaign of subtle denigration of Cripps, focusing on his plea for 'Austerity' – on the reckoning that Winston will fall by June, and that if Cripps loses ground with the public, he (Beaverbrook) will then be the only alternative as head of the government.[49]

The next piece of evidence comes from Ernest Bevin. He was approached by Beaverbrook in the week following the fall of Tobruk and asked much the same question put to Salter: Churchill was on the way out, and so what was Bevin's attitude to the formation of an alternative government? The implication was that it would be led by Beaverbrook. Bevin rejected the approach, but told Churchill who, according to Attlee's biographer, 'affected not to believe it, and also Attlee, who certainly did'.[50] Bevin also told the story to David Astor, then a Royal Marine but active on his father's paper, the *Observer*, who found no reason to disbelieve him, then or later.

Averell Harriman knew Churchill and Beaverbrook as well as most people; and it was part of his task, as Roosevelt's eyes and ears in London, to be an impartial observer of political behaviour. In May 1943, he wrote down this assessment of Beaverbrook's ambitions:

> At the time he left the government and for some time thereafter [he] felt that the days of Churchill's government were numbered and that there was a possibility, if he got out, that he would be called [to replace Churchill]. He believed, I think, that the situation would get so bad the public would call for him. Still, he personally made no public move to injure Churchill at any time. He based his hopes largely on the demand of the people for a man who would be sympathetic to Russia and had shown aggressive tendencies.

Of Beaverbrook's employees, George Malcolm Thomson believed that Nye Bevan approached Beaverbrook to lead an anti-Churchill move, and that Beaverbrook declined. Miss Bower was regularly at Cherkley at this time. She remembers herself and Beaverbrook on the floor of the library at Cherkley planning the second front:

> I told him he was wasting his time. We used for instance a rug as the English Channel. We didn't plan it in detail; just the idea of how it would work. He had a filthy habit of blowing his nose or spitting into tissues and dropping them on the floor; and he'd say, 'Put that tissue over there' – to represent some feature. I used to get fed up, exhausted, longing for bed, and ask if we'd finished. Then he'd say, 'Will you read to me?' He loved *Picture Post*, but it wasn't very readable out loud. 'Do put some expression into it,' he'd say. Then next morning the phone would go at six.

But Miss Bower did not notice any sign that her boss had an eye on the premiership. Michael Foot, however, asked years later whether it crossed his mind that Beaverbrook thought he might take over, replied, 'It did.'[51] Bruce Lockhart's diaries from March 1942 onwards made constant reference to Beaverbrook's depression about the progress of the war, his belief that the government would not survive, and that the British and the American people all wanted a second front. On 21 June, Bruce Lockhart recorded: 'I could see his mind working. Winston will fall on this [the Second Front]; Eden is not strong enough to be PM. Therefore I'll run him for the Premiership. Then, my chance will come.'

It might be argued that Beaverbrook's chances of supplanting Churchill were so slim as to be fantastical. He was a member of the House of Lords; he had no party behind him; most conclusive of all, Attlee and Bevin would not for a moment have considered serving under him, and nor would Cripps. Yet Churchill had expected Lord Halifax – who hated Beaverbrook and called him 'The Toad' – to become Prime Minister in 1940; Churchill had no party behind him in 1940; and there was a curious moment in May 1942 when the *Evening Standard* attacked Bevin and Attlee, and the *Express* began to praise Herbert Morrison, the Home Secretary, which caused Bevan to warn Beaverbrook that this use of his papers would give rise to the 'unwholesome impression' that 'a series of unpleasant intrigues are being set on foot'. Privately, Beaverbrook went further; he wrote flattering letters to Morrison, telling him that, 'Churchill apart, you are today by far the biggest figure in the country.'[52] Did he think he might detach Morrison – who was more sympathetic to Russia than Attlee or Bevin – from his Labour colleagues?

As Harriman observed, Beaverbrook did nothing overtly to injure Churchill. He defended him in the House of Lords after the fall of Tobruk. Yet he continued to press for an immediate second front, although he was in a position to know as well as anyone that the resources, particularly the shipping, to launch it with any hope of success did not exist. As Amery observed, once fixed on a goal, Beaverbrook ceased to pay rational attention to obstacles that stood in the way. He thought of himself as an inspirer: decide the ends, and, if the willpower and energy – 'The Rage' – are forceful enough, the means can be found. Foot's article about the shipping shortage represented Beaverbrook's view entirely: if a prime minister not afraid of the 'military trade union' truly made a second front his priority, then the shipping shortage would be solved and the timid excuses of the Chiefs of Staff overcome. In some moods Beaverbrook was immune to argument, even on technical military matters. When his star war correspondent with the Eighth Army, Alan Moorehead of the *Express*, reported after Tobruk that the British defeat had been caused by the inferiority of British equipment, especially tanks, Beaverbrook, who had told his editors to praise these tanks, simply refused to accept Moorehead's verdict. He was still trying to persuade Moorehead, without success, that he had been unfair and inaccurate about the tanks the following March.[53]

To Beaverbrook, the idea of a Beaverbrook government would not have seemed as outlandish as it seems in retrospect. Churchill indeed was, in the early summer of 1942, dangerously exposed. No agreed or obvious successor was in place, certainly not in Beaverbrook's eyes. He floated the idea of a general election, on the ostensible grounds that the government needed a new mandate; others thought the idea preposterous. Beaverbrook evidently wished to shake the political dice.

In August Churchill and Harriman, representing Roosevelt, went to Moscow to tell Stalin that a second front was impossible in 1942 and to explain why Britain and the United States had decided instead to land in French North Africa. Stalin, unlike Beaverbrook, accepted the arguments, though with reluctance. Churchill left Moscow on 15 August. On the 17th an 'expedition into Europe' of the kind that Beaverbrook had long advocated was mounted at Dieppe, resulting in large casualties, mainly Canadian. Later, Beaverbrook blamed the disaster on Mountbatten, the Chief of Combined Operations, calling him in an intemperate moment 'a murderer'.[54] But at the time the *Express* strongly defended Dieppe: 'Let us praise. When the army has carried out a bold operation do not let us criticise.' While the military planners saw Dieppe as powerful evidence that the Allies were far from ready to launch a big invasion in northern France, the *Standard* saw it (21 August) as almost a victory: 'The Germans cannot afford any more Dieppes either on land or in the air. . . . Two or three simultaneous raids on a large scale would be too much for the three solitary Panzer divisions in France. . . .'

Neither the Anglo–American decision to pursue 'a Mediterranean policy' as a prelude to a cross-Channel invasion nor the evidence of Dieppe shook Beaverbrook's belief that the invasion should be launched sooner rather than later. Liddell Hart went down to Cherkley on 26 September and found Beaverbrook sitting on the terrace with Jean Norton, who soon left. Bruce Lockhart arrived, and then Michael Foot.

> After dinner . . . we moved to Beaverbrook's private cinema, just off the entrance hall. On a dais at the back there were two large easy chairs; Beaverbrook put Kathleen [Liddell Hart's wife] in one and covered her up with rugs, and took the other himself. Behind this was a sofa, on which Bruce Lockhart and I ensconced ourselves under a rug together, while Michael Foot sat nearby. Then the household staff – remarkably large for wartime – filed in and sat in the seats in front. It reminded me of a kind of 'inverted family prayers' in the days before the last war. The film show was entitled 'Nothing is Sacred' [sic] – an American film showing how a newspaper made a popular heroine out of a girl who was supposed to be doomed by radium poisoning, and then had to keep up the pretence when it was found there was nothing the matter with her. I wondered whether Beaverbrook himself was responsible for this apparently cynical disclosure to his domestic staff of the darker side of sensational journalism. At any rate, nothing could have been better calculated to open their eyes.
>
> Later, the way that Beaverbrook 'chipped' Michael Foot about his ideals, reminded me of how Grigg [Sir James Grigg, Secretary for War] regarded him as 'the Anti-Christ', corrupting the young. Seen in such a light the cinema performance might well have been regarded as a kind of 'Black Mass'.
>
> . . . Much of the discussion that evening was concerned with the Second Front. On that question, Bruce Lockhart and I tended to line up, on practical grounds, against Beaverbrook and Michael Foot. . . . Beaverbrook argued that the problem of a 'fighter umbrella', and the limitation of its range, was no longer what it had been – that with the new 'Mosquitoes' and Beaufighters we could provide air cover at long range, even as far as the coast of Norway.

Liddell Hart noted that Fighter Command had only three squadrons of these machines; that Mosquitoes had not yet been tested against German single-seater fighters; and that Beaufighters 'would probably be shot down at once'.

Beaverbrook wore black patent leather boots, with the laces undone. 'He explained that he was using up his pre-1914 stock. Pulling up his trousers he also showed me that he was wearing white tennis stockings, his solution towards the problem of meeting the recent "cut" in the length of socks.'[55]

He stepped up the campaign, if anything, after November when the Russians surrounded a German army at Stalingrad, Anglo–American forces landed in French North Africa, and the church bells rang in England to celebrate the Eighth Army's victory at Alamein. To Beaverbrook, the North African campaign was always a misguided blunder that diverted resources from the prime objective of a second front. He did not then have access to the Ultra material that showed how effective North Africa was in drawing off German aircraft – especially transport planes – from the Russian front at a crucial moment in the battle for Stalingrad.

The argument – the central argument about Allied strategy in the Second World War – has continued ever since. Defenders of the

Mediterranean strategy argue that when the fateful decisions were taken, in June and July 1942, the Allied planners had no choice. A landing in northern France was the accepted goal; but nothing, to the Chiefs of Staff, would have been more damaging, perhaps fatal, than a failed attempt. The Germans had plenty of experienced troops in France and the Low Countries ready to oppose a landing, and would not have needed to draw off troops from the Russian front. A successful landing in 1942 would have required a steady flow of men and equipment across the Atlantic, where the U-boat campaign was inflicting heavy losses. Landing craft were few (it was only with difficulty that enough landing craft were assembled for the invasion in 1944, and even then some troops used converted Thames barges). Any second front would have meant diverting resources away from troops already fighting the Germans in the Middle East. Besides, a cross-Channel attack before the winter storms could not be compared to the much larger assault that could be mounted in North Africa later in the year.

In the event, the Allies failed to achieve their Mediterranean objectives in 1943, and the delay ruled out a cross-Channel invasion in that year. But by the end of 1943, greatly assisted by Ultra, the Mediterranean was again open to Allied shipping, Italy had collapsed, Sicily was cleared and the U-boat campaign decisively defeated, thus setting the stage for the final assault in 1944.

Against this, it has been argued that the Americans led by General Marshall thought an assault possible in 1943 if not in 1942, and so did Stalin. It was the will, not the material, that was lacking. The person who, after some wavering, stopped an early second front was Churchill; and he was inspired – one argument runs – as much by political as by military motives: he wanted to capture the Balkans before the Russians got there, to secure the lifeline to India.

No one can decide with authority between these two views, because no one knows what would have happened if a different decision had been taken. But the received view is that, once Anglo–American forces were committed to North Africa in 1942, it would have been impossible to redeploy them for a cross-Channel landing before 1944. Beaverbrook did not change his opinion that it could have been much earlier. When Michael Foot was writing his biography of Bevan in 1962, Beaverbrook lent him a book by the American Trumbull Higgins, published in 1957, that best states the anti-Churchill case. Foot based his justification of Bevan's second front campaign (which was also of course Beaverbrook's and Foot's) largely on Higgins. It should be noted that in all the argument about the second front in 1942 and 1943, neither Beaverbrook nor his allies, such as Bevan or Foot, produced any factual evidence to demonstrate that the operation could be mounted in such strength as to make success more likely than failure.

In retrospect, another argument against a second front emerged. The

American troops proved so raw that it seemed just as well they had a trial run in North Africa before tackling 'Fortress Europe'; in the desert, in late 1942, US battalion commanders were so inexperienced that they sought tactical advice from the *Daily Express* correspondent, Alan Moorehead.

RETURN TO OFFICE

By the autumn of 1942, when Churchill at last felt able to describe Allied military progress as perhaps marking 'the end of the beginning', any thoughts that Beaverbrook might have entertained about becoming Prime Minister had vanished. He told his overseas correspondents during the winter that Churchill was unchallengeable. In the following January, the prospect of a second front likewise receded when Churchill and Roosevelt, meeting in Casablanca – Stalin said he could not leave Russia – decided that the Mediterranean must be the focus of Allied attention in 1943. Nevertheless Beaverbrook continued his campaign. In February 1943, in the House of Lords, his violent advocacy of a second front aroused the wrath of both Lord Simon and Lord Trenchard.

Out of office, Beaverbrook kept open his lines to Roosevelt. He developed an informal, easy way of dealing with the President that Churchill never managed. Early in the war Beaverbrook sent him a Kipling manuscript, and he continued to bombard him with presents: first editions, colour prints, fifty-four Roosevelt family documents bought at auction in London by Miss Bower; besides, they were both admirers of Dorothy Schiff, and Beaverbrook was not a man to allow a link like that to go unexploited. The old magic worked with Roosevelt as it had worked with Bonar Law; their meetings, the President told him, provided 'the kind of real relaxation and fun which comes too rarely these days'.[56] In March 1943 Roosevelt invited Beaverbrook to Washington, at a time when both men were feeling impatient with the generals; in April, Churchill decided he needed another Anglo–American strategy meeting.

So in May the two men crossed the Atlantic together on the *Queen Mary*, Churchill once again showing his need for Beaverbrook's company at crucial moments. Harriman went as well. By this time he was closely linked to the Beaverbrook–Churchill circle. In 1939 Churchill's son Randolph had married the young Pamela Digby; their son Winston was Beaverbrook's godson. While Randolph was serving in the Middle East, Pamela and the baby often stayed at Cherkley, as did Harriman. By 1943, the Churchill marriage had broken down, Beaverbrook was helping Pamela meet her profligate husband's debts, and Harriman and she were often together. Harriman dealt with Beaverbrook and Churchill as an equal; and the voyage led him to provide an account of their wartime relationship that helps to answer the question which puzzled, and often disturbed, many in high places: why did Churchill, even against his wife Clementine's wishes, include Beaverbrook in his inner circle?

Harriman noticed the admiration that Churchill displayed towards Beaverbrook. He put it down partly to the fact that Churchill knew he could never have made a fortune from scratch. When the three men played poker during the voyage, Harriman and Beaverbrook agreed beforehand that they would not try to win at the expense of Churchill, who was not a good player. But Beaverbrook nevertheless played to win: 'This is typical of Beaverbrook's relationship with the Prime Minister,' Harriman wrote.

> The PM considers that Beaverbrook can do a lot of things which he cannot, such as building up his successful newspapers, financial acquisitiveness, gambling, etc., and he does not understand what is back of them. Beaverbrook realises this and never gives himself away. Winning from the PM at poker is an essential part of their relationship. . . .

It was Beaverbrook who had had a cinema installed at Chequers for Churchill's use, and arranged a regular supply of films; Churchill explained that 'Max knows how to do these things. I do not.'

Harriman also noticed Churchill's readiness to consult Beaverbrook about Russia. Stalin had complained that the British government had allowed the Polish government in London to launch an 'anti-Soviet smear campaign' over the Katyn massacres; Beaverbrook attacked the Poles and backed Stalin; and it was Beaverbrook who drafted the conciliatory reply to Moscow that so offended the Poles by minimizing Katyn, but seems to have appeased Stalin – rather as Beaverbrook's letters to Ribbentrop had done in 1938. Harriman strongly disapproved of Beaverbrook's 'appeasement' of Stalin; unless the Allies stood up to him during the war, he believed, they were storing up trouble for the future. Beaverbrook thought exactly the opposite: meeting Stalin's demands during the war would secure his goodwill afterwards. 'Beaverbrook is still an isolationist,' Harriman recorded, '. . . and doesn't give a hoot in hell for the small nations. He would turn over Eastern Europe to Russia without regard to future consequences, the Atlantic Charter, etc.'

Harriman went on to note illustrations of Beaverbrook's eccentricities and behaviour: his wild suggestion that on arrival in New York Churchill should show himself to the citizens by driving openly round Manhattan; another suggestion, which seemed equally wild to Harriman, was that Harriman must become a senator; his singing of hymns, loudly and tunelessly, 'exactly as one would have thought he did when a boy of twelve'; and his boredom when Churchill read aloud from Fowler's *Modern English Usage* – an example of Beaverbrook's impatience with rules not written by himself.[57]

In Washington, Churchill certainly seems to have feared that Roosevelt and Beaverbrook would combine against him over his Mediterranean strategy. He tried to stop Beaverbrook accepting an invitation from Roosevelt to the presidential retreat at Shangri La (later Camp David), and Beaverbrook went only after Roosevelt told him, through Harry Hopkins, that he was not in the habit of having his invitations refused. Churchill successfully insisted, however, that Beaverbrook should not attend any military talks.

Archie Rowlands's comparison of the relationship to a difficult marriage seems particularly apt. Churchill wanted Beaverbrook back in the government; Beaverbrook wanted to be back in the government. But he was still worried that Churchill was trying to cage him, and again demanded reassurances about a second front, like a separated wife asking her husband for an undertaking to change his behaviour before she returned to the matrimonial home. Churchill refused. Finally, Churchill was able to make the promise; on 23 September, after Beaverbrook had put down a motion about the second front in the House of Lords, Churchill asked him to drop it, telling him that an attack had been decided for the spring of 1944. Thus on 28 September Beaverbrook was sworn in as Lord Privy Seal, becoming automatically at the same time an honorary member of the United Services Club and a trustee of the British Museum. He waived his salary.

Three weeks before he returned to office, Beaverbrook learned that Valentine Castlerosse, who less than a year earlier had succeeded his father as Earl of Kenmare, had been found dead of a massive heart attack: he was fifty-one. Since the outbreak of the war neither of them had thought necessary, he and Beaverbrook had seen little of each other; during the phoney war Castlerosse had been in Ireland, building his dream golf course at Killarney. By the time he returned to London, Beaverbrook was in the government and had little time for amusement, although he had Castlerosse to stay at Cherkley after his former wife, Doris, took an overdose in the Dorchester Hotel in 1942. Castlerosse blamed himself; he had made it plain to Doris that he could not come to her rescue when she arrived from New York without money and with her beauty and social position damaged by the passage of time. Within weeks, however, he had recovered enough to marry another *femme fatale*, Enid Furness, who had already been widowed three times.

To the end, Beaverbrook paid his friend's medical bills and debts; after his death, Enid Kenmare continued to plead for money. In one of Castlerosse's last letters to his patron of nearly thirty years he wrote: 'If you could multiply the word "gratitude" by a billion I would be beginning to make a start – but there I had better leave it for I know that you like letters that end almost before they start. I don't suppose any man owed so much to another as I do to you.' Beaverbrook wrote affectionately in the *Sunday Express*: 'On the surface no two men could be more utterly different than Castlerosse and me. I had a talent for hard work and in consequence I made money. Castlerosse had a supernatural talent for getting rid of it. He was an enchanting and warm-hearted companion.'

DIVIDING THE WORLD

As Lord Privy Seal, based in Whitehall at Gwydyr House, a short stroll from Downing Street, Beaverbrook found himself handed by Churchill the sort of problem he relished. By 1943, flights across the Atlantic had become routine; and it was obvious that the end of the war would introduce a revolutionary new era of trans-oceanic air travel. The question was: how could Britain secure a fair – the civil service word for 'unfair' – share of this huge prospective market, given the superior power and resources of the United States?

Beaverbrook's calm and knowledgeable special adviser, Peter Masefield, who had been young Max's fag at Westminster School, gave him the documents and explained the problem. The Foreign Office had identified it as early as the autumn of 1942 – at about the time the British Eighth Army and the US First Army were linking up in North Africa – and it had put them in a high state of excitement. The United States was aiming at 'world domination' of post-war air routes and held a much stronger hand than Britain. The single British ace was a string of well-placed imperial airfields, whereas the Americans held two aces: more money and modern civil transport aircraft. Pan American Inc. and eight other US airlines were already operating, under charter to US Air Transport Command, a network of routes across Africa and into India. Pan American was flying to over sixty countries. Still more awkward, the Americans had built at great expense war bases on British territory, in Newfoundland, the British West Indies, Bermuda, and across central Africa, as well as in China and across the Pacific. Now they wanted to build airfields across North Africa, from Tripoli to Cairo. From Egypt, the Minister of State reported that the Americans were waging 'every form of propaganda and whispering campaign' against the inadequately equipped British Overseas Airways Corporation, with the object of securing a monopoly for themselves.

The Air Ministry and Foreign Office foresaw a grim future. At the end of the war, they said, the United Kingdom would be bound to let the Americans continue to use the airfields they had built on British Empire soil because it would be unable to satisfy the expected demand for air travel itself. The country would not have the machines. British bombers were not easily convertible to civil use, whereas the USA had a series of civil transport aircraft operating in military guise. Therefore the government must start planning a range of new civil aircraft, 'otherwise no amount of haggling by the Foreign Office and Air Ministry will prevent the Americans grabbing the air traffic of the world'.[58]

Faced with this threat, the British had dithered. A letter from Churchill to Roosevelt setting out British concerns was drafted and redrafted throughout the summer of 1943 and finally shelved. Meanwhile American production of military aircraft, some of them readily convertible to passenger aircraft, had risen to unimaginable heights: from 19,433 in 1941 to 47,838 in 1942 and 90,000 in 1943.

Beaverbrook's first move was to gather the reins into his own hands. He told C. D. Howe of Canada, who wanted to start bilateral negotiations with the Americans, that the best results would be achieved if the Americans had to deal with Britain alone 'when they need help or the grant of facilities'.[59] He tried, though he failed, to bypass the bureaucracies of both countries by dealing direct with Harry Hopkins. He opened negotiations for exclusive post-war landing rights in Abyssinia, to give himself an extra card in Africa. On 11 October, at a whirlwind and effective 'Empire Conference' in London, he secured an agreement to press ahead with a civil re-design of the Avro Lancaster IV bomber, and endorsement of the idea of a round-the-world air route operated in partnership by Commonwealth airlines. Five weeks after he returned to office he told Churchill what Britain's policy should be: she must stake 'overriding claims' to all traffic inside the UK and all traffic in the colonial Empire, invoking the principle of cabotage, 'which reserves to each country all traffic picked up at one point in its territories and set down at another'; and she must retain the right to fly all the 'great Empire routes'. (When Beaverbrook used the word 'cabotage' in the House of Lords he alarmed elderly peers who had never heard the word before and thought he was talking about sabotage.)

The problem was considered grave enough to warrant the creation of a War Cabinet Committee on Post-War Civil Air Transport, chaired by Beaverbrook and made up of all leading members of the War Cabinet, with Masefield as secretary. It met first on 11 November 1943 and thereafter almost every Thursday for the next fifteen months. Masefield found Beaverbrook 'surprisingly patient'.

In Washington the State Department negotiator was Adolf Berle, a brilliant forty-four-year-old Harvard lawyer who had helped to lay the intellectual foundations of the New Deal. Beaverbrook wooed Berle across the Atlantic, sending him a first edition of Cardinal Newman's *Occasional Hymns* under the impression that he was a Roman Catholic. Berle replied sardonically that a British intelligence dossier must have mixed him up with a former colleague who did turn Catholic, and that 'several generations of dissenting ancestors would turn in their graves if that happened' to him.

As usual, Beaverbrook's ambitions were large. In November, he unveiled a plan for dividing the air traffic of the post-war world between Britain and the United States, as if he and Berle were the modern successors of Octavian and Antony dividing the Roman Empire. Britain should make 'large concessions' to the United States in South America, where before the war the Germans had made considerable inroads. In return, the Americans would 'concede our claims' in Europe, the Mediterranean and Africa.

Left to themselves, Berle and Beaverbrook could have constructed a deal. Although the Air Ministry was alarmed by the very idea of letting the Americans enjoy traffic rights on British routes, Beaverbrook and Masefield were not; they thought that national airlines should be licensed to fly any route they wished, provided that competition between airlines was sensibly regulated. Pan American was as restrictive as the Air Ministry, hoping to establish its domination, but Berle wanted as few restrictions as possible. The American government, believing BOAC to be inefficient, opposed any monopoly, and were confident that the resulting competition would knock BOAC out of the skies.

Beaverbrook saw in the new year of 1944 in Marrakesh, where Churchill was convalescing after a bout of pneumonia. For a rich man who travelled so restlessly, Beaverbrook's horizons were curiously limited. Greece and Italy held no interest for him. He never went east of Moscow: not to the Far East, not to Australia, not even to India. Apart from brief stops on a yacht, his two-week stay in Marrakesh represented his only visit to Africa. Even then the circumstances were scarcely typical either of Africa or of wartime. The Americans had lent Churchill the luxurious Villa Taylor, with a fine French chef. Beaverbrook stayed there, as did Nockels, his valet. Churchill summoned and conferred with Allied military chieftains, but otherwise the atmosphere was that of a house party. Max Aitken – now Group Captain Max Aitken DSO, DFC – Randolph Churchill and Diana Cooper came and went; there were picnics in olive groves, riding, expeditions to admire the Atlas Mountains, rows between Randolph and his father that Beaverbrook tried but failed to douse, and poker at night. 'I made the mistake of trying to call Lord Beaverbrook's bluff,' Colville, the private secretary, recorded in his diary. He would have lost £2500 had not Beaverbrook and Churchill agreed to divide the gains and losses by 1000. Beaverbrook remained benevolent, taking Colville and Hollis, the military secretary, shopping, buying Hollis yards of useless gauze and Colville a magnificent white leather bag, and accepting from an antique shop owner in the market some revoltingly scented quince jam and mint tea for his companions, without asking them, while refusing for himself. Nockels, as usual, made an impression. The Villa Taylor featured an imposing courtyard. One morning the Spahi guards were drawn up for a visit to Churchill by the Allied Commander in Chief, General Eisenhower. Commands were shouted, rifle butts smacked. As the Commander in Chief walked slowly across the courtyard he passed an open window, and the party standing at attention to greet him heard a voice from within – Nockels, adopting his best Cherkley manner of welcome and condescension: 'How *are* we, sir, how *nice* to see you again!'[60] Beaverbrook's servants could always take liberties that his employees could not.

Back in London, the air negotiations hit turbulence. In April 1944 Berle and his team came to Gwydyr House, where on the second day they ran into head-on disagreement with Beaverbrook about traffic rights and the fixing of fares. Among those present at a final dinner at Claridge's was the

Oxford philospher Isaiah Berlin from the Washington Embassy, who was appalled by the way Beaverbrook went out of his way to humiliate Berle about wine in front of the wine waiter. In revenge, Berle said in his speech of thanks that his father had been a missionary in Persia where he had observed the oppressive brutality of the British Empire.

Three months later Beaverbrook and his advisers flew from London to Washington – the first non-stop flight (nineteen hours, forty-eight minutes) between the capitals – to take the talks a stage further. After three weeks Beaverbrook cabled Churchill to tell him that Pan American was still determined to dominate future air routes round the world and that the Americans were pouring dollars and energy into civil aircraft production. Unless Britain was prepared to produce new types of aircraft – converted bombers would not do – and subsidize British air transport, the mastery of world civil aviation would inevitably pass to the United States. The telegram ended: 'Arise O Israel!' On his return, Beaverbrook pressed the same argument in Cabinet Committee and in the House of Lords.

But he was becoming bored with the detail of civil aviation. When Roosevelt, without consultation with the British, called an international air conference in Chicago for November 1944, Beaverbrook 'laughed loud and long', saying it meant that the United States 'was determined to call the tune'. He told Churchill that a large international conference, which would need much time, effort and above all great patience, was 'not his cup of tea'; civil aviation needed a ministry of its own, and Lord Swinton was the man to head it. Churchill agreed. At lunch on the first day of the Chicago conference Swinton quarrelled violently with Berle – Swinton wanted 'a cosy parcelling out of traffic among nations' whereas Berle wanted a free-for-all – and in thirty-seven days the conference achieved nothing on traffic rights. Eighteen months later, in Bermuda, largely due to the disappearance of the hard-liners and to the good sense of Beaverbrook's protégé Peter Masefield, Britain and the United States signed a liberal, trail-blazing agreement on bilateral traffic rights; but by then Beaverbrook himself had moved on to other things.

Masefield had tried to persuade him to stay in charge of the civil aviation negotiations, but Beaverbrook said that with a general election pending he wanted to help Churchill prepare for post-war government rather than tie himself down with the details of international air transport.[61] Officially, as Lord Privy Seal he concerned himself with the development prospects for jet engines and the protection of British oil interests in the Middle East; unofficially he tried to make sure that the socialists kept their hands off capitalist interests in Britain. The Beveridge Report on post-war social reform had been published in December 1942; Beaverbrook concluded that capitalists were going to have to change their ways, but not by much.

With talk of post-war reconstruction in progress, he and his old socialist allies recognized that there had to be a parting of the ways. Foot handed over the editorship of the *Evening Standard* and became a leader writer on the *Daily Express*. Beaverbrook required him, against his will, to write a leader in December 1943 in support of Morrison's decision, as Home Secretary, to release the Fascist leader Oswald Mosley from prison. In June 1944 Foot told Beaverbrook he wanted to make a change: 'your views and mine are bound to become more and more irreconcilable'.[62] Driberg had been fired in the summer of 1943 for using information picked up in the *Express* office in a speech in the House of Commons; Blumenfeld wrote to Robertson to ask why he hadn't been got rid of years before. Frank Owen was editing a forces newspaper in South East Asia Command. Nearer to home, in Beaverbrook's old ministry in Shell-Mex House, a socialist who had always mistrusted Beaverbrook, Douglas Jay, was disturbed to learn that he was busily working at the highest levels of government to undermine all constructive discussion of post-war planning. Beaverbrook stated his views succinctly – with the *Daily Express* labour correspondent doing his research – when in January 1945 Bevin promoted a bill to set up wages councils: '. . . this is a constitutional change of the most sweeping character', he told Churchill, 'and with implications that lead to the nationalisation of wages'.[63] He told Leo Amery: 'I am not in favour of a controlled economy. I am against the supervision of our capital investment by civil servants. The only men who should control our money are the men who own it.'[64]

'I HAVE LOST MY MOORINGS'

Although Beaverbrook continued to see Mrs Norton during the war, especially at Cherkley, where she had her own room in the house as well as the cottage he had lent her, it seemed to those around them that he took her and the relationship more and more for granted and that Lily Ernst, although kept at a discreet distance, had displaced her. Jean Norton immersed herself in war work, first in London during the blitz and then taking a tough job in a factory near Leatherhead, where she operated a lathe and became a shop steward. In August 1943, on the death of her father-in-law, she became Lady Grantley, and celebrated by volunteering to clean out the lavatories at her factory. One regular guest at Cherkley thought Jean's looks were showing signs of age and hard work and that she was foolish, if she wanted to keep Beaverbrook, not to take more trouble with her appearance. But for Jean, as for her friend Edwina Mountbatten, the war brought out a sense of duty in a way that the bright social years had not. Both the Grantleys' children were caught up in the war, John with the Grenadier Guards like his father before him and Sarah in the Wrens; a letter from their mother to Beaverbrook survives, written after he had sent her a note congratulating her on their efforts. 'I value your appreciation of my children above all others. Perhaps because of the love I have and always shall have for you come what may – I can say no more but that I am and always shall be your ever loving Jeannie.'

In late January 1945, after an evening at Cherkley, she went back to her cottage, where her daughter Sarah and her sister Kitty Brownlow were staying with her, and during the night had a heart attack. A few days later Beaverbrook wrote in his own hand to Diana Cooper, then Ambassadress in Paris:

> Jean was very happy at the end of the year and the early days of Jan were filled with good news of her son and pleasant parties with her daughter Sarah.
>
> On Sunday she walked with me for a long time in the afternoon and her health was good and her strength was remarkable. In many ways she was better than in the days before the Factory.
>
> She left me at half after twelve on Sunday night after seeing a picture at Cherkley. Her car was standing under the Portico at the front door because of the rain. There was some fun about it – and away she moved in laughter and high spirits.
>
> At five o'clock on Monday morning a clot of blood reached her heart and she wakened in terrible pain. Kitty and Sarah were there and doctors were soon with her.
>
> When I was called by the local doctor he told me the illness would be grave but if she lived for a few days we might expect a respite – perhaps years. During the day I called in the specialists from London. They thought she had an even chance of life.
>
> About midnight on Monday I was told she was having a natural sleep. I went to her room very quietly and at a glance I could see that the end was soon to come upon her. The doctors came again. But at half after two she died.
>
> She was buried in a snow storm at Grantham. And I have lost my moorings.[65]

Jean Norton had loved Beaverbrook steadily for twenty years, despite his infidelities, and he must have known it. He remained on excellent terms with her husband, tried to help her children, and kept for the rest of his life, tucked into a blotter on his desk, a poem in her handwriting and inscribed, in his, 'By Mrs Norton, undated'.

> How should not absence from thy presence change me,
> Since in thy presence all my future is.
> And in thy absence all things do estrange me
> From that, and bind me to past miseries . . . .[66]

He made sure that she left nothing behind that could embarrass him. He arranged for a detailed inventory to be made of the contents of the cottage, and acquired several of her diaries.

THE END OF HOSTILITIES

The war was ending and the coalition had served its turn. Germany surrendered on 8 May 1945 and Churchill ended the coalition on 23 May,

Beaverbrook staying on as Lord Privy Seal in the caretaker government. He always enjoyed elections. In June, he made pro-Churchill speeches and became one of the Conservative Party's main election managers, sitting in on meetings chaired by Woolton (whom he disliked) and trusted by Churchill. Churchill told Willink, the Minister of Health, to be sure to consult Beaverbrook about health service policy 'as his political experience is very great and long' – though ten years shorter, he might have added, than his experience as a hypochondriac.

A revealing incident took place that May, on a Sunday evening at Cherkley. The 11th Marquess of Queensberry, Harold Balfour, Brendan Bracken and Colville were present. Colville recorded it as evidence of

> . . . the strong social chip on Lord Beaverbrook's shoulder. In the course of attacking Eden he said the latter owed his success to his birth and education. He then turned to the assembled company and said that true men of quality, like Harold Balfour, Brendan and himself, had worked their way up from nothing by sheer hard work and ability, whereas Lord Queensberry and I were like Anthony Eden and had only got where we were because of the circumstances in which we were born. Having made this attack, with flashing eyes, he then proceeded to send for the Scottish Psalter and read aloud to us several of the metrical psalms. I think he did this as a form of grace before dinner and a possible means of making amends to the Almighty.

Colville 'awoke to a glorious view through the Dorking Gap, a bath in a fantastically over-luxurious bathroom, and a single poached egg accompanied by the *Daily Express*'. He poked about in the library,

> . . . in the belief that books often tell one much about their owner. His were mostly dull, the lesser novelists and the standard biographies. But on a reading desk, by the side of two dictaphones, stood the Bible, open at the Psalms and in a nearby bookshelf was Wilkes's notorious *Essay on Woman*, an obscene parody of Pope's *Essay on Man*, which on publication was burned by the public hangman. Copies are therefore rare.[67]

After thirty-five years, five of them spent at war, working at the highest level, Beaverbrook still resented the English class structure and felt himself to be a social outsider; and he was still regarded with interest and amusement as an alien specimen by an insider like Colville. Like other visitors to Cherkley from a more orthodox English world, Colville enjoyed the racketeering, buccaneering atmosphere, but rightly foresaw that its fomenter would cause much trouble both during the coming election and after.

Michael Foot left the *Express* in the nick of time. The full force of Beaverbrookian campaignmanship was unleashed in the Conservative cause and directed against the 'socialists'. Churchill's famous and famously misjudged 'Gestapo' speech – with which Beaverbrook, though blamed for it, had nothing to do – was strongly featured and supported: 'GESTAPO

IN BRITAIN IF SOCIALISTS WIN', said the *Daily Express*. 'They would dictate what to do and say, even where to queue.' Socialism, which in its Communist form under Stalin had achieved such benefits in Russia, according to Beaverbrook's Waldorf speech three years earlier, would, it now appeared, if applied by Attlee to Britain, put the nation in chains. 'Mr Attlee is the decoy duck of socialism. . . . Cripps has outlined his party's technique for by-passing parliament and the courts of law. Attlee has publicly approved the method. And it is exactly the method used by Hitler to turn the Reichstag into a mockery in 1933. . . .' When Professor Harold Laski, the chairman of the Labour Party, made a speech apparently advocating the use of violence to achieve reform, Christiansen at the *Express*, and perhaps Beaverbrook too, thought the paper had been handed a weapon that would destroy Labour's chances. Attlee was hardly mentioned as the guns were turned on Laski and Laski-ism. 'SOCIAL-ISTS DECIDE THEY HAVE LOST', said the *Express* on 2 July.

Beaverbrook certainly expected victory. The puzzle is that the pro-prietor of Britain's most successful popular newspaper should have misjudged so completely the public mood. Still, the paper – no doubt surmising that many if not most of its readers had probably voted Labour – managed a certain dignity after the 'debacle' of the Labour landslide. 'There will be no captious criticism of the new government . . .,' said the *Express* of 27 July, '. . . no attempt to turn the nation's discontents into Party capital. The new government must be given its chance in this difficult period of the Aftermath.' Except in the case of Baldwin, Beaverbrook's instinct in politics was always to keep open the lines of communication to those in power.

CHAPTER 21

'THE MAN WHO
HAD TO KNOW'
1945–1956

ALMOST EVERY ASPECT of the post-war world order might have
been designed to frustrate and annoy Beaverbrook. The United States
emerged as the dominant power; Britain sank into dependence; new
international institutions were formed; imperial links grew weaker. He was
sixty-six in 1945 and unlikely to rethink his ideas. From Downing Street,
after Attlee replaced Churchill, Beaverbrook was more cut off than he had
been since the premiership of Baldwin. He had a low opinion of Attlee,
which was reciprocated, and, though well aware of the strengths of the
new Foreign Secretary, Ernest Bevin – he called him 'a formidable beast'
– disapproved of his foreign policy. He was against the Marshall Plan as
he had been against the American loan of 1945 (he thought the Empire
had been sold off cheap), against the rebuilding of Germany, against
Indian independence (he said Lord Mountbatten, the Viceroy, was
behaving like Santa Claus); in the Middle East, he thought Bevin had
achieved the impossible by being hated equally by Arabs and by Jews. He
clung firmly to his old ideas: imperial unity, freedom from foreign
entanglements, arm's length friendship with the United States. As for the
gravest foreign policy issue of all, relations between the West and Russia,
he took the position that he had taken after 1917: leave Russia to its own
devices. He had been honoured in 1944 with the Order of Suvorov, which
gave him the right to free travel in the USSR. The expansion of the
Russian empire and subjugation of European nations to a tyranny was
unfortunate, but did not affect Britain's vital interests. He was one of the
few influential voices in Britain who had no ideological sympathy with
Communism, yet believed the cold war unnecessary. He disapproved of

Churchill's Fulton Speech in 1946, in which he announced that an Iron Curtain had descended across Europe, as much as he disapproved of anything said or done by Bevin.

His attitude to Stalin's Russia echoed his attitude to Nazi Germany. In the spring of 1946 Ribbentrop's lawyer at the Nuremberg war crimes trials submitted a list of questions designed to elicit support for Ribbentrop's claim that he had always wanted peace between Germany and Britain and that Beaverbrook could confirm as much. George Malcolm Thomson formulated Beaverbrook's answers. The task was made easier by the fact that Ribbentrop got his dates wrong; he emphasized the years from 1937 to 1938, and Beaverbrook was able to reply that he had not seen Ribbentrop in 1937 or 1938. He acknowledged that he had visited Berlin in 1935 and met Ribbentrop and Hitler; but in answer to the suggestion that Ribbentrop had asked him to work towards 'friendly relations' between their two countries, the reply was: 'I have no recollection of this.' None of their contacts in 1936 or the visit to the Berlin Olympics came up. To the question: 'Are you of the opinion that von Ribbentrop devoted himself to this task many years of his life and . . . saw in the attaining of this goal the fulfilment of his life mission' Beaverbrook's answer was: 'I regarded Ribbentrop as a German official, bearing the German national aspirations, whatever they might be.'[1] The Beaverbrook responses were accurate as far as they went, but hardly reflected the nature of his dealings with Ribbentrop.

He was naturally hostile to the Labour government's nationalization programme, but little more in sympathy with the Conservatives, as they, in the wake of their rejection by the voters, set about rethinking their party's policies. The Conservatives were no better pleased with him than he was with them; some blamed him for helping Labour into office by employing left-wingers to write for his papers; others blamed him for alienating potential Conservative voters by being too violent in his attacks on the socialists during the election campaign – socialists who, after all, only yesterday had been loyal partners in the coalition that led Britain to victory. The one issue on which he agreed with the Labour government was its pursuit of full employment. Everyone had a right to a job. 'Beaverbrook wanted working people to prosper, so long as it didn't bother Beaverbrook,' said George Malcolm Thomson.[2]

Detached from British politics, he nevertheless remained, as one of his secretaries privately and accurately dubbed him, 'the man who had to know'; and he had one informant at the heart of the Labour government. Hector McNeil had become an MP during the war but remained on the *Express* part-time. When the Labour government was formed McNeil left the *Express*, with £500 from the paper and £500 as a personal present from Beaverbrook, and became first a junior minister and then in 1946 Minister of State (the title invented for Beaverbrook by Churchill) at the Foreign Office – Bevin's deputy. But he remained in close touch with Beaverbrook, despite the disapproval of Attlee and Bevin. In 1948 Beaverbrook offered to rent him and his wife, Sheila, a cottage on the Cherkley estate. McNeil was grateful: 'It is exactly what we have been looking for for some time – two bedrooms, water, and a garden where the boy can safely play.' McNeil suggested a rent of £100 a year unfurnished. Mr Millar, the head of Beaverbrook's private office at the *Express*, reported to Beaverbrook: 'I spoke to Robertson. He says it would be suicidal for the young man to take it. So near your own house, no one would believe in the inhabitant's absolute detachment. Further, he says it violates a cardinal rule – never to let a house to a friend. . . . Incidentally, you would have to pay 19s 6d in the £ on the rent.'[3] The proposal lapsed.

Beaverbrook's fierce public opposition to almost everything the Foreign Office was trying to do does not seem to have disturbed McNeil. He saw Beaverbrook in London; when he went to the United Nations in New York, he hoped he would see Beaverbrook there for a gossip. As often happened, Beaverbrook's friendly relations with a man were heavily influenced by his relations with the man's wife. Mrs McNeil liked his habit of singing Scottish psalms at dinner. Beaverbrook sent her brief, cheerful letters – 'I have no worries in this life and none about the life to come. For I believe in predestination. But I am in a bad way due to sunburn' – and hams from Canada, and warm boots, building bricks and an elaborate chemistry set for the young son. On Beaverbrook's seventieth birthday, in 1949, McNeil wrote: 'None of the adjectives usually attributed to old age fits you, Max. Serene? Definitely not. Tranquil? No. Passive? Anything but. Sober? Occasionally. Placid? Haven't noticed it. Patient? Heavens no.' For Christmas 1950 Beaverbrook gave McNeil a 'more than generous present. I don't mind telling you that it is exceedingly welcome.'[4] In 1950 McNeil became Secretary of State for Scotland and made enquiries about Scottish woodland suitable for Beaverbrook to buy.

After the Labour defeat in 1951 Beaverbrook asked McNeil to rejoin the *Express*, and McNeil would have done so 'without the slightest hesitation' had not his wife, without telling him, written to Beaverbrook to point out that 'a close association with the *Express* as a salary earner and a high position within the Labour party [are] incompatible'.[5] Instead, McNeil joined the *Encyclopaedia Britannica*; four years later, in New York, he was taken ill and, with shocking suddenness, died. Beaverbrook at once offered Mrs McNeil any comfort and help he could, and took responsibility for the boy's school fees at Westminster, sending him the occasional £25 tip.

ROYAL COMMISSION

In 1947, mainly under pressure from Labour Party journalists, the government set up a royal commission on the press, an act that Beaverbrook regarded as 'persecution' – as in its way it was, since

Beaverbrook was one of its main targets. To discredit him, his persecutors were trying to establish two points: first, that he ran his papers as personal fiefdoms, without giving their editors any freedom of action at all; second, that his papers operated a secret blacklist of people who were never to be mentioned – Beaverbrook's personal enemies, it was assumed. The *Express* team prepared carefully for their appearances before the Commission, and the Commission members, whose homework had been less thorough, failed to disconcert them. Two witnesses, both former Beaverbrook employees, led the attack. Michael Foot named Sir Thomas Beecham, Paul Robeson, Haile Selassie and Noël Coward as people on the banned list 'for personal and political reasons'. Tom Driberg added G. K. Chesterton and Hilaire Belloc.

In defence, Robertson put on an especially good performance. He explained that London Express Newspapers Ltd, of which he was chairman, owned the *Daily Express*, and through subsidiaries the *Evening Standard* and *Sunday Express*, and 51 per cent of the *Glasgow Evening Citizen*. Lord Beaverbrook 'never actually took any title; he has not been a director of the paper since 1920, but he was undoubtedly the paper . . . .' In mitigation of the charge that Beaverbrook was a dictator, he pointed to the existence of a Policy Committee of fourteen people, who did not include Beaverbrook. He freely admitted the existence of the lists, but said they were compiled by the lawyers. The Commission was given the lists.

Beaverbrook's appearance on 18 March 1948 was a triumph of apparent candour and genuine humour. For thirty years he had been answering, or dodging, criticisms about the way he conducted his papers. When asked why he owned newspapers, he gave one reply that became famous: 'I ran the paper purely for the purpose of making propaganda.' He explained that the propaganda went on in the leader columns only. 'The policy is that there shall be no propaganda in the news. There is a strong, stern rule, and the most tremendous attempt . . . to carry that rule into effect, but we do stumble. It is terrible how often we stumble; it is heartbreaking sometimes.' Of the lists, he said: 'Some people call it a blacklist. In the *Evening Standard* it is called the cautionary list, and in the *Daily Express* office it is called the warned list.' But there had never been a political name on it, and he had never put a name on it himself.

The most formidable member of the Commission was Lady Violet Bonham Carter, a fearless *grande dame* who regarded Beaverbrook as a malign influence in British public life, partly because he had helped to remove her father, Asquith, from Downing Street, and partly because she detested the appeasement policies Beaverbrook had pursued before the war. She particularly wanted to prove the existence of a secret blacklist, but she failed. Driberg alleged years later, as if making a revelation, that the reason why the Commission had been unable to discover the blacklist was because it was called a 'white list', to make it sound less menacing; but he had in fact talked about a 'white list' in his evidence. He also said he had got hold of a copy after the Royal Commission completed its work; Belloc was still on it, and other names included Noël Coward, Douglas Fairbanks Jr, Charlie Chaplin and Paul Robeson.[6]

But the Royal Commission concluded that the lists were unremarkable: they were 'for the most part a tangible expression of the risks of a libel action'. Both Beecham and Haile Selassie had brought libel actions. As for Robeson, there had been twenty-six references to him during Foot's association with the papers, and during Driberg's time Chesterton had been mentioned sixty-nine times and Belloc nine times.

Towards his critics, Beaverbrook adopted in his evidence the attitude of an indulgent parent to naughty boys: '. . . these lads, a splendid lot', he called them, had 'made up' their charges. He conceded that he issued what were called directives to his papers, but 'it was', he said,

> . . . really advice, particularly to Michael Foot. He is a very clever fellow, a most excellent boy. And then suddenly he was projected into the editorship of the paper before he was ready for it. . . . Michael Foot himself believed that I made him a journalist. He took the view that I allowed him immense freedom of expression, and he certainly thought that he had more freedom of expression with me than he could have had with anyone else.

This reply holed his main Labour critic below the waterline. Foot had fallen out with Beaverbrook after 1945, when the former editor became an MP, and had lambasted his proprietorship in the Commons during the 1946 debate that led to the setting up of the Royal Commission. But if he now replied to these personal references by saying that the directives were indeed directives, since they required him to write under orders, and were not merely 'advice', Beaverbrook had Foot's 1944 letter in his files to prove the opposite; Foot had written, 'I know you never ask me to write views with which I disagree.' Nevertheless, Foot's main point in that letter, and in an earlier letter in 1943, had been that he was frustrated precisely because he did not have 'immense freedom of expression'; on the contrary, it was because he had to suppress his own views that he wrote uninspired, non-committal leaders.[7]

SIR HARTLEY SHAWCROSS KC

Beaverbrook usually preferred, if he could, to outwit his critics rather than openly oppose them. The Labour Attorney General was Sir Hartley Shawcross KC. In the summer of 1946, when wartime food rationing was still in force, the Labour government found itself compelled to reduce the bread ration. The decision was violently attacked, and, as Shawcross thought, misrepresented by the capitalist newspapers. A by-election was in train in Battersea. On 19 July Shawcross made a bitter assault on 'the proprietors of the gutter press', named Kemsley and Beaverbrook, and said they had 'seriously abused the freedom which is accorded to them under the constitution'. He then went off to his yacht in the West Country, where he was telephoned by a barrister friend and advised that Kemsley was proposing to take a big libel action against him. 'I said, okay, I shall defend it.' This decision received immense publicity. Shawcross decided he would have to defend the action himself, not having the money to hire other lawyers, and that he would have to resign to do so. He drove to Chequers to tell Attlee he was going to resign. 'Oh no you're not,' said Attlee. 'You are going to apologise. It will be forgotten in a week. No argument. Now let's go and have supper.' Kemsley blazoned the public apology across all his papers. That did not settle matters with Beaverbrook. 'He had me defenceless. Having apologised to Kemsley, I couldn't fight Beaverbrook.'[8] Had Beaverbrook taken the matter to court, he would have been assured of substantial damages.

Beaverbrook sent Shawcross a message, and on 9 August the Attorney General sent back a handwritten apology. He had, he wrote,

> . . . learned with regret that certain words of mine . . . have given you the impression that I intended to impugn your business and professional integrity in the conduct of your newspapers, and in particular to allege that you were conducting a 'gutter press' and intentionally distorting and suppressing facts.
>
> I can assure you that I did not intend to make any of these imputations on you and if any words of mine appeared to make them I desire unreservedly to withdraw them and express my regret. . . .

On a separate sheet he added 'a personal note' in which he said: '. . . I realise and shall not forget that your present attitude has not been ungenerous.'

Beaverbrook's reply was delivered by Mr Millar in person to Sir Hartley's chambers in the Temple. 'I am obliged to you,' he wrote, 'for the generous and wholehearted manner in which you withdraw from the attack on me in your speeches.' The sting was in the tail: 'I see no need for bothering you with publication. If nothing further arises, the letter need never be referred to again.'[9] The warning was phrased with delicacy. Shawcross thought the letter clever; by keeping the withdrawal secret Beaverbrook earned the goodwill, and later the friendship, of a man who seemed likely to rise to the top in politics.

CHILDREN AND GRANDCHILDREN

After the war Beaverbrook's daughter Janet, now Mrs Kidd, decided to return with her husband to Canada with their two small children, leaving behind her older daughter and son, Jean Campbell and William Montagu. Jean had already, for some years, been spending more time at Cherkley with her grandfather than with her mother in Sussex; now, in her early teens, her relations with her mother were stormy and she made it quite clear that she would rather live with him.[10] Jean was a warm, intelligent, pretty girl and still the apple of Beaverbrook's eye. Bill, a quieter character, spent part of the time with his other grandfather, the Earl of Sandwich; nobody seemed to know quite what to do with Billy, and a story still circulates among the Montagus of how he was once found at a railway station with a label round his neck saying 'From Lord Beaverbrook to Lord Hinchingbrooke'. He was sent to Eton, and started to make frequent requests for extra pocket money, often fielded by the inscrutable Mr Millar.

Both Beaverbrook's older grandchildren were thought by his household to have suffered from their mother's casual attitude towards them, even before she remarried and went to Canada. Once Beaverbrook gave Miss Bower £100 and told her to take Jean and buy her some decent clothes, 'since her mother doesn't seem capable'; several outfits were purchased at Selfridge's, but Mrs Kidd was so angry that she sent everything back. The Kidds decided after about a year to come back to England after all, and with Beaverbrook's help eventually settled in the West Country to farm and breed horses; Jean continued to be based with her grandfather.

Max Aitken's first marriage broke up during the war; in 1946 he married Mrs Jane Lindsay and was to have two daughters, Kirsty and Lynda, before this marriage also failed. He was married for the third time in 1951, to Violet de Trafford, and had two more children; a son, Maxwell, born in 1951, and a daughter, Laura.

In 1947, off the coast of Sweden, Peter Aitken fell from a yacht and soon afterwards died in hospital. He was thirty-five, and had for some years been accident-prone and drinking heavily. His relations with his father had deteriorated; Miss Bower remembers being instructed by Beaverbrook to visit Peter in hospital after he had fallen off a motorbicycle and being told: 'You won't find him very agreeable, but go and see him.' When she arrived with her flowers and chocolates, Peter Aitken shouted at her: 'Who the hell are you? What does my father want?'[11] She did not stay long. According to Janet Kidd, Beaverbrook was in France when word came that Peter was dead. Her husband went to Sweden to bring back the body; Janet arranged the funeral at Mickleham church, where he was buried next to his mother. 'Perhaps Father's grief was silent, I don't know. He never spoke about Peter's death, either then or later.'[12] He did, however, take a great interest in Peter's two sons, who often stayed with him at Cherkley and at La Capponcina.

During the late 1940s Beaverbrook's love affair with Lily Ernst came to an end. According to her friends she still loved him as much as ever when the war ended, and hoped that perhaps, after Jean Norton's death, he might even marry her. One of her Viennese friends never forgave the way Lily was treated, believing that it was because she was foreign that Beaverbrook never brought her into the centre of his life, and that his maltreatment made her ill.[13] Michael Foot also remembered a long period of anxiety about Lily's health.[14] Certainly she became very unhappy; Lady d'Avigdor-Goldsmid has recalled that when after the war Beaverbrook resumed his regular trips to the West Indies or the Riviera, he also resumed his womanizing and Lily refused to tolerate it. But when she fell in love with Anthony Hornby, a cultivated and rich businessman who asked her to marry him, Beaverbrook was taken aback. He instructed Mr Millar to investigate Hornby's finances and asked Lady d'Avigdor-Goldsmid for advice.

> I got a call from Max: 'I gotta see you, Rose. I must see you today.' The chauffeur drove me up to that horrible flat in Arlington House and there he was, pacing up and down. 'Rose, you gotta stop this marriage.'
> So I said to him: 'If you buy a licence to marry Lily, and give me a cheque made out to her for £100,000, I'll try to persuade her, but I can't promise.'
> 'Oh Rose, don't you trust me? I can't do that. . . .'
> 'No, I don't trust you and I don't think Lily has any reason to trust you either.'
> He went on pacing up and down, more unhappy than angry. . . . Perhaps he genuinely loved her. She was as far as possible independent of him, and he respected that.[15]

According to Lord Granard, Beaverbrook did ask Lily to marry him and she refused. Granard has recalled meeting her around this time and finding her bitter at the shabby way she had been treated by Beaverbrook for ten years. Lily Ernst married Anthony Hornby in 1949. Janet Kidd remembered that the loss of the lovely girl he had rescued, and no doubt considered his property, reduced her father to tears.[16] He never liked to lose.

BACK TO NEW BRUNSWICK

Possibly because he felt alienated from British politics, possibly because he was bored and restless, soon after the war Beaverbrook began to add to his stock of houses and to settle into a pattern of annual travel between London, Jamaica, the Bahamas, the south of France, New York and Canada, like a medieval king touring his estates. There is no doubt, though he never spent a great deal of time there, that Canada was the most important of these way-stations, intricately connected both with his past and with the reputation he hoped to leave behind him. He had often been back to New Brunswick since he left, usually with a retainer. Castlerosse went with him in the early thirties and reported to Wardell that he had discovered a great secret, and Wardell must on no account tell Beaverbrook that Castlerosse had told it to him: Beaverbrook did not come from a poor background at all, as he pretended; the family home in Newcastle was the biggest in the place.

After the war, Beaverbrook chose his itinerary according to the tax laws and the seasons; and, always hating cold weather, took to visiting New

Brunswick in spring and particularly in the fall, when the province is at its best as the maple trees turn red and gold. He based himself in the provincial capital, Fredericton, a well-kept city that boasts handsome old houses and the University of New Brunswick on a fine sloping site looking across city and river to heavily wooded hills beyond, but undeniably remote, with a small-town atmosphere. When Beaverbrook arrived at the Beaverbrook Hotel, named after but not owned by him, everyone knew about it; and in case they did not, he heralded his own arrival by arranging to be interviewed by the local newspapers. Often he gave one interview in Montreal, and another when he reached Fredericton. In Fredericton, when the ritual was over, he invariably handed the reporter what was a substantial tip in the post-war years – $100.

In Montreal in the 1950s the ritual was on one occasion conducted by a journalist who later became a distinguished novelist. Brian Moore found him in a suite at the Windsor wearing a well-cut dinner jacket and thought him, with his tan and bearing, the model of an American rather than a Canadian tycoon. Beaverbrook delivered his usual discourse about imperial ties and the role of integrity on the road to success, and then asked Moore if he drank whisky. Moore, though he did, said he didn't. 'What do you drink? Do you drink champagne?' Moore said he did, though he didn't. Beaverbrook lifted the house phone. 'Bring a bottle of champagne for Mr Moore.' Champagne or cash for the reporter, and friendship with the reporter's proprietor, ensured Beaverbrook respectful coverage when he advanced on Canada.

Similar largesse, though on a more substantial scale, brought him in 1947 the chancellorship of the University of New Brunswick, which became the focus of his interest in the province. Dalhousie was the university with which his family had associations; his elder brother Traven had read law there; he himself had sat the entrance examination. Local legend says that he became the benefactor of the University of New Brunswick to get his own back at Dalhousie. After the war, he turned his attention to the library. Beaverbrook was not the sort of self-made millionaire who scorned learning; and he had his father's example before him. Dr Alfred Bailey was the university's first dean of arts, a historian by training, and the university librarian. His father had known and liked Beaverbrook, and at the turn of the century had once lent him $100 – a considerable sum; later, he had met the young Aitken on a train, and told his son that Aitken had said to him, 'I have just made my first million. I'm on the pig's back. Now watch me!'[17]

Dr Bailey used to see Beaverbrook almost every day when he was in Fredericton; one of his first post-war memories was of entering the 'Vice-Regal Suite' on the seventh floor of the Beaverbrook Hotel and finding the occupant in the act of getting dressed, giving orders to a valet and to a maid about the shirts to be packed for his next stop, which was Jamaica. Bailey soon found himself, as librarian, at the Canadian end of a cornucopia. For three and a half years, he and three assistants spent most of their time drawing up and despatching lists of books that the university needed, and cataloguing them as they arrived. In that short time, the number of books held by the university rose from fifteen thousand to fifty thousand. After 1952 some of them were sent off to the public library in Newcastle that Beaverbrook was establishing at the Old Manse, which he bought that year after the presbyters decided it no longer suited their purposes.

Literary editors on the Beaverbrook papers required reviewers to send back the books they reviewed; many of them ended up in New Brunswick, as did books from Beaverbrook's own shelves. Thus the university library was surprised to receive Dale Carnegie's best-seller *How to Stop Worrying and Start Living*, and on the shelves of the Old Manse Library the memoirs of Tallulah Bankhead inscribed in flamboyant handwriting 'Max with love from Tallulah' now stand alongside volumes of sermons that belonged to his father. He sent over the proofs of Churchill's *Marlborough*, with marginal notes in Churchill's hand. Sometimes he sent manuscripts; he was proud of a letter from Nelson to Lady Hamilton that Beaverbrook characteristically insisted accused her of infidelity to Nelson.

Beaverbrook set out not only to equip the university with a decent library, but also, as Dr Bailey understood him, to make it the repository for the principal collection of modern British political papers. As an executor of Bonar Law's estate Beaverbrook had inherited his papers; after the war he bought the Lloyd George papers for £15,000; and he was left the papers of the former Canadian Prime Minister, his old friend R. B. Bennett. All these were intended for a new building called the Bonar Law–Bennett Library and opened with much publicity; one room was named, in anticipation, the Lloyd George Room. But the hope was not fulfilled. The Bonar Law papers arrived, but had to be sent back to England when the British government objected to Cabinet papers being shipped out of the country. The Lloyd George papers never arrived at all. The Bennett papers arrived, but not in the condition that Dr Bailey would have wished. They seemed to have been stored in a brewery, and smelled of beer. He was horrified to see the two women who had arrived with the papers throwing away and burning 'very large quantities'; he could not forbid them to do so, because the papers had not yet been formally handed over to the university; and when he remonstrated with Beaverbrook, saying that the destruction meant that an adequate biography of Bennett could never now be written, he received the reply that the women, one of whom was Bennett's devoted secretary, Miss Alice Millar, were merely trying to protect Bennett's reputation and were acting out of loyalty to his memory. Though greatly admiring of Beaverbrook, Dr Bailey found his notion of scholarship wayward in other instances; having identified the need for a dictionary of Canadian biography, Beaverbrook suggested that a set of volumes could easily be produced by Dr Bailey's graduate students working under his supervision.

In New Brunswick Beaverbrook – the son of the manse made good, with the other sides of his character well concealed – became, especially in Fredericton, the father of the community, with his benefactions to the university, his Overseas Scholarships, his pensions for retired Presbyterian ministers and paid trips to the Caribbean or Britain for New Brunswick politicians. He knew many, and was polite to all. He had a way, Dr Bailey has recalled, of mingling on easy terms with the ordinary local people, of conveying the impression that they were the main concern in his life – 'hard to express . . . and not quite the same as the common touch'. He could create the impression, Dr Murray Young has said, 'that the person with whom he was dealing had a special place in his affections. When the spirit moved him, he could improve the self-esteem and raise the sense of worth of any man or woman, from the lowest to the highest in the land.'[18] He sat on the veranda of the old Fredericton Canoe Club one day with his bare feet on the grass. A man approached and asked for an appointment. 'Yes,' said Beaverbrook, 'tomorrow morning at ten o'clock in my office.' But where was his office? 'Right here,' said Beaverbrook. He was treated like a tribal chief, and he behaved like one, too. When the university president resigned in 1953 Beaverbrook appointed a successor, which he was not empowered to do; after the university council demurred, Beaverbrook resigned himself. The problem was solved by the passing of an act by the provincial legislature making him Honorary Life Chancellor. The new president, Colin Mackay, and Bailey drafted the law; Bailey suggested it should describe him as 'a native son of New Brunswick', to counter his professed regret at having been born in Ontario; later, when the university adopted a new coat of arms, beavers were incorporated as a further compliment.

Bailey observed Beaverbrook more closely than anyone in Canada and with fascination. Beaverbrook said to him one evening when Bailey was smoking, 'Alfred, those things are not doing you any good. Why don't you give them up?' Bailey stubbed out his cigarette and never smoked again. He was treated as if he were on Beaverbrook's staff. Beaverbrook rang him at one o'clock in the morning: 'Doctor professor, what is that inscription at the front of the university library?' He had had it placed there.

'*Ne derelinquas me domine.*'

'Thank you. Goodbye.'

Once Bailey was in the office of the professor of civil engineering. The phone rang; it was Beaverbrook.

How did he know I was there? I hadn't told anyone where I was going. He wanted some references looked up, a dozen or more. I hadn't heard of most of them. But I performed a kind of miracle. I started at 10 a.m. and found the last of them at 10 p.m., and rushed off to the suite in the Beaverbrook

Hotel. Beaverbrook sprang up and took hold of one after the other. Yes, yes, yes, he said, going through them all. 'Thank you Alfred, will you have a drink.' He was sitting with premier McNair drinking Johnny Walker Black Label whisky.

Dr Bailey had another memory. He was with Beaverbrook in his suite at the Beaverbrook Hotel when

> . . . he began taking rolls of dollar bills out of his pocket, flicking them over and transferring them to other pockets. All the while he looked me intently in the eye. I don't think there was anyone else there, except perhaps the two menservants, Raymond and Charles, but when someone came in, Colin [Mackay] or Brigadier Wardell perhaps, he said, 'Bailey is not interested in money'. . . . He thought he could size a person up by watching his reaction to that dollar-transfer act.

Beaverbrook was beginning to think about his past. He was pleased when the Chatham authorities put up a plaque on the little wooden building where he had worked with Tweedie and Bennett. He thought about commissioning a biography of Bennett.[19]

Also in 1947, through the Newcastle lawyer Harold Davidson, he gradually bought up the 'Wilson property and graveyard', a historic and beautiful spot on the Miramichi, to turn it into a public park. He sold his parents' house in Newcastle for $7500 and distributed the money – $2000 of it to St Mary's Roman Catholic church in Newcastle in memory of his father's chess opponent, Father Dixon, one of the few adults who, half a century earlier, had seen any good in the young Max.

As Beaverbrook's devotion (Dr Bailey's word) to New Brunswick grew and his activities there expanded, he secured the services of two men who danced attendance on him during his visits and performed odd jobs for him when he was elsewhere. One of these was R. A. (Bob) Tweedie, the cousin of the head of the Chatham law firm, who knew his way round Fredericton politics and had served in the Premier's private office; at one stage Tweedie was working for the government and Beaverbrook at the same time. The other was Wardell.

His relations with Wardell show Beaverbrook at his most manipulative and cast an odd light on his notions of friendship. He described Wardell as one of his most intimate friends, and Wardell constantly described Beaverbrook in similar terms. Not everyone liked Wardell. Some found him snobbish – he was inclined to mention too often his connection with the Duke of Windsor – erratic, with his divorces and womanizing, and arrogant. Yet other members of the Beaverbrook circle would certainly have listed him as one of Beaverbrook's closest friends; after all, he had started to work for Beaverbrook in 1926, become the business head of the *Evening Standard*, travelled with him, stayed with him. Though he had achieved the rank of brigadier in the Second World War, Beaverbrook always called him, with apparent affection, 'the Captain'.

After the war Wardell returned to Express Newspapers as a senior executive and member of the board. In 1951, rather suddenly and to his own surprise, he found himself, entirely because of Beaverbrook, in Fredericton, very much a backwoods town to someone of Wardell's metropolitan tastes. He believed he was there because Beaverbrook had spotted a promising local commercial opportunity and generously wanted Wardell to benefit from it. So the brigadier laid his plans, all the more confidently because of Beaverbrook's backing: he would set up a university press, buy the local paper, the *Daily Gleaner*, from two old gentlemen who wanted to sell, acquire a book and stationery chain and a jobbing printers, and undertake contract printing.

He was counting on Beaverbrook, and used his name when he sent out circulars to potential investors. But he had scarcely bought the *Daily Gleaner* and the printers when things started to go wrong. He applied to Beaverbrook for loans and, after argument and delay and criticism, usually got them. The loans, naturally, made him Beaverbrook's dependant. He accused Beaverbrook of backtracking; of having led him to believe that they were to be genuine partners, and then behaving as if the enterprise was solely Wardell's responsibility. He said he would never have 'dreamed of coming into Fredericton to do business except it was in partnership with you and because you wished it'. Although he marked some of his letters about business or his own finances 'private and personal', Beaverbrook always passed them on to Mr Millar for advice and comment.[20]

Wardell did his utmost to please Beaverbrook. He sent him copies of the *Gleaner*, and accepted all suggestions for improvement. Some were minute; all were sensible. 'A local picture is better than an Ottawa picture. . . . Strike out the words per copy after the price. . . . Put number of paper not vol. 6 no. 130. That is number 18,000 or whatever is the correct number. . . . Stop describing the address of the *Gleaner* as Phoenix Square: everybody knows the address of the *Gleaner*. . . . You do not pay enough attention to finance.'

Before long, Wardell was less a Beaverbrook partner than a Beaverbrook agent. When Beaverbrook bought a house – one of the handsome old houses near the river – Wardell was put in charge, and duly harried. 'Will you please let me know why we had a nightwatchman for the month of November?' How was the house being furnished? For tax reasons it was most important that only the housekeeper's quarters were furnished. The Beaverbrook Hotel needed a fire escape and a skylight in the bathroom; Wardell must see to it. What had happened to the drums and fifes he had presented to the Sea Scouts? Were they in use or stored? Wardell attended to the smallest detail: did Beaverbrook want his name listed in the local telephone book? (He did not.) When Beaverbrook, in Jamaica, wanted to buy a camera as a Christmas present, Wardell was required to find out whether cameras and films were cheaper in Canada. He was chivvied for sending Beaverbrook parcels on which duty had to be paid. Fear of being thought extravagant made Wardell nervous. He and friends arranged to send Beaverbrook some salmon as a present, and warned him to expect it; when Wardell discovered that it would cost $95.25, he cancelled the order and wrote Beaverbrook a long letter of explanation. At that time, Beaverbrook had a balance in his current account at the Bank of Nova Scotia – only one of his Canadian accounts – of $408,714.

Wardell was in debt to Beaverbrook, but Beaverbrook set up trust funds for Wardell's mother and two of his sons, increasing Wardell's moral dependence. Disputes were common, usually about business. It was small consolation that when the Duke of Windsor wrote his memoirs he sent Brigadier Wardell a copy inscribed, 'To Mike, with kind regards, David'. At first Wardell lived in the Beaverbrook Hotel; then he rented rooms over a dry cleaners, where he lived in some squalor.

His business did not go well, though Beaverbrook's friends put money into it: Lord Rosebery £10,000; Ben Smith, the US financier, $25,000. In August 1952 Smith sued Wardell for 'fraudulent misrepresentation', on the grounds that Wardell had misled him about the nature of the business. Wardell was in despair; Beaverbrook got his old wartime colleague Sir Patrick Hennessy to speak to Smith, but to no avail. Wardell borrowed another $100,000 from Beaverbrook, without revealing that he was going to use part of it to pay off Smith. Beaverbrook was furious. He was still more furious when he discovered that Wardell had spent $50,000 on an extension to his printing plant: 'This is quite contrary to the basis on which I lent the money.' Yet Wardell was regularly given free air tickets so that he could spend Christmas or a holiday with Beaverbrook. 'A message has come here that you are to spend Christmas with Lord Beaverbrook,' Mr Millar wrote drily. 'I am to make the arrangements for your journey. . . . At the same time, if you know where Lord Beaverbrook is spending Christmas I should like this information.' It became a characteristic of Beaverbrook's peripatetic life that letters were always arriving at the wrong place.

Wardell never discovered the real reason why he was in Fredericton. It was that the senior management at the *Express* could not get on with him, and found him in any case disorganized. Because he was always ready to talk about his prowess as an amateur rider when he was in the Army, he was known behind his back as 'The Great Military Handicap', which he did not like when he heard about it. The senior managers told Beaverbrook privately that either Wardell went or they did. It was then that Beaverbrook took Wardell on his next trip to Fredericton and expounded to him the great opportunities in local publishing.[21]

At first, Wardell remained on the *Express* board with fees of £3000 a year. Then one day out of the blue Beaverbrook told him he must resign, because he was living in the wrong country and could not properly attend to his board duties. Wardell was appalled. He was in the wrong country because of Beaverbrook, he protested, '. . . to carry out your will and intention'. Beaverbrook told him not to make such a fuss; the new arrangement had 'obvious advantages' for Wardell, he said, though he did not explain how.

THE JOURNALISTS

In 1951 Beaverbrook was seventy-two. In 1950 Labour had narrowly won one general election, and in 1951 narrowly lost another, when Churchill returned as Prime Minister. Even then Beaverbrook showed little of his old zest for British politics. He was feeling increasingly isolated. Churchill was no longer an Empire Man; Eden and the rest were free traders. The Beaverbrook papers were as lively as ever, but taken less and less seriously by the political world. The Crossbencher political column in the *Sunday Express* printed regular paragraphs, written in what had become a pastiche of Beaverbrook's own prose style ('And for why?'), about the financial interests of socialist MPs, and collected and published the paragraphs in a little blue booklet, with accompanying photographs. The booklets were intended to demonstrate the hypocrisy of Labour politicians, but since at the same time Express Newspapers continued to encourage everyone to improve their lot, it was unclear where the hypocrisy charge finally lay. Beaverbrook was introduced to the staff of the Crossbencher column at an office party. He gazed at the line-up: 'So these are the men they all fear,' he said.[22] In truth, no one feared them. In 1951, the crusader on the *Daily Express* masthead was put in chains: it looked like eccentricity, but reflected accurately how Beaverbrook saw himself. The chained crusader could also be taken as a symbol of Beaverbrook's frustrations, as he continued, spasmodically, to advance his old protectionist and imperialist panaceas.

He was far too good a journalist, however, to allow the sour taste of disappointed politics to contaminate his papers. Meeting the new editor of the *Observer* at the Albert Hall, he gave him some advice: 'Sprinkle a little politics with it,' he said – a master-chef recommending the addition of an optional extra ingredient, like paprika. Politics should not dominate or bore. The *Express* gave the readers a surprise every day, and was never dull: like the first cigarette at breakfast, said a rival editor. It was bright all the way through, well subbed, well written, classless, newsy and snappy; Beaverbrook recommended a smorgasbord of at least twenty-two stories daily on the front page. The *Sunday Express* found a winning formula and stuck to it: right-wing tub-thumping by the highly professional editor, John Gordon; a patriotic adventure serial, often about the recent war, for armchair reading after Sunday lunch; unmalicious gossip about well-known people; malicious gossip about socialist politicians (Crossbencher); the cartoonist Giles; and comprehensive sport. The *Evening Standard* remained, as it had always been, the one Beaverbrook paper that

Beaverbrook's friends read, and was therefore allowed to be more sophisticated and less profitable than its stablemates. In the drab years after the war Express Newspapers were the most successful and most talked about newspaper group in Fleet Street, and no one doubted who should take the credit – even if he was never seen in Fleet Street.

Michael Foot came back into Beaverbrook's life in 1948. He had succeeded Nye Bevan as the leading light of the left-wing *Tribune* when Bevan joined the Labour government as Minister of Health. On 19 January 1949 Beaverbrook told him that 'the separation that has lasted so long has depressed me. The reunion will give me great joy.'[23] Beaverbrook's relations with left-wing members of his staff were less happy. In 1950, James Cameron resigned from Beaverbrook newspapers altogether when the *Evening Standard* 'engaged in what he justly believed to be a shameful slur' – as Foot later wrote – against the Labour Minister, John Strachey.[24] In spring 1951, though no longer Minister of Health, Bevan after much hesitation resigned amid acrimony when the government decided to impose charges on false teeth and spectacles. Almost all Bevan's associates thought this the wrong issue on which to resign, since in 1949 he had conceded the principle of health charges on prescriptions. Bevan's wife and Foot alone urged him on to resignation, and, as Bevan's criticisms of the Labour leaders became more and more violent, so did those of *Tribune*. Later, Gaitskellites – it was Hugh Gaitskell's budget that imposed the health charges – said that *Tribune* had poisoned Labour's debate by their vitriolic journalism.

At the time of Bevan's resignation, on 21 April 1951, *Tribune* was on the edge of extinction. Foot wrote to Beaverbrook from the House of Commons on 30 April saying: 'Dear Lord Beaverbrook, I had no right to ask it. But the fact that I did is an indication of the way you have always treated me. Thank you so much. It has meant a great deal to me at a most critical moment!' Beaverbrook wrote to Foot on 3 May: 'Do not undertake burdens greater than you can bear. Send me a message when you must have £1200. . . .' On 18 May Foot wrote to say he was 'resolved not to get into the same scrape again . . . It would, however, be a great assistance if I could have the further amount in, say, the next three weeks. . . .' Beaverbrook told him from Toronto on 21 May: 'You may draw balance at any time stop I will be back June 13 do you require funds before then?'

Altogether, Beaverbrook supplied Foot with £3000. It was forty years since he had secretly subsidized Blumenfeld and the *Daily Express*. 'The transaction', Foot wrote later, 'was creditable to Max, and most convenient to me: at that moment it saved *Tribune* from extinction.'[25] But Foot did not give Beaverbrook the credit for saving *Tribune* at the time; and Beaverbrook appears to have been aware of the need for secrecy, judging by the fact that he kept the exchange of messages between Foot and himself not among his normal correspondence files but in its own brown envelope marked 'Mr Michael Foot. Private to Lord Beaverbrook'.

Journalists working on *Tribune* knew nothing of the matter, and would have been shocked if they had; nor would rank-and-file left-wingers have found it easy to understand, or to forgive, an alliance between a socialist journal and a proprietor whose own papers were consistently anti-socialist. Some Bevanites would have welcomed the paper's passing; in 1954 Harold Wilson, a moderate Bevanite, thought that Bevan 'would be far better without the *Tribune*'. What was Beaverbrook's motive? Affection for Foot was no doubt part of it; but it would have been out of character for him not to have been excited by the chance of keeping alive, covertly, a principal source of discord inside the Labour Party.

The relationship between Foot and the man whom most of the Labour Party regarded as pernicious took another turn when Beaverbrook offered, and Foot and his wife Jill Craigie accepted, the use of a tumbledown cottage on the Cherkley estate: the offer that both Bevan and McNeil had declined for reasons of political prudence. Foot's acceptance bewildered and confused his left-wing colleagues. Again, Beaverbrook developed a friendship with his friend's wife. Jill Craigie wrote to him often, when he was abroad, sometimes thanking him for presents and passing on Labour Party news, or inviting him to drop in when he was at Cherkley.

When Robertson questioned the *Tribune* loan, Beaverbrook replied that it would be a pity to let the paper die since it was a valuable recruiting ground for *Express* journalists. So it was. Good right-wing journalists were rare; so Beaverbrook hired left-wing journalists and turned them, or they turned themselves, into right-wingers. Robert Pitman from *Tribune* made the change; so did Robert Edwards, who became editor of the *Express*. Woodrow Wyatt had been writing leaders for *Tribune*, as a Labour MP, when he came to Beaverbrook's notice. Wyatt thereafter dined with him and occasionally wrote for the *Evening Standard*; and he was grateful when Beaverbrook in person devised a 'very helpful' formula 'to save political embarrassment', whereby Wyatt sold a series of articles not directly to the *Standard* but to the *Express* syndication service, which sounded politically neutral. Wyatt also wrote a profile of Beaverbrook for the American journal *Harper's*, which he submitted to Beaverbrook before filing; after approval by Beaverbrook and publication by *Harper's*, Beaverbrook Newspapers bought the serial rights for £750.[26] One *Tribune* journalist, Mervyn Jones, became so irritated by the drain of talent from *Tribune* to Beaverbrook that when he himself was approached by the *Evening Standard* he wrote to Michael Foot saying the process had gone on long enough.

Beaverbrook recaptured Foot and made him the *Evening Standard*'s chief book reviewer, the slot once occupied by Arnold Bennett. But Beaverbrook also lost a few good journalists. After the war Alan Moorehead left him, despite invitations to Cherkley and offers of a large salary; Beaverbrook never spoke of him again. James Cameron resigned. David Low went to the *Daily Herald*. Beaverbrook also failed to recruit a few. He knew that the brilliant wartime despatches from the Washington Embassy to Churchill had been written by the Oxford philosopher Isaiah Berlin; after the war he wooed Berlin, making one of his rather rare misjudgements of character. Berlin was not disposed to admire Beaverbrook. He had shared the Embassy's wry amusement when the cypher clerks circulated their decode of a message from London saying that Lord Beaverbrook was about to arrive with a 'corrupt group' – the term used to denote indecipherable figures. In August 1945 Berlin was about to take up an appointment at the British Embassy in Moscow when he was summoned by Beaverbrook to Arlington House. 'Beaverbrook said, "I want you to write for the *Evening Standard* two columns a week on anything you please." I behaved like a Swiss governess an attempt on whose virtue was being made. I said, "I'm afraid I'm no good at that sort of thing." Beaverbrook said, "Well, and what are you going to do?"' Take up the post in Moscow, Berlin replied. Beaverbrook said, 'If you do, you will end up in a backroom in the British Embassy and no one will take any notice of you. If you write for me, you can live at Claridge's Hotel and have all the money, all the drink, and all the women you want. This is a privilege I reserve for very few.' Some time later, having left the Foreign Service, Berlin gave a talk on the BBC about Anglo–American relations, which he compared to a marriage that had its ups and downs but contained no prospect of divorce; the *Listener* reprinted the broadcast. At once the *Evening Standard* reacted with an article headlined: 'Who is Mr Berlin?' He was forty and unmarried; what did he know of marriage? As a foreigner what did he know of the British Empire, its glories, its agonies? 'It was an attack from beginning to end,' Berlin has said, 'and I was surprised and annoyed by it until friends rang up to congratulate me.'[27]

Beaverbrook did not understand the attractions of all his stars. What, he asked Christiansen, was the point exactly of the Osbert Lancaster pocket cartoons in the *Express*? They sprang from an upper middle-class section of English life, a non-political world of clubs and archdeacons, dons and gymkhanas, of which Beaverbrook after forty years in England had no knowledge. Lancaster used to refer to him as 'the old brute', and steered clear of his social invitations.

An old man, somewhat more mellow, and rarely visiting his papers, Beaverbrook became a fertile source of journalists' anecdotes and legends. One popular *Express* story described how at an office party Beaverbrook overheard a reporter comparing his working life to that of a galley slave: 'Set the slave free, Mr Christiansen,' said Beaverbrook. Robert Edwards was invited to dine at Cherkley and told that it would be quite informal as nobody else was coming, except Onassis and Churchill: Edwards thought it was a Beaverbrook joke, but both were present. Sometimes Beaverbrook played the joke in reverse. Miss Bower was told nobody was coming to lunch, and found herself seated next to Field Marshal Montgomery. Less well-attested stories were told. He was said to have offered Merle Oberon – or in some versions Marlene Dietrich – £1000 to spend a night with him at the Dorchester Hotel.

There was a sad ending to Christiansen's long editorship of the *Express*. In 1956, while staying with Beaverbrook in the south of France, he suffered a heart attack. Without telling Christiansen, before long Beaverbrook appointed a new editor, Edward Pickering, and a new second-in-command, Charles Wintour from the *Standard*. Unsuspecting, Christiansen returned to the office to find, when the confusion caused by his return was cleared up, that his career was over. Christiansen told people that Beaverbrook saw him into a lift and said, 'I am sorry to see you going down.' That does not sound like Beaverbrook. Nevertheless, Wintour thought the manner of Christiansen's removal 'very cruel'.[28] It was also strikingly similar to the way Beaverbrook had treated Blumenfeld.

He knew better than to depose the two key people at Beaverbrook Newspapers who were prepared to cope with his vagaries while continuing to give him unswerving loyalty and objective advice. Journalists and politicians might fall out and quarrel with him; Robertson and George Millar never did, partly at least because they never became involved in his social life. Robertson still addressed him as 'Lord Beaverbrook' fifty years after they met, and was always himself addressed as 'Mr Robertson'; the same was true of Mr Millar. The management was strengthened by the addition of one or two wartime heroes, friends of young Max, including Group Captain Hugh Dundas DSO, DFC; but although Max became a Conservative MP after the war and was on the board, he found it difficult to adjust from the excitement of the air force to the responsibilities of the newspaper business – particularly as his father constantly, and often publicly, criticized his performance. Max bought a house at Cowes, and escaped as often as he dared to the pleasures of what Beaverbrook scornfully described as 'yatting'. Robertson and Millar remained the keys. At the *Express* Mr Millar was to the rest of the building totally unknown and obscure, unrecognized as he came and went past the journalists in the exuberant art deco lobby with its Epstein bust of Beaverbrook. This Edinburgh accountant of absolute discretion was at the centre of all Beaverbrook's personal finances: the houses, the often contentious family payments, the presents to women on his birthday and at Christmas – not all of them old girlfriends, by any means – bonuses for staff, the travel arrangements for Beaverbrook's guests, the trust funds. He was a strict Presbyterian and believed that 'there was right and there was wrong, and never the twain shall meet', as Mrs Ince, his assistant for many years, put it; he did not think Beaverbrook was always right, but kept such thoughts to himself. He placed only two conditions on his service, which Beaverbrook accepted: he insisted on keeping precisely regular office hours – he was the only employee whom Beaverbrook did not telephone at home – arriving at nine and leaving on the stroke of six; and he never worked on Sundays. Mrs Ince said: '. . . he had the most terrible ulcers;

he must have suffered hell'.

As an absentee proprietor – the worst kind of proprietor, he cheerfully told the royal commission on the press – Beaverbrook dominated his papers by telephone and by his Soundscriber dictating machine. The discs from the machine, if Beaverbrook was abroad, were sent to London for transcription and the rambling messages on them distributed. He avoided the office, Mrs Ince observed, because 'he didn't want to get involved in the rough and tumble. When he did come down, the whole building shook.' Robertson had a heart attack in the mid-fifties and was replaced as business head of the *Express* group by Tom Blackburn. Blackburn loved golf, but found little time to play. One Sunday morning he arranged a game. Beaverbrook tracked him down by telephone and asked the club steward to tell Mr Blackburn that Lord Beaverbrook wished to speak to him. Blackburn trudged back to the club house. 'Mr Blackburn. This is just to remind you that you are working for me twenty-four hours a day' – and bang went the receiver.[29] Beaverbrook paid the highest wages on Fleet Street to his managers and journalists, but not to the rest of his employees. Mrs Ince only had one typewriter the whole time she worked for Beaverbrook, and was required to look after it herself. When Beaverbrook was young, envelopes were expensive; in old age he continued to insist that new envelopes must not be used for inter-office communications or for communications to him, and that every inch of space on old envelopes must be filled, which sometimes meant that confused messengers took mail to Cherkley when Beaverbrook was in London and vice versa. Used envelopes, some of them years old, cascaded out of the Ince office cupboards when opened. Even in retirement Mrs Ince could not break the habit; drawers in her house were stuffed with old envelopes.

FARMS AND HOUSES

Beaverbrook, as all his employees agreed, did not have enough to do after the war. His post-war restlessness was prefigured when he was out of office in 1942–43. He started acquiring houses. Miss Bower, originally engaged as a secretary at the Ministry of Aircraft Production, found herself appointed house finder. He told her he wanted somewhere in Cornwall; she leased a house where he never stayed and abandoned after six months. Next he wanted a place in Brighton; she bought a six months' lease on a flat on the front – he never went there. At one time after the war he had thirteen places of residence, not counting a house in Canada that he bought in Fredericton for tax reasons but which, also for tax reasons, he could not live in; and The Vineyard in Hurlingham which he had long since turned over to his sister, Mrs Stickney.

1. Cherkley Court, Leatherhead.
2. A flat in Brook House, Park Lane.
3. A flat in Arlington House, St James's Street.
4. A flat on the second floor of the *Evening Standard* building, air-conditioned and fortified, where he spent many nights during the war.
5. An estate in Norfolk.
6–8. Three farms in Somerset.
9. La Capponcina at Cap d'Ail, France.
10. Cromarty in Montego Bay, Jamaica.
11. Aitken House in Nassau, Bahamas.
12. Pancake House in Nassau.
13. Spanish Wells, a house on a nearby island.

From house finder, Miss Bower was appointed interior decorator, and did not think much of her employer's taste. He insisted, despite the heat of Nassau, on installing a scarlet carpet and bedspread in what became known as the Scarlet Bedroom at Aitken House. In the salon, he made Miss Bower plaster over the wooden ceiling because he did not like the 'boards'.

During the war, Beaverbrook had turned farmer, following his grandparents, though on gentler terrain. He bought two substantial houses in the Somerset hamlet of Cricket Malherbie, and the land that went with them. The first, Cricket Court, an eccentric early nineteenth-century building with an alleged bear-pit, housed an elderly lady, who was allowed to remain; the second, a pretty Elizabethan manor house known as Manor Farm, Beaverbrook instructed Miss Bower to furnish from the store of motley furniture, which included a chair he had once had made for F. E. Smith, that he kept at the *Evening Standard*. He refused to allow Miss Bower to visit Manor Farm; what was the need, when he could give her the measurements? Two huge removal vans left Fleet Street for the narrow lanes of Somerset. The measurements had not mentioned ceiling heights; the vans, laden with tallboys, returned almost as full as they went.

To manage the farms, which were in a sorry state, Beaverbrook poached from the Ministry of Agriculture in 1943 a hard-headed and knowledgeable young New Zealander, 'Sandy' Copland, who was told to buy additional derelict farms, build up the livestock, show other farmers how a farm should be run, install lavatories in the farm cottages and make money. Over the years prize bulls and heifers named Cherkley this and Cherkley that were duly bred, and prize Ayrshire and Guernsey herds established. Beaverbrook did not like pigs; but pigs were kept. He was interested in cheese, so cheesemaking was started; every Christmas off went 10lb cheeses to twenty or thirty Beaverbrook friends. Every now and again, at short notice, Beaverbrook and party would arrive at Cricket Malherbie for the weekend and tour the estates, with Beaverbrook in his city clothes, attended by a Rolls Royce, taking an interest in all that was going on and asking awkward questions.

At one point he decided that for touring the estates a caravan would be more efficient than a motor car; so a London bus was gutted and equipped with a bedroom, lounge with table and chairs, built-in cupboards, radio, telephone, dictaphone, lavatory, hot and cold water, shower, washbasin, refrigerator stocked with wine, kitchen and carpets. In this monster, on its maiden voyage, Beaverbrook set off from Cricket Malherbie one day at 8 a.m., accompanied by Copland and the politician W. J. Brown, to inspect the three farms he had acquired near Liskeard in Cornwall, a hundred miles away, with the Rolls driven by a chauffeur following behind. No vehicle could have been less suited to the tortuous roads of the West Country; oncoming cars were forced to back long distances to find lay-bys; water in the vast tank on the roof swished about as the driver slowed down or changed gear on the many hills; frequently the bus was held up behind farm vehicles. Determined nevertheless to demonstrate the advantages of his invention, Beaverbrook sat at the table and dealt with papers, dictated to two secretaries, then lay down on his bed. Villagers stopped to stare.

At last the caravan, having lumbered across Bodmin Moor, constantly changing gear, reached Pengelly, where the famous award-winning Cherkley herd of Devons, brushed and polished, were paraded for inspection. The chauffeur laid out a lunch of cold chicken and lettuce hearts. Beaverbrook purred. Alas, on the return journey the weather changed; Bodmin Moor became first misty, then enveloped in thick fog. The impatient Beaverbrook transferred to the Rolls. He was always keen on maps; the chauffeur was on course for Launceston when Beaverbrook decided they were on the wrong road. The chauffeur demurred but was over-ruled. In the fog Beaverbrook, Brown and the chauffeur now drove slowly off in exactly the wrong direction. The caravan, like the tortoise in the fable of the tortoise and the hare, crawled back to Cricket Malherbie, arriving at 11 p.m. to find no sign of the others. Long after midnight, the lights of the Rolls were observed in the driveway and Beaverbrook and Brown emerged. That was the end of the caravan; Beaverbrook never made a second journey, telling Copland that the caravan would be ideal for his own use and he could sleep in it overnight if necessary. Copland stored the monster in a covered yard where it took up the space of a combine harvester; later it was taken over by the *Daily Express* for publicity work at agricultural shows.[30]

Beaverbrook's farming employees concluded that he did not know a great deal about farming, enjoyed rows and possessed a dangerously good memory. Poking about behind a barn, he came across a heap of tiles. Copland explained that they were needed to repair a roof. 'That's what you told me five years ago.' The farms were a success; before Copland had finished, Cricket Malherbie Ltd owned thirteen farms on 2500 acres and milked 1000 cows. Apart from Beaverbrook's phenomenal energy and sometimes alarming methods of detailed control, it was his kindness to farm workers that impressed Copland.

Removed from daily politics, and often abroad, Beaverbrook was no longer one of Churchill's regular cronies, and he was suspicious of Churchill's support for a federal Europe. In August 1949 Churchill was staying at La Capponcina when he had his first stroke, playing cards with Wardell at one o'clock in the morning; Beaverbrook took it upon himself to keep the incident quiet. He presented Churchill with a lift for Chartwell; but the main link between the two men was Brendan Bracken, now chairman of a South African mining company as well as a Conservative MP and newspaper owner. Bracken wrote regularly to Beaverbrook with the political gossip, and kept him up to date about Churchill's morale, health and the progress of his war memoirs. Neither Bracken nor Beaverbrook was in sympathy with the post-war Conservative Party, even though it was led by Churchill, and they reinforced one another's prejudices. Bracken described Macmillan and R. A. Butler as 'neo-socialists'; Beaverbrook wrote from New Brunswick: 'This is the place for free enterprise and no nonsense. It is the home of liberty.'[31] Then he left for Jamaica. He sent Bracken ham and cheese from Cricket Malherbie, cases of the best Scotch whisky, Alsatian wine, caviar, and Blue Mountain coffee from Jamaica. Bracken asked Beaverbrook if Copland could look at some land in the West country that the Churchill Trustees, of whom Bracken was one, were thinking of buying.

For the second general election in 1951 Beaverbrook returned to London and was invited by Churchill to give him campaign advice, despite the disasters of 1945. When Churchill was elected he did not offer Beaverbrook a job, though he brought back other wartime associates. Beaverbrook wanted direct negotiations between Churchill and Stalin, and opposed Churchill's acquiescence in German rearmament; otherwise, though eager for political gossip, he showed little interest in political issues. But he was, as always, interested in his relations with Churchill. After Churchill visited the United States in January 1953, he lunched with Beaverbrook in Jamaica; Beaverbrook wrote to Bracken: 'I was warmly received by Clemmie, and was gratified.' Five months later Churchill had a massive stroke; Colville, his private secretary, told only three men outside the government – Beaverbrook, Camrose and Bracken – with the aim of silencing Fleet Street. In September, Churchill recuperated at La Capponcina. This marked the opening of the last phase of their long association: henceforward Beaverbrook, always protective, could play host to the ailing hero with, at last, the gratitude instead of the hostility of his wife. In 1955, the year that Churchill finally resigned, Beaverbrook, using Bracken as the intermediary, told Churchill that he could have La Capponcina 'each and every year' between 1 December and 1 April, and the resident staff would be at his disposal.

MAKING HISTORY

The Beaverbrook energy, still phenomenal, released by his retreat from present-day politics was concentrated instead on the past. He brought in other people to write history, in an audacious attempt to influence the historiography of the twentieth century by granting access to the important papers he owned only to writers approved by himself; he went back to his own history-writing; and he attended to the story of his life. He was always torn between his desire to be a participant in great events and his urge to be an observer and recorder of them. Even during the war he had made Farrer find time to write a book about his achievements at the Ministry of Aircraft Production. He sent memorandums about his meetings with Stalin not only to the British government but also to Mr Millar at the *Express* for safekeeping. After the war, he invited the playwright and Roosevelt's speechwriter, Robert Sherwood, author of *The White House Papers of Harry Hopkins*, from which Beaverbrook emerged well, to write the life of Lloyd George; when Sherwood declined, he gave the job to Frank Owen. He arranged for a young Oxford don, Robert Blake, to write the life of Bonar Law. He toyed with the biography of R. B. Bennett. He controlled the access to the papers of all three Prime Ministers; and in the case of Owen's life of Lloyd George, he controlled the text as well. The procedure was straightforward. Owen sent him chapters; Beaverbrook made suggestions; Owen incorporated them. A year or so after the book, *Tempestuous Journey*, was published, Beaverbrook not for the first time congratulated Owen on its quality; 'I frequently turn to it,' he wrote with no trace of irony, 'as a work of reference.'[32]

Blake's biography of Bonar Law was based on the papers Beaverbrook had inherited in 1924. Since then, Beaverbrook had guarded them closely; when Viscount Davidson asked him to allow Tom Jones to use them in preparing the entry on Bonar Law for the *Dictionary of National Biography*, Beaverbrook declined on the grounds that Richard Law was planning to write a biography and any prior use of the papers 'would damage the project'. By the early 1950s Law, now Lord Coleraine, decided after writing two chapters that he could not finish the task; Blake was recommended to Beaverbrook by his colleague at Christ Church, Hugh Trevor-Roper.

During 1952 and 1953, Blake worked on the papers at Cherkley during the university vacations. Frank Owen was working at the same time on Lloyd George, but Blake 'was not encouraged to meet him. Beaverbrook liked to deal separately with the historians on whom he conferred his patronage.' Blake was wary of Beaverbrook from the start – 'I knew I had to take what he told me with a pinch of salt . . . he was not trying to falsify history, but he put his own place in history pretty high.' Nevertheless, he found his patron's memory remarkable and his reminiscences stimulating. Beaverbrook did not tell him that he had held back some of the Law material, in particular all reference to their financial dealings. When Blake's book came out in 1955, to general acclaim, Beaverbrook was dissatisfied. He had hoped, Blake thought, for a more dramatic portrait of his hero, and felt that his own role in Bonar Law's life was not sufficiently emphasized; he was not pleased to be referred to in the acknowledgements as Bonar Law's literary executor. 'He wanted it known that he owned the papers.'[33]

Beaverbrook took up his own writing again, planning the continuation of *Politicians and the War* beyond 1916 and tinkering with a projected demolition of his old enemy provisionally entitled *The Age of Baldwin* He started to organize material for a book on Churchill. Beaverbrook's methods were idiosyncratic. The files are crammed with research notes and drafts, mostly undated, prepared by different assistants, sometimes corrected in his own hand. Often there is an early account written by him soon after the events described, which reappears embellished and extended through the decades; thus in the early 1950s he dug out his original account of the abdication crisis of 1936 and reworked it into a book, but the illness and death of George VI in 1952 led him to leave it unpublished. He also had a hand in the Duke of Windsor's autobiography, *A King's Story*; while the book was being written he was in close touch with the ghost writer, Charles Murphy, a seasoned American reporter provided by the project's chief backer, Henry Luce of *Time-Life*. When the Duke's book appeared in 1951, it struck some readers that Baldwin was treated with less than justice. Many of Beaverbrook's employees over the years found themselves set to work to help him with his writing, as researchers, ghosts, critics or editors. When he turned to writing history again in earnest, three women in particular helped him: Rosemary Brooks, Sheila Lambert, who acted as archivist, and a young Australian history graduate, Ann Mozley, who became Beaverbrook's research assistant in 1954. She helped him to write the book that began as *Politicians and the War*, Volume III, and became *Men and Power*.

Ann Mozley was aware that Beaverbrook's control of important documents had not endeared him to professional historians, who regarded him with mistrust; one friend advised her strongly against helping Beaverbrook with his 'brainwashing'. She was, however, captivated by Beaverbrook and impressed with his energy, application and powers of recall; she would often find, after laborious checking, that Beaverbrook, to her surprise, was right. 'There were, indeed, many occasions when his memory of an incident, persisting fiercely in the face of conflicting published evidence, would triumph over the united resistance of the archivist and myself when the corroborating evidence would turn up among the files.' She noticed that he was oddly nervous at presenting himself as an historian, and thought she detected a 'slight chip on the shoulder'; he deliberately avoided employing established academics to help him. 'By normal research methods, we operated in reverse,' Ann Mozley has recalled. First, Beaverbrook would talk at length about incidents and personalities; then she would consult published sources and Beaverbrook's archives and prepare a draft; then Beaverbrook would work and rework the text.[34]

He also kept an eye on his own biography. It was in 1952 that he started to collect material for the account of his early life eventually published by the *Atlantic Advocate*, and the following year that the first would-be biographer of the post-war years stepped forward: Tom Driberg. A more disreputable candidate could scarcely have been found, even among former *Express* journalists. Driberg had caused extreme alarm in the Bevanite camp at the Labour Party conference in 1952. It was a critical conference, with the tide running strongly towards Bevanism and the Left; the night before the conference opened, word reached the Bevanite hotel that Driberg, one of the group's most prominent members, was seducing someone on the beach and that police were not far away. Beaverbrook knew that Driberg was an active homosexual, and thus liable to arrest at any time. He did not know that Driberg's biography of himself would preoccupy both author and subject for eighteen months.

Driberg, still an MP, was as usual in debt. He secured an advance from the publishers Weidenfeld and Nicolson for a life of Beaverbrook of eighty thousand words, and Beaverbrook said (later) that he agreed to co-operate 'to help him make some money'. He took Driberg off to Canada and showed him the Birthplace and the Boyhood Home. In Newcastle, he invited Driberg to advise the Old Manse Library on modern poetry. Relations were friendly. From Nassau Beaverbrook asked for London gossip; Driberg told him that 'Bob Boothby (who works for the *News of the World*) says there is a swing of public opinion against the fantastic and irregular methods used by the police in prosecuting homosexuals' – an item of more interest to Driberg perhaps than to Beaverbrook. Beaverbrook made the deal himself: the *Daily Express* would pay Driberg £4000 on submission of the first twenty thousand words, which were to be delivered by 7 April 1954, and the rest by 1 September. Mr Millar was told to inform Driberg's creditors about the arrangement. Thus Driberg's debts were in effect transferred to Beaverbrook. His financial dependence was increased when he missed his first deadline. 'You had ten days before you,' Beaverbrook told him. 'And you can easily write 2000 words a day when you have your material before you.'[35]

Beaverbrook asked Driberg to Cherkley and to the south of France. Driberg unwisely failed to respond. Beaverbrook said he was 'quite willing to drop the whole project, but not agreeable to being pushed around'. He had never for a moment intended to give Driberg any serious help; he had of course confined his help, he assured Robertson, who had been opposed to the project from the start, 'to matter already printed. I have never opened my files to him at all.' Finally, in November, Beaverbrook wrote to Robertson from Nassau: 'I have received this Driberg stuff. It is very wicked indeed.'

Beaverbrook was genuinely angry. He was especially furious over Driberg's speculations about his relationship with Gladys. Driberg had written: '. . . she may well have had a good deal to make allowances for'; the people that 'gathered around her millionaire husband' were a 'motley set of financial and political adventurers, ruthless business men, and glittering mondaines'. After a wife's death, Driberg went on, even the best of husbands may feel 'a self-reproaching regret that is almost remorse'. In Beaverbrook's case 'the fury . . . turned inward on himself . . . seeking not so much comfort in sorrow as reassurance against a curious itching of his calloused conscience'. Beaverbrook told Robertson that this passage 'will not be tolerated by me, but resented to the furthest extent and with the utmost possible resources'. He found almost equally offensive a story alleging that he had made heartless references, 'with a wild leer', to a child in Fredericton who had polio. He also strongly objected to being labelled an appeaser.

The manuscript, however, presented Beaverbrook with a problem. He had been holding out the carrot of serialization in the *Daily Express*. He could cancel the *Express*'s interest and demand his money back, on the grounds both that Driberg was late in delivery and that his manuscript was libellous (of others as well as Beaverbrook); or he could require the libels to be removed. But either course would still allow Driberg and Weidenfeld to publish a libel-free text, and not all Beaverbrook's objections – for instance to the appeaser label – were based on libel.

Driberg was summoned to Nassau and put up in a hotel. He produced an ingratiating seven-page handwritten memorandum in which he said he had, 'even in left-wing circles', always stressed the contrast between his regard for Beaverbrook personally and his political disapproval of what Beaverbrook and the *Express* stood for. He had, he claimed, 'tried to be fair'. Hector McNeil once said that Beaverbrook could be 'terrifying'. Beaverbrook now barred Driberg from the house. Driberg was evidently shaken.

Many people, confronted with the Driberg text, would have demanded changes. Beaverbrook was more cunning. He told Driberg about the polio story. 'I do not ask you to cut the passage out. You must take your own decisions. No doubt your publisher will take his decisions too.' He knew he had rumbled Driberg's strategy. Driberg wanted to get Beaverbrook to make changes so that he could go back to George Weidenfeld and tell him that he now had a revised text to which Beaverbrook had agreed. Instead, Beaverbrook worked to acquire full control of the text. A leading lawyer, Helenus Milmo KC, was asked to read it for libels and found many: Churchill, the Duke of Windsor, Beaverbrook's trainer and jockey, and various members of the staff of Express Newspapers. Thus armed, Beaverbrook's son Max saw Weidenfeld. Weidenfeld, not unnaturally, Max reported, was 'deeply distressed and horrified', and not only because of the libels, which could be easily rectified. He wanted to stay on good terms with the *Express*, with which he had other business pending. In addition, he had sunk £500 in the book; and he felt he would not sell many copies unless the book was serialized, which required Beaverbrook's acceptance of the entire text. Weidenfeld asked Randolph Churchill's advice; Randolph Churchill asked Max Aitken how he should respond; then he advised Weidenfeld to 'seek agreement with the other side'. Weidenfeld said he was ready to meet all objections; in that case, Max told him, 'we might even consider serialisation'.

Driberg was cornered. He made changes, and more changes, by no means all for libel reasons: 'I have . . . put in your interesting point that Empire Free Trade might have been accepted but for the 1931 crisis.' In June 1955 he wrote to Beaverbrook saying he was glad to hear from the publisher that 'you have, in principle, passed the revised version of the book'. The response came not from Beaverbrook but from Mr Millar: 'He [Lord Beaverbrook] asks me to inform you that he has not passed the text of your manuscript in principle or otherwise. I must also inform you that Lord Beaverbrook takes no interest in your manuscript. . . .' Finally, Beaverbrook was satisfied. The book was called *Beaverbrook, a Study in Power and Frustration*. Christiansen, the *Express* editor, sent him proposed extracts, and Beaverbrook cabled back footnotes to be published at the same time, pointing out inaccuracies and showing that Driberg had sought and been given generous special payments when he worked on the *Express*. Christiansen also sent Beaverbrook the proposed introduction. 'It is a hostile biography. It is also inaccurate. Nevertheless the *Express* will publish extracts in accordance with its custom to suppress nothing.'

In 1977, in his autobiography, Driberg said that the book had been 'mutilated by Lord Beaverbrook's libel lawyers'. He failed to mention that his work had been largely financed by Beaverbrook and that he had made all the changes Beaverbrook demanded, whether for reasons of libel or not. Thus a book controlled by Beaverbrook has been regarded sometimes as the single 'hostile' Beaverbrook biography. Weidenfeld promoted it as such.

One person was not taken in. Evelyn Waugh wrote to Driberg on 23 February 1956:

I opened it with eagerness as I had seen it advertised as a 'hostile' biography. What do I find? A honeyed eulogy. You mention a few of Beaverbrook's more notorious public aberrations but you give little impression of the deep malevolence of the man. Instead you exalt him to the dignity of a St John – a brilliant statesman who just failed. Was all the story of your tiff with him a 'publicity stunt' devised by the pair of you? If Beaverbrook really thinks your book hostile, he must have singularly little sense of his true position. . . . While you fail to give the full villainy of the man, you fail to give his superficial charm. He is, or was, at his best among women. Yours is an all-male cast.[36]

CHAPTER 22
BENEFACTOR AND BRIDEGROOM
1956–1964

BEAVERBROOK SAID IN 1956 that he derived more pleasure from establishing the Beaverbrook Art Gallery in Fredericton than from anything else, but he was one of the few who did. Everything went wrong. The architect originally engaged died and left no drawings. The all-important lighting was installed by a highly recommended Montreal firm. Beaverbrook, surrounded by local celebrities, supervised the dusk switching-on ceremony, which, wrote Tweedie, the secretary of the gallery's board of governors, 'had many of the characteristics of a seance: expectations were high; results, non-existent. The great moment arrived. Beaverbrook gave the command to light up. Disaster! Complete and unmistakable.' Paintings and walls were bisected by shadows. Experts were summoned from Montreal, New York and Boston. Adjustments were made, but 'failed to please'. Beaverbrook's 'temper became shorter, his tongue sharper'. Finally, the problem was solved by the use of 'diffusing glass'.[1]

With his usual distrust of experts, Beaverbrook started buying paintings first through Betty Bower and then through Mrs Ince in the *Express* office. In 1952, having originally hired Marie-Edmée Escarra to teach him French, he made her first his mistress and then his art expert. She was not the only adviser. 'The art galleries of London, Paris, New York, Toronto and Montreal are littered with the bodies of discarded experts,' Wardell wrote, 'some in chagrin, some in anger, and some, it must be said, in relief.' The most remarkable of them was undoubtedly a dark, good-looking South African, Le Roux Smith Le Roux, who claimed to have been dismissed from the Pretoria art centre because of his anti-apartheid views and who was appointed by Sir John Rothenstein to be his assistant keeper at the Tate Gallery in London.

In the second volume of his memoirs Sir John devotes 145 pages to his troubles at the Tate, most of them stemming from the alleged attempts of

Le Roux to capture his job. 'He succeeded in inflicting on me more harm and more distress than I have suffered from all others together who have wished me ill,' Rothenstein wrote. The dispute became public knowledge; newspapers took sides; the *Evening Standard* backed Le Roux. Rothenstein won; and in May 1954 Beaverbrook hired Le Roux to write for the *Standard*. Beaverbrook suggested an article on the fluctuation of art prices; Le Roux submitted it to Beaverbrook in person; Beaverbrook shortened it; Le Roux thanked him for his patience and advice and said he must learn to shed his 'museographic love of detail'. He had barely got his first piece in shape – 'I have stripped the story to its bones and I realize how that increases the impact' – before he was drawing up a list of 'desirable' twentieth-century British artists who ought to be represented in Fredericton. By the end of June he was acting as a go-between for Beaverbrook with the dealers, sending round a dozen paintings to Arlington House: a Wilson Steer from Agnew's; a Matthew Smith, a Wadsworth, a Paul Nash ('I think that we can find a better one') and two Stanley Spencers from Tooth's; a Christopher Wood ('a bargain') and a Wyndham Lewis from the Redfern Gallery; a Ben Nicholson, an Ivon Hitchens and a Francis Bacon (*Yawning Man* – 'a bargain') from Gimpel; and a Peploe still life from Lefevre. On 28 June he was in Oxford buying a Paul Nash landscape from Nash's widow for £400.[2]

By the autumn of 1955, after Le Roux had been at the heart of Beaverbrook's buying operations for over a year, things began to go sour. Returning to England aboard the *Queen Mary*, Le Roux wrote to tell Tweedie that 'my senior partner' was feeling disenchanted by his gallery, threatening to abandon the whole scheme and 'complaining pointedly that he lacked reliable advice. So I told him that he had too many advisers and from my point of view seemed only interested in advice which agreed with his own preconceptions. That cleared the air considerably but may also hasten my own demise as a member of the set-up!'[3]

Through Le Roux, Beaverbrook bought a Constable painting of Flatford Mill and a Turner. On 4 April 1956 Le Roux wrote to say that he was in bed with malaria. On 26 May he said that his recovery would be slow, and abruptly resigned, saying he must go to the continent. Beaverbrook then began to worry about the authenticity of the Constable and the Turner. On 16 June Beaverbrook was in pursuit of the Constable Flatford Mill papers. Where were they? Where was that record? Of course Le Roux had got it somewhere. Three days later Beaverbrook wrote: 'We are now wanting the papers relating to the authenticity of the Turner.' After a delay, Le Roux wrote to Mrs Ince in reply to 'various communications'. The Constable papers had not been in his possession since they were taken to Arlington House, he claimed. As for the Turner papers, they were merely photostats of letters in the possession of the previous owner, Mr Elmaissian. By now Beaverbrook's suspicions were thoroughly aroused. He sent for the *Daily Express* crime reporter, Percy Hoskins, who duly

485

provided a report: 'The above named [Le Roux Smith Le Roux] was born in South Africa. He is now living at 13 Chapel Street S.W.1. with a woman known as Lois Le Roux. They are regarded as man and wife but they are not – at least, there is no record of any marriage. . . . The woman known as Lois Le Roux was born in December 1926 at Dollis Hill, London, and was christened Winifred Gates.'[4] Beaverbrook did not pursue Le Roux, but in 1961 he told Rothenstein that Le Roux had swindled him out of £40,000 and 'added that the investigation he had caused to be made had very strongly suggested that, in addition, Le Roux had been drawing secret commissions from many dealers – including some reputable ones'.[5] Le Roux was found dead on the floor of a conservatory in 1963. Everyone had liked him.

The gallery, opened in 1959, was, in a way, Le Roux's memorial, since it was built not as Beaverbrook had originally intended, on the university campus, but on the riverbank site of the old Fredericton Canoe Club, as suggested by Le Roux. Later, when the gallery was flooded, the suggestion seemed less inspired. On the whole, considering that the collection had been so rapidly put together, 'the batting average was rather high', in the opinion of a later director, especially as Beaverbrook wavered between lack of respect for professional scholars and mistrust of his own judgement.[6]

One artist he knew he liked was Graham Sutherland, who had painted his portrait during 1950 and 1951 and given him a purple suit; he looked, the eminent art historian Quentin Bell wrote, 'very much like a diseased toad bottled in methylated spirits'. He promoted Sutherland in the *Daily Express* and encouraged the Houses of Parliament to commission him to paint the famous eightieth birthday portrait of Churchill in 1954 – the painting that Lady Churchill destroyed. Beaverbrook tried to buy that portrait and failed, before he knew its fate; but he succeeded in buying Sutherland's much-admired portrait of Helena Rubinstein, which pleased her because she thought that in Fredericton no one would ever see it. He had a passion for Etty nudes, a genre about which he did not need advice. He fell in love with Fragonard's painting of Mademoiselle de Honoré and travelled with it sometimes; it had cost him £17,500. He acquired several Sickerts, including portraits of Sir James Dunn, the Prince of Wales and Castlerosse. The doyen of Canadian dealers found him high-quality nineteenth-century Canadian paintings. He bullied people into giving pictures to the gallery; a small Krieghoff presented by 'Mr Roy Thomson', the Canadian newspaper owner, was one of them. When he became aware that he ought to own a Gagnon, a well-known Canadian painter, he wooed Mrs Gagnon by letter and she eventually sold him a French scene; Beaverbrook was very pleased, until he was told that it was Gagnon's Canadian paintings he should have. He wrote to Mrs Gagnon again, saying the French picture was wonderful and he now wanted a Canadian one; he did not get it. He asked Stanley Spencer for an explanation of the iconography in one of the Spencers bought by Le Roux. Spencer wrote back using a ballpoint pen on both sides of thin paper. Beaverbrook asked him to rewrite the explanation on thicker paper.

The gallery was not run on orthodox lines. Beaverbrook called himself the Custodian. He took up a young local artist with no museum or art training, bought him a little house, found him a part-time job as the *Gleaner*'s cartoonist, and put him in charge of showing schoolchildren round the gallery. But the young man was subject to epileptic fits, which the children misinterpreted as part of the show. To get him off the floor, Beaverbrook appointed him registrar, but he had no notion of the proper way to document the paintings that Beaverbrook shipped over. London rarely sent complete papers or the history of ownership. 'It was', said a gallery official, 'almost like you were receiving hot merchandize.' Beaverbrook's curiosity was undiminished; was not the name of the miniaturist Hilliard spelt, in Elizabethan times, Hillyarde, and should not the gallery therefore adopt that spelling? 'The Gallery is my affair,' he told Wardell – and it was, with every decision referred to him. He knew what he did not like. 'I certainly would not pay $500 for [an exhibition of] some Yugoslavian medieval frescoes,' he wrote; and: 'I send warning of the insidious cunning of the picture groups pushing abstract art.'

MADAME ESCARRA AND OTHERS

Beaverbrook met Marie-Edmée Escarra, the Frenchwoman who was his companion during the mid-1950s, through Lady d'Avigdor-Goldsmid. He wanted to learn French, and asked her to find him someone suitable, 'not too pretty or they'll all say she's my mistress, but someone I can take anywhere'. Madame Escarra, from a prosperous banking family, was elegant rather than beautiful, small and fair, and had once been a model; she then became involved with Philippe de Rothschild, an affair that ended badly. She first met Beaverbrook in France in 1952, returned to England with him and was soon so much in love with him that she was prepared to put up with his cavalier and domineering treatment of her. Beaverbrook was widely reckoned to be remarkably mean with his women, in circles where a fur coat and some good jewellery were thought to be the least that a millionaire should provide for his latest mistress. Lady d'Avigdor-Goldsmid has recalled with glee an occasion when she took Marie-Edmée to Fortnum & Mason, bought her a mink coat and sent the bill for £7000 to Beaverbrook. She also believed that it was through Marie-Edmée that Beaverbrook first became interested in paintings. Tired with always walking in Green Park, she took him one day to the National Gallery. 'He sat outside and saw all the people going in and he couldn't believe that they didn't have to pay.'[7]

But Madame Escarra's devotion came to bore Beaverbrook. The *Express* journalist Geoffrey Bocca thought his aim 'was to break her spirit, destroy her'.[8] When she started to drink he lost all interest in her; she went back to Paris, where for a time he sent her a small allowance. One of his later secretaries, Josephine Rosenberg, remembers that he was always trying to cut the allowance down. She also remembers that he would send Helen Fitzgerald, who also drank too much as she grew older, a single red rose every week when he was in London.[9]

Beaverbrook was always able to surround himself with amenable young women by employing them. Sometimes they were his secretaries; one joined his staff as a nurse, although he was not ill at the time; or he would single out a promising girl from one of his newspapers. Anne Sharpley, a reporter on the *Standard*, was one of his favourites and she became deeply fond of him, although she soon realized that he usually contrived to summon her when she had a previous engagement or to arrange a foreign posting when a relationship with a boyfriend began to get serious. He would hold her hands for hours, she remembered, and gaze at her, saying, 'Let me look at you. You are a woman in her prime.'[10] According to her journalistic colleagues, things went further; if she accompanied him on a plane journey, he enjoyed her discreet attentions under a rug on his lap.[11] Well into his late seventies, Beaverbrook would look out for new opportunities with women and was capable, one way or another, of making the most of them. He courted a young doctor, Christian Carritt, whose twin brother David, a brilliant art historian, wrote for the *Standard* and acted as one of Beaverbrook's advisers; she remembers how he tricked her into dining with him alone, evidently for seduction purposes. He sent her masses of flowers and often bought her presents – a new dress or an evening bag.[12]

Sometimes these young women were the same age as, and friendly with, his granddaughter Jean, and it struck some observers that he might have been looking for such companionship partly as a result of a period of estrangement from her. After living with her grandfather and travelling with him for several years, Jean's own romantic life became complicated during her twenties; when she had love affairs with older men such as Sir Oswald Mosley whom her grandfather knew, he was outraged. For a time they were on bad terms, although he was always proud of her, especially when she became a successful New York reporter for the *Evening Standard* in the late 1950s. In 1961, Jean had a love affair with Norman Mailer and became pregnant. She was undecided for some time whether or not to marry him, and this was also hard for Beaverbrook to accept. When Rebecca West learned of her dilemma she wrote to her begging her not to have a child out of wedlock.[13] Acting on impulse, the pregnant Jean took Mailer to La Capponcina. Mailer has recalled:

> As I was saying goodbye to Beaverbrook at the end of the surprise visit Jeannie and I afforded him (for we did land without warning), I said to him in parting, 'Well, sir, under the circumstances you've been gracious,' at

which point the, I suspect, famous gleam came into his eyes and he repeated in an evaluative voice, half statement, half question, 'Under the circumstances'. I would like to think it amused him but I can't bet on it.[14]

'KING OF NEW BRUNSWICK AND QUEEN'

To New Brunswick at large, the supply of memorials of and by its most famous son gradually speeded up. The Newcastle ice rink named after Beaverbrook's early benefactor, the lumberman Edward Sinclair, opened in 1956; the Newcastle town hall and theatre, named after himself, opened in 1957, built 'at a price that seems to me unbelievably low in view of the product', Roy Howard of the Scripps-Howard newspaper chain told him, ambiguously, after a visit.

One memorial caused embarrassment. Wardell reported that the grateful schoolchildren of Fredericton wished to erect a statue of him; reluctantly, Beaverbrook allowed an appeal to be launched in the *Gleaner*. Extensive searches were made for his peer's robes; the sculptor appeared at La Capponcina and drew sketches. Time passed. Discreetly, Beaverbrook enquired about the progress of the appeal. The schoolchildren had proved less grateful than Wardell had anticipated. An anonymous donation followed – one of the few occasions on which a Beaverbrook contribution to a public cause was kept quiet. Dr Alfred Bailey had earmarked a site in Fredericton for a much-needed repository for the New Brunswick archives, which he hoped and expected Beaverbrook to finance; instead, the city was given a Beaverbrook theatre. In 1960, Newcastle erected a bust of him in the town square.

He ceased to stay at the Beaverbrook Hotel, where stepping on the word 'Beaverbrook' marked on a bathmat had once given Le Roux an unsettling moment. His tax needs having changed, he stayed instead either in his mansion, Somerville House, which later became the official residence of the Lieutenant Governor, or in his small flat in the gallery, where his own chef cooked for him.

Everyone had to put themselves out for Beaverbrook on his visits. Successive premiers, Liberal and Conservative, worked hard to accommodate the province's most munificent benefactor. He liked, in his phrase, to get them 'jumping'. If he felt thwarted, or – still worse – if he imagined that he was being slighted, he would threaten to pull out altogether: ' . . . they don't want a man like me around here'. Rows with Tweedie and Wardell were habitual. 'Whenever his lordship departed for other climes', wrote Tweedie, 'I thanked God with a humble and contrite heart for His mercy.' Wardell thought he had been promised $15,000 to print the gallery catalogue and raged at Beaverbrook in Tweedie's presence when Beaverbrook back-pedalled; later Wardell told Tweedie, 'How angry he could make me and how he enjoyed doing it.' Later still Tweedie asked Beaverbrook how many people he allowed to talk to him like that: 'Not many. Churchill could and Brendan Bracken could . . . but not many, not many.'

Despite or because of the rows, and with Beaverbrook always keeping Wardell on a string about money, Wardell became even more Beaverbrook's creature, defending him in print against any public criticisms – always sending him proofs for approval – and reprinting, at Beaverbrook's suggestion, pro-Beaverbrook articles that had appeared elsewhere. When Wardell's *Atlantic Advocate* published Beaverbrook's series about his early life, every line and picture was exhaustively checked with the author. Word came from London: 'Lord Beaverbrook says that surely you can find snapshots of him which are of lively interest – where he is grimacing, looking ugly, etc? . . . Lord Beaverbrook remembers a picture of himself very tight, which was taken at the Albert Hall?' The autobiographer attended to the biblical cadences of his prose. ' "When night fell I asked Heber for news" should read "And when the day was done I asked Heber for news".' At last the proof-reading drew to an end. Lord Beaverbrook, Wardell was told, had decided to conclude with the words, 'I knew the wickedness that is in the heart of man.'

Beaverbrook was eighty in May 1959, but his lifelong alertness to real or imagined slights increased rather than diminished with old age. He was capable of becoming agitated even about his relations with the royal family. Eight years earlier, when Princess Elizabeth and the Duke of Edinburgh had been due to visit the Bonar Law–Bennett Library during a royal tour, Dr Bailey asked him if he would be present. 'Don't you know, my friend, that Presbyterians are not monarchists?' said Beaverbrook, and left town. In 1959 the Queen was again due to visit Fredericton, and Beaverbrook's admirer Anne Sharpley of the *Evening Standard*, a royal tour reporter, complained to the Premier of Newfoundland that 'they' were making a 'stupid mess' of the visit by not inviting Beaverbrook to meet Her Majesty.[15] Premier Smallwood remarked that the cleavage was due to Beaverbrook's backing of Edward VIII, was it not? Yes, said Anne Sharpley, which was all the more reason to close the gap, and it could be done well in Canada. Smallwood undertook to intercede.

Sitting next to the Queen at dinner, he said he had heard that the New Brunswick authorities had not invited Beaverbrook to meet her. 'Why, he's the King of New Brunswick, and you, Your Majesty, are the Queen.' According to Smallwood, the Queen replied, 'I'd be happy to meet Lord Beaverbrook, happy to meet him. You see, I don't arrange these things. Someone has to arrange them.' Smallwood thereupon talked to the Queen's Private Secretary, Sir Michael Adeane, who told him the Queen never asked to meet anyone; that was something for the Governor or Lieutenant Governor to arrange. However, Adeane was in favour of bringing the pair together. He and Smallwood agreed that Wardell, as Beaverbrook's henchman, should be notified. Wardell saw Adeane on the royal yacht in Montreal: did Adeane want Wardell to 'intervene' with Beaverbrook? Yes, said Adeane, to the extent that the meeting was 'most desirable'; but Wardell must not say that he, Adeane, had instigated it, as a request from him was the equivalent of a request from the Queen. Wardell told Adeane to assume that Beaverbrook would be in Fredericton at the same time as the Queen, and Adeane replied that the news was 'most welcome'.

The assumption proved false. When Beaverbrook heard about the elaborate quadrille being danced for his benefit he was not pleased. He wrote to Wardell on 17 July:

My dear Captain,
Many thanks for your letter of 12th July and for your very generous interest in my problem.
Briefly, here is the story.
1. I am fourth in order to serve among the Privy Councillors.
2. I served two monarchs in high office.
3. When the Coronation tickets in the Abbey were being issued a device was practised to refuse me a place, claiming that I was too late. Of course, I had just come back from the West Indies. Subsequently, I was offered a place and necessarily declined it.
4. Sir Michael Adeane visited me before the Palace entertained the Maritime Premiers. I don't think I looked good to him as he did not suggest that I should take my guests to the Palace.
5. The *Evening Standard* informed me that Commander Colville [the Palace press secretary] had said Her Majesty hoped I would be at Fredericton.
6. I wrote the following letter to Commander Colville on the 15th June:-
'Dear Sir,
I have received your message through the *Evening Standard*.
If it is Her Majesty's wish that I should be at Fredericton during her visit I will, of course, go there.
It is my hope that I may be allowed to serve the Queen at all times.
Yours sincerely (Beaverbrook)'
7. I receive an answer by telephone to the effect that I misunderstood the message.
8. Now I get this very kind letter from you. Evidently Sir Michael Adeane expects me to go to Fredericton for the Queen's Reception on this very indefinite, and even nebulous approach.
Now I take it all this difficulty arises from my support of the Duke of Windsor when he was the Monarch.
Again my gratitude to you for taking so much trouble about my unhappy relations. Maybe the situation arises through my hostility to the Earl Mountbatten over what I believe to be the betrayal of Burma, refusal to let the Dutch back into Indonesia. And over everything the sack of India. The bright jewel in Queen Victoria's Crown. Yours ever, Max.

No meeting between the Queen and Beaverbrook took place.

PUBLIC LIFE AND VENDETTAS

In his conduct of the most trivial affairs of life, Beaverbrook even in old age continued to be irrationally concerned by what he considered to be needless expense, especially when he thought other people were presuming to waste his money. When Miss Bower's accounts for her interior decoration of Aitken House in Nassau failed to add up by a very small sum, she was forced, despite her readiness to fund the deficit herself, to review every expenditure until she balanced her books. Wardell sent Beaverbrook what were considered to be unnecessary telegrams; he was told that in future, to impress on him the importance of economy, Lord Beaverbrook's letters to him would be unstamped. The director of the art gallery was instructed to stop stapling documents together – without being told why; the obvious explanation was that the Custodian found staples a nuisance; but the director could not entirely rule out the possibility that the Custodian regarded them as a luxury and evidence of the gallery's profligacy.

Beaverbrook's extreme touchiness when he thought anyone was exploiting or scoring off him was connected with his much-discussed vendettas. George Malcolm Thomson thought his greatest fault was his 'vindictiveness'. Often the cause was known only to himself. He vehemently denied that he engaged in vendettas. In the fifties, his newspapers consistently attacked the Arts Council; his staff put it down to his hostility to the head of the Arts Council, Lord Lloyd. In the margin, however, of the proofs of Driberg's biography, when he came across this interpretation, he wrote, ' . . . untrue. My relations with him were always friendly.' He pursued, as has been seen, the Duke of Hamilton apparently for no better reason than that he had rejected Beaverbrook's invitation to fight an election as an Empire Free Trade candidate. He persecuted the rich recluse Sir John Ellerman for reasons that nobody ever discovered – including Hugh Cudlipp, who tried without success to persuade Beaverbrook to 'loosen the talons from the prey'.

He had a long feud with the Astor family. He also attacked the National Trust over many years, evidently because the 2nd Viscount Astor had handed over Cliveden, his country house, to the Trust; his motive, Beaverbrook alleged, was to escape death duties – though why this motive should have seemed disreputable to Beaverbrook, who had himself taken steps to avoid death duties, is obscure. As soon as Garvin was fired by the Astors as editor of the *Observer* in 1942, Beaverbrook hired him for the *Sunday Express*. The feud was exacerbated in 1949 by a dismissive seventieth birthday profile in the *Observer* that described him as 'a golliwog itching with vitality' and his *Express* leaders as 'political baby talk'. Every now and again thereafter the *Evening Standard* ran paragraphs in the Londoner's Diary about the transference of the ownership of the *Observer* from the Astors to a Trust; the Trust provided that the higher direction of the paper must be exercised by persons of the Protestant religion, which was an odd stipulation no doubt, but not a sign of the paper's prejudice against Catholics and Jews, as Beaverbrook often implied; 'I believe we touch you up about it once in a while,' he remarked to an *Observer* reporter in 1956; and the touching up continued until the terms of the Trust were changed. When Jean Norton's daughter, Sarah, married the 3rd Viscount Astor, Beaverbrook refused to attend the wedding.

But his most striking vendetta – once again, he strongly repudiated the word – was against Mountbatten. Edwina Mountbatten had been part of his social circle. His alleged close friend Wardell was a friend of the Mountbattens, and a former lover of Edwina. But from the end of the war onwards 'Laard Mountbatten', regarded by most ordinary people as a war hero, became a regular Beaverbrook newspaper target. After Mountbatten, as the last Viceroy of India, had negotiated Indian independence under instructions from the Attlee government, the *Express*, writing about Nehru but also mentioning Mountbatten, used the phrase, 'in all the world we have few more dangerous enemies'. Mountbatten alleged that he had been called a traitor, and told Wardell that his counsel said he could get libel damages of £100,000 for that phrase alone, but he did not intend to bring an action. Beaverbrook told Wardell: 'If the Lord Mountbatten is under the impression that the phrase which related to Nehru also applied to him, then it is just another reason why he should not be First Sea Lord' – the post on which Mountbatten had set his heart and which Beaverbrook wished to deny him.

Various explanations have been put forward, publicly and privately, for this vendetta – a word that does not seem inappropriate. Some pointed to a scene in Noël Coward's wartime film *In Which We Serve*, inspired by Mountbatten, when a destroyer is sunk and the survivors notice, floating on the waves, a copy of the *Daily Express* headlined 'No War This Year'. Others thought it stemmed from the Dieppe raid, of which Mountbatten was in overall command, and the massacre there of Canadian soldiers. Beaverbrook's vehemence, some thought, might have been connected with his advocacy of precisely that type of raid to relieve German pressure on the Russian front. Beaverbrook himself said that Mountbatten was merely subject to the same measure of attack as any other public man who, like Mountbatten in India, 'might transgress the high principles which the *Express* sets in all matters concerning the British Empire'. George Malcolm Thomson reflected the view of people inside Express newspapers at the time when he said, with confidence, though forty-five years after the event, that the cause of the vendetta was personal. After Jean Norton's death in 1945 at her cottage on the Cherkley estate, Beaverbrook learned from her papers that, while she was his mistress, she had also had an affair with Mountbatten. This coincided with the view of Edwina Mountbatten's friends, who remembered an earlier time when both the Mountbatten marriage and the Beaverbrook–Norton relationship had been under strain, and the two had seen much of one another.

These particular hostilities, more obviously inspired by the private grudges of an old man than, for instance, the sustained political campaigns against Baldwin in the thirties, weakened the authority of Beaverbrook's papers after the war, though without affecting their circulation. Mockery damaged their standing also, particularly when lightweight *Express* writers took on heavyweights such as Evelyn Waugh (a former employee and a special correspondent for the paper at the coronation of Haile Selassie in 1930) and Graham Greene. Waugh derided the intellectual pretensions of the Beaverbrook press and in 1957 won two libel actions against it; Greene inflicted a more damaging wound when, intermittently between 1956 and 1959, he held up the editor-in-chief of the *Sunday Express*, John Gordon, to national ridicule. Greene named Nabokov's *Lolita*, then scarcely known, as one of his 'books of the year'. Gordon, a stern moralist, attacked both the book ('sheer unrestrained pornography') and Greene in his *Sunday Express* column, which inspired Greene to found the John Gordon Society 'against pornography', of which he became president and which prominent social and literary figures happily joined. At a packed meeting in a Tottenham Court Road hotel Gordon was duly insulted and mocked; the *Daily Express* reported the uproar at length.[16] Controversy, Beaverbrook believed, was good for newspapers.

Secure in the citadel of his own fixed beliefs, his ammunition locker well stocked with documents and by his own long and formidable memory, his spies everywhere, and a marauding force of researchers and reporters on standby, he could humour himself by taking pot shots at his enemies and keep boredom at bay at the same time. Rows or criticisms of himself he invariably promoted or reprinted in his own papers. Some newspaper proprietors, he told Stanley Morison, 'think there is more fun in printing criticism than praise'.[17] Beaverbrook printed both.

But his influence as a press baron was in decline. His newspapers had carried most weight and caused most trouble when he was himself engaged in a political intrigue or campaign and deployed his papers in support. The Suez crisis of 1956 showed the extent of the change. Churchill retired, against Beaverbrook's advice, in April 1955, and Eden, who had thought of himself as the crown prince since 1940, became Prime Minister. In July 1956 Nasser seized the Suez Canal. Beaverbrook still knew personally the men in power: Eden and Macmillan, the Chancellor of the Exchequer, the main advocates of armed intervention against Nasser; and he knew also the leading sceptics, Walter Monckton, the Minister of Defence, and Mountbatten. His main London informant was Brendan Bracken, an Eden supporter.

Even so, there was no personal role for Beaverbrook to play. He supported Eden fully. He had told Stanley Morison three years earlier that his fourth volume of the *History of the Times* was also a history of the decline of the British Empire; like Eden, he thought it intolerable that Nasser should have, in Eden's phrase, 'his thumb on our windpipe': were not a third of the ships using the Canal British? But he did not interrupt his routine. He thought his old forebodings were coming true. The United States, not Britain, was now the arbiter of peace or war. He had also predicted that Macmillan would make trouble for Eden, as he did when he successfully urged withdrawal to save the pound. Beaverbrook, on the contrary, thought Eden wrong to pull out. When Eden, a sick man on the brink of resignation, went to Jamaica to stay in Ann and Ian Fleming's house in December 1956, Beaverbrook declined to make the journey from Nassau to see him. With the Suez fiasco, the old imperial hopes disappeared from view also. Eden spent part of his convalescence as Beaverbrook's guest at the Manor Farm in Cricket Malherbie, looked after by Copland. Less than two years later Bracken was dead, and Beaverbrook was left to ponder what had gone wrong.

PRIVATE FACES

Beaverbrook's calendar, in later life, became fixed. From 15 December to the end of February he spent in Nassau. For a week or so in March he went to New York, staying at the Waldorf Towers on Fifth Avenue. In spring and most of the summer he was in England: Cherkley, Arlington House and, for two or three days, Cricket Malherbie. For August he transferred to La Capponcina. Towards the end of September he went to Canada, and then put in a month or so in New York before the round started again with Christmas in Nassau.

His habit was to rise at about a quarter to eight, and, if not in a hotel, to breakfast downstairs. In England he might have an egg, or half a partridge – never bacon. While he ate, he read. From 8.30 or 8.45 a.m. he worked, always standing at a lectern, dictating to a secretary or talking into his Soundscriber dictating machine. He maintained the same routine in Jamaica, the Bahamas, Cap d'Ail and Canada. Wherever he was, he was impatient for the arrival of the newspapers and his mail, with its regular stack of nasty little reused envelopes from Mr Millar. Having read the *Express* and the *Standard*, he fired off criticisms.

In Nassau, the morning's work done, there would often be an expedition in his luxurious boat; he liked to fish, sitting in a chair. The expedition might go to Spanish Wells for the night, where he had his own house, but he declined to sleep ashore because of the sandflies, though others of the party did; he slept on the boat. In earlier days, confusion had arisen about his nocturnal whereabouts; on one occasion the actress

Hermione Baddeley, believing him to be in his shipboard bunk, entered the cabin, bared her breasts and climbed in; but the sleeping figure was Albert the butler, a nervous man, who nearly jumped through the porthole, or so the story went.

Lunch was served on the boat, and the menu was always the same: each person was allocated one lettuce heart, one tomato, one slice of roast beef and one wing of chicken. Cheese was never served; usually there was a Danish pastry. Those who wanted more went without. Beaverbrook drank whisky. Alsatian white wine and champagne were freely available.

In Nassau, during the afternoon, Beaverbrook rested or pottered off to the end of his garden in a golf cart and talked to the gardener. He was safe driving a golf cart, but not a car. Afterwards he awaited with impatience the six o'clock post. At 8 p.m., the company would assemble for daiquiris made by himself. At dinner, the champagne was always especially good: often a Louis Roederer 1947.

The host drank less than he urged on his guests. Sir Patrick Hennessy likened the opening of bottles at Beaverbrook dinners to the firing of guns. After Hennessy borrowed La Capponcina for a holiday Beaverbrook wrote to him:

> While you were here the book shows you consumed, along with your immediate associates (Madame Escarra, Mr Frederick Lonsdale, and Mr Stanley Morison):–
> 70 bottles champagne
> 56 bottles red and white wine
> 2 bottles brandy
> 3 bottles gin
> 9 bottles rum
> 10 bottles whisky
> A record, and I will award Medals.[18]

Four courses were always served, the main course being invariably local fresh fish, charcoal-grilled steak or chicken. Beaverbrook only wanted the food he liked, and it was chosen to suit his own restricted tastes. Garlic was banned. Tea was not served because it wasted time. When Morison, after a thirty-eight-hour journey from London to Nassau, asked for tea, Beaverbrook said: 'Bring a bottle of champagne for the holy father.'

In London, he would go for a walk in Green Park at about 11 a.m., always accompanied, often by Robertson or Christiansen. He rarely went to other people's houses, where it was less easy for him to control proceedings. In New York he usually looked up his old favourite Dorothy Schiff, now the owner of the New York Post, and occasionally lunched at the Chambord or Le Pavillon, where to the dismay of first-time guests he would growl at the waiter, 'Bring us some soup and some beef.' He never booked at any restaurant, assuming that for him a table would always be free – as it was. He enjoyed the theatre in New York, and wanted to see the hits: two favourites were *My Fair Lady* and *Tea and Sympathy*.

He had established his sartorial style early in life and retained it: brown shoes with navy serge suits, a blue cashmere cardigan instead of a waistcoat, white shirts, blue tie usually, with a loose knot, black hat, black coat. In summer he wore white linen trousers, sometimes holed at the knee, and often a short-sleeved shirt. He was not vain about his appearance; yet in Nassau he would take sly looks at himself in the mirror opposite his lectern. His capacity for sustained work was unaffected by age. To finish urgent work, he would rise before 5 a.m. Copland found himself invariably given appointments at 7 a.m., which he put down to a Beaverbrookian belief that that was a normal business hour for farmers. At Cherkley, Copland was particularly impressed by his employer's economical use of time when he found himself one of a series of visitors reporting to Beaverbrook at intervals while he splashed and gasped up and down the indoor pool.

He cultivated the rich. The French millionaire and racehorse owner Marcel Boussac dined at La Capponcina, with Madame Escarra translating. The financier Ben Smith supplied Beaverbrook with PanAm tickets and, during the years of exchange control, US dollars. The most brazen flatterer was Arpad Plesch, a millionaire neighbour in the south of France (a collector of rare pornography, in which Beaverbrook was not interested). Plesch was entranced by meeting Beaverbrook; and Beaverbrook wanted something from him – books for the University of New Brunswick and prints for the Fredericton art gallery. So Plesch showered books and prints on New Brunswick and Beaverbrook in return handed out an entrance ticket to the Beaverbrook circle. Another very rich man was K. C. Irving, the New Brunswick industrialist; tapping him for university contributions, Beaverbrook said, was like getting blood out of a stone.

He cultivated rich women as well as men. Izaak Walton Killam, Beaverbrook's 'first employee and oldest friend', who bought him out of Royal Securities in 1919, died in 1955, leaving his entire fortune, $83,000,000, to his American wife, a glamorous woman interested in baseball and diamonds (she also owned the pearls handed by Colonel John Jacob Astor to his wife before he went down in the *Titanic*). She had a house in Nassau. Beaverbrook invited her to dinner and surrounded her with men of distinction, explaining to them beforehand that his aim was to extract Killam money for the University of New Brunswick. The dinner developed into a battle of wits, and Mrs Killam left without promising a dime. 'She beat us all,' said Beaverbrook. (When she died, in 1965, she left $87,000,000, tax-free, to institutions that included the universities of Dalhousie, Alberta and British Columbia, but not New Brunswick.)

Among newspaper people he saw Roy Howard, who told Tweedie that Beaverbrook's newspapers were 'awful, not worthy of being called newspapers'; Jean Provoust of *France Soir* and *Paris Match*; Clare and Henry Luce of *Time-Life*; and sometimes William Randolph Hearst Jr. Lord Kemsley was his favourite newspaper proprietor, and Beaverbrook eventually sold him his house in Nassau. He quite liked Roy Thomson, who imitated Beaverbrook by buying a house at Cap d'Ail and shocked Miss Rosenberg by saying, 'I'd go to hell if money was there'; Beaverbrook called Thomson 'a little fellow who owns a lot of little newspapers'. His Cap d'Ail circle included Emery Reves, Churchill's literary agent, and his much younger wife, Wendy Russell, a former New York model.

Showbusiness people occasionally appeared. The actress Elizabeth Taylor and Mike Todd, her producer husband, dined with Beaverbrook; Todd, having flattered Beaverbrook relentlessly all evening, presented him as they left with a new tape recorder. 'Raymond can set it up and tomorrow I can use it,' said Beaverbrook, and went to bed. Raymond and Miss Rosenberg plugged it in and played a tape the Todds had left with the machine. It was of Todd and Taylor making love. Next day Miss Rosenberg told Beaverbrook. He listened, and said, 'They did it deliberately. They did it to heat me up for the night.' Todd wanted to give both Beaverbrook and Miss Rosenberg each a vicuna coat. 'I'm not accepting,' he told Miss Rosenberg, 'and you're not to accept either.'[19] Few people understood better than Beaverbrook the delicate mechanism that links the acceptance of presents to obligation.

He was loyal and hospitable to Bonar Law's descendants, and to his Canadian associates, offering invitations and free tickets to favoured New Brunswick premiers. He liked and kept up with Joseph Kennedy, lending him Aitken House to stay in with his nurse and mistress. Edward Kennedy spent the first night of his honeymoon there. (Beaverbrook sent Miss Rosenberg to report the 1960 US election primaries for the *Evening Standard*, but she thought it prudent not to report the 'flick, flick, flick' of the $20, $10 and $5 bills as Joe Kennedy's money was handed out to encourage the recipients to vote for his son Jack.) Randolph Churchill came and went as he pleased, shouting and getting drunk and burning the parquet floors with his cigarette ends. His son Max came and went only by invitation; Beaverbrook's children did not have keys to any of his houses. Lord Rosebery was one of the few visitors who paid his own fare. An advantage of this generosity was that guests could not object when Mr Millar, having arranged their tickets, asked them to take provisions to Beaverbrook that he could not buy on the spot: limes, Black Label whisky, maple syrup, Barker and Dobson fruit drops.

He hated to be alone. He liked his houses to contain one or two visitors, though he did not always see much of them. But his hospitality had curious limits. His guests could not help themselves; everything was kept locked until he decided it should be unlocked; and he had first call on the newspapers. He liked nothing better than to be seated opposite a political opponent. His dislike of eating out increased; he feared he might find his neighbours disagreeable. This policy was confirmed after he dined next to a French woman, the wife of an employee, who was ugly, smoked Gitanes, and smelled of red wine and garlic: Beaverbrook's idea of true suffering.

John Junor of the *Sunday Express* could never understand Beaverbrook's tolerance of homosexuals. Nor could John Gordon, who in his *Sunday Express* column described the Wolfenden report on homosexuality as a 'Pansies' Charter'. When on one occasion Tom Driberg asked for $500 so that he could go to New York to see a woman, Beaverbrook was 'so intrigued by the mission', he told Bracken, that 'I handed out the money.'[20] Jean Cocteau and his partner were received without comment at La Capponcina. So was Somerset Maugham, a neighbour. A succession of Beaverbrook's menservants were homosexual or bisexual. He startled one of them, when he was cleaning a bath, by putting his head round the door and rasping: 'Are you a homosexual?' Hiring a homosexual for the *Express*, he arranged for him to be given a desk next to a handsome young reporter. He called homosexuals 'bugger-boys'.

To the end of his life Beaverbrook maintained a keen interest in sexuality – his own and other people's. Rumours were rife about the attentions he preferred – fellatio, as A. J. P. Taylor later told his future wife, or, as others said, the arrival in his bedroom of a young woman naked under a fur coat.[21] He also liked to reminisce about past adventures; Miss Rosenberg was once given an account of how he and some friends had hidden in the garden at Cherkley to peer through a bedroom window to watch Castlerosse perform. On another occasion, Beaverbrook showed her a hollow yew tree in the grounds where, he told her, bottles of champagne used to be secreted to encourage outdoor trysts.

To two of the young women closest to him in his old age, Josephine Rosenberg and his granddaughter Jean, it was clear that Beaverbrook's attitude to women had a dark side; it became increasingly marked as the influence of the two women – apart from his wife – whom he had perhaps in his way both loved and respected, Jean Norton and Lily Ernst, faded into the distant past. Miss Rosenberg disliked the contemptuous way he referred to Marie-Edmée Escarra; and Jean Campbell never forgot a moment in the south of France when, after an angry exchange about her conduct and what he regarded as her wilful, extravagant habits, he pointed to a maid on her hands and knees scrubbing the floor and told his granddaughter that she should be more like that, more like 'a real woman'. 'His great flaw was his inability to treat his women with dignity,' Jean Campbell has said. 'Slowly he would turn on them and devastate them. He made them feel they had no right to exist.' To her, there was evidently self-hatred involved in his maltreatment of the women he controlled; he despised them for being available, and himself for needing them.[22]

Yet he never stopped sending loving letters and presents to his old favourites, such as Diana Cooper, Helen Fitzgerald and Daphne Fielding; and Lily Ernst – Lady Hornby after her husband was knighted in 1960 – was sent a case of the best champagne every Christmas. 'I call it my pension,' she wrote. Mr Millar would remind him about birthdays, including hers; in 1954 he sent her a particularly romantic telegram; 'What is lovely never dies all that is beautiful shall abide.' She in her turn never forgot his birthday in May, because it fell just after the anniversary of her rescue from the Nazis in 1938. 'Thank you for getting me out of hell and bringing me here twenty-two years ago,' she wrote in 1960.[23]

In 1957 Beaverbrook discovered the pre-war Italian Ambassador to London, Count Grandi, living in Sao Paulo, Brazil; Grandi became a regular and feted visitor to Cap d'Ail and Nassau, where he liked to claim that, when Ribbentrop complained about Londoners throwing stones through the windows of the German Embassy, he had replied, 'My dear Joachim, we just leave our windows open.' In Jamaica and London Beaverbrook liked to gossip with Ann Fleming, though he did not particularly like her third husband, Ian, the inventor of James Bond.

He travelled with a valet and a secretary. Chefs were important. In England, his chef was a Dutchman. Beaverbrook asked: 'Chef, are you honest?' The answer was: 'As honest as a chef could be.' Beaverbrook loved maple sugar and maple syrup; fiddlehead ferns, a seasonal Canadian vegetable rather like asparagus, he always had sent to him for his birthday on 25 May. The other birthday ritual, the presents to other people, continued: $500 to some members of his staff and to his favourites. Lily Ernst, after she married, enjoyed a covenant for life of £3000 a year. His sister-in-law Helen Fitzgerald could draw money on request. Mrs Graham Sutherland mentioned a desirable white house that she and her husband had seen in Menton; Beaverbrook gave them the purchase price of £5000.

Among the regular visitors were 'the two black crows', as the staff called them: dark-suited bankers from the Montreal Trust Company and the Eastern Trust Company of St John. Allan Aitken, Beaverbrook's stockbroker brother, was constantly in action on Beaverbrook's behalf on the Montreal stock exchange, buying and selling Canadian and US stocks, but he was more often the agent than the inspiration of the deals; usually Beaverbrook saw an opening, or was given a tip by an industrialist or fellow financier, and asked his brother to investigate further and report back. Most of Beaverbrook's serious investments were in North America. Dr Bailey was present in the Waldorf Towers when Beaverbrook made a telephone call and, without troubling to identify himself, gave orders to buy a particular stock, and US Treasury bonds, worth $750,000. In England, lesser financial matters were handled, though always on a tight rein, by Millar. It may be doubted whether, in sixty years of constant financial activity, Beaverbrook ever allowed anyone to invest or spend a cent on his behalf without his express authority – whether on a heifer for Cricket Malherbie Ltd, a roof for a Cherkley outhouse, a printing press for his newspapers or mineral water for La Capponcina.

Apart from the bankers, the most important visitor was always Churchill, and Beaverbrook treated him with solicitude. In 1955, Wardell wanted to know if Beaverbrook had sent a message on his retirement; no, he had not; Churchill had had enough messages, and in any case he had seen him the day before he left Downing Street. It was true, though it was their first meeting for a long time. In 1958, Wardell wondered whether Churchill might be asked to write an introduction to the Beaverbrook Art Gallery catalogue; no, he might not: 'I could get him to do many things out of friendship. He had three intimate friends – the Prof [Professor Lindemann], Bracken, and me. Now he regards me as the only intimate friend and expects to outlive me. But I must be sure not to impose on him.'

At La Capponcina, a lift was installed for Churchill. He occupied the master bedroom; and, to the envy of others, was served foie gras and claret. He and Beaverbrook dined together, but never lunched, because Beaverbrook was out on his boat. One day Churchill wanted to go on the boat. 'No,' said Beaverbrook, being protective, 'you are not coming.' Off went the Beaverbrook party and tied up in Monte Carlo harbour. At lunchtime, a limousine drew up containing a detective and Sir Winston. 'What's he doing?' Beaverbrook asked. Churchill could not walk and clambered aboard on all fours. Someone aimed a camera. No, said Beaverbrook. Churchill was pleased with himself; Beaverbrook scowled. He did not like to be outwitted.

BOOKS AND A. J. P. TAYLOR

For the last ten years of his life Beaverbrook was busy not only with his art gallery but with writing books, which came to take precedence over his newspapers. In 1956 he published *Men and Power, 1917–1918*. The book was printed in large type and the sentences were short: there were only seven commas on the first two pages. 'Complete impartiality' was Beaverbrook's description of his authorial stance, but he stuck his pin into old targets just the same. A photograph of Asquith in court dress is captioned 'Uniformed Indolence'. Baldwin is captioned: 'Mrs Baldwin called him "Tiger" '. Many episodes involved Beaverbrook. 'It may be

501

asked "Were you there?" I was there!'

Men and Power led to one of the most curious alliances of Beaver-brook's life. By the mid-1950s the fame of the historian A. J. P. Taylor had spread far beyond Oxford through his journalism in the *Sunday Pictorial* and his appearances on television: wearing a bow tie, looking puckish and sounding intellectually fearless. The two men first exchanged letters in 1955.[24] Beaverbrook – 'I am not writing in a controversial spirit' – had asked Taylor his authority for two statements in his 'splendid' book *The Struggle for Mastery in Europe*. Taylor supplied the evidence and went on: 'I am very flattered by your kind words about my book. It is agreeable to please historians; but even nicer to satisfy those who have made history.'

The mutual flattery did not survive the publication of Driberg's biography the following year. Taylor reviewed it in the *Observer* and wrote about Beaverbrook with disdain, almost contempt, comprehensively dismissing any suggestions that he should be taken seriously as a newspaper proprietor, as an historian or as a politician.

> . . . Max Aitken once played some part in politics when he brought Lloyd George and Bonar Law together against Asquith: but the only person who supposes that this part was decisive is the author of *Politicians and the War*. As to Lord Beaverbrook's later incursions into politics, the Empire Crusade was a knockabout comedy, not worth a footnote in the textbooks. In 1940 the Minister of Aircraft Production may have inspired his colleagues; but only plans made years before could mature into aircraft. The Battle of Britain was won by Chamberlain, or perhaps by Lady Houston,* not by Lord Beaverbrook; a melancholy reflection. Lord Beaverbrook has counted for something in politics now and then – counted from his personality, not as a newspaper proprietor; but he has never counted very much. . . . He likes to be accused of seeking power – even power without responsibility. In reality he loves energy, which is something quite different . . . though Lord Beaverbrook has often made news, it has not been news of any significance.

Later that year Taylor was sent *Men and Power* to review. To his surprise, and that of his readers, he found it 'one of the most exciting works of history' he had ever read; Beaverbrook was 'a great historian'. Michael Foot was with Beaverbrook when he read the review, and observed his satisfaction, though it is not clear from Foot's account whether Beaverbrook was or was not surprised to find himself compared with Tacitus. Taylor's praise was 'quite uncalculated', he said later; but it changed both his and Beaverbrook's life.

---

*Lady Houston (1857–1936) was an eccentric philanthropist who financed a British team that entered the Schneider Trophy air race in 1931, after the government refused support. The trophy was won by Flight Lieutenant G. H. Stainforth flying a Supermarine Rolls Royce S6, direct predecessor of the Spitfires and Hurricanes of the Battle of Britain.

A year after the review, Taylor wrote to ask Beaverbrook about his assertion in *Men and Power* that at one of the most dramatic moments of the First World War Lloyd George, when he was imposing convoys on the admirals, had 'descended upon the Admiralty and seated himself in the First Lord's chair'. Beaverbrook sent back references and the copy of a letter from Carson to Curzon, adding firmly, 'The copyright of the Curzon papers belongs to me . . . the Lloyd George papers are under my control.' Taylor might be the professional historian, but Beaverbrook owned the raw material. Beaverbrook added that he would ask Churchill about the incident, but he never did, and Taylor concluded that it had been invented. Soon Beaverbrook sent Taylor more documents, this time about George VI. They met and lunched. In July 1958, Beaverbrook wrote to say that he was sorry Taylor had not been able to dine with himself and Churchill: 'I had hoped you would be there too, to entertain him, or he you.'

It was as if Taylor's Driberg review had never been written – or perhaps Beaverbrook set out to woo Taylor because of it. Taylor made no bones about what he saw in Beaverbrook. 'Of course Max bribed me as he did everyone else,' he wrote cheerfully in his autobiography. Taylor was a contributor to the *Sunday Express*. Beaverbrook sent him cheese and claret, having learnt that Taylor preferred claret to champagne. Taylor was particularly grateful to Beaverbrook for one service. Halfway through his *English History 1915-1945*, he got stuck and talked of giving up; Beaverbrook revived his enthusiasm and was thanked for his 'unfailing stimulus'. Taylor was fascinated by Beaverbrook's 'fantastically vivid' recollections, 'though no doubt sometimes overdrawn or even fabricated'. He was not the first to understand how the trick was done, and yet find it irresistible. 'He had a gift for making you feel when you were with him that you were the most important person in the world. Of course I knew he forgot about me the moment I left the room but it was magical all the same. Max Beaverbrook well knew how to steal the hearts of men. He certainly stole mine.'

What was Beaverbrook's interest in Taylor? He became the patron of an outstanding historian who was also a mischief-making *Sunday Express* columnist of the sort he had always liked to employ. But there was more to the relationship than that. Taylor himself believed that what Beaverbrook sought from him was self-confidence. Beaverbrook was seventy-seven when he published *Men and Power*, and, though still packed with energy, less interested than for half a century in current politics. He was more interested in looking back. He was excited by the idea of success in a field not his own, and Taylor assured him that he had achieved it. The flattery again became mutual, as they praised one another's writings and activities. Taylor changed his mind about the Empire Crusade not being worth a footnote in the textbooks. 'Your campaign against Baldwin in 1929–31 . . . deserves a book,' he told

Beaverbrook on 9 December 1961.

They shared to some extent the same attitude to historiography. The great L. B. Namier, professor of history at Manchester when Taylor was a lecturer, thought that Taylor possessed extraordinary gifts, but disapproved of his journalism; responsible historians, Namier believed, should eschew journalism, characterized as it was by 'the desire to *épater*, to entertain, to be brilliant'. But it was precisely this desire that excited Taylor and Beaverbrook alike when they wrote history. To enliven a narrative, Beaverbrook, as Taylor knew, engaged in 'balancing', which was a polite term for making things up. If one authority said one thing, and Beaverbrook said the opposite, Beaverbrook, if challenged, would explain that he was giving 'another version of the same'. 'But what did I care?' said Taylor. Taylor himself was equally intent on entertainment, though of course he enlightened as well as dazzled and amused his readers. The two men discussed men and motives, exchanging gossip, not ideas. That Taylor became an active member of the Campaign for Nuclear Disarmament in 1957, in the early days of the friendship, did not trouble either of them. Beaverbrook gave his friend an honorary D.Litt. (New Brunswick) in 1961 and took him to Fredericton to lecture, Taylor's only transatlantic trip. 'Dr Taylor has come a long way to address you, so listen carefully to what he has to say,' said the Chancellor. He then sat down and went to sleep.

Taylor became Beaverbrook's main historical adviser. After Beaverbrook drafted *The Decline and Fall of Lloyd George: And Great was the Fall Thereof*, he sent the manuscript to Taylor, saying he was 'anxious' about its quality and would not publish it without Taylor's approval. He offered Taylor £500 for the task, which Taylor refused, saying 'it will be a little, and inadequate, tribute of friendship. A box of cigars perhaps if my verdict is favourable.' Two days later Mr Millar sent him a box of cigars from Beaverbrook and renewed the offer of £500, which Taylor again refused; but an alternative would be for Beaverbrook to pay for an operation on Taylor's wife's leg, costing about £50. Taylor approved of the book; he corrected details, noted repetitions and recommended cuts. Beaverbrook confessed that 'it is unfortunately a bad habit with me to engage in repetition and also to use the same words too often'. Taylor asked to read the proofs: 'I am a reliable proof reader.' Cheese, wine and more cigars followed. On 19 February Taylor assured Beaverbrook: 'It is a magnificent book.' Beaverbrook said he was encouraged to press ahead with his long-projected work on the Age of Baldwin. People do not usually review books that they themselves have helped to bring to birth; but Taylor reviewed *The Decline and Fall of Lloyd George* in the *New Statesman*, and was thanked for his 'learned and generous review' by Beaverbrook, who was the only person who had known in advance what Taylor's verdict would be. It was an improvement on his 1956 verdict. Beaverbrook, he said, 'has been at the heart of events for over 50 years, at once observer and doer. . . . He has been the greatest newspaperman since Northcliffe. Now, on top of this, he writes books which are the admiration and envy of the professional historian.'[25] While Taylor grew steadily closer to Beaverbrook, Robert Blake drew away. He too reviewed *Men and Power*, for the *Sunday Express*; he praised the book but mentioned some minor mistakes. When he saw that 'some toady' had cut all his critical references he decided 'enough was enough'. Blake never knew whether Beaverbrook himself had ordered the changes, but it is hardly likely that the paper failed to submit the review to him in advance.[26]

FRIENDS

Beaverbrook's zeal in old age for recording aspects of his past was not confined to his experience of British politics. New Brunswick had produced in one generation, besides himself, three men of outstanding achievement: Bonar Law, R. B. Bennett, and Sir James Dunn. All were friends of Beaverbrook. In the 1930s, a *Daily Express* sports writer named Trevor Wignall, possibly the first of the sports writers to promote himself as well as his subject, published a successful book called *I Knew Them All*. Beaverbrook wrote in the same spirit. His memoir of Bennett, published in 1959, was called *Friends: Sixty Years of Intimate Personal Relations with Richard Bedford Bennett*. It is consistently entertaining. Beaverbrook contrived both to assert that his old friend was a heroic Prime Minister who had saved Canada during the depression and yet at the same time to portray him as pompous and absurd: a teetotaller, for instance, whose rigid principles nevertheless allowed him to drink crème de menthe and to add sherry to his soup. Bennett's career is shown to have depended on Beaverbrook's patronage: it was Beaverbrook who pushed him into politics, made his fortune by cutting him in on Beaverbrook-sponsored power and grain enterprises in western Canada, and organized his retirement to England by installing him next to Cherkley and by putting him forward for a viscountcy, which he was given in 1941. 'Thereafter he showed an immense interest in the practice and proceedings of the noble lords who sit at Westminster, wielding neither influence nor power and as absurd as an hereditary Medical Council would be.' In his will, Beaverbrook recorded, Bennett left the Royal Society for the Encouragement of Arts 'sixty-seven volumes of the works of Elbert Hubbard, the American writer, not widely read in Great Britain'.

Beaverbrook sent a copy of *Friends* to A. J. P. Taylor, drawing his attention to its attacks on Baldwin as a liar. Indeed, it could be argued that the true aim of the book was to bestow a high posthumous political reputation on Bennett and contrast it with the decline of Baldwin's. References to Baldwin are malign. More and more, as he got older,

Beaverbrook became obsessed by his own 'greatest blunder' in 1930 when he failed to back Bennett in the Canadian general election, and thus was not invited to attend the Ottawa Conference at his friend's right hand when Baldwin, the leader of the British delegation, was scuppering the conference – and Bennett – and sinking forever all prospects of Empire Free Trade.

SIR JAMES AND LADY DUNN

Beaverbrook's memoir of another friend, Sir James Dunn – *Courage*, published by Collins in 1961 – was on the face of it the least self-serving book he ever produced. He knew Dunn for nearly three-quarters of a century, but although they were both financiers from the same distant quarter of New Brunswick they never did business together, apart from swapping share tips. Beaverbrook was thus free to tell, with only an occasional pause for self-promotion, the story of the triumphs and near-disasters of 'Canada's foremost industrialist', and to describe the wild eccentricities of a man who 'lived more splendidly and spent more lavishly than any other I have ever known'. Beaverbrook placed a quotation from Deuteronomy opposite the preface, and further quotations from Cicero, Bret Harte, S. Baring Gould, C. S. Lewis, Disraeli and so on at the head of each chapter, including 'All things are done magnificently by the rich – from the Latin'. He gravely explained that Dunn's life was ruled by the Shorter Catechism, though 'he was possibly unaware of it'. In amassing net assets of $65,825,000, mainly in the shares of the Algoma Steel Company he controlled, Sir James had been obeying, Beaverbrook explained, the Shorter Catechism's questions and answers to the eighth commandment, which lay down that this commandment 'requires the lawful procuring and furthering of the wealth and outward estate of ourselves and others'. Beaverbrook added: 'That is a positive injunction.' He often had recourse to these comforting questions and answers when he felt the need to justify great wealth, his own included. The Shorter Catechism, however, was silent about the concerns, apart from money, that more consciously affected Dunn's life. Beaverbrook publicized and revelled in them.

> He was always suspicious that his health might be affected by the wrong food cooked in the wrong way. When he sailed from New York to Southampton in a strange liner, not a Cunard vessel, he had grievances on the first day out. He claimed the blankets were made of some form of fibre glass and were disagreeable to him.
>
> This provoked alarm in his mind about what he was being given to eat. He visited the kitchens. What he saw did not dispel his fears.
>
> Fish was being cooked on a production line where the chef held a hot swatter, and attacked every piece of fish with it to give the impression that the cooking had been done on a grill, when, in fact, it had been cooked

by electricity.

In Dunn's view, all the food on the ship was electrocuted. For the rest of the journey he would eat nothing but honeydew melons and yoghourt. He had five days of this restricted diet.

Dunn forbade the use of electric razors in his house, believing them to disseminate stubble that filled the air and might promote cancer. Hatred of noise and fear of marauders led him to build a nine-foot fence around his property at St Andrew, New Brunswick. On his constant travels he was accompanied by hat-boxes packed with cooking equipment, specially blended teas, pots of honey, glucose, molasses, oatmeal and boot-polishing material, 'for James attached great importance to his shoes being polished until they shone like glass. Sometimes he would discard as many as five pairs before he found a pair polished to his liking.' His shoelaces were ironed before use. The maid at his Waldorf Towers apartment, which was protected by locks and chains 'like an ancient keep', was instructed, when cleaning the rooms in Dunn's absence, to brush the carpet at the entrance while walking backwards. 'Thus any intruder would be betrayed by his footprints.'

The reader finishes *Courage* with the impression that Canada's foremost industrialist, had he not been so rich, would have been lucky to escape confinement in an institution. It was this aspect of the book that infuriated Dunn's children by his first two marriages, who seriously considered taking out an injunction and wrote letters of protest to newspapers. They were sure the book was motivated less by Beaverbrook's affection for their father than by long-standing rivalry and malice – a calculated attempt to belittle him. Nor was their anger lessened by the fact that the book had been cleared for publication by Dunn's third wife, who allowed Beaverbrook unrestricted access to Dunn's private papers.[27]

Courage is notable for another reason. It is the prime source of information about Dunn's third wife, who became Beaverbrook's second: Marcia Christoforides, generally known as 'Christofor'. She was born in Sutton, Surrey, on 27 July 1910, and, according to Beaverbrook, went to work for Dunn in 1930 after she applied unsuccessfully for a job on the *Sunday Express* city pages, whose editor knew that Dunn was looking for a junior secretary. She was a keen Empire Crusader. 'A long neck, high cheekbones and hair of a slightly golden hue gave her an exotic appearance,' Beaverbrook wrote (she was half-Greek). She became rich through the patronage of two rich men. Dunn gave her shares as an investment. Unknown to him she sold the shares and put the proceeds on a horse tipped to her by her friend Sir Hugo Cunliffe-Owen, chairman of the British American Tobacco Company and an old Empire Crusader; the horse won at 8–1. She reinvested her winnings on the rising New York stock exchange. By twenty-five she was 'a woman of fortune', assistant secretary of Algoma Steel and Dunn's confidante. In 1942, Dunn fell seriously ill in Canada and Christofor nursed him back to health; soon afterwards Dunn's second wife divorced him and he and Christofor married. When he died in 1956 Christofor, 'who was in her own right already a wealthy woman', inherited $15 million. Beaverbrook ended his book by noting Lady Dunn's bequest to Dalhousie University.

Dunn's death left her inconsolable. Beaverbrook told Bracken that she wanted to go to a convent. If she did, said Beaverbrook, she would not like the food and would 'certainly quarrel with the Mother Superior'.[28] Wardell told Beaverbrook in July 1958 that 'she talked of you, said she heard from you frequently, evidently relies on you'.[29] Beaverbrook tried to distract her by encouraging further bequests, this time in Fredericton, and by persuading her to finance with him the new theatre, of which she took charge. Dunn had been a considerable art buyer and patron in his time; in 1914, after his business partner defaulted and fled, Dunn sold Knoedlers, the art dealers, thirteen paintings, including three Goyas, a Holbein, a Bronzino, an El Greco and a Manet; he sold the Frick Collection in New York paintings by Gainsborough, Hogarth, Goya and Manet. Later, back in the money, he commissioned a dozen portraits from Sickert, and portraits of himself and Lady Dunn from Dali – one of which shows him, quite appropriately in Dunn's view, as Augustus Caesar. Lady Dunn gave or lent some of her late husband's paintings to the Beaverbrook Art Gallery, and began to spend more time with Beaverbrook himself.

WRITING THE RECORD

He produced three more books: another reprint of *Success*, the brief homily that he wrote first in the twenties to assist the circulation of the *Sunday Express*; the collection of his *Atlantic Advocate* articles called *My Early Life*; and a strange long essay called *The Divine Propagandist*, a new version of the work he had started in 1926. The argument is that St Paul and the Churches were mistaken in proclaiming that the wages of sin is death. 'What did Jesus consider to be sin according to the Gospels? It would appear to me that He thought of it simply as an unregenerate state of mind which preferred pride, selfishness, materialism and lust to the ideals of life of the Kingdom of God – and did so deliberately and persistently. But apart from this general conception Jesus drew up no code of morals whatever.' Beaverbrook singles out for special mention Jesus's forgiveness of the woman taken in adultery. He also points out that Jesus laid down no bar to the making of money – in fact, in the parable of the talents it is the servant who fails to get a good rate of interest on his money who is blameworthy. The book is a continuation of a lifelong argument with his father. 'My remarks on the Church and the Apostle Paul . . . may be, in some measure, the result of a reaction from my early life in the Manse . . . this is not an evangelical book. It is not according to the teaching of my father. . . .' It may also be read as a rehearsal of the arguments Beaverbrook will deploy in forthcoming negotiations at the pearly gates if St Peter shows any sign of refusing him admission.

The Divine Propagandist came out in 1962. In the same year Peter Howard, who had recently succeeded the American evangelist Frank Buchman as head of the worldwide movement for spiritual renewal, Moral Rearmament, told Beaverbrook he wanted to write another biography of him, partly to counter Driberg. 'Nobody sees your size. . . . If Asquith had not gone down, we might have lost the first world war. If the fighters had not gone up, we would have lost the second. Twice you have helped to save this land by your exertions. It is time everybody understood this.' Beaverbrook agreed. He entertained Howard and his wife at La Capponcina, and supplied many helpful notes and comments. When Howard sent him the final manuscript to approve he thought Beaverbrook might object to a story about the way his former valet, Albert, when asked who was attending a Beaverbrook party, would invariably reply 'parasites and prostitutes'. But he did not, though he made other comments and corrections. Howard told him: 'I have adopted all your invaluable suggestions, additions, and subtractions.'[30]

Here was the last instance of Beaverbrook's hidden hand at work. The tally of books about his own life and times that he had written, controlled, influenced, financed, or interfered with during his lifetime now read as follows:

Politicians and the Press (1925). By himself.

F. A. Mackenzie's biography (1931); involvement kept quiet.

Politicians and the War. Two volumes (1928 and 1932). By himself.

Farrer's story of the Ministry of Aircraft Production, *Reach for the Sky* (1943). Written under Beaverbrook's direction.

Duke of Windsor's account of the abdication, *A King's Story* (1951). Sub-edited and influenced by Beaverbrook.

History of The Times, Vol. IV (1952), written anonymously by Stanley Morison. Beaverbrook's involvement kept quiet. Morison met Beaverbrook on board the *Queen Mary*, when he asked him for help with the history, which Beaverbrook gave. Later, Morison became part of the inner circle. One day Morison mentioned to Beaverbrook that he had examined a large collection of Lloyd George papers in the possession of his widow, and that she might sell them to *The Times*; Beaverbrook bought them instead. When Morison sought permission to quote from papers he had seen before they changed hands, Beaverbrook refused it. Morison was incredulous, but nevertheless he had to remove much Lloyd George material from his history, which was already in type. Tom Blackburn, general manager of London Express Newspapers, informed Morison of Beaverbrook's conditions for allowing publication to proceed: ' . . . no acknowledgement in Preface or elsewhere, or any reference whatever to him as a source of information or to the papers which he owns'.[31] Beaverbrook reviewed the book on television, standing at a lectern ('What a show ! ! !', Morison told him), and he gave another talk on the radio. His account was disputed by Wickham Steed, a former editor of *The Times*.

Geoffrey Bocca's *She Might Have Been Queen* (1953), about Mrs Simpson and the abdication. Commissioned by Beaverbrook; published by Express Books.

Frank Owen's life of Lloyd George (1954). Commissioned by Beaverbrook, edited by Beaverbrook.

Blake's *Bonar Law* (1955). Commissioned by Beaverbrook. Material withheld from Blake by Beaverbrook.

Driberg's biography (1956). Controlled by Beaverbrook.

Men and Power (1956). By himself.

Castlerosse (1956), by Leonard Mosley. Information supplied by Beaverbrook.

War at the Top (1959), by Lieutenant-General Sir Leslie Hollis and James Leasor. During the war Hollis, a Royal Marine, was one of the three military secretaries to the War Cabinet. After the war, he became Commandant General of the marines. In retirement, he set out to write his wartime memoirs in collaboration with a former *Daily Express* journalist and novelist, James Leasor; they sought Beaverbrook's help, Hollis informing Beaverbrook that his 'great contribution' to the war effort had not been fully represented. Having first enquired 'what case General Hollis intends to make about the Second Front', and having sent Leasor the pro-Second Front book by Trumbull Higgins that he also lent to Michael Foot while Foot was writing his biography of Bevan, Beaverbrook decided to help. On 28 July 1958, Leasor sent Beaverbrook the manuscript. On 22 August Leasor told Beaverbrook that the publishers had agreed to hold up publication 'so that we can reshape the book entirely to your excellent suggestions'. On 27 August Beaverbrook told Hollis: 'The *Express* is taking your book'. In October Hollis asked for 'instances from the granary of your memories of failures in duty or villainy' that he could work in; Beaverbrook encouraged him to criticize Montgomery, 'the egotistical monkey'. On 14 January 1959 Hollis thanked Beaverbrook for a 'very handsome cheque from the Express Newspapers'. In March, the *Sunday Express* serialized the book.

Hollis and Leasor next proposed to write Beaverbrook's biography, with his co-operation, and Beaverbrook agreed. Hollis's wartime colleague, Sir Ian Jacob, at this time director general of the BBC, was appalled when Hollis told him about the project; he concluded that Beaverbrook had corrupted Hollis, who was drinking heavily. But the book was never written and Hollis died in 1963.

James Cameron's *1916*, an account of the overthrow of Asquith (1962). Suggested and financed by Beaverbrook.

Rudolf Hess, The Uninvited Envoy (1962), by James Leasor. Suggested and greatly helped by Beaverbrook. He told Mr Millar to tell Leasor: 'I think I have given so much to the Hess production he had better leave me out of his sources of information altogether'. Leasor replied: 'I will bow to your wishes'. Serialized by the *Sunday Express*.

The Peter Howard biography (1964). Sanctioned and final manuscript approved in detail by Beaverbrook.

Before the Second World War, Castlerosse began a biography of Beaverbrook. After the war, Beaverbrook gave Gerhardie, now poor and obscure, a £300 commission to write his life; nothing came of it.

POSTHUMOUS:

Kenneth Young's *Churchill and Beaverbrook* (1966). Dedicated to Sir Max Aitken, Bt.

Beaverbrook's story of the abdication, *The Abdication of King Edward VIII* (1966). Edited by A.J.P. Taylor.

Frances Stevenson's *Lloyd George: A Diary* (1971). Edited by Taylor.

A. J. P. Taylor's biography (1972). Proposed and agreed before Beaverbrook died. Jonathan Aitken was deputed by Robert Blake to tell his great-uncle that Blake thought Taylor would not be an appropriate biographer because he would be too favourable. Beaverbrook did not take this advice kindly.

THE CLATTERING TRAIN

Outwardly, Express Newspapers – renamed Beaverbook Newspapers in 1954 – was run like an orthodox business, with a board and various departments and editors underneath. In practice, Beaverbrook continued to be a dictator. He rarely attended a board meeting, though he made his 'suggestions'.

Other newspaper proprietors regarded him as a menace. Throughout the 1950s and into the 1960s the power of the print unions grew, marked by extravagant wage demands, spasmodic attempts to censor editorial content, acts of individual sabotage and gross overmanning. The proprietors agreed that the only way to resist the unions must be to form a united front through their own trade union, the Newspaper Proprietors' Association, later renamed the Newspaper Publishers' Association. For seven years the Association's chairman was Cecil King, head of the Mirror group and Northcliffe's nephew. He wrote later: ' . . . whatever pledges were made or undertakings signed, when the crunch came it was the *Express* that broke the united front'.[32] Beaverbrook's strategy was to buy industrial peace for himself and leave the rest of Fleet Street to manage as best it could.

Newsweek made Beaverbrook its cover story in 1952, and calculated that he was selling more papers per day – five million – than anyone else in the world. Thereafter his circulations rose still higher. In 1960, the *Daily Express* was selling 4,300,000 copies. The *Sunday Express* was selling almost as many. The *Evening Standard* was far outsold by the *Evening News*, and it was never a financial success, but it was the evening paper that anyone who mattered read.

All this was achieved by a man in his seventies and eighties. It was not done by following an orthodox political line. In the last two decades of his life, it is worth recalling, Beaverbrook was anti-socialist, anti-Marshall Plan, anti-independence for India, pro-Suez; he was against the United Nations, against the Cyprus Settlement, against decolonization in Africa, against German rearmament, against the Common Market. On lesser issues he was unpredictable: he was against higher service pensions. His only consistent themes were prosperity for all, and imperial unity.

It would have been difficult to find anyone else in politics who supported all these positions, apart perhaps from Brendan Bracken. The streak of political nihilism in Beaverbrook culminated in 1963, when he greeted the accession to the premiership of Sir Alec Douglas-Home by singing down the telephone to the *Express* 'We'll Sow the Seeds of Discord' to the tune of 'The More We Are Together'. Watch where Sir Alec is going, and go the other way, he told his editors.

How did he find editors willing to collaborate with him in promoting his whimsical ideas? Some of them followed Christiansen's policy of having no political views: Percy Cudlipp and Percy Elland at the *Evening Standard*, for example. At the *Sunday Express*, Beaverbrook was lucky to find, in John Gordon and his successor John Junor, two of the handful of able journalists in the country who thought his ideas more or less sensible. One editor, when he was fired, threw a pot of ink at the Beaverbrook portrait in his office, but such outbursts were rare. Charles Wintour, editor of the *Standard* after 1959, was fascinated by outsize figures with strong wills – during the war he had been on the staff of Field-Marshal Montgomery – and sensibly saved himself much anguish about editorial independence by regarding Beaverbrook not as his proprietor but as his editor-in-chief.

Robert Edwards, a socialist, was a former editor of *Tribune*, and yet twice appointed by Beaverbrook editor of the *Daily Express*. Edwards was against Suez, and shocked by Beaverbrook's prejudice against blacks. When he came to write his autobiography, he justified himself by being amusingly cynical on the one hand – editors, after all, had the freedom to agree with Beaverbrook – and saying on the other that he found areas of agreement with his proprietor and that the *Express* support for the Conservatives in the 1959 election was lukewarm.[33]

Beaverbrook patronized, fought, protected, rewarded and sometimes befriended his editors, but always regarded them as his instruments.

Robert Blake once observed Beaverbrook and Bracken, by this time proprietor of the *Financial Times*, in action. On 21 April 1951 he was sitting on the terrace at Cherkley and listening while the two potentates

> ... began a sort of cross-talk evidently for my benefit. Beaverbrook declared that it was essential to leave editors with complete freedom and never interfere. 'I have no idea what is going to be in the *Sunday Express* tomorrow,' he said. 'It will be as entirely fresh to me as to any of the readers'. 'I entirely agree, Max,' said Brendan Bracken. 'I never interfere in the *Financial Times*. The Editor must be free to make up his own mind'. And so on ... I listened drowsily till there was the sound of the french door being opened, and the butler came out bearing a piece of ticker tape on a silver salver. Cherkley was wired to Fleet Street, rather like a London club. He went up to my host and said, 'There's a message, my lord'. Beaverbrook looked at it. It was the news that Aneurin Bevan and Harold Wilson had resigned from Attlee's cabinet. The terrace had at least two telephone lines. Before I could draw breath, Beaverbrook was telephoning instructions on the treatment of this startling development to John Junor, the political correspondent of the *Sunday Express*, and Bracken was doing the same to a man called Grimes who, presumably, had a similar role at the *Financial Times*. When they had finished – and it took quite a time – they resumed their discussion on editorial freedom as if nothing at all had happened.[34]

The post-war editors saw themselves as working for a legend, a constant source of stories in Fleet Street pubs, his voice imitated and his sayings repeated: 'Who is in charge of the clattering train?' 'What's the news?' 'Goodbye to you.' To the editors, Beaverbrook, whatever his views, was the greatest journalist of his time: someone who knew as much if not more about popular journalism than they did: a man of endless curiosity and zest, a brilliant talent-spotter and encourager of talent, who knew what was lively and what was dull, and what was news and what was not. As a proprietor he spent money: the *Express* in the 1960s employed fifty photographers and numerous foreign correspondents, and hired aeroplanes without thinking twice. Besides, he brought his editors, and selected members of his staff, into touch with the rich and the mighty. Anyone who went to work for him knew, or thought they knew, what they were getting into. There was never any question that the opinions of his papers were his and his alone. When John Junor was a leader writer on the *Evening Standard* he was summoned to the south of France and put up in a hotel in Monte Carlo; every day he wrote leaders to Beaverbrook's directions, which went straight into the paper without being touched by the editor. Beaverbrook enjoyed noisy political argument, but he rarely engaged in serious discussion with his editors or leader writers about the papers' policies; and they knew it was a waste of time, or possibly the waste of a job, if they tried to have one. He told George Gale, in an interview published in the *Daily Express*, that

' . . . we have a system, you know. I speak at this end and there is a machine at the other end and it comes out as a leading article.'

Editors and leader writers soothed their pride as best they could. George Malcolm Thomson, who wrote hundreds of leaders for the *Express*, regarded leader-writing for Beaverbrook as a form of prostitution, but comforted himself with the thought that he wrote nothing under his own name that he disagreed with. Beaverbrook did not object if someone jibbed at writing a particular leader; there was always someone else who would comply; and in any case someone who agreed with him was likely to write a stronger piece. His notion of what was suitable for a leader was highly personal. Robert Edwards knew he must be seriously out of favour at Cherkley when he was not required even to write leaders about the need for an underpass at Tolworth junction on the A3 near Leatherhead. Wintour at the *Standard* was advised to have 'fun' in his leader column about 'the need for sending deputations of British women to inspect American kitchens'.

His editors were usually in a nervous state, which was understandable, since his directives were continuous. He liked to keep people off balance. The record number of directives, in a single day, was said to be 147. To preserve a show of independence, his editors sometimes disguised his decisions as their own. He pursued them day and night. When Alfred Hinds escaped from gaol and every paper in Britain was hunting for him, Beaverbrook tracked down Wintour to El Vino's wine bar. Wintour bravely admitted where he was. 'Well,' said Beaverbrook, 'you won't find Alfie Hinds in there.' He had a habit of interrupting conferences to talk to his editors, showing his dominance. Edwards installed two tape recorders to record Beaverbrook's instructions. And he used other, more subtle methods of control. He asked subordinates what they thought of their paper and then relayed their criticisms to the editor, saying that of course they were Mr X's views, and he was passing them on without comment. He secretly appointed John Junor editor of the *Sunday Express* months before the current editor learned his fate; such tactics did not make editors feel secure. Junor had an ulcer, and champagne caused him agonies; but Beaverbrook 'had a tendency to write off anyone who had anything except the most trivial of illnesses', and he insisted on his guests drinking champagne; all summer at Beaverbrook's table, after he had been given the editorship but before it had been announced, Junor drank champagne.[35]

At the newspapers, as in other matters, Beaverbrook hated to be worsted. When the rivals had stories that his papers did not, he caused trouble. Editors soon learned that they could usually justify complaints about extravagance by saying the money had had to be spent to beat the *Daily Mail*. When the up-and-coming Tom Stacey was hired away from the *Express* by the *Sunday Times*, Beaverbrook instantly identified an up-and-coming reporter on the *Sunday Times* and hired him, doubling his salary, for the *Express*. His employees were forbidden to work for anyone else. When commercial television was starting, Richard Baerlein, the *Standard*'s racing writer, was employed as a commentator; on the eve of the launch, Baerlein was told to withdraw. Many members of Beaverbrook's London staff never saw him, but they 'felt his eyes burning along every line' they wrote. Beaverbrook knew that most journalists yearn for a response to their copy, disliking silence most of all. He was never silent, but constantly stirred up excitement with messages of praise or blame or sudden calls. 'What is a lug?' rasped a voice down the telephone the day after Eve Perrick used the word in a story. Favoured writers would be summoned to walk with Beaverbrook up Bond Street, or find themselves with a ticket to La Capponcina; Angus McGill was advised by his editor to take a taxi from Nice airport and tell Beaverbrook he had used the bus.

The New York reporters were part-journalists and part-servants, required to buy theatre tickets, or medicines, or books, or coffee. Unlike Mrs Ince with her cupboards stuffed full of used envelopes, the New York staff kept only new envelopes, but skidded them to and fro across the floor to make them look used before they went to Beaverbrook. A dozen tins of Campbell's tomato soup were kept in a cupboard, Alan Watkins learned, because Beaverbrook had once wanted some and might do so again. Walking in Central Park, Beaverbrook pointed to a faint sheen on the lake and told Alan Brien of the *Standard*: 'Some day – make a note of it – they will find oil wells under here, in Central Park.' Next day Brien questioned a man who looked after the boats. Yes, the man said, that's the grease from my rowlocks. Who was fooling whom, Brien wondered. He told Brien that they would visit the antique shops on Third Avenue. Brien said they had all shut down. Nonsense, said Beaverbrook. Finally they found one junk shop with an old chair in the window. There, said Beaverbrook, that must be a very expensive chair to be alone in the window.

He had to know best. At La Capponcina, Angus McGill told him that his colleague Maureen Cleave on the *Standard* wrote wonderful interviews. Next morning a Cleave interview with Nana Mouskouri was on Beaverbrook's desk. Had McGill heard of Mouskouri? He said he had. Miss Kits, a secretary, said she had. 'Lord Beaverbrook switched on his recording machine. "Mr Wintour", he said. "Why does the *Evening Standard* devote a whole page to a Greek singer no one has heard of?" '

Beaverbrook continued the unpleasant trick of showing his staff who was boss by receiving them naked, or leaving the lavatory door open when he was inside. He had other tricks. He held out the possibility of editorships. He tested the social aplomb of young new recruits at dinner parties. He teased: he told the political editor of the *Express* he was going to see Churchill, and they both got in the car; then he dropped off the political editor at a bus stop. His method of suppressing pieces was usually indirect. Anne Sharpley wrote a hostile review of Lady Diana Cooper's memoirs. Beaverbrook rang her up and said that 'you beautiful women' caused him problems; he would have to jump out of the window if she did not change the review. Sharpley, won over, said he could spike it. A favourable review by someone else was published. Beaverbrook sent Sharpley a note saying her review was so brilliant that he had 'ordered it to be put in the archives'.

Even humble, servant-like tasks gave the journalists a feeling of intimacy with Beaverbrook. He created an atmosphere that reflected his own combative nature: here on the sunny side of the street was the Beaverbrook press, and on the other side was the rest of the world. His staff knew they had to satisfy one reader only, and they liked the notion that he was an outsider who called the House of Lords the 'House of Make Believe', was no respecter of persons, even the royal family, and wanted, like them, to stir things up. They believed, with some cause, that although they were subject to his whims and absurdities, he would protect them against complaints from outside and rescue them if they were in trouble. He cared little about what people's views were or where they came from. On the *Sunday Express*, at the height of its success, no member of the senior staff had been to a public school. He was the one proprietor who gave his journalists the feeling, even if they were fifty years younger, that he depended on them – as a target for his restless energy, and as a source of private information and gossip – as much as they depended on him. Proprietor and staff shared a common interest in the product. The daily fusillade of ideas, questions, extravagant flattery and blame seemed to prove it. So did the invariable courtesy – the way he would see the most junior reporter to the door – the level of salaries and the sudden arbitrary rises.

Sometimes the charm and excitement failed to last, breeding disillusion. Christopher Dobson was the *Express* correspondent in Russia when Khrushchev was in power. He concluded that Beaverbrook's wartime mission to Moscow, far from being a success, had achieved agreement only because Beaverbrook had given in to all Stalin's demands, 'thus serving as a prototype for the sell-outs at Yalta and Potsdam'. When Dobson left Russia, he wrote an angry article revealing some of the facts the censors had prevented him from writing while he was *en poste*. *Pravda* published a rebuttal headed 'Mr Dobson is a liar'. 'Beaverbrook hated it because at that time he had come to believe that the only way he could leave his mark on the world was by bringing about a rapprochement between the Soviet Union and the West, and he saw the *Daily Express* as his catalyst. . . . He never forgave me, never spoke to me again, put me in cold storage in Washington . . . and after a year I was brought home and fired.'

William Davis was the *Sunday Express* City editor. He respected Beaverbrook's financial acumen: he was dining at Arlington House when Kennedy was shot, and Beaverbrook told him that Wall Street would have a boom; he had better get over there at once. Beaverbrook was right. But Davis became aware of the limits to his freedom. He was sacked from the *Express* after he had criticized a new unit trust that had advertised in the same issue. Taken on nevertheless by Charles Wintour at the *Standard* as City editor, he was asked by Beaverbrook to write a diary paragraph about Roy Thomson's financial manipulations. Having discovered that Thomson's empire was in effect controlled by his grand-children, Davis wrote a feature saying so. 'It was sent to Beaverbrook, who exploded. This was not at all what he had in mind; it made Thomson look *good*. The article was not to be published. Charles tried to argue with him but was curtly informed that the proprietor's decision was final.' Davis had overstepped the mark again; why couldn't he obey orders? Davis, 'disillusioned with the Beaverbrook group', soon transferred to the *Guardian*, at a lower salary.

THE LAST HURRAH

Beaverbrook's last hurrah was his campaign against the Common Market, which featured the launch of a new journal, the *Farming Express*, and months of tirades that sometimes read like self-parody, ending with a call for Commonwealth trade. After Eden resigned, Beaverbrook told Bracken: 'It is my view that Macmillan was the wrong choice for Prime Minister. If Butler was to be turned down, then a younger man should have been chosen.' Nevertheless he had written a hypocritical letter of congratulation to Macmillan, saying he had always hoped and prophesied that he would become Prime Minister. When the Common Market loomed Macmillan made one or two overtures to Beaverbrook, hoping to modify his opposition, but without success: Beaverbrook told him he would support him on 'everything but that blasted Common Market, which is an American device to put us alongside Germany. As our power was broken and lost by two German wars, it is very hard on us now to be asked to align ourselves with those villains.' In 1961 Macmillan privately included him in a list of newspaper proprietors whom he found 'rather unpleasant'.[36]

The Common Market campaign produced the last of Beaverbrook's strange alliances. For years Hugh Gaitskell had steered well clear of Beaverbrook, suspicious of his association with Bevan and Foot, his bitter enemies inside the Labour Party. Now the Labour leader was opposing the terms on which Macmillan was seeking entry into Europe; and the press, apart from Beaverbrook, was solidly pro-Market. For once, Beaverbrook and a Labour leader were, at least superficially, on the same side: emotionally unsympathetic to Europe, and unwilling to abandon the Commonwealth. It was exactly half a century since Beaverbrook had backed Bonar Law against Balfour on the issue of Tariff Reform and imperial economic unity; he had not budged. But the Commonwealth that Gaitskell and Beaverbrook had in mind was not the same institution. Gaitskell saw it as a unique group of nations both white and black. Beaverbrook saw it as the white dominions. Still, Britain failed to enter Europe, much to Beaverbrook's satisfaction. One of Gaitskell's young supporters, the Labour MP and journalist Woodrow Wyatt, wrote him a comforting letter in early 1964. He said that Beaverbrook's wish not to be dependent on politics

> may have prevented you from becoming Prime Minister – probably did – but does that matter in the long run? Eden, Attlee, Macmillan were PM for a short time but minus the office they are nothing. None of them – or all of them together – could have as much influence as you in stopping Britain joining the Common Market. . . . You were almost certainly the deciding factor against. . . .[37]

Beaverbrook's private as well as his political life had entered its last phase. He made a better grandfather than father, although as his grandchildren grew up they often discovered that he resented any departure from his plans for them. His eldest grandson, Bill Montagu, fell from favour when he abandoned farming to join his mother in Barbados. The rows with his daughter Janet, usually over money, continued, but he remained aware that her strong character, even her wild streak, perhaps came from him. He wrote to her about her younger daughter, Jane Kidd: 'You must look after that child and see that she gets a fine example, so that she will grow up to be a woman after the manner of her grandmother. Not her grandfather, nor her mother.'[38]

Sometimes all the younger generation would gather at Cherkley for a party and lavish presents. His youngest grandson, Max Aitken's only son and heir Maxwell (later the 3rd Lord Beaverbrook), was living with his parents at the Garden House on the Cherkley estate; his mother remembers that Beaverbrook used to make the little boy sick by stuffing him with chocolate. Tim Aitken, who was especially devoted to his grandfather, recalls the glee with which Beaverbrook won a bet about whether or not they would get into the film *I'm All Right Jack* by secretly arranging a private screening.

If any young Aitken showed an interest in following in his footsteps he was pleased. 'I hope you will not be led into finance or commerce,' he wrote to a Canadian nephew after the boy had won an essay prize. 'There are only two paths for genius. One is politics. The other, journalism.' When Tim asked for a job as a reporter while waiting to go to university in Canada Beaverbrook fixed it for him, despite Max Aitken's resistance. Tim Aitken covered the court case for the *Standard* when the prostitute Christine Keeler was shot by her lover Lucky Gordon; and was in the library at Cherkley when the Prime Minister, Macmillan, telephoned in a rage to complain about that day's *Express*, which had juxtaposed stories about Keeler and the Minister of Defence, John Profumo, in a way that unmistakably suggested an intimate link between them – a link not then admitted. Beaverbrook responded sadly that he was an old man, and that no one at the *Express* paid any attention to him any more. As soon as the Prime Minister rang off, Beaverbrook picked up the phone to the *Express* editor and barked: 'It was a fine front page today. Give us more of that.'[39]

A great-nephew, Jonathan, decided after he went up to Oxford to read history in 1960 that it was time he met his historic great-uncle. He wrote him what he has described as a clever letter, expressing his keen interest in politics and admiration for Beaverbrook's writings, and was summoned to Cherkley by return. Thereafter he became a frequent visitor, fascinated by Beaverbrook's charm and energy despite his age and poor health. 'I'm thinking of marrying Christofor,' Beaverbrook told him one day. Why? 'Never be ashamed to marry a rich woman. She has eighty – eight, zero – million.' Like many rich old men, Beaverbrook played games over his will. He told Jonathan one day that he was reconsidering his legacies, and went on to praise his great-nephew to the detriment of all his children and grandchildren. Finally he said: 'I'm going to do the greatest thing I can for you – the greatest thing of all. I'm not going to leave you any money.'[40]

Lady Dunn became his constant companion. In Canada, she commuted between the old Dunn fortress at St Andrew and Fredericton. They stayed at the Waldorf together where, during a strike, she offered $100 to any member of the staff who would bring her breakfast. Beaverbrook liked to tell people: 'She is richer than I am.' Sir James Dunn's dietary concerns were inherited by his widow. Aboard the Beaverbrook yacht in the Mediterranean, she lunched off sixteen small boiled new potatoes. One result of her association with Beaverbrook was to separate him from his family, or so they saw it. Janet Kidd spent an idyllic few weeks with her father when Lady Dunn was away from Cherkley, but saw little of him thereafter. When Beaverbrook needed a new secretary a young man, not a young woman, was employed. Raymond the valet was dismissed. Anne Sharpley still received sudden summonses to tea, but they were secret meetings. Aitken House in Nassau was sold.

Beaverbrook wrote to Wardell in January 1963, saying that his heart was all right, but 'unfortunately, my lungs have considerable defects manifested in asthma attacks of a most violent nature. Then again I cannot walk.' He had stiffness in both feet due to prolonged gout which began, he noted with precision, on 23 May 1962. He was seeing two doctors, who gave him contradictory advice.

Beaverbrook had shown signs of a preoccupation with death, not constant but often intense, ever since he had been obliged, as a small boy in New Brunswick, to take part in funerals conducted by his father. His life had been marked by the premature deaths of several of those closest to him, including his wife, his younger son, and his first great political friend and mentor, Bonar Law. He worried endlessly about his own health, and was much given to predicting that his life was nearly over. It was not merely death as the end that preoccupied him, but what might come afterwards. In his prime he would joke about the fires of hell that, according to his father's faith, awaited wrongdoers; Lady Diana Cooper, among others, always remembered one particular hymn he would chant with relish:

> I know that God is wrath with me
> For I was born in sin.
> My heart is so exceeding vile
> Damnation dwells therein,
> Awake I sin, asleep I sin,
> I sin with every breath.
> When Adam fell
> He went to Hell
> And damned us all to death.

'Beautiful, isn't it?' he always added.

As he became very old, his thoughts increasingly turned at times to what might be in store for him. He would occasionally talk about what was on his mind to the young women around him. To Christian Carritt he said more than once that he was a very wicked old man and that he knew he would go to hell; but he would add that as it was too late to change his ways he might as well enjoy life to the end. She felt that both the fear and the defiance were real. With Dr Carritt and with Anne Sharpley Beaverbrook would sometimes expose his sadness that his life was coming to a close, telling them how lucky they were to be young and attractive with so much ahead of them; he would hold their hand and gaze at them as if he could thereby recapture youth, vitality and promise. In the last year of his life, when he summoned Anne Sharpley to Cherkley for what turned out to be the last time, she felt he needed her: 'I sat with him on the sofa putting, and keeping, my arms around him, trying to save him from pain and death.' To his granddaughter Jean, on one of the last times she saw him, he seemed close to panic. He was in bed and feeling ill; he kept asking her, 'Am I among the elect? Do you think I shall be saved?' Even so, a joke he made at his last birthday party shows he was not always afraid. Each guest was presented, rather oddly, with a glossy cookbook produced by one of the Thomson companies. Beaverbrook said: 'Roy Thomson obviously believes there are good cooking facilities where I'm going.'[41]

On 7 June 1963 – the anniversary of Lady Dunn's wedding to Sir James – he left Cherkley by car accompanied by her, his son Max and Mr Millar. A week later, it was revealed that he and Lady Dunn had got married.[42] He had been a widower for thirty-six years; he was eighty-four, she fifty-three, born in the year he was elected at Ashton-under-Lyne.

It is not clear when Beaverbrook knew he had cancer. He told his young secretary, Colin Vines, that Sir Daniel Davies had diagnosed cancer of the bladder in July 1962, but that a week later a well-known surgeon had ridiculed the diagnosis. In the summer of 1963 he told Robert Edwards that Churchill was dying from the head down, and he was dying from the feet up, by which, Edwards later thought, he meant that he was dying from cancer. He continued to receive visitors. Colin Vines overheard a conversation with the Canadian food magnate Garfield Weston, owner of Fortnum & Mason, about staff; Weston had apparently taken to heart some advice given him by Beaverbrook, and now he was was always thinking up something to keep his staff on their toes, always giving them something new to think about. Vines concluded that when Beaverbrook asked his constant questions, ' . . . it was not the *question* that mattered, it was the asking of it!' Churchill still visited La Capponcina, not always coherent; Beaverbrook was determined, in a competitive spirit, to outlive him. He could still become angry. Lord Rosebery dripped salt water on to a rug on the yacht; Beaverbrook abused him with such force that Vines was shocked.

Perhaps the publication of *The Divine Propagandist* had made him think about repairing his fences on earth. He effected a reconciliation with Tom Driberg without difficulty by sending him a case of the old champagne that Driberg preferred. He finally put Wardell out of his financial misery by writing off his debts; Wardell was overcome with relief and gratitude.

His dealings with his editors became more erratic, but the energy was still there. Two memos dictated to Wintour at the *Standard* ran as follows:

Mr Wintour, it would be a very good thing if you took up the cause of Turner, J. W. M. Turner, the painter. He left I think 11,000 Turners, or some other number, probably 11,000 paintings to the National Gallery. He left these paintings to the National Gallery on condition that they built a wing and carried his work in the gallery. His work alone, as I understand it.

Now the National Gallery accepted the pictures but instead of building a wing and showing them they were sent over to the Tate Gallery. What then – a great majority of them are down in the basement, put away, never seen, never let out, never dealt with at all, just lying there like in a morgue, dead. And furthermore a great many of them were damaged, some of them irreparably damaged by a flood about four or five years ago when the Thames overflowed if you remember.

I think you ought to do not just one article about it, but you want to have a hell of a row about it, it is sheer dereliction of trust and those gentlemen of high reputation and great purpose and splendid examples of conduct to their fellow men should be ashamed to allow the Turner position to remain where it is at present.

Mr Wintour – very many thanks for your note about Mr Macmillan. I think his speech was extremely bad and I think the fire is out of his belly. I don't think he's got any more there. I think the fire was out of his belly some time before he ceased to be Prime Minister. I don't expect any performance whatsoever in the future from Mr Macmillan. He says he is going to write a book on philosophy. I don't think he could give us anything on philosophy that you or I would be willing to read, at this stage of his life. But he is a wealthy man of course, a very wealthy man. You want to look up the Macmillan fortune and you will find it very big. They sold their business to America for a very big sum indeed. While he was Prime Minister most of his fortune was made. . . .

Visitors found Beaverbrook smaller, and the spots on his hands browner. Machines attached to bannisters carried him upstairs and downstairs at Cherkley and La Capponcina. An improvised sedan chair carried him up the steps to his car. When he walked, he needed a stick. Occasionally he fiddled with his book on Baldwin. When Colin Vines read to him, he paused when he thought Beaverbrook had gone to sleep. But he could still enjoy making mischief, insisting, at La Capponcina, on getting a new building painted before the plaster had dried, knowing full well that the paint would peel, which would provide an opportunity for a row with the painters. He took out a writ against Alan Brien and the *Spectator* for accusing him of arranging that the modern history of Britain 'should be written, or rather rewritten, to make him a key figure in our island story'.

In January 1964 he made his last will. He did not leave Lady Beaverbrook any money, because she had 'ample resources of her own', but left her his portrait by Graham Sutherland, a bronze head by Oscar Nemon, and 'all gold and silver boxes and all musical boxes of which I die possessed'. He left Sir Patrick Hennessy $3000 to finance parties for the Other Club. His personal papers were to be given to his son Max and his daughter Janet for six months, during which time they were 'to examine all such papers and to destroy such as they in their absolute discretion shall think fit'; surviving papers were to be added to the archives of the First Beaverbrook Foundation, a charity he had established in 1954. He left various sums to relations and to his secretaries and to household staff. He left nothing to Max and Janet 'because I have amply provided for them both in my lifetime'. The main beneficiary was his favourite granddaughter, Jean, who was left the income from a trust fund of $500,000.

There was one last grand occasion. His fellow Canadian Roy Thomson organized a banquet at the Dorchester Hotel on 25 May 1964 for his eighty-fifth birthday and invited everyone Beaverbrook had ever known, apart from the women. Even Driberg received an invitation. Beaverbrook tried to record his speech in case he was not strong enough to deliver it in person; but the result was unimpressive. On the day, he struggled to the Dorchester in his dinner jacket and entered the hotel, where specially imported Mounties and Indians were drawn up in his honour, on the arm of his handsome son. The night was a triumph: a final act of showmanship, spiced with malice. In his speech, delivered with almost all his old force and all his old charm, he mocked his host for his choice of title, Lord Thomson of Fleet, and ended with a peroration that brought some members of his large audience to the verge of tears. 'It is time for me to become an apprentice once more. I am not certain in which direction, but somewhere, sometime, soon. . . .'

Back at Cherkley, he gave instructions that anyone who asked after his health was to be told he was 'very well'. He was not quite finished. An over-zealous *Express* manager sent him an account of the expenses racked up by *Express* journalists: a very large sum, featuring much first-class travel and many expensive lunches. *Express* expenses had for years been one of the wonders of Fleet Street. Sam White, the *Standard*'s Paris correspondent, spent much of his time in the Crillon bar; he sent all his bills, scarcely looking at them, still less justifying them, to London.

Sitting out of doors on a wickerwork seat at Cherkley, wrapped from head to foot in an old-fashioned car rug, Beaverbrook asked Edwards if he would support 'a reign of terror' against expenses. Mr Blackburn, he said, planned to send a letter to all the staff to crush the racket. 'Anything to say about that?' Edwards said that perhaps he might not wish to have such a note sent to key members of his staff – naming his favourites. Beaverbrook picked up his Soundscriber. 'Mr Blackburn, Mr Blackburn, Mr Blackburn. Check every name on that list with Mr Edwards before sending out the letter.' The letter was never sent.

He moved in and out of the house on to the terrace, with paraphernalia: cushions, a heavy rug, a light rug, his telephone, his dictaphone, papers, footrest. When he was settled, Vines removed his shoes for him. He fumbled with the telephone, sometimes getting through to the *Express*, sometimes not. On 7 June, the first anniversary of his wedding, he lay in bed all day, exhausted. Vines noticed the way his lower lip protruded; and observed that the newly acquired oxygen cylinder did not ease his constant pain. Vines told him he needed to rest for a week, and then he would be all right. 'But maybe I wouldn't wake up.'

He died on the afternoon of 9 June. Next morning, Lady Beaverbrook telephoned selected friends and employees and invited them to view the body. It was a bright summer's day. In the garden, put out for the birds and being attacked by crows, was a vast cake sent by Garfield Weston for the birthday. Lady Beaverbrook told Mead the butler to be sure to remove it before Mr Weston arrived.[43]

In the valedictory *Daily Express* that morning George Malcolm Thomson had written a farewell leader, and Jean Campbell had recorded the lessons her grandfather had taught her about journalism: 'Emphasise human interest. Put the best strawberry on top of the basket. Write short sentences. Cut, cut, cut. Always interview people face to face. Never rewrite from another newspaper. Keep widening your circle of acquaintances – even if it means accepting the invitations of bores. Use your feet.' William Barkley, on Beaverbrook's staff since 1925, rehearsed old myths. The most startling obituary item was a photograph of Beaverbrook with Stalin. 'Mutual respect', the caption read. The photograph was a fake.

Most obituarists compared him with Northcliffe; others, less complimentary, with the megalomaniac Citizen Kane. In private, one or two verdicts were less complimentary still. Clement Attlee had declined to write an appreciation, saying, 'He was the only evil man I ever met. I could not find anything good to say about him'.[44] The editor of the *Observer*, David Astor, said he had always thought that if Britain had made peace with Hitler in 1940, Beaverbrook would have been the British Laval. After he died, he lay in state at Cherkley for five days, a most unusual procedure in England. It was the new Lady Beaverbrook who arranged for his body to be laid out in the Cherkley drawing room. Not all the mourners had met her before, and some of the Aitkens took her for the housekeeper, misled by her plain black dress and the bunch of keys at her waist, as she unlocked the drawing room door and showed them in to pay their respects. 'Uncle Max was lying on a table, with a covering like a table-cloth drawn up to his chin. He looked minute,' said one of his nieces.[45]

The funeral was equally unorthodox. It took place on a glorious summer's day; and the twenty or thirty people invited had been asked to assemble at Cherkley at noon. Few of the usual visitors of Beaverbrook's last years were present: Michael Foot, A. J. P. Taylor, John Junor. Mead, the butler, serving drinks to the mourners, handed one of them a full pint glass of whisky and water. The party then moved to the dining room for a magnificent buffet, with German wine flowing, and thence to the front of the house, to prepare to set off for the crematorium. There was no sign of a coffin or a hearse.

Outside, the drive was packed with cars facing in all directions. The mourners began to back and turn. One or two, having turned, disappeared up the drive. The rest, not knowing the route to the chapel, quickly followed, fearful of losing the car in front. Near the end of the drive at Cherkley is a roundabout. Colin Vines recalled:

> We all sped round this roundabout at tremendous speed and proceeded to the crematorium at forty miles an hour at least, dashing to Beaverbrook's funeral. It was just so typical of Beaverbrook that the funeral would be like this. We had the service, a lovely service, conducted by an old man, and then we came out of the chapel into the sunlight and dispersed, and that was the end of Beaverbrook.[46]

A memorial service was held on 24 June, in a packed St Paul's, with an address by Lord Rosebery, with whom the young Max Aitken used to 'hunt women'.[47] Churchill was not well enough to be present, but word spread about his reaction to Beaverbrook's death. He was reported to have said nothing, 'but his chin sank on his chest'. Word also went round that a member of the Astor family had attended the service and had explained, when asked to account for his presence, that he had come to make sure that Beaverbrook really was dead; but that report, though plausible, was denied.

On 25 September a final, open-air ceremony took place in Beaverbrook Town Square, Newcastle, New Brunswick, in the presence of members of the family and a crowd of local citizens. The square, the site of Newcastle's foundation in 1790, had been presented to Beaverbrook in 1958 in return for his many benefactions to the town where he spent his early years. Evidence of his bounty surrounded the mourners: the Beaverbrook Theatre and Town Hall at the side of the square; the monument of a sailing ship erected by Beaverbrook to commemorate his youthful hero, Peter Mitchell; the seventeenth-century gazebo brought from a dismantled English stately home, Bramshill; the eighteenth-century sundial from Copt Hall in Essex; the six Victorian street-lamps, former adornments of Admiralty House in London, said to be made from cannon captured in the Crimean War. Up the hill stood the Old Manse public library; and St James church with the eleven bells and pipe organ presented by Beaverbrook. Nearby stood the church's Sunday School, built with the aid of Beaverbrook funds. In 1960, he set up a tax-exempt Canadian Beaverbrook Foundation to finance his Canadian benefactions.

Shortly before he died, Beaverbrook estimated that he had given $16 million to various causes and structures in New Brunswick. Many of them bore his name, leading Malcolm Muggeridge to write a mocking article for a Canadian magazine saying that his former employer had memorialized himself in his own lifetime 'to a degree which might have been considered excessive if accorded to Napoleon in Corsica or Shakespeare in Stratford-upon-Avon' – a quip disputed in the *Atlantic Advocate* by Wardell, who indignantly pointed out that there were only three memorials of Beaverbrook in the entire province: the statue in Officer's Square, Fredericton; the bronze head on the terrace of the Beaverbrook Art Gallery in Fredericton; and the bronze bust by Oscar Nemon in Newcastle.[48] It was the bust that formed the centrepiece of the last posthumous ceremony: a larger-than-life head of a man with his coat collar turned up, frowning into space, mounted on top of a rough sandstone plinth near the middle of the square, and identified by a plaque reading simply 'Beaverbrook: Born 25th May, 1879: Died 9th June, 1964'.

It was into the base of the plinth that, at the climax of the ceremony, Lady Beaverbrook placed an urn reported to contain Beaverbrook's ashes. Later, some of Beaverbrook's relations as well as a long-standing employee expressed doubt about the authenticity of the remains. Had the urn contained anything at all? Lady Beaverbrook kept the ashes of her first husband, Sir James Dunn, buried under a tree at the Dunn estate in St Andrew, New Brunswick, enclosed in a casket of Algoma steel. They thought it improbable that she would deposit the ashes of her second husband, to whom she had been devoted, in such an exposed and public place, defenceless against vandals and 'not even in a cemetery', as one of them put it.[49] Other family members believed that Lady Beaverbrook had placed half the ashes in the plinth and retained half as her private memorial.

Luckily for the Beaverbrook estate, however, this scepticism did not come to the attention of the British tax authorities. For the ceremony was part of a long-planned coup. On 4 August Vincent J. McEvoy, the registrar for probate in and for the County of Northumberland, Province of New Brunswick, had granted probate 'unto Lady Marcia Beaverbrook, G. Kenneth McKenzie and the Acadia Trust Company', in respect of the 'last will and testament of me The Right Honourable William Maxwell Baron Beaverbrook of McTavish Farm South Esk Miramichi in the Province of New Brunswick made 10 Jan 1964'. 'Lady Marcia Beaverbrook', properly 'Lady Beaverbrook', was the second wife; the Acadia Trust Company was a Beaverbrook company; and McKenzie was a chartered accountant with Touche, Ross, Bailey and Smart in St John. Paragraph two of the will read: 'I declare that I was born in Canada and have at all times during my life been domiciled within Canada in the province of New Brunswick and I desire this will to be construed and to take effect according to the laws of that province'.

Beaverbrook's statement that he had 'at all times been domiciled within Canada' might seem startling to the lay mind. His 1935 British passport stated: 'Domicile: England'. He had lived outside Canada, mainly in England, for fifty-four years. His 1943 British passport stated: 'Residence: England'. Commonsense would have required him to describe himself in his will as Baron Beaverbrook of Cherkley Court, Leatherhead, since he had occupied that house continuously for over half a century, whereas he had never spent a single night at McTavish Farm, South Esk. Commonsense and the laws of domicile are, however, strangers. During the 1950s, with the avoidance of Britain's severe death duties in mind, he and his advisers drew up a series of documents defending his claim to Canadian domicile. True, he had become an MP at Westminster in 1910, but he had intended to go into Canadian politics, and possessed letters from Sir Robert Borden to prove it. In the First World War he had represented the Canadian government. Later he had lived outside Canada to be in easier reach of his medical advisers. He had given Cherkley to his son Max in 1950, and on visits to England stayed there at his invitation. In 1954 he had set up two charitable organizations, the First and Second Beaverbrook Foundations, and transferred to them all his shares in Beaverbrook Newspapers. His farms were let to his daughter and grandson. All his fortune was in Canadian or United States securities. His yacht in the Mediterranean was Canadian-registered. On 17 December 1951 he had formally renounced UK citizenship.[50] The impression created by these documents is that, but for chance and ill-health, Beaverbrook would never have left Canada.

Paragraph three of his will stated: 'I wish to be buried in the province of New Brunswick.' The effect of this clause, from a legal standpoint, was to reinforce the statement that he was domiciled in Canada by asserting his intention, despite his prolonged absences in life, of returning there in death. His last instruction to his younger sister Mrs Stickney was to make absolutely sure that the terms of his will were obeyed; he told her that 'they' would want to bury him in England, but she must make certain that he was buried in New Brunswick.[51] His wiliness, not for the first time, though presumably for the last, was rewarded. The Inland Revenue, not often confronted with a scheme for avoiding English tax that featured the interment of ashes in a public square as evidence of domicile, was persuaded to accept the legality of these arrangements. Had the surmise that only half the ashes were in the plinth turned out to be capable of proof, Regina *v*. Beaverbrook Estate might well have joined the list of other tangled cases heard before Mr Justice Cocklecarrot in Court Four of the Probate and Fisheries Division. As it was, the prominent Montreal lawyer who negotiated with the Revenue on behalf of the estate regarded his victory as a high point of his career – with reason. Beaverbrook paid virtually no death duties at all. In the United Kingdom, he paid a mere £100,000. All the elements of this final success story were Beaverbrookian: money, ingenuity, semifarce, mystery, and affection for the colonial backwater whence he came.

THE CANADA
CEMENT AFFAIR
1909–1913

To reconstruct the Canada Cement affair is not easy: records were moved and destroyed on Aitken's instructions; participants lied about their role. It is possible nevertheless to illuminate to some extent the merger's cloudy depths and to observe Aitken in action among them.

The story began with the establishment of the Western Canada Cement and Coal Company in Exshaw, Alberta, in 1905, though its cement 'mill' did not start operating until 1908. From the beginning, the enterprise was plagued by strikes. It had also – Aitken later maintained – been set up on an insecure and even fraudulent basis because one of the founders, Joseph Irvin, had bought parcels of useless land in the back country and sold them to the company at an exorbitant price. By early 1909 Exshaw, as it was called for short, was virtually bankrupt.

In the preliminary hearings of the action that the Bank of Montreal later brought against Irvin and his associates for the repayment of debt, Irvin (under oath) gave the following account of his next moves. He had, he said, for some years before 1909 thought it would make financial and commercial sense to merge the three companies for which he was responsible, and to add one or two others. A merger would protect Exshaw's creditors and shareholders and take care of the company's debts to the Bank of Montreal. Accordingly, early in 1909 he formed a syndicate to bring about the merger: himself; a prominent financier, Rodolphe (later Sir Rodolphe) Forget; and a company promoter, W. Grant Morden.

Irvin went to see Clouston at the Bank of Montreal, and pointed out the advantage to the Bank if Exshaw's debts became a charge against a large merged company – which would include Irvin's two profitable mills – instead of against a small company on the verge of bankruptcy. Sir Edward, in Irvin's account, liked the plan, but thought it might be rather hard to finance because of the amount of money involved. Clouston then asked Irvin if he knew 'one Maxwell Aitken'. Irvin, a stranger to the financial world of Montreal, did not; and when he mentioned the name to the other members of his syndicate they said they did not want to be mixed up with Aitken. 'They gave me to understand that he was not to be trusted.'

Next day, in the Rotunda of the Windsor Hotel, a man approached him and introduced himself as Aitken, saying he had been asked by Clouston to see Irvin about the proposed merger. Irvin swallowed his doubts. They went to Irvin's room, where, until a late hour, Irvin 'laid the whole proposition before him'. Aitken asked if he could pay in $200 to join the syndicate; his membership, he persuaded Irvin, would cause the Bank of Montreal, including its leading officials, to look favourably on the deal. The other members of the syndicate agreed reluctantly to Aitken's participation. Next, Aitken persuaded them that the syndicate would be strengthened by an experienced lawyer; he suggested C. H. Cahan, his old associate; Cahan duly paid his $200 and joined. Next, to Irvin's considerable surprise, Aitken said he wanted to bring in yet another partner. At first he wanted the name kept secret, but finally revealed that his other candidate was A. R. Doble, Clouston's confidential private secretary at the Bank. 'You know we cannot put this thing through without the Bank of Montreal behind us,' Aitken told Irvin. He also told Irvin that it would be necessary for him, Irvin, 'to help with other members of the Syndicate to secure at least $250,000 worth of stock for Mr Doble in order to pay him for his services and so that he would handle matters in the Bank for us in a proper manner'.

For a time, matters proceeded smoothly. Clouston agreed that the Bank of Montreal should act as bankers to the merger, and Irvin travelled about assembling options from other cement companies – agreements in principle to sell at a certain price. Aitken then announced that it would be advisable if all options were transferred to or taken in the name of the Bond and Share Company. Irvin had never heard of it. It was, Aitken explained, a small company capitalized at $100,000 and owned by himself, Sir Edward Clouston and Mr Stavert, a senior official in the Bank. The original members of the syndicate warned Irvin that this switch 'would no doubt furnish the way by which Mr Aitken and those interested with him could secure a large amount of the stock of the merger company if they felt disposed to do so'. Nevertheless they agreed to the change, always with the thought in mind that they must keep in with the Bank of Montreal if the merger was to be a success.

The Bond and Share Company (usually referred to as the Bond Company) had been incorporated in 1908 with Aitken as president, one of his employees, Fred C. Clarke, as company secretary, his secretary Miss de Gruchy as one director and Victor M. Drury as the second. Drury, who worked for Aitken at Royal Securities, was his wife's brother.

From then on, Irvin claimed, he and his advisers were frightened that

Aitken and his Bond Company would have the right to reject one option while taking up another – and especially feared that Aitken might 'play fast and loose with the Exshaw option'. Irvin was not worried about Aitken honouring his agreement to take up the two other options – on International Portland and Eastern Canada – since these were strong firms that any merged company would need to include.

Aitken now tried to separate Irvin from his associates. According to Irvin, he told him that he, Aitken, would take care of anything that was owed to Irvin personally by Exshaw if he would cut adrift from another Exshaw director who was also one of its principal creditors, a Mr F. B. Dunsford. The syndicate could thus renege on the Exshaw option and leave Dunsford out in the cold, while Irvin would still get his money. 'He was trying to bribe me,' Irvin told the court. He and Dunsford were now certain that Aitken had no intention of honouring the agreement to buy Exshaw. Accordingly, they decided they would not proceed with the merger – would in fact sink it – unless the Bank of Montreal exerted its authority to guarantee that all the options prepared by Aitken were taken up. This guarantee, said Irvin, was given in unequivocal terms by Stavert, who assured them that he spoke for Clouston. No written undertaking was given, however.

Aitken himself travelled the country collecting more cement company options. The owners he approached naturally sought advice from their bankers – who were in many cases the Bank of Montreal. So the combine came together; and in C. H. Cahan's office between 27 August and 10 September 1909 'agreements' were signed between the Bond Company and all the participating cement companies.

It later emerged that the Bond Company bought eleven of the twelve properties (the one option not yet taken up was Exshaw) for:

	$
Cash	7,001,600
Cement Company bonds	1,348,000
Preferred stock	4,316,800
Common stock of the Cement Company	2,155,850
Total	14,822,250

On the day the last of these agreements was signed, 10 September, the Canada Cement Company was floated – in an hour, according to one account. Three provisional directors were named: Senator W. C. Edwards, Senator Robert Mackay and Aitken. Edwards was represented by a proxy. Shares were then voted to seven office clerks. A second meeting, regarded as a shareholders' meeting, ratified an agreement previously prepared between the Bond Company and the new Canada Cement Company. At a third meeting, the directors adopted the agreement.

Under the deal, the Bond Company transferred to the Cement Company the properties covered by the options and agreed to pay the company $1,770,000 in cash, in return for:

	$
Bonds	5,000,000
Preferred stock	10,500,000
Ordinary shares	13,498,400
Total	28,998,400

Thus the total amount (at par value) of the bonds and shares delivered to the Bond Company by the Cement Company was considerably greater than the total amount of cash and securities that the Bond Company was called upon to pay to meet its contracts with the selling companies and the Cement Company. The agreement between the Bond Company and the Cement Company was signed for the Bond Company not by Aitken, but by his secretary Miss de Gruchy and his brother-in-law Victor Drury. On the same day, the Bond Company sold to the Canadian Agency of London, represented by Major Guy Stewart St Aubyn, 11,832 preference shares with a par value of $1,183,200 and 8874 ordinary shares with a par value of $887,400. The Agency paid $1,064,880.

THE COMPANY PROSPECTUS

On 14 September, in Montreal, the new Canada Cement Company issued a prospectus. It announced that the new company had been incorporated in order to take over ten companies and acquire control of two additional companies (one of which was Exshaw). It announced 'the issue of $5,000,000 seven per cent cumulative preference shares of $100 each'. The company had an authorized capital of $30,000,000 and was issuing $10,500,000 of preference shares and $13,500,000 of ordinary shares. 'The Royal Securities Corporation Limited', the announcement continued, 'is prepared to receive subscriptions for $5,000,000 of the above 7 per cent cumulative preference shares at the price of $93 for each share; with a bonus of ordinary shares equal in par value to 25 per cent of the par value of the preference shares allotted, to be delivered on payment of the subscription in full'. The Royal Securities Company, of course, was Aitken.

The Bank of Montreal was named as the new company's banker, and reasons for the merger were given. Demand for cement had nearly doubled in the preceding five years, the prospectus said, and was certain to increase because of the 'enormous public works in progress and in contemplation, including Railways, Canals, Bridges, Harbor Improvements, Piers, Wharves, Docks, Piles, Pavements, Building Foundations, and Buildings, etc'. Despite the boom, the document candidly went on, in 1908 the average price per barrel had been $1.39, whereas in 1907 it had been about $1.60. 'The large competing companies', in other words, were cutting one another's throats; they had 'realised' that 'the business could be rendered much more profitable by a merger'. The list of fifteen directors was headed by Sir Sandford Fleming KCMG, Ottawa, director of the International

Portland Cement Company and the Canadian Pacific Railway. J. S. Irvin was among them, and three senators, and at the end of the list, 'W. M. Aitken, Montreal, Director Montreal Trust Company' (his connection with the Royal Securities Corporation was not mentioned), followed by Charles H. Cahan. On 15 September, the Bond Company sold its Canada Cement bonds and shares to Royal Securities. Fred C. Clarke and Drury signed for the Bond Company, and Aitken for RSC, with Miss de Gruchy as a witness.

The new full board of Canada Cement met for the first time on 18 October, under the chairmanship of C. H. Cahan. Fleming was surprised to find himself named honorary president. Thinking he should inform himself more fully about the company – of which he knew very little – he asked, by letter and telegram, both the general manager and the secretary to send him copies of any documents explaining the company's origins; but he got no reply.

Eventually, at the end of another board meeting on 4 March 1910, he saw briefly among a pile of other documents the agreement – the cement Magna Carta, he called it – signed between the Bond Company and Canada Cement the previous September. He at once wrote to Canada Cement's vice-president. He said he had discovered that 'an organisation known as the Bond & Share company' had been given securities with a face value of $27,228,000 when eleven of the twelve companies mentioned in the prospectus had cost $14,629,000. Thus 'the capital over-issued to the Bond and Share company now stands at between $12,000,000 and $13,000,000'. Five days later the Board of Directors met to approve a Report to the Shareholders. Fleming was asked to move its adoption. He declined, saying he objected to a sentence reading, 'Cost of properties at dates of acquisition, together with additions to Dec. 31st, 1909. $27,134,786.92.' Nevertheless the report was approved.

On 11 March Fleming wrote to the vice-president again, saying he thought the greater part of the Bond Company's stock should be returned to Canada Cement, while adding that the Bond Company should be liberally dealt with and 'fully and adequately compensated'. On 15 March he wrote a third letter to the vice-president with 'additional facts'; this time he pressed for an internal inquiry into the Bond Company's dealings 'in the interests of business morality'. Canada Cement, he said, owed a duty to its ordinary investors in Canada and England to conduct such an inquiry. (The Duke of Portland, Lord Hinchingbrooke and Edmund Gosse were early investors in England.) On 24 March, four Canada Cement directors – Senator Cox, Senator Edwards, Senator Mackay and J. M. Kilbourn, former president of one of the merged companies, Lakefield Cement – wrote to tell Fleming that the Bond Company deal was 'legal and binding', without sending him any of the documents he had asked to see.

By this time, unknown to Fleming and perhaps almost everyone except Aitken's immediate staff, the Bond Company had been sold and was well on the way to dissolution. On 17 February the Utilities Securities Corporation – president, W. M. Aitken, secretary, V. M. Drury, and with two others present (one of whom was the useful Fred C. Clarke) – authorized the sale of the Bond Company to the Corporate Organization and Audit Company of New York. On 19 February, Drury sent certificates for 950 shares of Bond Company stock to Messrs Curtis, Mallet, Prevost and Colt at 30 Broad Street, New York. Of these shares Aitken held 945. The remaining five were held – one apiece – by Drury, Izaak Walton Killam, Miss de Gruchy, H. G. Boyle and, of course, Fred C. Clarke. The Corporate Organization and Audit Company paid $95,000 for these shares: the total Bond Company assets. The Bond Company sent them a cheque for $95,000 and the Corporate Organization sent one back for the same amount. The New York lawyer reminded Drury that the cheques must not be cashed separately; he had put their cheque in his own office safe.

To finish the story of the winding up: on 20 June 1910 the Toronto lawyers who had originally incorporated the Bond Company wrote to Drury to say they had received a letter from the Ontario government addressed to the company. The Assistant Provincial Secretary stated that the company had failed to comply with section 131 of the Ontario Companies Act; that is, it had not filed an 'Annual Summary' of its affairs for 1909. Drury wrote back to Johnston, a partner in the Toronto law firm: 'I am no longer an officer of this company.' He added: 'I would kindly ask you to inform the Assistant Provincial Secretary that your clients know nothing concerning this company.' He asked Johnston what previous reports the company had filed. Johnston said it had never filed any. On 30 June Drury wrote to Johnston again: 'I know nothing about this company. . . . I don't suppose you will be able to give any information in connection with the affairs of this company if any requests to do so are made.' On 29 July Drury asked the New York lawyers to send the Bond Company charter to the Toronto lawyers. They in turn would surrender it to the Ontario authorities and 'cover up any irregularities that may exist, particularly as to the annual reports which every Ontario company is supposed to make to the Provincial Government'. This was done, and the Provincial Government fixed 12 January 1911 'as the date upon and from which the company shall be deemed to be dissolved'.

Drury had a final tremor of anxiety. On 4 January 1911 he informed Johnston that an unidentified lawyer was trying to extract Bond Company documents from F. P. Jones, the general manager of Canada Cement. On 6 January Johnston wrote a soothing reply. All that was necessary to block the lawyer was for the president of the company that had bought the Bond Company, Mr Albert S. Rockwood of New York (all five directors lived in New York, and all owned one share), to send Jones a telegram giving him permission to hold on to any Bond Company documents he might have. That would deny access to the lawyer. 'Of course,' Johnston added, 'after the 12th inst. there will be no such thing as the Bond and Share Company.'

To return to the main narrative: Aitken knew that the Bond Company was in the process of disappearing, like the smile on the Cheshire Cat, when on 4 March 1910 he proposed a deal over Exshaw. It is unlikely to have been a coincidence that this was the very day that Fleming first sighted the agreement between the Bond Company and Canada Cement. Aitken wrote to F. B. Dunsford saying he would help financially with Exshaw's reorganization on condition that Fleming wrote to his Canada Cement co-directors accepting 'the legality of the proceedings connected with the organisation and capitalisation of the Canada Cement Co. Ltd'. At the same time Aitken sent a Montreal lawyer, Gordon Macdougall, to see Fleming in Ottawa. Macdougall told Fleming that Aitken controlled and 'practically is' the Bond and Share Company (which by then had been sold to the New Yorkers), and tried to persuade Fleming to stop pressing for an investigation.

Fleming half capitulated. He wrote a letter, but Aitken said it did not comply with his conditions and refused to accept it. Aitken then tried another tack. On 2 April he lent Exshaw, via Dunsford, $50,000 on the understanding that the loan would be withdrawn if Fleming took any legal action against Aitken or made any public criticism of the merger. Meanwhile the Canada Cement board, inspired by Aitken, refused to take over Exshaw at the price stated in the option, on the ground that Exshaw had not reorganized itself as promised. Exshaw protested that they had not had time.

On 10 May 1910 Fleming returned to the attack, having gathered further information about the way the merger had been handled – allegedly from an unnamed person present at the original meetings. He repeated, to the company president, Senator Edwards, his contention that there had been an over-issue of some twelve million shares to the Bond Company. If these shares, or the bulk of them, were returned to Canada Cement, he said, all the shareholders would benefit – both the shareholders of the original companies who were paid with the new company's shares, and the new shareholders. 'With restitution voluntarily entered into, the difficulty would be set aside, and as dividends would be payable on the surrendered securities, the whole earnings of Canada Cement would be available for dividend purposes on the greatly reduced capital. By this means, the yearly profits of the shareholders would be much augmented.' He warned Edwards that one day the facts were bound to become public.

The board this time did not dismiss Fleming's attacks out of hand. Instead, with his agreement, two lawyers, H. A. Lovett of Montreal and J. F. Orde of Ottawa, were instructed to consult the documents, investigate the circumstances of the deal and report on whether an action could be successfully maintained by the Cement Company against the Bond Company.

On 18 July 1910 they reported that it could not. Since the Bond Company, set up and dominated by Aitken, and the Cement Company, set up and dominated by Aitken, were on both sides of the bargain, and no one else was financially interested, these parties had a right to place whatever figure they thought appropriate on the properties being acquired by their own company. They could issue themselves as much stock in their corporation as they thought fit in return for the assets it was acquiring. The lawyers added, however, that 'the magnitude of the transaction, the large issue of securities made to the Bond Company in connection therewith, and the difficulty of applying legal principles to transactions of this nature make it essential in the interests of everyone concerned that the contracts should be carefully considered and both the facts and the law applicable thereto ascertained'.

This was a less than wholehearted endorsement of the merger deal; and from the report Fleming and his associates learned for the first time exactly what had been paid and how for each property. The lawyers put the total price paid at $14,822,250, which confirmed – near enough – the original Fleming allegation.

Fleming continued to press his co-directors to act, without success. Finally, on 13 February, he resigned as honorary president of the company and sent all his fellow directors a long letter, by registered post. He particularly wondered why Canada Cement's balance sheet of 31 December 1910 prepared for shareholders again valued its properties at $27,134,786.92. 'Since the properties have apparently not cost more than $14,822,250 at the outside,' he wrote, this discrepancy 'needs explanation'. He still hoped for a private resolution of the dispute; he suggested arbitration. Five weeks passed. Only one director, an American, wrote back. Accordingly, on 3 April, he wrote to the Liberal Prime Minister, Sir Wilfrid Laurier, appealing for a government investigation.

Meanwhile, a Canadian general election was in the offing. Aitken by now had been living in London for ten months and had been a member of the House of Commons for four. Nevertheless he was thinking about entering political life in Canada, at the urging of the Conservative leader, R. L. Borden. He wrote to Macdougall on 3 April saying that Borden wanted him to lead the Conservative Party in New Brunswick and to accept office if the Conservatives won the election. 'I have practically decided to accede to his request.'

FLEMING GOES PUBLIC

On 12 May Fleming went public with his charges, which made news from the Atlantic to the Pacific. Asked by the Toronto *Daily Star* for a comment, F. P. Jones, the general manager of Canada Cement, who had been appointed by Aitken, said that Fleming was prompted by spite. There had been no difficulties until Canada Cement refused to buy the company of which Fleming was president, Exshaw; such a deal would have been to Fleming's 'personal and financial advantage', but to the detriment of Canada Cement's shareholders.

On 21 May Jones wrote cheerfully to Aitken in London saying he would go to Ottawa and get Senators Edwards and Cox to see the Prime Minister. Parliament, in any case, could not investigate the Bond and Share Company since it no longer existed. Aitken thought, or pretended to think, that Fleming's campaign was politically inspired. At any rate, he changed his mind about taking part openly in the Canadian election. He told Borden on 4 July that as 'the principal figure in the anti-Trust agitation' he had best keep clear; however, he had told Allan Davidson in Newcastle that he would 'provide the entire election expenses' for the local Conservative candidate; 'I have made it a condition that he shall deny that the money comes from me.'

On 27 July he wrote from London: 'Decent Liberals are resenting the conduct of their newspapers. The *Montreal Herald* refused to follow the inspired campaign any further. . . .' He did not mention that six weeks earlier he had lent the owner of the *Herald* $150,000 and saved him from ruin. He did complain, however, that the Conservative press had 'made no defence whatever' of him during the 'inspired' attacks.[1]

The election took place on 21 September 1911, and the Conservatives, helped by Aitken's secret payments, duly won. On 25 October Fleming wrote to the new Prime Minister, Borden, restating and expanding his complaints and proposing a Royal Commission. In reply, Borden said that aggrieved shareholders could seek remedies in the courts, and that the government was considering 'the question of providing some check upon over-capitalization'. On 15 November 1911 Fleming published a twenty-two-page document containing an account of 'capital having been misappropriated on an enormous scale', with copies of various letters.

On 23 November, the *Ottawa Evening Journal* characterized the dispute as 'a millionaire of 84 pursuing with a sharp stick a multi-millionaire of 32'. Two days later, R. B. Bennett, who had been one of the original investors in Canada Cement with a borrowed $100,000, and had made a 'substantial' killing as a result, informed Aitken that he had had a long conversation with the Prime Minister; Borden had said there would be no investigation and no parliamentary inquiry; there was accordingly no cause for worry.[2] The newspapers had reported the dispute without going into the figures, and Canada Cement stock was unaffected.

Aitken wanted to counter-attack. Through Bennett and Drury, he had established to his own satisfaction that Irvin, Fleming and Fleming's son had all acted illegally by selling Exshaw shares, to their own financial benefit, when they knew the company was insolvent. Aitken cabled Montreal in code saying he wanted to expose 'Fleming reasons for present blackmail'. He was prepared to sign a statement about watered stock in Exshaw. On 26 November he cabled again: 'Will F. P. Jones agree that I give out interview about Exshaw swindle and charging Sir Sandford Fleming with blackmailing me.'

The Montreal lawyers tried to calm him down. On no account should he say anything about Exshaw, 'as would have appearance weakness on main issue'. He could, however, make the point that the last government had seen no grounds to take action over the merger. Drury cabled on 1 December, 'Absolutely no agitation or attention being paid to charges by anyone. Current street gossip says old man must be crazy.'

On 5 December, Aitken wrote to his old friend J. L. Stewart of the *Chatham World* to thank him for a helpful article.

> My own profit on the transaction amounted to 6000 shares, and the profit of my company amounted to 20,000 shares. For these two commissions, our joint and several liabilities amounted to $9,000,000. Assuming the stock was worth $20 a share, the commission to us was less than $600,000 for a liability of $9,000,000. I do not think any Bank would undertake the liability for less commission. . . .
>
> The difficulty lies in the fact that Sir Sandford Fleming's associates owe the bank of Montreal $100,000, on account of the Exshaw Cement Company. I would not take the Exshaw Company over at Fleming's price, and he not only lost his prospective profit but in addition the $100,000, which he will have to pay the Bank of Montreal. He is trying to blackmail me into inducing the Bank of Montreal to withdraw its claim. I am not prepared to do so.
>
> Sir Sandford Fleming, of course, is thoroughly experienced in stock watering operations. He created $3,000,000 watered stock in the Exshaw Company, and in addition his friends and himself filched $200,000 of the bond money. The company naturally failed. A reason contributing to the failure was the engagement of Sir Sandford Fleming's useless son as Secretary.

Canada Cement, Aitken concluded, 'will be the biggest industrial company in Canada in the near future'.

On 21 December 1911 Drury wrote to say that 'I think we [Bennett and himself] have proved that in 1905 Irvin had bought land for the express purpose of handing it over to Exshaw at exorbitant prices when the company was incorporated, and stock, bonds, and cash handed over to Fleming, Hugh Fleming, et al.'

Before Christmas 1911, the Bank of Montreal brought a suit against Fleming and Irvin for the repayment of the $100,000. Aitken thought the suit would give 'the old blackmailer enough to think about for the present', but added that Fleming was 'very likely to try to force my hand by further blackmailing tactics'. Aitken always believed that attack was the best form of defence. A document dated May 1912 survives in the Aitken files that reads like an article intended for publication in case of need; it concentrates on the crookedness of Fleming and Irvin and is evidently based largely on Bennett's researches. However, Aitken concedes that with Canada Cement there had been 'a very large creation and issue of watered capital . . . but its $100 shares have never been sold at more than $30 and the project was sound, and not incompatible with the capitalisation of the company'.

MOVING THE DOCUMENTS

The confident tone adopted by Aitken with correspondents outside the inner ring was not reflected in his actions. The Bank of Montreal's suit against Fleming might lead to enquiries about his own operations two years earlier. He asked Drury to send him exact copies of all documents filed by the Bond Company with the Ontario government since its incorporation. Then he suggested to Drury that all relevant documents still in Montreal should be moved elsewhere. Drury wrote to him at his Knightsbridge flat on 15 December: 'If suit is taken the first thing Fleming will ask for are our books and as soon as they find every trace of every cement transaction gone they will at once make a big howl that we had something to hide and should think they could make a great deal of capital out of the fact. It seems to me your suggestion to take the books to Halifax is the best, that is of course if you want them to disappear.'

Drury had another anxiety. Should not the directors of the Bond Company – Miss de Gruchy and himself – have been paid? Otherwise, it looked a 'bit odd'. He suggested a fee of $5 a meeting, adding that there had only been about ten meetings in all. He had closed one loophole. 'I had a long talk with Miss de Gruchy today. She is getting married at 8 am Wednesday 20th inst. She is prepared to do anything or go any place that may be necessary, she advises me she has absolutely forgotten everything that occurred during the cement transaction.'

By 19 December Drury was preparing to ship Royal Securities Corporation documents to London. 'There is no reason why the books of the company should not be in the custody of the London office [of RSC] in view of the fact that the President and Managing Director are there.' On 6 January 1912 he told Aitken that he had sent over by express an old minute book of the RSC and stock certificate book of the Utilities Securities (Aitken had sold Bonar Law shares in this firm). He had shipped by freight all the old books and vouchers of RSC up to 31 December 1910.

> It was thought better not to mention it in the minutes but just to treat it as the natural thing that the books as far as possible should be with the President.
> Regarding the correspondence of the RSC previous to 1911 I am going over it carefully and eliminating anything which I think necessary. I have taken out the whole of the Royal Trust file as it gives very full information regarding the cement agreements.

Royal Trust was in effect a subsidiary of the Bank of Montreal.

On 1 April 1912 Aitken wrote to Doble about the personal profit made out of the cement merger by Sir Edward Clouston.

> The books and accounts of the Royal Securities Corporation clearly show that Sir Edward Clouston was paid for his services in guaranteeing the sale of Canada Cement Bonds in Ordinary Shares of Canada Cement stock. Also that these shares were subsequently sold to the Royal Securities Corporation at $15.50 per share. Also that the proceeds paid for Sir Edward Clouston's stock in the Royal Securities Corporation.
>
> My own books and my Bank balances show that several months afterwards Sir Edward Clouston paid me by cheque the sum of $25,000, and this sum was credited to Sir Edward Clouston's account and so remains at the present time.

He went on to say that 'sooner or later I may go into Court with the books of the Royal Securities Corporation and my own books. Under such circumstances it will be entirely necessary to give a full disclosure of the whole transaction.' He told Doble to send the letter back.

He had Clouston by the throat. Doble replied on 22 April: 'Sir Edward Clouston has made a statement that he did not in any way participate in the promotion profits of the Canada Cement Co. other than by underwriting or purchasing in the open market and therefore' – here Doble became ironic – 'the contentions set forth in your letter to Mr Doble would be of no use unless you wish to contradict Sir Edward's statement which I am sure you would never think of doing.'

As the Bank v. Fleming suit approached, Aitken resumed his aggressive stance. A Fleming lawyer had been poking around. On 12 May Aitken wrote to his Toronto lawyer, A. M. Stewart: 'If Mr Osler persists in looking for trouble then it seems to me the proper course is to make peace no longer but to pursue his whole gang constantly and relentlessly. I am tired of this thing dragging along interminably. I have less to lose than anybody else. I have already told you I was a minority shareholder in the Bond & Share Company. You know full well the conduct of that Company can be defended.'

Stewart calmed him down. He was sure, he said, that 'the transactions relating to the organisation of the Canada Cement Company are not only not open to legal attack, but are entirely meritorious in a business sense'. In any case, Fleming was showing no signs of attacking Aitken, being himself under attack by the Bank of Montreal. Nevertheless Aitken was anxious about the course the proceedings might take. Stewart advised him on 3 June that R. B. Bennett had told him that 'under these pleadings the defendants cannot possibly rake up the distribution of the ordinary stock'.

Preliminary hearings began in the autumn of 1912 in the Ontario High Court. By then, Clouston was dead. In his examination for discovery, on 23 November, Irvin said he thought in retrospect that the Exshaw option had been deliberately drawn up with holes in it by Aitken, 'which resulted in them getting the Exshaw property direct from their bondholders at their own price'. About Clouston, he said that Aitken had 'made no bones' about Clouston's profit.

He drove me out in his motor car on a Saturday afternoon. . . . He says, 'I must take care of the General Manager at the big pillars'. He frequently spoke of the Bank of Montreal as the place with the big pillars.

Q: How was that taken care of?

Irvin: He simply said to me he would have to give him a million dollars worth of the stock, that is what he said, take it for what it is worth.

Clouston's successor as general manager of the Bank was H. V. Meredith. He had not been involved in the merger. He told the court that Aitken was regarded by Clouston as 'a very clever man and a very successful one' and that Aitken had had an account with the bank. During the questioning of Meredith, the Bank of Montreal intervened to say, on behalf of Doble and Stavert, that they had no connection 'direct or indirect' with any syndicate or merger. The lawyer also said, on Cahan's behalf, that he and Clouston had had no connection with Aitken; Cahan had simply been asked by Clouston to look into Exshaw and had found it to be insolvent.

The 'hopeless' Hugh Fleming said that Doble and Stavert had in fact been in on the merger. Irvin, Morden and Forget – the original members of the merger syndicate – had been moved out and Aitken, Cahan and Doble had moved in and taken control. The result was that other cement firms had been taken in, the issue of stock changed and the capitalization of the company greatly increased.

He said that Aitken was always purporting to be the agent of the Bank of Montreal; 'He always put that before us.' Certainly, everything that Aitken did, Doble knew in five minutes. Hugh Fleming thought the shareholders of Exshaw had been done down. The bondholders transferred their assets to the merger company, but 'that didn't pay the shareholders'.

During the examinations, Stewart wrote to Aitken saying that the Bank's lawyer 'thinks it advisable that I should attend the trial in your interest, though nominally as though briefed with him by the Bank, which latter detail he thinks he will have no difficulty in arranging'. However, Aitken would pay his fees. 'I should not care to put you to this expense without specific instructions.'

CAHAN AND 'BLACKMAIL'

As the trial approached, though no date was yet fixed, Stewart told Drury on 17 February 1913 that he had gone over all the pleadings in the action, and did not think Aitken 'need concern himself very much'. Irvin's statements were for the most part 'mere expressions of opinion'. He was 'somewhat against submitting Mr Doble for examination for discovery', and he was also against Aitken 'going into the box unless it is quite necessary'. In giving evidence 'it is not always possible to start just where you want to and stop just where you want to'. Besides, 'we are concerned here with the verdict, not of the Court, but of the newspapers'. The court in this case would not pass judgement on any issue affecting Aitken, none such being raised. But 'a certain section of the press is always ready to gain popularity by attacking large companies and prominent capitalists'. The evidence given 'may be absolutely satisfactory for us', and yet 'may be made the basis of newspaper agitation and unfavourable comment. The public can never understand a transaction involving the creation of stock values, and that gives an unscrupulous or ignorant newspaper its opportunity.' The course they had hitherto adopted of letting newspaper comment 'die out for want of fuel' had been 'very successful' and 'I think it should still be pursued.' Stewart wrote to Aitken direct on 4 March: 'The proposal to attack the organisation of the Cement Company is, to all appearances, dead.' Exshaw had gone out of business.

The trial date was tentatively fixed for 17 November 1913 in Toronto, and the question of Aitken being called as a witness on behalf of the Bank was raised once again. On 20 October Aitken cabled that he would 'sail November 8th providing they realize I will give complete record of common stock distribution if called for in evidence'. Ten days later he was in search of a settlement. Orde had written to him on 21 May offering a settlement for $50,000. He had never answered 'as I was ill'. Now he wanted Stewart to procure a settlement. Canada Cement would pay something, and 'I am willing to contribute'. By 6 November the deal was done. The Bank's total claim amounted with interest to $115,000. The Fleming interests paid $75,000, and Aitken $20,000. The Bank stood the remaining loss. Neither Cahan nor the Fleming interests were told that Aitken had contributed to the settlement. Stewart cabled: 'Defendants [i.e. the Fleming interests] and Cahan ignorant of contribution. Otherwise reasonable settlement impossible and attacks encouraged. Settlement removes motive to attack. Keep contribution secret.' Next day Stewart drew a line under the story. Aitken had presumed that the deal included an undertaking from Sir Sandford Fleming not to attack Canada Cement or himself. Now Stewart reported that Fleming had 'so far lost his capacity for attending to business that his property is being placed in the hand of trustees. This renders any further attack from him improbable, and at the same time would have made it extremely difficult, if not impossible, to negotiate with him on the subject of any pledge.'

What are we to conclude from this complex tale? Something troubled Aitken about the merger. Why otherwise were the tracks of the Bond and Share Company obliterated? Why did he oversee the concealment and destruction of company records? In his short book *Success*, published in 1921, he included four imprecise paragraphs about the affair, congratulating himself on his moral fortitude. In old age, when he wrote his reminiscences for the *Atlantic Advocate*, he promised in one article to tell the Canada Cement story in a later one. He did not do so. In 1958 a researcher, Rosemary Brooks, assembled for him a 'rough draft' narrative from the records. Beaverbrook sub-edited and corrected two pages, and then stopped. She noted that the narrative, 'on Lord Beaverbrook's instructions, was abandoned before it was completed'.

In one of his additions to the Brooks draft, Aitken scribbled a phrase saying that he 'had no account' at the Bank of Montreal 'and no business relations with that institution'. Meredith, who had been manager of the Montreal branch of the Bank, testified that he had. Why, half a century later, would Beaverbrook have denied it? Was it a lapse of memory? Or did he want to minimize his links with the Bank at the time of the merger? Why, when he wrote to someone in Ashton-under-Lyne in 1911, at a time when the Bond and Share Company was under criticism, did he say that he had consulted his records and found that he had never been a shareholder in the company, and then tell his Toronto lawyer the following year that he had been a 'minority shareholder'? He virtually owned it.

Drury lied when he claimed he had no knowledge of the Bond Company. Doble lied when he claimed he was not involved in the merger. Cahan lied when he claimed that his only connection with the merger was an inquiry into Exshaw he made for Clouston. Clouston seems to have lied when he claimed to have made no personal profit out of the merger.

Irvin – as the evidence collected by Bennett and Drury powerfully suggests – operated a 'swindle' (Aitken's word) when he bought worthless land cheaply and sold it to Exshaw at an exorbitant price. Was it Irvin's fear of exposure by Aitken – he would have known that Aitken had employed Bennett to investigate that deal and others – which caused him to settle with the Bank of Montreal just before the case came to trial?

Aitken's method of dealing with the criticisms is illuminating. He did not answer directly the Fleming–Irvin charges about his profits, or about the watering of stock, or about the wide discrepancy between the stated assets of the cement company and the price it had paid for them. Instead he dug into Irvin's land deals, threatened to reveal the distribution of the common stock, and claimed that the attacks were political.

He said he made little out of the merger: 'not one tenth, not one twentieth, not one fortieth' of the amount he was accused of making; but he had fifty years to complete the destruction of the evidence. His defence against the charge of over-capitalization was that the company was not over-capitalized in relation to its prospects, and that in any event it was an outstanding success; early buyers of Cement common stock would have made a fortune if they had hung on over the decades. Still, in the 1930s the company spent years squeezing the water out of the stock.

Aitken showed great skill in deploying others to assist his purposes. The support of the Bank of Montreal was essential: to give the merger solidity, to give the investors confidence and to encourage all the various owners to join in; and Aitken had both Stavert and Doble on his side, one of them a high official and the other, in the general manager's office, in a position to supply Aitken with inside information about every move made. Aitken evidently cut Sir Edward Clouston in on the merger. The evidence of Clouston's successor, H. V. Meredith, is of particular interest. He told the court that the Bank's board minutes for the relevant period contained no mention of the merger, which is strange, since it was an exceptionally large undertaking. Again, Meredith told the court he was surprised that Stavert had been put in charge of the merger negotiations; true, he was a high official, but he was responsible for the Maritimes, and not the obvious person for Sir Edward to have chosen. Stavert was employed by Aitken at Royal Securities, as was Doble, and though such outside jobs were not absolutely forbidden by the Bank, some senior people there strongly disapproved, as Doble told Aitken at the height of the row. Another person whom Aitken handled with dexterity was the financier Rodolphe Forget, who was a member of Irvin's original syndicate: he threw his hand in with Aitken and was rewarded with a large amount of stock.

Cahan is an odd case. He pursued Aitken in London in 1910 and 1911 for money that he said Aitken owed him. He had been much more than Aitken's legal adviser, he argued, and deserved much more than legal fees; in the cement merger, he insisted, he had been Aitken's 'partner'. His demands added up to hundreds of thousands of dollars. In a note written years later and attached to this correspondence Beaverbrook described Cahan's letters as 'blackmail'; and Cahan in one letter certainly wrote in threatening tones that if Aitken did not pay up he, Cahan, would have only one course left open to him. The 'blackmail' was at least partially successful; Aitken sent him $40,000, whereupon Cahan climbed down.

Irvin and Hugh Fleming claimed that Aitken tried to 'bribe' Irvin at one stage. Half a century later, Aitken's offer to pay Dunsford $50,000 if he silenced Fleming worried Miss Brooks. In a memorandum to Beaverbrook attached to her draft narrative she said she was 'particularly uneasy' about this story, though it was taken from Aitken's own letters of the period; 'at this distance of time, it looks a little bald'.

Possibly Aitken was lucky that the case between the Bank of Montreal and the Fleming interests did not come to trial; that Clouston died and Sir Sandford became senile. But even if it had, his tracks were well covered.

BEAVERBROOK AS HISTORIAN

BEAVERBROOK REMARKED MORE than once that he would be remembered more for his books of political history than for his newspapers; and perhaps he was right. For students of the period 1914–23, his accounts remain essential reading, and will continue to be so because they are an excellent and often the only source for certain transactions. Besides, he never wrote a boring paragraph. His position as eye-witness gives his historical writings unusual freshness and the ring of authenticity; he was undoubtedly there, so that to disprove him is not easy, especially given his habit of consulting his contemporaries before publication and his skill in deploying his private hoard of documents. Professional historians are still obliged to confront Beaverbrook and take him seriously.

Until several years after his death criticism of Beaverbrook's version of events was directed at his general picture rather than at particular incidents. His placing of himself, as Bonar Law's lieutenant and motivator, in a crucial position between 1914 and 1916, came as a surprise to some of the other protagonists. In June 1931, when his account of the political crisis of December 1916 appeared in the *Daily Express*, Leo Amery noted in his diary for 24 June after a visit to Carson, one of the key conspirators: 'He . . . was full of talk about Beaverbrook's story of the fall of the Asquith government. He told me that he was quite unaware that Beaverbrook was playing so important a part as he, Beaverbrook, now makes out . . . .' Privately, some of his correspondents, including Churchill, queried his glowing picture of the strength and wisdom of his self-proclaimed hero, Bonar Law, but his unflattering portrait of Asquith as an extinct volcano, his mind not fully on his job, although fiercely resented by Asquith's daughter Lady Violet Bonham Carter, was hardly challenged before the publication of Roy Jenkins's biography of 1964. Jenkins pointed out that Beaverbrook's account of 1916, although evidently partisan, had been treated as source material by most subsequent writers. 'Even J. A. Spender', notes Jenkins, 'in the relevant chapter of Asquith's official biography, used a great number of Beaverbrook's facts. It is therefore often the case that, at first sight, a statement appears to be overwhelmingly confirmed from about six different sources; but on closer examination the six sources all turn out to be subsidiaries of the central Beaverbrook fount.'

When Asquith was preparing his own memoirs, he asked Venetia Montagu to lend him his wartime letters to her as an *aide mémoire*; she sent him an edited selection, 'leaving out all sentimentalities' as she put it to Beaverbrook. Nearly ten years earlier she had shown much of this material to Beaverbrook himself. Michael and Eleanor Brock discuss Beaverbrook's use of the letters, with examples of how he transposed and altered passages to suit his narrative, in an appendix to their edition of the correspondence.

As for Lloyd George, who whether Beaverbrook intended it or not, emerges as the real hero of the Beaverbrook version of the political crises of 1915 and 1916, he read the first volume of *Politicians and the War* in 1928 with 'great enthusiasm', according to Frances Stevenson, who wrote to Beaverbrook to say how flattering she thought his portrait of Lloyd George. When Lloyd George's own *War Memoirs* appeared in 1933, after Beaverbrook's second volume, his debt to Beaverbrook for the story of December 1918 was plainly stated. 'The story is told in detail by Lord Beaverbrook. Much of what he relates I learnt for the first time when I read his book.' Lloyd George's latest biographer, John Grigg, also relies heavily on Beaverbrook as a primary source. The way in which A. J. P. Taylor, through his relationship with Beaverbrook, developed and substantiated the elevation of Lloyd George's reputation at the expense of Asquith's has been delineated by Stephen Koss in his essay 'Asquith versus Lloyd George; the Last Phase and Beyond' in *Crisis and Controversy, Essays in Honour of A. J. P. Taylor*, published in 1976. Earlier Martin Gilbert and Cameron Hazlehurst had been re-examining the politics of the First World War and subsequent episodes, raising questions about Beaverbrook's version in detail as well as in outline; their approach was to place his narrative in a more comprehensive context rather than merely to dispute him on specific events. Hazlehurst observed in 1971 in his book *Politicians at War* that Beaverbrook's account was 'not a dispassionate analysis. Nor does it attempt to set the problems of Lloyd George and Asquith, Bonar Law and Lansdowne, in the context of parliamentary opinion and loyalties'.

Other historians have been more hostile. Lloyd George's reliance on Beaverbrook was noted by Peter Fraser of Dalhousie University, one of the most pugnacious of the historians who have in the last ten years put the Beaverbrook narratives under the microscope. His article entitled 'Lord Beaverbrook's Fabrications in *Politicians and the War, 1914–1916*', in the *Historical Journal* for 1982, surveys a series of what he and his colleague J. M. McEwen call 'numerous and flagrant instances [of] inaccuracies, biases, disregard of fact, and elevation of fancy to the level of truth'. He compiles an impressive dossier of Beaverbrookian falsehoods: the diary on which Beaverbrook claimed to have based his account never existed; the misuse of the Bonar Law narrative (it is worth pointing out that Bonar Law was dead well before Beaverbrook published his account); the attempts to support the bridge game story ('Beaverbrook was more interested in justifying his story as something that should have happened than in debating whether it did'). Fraser suggests, moreover, that even when Beaverbrook has documentary evidence that appears to support his own key role in events another reading of the document is possible.

The matter of the Beaverbrook Memorandum of 25 November 1916 provides a good example of Fraser's attitude to Beaverbrook and his use of material. The memorandum, which Beaverbrook claimed to have 'drafted out . . . for the approval of the triumvirate', was printed in facsimile in *Politicians and the War*; it is indeed clearly in Beaverbrook's handwriting with corrections in Bonar Law's. Thus it seems to prove incontrovertibly that Beaverbrook 'was the virtual author of this vital and crucially instrumental document'. But, Fraser continues, 'The document was manifestly dictated to Beaverbrook, however, for it contains the slip "provide" for "preside", duly amended seriatim in his hand, in a context where the former word could hardly be accommodated by any likely alternative text. One's suspicions on this point are confirmed when one finds that he [Beaverbrook] had originally written about Bonar Law and the memorandum: "He had written it out himself before the meeting and it was finally adopted without alteration".' Fraser concludes: 'Law's handwriting was abominable, and it is most likely that Beaverbrook's handwritten version was taken down as the copy for the typist.' In other words, Beaverbrook played the part more of a secretary than co-author.

Fraser is also critical of other historians, notably A. J. P. Taylor, for allowing Beaverbrook's claims to go largely unchallenged. In particular he and J. M. McEwen ('The Press and the Fall of Asquith', *Historical Journal,* 1978) have demonstrated that some of Beaverbrook's statements about the role of the press in December 1916 are not borne out by examination of the files. Beaverbrook, they indicate, exaggerated the importance of his efforts to orchestrate support for Lloyd George by direct pressure on the *Daily Chronicle* and the *Daily Express*. 'Both papers came out against Asquith's direction of the war on Saturday morning', Beaverbrook wrote in 1931. Fraser points out that '. . . both papers did nothing of the kind, but included Asquith and Balfour in their conjectural list of the possible composition of the new war committee'.

Nevertheless, it has proved impossible to dismiss Beaverbrook altogether as an historical source. In *British Politics and the Great War*, published in 1992, John Turner pays tribute to the lasting impact of Beaverbrook's account. 'The transition from polemical memoir to the party history of the First World War was made, but only just, by Lord Beaverbrook . . . Although Beaverbrook knew the principal actors and in his later work had the advantage of exclusive access to the papers of leading figures including Lloyd George, he was interested in powerful men rather than in the uses of power. A large body of scholarship, reaching into the minutest detail, has grown up to refute his accounts of political interaction at the top. The result is that historians now know in greater detail than ever before who ate whom for breakfast, but few historians of Cabinet-level politics have succeeded in breaking away from Beaverbrook's pattern of thought, which was to see the rise and fall of ministries as the ultimate *explanandum*.' In his own account of the 1916 crisis, Turner demonstrates several errors and inventions of Beaverbrook, but is nonetheless obliged to cite him as a source no less than seven times.

Beaverbrook himself would not be displeased to be still at the centre of debate and reappraisal by historians of his times, nor to learn that for readability and shrewd assessment of human nature he is still regarded as hard to beat. In 1928 H. G. Wells wrote to him in praise of the first part of *Politicians and the War*: 'There but for the grace of God goes a fine novelist – not a fictionist I mean but an appraiser of conduct and character.' Beaverbrook wrote back: '. . . you say I can interpret character. That is exactly the claim I should have made for my own book myself had I dared.'

Martin Gilbert has said that Beaverbrook's great contribution to the writing of twentieth century political history was his introduction of personality and character to explain the course of events, and his use of anecdote and detail to bring his story to life. 'We write contemporary history in a new way because of Beaverbrook.' But Gilbert also issues a warning. On the events of his times, Beaverbrook, he says, 'is on the one hand indispensable; on the other, never quite right'.

SOURCE NOTES

The main source for any biography of the 1st Baron Beaverbrook must be the approximately 900 boxes and 109 volumes of his papers in the House of Lords Record Office. House of Lords Record Office Memorandum No. 54 is a guide to the collection. The visitors' books for Cherkley Court for 1911–64 and Beaverbrook's engagements diaries for 1922–64, kept by a secretary, have survived; so have sixty-five volumes of press cuttings and ninety boxes of material collected for his books. All this material was housed at Cherkley during Beaverbrook's lifetime; it was transferred in 1967 to the Beaverbrook Library in St Bride Street, off Fleet Street, and then in 1975, through A. J. P. Taylor, who had been Honorary Director of the Beaverbrook Library, to the House of Lords Record Office. Taylor's autobiography, *A Personal History* (Hamish Hamilton, 1983), describes the way the papers moved from Cherkley to Fleet Street to the House of Lords; and his biography *Beaverbrook* (Hamish Hamilton, 1972), contains, under the heading 'Sources', what amounts to an essay on the collection. Beaverbrook himself evidently destroyed some documents and letters. His 1902 diary has been tampered with, and the entries from 14 to 17 September apparently cut out. On the day he died at Cherkley, he gave his son Max Aitken a box of papers, which Aitken and A. G. Millar took outside and burned. 'There is really no mystery about what it contained,' Taylor wrote; but he did not explain the reasons for his confidence. Taylor's successors who tackle Beaverbrook's biography have a legitimate cause for complaint in that he provided no source notes. Where we have been unable to find among the 900 boxes the source of a quotation or significant fact, we have ascribed it to Taylor in the notes that follow.

Under Beaverbrook's will, his surviving children inherited the papers for six months and were charged to destroy whatever they thought fit; whether they did or did not destroy material in those months is not known. Not all the Beaverbrook papers found their way to the House of Lords Record Office; the family retained letters (though not all of them) exchanged between Beaverbrook and his children and other family members, as well as sixty-one albums of photographs. This material has not been available to us. In 1964, the Dowager Lady Beaverbrook closed to researchers the files relating to Sir James Dunn – the documents on which her second husband based his biography of her first.

Albums of original letters from politicians, writers and artists were sold. Individual items have appeared at salerooms. Transcripts of these form a large part of the C Series in the Beaverbrook Papers. Correspondence files with lawyers, partly concerning petty litigation, were destroyed on A. J. P. Taylor's orders.

The University of New Brunswick holds much Beaverbrook material relating to Canada, including, for the biographer, a valuable collection of letters exchanged by Beaverbrook and Brigadier Michael Wardell. The Bonar Law–Bennett Library, built at Beaverbrook's expense on the campus of the university to house the papers he had acquired of these old friends, as well as those of Lloyd George, now contains the archives of the province of New Brunswick. A few family records are held by the Old Manse Library at Newcastle, New Brunswick.

Abbreviations used in notes:

BBK: Beaverbrook Papers in the House of Lords Record Office.

RBL: *The Diaries of Sir Robert Bruce Lockhart*, edited by Kenneth Young, Vol. I (Macmillan, London, 1973); Vol. II (1980).

BLP: Bonar Law Papers.

DF: Lord Beaverbrook, *The Decline and Fall of Lloyd George* (Collins, 1963).

HIL: Harriet Irving Library, University of New Brunswick.

HLRO: House of Lords Record Office.

LH: Liddell Hart Papers, Liddell Hart Centre for Military Archives, King's College, London.

MP: Lady McLintock Papers.

OML: Old Manse Library, Newcastle, New Brunswick.

PP: Lord Beaverbrook, *Politicians and the Press* (Hutchinson, 1925).

PW (1): Lord Beaverbrook, *Politicians and the War*, Vol. I (Thornton Butterworth, 1928).

PW (2): Lord Beaverbrook, *Politicians and the War*, Vol. II (The Lane Publications, 1932).

Chapter 1
Son of the Manse, 1879–1900

Unless otherwise noted, all Beaverbrook quotations in this chapter are from the two series of articles he sent to the *Atlantic Advocate* in Fredericton, New Brunswick: 'My Early Days in New Brunswick' was published in 1956, and 'My Early Life' in seven instalments from February to August 1964 (the last article came out after his death). The articles were collected into a book, *My Early Life* (1964).

The letters of the Reverend William Aitken, quoted passim, are held by the Old Manse Library, Newcastle, New Brunswick.

Aitken family information, unless otherwise noted, derives from interviews with Lady McLintock from 1987 to 1991 and with Mr Alan Ramsay from 1989 to 1991. Jean McLintock's father was Beaverbrook's eldest brother, Traven Aitken, and she was partly brought up in Newcastle by the Reverend William and Mrs Aitken. Alan Ramsay's mother, Laura Ramsay, was Beaverbrook's youngest sister.

1. Wardell, J. M. S. Introduction to *My Early Life*.

2. Interview, Lady McLintock, 1988.

3. Papers of the Marquess of Linlithgow, Hopetoun House. See also Cadell, H. M., *The Rocks of West Lothian* (Oliver & Boyd, 1925). The Scottish Genealogy Society published in 1969 a series of Monumental Inscriptions (pre-1855) in West Lothian churchyards, by John Fowler Mitchell CIE and Sheila Mitchell, which included Torphichen churchyard. Seven Aitken tombstones could be identified at that time. The

tombstone of John Aitken, Beaverbrook's great-grandfather, is the only one that names Silvermine.

4. MP, *Aitken Family Connections with Tartraven and Silvermine*.

5. Interview, Alan Ramsay, 1989.

6. Hoddinott, D. F., *From Whence We Came*, Commemorating the 150th Anniversary of St James and St John's United Church, Newcastle, New Brunswick, 1829–1979 (Walco Print & Litho Ltd, n.d.), p. 215.

7. ibid, p. 5.

8. ibid, p. 181.

9. ibid, p. 28, quotes a description of the church by an Irish historian and journalist, Robert Cooney, in 1832.

10. ibid, p. 190.

11. BBK/G/17. File marked 'Material collected under care Brig. Wardell in 1952'.

12. Interview, Lady McLintock, 1990.

13. OML, Harkins Academy School Register.

14. BBK/G/17/IV.

15. BBK/G/18/XIV.

16. BBK/G/17/IV.

17. BBK/G/17/IV.

18. BBK/G/17/IV.

19. Young, Dr Murray, *A Tribute to Lord Beaverbrook*. An address presented on Founders' Day, October 18, 1979 at the University of New Brunswick (University of New Brunswick, 1980).

20. Tweedie, R. A., *On with the Dance* (New Ireland Press, 1986).

21. MP, H. E. Borradaile Memorandum.

22. BBK/G/18/X.

23. BBK/G/18/X.

24. BBK/G/19/XVI. Montgomery to Ait-

ken, 10 February 1897.

25. Cartland, Barbara, *We Danced All Night* (Arrow Books, 1973), p. 271. Interview, Barbara Cartland, 1989.

26. West, Rebecca, *Sunflower* (Virago, 1986), p.209.

Chapter 2
The Money Spinner, 1901–1906

In this and the following chapter we have relied heavily on Armstrong, Christopher, and H. V. Nelles, *Southern Exposure, Canadian Promoters in Latin America and the Caribbean, 1896–1930* (University of Toronto Press, 1988). This is a pioneering and highly entertaining study of 'international financial adventurism' and the methods used by Canadian entrepreneurs, including Max Aitken and James Dunn, to channel investments into the Caribbean, Mexico, Brazil and later Spain, mainly into urban public utilities – trams, telephones, light, power, gas and hydroelectricity.

No thorough biography of the uncommunicative Izaak Walton Killam has yet been published (he left no papers), but useful information is contained in How, Douglas, *A Very Private Person*, copyrighted by the 'Trustees of the estate of the late Dorothy J. Killam, 1976'. The book does not mention either publisher or date of publication.

Few records of the Royal Securities Corporation survive.

As in Chapter 1, Beaverbrook quotations, unless otherwise noted, come from *My Early Life*, and those of the Reverend William Aitken from his letters in the Old Manse Library, Newcastle.

1. The diary is held in the House of Lords Record Office.
2. Armstrong and Nelles, p. 25.
3. MP, Borradaile Memorandum.
4. BBK/G/1/III.
5. See *My Early Life*, and diary entries for October 1902.
6. BBK/A/7.
7. BBK/A/14.
8. *Atlantic Advocate*, April 1964, p. 25.
9. BBK/A/16.
10. How, p. 23.
11. BBK/A/28.
12. HIL, Bailey, Dr A. G., unpublished memoir.
13. MP, Borradaile Memorandum.

14. BBK/A/35.
15. BBK/A/31.
16. BBK/A/27. Aitken to James Riley, 24 June 1903.
17. BBK/A/27.
18. BBK/A/44. Aitken to George Abbott, 22 October 1907.
19. BBK/A/16.
20. Armstrong and Nelles, p. 118.
21. BBK/A/36.
22. BBK/A/29.
23. BBK/A/6. Aitken to W. D. Ross, 11 December 1903.
24. BBK/A/45-46.
25. BBK/A/29. F. T. Burrill to Aitken, 4 October 1906.

Chapter 3
Marriage and Mergers, 1906–1910

1. BBK/G/18/X-XIV contains family letters and details of payments from this period.
2. BBK/A/8.
3. BBK/A/20.
4. Kidd, Janet, *The Beaverbrook Girl* (Collins, 1987), p. 14.
5. BBK/B/30. Arabella Languedoc (*née* Drury) to Beaverbrook, 21 August 1928.
6. BBK/A/17 and BBK/A/19.
7. BBK/A/30.
8. Wardell, J. M. S., *Atlantic Advocate*, November 1963.
9. BBK/A/79.
10. BBK/A/41.
11. BBK/A/42.
12. BBK/A/29. R. A. Betancourt to Aitken, 27 June 1906.
13. BBK/A/35.
14. BBK/A/32.
15. BBK/A/38.
16. Kidd, p. 12.
17. BBK/G/18/XII.
18. BBK/G/18/XIII.

Chapter 4
The Plunge Into Politics, 1910–1912

All Beaverbrook quotations in this chapter, unless otherwise indicated or from his letters, are taken from *My Early Life*.

For Bonar Law's background and career we have relied on Blake, Robert, *The Unknown Prime Minister* (Eyre and Spottiswoode, 1955).

The letters and telegrams from Edward Goulding (later Lord Wargrave) to Beaverbrook, and vice versa, are from BBK/C/317–20.

The letters and telegrams from Rudyard Kipling to Beaverbrook, and vice versa, are from BBK/C/197–9. For Kipling's life and work, see Carrington, Charles, *Rudyard Kipling* (Macmillan, 1955) and Wilson, Angus, *The Strange Ride of Rudyard Kipling* (Secker and Warburg, 1977). For his political attitudes, see *Outside his Art: Rudyard Kipling in Politics*, the Stephen Graham Memorial Lecture given by Michael Brock in 1986 and published by the Royal Society of Literature and the Boydell Press, 1988.

Details of the Ashton-under-Lyne election campaign of November–December 1910, including Beaverbrook's speeches, and its immediate aftermath, are taken from contemporary newspaper reports collected in a scrapbook in the House of Lords Record Office, and from Mackenzie, F. A., *Beaverbrook, An Authentic Biography* (Jarrolds, 1931) and Wood, Alan, *The True History of Lord Beaverbrook* (Heinemann, 1965).

The account of Beaverbrook as MP for Ashton-under-Lyne is based on the constituency correspondence, BBK/B/35–87 in the House of Lords Record Office, which is arranged by year and filed alphabetically. The correspondence with his lawyer, J. Ratcliffe Cousins, in January 1911 over allegations of corrupt practices is in BBK/B/49.

Recollections of life at Cherkley in her childhood are taken from Kidd, Janet, *The Beaverbrook Girl*.

1. PW(1), p. 39.
2. Blake, p. 43.
3. PW(2), p. 57.
4. ibid, p. 59.
5. Taylor, A. J. P., *Beaverbrook* (Hamish Hamilton, 1972), p. 45. Evidence of Bonar Law's extensive financial dealings with Beaverbrook and Royal Securities can be found in the business correspondence section of his personal papers in the HLRO, starting with Box 7, File 9.
6. BBK/C/201.
7. Obituary of Lord Wargrave, the *Observer*, 19 July 1936.
8. Blumenfeld, R. D., *All in a Lifetime* (Benn, 1931), quoted Wood, p. 47.
9. Taylor, p. 44.

10. Carrington, Charles, *Rudyard Kipling* (Macmillan, London, revised edition 1978), p. 476.
11. BLP, 18/8/13.
12. BBK/C/201–14.
13. BBK/C/148.
14. Wood, p. 49.
15. Taylor, p. 49.
16. Mackenzie, p. 18.
17. Beaverbrook, BBK/C/85 (copy from Churchill Papers, Churchill College, Cambridge).
18. Gilbert, Martin, *Winston Churchill*, Companion Vol. II, Part 2 (Heinemann, 1965), pp. 1362–4.
19. BBK/C/50.
20. BBK/C/50.
21. BLP, 18/7/181.
22. BBK/J/7.
23. BBK/C/201.
24. HIL, Wardell Correspondence File.
25. Extracts from Mrs Kipling's diary, afterwards destroyed, were taken by Charles Carrington and are now held with the Carrington Papers in the University of Sussex Library.
26. BBK/C/198.
27. BBK/C/317–20.
28. BBK/B/309.
29. Carrington, p. 472.
30. Brock, p. 116.

Chapter 5
'The Giddy Heights of Journalism', 1910–1912

Accounts of Blumenfeld's career and views are contained in his four books: *RDB'S Diary* (Heinemann, 1930); *All in a Lifetime* (Benn, 1931); *The Press in My Time* (Rich & Cowan, 1933); and *Home Town* (Hutchinson, 1944).

1. BBK/G/19/XX.
2. BBK/G/19/XX.
3. Blumenfeld interview, *Evening Standard*, 1945.
4. *Sunday Express*, 10 November 1963.
5. *Dictionary of National Biography 1961–1970*. Aitken, William Maxwell, by Sir John Elliot (Blumenfeld's son).
6. Kluger, Richard, *The Paper* (Alfred A. Knopf, 1986), p. 145.
7. *Sunday Express*, 10 November 1963.
8. HLRO/Blumenfeld (Additional) Papers/Box 1. Sir John Elliot to John Gordon, 11

May 1953. 'He always told me he educated Lord Beaverbrook in the matter [Tariff Reform].'

9. *New York Evening World*, 7 January 1927. Blumenfeld at the *Express* spoke to Ralph Pulitzer, publisher of the *New York World* and the *New York Evening World*, which reported the conversation verbatim.

10. BBK/G/19/XX and BBK/G/2/IV contain the Aitken–Doble exchanges.

11. BBK/C/317.

12. The authoritative account of the financing of newspapers by political parties is to be found in Koss, Stephen, *The Rise and Fall of the Political Press in Britain*, 2 vols. (Hamish Hamilton, 1981 and 1984).

13. BBK/C/197–9.

14. BBK/G/19/XX.

15. BBK/B/2.

16. BBK/B/4 and BBK/B/5 contain the various proposals put to Aitken at this period.

17. BBK/G/19.

18. BBK/B/9.

19. BBK/C/197–9.

20. BBK/C/197–9.

21. BBK/C/197–9.

22. The dealings between Blumenfeld, Conservative Central Office and Aitken are detailed in Parisi Jr, Frank Joseph, *From Main Street to Fleet Street: R. D. Blumenfeld and the London Daily Express, 1887–1932*, a dissertation submitted to George Washington University, Washington, DC, 5 May 1985. Copy in HLRO.

Chapter 6
The Hermit Crab, 1911–1914

The letters and telegrams from Rudyard Kipling to Beaverbrook are from BBK/C/197–9.

Beaverbrook's descriptions of the Irish negotiations of 1913–14, and of the onset of the First World War in July–August 1914, are taken, unless otherwise noted, from *Politicians and the War*, Vol. I, 1928.

1. BLP, 18/7/198.

2. BLP, 24/1/1.

3. Lord Rankeillour's Papers, quoted Blake, p. 82.

4. Blake, p. 85.

5. ibid, p. 85.

6. A. J. Balfour's Papers, Sandars to Balfour, quoted Blake, p. 90.

7. Correspondence between Hazen, Borden and Bonar Law: Taylor, p. 71.

8. BLP, 33/3/32.

9. Campbell, John, *F. E. Smith, First Earl of Birkenhead* (Cape, 1983), p. 266.

10. DF, p. 231.

11. PP, p. 121.

12. Crawford and Balcarres Papers. We are indebted to Dr Cameron Hazlehurst of the Australian National University for drawing this fact to our attention.

13. Gollin, A. M., The *Observer and J. L. Garvin* (OUP, 1960), pp. 383–5.

14. Mackenzie, p. 85.

15. BBK/C/201.

16. Interview with Dr Murray Young, University of New Brunswick, 1988.

17. Asquith Papers, quoted Jenkins, Roy, *Asquith* (Collins, 1964), p. 288.

18. Draft for PW, BBK/5/5–11.

19. Kipling Papers, University of Sussex.

Chapter 7
A Canadian in Flanders, 1914–1916

All extracts from the telegrams and letters between Beaverbrook and Sir Samuel Hughes, and between Beaverbrook and Sir Robert Borden, together with details of Beaverbrook's appointments and operations as Canadian Representative Overseas and War Records Officer, are taken from BBK/E/1.

1. Taylor, p. 86.

2. BBK/C/39.

3. PW (1), pp. 50–1.

4. BBK/C/39.

5. Campbell, p. 374.

6. Mosley, Leonard, *Castlerosse* (Arthur Barker, 1956).

7. Carrington Papers, University of Sussex.

8. BBK/C/199.

9. PW (2), p. 39.

10. Taylor, p. 90.

11. Harcourt Papers, quoted Taylor, p. 90.

12. Parisi.

13. ibid.

14. BBK/B/20.

15. The final version of a story Beaverbrook told many times was published in the *Sunday Express*, 10 November 1963.

Chapter 8
The Ousting of Asquith, 1916

This account of the political manoeuvres of 1915 and 1916 is based on Beaverbrook's, as published in *Politicians and the War*. His version went through many drafts and revisions between 1917 and 1932; where these show significant differences from the published text, we have pointed them out. Subsequent historians have taken issue with Beaverbrook on a number of points; we have surveyed some of these in Appendix B.

Unless otherwise noted, the quotations from Beaverbrook himself are taken from *Politicians and the War*. The material collected by Beaverbrook from 1916 onwards, and his earlier drafts and proofs can all be found in BBK/G/5–11.

1. BBK/C/39.
2. Taylor, p. 95.
3. BLP, 53/6/21.
4. Jenkins, p. 373.
5. Blake, p. 260.
6. Jenkins, p. 369.
7. Gilbert, Martin, *Winston Churchill, Companion* Vol. III, Part 2 (Heinemann, 1973), p. 2.
8. ibid, p. 1338.
9. Gilbert, Martin, *Winston Churchill,* Vol. III (Heinemann, 1971), pp. 697–8.
10. Soames, Mary, *Clementine Churchill* (Cassell, 1979), p. 176.
11. Gilbert, Martin, *Winston Churchill, Companion* Vol. III, Part 2 (Heinemann, 1973) p. 1469.
12. Blake, p. 289.
13. Dr Cameron Hazlehurst of the Australian National University has shown us his unpublished paper *Biographical Propriety and the Historical Asquith*, in which the circumstances surrounding the alleged bridge game are thoroughly and entertainingly dissected.
14. Jenkins, p. 410.
15. Taylor, pp. 98–9.
16. ibid, p. 102.
17. See Asquith, H. H., *Letters to Venetia Stanley*, selected and edited by Michael and Eleanor Brock (Oxford University Press, 1982), Appendix 1.
18. Stevenson, Frances, *Lloyd George: A Diary*, edited by A. J. P. Taylor (Hutchinson, 1971), p. 124.
19. ibid, p. 130.
20. Ten years later, Beaverbrook sent Churchill a set of proofs which included the following lines (not in the published version) on Bonar Law's attitude to the Beaverbrook press campaign: 'A mere additional fling about the press did not matter. He did not blame anyone – myself or Lloyd George – for letting the country know what was happening.' Churchill commented: 'I thought then, and still think now, that Bonar Law was wrong in treating the moral side of the question so casually. The charge that Lloyd George inspired the Press to attack his chief in this crisis is on the way to pass into history – and the historian will certainly quote this Conservative resolution as supporting the accusation.' BBK/G/9/XIV.
21. Stevenson, p. 131.
22. BBK/G/8.
23. Churchill asked Beaverbrook to omit the whole story; Beaverbrook refused.
24. All these accounts can be found in BBK/G/5–11.
25. BBK/C/261.

Chapter 9
The Propaganda Period, 1917–1919

Beaverbrook told the story of his political activities in 1917 and 1918 in *Men and Power* (Hutchinson, 1956), and included letters and other original documents; this chapter is partly based on his account, and quotations from it are noted. Other source material, including his draft letters to Lloyd George, is in BBK/G/46–9. The HLRO also holds the papers relating to his work on the Cinematograph Committee and the Pictorial Propaganda Committee in 1917 and 1918 (BBK/E/2) and to his time as Minister of Information and Chancellor of the Duchy of Lancaster in 1918 (BBK/E/3); all quotations from letters and memorandums concerning the aims and problems of the Ministry are taken from these files.

For Arnold Bennett's background we have relied on Drabble, Margaret, *Arnold Bennett* (Weidenfeld and Nicholson, 1974). Extracts from his letters are taken from *The Letters of Arnold Bennett, 1916–1931*, Vol. III, edited by James Hepburn (Oxford University Press, 1970), reproduced by permission of A. P. Watt Ltd. on behalf of Madame V. Eldin.

1. *Men and Power*, p. 43.
2. ibid, p. 47.
3. ibid, p. 101.
4. ibid, p. 136.
5. Blake, p. 356.
6. *Montreal Star*, May 1917: cutting pasted

554

in Beaverbrook's sister Rahno's diary, in the collection of Lady McLintock.

7. BBK/G/57.

8. Woolf, Virginia, *Diary*, Vol. II (The Hogarth Press, 1978) p. 290.

9. *Men and Power*, p. 266.

10. ibid, p. 265.

11. Information about the Department of Information under Masterman and Buchan is taken from Adam Smith, Janet, *John Buchan* (Rupert Hart-Davis, 1965), and from Buitenhuis, Peter, *The Great War of Words* (Batsford, 1989).

12. *Men and Power*, p. 275.

13. ibid, p. 266.

14. ibid, p. 278.

15. BBK/B/309.

16. Carrington Papers, University of Sussex.

17. *Men and Power*, p. 279.

18. ibid, p. 279.

19. ibid, p. 285.

20. ibid, p. 288.

21. Adam Smith, p. 211.

22. Mosley, p. 52.

23. *A Durable Fire, The Letters of Duff and Diana Cooper*, edited by Artemis Cooper (Collins, 1983), p. xiv.

24. Cooper, Diana, *Autobiography* (Michael Russell Publishing, one-volume edition, 1979), p. 138.

25. ibid, p. 172.

26. Interview, Mrs Daphne Fielding, 1988.

27. Cooper, Diana, p. 177.

28. Drabble, p. 236.

29. Cooper, Diana, p. 189.

30. BBK/C/258.

31. *A Durable Fire*, p. 76.

32. Beaverbrook's unpublished letters to Lady Diana Cooper were kindly made available to us by Artemis Cooper.

33. Information about Lady Diana Cooper comes from Ziegler, Philip, *Diana Cooper* (Hamish Hamilton, 1981).

34. *Men and Power*, p. 299.

35. ibid, p. 301.

36. Bennett, Arnold, *Lord Raingo* (Cassell, 1926).

Chapter 10
'Bring Bonar Back', 1919–1922

In *The Decline and Fall of Lloyd George* Beaverbrook wrote his own account of the crumbling of the coalition, the negotiations leading to the Irish Treaty, and the crisis that made Bonar Law Prime Minister. Unless

otherwise noted, quotations from him, and from material concerning him, are taken from that book.

The correspondence between Beaverbrook and Tim Healy is in BBK/C/161–3.

The correspondence between Beaverbrook and Edwin and Venetia Montagu is in BBK/C/246.

1. Kidd, p. 35.

2. *A Durable Fire*, p. 131.

3. Asquith, p. 262.

4. BBK/C/86.

5. Beaverbrook's connections with the British film industry are described in Low, Rachael, *The History of the British Film*, Vol. I, 1914–18, and Vol. II, 1918–29 (Allen and Unwin, 1950 and 1971).

6. Young, Kenneth, *Churchill & Beaverbrook* (Eyre & Spottiswoode, 1966), p. 55.

7. Cooper, Duff, *Old Men Forget* (Hart-Davis, 1953).

8. Blake, p. 419.

9. Jones, Thomas, *Whitehall Diary*, Vol. III, edited by K. Middlemas (Oxford University Press 1971), p. 50.

10. Lord Beaverbrook, *Politicians and the Press*, p. 41.

11. Jones, p. 147.

12. PP, p. 40.

13. Campbell, p. 713.

14. Jones, p. 218.

15. Taylor, p. 240.

16. Private information.

17. Interview, Gwen Ffrangçon-Davies, 1990.

18. Interview, Mrs Margaret Gordon, 1990. Born Margaret Guthrie, she became first Mrs Ince, and second, in 1972, the wife of John Gordon, editor-in-chief of the *Sunday Express*.

19. Kidd, p. 17.

20. Private information.

21. Salvidge, Archibald, *Salvidge of Liverpool* (Hodder & Stoughton, 1934), p. 225.

22. BBK/G/50/6.

23. Kidd, p. 24.

24. Young, pp. 60–1.

25. PP, p. 49.

26. Blake, p. 448.

27. BBK/G/46/IV.

Chapter 11
Prime Minister's Friend, 1922–1924

Unless otherwise noted, Beaverbrook quotations in this chapter are taken from his

Decline and Fall of Lloyd George. Some additional material is in the HLRO, BBK/G/50–63, and where used is noted. The story of Bonar Law's administration, decline and death are dealt with in Beaverbrook's published version only in outline, although over the years Beaverbrook drafted and redrafted a fuller account; material from this draft is also noted.

Victoria Glendinning first told the story of Rebecca West's infatuation with Beaverbrook in *Rebecca West* (Weidenfeld and Nicolson, 1987).

1. BBK/G/12–13.
2. Salvidge, p. 238.
3. Wickham Steed, letter to *The Times*, 17 December 1947.
4. Blake, p. 456.
5. See Davidson, J. C. C., *Memoirs of a Conservative* (Weidenfeld and Nicolson, 1969).
6. BBK/G/12–13.
7. BLP 107/2/78.
8. Copies of the letters exchanged by Guest and Beaverbrook are in BBK/G/12–13.
9. Beaverbrook told A. J. P. Taylor that Churchill had given him *The Prince* in 1922, and Taylor told his third wife, Eva Haraszti Taylor, as she records in *A Life With Alan* (Hamish Hamilton, 1987), p. 4, adding that after Beaverbrook's death Lady Beaverbrook gave the copy to Taylor.
10. BBK/G/12–13.
11. All Beaverbrook quotations in the rest of the chapter concerning Bonar Law's health and his resignation are taken from *Bonar Law: The Last Phase*, BBK/G/57 unless otherwise noted.
12. BBK/C/163.
13. The complex chain of events whereby Baldwin succeeded Bonar Law has been exposed by Dr Cameron Hazlehurst in his unpublished paper *The Baldwinite Conspiracy*, which strongly indicates that J. C. C. Davidson, Ronald Waterhouse and Thomas Jones actively conspired to promote Baldwin and block Curzon, with Bonar Law's connivance, and that at the time Beaverbrook was kept in the dark.
14. Blake, p. 517.
15. ibid, p. 529, and in interview with Anthony Howard for BBC Television, 1981.
16. Taylor, p. 210.

Chapter 12
Northcliffe's Successor, Baldwin's Foe, 1918-1929

1. Kluger, p. 208. See also Blumenfeld, *Home Town*.
2. Baxter, Beverley, *Strange Street* (Hutchinson, 1935), p. 142.
3. Mackenzie, p. 145.
4. BBK/B/30.
5. BBK/B/20.
6. Blumenfeld, R. D., *The Press in My Time* (Rich & Cowan, 1933), p. 199
7. Christiansen, *Headlines All My Life* (Heinemann, 1961), p. 126.
8. BBK/G/15/III.
9. BBK/B/20.
10. BBK/B/30.
11. Camrose, Viscount, *British Newspapers and Their Controllers* (Cassell, 1947), p. 52. 'Lord Rothermere used to say that it was not such a bad thing for his shareholders if the *Express* went ahead of the *Mail* as they had a foot in both camps.'
12. Blumenfeld, p. 72.
13. *Dictionary of National Biography*. Aitken, William Maxwell, by Sir John Elliot.
14. Parisi.
15. Beaverbrook sometimes claimed to have recommended Baldwin to Bonar Law. But see Keith Middlemas and John Barnes, *Baldwin* (Weidenfeld and Nicolson, 1989), p. 58; and Hazlehurst, Cameron, in *The Times*, 30 August 1969.
16. PP, p. 75.
17. ibid, p. 77.
18. *Arnold Bennett's Letters to his Nephew* (Heinemann, 1936), p. 109.
19. BBK/C/64.
20. The *People*, 18 May 1924.
21. PP, p. 63.
22. BBK/C/334.
23. BBK/C/283.
24. Young, pp. 71–3.
25. ibid, p. 76.
26. ibid, pp. 78–9.
27. ibid, p. 93.
28. Parisi.
29. Christiansen, p. 92.
30. RBL, 11 May 1931, p. 165.
31. BBK/H/17.
32. Parisi, quoting Sir John Elliot, 1982.
33. *World's Press News*, 1931.
34. Christiansen, pp. 86–7.

35. Interview, George Malcolm Thomson, 1989.
36. Christiansen, p. 102.
37. BBK/B/20.
38. Christiansen, p. 101.
39. Lees-Milne, James, *Harold Nicolson*, Vol. I (Chatto & Windus, 1980), p. 376.
40. RBL, Vol. I, 4 May 1931, p. 165.
41. Lees-Milne, Vol. II (1981), pp. 18–19.
42. Interview, Mrs Margaret Gordon, 1990.
43. BBK/B/18.
44. BBK/B/19.
45. BBK/B/27.
46. BBK/B/11.
47. BBK/B/14.
48. BBK/B/19.
49. BBK/B/109.
50. Bruce Lockhart, R. H., *Retreat From Glory* (Putnam, 1934), pp. 28–9.

Chapter 13
Writers and Women, 1924–1928

William Gerhardie (who until 1967 spelled his name Gerhardi) described his meeting with Beaverbrook and its consequences in his autobiography, *Memoirs of a Polyglot* (Duckworth, 1931). His letters to his mother and other papers are in the Gerhardie collection at the Cambridge University Library; his correspondence with Beaverbrook is also in BBK/C/142. For Gerhardie's background and eccentricities we have relied on his biography by Dido Davies (Oxford, 1990).

1. Keyishian, Harry, *Michael Arlen* (Twayne Publishers, Boston, 1975), p. 82.
2. Davies, Dido, *William Gerhardie* (Oxford, 1990), p. 155.
3. Dame Barbara Cartland has written about her friendship with Beaverbrook in *The Isthmus Years* (Hutchinson, 1943), and in *We Danced All Night*. This account is based on hers, and on an interview in 1989.
4. Private information.
5. *A Durable Fire*, p. 258.
6. The correspondence between Arnold Bennett and Beaverbrook is in BBK/C/31–5; letters are taken from *The Letters of Arnold Bennett, 1916–1931*, Vol. III, edited by James Hepburn (Oxford University Press, 1970), and diary extracts from *The Journals of Arnold Bennett*, Vol. III, edited by Newman Flower (Cassell, 1933).

7. The draft of *The Life of Jesus* and Beaverbrook's correspondence about it with Tim Healy are in BBK/C/164–5.
8. Harriet Cohen's friendship with Rebecca West, Arnold Bennett and Beaverbrook is recounted in her autobiography, *A Bundle of Time* (Faber, 1969), which also quotes from Bennett's letters to her.
9. Harriet Cohen's letters to Beaverbrook are filed with his general correspondence for the 1920s, BBK/B/27.
10. Wood, p. 170.
11. Gerhardie, p. 303.
12. *Jazz and Jasper* was republished under the title Gerhardie had originally wanted, *Doom*, by Macdonald in 1974. Quotations are from that edition, reproduced by permission of Curtis Brown Ltd, London.
13. Castlerosse quotations are taken from Mosley, Leonard, *Castlerosse* (Arthur Barker, 1956).
14. RBL, p. 391.
15. Taylor, p. 242.
16. Janet Aitken's upbringing, her own and her brothers' relationship with her parents and her reaction to her father's conduct is described in her autobiography, *The Beaverbrook Girl*, and recalled in our interviews with her contemporaries Lady Sibell Rowley (*née* Lygon) and Lady Bowater (*née* Dawson) in 1989 and 1990. Information about Mrs Richard Norton comes from her husband's (Lord Grantley's) autobiography, *Silver Spoon* (Hutchinson, 1954), and from an interview with her daughter, the Hon. Mrs Sarah Baring, 1989.
17. Soames, p. 251.
18. Private information from members of the family.
19. The programme for the New Brunswick teachers' tour of 1926 survives in the collection of the HIL, University of New Brunswick.
20. Interview, Mrs Margaret Gordon, 1990.
21. BBK/B/22.
22. Taylor, p. 241.
23. Carrington Papers, University of Sussex.
24. Beaverbrook removed almost all traces of his first wife's illness and death from his records. These fragments remain in his general correspondence files, BBK/B/21–5.
25. Interview, Mrs Margaret Gordon, 1990.
26. Wood, p. 181.
27. BBK/B/21–25.
28. BBK/B/21–25.
29. Beaverbrook to Frank Wise, BBK/B/34.

Chapter 14
The Great Campaign, 1928–1929

The diaries of Jean Norton (Lady Grantley) for 1928–31 are in BBK/K/20.

1. BBK/C/247.
2. Taylor, p. 246.
3. Private information.
4. BBK/B/25.
5. Bennett, Arnold, *Journal 1929* (Cassell, 1930), p. 8.
6. Information about Doris Delavigne from Mrs Daphne Fielding, 1989.
7. Mosley, p. 90.
8. BBK/C/71.
9. Wardell, *Atlantic Advocate*, June, 1957.
10. BBK/C/255.
11. RBL, 2 March 1931, p. 155.
12. BBK/C/259.
13. BBK/C/259.
14. Ziegler, Philip, *Diana Cooper* (Hamish Hamilton, 1981), p. 164.
15. Unpublished letter, made available by Artemis Cooper.
16. Fielding, Daphne, *Mercury Presides* (Eyre and Spottiswoode, 1954), p. 134.
17. This account of the troubled Campbell marriage, including correspondence, is taken from *The Beaverbrook Girl*.
18. BBK/B/30.
19. Jones, Thomas, *Whitehall Diary*, Vol. II, edited by Keith Middlemas, p. 167.
20. BBK/C/173, and Taylor, pp. 256–8.
21. Young, pp. 96 and 106.
22. BBK/C/41.
23. Fielding, p. 136.
24. Castlerosse's finances are revealed in BBK/C/189–92.
25. Kidd, pp. 110–11.
26. RBL, pp. 88–9.
27. The indispensable account of Conservative politics in these years is Dr Stuart Ball's *Baldwin and the Conservative Party, The Crisis of 1929–1931* (Yale University Press, 1988). Among other merits, the book contains a detailed analysis of the geographical spread of support for the Empire Crusade.
28. BBK/C/284.
29. BBK/C/284.
30. BBK/C/284.
31. BBK/C/284.
32. Wells, H. G. *The Autocracy of Mr Parham* (Heinemann, 1930), p. 6.
33. Horne, Alastair, *Macmillan, 1894–1956* (Macmillan, 1988), p. 84.
34. BBK/B/120.
35. BBK/B/200.
36. RBL, 30 May 1929, p. 89.
37. BBK/C/126.
38. BBK/C/284.
39. BBK/B/120.
40. RBL, 22 November 1930, p. 135.
41. Carswell, John, *The Exile: A Life of Ivy Litvinov* (Faber, 1983), p. 124.
42. RBL, p. 106.
43. Morgan, Janet, *A Life of Her Own* (Collins, 1991), p. 211.
44. BBK/C/247.
45. *Letters of Arnold Bennett*, p. 327.

Chapter 15
Frustrations of a Crusader, 1929–1935

1. BBK/B/115.
2. RBL, 9 August 1929, p. 105.
3. BBK/B/108.
4. BBK/C/229.
5. RBL, 14 April 1930, p. 118.
6. BBK/B/88.
7. BBK/B/108.
8. BBK/B/114.
9. *The Empire at Bay, The Leo Amery Diaries, 1929–1945*, edited by John Barnes and David Nicholson (Hutchinson, 1988), p. 4.
10. James, Robert Rhodes, *Victor Cazalet* (Hamish Hamilton, 1976), p. 131.
11. BBK/C/284.
12. BBK/C/126.
13. BBK/B/88.
14. *Amery Diaries*, 13 November 1929, p. 54.
15. Gerhardi, p. 250.
16. *Amery Diaries*, 30 March 1930, p. 65.
17. RBL, 21 January 1930, p. 113.
18. BBK/C/284.
19. BBK/C/284.
20. *Amery Diaries*, Buchan to Baldwin, 13 January 1930, p. 12.
21. RBL, 12 February 1930, p. 115.
22. BBK/C/284.
23. *Amery Diaries*, 5 May 1930, p. 68.
24. ibid, 19 June 1930, p. 73.
25. BBK/B/108.
26. Acton, Harold, *Nancy Mitford* (Hamish Hamilton, 1975), p. 42.
27. Waugh, Evelyn, *A Little Learning* (Chapman and Hall, 1964), p. 204.
28. BBK/B/123.
29. Letter to authors from Lord Young of

Dartington, 21 March 1990.
30. Middlemas, Keith, and John Barnes, *Baldwin* (Weidenfeld and Nicolson, 1969), p. 574.
31. Beaverbrook, Lord, *Friends* (Heinemann, 1959), p. 64.
32. RBL, 22 November 1930, p. 135.
33. Gerhardi, p. 251.
34. *Amery Diaries*, p. 38.
35. Winterton, Earl of, *Orders of the Day* (Cassell, 1953), p. 166.
36. *Amery Diaries*, p. 91.
37. Middlemas and Barnes, pp. 579 and 582.
38. Interview, Lord James Douglas-Hamilton MP, 1990.
39. James, p. 133.
40. BBK/B/189.
41. BBK/C/286.
42. RBL, 9 February 1931, p. 152.
43. RBL, 5 February 1931, p. 151.
44. BBK/B/206.
45. James, p. 133.
46. BBK/B/200.
47. Middlemas and Barnes, pp. 588–9.
48. BBK/B/189.
49. Charmley, John, *Duff Cooper* (Weidenfeld and Nicolson, 1986), p. 64.
50. Middlemas and Barnes, p. 598.
51. BBK/B/189.
52. BBK/B/189.
53. BBK/B/200.
54. BBK/B/187.
55. BBK/B/195.
56. BBK/B/195.
57. Campbell, pp. 820 and 837.
58. BBK/B/168.
59. Drabble, p. 350.
60. RBL, 26 May 1931, p. 168.
61. RBL, 24 June 1931, p. 176.
62. Interview, Janet Morgan, 1988.
63. RBL, 27 and 28 July 1931, pp. 179–80.
64. BBK/C/231.
65. BBK/C/231.
66. BBK/B/200.
67. BBK/B/200.
68. The story of Beaverbrook's affair with Dorothy Schiff is taken from Potter, Jeffrey, *Men, Money and Magic, The Story of Dorothy Schiff* (New American Library, 1976), which was based on her records and on taped interviews with her.
69. RBL, 30 November 1931, p. 193.
70. Interview, Sir Max Aitken's widow, Lady (Violet) Aitken, 1990.
71. Argyll, Margaret, Duchess of, *Forget Not* (W. H. Allen, 1975), p. 61.
72. Roberts, Brian, *Randolph* (Hamish

Hamilton, 1984), p. 95.
73. ibid, p. 98.
74. Interview, Lady Sibell Rowley, 1988.
75. *The Beaverbrook I Knew*, edited by Logan Gourlay (Quartet Books, 1984), p. 23.
76. Private information.
77. Interview, Lady d'Avigdor-Goldsmid, 1990.
78. Interview, Miss Toto Koopman, 1991.
79. Interview, Lady (Penelope) Aitken, 1991.
80. Kidd, p. 146.
81. *A Durable Fire*, p. 280.
82. *The Diaries of Evelyn Waugh* (Weidenfeld and Nicolson, 1976), p. 284.
83. Morison Papers.
84. *Sunday Telegraph*, 17 September 1989.

Chapter 16
Appeasement and Abdication, 1931–1939

1. BBK/B/202.
2. BBK/B/201.
3. RBL, 1 May 1931, p. 164.
4. RBL, 6 March 1933, p. 248.
5. Kidd, p. 137.
6. RBL, 7 July 1933, p. 260.
7. RBL, 6 July 1934, p. 299.
8. Beaverbrook's correspondence with Mittelholzer about his trip to Germany is in BBK/B/260.
9. RBL, 27 November 1935, p. 333.
10. HIL, Wardell Correspondence File.
11. BBK/C/275.
12. Taylor, p. 346.
13. Beaverbrook's correspondence with Patterson about isolation is in BBK/C/268.
14. For Beaverbrook's impact on Hoare's political career, and a full account of the Hoare–Laval Pact, see Cross, J. A., *Sir Samuel Hoare, A Political Biography* (Cape, 1977). All correspondence between Beaverbrook and the Hoares is from BBK/C/307–8.
15. BBK/G/56.
16. Ribbentrop's operations in Britain in the mid-1930s are described in Griffiths, Richard, *Fellow Travellers of the Right* (Constable, 1980).
17. Beaverbrook's correspondence with Ribbentrop and Von Durkheim-Montmartin is in BBK/C/275.
18. Kidd, pp. 148–54.
19. BBK/C/218.
20. RBL, 30 November 1929, p. 110.
21. Aird and Lascelles as quoted by Ziegler,

Philip, *King Edward VIII, The Official Biography* (Collins, 1990), p. 282.

22. For the background to the abdication crisis see Ziegler; also Donaldson, Frances, *Edward VIII* (Futura, 1978).

23. Beaverbrook collected material for his book on the abdication for twenty-five years; it is now in BBK/G/23-7. All quotations from Beaverbrook, unless otherwise noted, are taken from his early account, entitled 'The Beaverbrook Narrative', marked 'Revised December 16, 1936'.

24. *Chips, The Diaries of Sir Henry Channon*, edited by Robert Rhodes James (Penguin, 1970), pp. 97-8.

25. A reference to 'my first attack of asthma' appears in a letter of 29 March 1936, BBK/B/260. His mother, his sister Rahno and his daughter Janet were fellow sufferers.

26. Cables to and from the *Bremen*, and all Beaverbrook's communications with Whelan and Monckton, are in BBK/G/23-7.

27. RBL, 22 November 1936, p. 358.

28. Interview, George Malcolm Thomson, 1989.

29. Christiansen, p. 135.

30. A copy of Churchill's letter is in BBK/G/23/7.

31. RBL, 4 December 1936, p. 359.

32. Wood, p. 234.

33. BBK/G/23/7.

34. Donaldson, p. 281.

35. RBL, 10 December 1936, p. 361.

36. Ziegler, p. 315.

37. Colville, John, *The Fringes of Power* (Hodder and Stoughton, 1985), p. 716.

38. Ziegler, p. 274.

39. Griffiths, p. 240.

40. HIL, Wardell Correspondence File.

41. The story of Beaverbrook and Lily Ernst is based on interviews with Lord Granard, 1989; Michael Foot, 1991; Lady d'Avigdor-Goldsmid, 1990; the Hon. Mrs Pamela Harriman, 1989; Mrs Zenia Lester, 1991; and Lady Sibell Rowley, 1989. Michael Foot has also written about her in *Debts of Honour* (Davis-Poynter, 1980).

42. Lily Ernst's letters to Beaverbrook, and his cables concerning her, are in BBK/B/261.

43. Interview, Mrs Betty MacArthur (Miss Bower, later Mrs May), 1990.

44. BBK/B/255.

45. BBK/B/257.

46. BBK/B/262.

47. BBK/B/261.

48. BBK/B/261.

49. BBK/C/275.

50. Taylor, p. 377.

51. RBL, 12 April 1938, p. 391.

52. A copy of the summary is with the Ribbentrop correspondence, BBK/C/275.

53. Gilbert, Martin, *Winston Churchill, Companion* Vol. V, Part 2 (Heinemann, 1979), pp. 957-8, 987.

54. Campbell, Patrick, *My Life and Easy Times* (Michael Joseph, 1988 edition), p. 144.

55. Low, David, *Low's Autobiography* (Michael Joseph, 1956), p. 279.

56. For a full account of how Chamberlain, Halifax and Hoare manipulated the press in 1938 and 1939 see Cockett, Richard, *Twilight of Truth* (Weidenfeld and Nicolson, 1989).

57. BBK/C/152.

58. BBK/C/80.

59. Nicolson, Harold, *Diaries and Letters 1939-1945* (Collins, 1967), p. 355.

60. BBK/C/89.

61. Apart from this last letter, and the dates and amounts of the cheques, for which the only source is Taylor, p. 386, the Hoare-Beaverbrook exchange is in BBK/C/308.

62. BBK/C/308.

63. Watt, Donald Cameron, *The Independent*, 9 April 1991.

64. RBL, 7 November 1938, p. 408.

65. Quoted Cockett, p. 81.

66. RBL, 6 December 1938, p. 412.

67. See Watt, Donald Cameron, *How War Came* (Mandarin, 1990), p. 186.

68. Christiansen, p. 143.

69. See Cox, Geoffrey, *Countdown to War* (Coronet, 1990).

70. Christiansen, pp. 180-1.

Chapter 17
Patron of the Left, 1929-1939

1. Christiansen, p. 252.

2. Williams, Philip M., *Hugh Gaitskell* (Oxford University Press, 1982), p. 163.

3. Foot, Michael, *The Beaverbrook I Knew*, edited by Logan Gourlay (Quartet Books, 1984), p. 80.

4. BBK/B/121.

5. BBK/B/121.

6. Lee, Jennie, *My Life with Nye* (Penguin, 1981), p. 111.

7. ibid p. 77.

8. BBK/C/37.

9. BBK/C/37.

10. Lee, p. 99.

11. Nicolson, Harold, *Diaries and Letters, 1930-39* (Fontana, 1969), p. 56.

12. BBK/C/254.
13. RBL, 1 May 1931, p. 164.
14. BBK/C/37.
15. BBK/C/37.
16. BBK/C/37.
17. Lee, p. 117.
18. BBK/C/37.
19. Foot, Michael, *Aneurin Bevan*, Vol. I (MacGibbon and Kee, 1962), p. 183.
20. Christiansen, p. 177.
21. Lee, p. 83.
22. Foot, p. 183.
23. HLRO, Blumenfeld (Additional) Papers, Box 2, Gordon to Elliot, 23 May 1953.
24. Edwards, Robert, *Goodbye Fleet Street* (Jonathan Cape, 1988), p. 95.
25. BBK/C/124.
26. Driberg, Tom, *Ruling Passions* (Jonathan Cape, 1977), p. 133.
27. BBK/C/124. Driberg to Beaverbrook, 7 March 1940: 'You have always been so kind to me personally that I regard you as, in a sense, in loco parentis . . . I need £2000.'
28. Driberg, p. 150.
29. *Daily Express*, 23 March 1935.
30. Driberg, p. 103.
31. BBK/C/124.
32. Interview, Michael Foot, 1990.
33. ibid.
34. Interview, Mrs Döe Howard (Mrs Peter Howard), 1990.
35. Interview, Michael Foot, 1990.

Chapter 18
'This Was His Hour', 1940

1. Peter Howard Papers, 1962.
2. *DNB, 1971–1980*, Owen, Frank, by Michael Foot.
3. Dennis Morgan Griffiths Papers.
4. *Amery Diaries*, 8 October 1939, p. 574.
5. *The Diplomatic Diaries of Oliver Harvey, 1937–1940*, edited by John Harvey (St Martin's Press, New York, 1971), p. 326.
6. Cockett, p. 140.
7. Bradford, Sarah, *George VI* (Weidenfeld and Nicolson, 1989), pp. 433–4.
8. Cockett, p. 157.
9. LH/11/1940/15.
10. BBK/C/37.
11. Griffiths Papers.
12. Cudlipp, Hugh, *The Prerogative of the Harlot* (Bodley Head, 1980), p. 295.
13. Griffiths Papers, Robertson to Beaverbrook, 2 October 1939.
14. Hore-Belisha diary, 17 September 1939; Minney, R. J., *The Private Papers of Hore-Belisha* (Collins, 1960).

15. BBK/C/308.
16. *My Dear Max, The Letters of Brendan Bracken to Lord Beaverbrook*, edited by Richard Cockett (The Historians' Press, 1990), p. 50.
17. Taylor, p. 407.
18. ibid.
19. BBK/D/96.
20. *Sunday Express*, 1 December 1963.
21. Gilbert, Martin, *Finest Hour, Winston S. Churchill, 1939–1941* (Heinemann, 1983), p. 301.
22. ibid, p. 302.
23. ibid, p. 316.
24. Bradford, p. 219.
25. BBK/D/440.
26. Gilbert, p.204.
27. Churchill, Winston, *The Second World War*, Vol. II, p. 12.
28. Young, p. 141.
29. BBK/D/438.
30. Churchill, pp. 286–7.
31. Interview, Kenneth Harris, 1987.
32. Colville, p. 153.
33. Gilbert, p. 534, quoting Major-General Sir Edward Spears, *Assignment to Catastrophe*, Vol. II (1954), pp. 213–15.
34. BBK/C/308.
35. BBK/D/96.
36. BBK/C/137.
37. BBK/C/137.
38. *DNB, 1971–1980*, Owen, Frank, by Michael Foot.
39. Griffiths Papers.
40. Wolrige-Gordon, Anne, *Peter Howard, Life and Letters* (Hodder and Stoughton, 1969). The author, Peter Howard's daughter, refers to 'the unspoken hatred which he felt for men in positions of power'.
41. Young, p. 149.
42. ibid, p. 150.
43. *DNB 1971–1980*, Owen, Frank, by Michael Foot.
44. Farrer, David, *G for God Almighty* (Stein and Day, New York, 1969), p. 28.
45. Interview, Michael Foot, 1990.
46. Taylor, p. 435.
47. Interview, Michael Foot, 1990.
48. Interview, Sir Isaiah Berlin, 1991.
49. BBK/D/438.
50. Farrer, p. 58.
51. Lee, pp. 148–51.
52. LH/11/1940/101.
53. Taylor, p. 423.
54. Farrer, p. 51.
55. Interview, Mrs Betty MacArthur (Miss Bower, later Mrs May), 1990.

56. Farrer, p. 62.
57. BBC TV, 17 September 1989.
58. *Friends*, pp. 103–5.
59. BBK/D/22.
60. Interview, J. R. A. Bailey, 1989. See also Bailey, Jim, *The Sky Suspended, A Fighter Pilot's Story* (Bloomsbury, 1990).
61. BBK/D/22.
62. BBK/D/171.
63. BBK/D/171.
64. *Evening Standard*, 26, 27, 28 November 1940.
65. Interview, General Sir Ian Jacob, 1990.
66. Farrer, p. 47.
67. Young, p. 235.
68. LH/11/1943/18.
69. LH/11/1942/94.
70. Churchill, Vol. II, pp. 286–7.
71. BBK/D/440.
72. Taylor, p. 415.
73. PRO, Cabinet papers, 65/7.
74. Richards, Denis, and Hilary Saunders, *Royal Air Force 1939–1945*, Vol. I (HMSO, 1974), p. 19. See also Richards, Denis, and Richard Hough, *The Battle of Britain* (Coronet Books, 1989), pp. 102–3.
75. Terraine, John, *The Right of the Line, The Royal Air Force in the European War 1939–1945* (Sceptre, 1988), p. 192.
76. ibid.
77. ibid. A discussion of why a 'priority system' of producing aircraft, as operated by Beaverbrook, was bound to break down in the long run will be found in Cairncross, Sir Alec, *Planning in Wartime, Aircraft Production in Britain, Germany and the USA* (Macmillan, 1991), pp. 13–14, and p. 164.
78. Young, p. 183.
79. BBK/D/171.
80. Young, p. 168.
81. ibid, p. 181.
82. *Amery Diaries*, 18 April 1941, p. 684.
83. Young, p. 185.
84. Moran, Lord, *Winston Churchill, The Struggle for Survival, 1940–1965* (Constable, 1966), pp. 29–30.
85. Young, p. 185.

Chapter 19
Red Wolves in the Kremlin, 1941–1942

1. The leader galleys survive in BBK/C/136.

2. Young, p. 186.
3. ibid, pp. 187–8.
4. Interview, Sir Ian Jacob, 1990.
5. Young, p. 191.
6. ibid, pp. 195–6.
7. LH/11/1942/14.
8. Colville, p. 395.
9. Young, p. 232.
10. ibid, pp. 186–7.
11. *Amery Diaries*, 11 December 1940, p. 668.
12. Colville, p. 394.
13. Michael Foot, *Debts of Honour* (Davis Poynter, 1980), p. 99.
14. BBK/D/96. A narrative entitled 'The Second Front' written by Farrer 'after the war' and evidently based on material collected in consultation with Beaverbrook; but the draft was not corrected by Beaverbrook and got no further. An attached note says, 'GMT (George Malcolm Thomson) confirms.'
15. Colville, pp. 404–5.
16. Interview, Lord Jay, 1990.
17. Horne, pp. 143–5.
18. Harriman, W. Averell, and Abel, Elie, *Special Envoy to Churchill and Stalin in 1941–1946* (Random House, New York, 1975), p. 61.
19. Interview, the Hon. Mrs Sarah Baring, 1989. The story, using the pseudonym 'Mary Fitzmaurice', was filed to the *Baltimore Sun*, 21 August 1941.
20. Harriman, p. 79.
21. BKK/D/96.
22. Young, p. 206.
23. BBK/D/443.
24. BBK/D/443 contains the Beaverbrook–Hess letters and a twenty-two-page verbatim transcript of their conversation headed 'Dr Livingstone and Jonathan' and stamped 'Most Secret'.
25. Interview, Lord James Douglas-Hamilton MP, 1990. See also Douglas-Hamilton, Lord James, *Motive for a Mission* (Macmillan, London, 1971).
26. Colville, p. 388.
27. Douglas-Hamilton, p. 174.
28. Interview, Lord James Douglas-Hamilton MP, 1990.
29. Cockett, pp. 50–1.
30. BBK/C/238.
31. BBK/D/96.
32. BBK/D/96.
33. Gilbert, Vol. VI, pp. 1183–4.
34. Young, p. 208.

35. Gilbert, Vol. VI, p. 1178.
36. Harriman, p. 82.
37. BBK/D/97.
38. Griffiths Papers.
39. BBK/D/98.
40. The Moscow Mission is described in Beaverbrook's scribbled contemporary notes to himself; in his memorandums and despatches to the War Cabinet; and in an undated draft written in pencil, marked 'secret', entitled 'Relations with Russia – Full Story based upon documents in Lord Beaverbrook's archives', and typed up apparently on 25 June 1945 as 'Moscow Narrative'. All these are in BBK/D/96/98/99/100. Harriman's account is to be found in his despatches to Washington, and in *Special Envoy*.
41. Howard Papers.
42. BBK/D/99.
43. Howard Papers.
44. BBK/D/99.
45. LH/11/1942/14.
46. Harriman, p. 104.

Chapter 20

Champion of Russia, 1941–1945

1. Harriman, p. 105.
2. *Daily Express*, 13 October 1941.
3. BBK/D/439.
4. PRO, Cabinet papers, 69/8.
5. Interview, Sir Ian Jacob, 1990.
6. *Evening Standard*, 6 October 1941.
7. Interview, Lord Jay, 1990.
8. BBK/D/96.
9. Interview, Lord Jay, 1990.
10. Horne, pp. 144–5.
11. BBK/D/77.
12. Farrer, p. 77.
13. Young, p. 214.
14. Gilbert, Vol. VI, p. 1227.
15. BBK/D/125.
16. BBK/D/125.
17. LH/18/3/14.
18. BBK/D/123.
19. BBK/D/97.
20. BBK/D/97.
21. BBK/D/96.
22. BBK/D/435.
23. Harriman, pp. 125–6.
24. BBK/D/96.
25. Nicolson, pp. 189–90.
26. Harris, Kenneth, *Attlee* (W. W. Norton, 1982), p. 194.
27. *Tribune*, 27 February 1942.
28. Soames, pp. 313–14.
29. BBK/D/96.
30. LH/11/1942/43.
31. LH/11/1942/15.
32. LH/11/1942/15.
33. Farrer, p. 86.
34. ibid, p. 89.
35. BBK/D/123.
36. Harriman, p. 133.
37. Farrer, p. 92.
38. BBK/C/137.
39. LH/11/1942/43.
40. BBK/C/137, 10 June 1942.
41. Wheen, Francis, *Tom Driberg* (Chatto and Windus, 1990), p. 170.
42. BBK/D/451.
43. LH/11/1942/82.
44. BBK/C/308.
45. Wheen, p. 171.
46. Koss, Stephen, *Fleet Street Radical, A. G. Gardiner and the Daily News* (Allen Lane, 1973), p. 246.
47. *Amery Diaries*, 23 July 1942, p. 821.
48. Farrer, p. 84.
49. LH/11/1942/33.
50. Harris, p. 199. The account of the Bevin-Beaverbrook meeting is contained in Bullock, Alan, *The Life and Times of Ernest Bevin*, Vol.II (Heinemann, 1967) p. 177. A. J. P. Taylor (p. 530) is sceptical about both the Salter and the Bevin stories.
51. Interview, Michael Foot, 1989.
52. BBK/C/37.
53. Pocock, Tom, *Alan Moorehead* (The Bodley Head, 1990), p. 143.
54. Wheen, p. 285.
55. LH/11/1942/82.
56. BBK/C/277.
57. Harriman, pp. 206–10.
58. BBK/D/267 and 293.
59. BBK/D/151.
60. Farrer, p. 125.
61. For an authoritative account of these negotiations, see Masefield, Sir Peter, 'From Paris to Chicago, 1919–44: the Civilisation of Air Transport' (*The Putnam Aeronautical Review*, March 1990).
62. BBK/C/137.
63. BBK/D/167.
64. BBK/D/343.
65. Unpublished letter, made available by Artemis Cooper.
66. Taylor, p. 245.
67. Colville, 27 May 1945, p. 603.

Chapter 21
'The Man Who Had to Know', 1945–1956

1. BBK/C/275.
2. Interview, George Malcolm Thomson, 1988.
3. BBK/C/236 and 237.
4. ibid.
5. ibid.
6. Driberg, p. 98.
7. BBK/C/137.
8. Interview, Lord Shawcross, 1989.
9. BBK/C/294.
10. Interview, Lady Jean Campbell, 1988.
11. Interview, Mrs Betty MacArthur (Miss Bower, later Mrs May), 1990.
12. Kidd, p. 205.
13. Interview, Mrs Lester, 1991.
14. Interview, Michael Foot, 1991.
15. Interview, Lady d'Avigdor-Goldsmid, 1990.
16. Kidd, p. 204.
17. Interview, Dr Alfred Bailey, 1988.
18. Young, p. 11.
19. HIL, Beaverbrook Papers, Case 45 Canada General A–M.
20. HIL. The Beaverbrook–Wardell letters are in the Wardell Correspondence File.
21. Interview, John Sancton, formerly Wardell's managing editor at the *Gleaner*, 1988. His source was Sir William Aitken MP, Beaverbrook's nephew.
22. The story was often told by the late John Gale.
23. BBK/C/136.
24. *DNB 1981–1985*, Cameron, James, by Michael Foot.
25. Taylor, p. 598.
26. BBK/C/332.
27. Interview, Sir Isaiah Berlin, 1991.
28. Interview, Charles Wintour, 1991.
29. John Sancton heard the story from Sir William Aitken MP.
30. Copland, A. A., *The Press Baron and the Kiwi* (Springwood Books, 1985), pp. 158–60.
31. *My Dear Max*, p. 91.
32. BBK/C/264.
33. Interview, Lord Blake, 1991.
34. Mozley, Ann, *Journal of the Royal Australian Historical Society*, Vol. 5, March 1965, pp. 1–9. Interview Ann Mozley (Mrs Moyal), 1991.
35. BBK/C/123 and 124 contain correspondence and material about the Driberg biography.
36. *The Letters of Evelyn Waugh*, edited by Mark Amory (Weidenfeld and Nicolson, 1980), p. 467.

Chapter 22
Benefactor and Bridegroom, 1956–1964

1. Tweedie, pp. 171–2.
2. HIL/Box 1/File 5.
3. Tweedie, p. 173.
4. HIL/117/5.
5. Rothenstein, John, *Brave Day, Hideous Night* (Hamish Hamilton, 1966), pp. 372–3.
6. Interview, Ian Lumsden, 1988.
7. Interview, Lady d'Avigdor-Goldsmid, 1990.
8. *The Beaverbrook I Knew*, p. 175.
9. Interview, Mme Champsaur (Miss Rosenberg), 1990.
10. *The Beaverbrook I Knew*, p. 220.
11. Private information.
12. Interview, Dr Christian Carritt, 1991.
13. Interview, Lady Jean Campbell, 1988.
14. Letter to the authors from Norman Mailer.
15. HIL. The exchanges and letters about the Queen's visit are in the Wardell Correspondence File.
16. Greene, Graham, *Yours etc. Letters to the Press 1945–89*, selected and introduced by Christopher Hawtree (Reinhardt Books, 1989), pp. 76–88.
17. Morison Papers.
18. ibid.
19. Interview, Mme Champsaur (Miss Rosenberg), 1990.
20. *My Dear Max*, p. 173.
21. Taylor, A. J. P., *Letters to Eva* (Century, 1991), p. 271.
22. Interview, Lady Jean Campbell, 1988.
23. BBK/K/17.
24. BBK/C/305 contains the Beaverbrook–Taylor exchanges.
25. *New Statesman*, 8 March 1963.
26. Interview, Lord Blake, 1991.
27. Interview, Mrs Anne Moynihan (*née* Dunn), 1991.
28. *My Dear Max*, p. 188.
29. HIL. Wardell Correspondence File.
30. Howard Papers.
31. Morison Papers.
32. *The Beaverbrook I Knew*, p. 41.

33. Edwards, passim.
34. *The Beaverbrook I Knew*, p. 31. This is the richest source of published Beaverbrook anecdotes. The quotations from Alan Brien, William Davis, Christopher Dobson, Angus McGill and Anne Sharpley are taken from this book.
35. Junor, John, *Listening For a Midnight Tram* (Chapmans, 1990), pp. 80–1.
36. Horne, Vol. II, p. 264.
37. BBK/C/332.
38. BBK/K/6.
39. Interview, Timothy Aitken, 1991. In 1974, when he stood as Conservative candidate in Ashton-under-Lyne, an old man shouted at him, 'I didn't vote for your grandfather and I'm not going to vote for you!'
40. Interview, Jonathan Aitken MP, 1989.

41. *The Beaverbrook I Knew*, p. 162.
42. Vines, C. M., *A Little Nut-Brown Man* (Leslie Frewin, 1968), pp. 202–3.
43. Edwards, pp. 148–9.
44. Harris, p. 194.
45. Interview, Lady McLintock, 1990.
46. BBC2 television programme, *Reputations: Lord Beaverbrook*, 28 June 1981.
47. Interview, George Malcolm Thomson, 1990.
48. Muggeridge's article was published in *McLean's* magazine. Michael Wardell replied in the *Atlantic Advocate*, published in Fredericton, New Brunswick, November 1963.
49. Interviews, Lady McLintock, 1989, and Mrs Margaret Gordon, 1990.
50. BBK/K/13.
51. Interview, Lady McLintock, 1989.

APPENDIX A: NOTES

THE EARLY HISTORY of the cement industry in Canada is told from the viewpoint of the producers in *The Canada Cement Lafarge Story*, a booklet produced by Canada Cement Lafarge, the company created by the merger of the Canada Cement Company and Lafarge Canada in 1970. The booklet describes the 'vicious competition' that existed in 1908, before Max Aitken's organization of the industry in 1909 produced 'economic efficiency'.

The documents quoted in this appendix, including the Canada Cement prospectus of 14 September 1909, are to be found conveniently in BBK/G/2 and BBK/G/3, which contains the Preliminary Hearings of the High Court case between the Bank of Montreal, and Sir Sandford Fleming and Joseph Samuel Irvin. The evidence of the dispersal and destruction of documents is to be found in BBK/G/2.

1. BBK/G/19/XXI.
2. Lord Beaverbrook, *Friends* (Heinemann, 1959), pp. 44–5. The pertinent sentences read: 'He borrowed $100,000, no doubt from his bank in Calgary, and invested the sum, with me, in financing the Canada Cement Company. I cannot recall his share of the profits, but, since he took part in the original syndicate, the amount was substantial. With the proceeds of this successful investment Bennett was established as a man of small but real wealth.' This statement is hard to reconcile with Beaverbrook's contention after the storm broke in 1911 that his own 'total personal profit, directly or indirectly' was not substantial at all – in fact 'did not exceed $350,000'. See BBK/G/2, Aitken to H. A. Gwynne, 2 August 1911. Gwynne had sent Aitken a letter from P. D. Ross of the *Ottawa Journal* dated 24 July saying:

> The Cement merger doubled the fair capitalisation of the properties included; and the properties included control of the business in Canada; and the merger has greatly increased the price of cement. Mr Aitken's brains went into the establishment of a monopoly under conditions practically compelling an otherwise unnecessary increase in the price of a great public staple. And Mr Aitken profited personally. . . . I would not like myself to be tempted by opportunity of inciting or sharing in such enterprise. But it isn't any more moral than the business of the old feudal bandit, who swooped down from his advantageous eyrie over a highway and plundered travellers.

INDEX

Note: Ranks and titles are generally
the highest given in the text

INDEX

A NOTE ABOUT THE AUTHORS

Anne Chisholm is the author of a biography of Nancy Cunard and *Faces of Hiroshima,* a book about the Hiroshima Maidens. Michael Davie is a leading British journalist, a longtime reporter, editor and columnist for the *Observer.* He has written books on Lyndon Johnson, the *Titanic,* and California, and edited *The Diaries of Evelyn Waugh.*

DATE DUE

WITHDRAWN

GAYLORD   PRINTED IN U.S.A.